THE ONLY BOOK THAT TELLS YOU ALL ABOUT WHAT YOU *DON'T* EXPECT WHEN YOU'RE EXPECTING

PREEMIES:
THE ESSENTIAL GUIDE FOR PARENTS OF PREMATURE BABIES

Dana Wechsler Linden and Emma Trenti Paroli, both mothers of children who were born prematurely, have joined neonatologist Mia Wechsler Doron, M.D., to write the book they wish had been available to them during their pregnancies and beyond. *Preemies* is an engaging and fact-filled reference that guides new parents through the many questions and uncertainties of anticipating and caring for a premature baby. Read all about . . .

* why premature births happen, and what can be done to prevent them
* premature delivery: getting ready for it
* seeing your preemie for the first time
* questions to ask your doctors and nurses
* settling down in the hospital
* taking your preemie home
* your baby's first year
* the loss of a baby
* special-needs children

. . . and much more. Reassuring yet realistic, the advice in *Preemies* constitutes the ultimate companion to caring for your very special child.

PREEMIES

The Essential Guide for Parents of Premature Babies

Dana Wechsler Linden,
Emma Trenti Paroli, and
Mia Wechsler Doron, M.D.

POCKET BOOKS

New York   London   Toronto   Sydney   Singapore

The sale of this book without its cover is unauthorized. If you purchased this book without a cover, you should be aware that it was reported to the publisher as "unsold and destroyed." Neither the author nor the publisher has received payment for the sale of this "stripped book."

The ideas, procedures, and suggestions in this book are not intended as a substitute for the medical advice of your trained health professional. All matters regarding your health require medical supervision. Consult your physician before adopting the suggestions in this book, as well as about any condition that may require diagnosis or medical attention. The author and publisher disclaim any liability arising directly or indirectly from the use of the book.

An *Original* Publication of POCKET BOOKS

POCKET BOOKS, a division of Simon & Schuster Inc.
1230 Avenue of the Americas, New York, NY 10020

Copyright © 2000 by Dana Wechsler Linden, Emma Trenti Paroli, and Mia Wechsler Doron, M.D.

Illustrations by Daniela Rossato

All rights reserved, including the right to reproduce
this book or portions thereof in any form whatsoever.
For information address Pocket Books, 1230 Avenue
of the Americas, New York, NY 10020

Library of Congress Cataloging-in-Publication Data

Linden, Dana Wechsler.
Preemies : the essential guide for parents of premature babies / Dana Wechsler Linden, Emma Trenti Paroli, Mia Wechsler Doron.
p. cm.
ISBN 0-671-03491-X
1. Infants (Premature) 2. Infants (Premature)—Care. 3. Birth weight, Low—Complications. 4. Pregnancy—Complications. I. Paroli, Emma Trenti. II. Doron, Mia Wechsler. III. Title.

RJ250.L56 2000
618.92'011—dc21 00-028554

First Pocket Books trade paperback printing August 2000

10 9 8 7 6 5 4 3

POCKET and colophon are registered trademarks of
Simon & Schuster Inc.

Book design by Pagesetters, a division of Stratford Publishing Services
Cover design by Anna Dorfman; front cover photo by Elizabeth Hathon

Printed in the U.S.A.

RRDH/

To our children,
and to all preemies

Acknowledgments

We feel deeply grateful to our families, who all made sacrifices for this book; to a few, extraordinary doctors — Kathryn Crowley, Joelle Mast, Barney Softness, and Mark Souweidane — who took care of Dana's and Emma's babies with a rare combination of clinical skill and compassion; to the families of the preemies Mia has cared for, who shared their joys and fears and were examples of courage and strength; and to the experts who generously contributed their time and expertise to this book:

Heidelise Als of Harvard Medical School

Marie Anzalone of Columbia University

Ronald Ariagno of Stanford University School of Medicine

Grace Baranek of University of North Carolina

Jane Barlow of University of North Carolina Hospitals

Judy Bauman of University of North Carolina Hospitals

Frank Chervenak of New York Presbyterian Hospital

Martha Collette of Massachusetts General Hospital

Rosalyn Benjamin Darling of Indiana University of Pennsylvania

Barry Fleisher of Stanford University School of Medicine

Sharon Freedman of Duke University Eye Center

Miriam Mazzoni Frigerio of Ospedale Sant'Anna, Como, Italy

Carol Gilmer of University of North Carolina Hospitals

Stanley Graven of University of South Florida College of Public Health

Victor Groza of Case Western Reserve University

Ruth Eckstein Grunau of British Columbia Children's Hospital, Canada

Wendy Hansen of University of Iowa Hospitals and Clinics

Melissa Johnson of WakeMed, Raleigh, North Carolina

Emily Pearl Kingsley of Children's Television Workshop

Susan Shier Lowry of Governor Morehead School, Raleigh, North Carolina

Jane Madell of Beth Israel Medical Center, New York

Joni McKeeman of University of North Carolina Hospitals

Florence Milch of New York Eye and Ear Infirmary

Management of Pediatric Services of America, Inc.

Jonathan Roth of Kaiser Permanente, Denver, Colorado

Lynn Spivak of North Shore/Long Island Jewish Health System

Judith Stadler of New York Presbyterian Hospital

Robert Strauss of University of North Carolina Hospitals

Stuart Teplin of University of North Carolina Hospitals

Mary Tully of Mother's Milk Bank,
WakeMed, Raleigh, North
Carolina
Steven Wells of University of North
Carolina Hospitals

Rhonda Weiss of Office of Special
Education and Rehabilitation, U.S.
Department of Education
Randah Whitley of University of North
Carolina Hospitals

We also want to thank Tracy Berran of New York Presbyterian Hospital, for reaching out to us and other parents of preemies; Lisa Gubernick, for always pointing us in the right direction; the doctors and nurses at UNC Hospitals, whose lessons fill the pages of this book, and especially Carl Bose, for his unwavering support; and our editor, Nancy Miller, who believed in this book from the minute she heard about it.

Contents

Introduction   xi

A Note to the Reader: How to Use This Book   xiii

Part I
BEFORE BIRTH

1   In the Womb: Why Premature Birth Happens and What Can Be Done to Prevent It   3

For parents trying to grasp the extent of their risk, and what they can do to minimize it. Also for parents looking back, trying to make sense of what happened.

Part II
IN THE HOSPITAL

2   Welcome to the World: Your Baby's Delivery   41

Your baby's transition from the womb to the world. Preparing for, and understanding, a premature birth.

3   The First Day   76

Entering the foreign world of the neonatal intensive care unit. Why it's the best place for your baby to be.

4   The First Week   129

A time of crucial test results and waiting. Understanding that things sometimes get worse before they get better.

5   Settling Down in the Hospital   206

Making the NICU the best possible home-away-from-home for you and your baby.

6   If Your Baby Needs Surgery   303

Guiding parents through an event that is usually scarier than it needs to be.

Part III
A LIFE TOGETHER

7 Finally Taking Your Baby Home   329

Decisions and preparations for the moment you've been waiting for.

8 From Preemie to Preschool (and Beyond)   394

A time to watch your baby's health and development—and gradually begin to relax and enjoy!

9 When Parents Have Something Special to Worry About   440

Learning more about some possible consequences of prematurity.

Part IV
OTHER CONSIDERATIONS

10 Losing a Baby   483

Helping you deal with a profound grief, and guiding you through the necessary arrangements.

11 I Was a Preemie, Too   504

Famous people who were born premature and thrived, even before the recent advances in neonatal medicine.

APPENDICES

Appendix 1: *Conversion Charts*   511

Appendix 2: *Growth Charts*   513

Appendix 3: *A Schedule for Multiples*   519

Appendix 4: *Cardio-Pulmonary Resuscitation—Birth to One Year*   520

Appendix 5: *Resources for Parents of Premature Babies*   521

GLOSSARY
535

INDEX
545

Introduction

Preemies was conceived a few years ago, when our lives took turns that we never could have predicted.

Dana and Mia were two sisters with professional lives that had never overlapped: Dana was a journalist writing for a business magazine in New York, and Mia a doctor who specialized in the care of premature and sick babies at the University of North Carolina at Chapel Hill. They hadn't met Emma, who lived a few miles from Dana and was also a journalist, writing about medical issues for the leading publications in Italy, where she grew up.

Dana and Emma were pregnant. Dana had a two-year-old daughter already, but this time she was expecting twins, so she had much to discover about the extraordinary experience of a multiple gestation. Emma was in her first pregnancy, the result of six years of infertility treatments. She was finally allowing herself to believe that, after all, she would become a mother.

It was for both expectant mothers a wonderful time in our lives. We expected our pregnancies to last nine months, of course, and felt safe as our favorite pregnancy books led us by the hand. But we never got to read the last chapters as we had pictured: lying on the sofa with swollen feet and giant bellies vibrating from vigorous baby kicks. Instead, Dana's water broke suddenly one night, and Emma developed an infection. We leaped over the last trimester of our pregnancies in a matter of days, delivering our babies almost three months before term.

Before we had even started to think about cribs and baby clothes, we were hurled under the glaring lights of the neonatal intensive care unit, where our children would spend the first months of their immature lives. We met in the nursery—in that high-tech world of frail, tiny babies, attached to machines that set off loud alarms whenever breathing or heart rate faltered for a few seconds, where our children were fighting for their lives.

And we were hardly alone. Our children had become part of a growing crowd—the one out of ten births in this country that are premature.

In the beginning, we didn't know anything about prematurity. We had to learn a great deal just to understand what was happening to our babies, and what it might mean for their futures. We asked questions of the medical staff. We called our friends' doctors for further explanations. Dana's sister Mia—how fortunate that she was a neonatologist!—left her family and job to be with Dana and Dana's husband during the most difficult days of their twin daughters' hospitalization.

But every day we needed more information, and the conversations with doctors and nurses were never enough. Sometimes the professionals taking care of our babies gave us conflicting answers to crucial questions. Sometimes they delivered news in callous or terrifying ways, adding unnecessary worries. There were many times when we were told things that we were simply too distressed to remember a few hours later.

Emma's son, Luigi, was diagnosed with a brain bleed and soon developed hydrocephalus, a buildup of fluid in the brain, which required surgery—how could he withstand it, at his tiny size, and what would this mean for his development? Dana's daughter Elena was breathing vigorously in the delivery room—did that mean she was out of danger? Why did Maya's ears fold over in a funny way? Were our babies as aware as they seemed? Were they in pain? We had hundreds of questions; some profound, others so seemingly trivial that we didn't dare ask.

As a neonatologist, Mia had counseled many parents about their premature babies over the years. She knew that even the most empathetic doctor, when charged with caring for dozens of tiny or critically ill babies in an intensive care nursery, doesn't have enough time in the day to give each parent all of the information he or she so desperately wants. She bought Dana and her husband, as a "birthday" gift, a book about premature babies, the only guide she knew of for parents. But even though the time she spent with them, explaining and advising and comforting, was invaluable, the book terrified them, emphasizing all of the things that can go wrong in premature babies (but that most parents really don't have to worry about). At the hospital where Dana and Emma met, the doctors said regretfully that there was no book they could wholeheartedly recommend.

A few months later, memories from the NICU brought us together, and so, from our experiences, *Preemies* was born, as the book Dana and Emma wished they could have had, and Mia wished she could have given—a companion and resource, guide and teacher, realistic but reassuring. It is a book that parents can keep on their nightstand, or keep handy as they travel back and forth to the hospital, to consult briefly and frequently, as new questions and doubts arise almost every day. It is a book for all future parents, and those close to them, who will both suffer and rejoice in their children's premature births.

What happened to our preemies in the NICU and after is the personal legacy we carry into this book. Luigi had his surgery, came out of it stronger than ever, and went home a few days later. Maya had some serious ups and downs—including a sudden illness and rehospitalization just a few days after she got home—but grew gradually healthier, and came home for good before her due date. Elena, although she was slightly bigger than her twin sister at birth, suffered much more. She developed a tear in her lung, and a spiral of complications followed. She died in the hospital. Her parents miss her badly.

Our inspirations in writing *Preemies* have been Mia's little patients and their parents, whose bravery and openness she admires and finds constantly amazing, and Dana's and Emma's preemies: the memory of Elena Linden, and Maya Linden and Luigi Trenti Paroli, who are now normal, beautiful, thriving preschoolers, so happy to be alive.

A NOTE TO THE READER:

How to Use This Book

There are a few things you need to know, as a reader of *Preemies*. This book cannot, and is not intended to, replace conversations with your baby's doctors. Every baby is different, and each case has its own subtleties. In fact, we hope *Preemies* will encourage more meaningful conversations with your baby's doctors, by giving you background knowledge and helping you to know what questions to ask.

Very important: Don't read all of this book! We purposely wrote it in bite-sized pieces, with each question-and-answer or box addressing a separate topic, so that you can read about the specific issues that are relevant for you and your baby—and skip all of the rest. Every preemie's story is different, and if you read about the wide range of problems that occur in different children—most of which you'll never have to deal with—you'll develop a scary, highly distorted image of what to expect for your baby. Most babies who are born premature today grow into healthy, happy, normal children and encounter only a fraction of the hurdles you can read about here. So, browse through each chapter, or use the index, to follow your baby's own unique experience.

Use the table of contents at the start of each chapter to find the questions or topics you may encounter during that period of your baby's life. Read "The Parents' Perspective" if you are interested in reflecting on your emotional reactions, and on some ways that other parents of premature babies respond to this experience. In each chapter, "The Doctor's Perspective" gives you a special insight into something we found frustratingly mysterious: what your baby's doctor might be looking for at that stage. This section also provides a good overview of the whole chapter, if you want one. If you would like some statistics on the outcomes and paths of premature babies in general, you can find them in "A Different Story for Different Preemies." Look under your baby's gestational age for the information that would apply to him.

Keep in mind that different nurseries do things differently. Our descriptions cover some of the most common ways of doing things, but not all, so if the medical staff at your hospital does things in ways that diverge from our descriptions, that doesn't mean they're wrong. That's also true for services that are available to preemies after they leave the hospital. State-run organizations, in particular, vary widely across the country.

Thankfully, neonatal care is changing and progressing all the time. We'll update this book periodically, but for information on the most recent research and developments, you should rely on your baby's doctors. For all of the general parenting issues that aren't unique to preemies, and relate just as much to term babies (there are lots of things that are not different for a premature baby, and we'll be pointing many of these out to you in the text), you should turn to the many excellent pregnancy and childcare guides in print.

Part I

BEFORE BIRTH

1

In the Womb

Why Premature Birth Happens and What Can Be Done to Prevent It

▶ *For parents trying to grasp the extent of their risk, and what they can do to minimize it. Also for parents looking back, trying to make sense of what happened.*

INTRODUCTION   4

QUESTIONS AND ANSWERS
  Bed Rest   5
  Bed Rest Survival Tips   6
  High Blood Pressure and Preeclampsia   8
  Predicting the Birth Date   10
  Diagnosing and Treating Preterm Labor   12
  Are You in Preterm Labor?   13
  Drugs for Preterm Labor   14
  Cerclage   15
  Diagnosing an Incompetent Cervix   16
  Hidden Infections and Preterm Birth   17
  If Your Water Breaks   19
  If Your Water Breaks before Your
    Baby Has Reached Viability   21
  When Baby Needs to Be Delivered Early   22

Checking on a Baby's Well-Being before
    He Is Born   23
  Baby's Fighting Spirit   26
  Steroids   26
  Are There Medications other than Steroids
    You Can Take to Help Your Baby?   27

MULTIPLES
  Likelihood of Prematurity   28
  A Note If You Considered Multifetal
    Pregnancy Reduction   29
  Twin to Twin Transfusion Syndrome   30
  One Twin Needs Early Delivery   31

IN DEPTH
  Risk Factors for Prematurity:
    Are You at Risk?   33

Introduction: In the Womb

A normal pregnancy that leads, nine months later, to the birth of a healthy baby is a natural life experience in which doctors are mostly watchful bystanders, until the time of delivery comes. But if you're at risk for a premature birth, your experience is going to be different. Some women will be aware of their risk before they conceive. For many others, suddenly becoming a patient comes as a shocking surprise.

If you're likely to have a preterm birth, you'll probably get assistance from an obstetrician who specializes in high-risk pregnancies (called a perinatologist). Your doctor's efforts will be directed at preventing a premature birth, or postponing it as much as is possible and advisable.

Why prematurity happens is still a puzzle. In fact, experts believe most preterm births result not from a single cause, but from several risk factors interacting throughout pregnancy. Doctors know many reasons for preterm birth (as you'll see from the list on page 33), and can identify many pregnancies at risk. But about half of the expectant mothers who go into preterm labor have no known risks for it. If you've already given birth to a preemie, and you never suspected that it might happen to you, you're certainly not alone.

Perhaps even more frustrating is that in many cases, premature birth cannot be prevented, even when mothers are known to be at risk. Still, even if a premature delivery cannot be avoided, a lot can be done to delay it for at least a few days (and sometimes much longer)—enough time to take some precautions that can greatly reduce the health risks for both you and your baby. For example, you may be admitted to a hospital, where you and your baby can be monitored twenty-four hours a day, or transferred to a facility with more expertise in perinatology and newborn intensive care. If you have an infection, you'll be started on antibiotics, to help prevent your baby from getting it, too. And you may be given steroids to help your baby's organs mature faster before birth.

Sometimes, your doctor may decide to purposely deliver your baby before term, because he is not growing or doing well in the womb, or because it has become too dangerous for your own health to continue the pregnancy. About 20 percent of all preterm births are such so-called "elective," or medically indicated preterm births. The rest occur spontaneously—about 30 percent after a woman's water breaks too early, and about half after preterm labor.

As you read through the information below, remember that only an experienced obstetrician can evaluate your own individual case. It's important for you to develop a good, trusting relationship with your obstetrician, so that you can count on her for support, as well as for state-of-the-art medical care, as you travel the demanding road of a high-risk pregnancy.

Questions and Answers

Bed Rest

My doctor told me to go on bed rest, but I have so many things in my life I need to do. Will bed rest really help prevent an early birth?

Nobody knows for sure. Bed rest is probably the oldest prescription for a high-risk pregnancy. Yet despite its widespread use—one out of every five pregnant women in the United States is put on bed rest—it has not been studied extensively. Although more research is needed before anyone can answer your question for sure, so far, the few studies that have been done have produced no convincing evidence that bed rest helps reduce preterm births.

So, why do almost all obstetricians prescribe it to women with preterm labor, premature rupture of membranes, preeclampsia, bleeding, or other pregnancy problems, and sometimes even as a preventive measure to women who are expecting multiples? Because even without proof, there are situations where bed rest makes sense to doctors, for some solid, scientific reasons.

For example, say your baby isn't growing as well as she should in the womb. Fetuses depend entirely on blood flowing through the placenta for their supply of nutrients and oxygen, and a mother's blood flow to the placenta is greatest when she is lying down. So, it makes sense that your baby will have the best chance of growing better if you spend a few extra hours in bed each day.

Or say your water has broken early. It makes sense that you could maximize the amount of fluid remaining around your baby by spending more time off your feet, since increased blood flow to the baby leads to greater production of amniotic fluid. Also, the fluid is less likely to drip out when you're lying down.

Bed rest also makes sense when gravity may be dangerous for a pregnancy. For example, once a woman's membranes have ruptured, there is a risk that the umbilical cord could slip down through her cervix—an absolute emergency, because the cord could get caught there and squeezed, cutting off blood flow to the baby. Gravity also can be risky when a woman has a weak, or "incompetent," cervix, which could open if the fetus presses down on it too hard.

There is also good evidence that blood pressure is higher in women who are walking around. So, it is assumed that bed rest is helpful to pregnant women with preeclampsia, a condition involving high blood pressure which, when it's severe, can necessitate a premature delivery. Although research hasn't demonstrated so far whether bed rest itself makes the difference, we know there has been a dramatic improvement in the outcomes of pregnancies with preeclampsia. It may well have to do with the increasing use of hospitalization, which allows for both intensive monitoring and more bed rest than most women can get at home.

But if sometimes there is sound reasoning behind the prescription of bed rest, other times there is simply a mixture of observation and wishful thinking. Take preterm labor. Many doctors believe that women who remain active in the third trimester of pregnancy have more Braxton-Hicks contractions—the normal, "false" labor contractions that don't lead to cervical change and delivery, and are of no concern. It's natural for obstetricians to extrapolate from that and assume that bed rest might reduce the risk of real labor, too. Nobody knows whether the initial observation itself, about Braxton-Hicks contractions, or the extension of it to real labor, is valid.

So far, studies on pregnant women haven't found that bed rest decreases preterm labor. (Monitoring contractions with a home monitor—another intervention that seems like it should work—doesn't appear to make a difference, either. Research suggests that home monitors don't improve pregnancy outcomes, although they do increase the number of doctor visits—probably meaning they cause a lot of preterm labor scares.) But well-meaning obstetricians want to do *something* for women with preterm labor, so as long as there is a possibility that bed rest might help, many suggest it.

Some obstetricians also have observed that a prescription of bed rest can bring a helpful focus to a pregnancy. The thinking is that your pregnancy may have the best chance of succeeding if you, your family, and even your doctor focus more attention on your needs, concerns, and symptoms. Some women say this worked for them: that after trying to juggle a lot of things during the early part of their pregnancies, bed rest actually reduced their stress by allowing them to shift their emphasis away from their many other daily obligations.

Undoubtedly, obstetricians also prescribe bed rest partly as a holdover from past medical practice. As recently as a decade ago, nearly every

woman with a pregnancy risk or problem was put immediately to bed, and told to stay there twenty-four hours a day.

Today, however, on top of a lack of proof of bed rest's effectiveness, there's a growing awareness of its potential costs. Total bed rest quickly causes bone and muscle loss (much of which is regained after a woman becomes active again). And for plenty of women it causes more stress, rather than less. In fact, it can be really hard on an entire family, especially when there are older children, or job and financial concerns. So, more and more doctors are recommending reduced activity—lying down for a few hours each morning and a few hours each afternoon—rather than complete bed rest, except in a few situations like an already open cervix, ruptured membranes, or severe preeclampsia.

Thankfully, you'll rarely see the once-common Trendelenburg position, in which a woman lies with her feet raised higher than her head. There's no evidence that it makes a difference, and a general consensus that no one can tolerate that position for long!

While you nestle in bed, try to stay as optimistic as possible (remember that medical treatments often work best when patients believe they will), and take a look at the practical tips below to make that experience more tolerable.

BED REST SURVIVAL TIPS

OK. You've been put on bed rest, and you're feeling understandably miserable. How are you going to make it through the long weeks ahead? These survival tips may help:

❋ *Recognize that you are performing a job, one of the hardest you'll ever do.* If you are an active person with a tendency to ask "What have I gotten done?" each day, it's easy to feel frustrated and inadequate while on bed rest—unless you give yourself credit for a daily achievement: an investment in your child's and family's future. Whenever you feel like you can't take it anymore, or are about to give in to the many temptations to get up, remind yourself of the job you have to do, and focus on your goal!

❋ *Make your physical comfort a priority.* Lying down for long stretches at a time can be very uncomfortable, and aches and pains are going to make your job far more difficult. You may have heard that you should lie on your left side, because blood flow to the placenta will be greatest—but your right side is good for your baby, too. What's most important is simply to avoid lying flat on your back, because blood flow is reduced that way. Rest a pillow under one side of your tummy or back, so you're on a slight tilt. That's fine!

❋ *Do light exercises in bed.* To avoid muscle and bone loss, some obstetricians now arrange for a physical therapist to visit their patients on complete bed rest. If your doctor doesn't mention this, don't hesitate to ask. The therapist can teach you light, isometric exercises you can do while lying down. Or you can try to make up your own, very light exercise regime: point and flex your toes, do head rolls, rotate your hands, tense and relax the muscles of your arms and legs.

❋ *Stay clean and attractive.* It's amazing how this can affect your mood. Many hospitals have arrangements with hairdressers who will come to your room and expertly wash your hair without ever asking you to sit up. If you're at home, ask friends or the staff of your hair salon if they know of a hairdresser who makes house calls. Put on makeup every morning. Some women find that when they're feeling down, it lifts their mood to pamper themselves with manicures, pedicures, or facials.

❋ *Make your environment attractive, too.* It will just take a couple of minutes for a friend or your partner to tape up some family photos or art works by your children. When you're feeling imprisoned, warm touches go a long way!

❋ *Don't expect the household to run as smoothly, or cleanly, as usual.* It's a fact of life: women on bed rest don't have clean houses! If your family eats pizza for the seventh time in a week, you're not alone, either. The best thing is to lower your expectations, recognize that these things aren't a priority right now, and plan to fix them later, when you're up and about.

❋ *Organize your space.* It's terrible to have to ask for every little thing you need. Instead, ask your partner to put a table next to your bed, with the following items within easy reach: a telephone, books and magazines, grooming items, tissues, and disposable cleansing wipes (to wash your hands), the television remote control, paper and pencil, things you need for your hobby, a water pitcher, and a lunch that your partner sets out for you each morning. No matter how much your partner wants to help, it will minimize tension between you if he doesn't have to act as your constant gofer.

❋ *Be understanding that bed rest is hard on your partner and children, too.* Your partner's life is also disrupted. He may be as worried and distressed as you are, and he's probably picking up lots of extra tasks while holding down his usual responsibilities. Try not to be resentful of him for still being able to move around, or for not being able to meet your every need. And give him as much time off as you can. It's important to keep supporting each other.

It's normal for your children to show some reaction, either behaving badly toward others or toward you. It's also normal for you to worry about them, and to think how long this period feels to them. But believe us, they will forget about it soon afterward. In the meantime, encourage them to spend time with you by making your bedside into a play area with their toys, and putting up a little table where they can eat some meals. Try to arrange special time for them with grandparents. Some mothers say it helped a lot for their child to be present when the doctor explained the need for bed rest; hearing it from an outside authority made the child understand better, and even eager to cooperate.

❋ *If you were working, make sure to discuss financial arrangements with your employer.* Find out if you are eligible for disability payments, and whether this time is being counted as part of your maternity leave or sick leave. Remember that the Family and Medical Leave Act requires employers with 50 or more employees to give up to 12 weeks of unpaid leave related to pregnancy problems or childbirth. You are eligible if you have been working for your employer for 12 months, and have worked at least 1,250 hours during the last year.

❋ *Get some easy things done from bed.* You haven't bought furniture or linens for the nursery yet? There are childcare books you wanted to read and don't have? Shop by catalog or computer. Or give your mother-in-law a list of all of the layette items you need—she'll probably be thrilled to help, and it's like having a personal shopper!

❋ *Don't be surprised if you get depressed, or have ups and downs.* Many women say that some days their spirits are up, and then suddenly they find themselves in tears. Irritability, lots of anxiety, anger, and inability to concentrate are all normal reactions. You can expect a few naïve comments from friends, like "I'd love to be on bed rest and catch up on my reading." But most people who have been on bed rest themselves will tell you that it's hard. When you think what you're doing it for, though, it's worth it.

High Blood Pressure and Preeclampsia

I've always eaten right and exercised. But now, in my pregnancy, I suddenly have high blood pressure. I'm stunned.

Because high blood pressure is often associated with an "unhealthy" lifestyle, it can be a real shock for a health-conscious pregnant woman to find out that she has it. But there is a kind of high blood pressure that occurs only during pregnancy, and can strike out of the blue. When it is accompanied by other signs and symptoms, like protein in the urine and fluid retention (which shows up as very rapid weight gain, or a puffy face and hands—not the normal leg swelling that many pregnant women have), doctors call it preeclampsia. Luckily, the prognosis is usually very good. Upward of 90% of all women who develop high blood pressure during pregnancy will deliver a healthy baby at term. And because preeclampsia always goes away after delivery, the vast majority of mothers are back to their previous state of health within a few days of their baby's birth.

Despite the fact that most people haven't heard of it, preeclampsia is actually quite common, affecting nearly 10% of pregnant women. Some women are more at risk for it: those who are pregnant with multiples, are overweight, already have high blood pressure, or have kidney disease or diabetes. Preeclampsia also runs in families, so if your mother or sister had it, the likelihood that you'll get it is increased. But an enormous 70% of women with preeclampsia don't have any risk factor for it at all.

Most of the time, preeclampsia is an easy diagnosis for your obstetrician to make. He'll measure your blood pressure, check your weight, and possibly do some simple urine and blood tests. But sometimes, it isn't clear whether preeclampsia or some other medical condition is causing the problem. It is important for your doctor to figure that out, because the cure for preeclampsia is delivery. If you have a severe case of it, a time may come when it's best to deliver your baby prematurely.

The reason preeclampsia is dangerous is that it causes changes in the body that are the opposite of what should happen during pregnancy. Normally during pregnancy, the amount of circulating blood in a woman's body increases, to provide for both her and her fetus, and her blood vessels open wider to accommodate it. But in preeclampsia, a mother's blood vessels tighten, and not as much blood can flow through them. Her blood pressure rises, and all of her organs, including her uterus, receive less blood.

When preeclampsia is mild, the amount of blood flow is slightly decreased but still adequate. But when preeclampsia is severe, a mother's vital organs may not get enough blood, and serious complications can result. Your doctor will watch you closely for kidney, liver, or intestinal problems (be sure to tell him if you have pain in your belly), and symptoms like blurry vision and headaches, which could indicate that your eyes or brain are suffering. In a very small minority of women with preeclampsia (only about 5%), the symptoms progress to seizures (called eclampsia) or dangerous abnormalities of blood clotting with liver damage (called HELLP syndrome, for *hemolysis*—destruction of red blood cells—*elevated liver* enzymes, *low platelets*). Women with these most severe forms of preeclampsia occasionally have strokes, or even die—that's why your obstetrician takes it so seriously.

For a fetus, the main consequence of preeclampsia is receiving less blood flow through the placenta and, therefore, getting less oxygen and nutrients. For that reason, babies of mothers with preeclampsia are often small for their gestational age. (See page 70 for what that can mean for a child.) If the restriction of blood flow becomes extreme, or if the placenta separates from the wall of the uterus (a complication called placental abruption, which is more common in pregnant women with high blood pressure), there's a risk of fetal death. But thanks to alert doctors and good fetal monitoring, this is an uncommon tragedy today.

The earlier that preeclampsia occurs during pregnancy, and the more severe its symptoms, the more it can affect a mother's and fetus's well-being. Most women with mild preeclampsia continue their pregnancies until term, but women with severe preeclampsia usually deliver within a couple of weeks of being hospitalized for it. Some, however, are luckier, and are able to continue their pregnancies for much longer. Your doctor will tell you what you should expect in your own particular case.

The simplest and most commonly prescribed treatment for preeclampsia is rest, which can lower an expectant mother's blood pressure, and help her baby to get more blood flow. Your doctor may recommend bed rest at home, or admit you to the hospital. You may also get medications to lower your blood pressure, and to prevent seizures. The usual drug to prevent seizures is magnesium sulfate, which is generally safe for both mother and fetus, although it can have bothersome side effects (like making some mothers feel sick, and sometimes, temporarily depressing a newborn baby's breathing. Don't worry about that, though—if necessary, a ventilator can help your baby breathe until the magnesium wears off).

If it looks like your pregnancy is becoming too risky to continue, your obstetrician will decide to deliver your baby prematurely. In fact, preeclampsia is the most common cause of elective preterm deliveries, done most often to protect the mother's health. When you hear that, you may think, "I don't care about myself, if it would help my baby to stay longer in my womb." It's heroic to be willing to take such risks for your child. But your family, including your baby, needs you. And when preeclampsia gets so severe in a mother, her fetus usually begins to suffer severely too, and is in real danger of dying soon in the womb.

Women who have had early, severe preeclampsia in a previous pregnancy have about a 40% chance of getting severe preeclampsia again. Unfortunately, efforts to prevent preeclampsia by using medications such as aspirin or calcium, on which researchers once pinned their hopes, have not been very successful. Although these drugs have not proved helpful when prescribed to a wide range of pregnant women, your obstetrician may still use them. They are safe, and there is some evidence to suggest that they may possibly be of benefit to women who are at the highest risk.

Predicting the Birth Date

My doctor says I'm at risk for having a premature baby. Is there any way of telling how long my pregnancy will last?

If pregnancy researchers had a Holy Grail, it would be the ability to predict whether an expectant mother would deliver her baby early, and if so, when. That crucial information would allow doctors to intervene early, when therapies are most effective, and only treat women who really need them. Tests of fetal well-being (see page 23) can help determine how long a pregnancy might last when there's a known medical complication. But those screenings can't predict whether preterm labor, or preterm rupture of the membranes, might cut short a pregnancy that is otherwise proceeding well.

Most methods adopted so far to help forecast the likelihood of a preterm birth—such as adding up and scoring a mother's risk factors, or closely monitoring the opening of her cervix or her uterine contractions—have had disappointing results. In recent years, though, researchers have been looking at a whole new set of tests that seem to be more useful and effective.

Many obstetricians have started using ultrasound, in addition to their traditional exam, of the cervix. Doctors traditionally examine a pregnant woman's cervix with their fingertips, to see if it is starting to open (or "dilate"). But this technique evaluates only the outer part of the cervix. Ultrasound can be used to look at the inner part of the cervix, where the earliest sign of dilation—a shortening of its length—can be detected.

An early answer as to whether the cervix is opening can provide a doctor with useful information. For example, if your cervix is shorter than it should be, your doctor may decide to give you a cerclage (a simple surgical procedure in which your cervix is sewn shut) to try to keep it from opening further. On the other hand, if you're having contractions, but your cervix looks normal on ultrasound, your doctor may decide that you're not in true labor, and instead of prescribing medication to stop contractions, may simply observe you for a while. Ultrasound measurement of cervical length is a quick and painless test that can be done at the same time as a routine vaginal exam.

One of the most exciting new tests for prematurity measures a pregnant woman's saliva for the presence of the hormone estriol: a kind of estrogen that has an important role in preparing the uterus for labor and delivery. One version, called SalEst (Sal for saliva, Est for estriol), has already been approved by the Food and Drug Administration. In the studies done so far, this test was used weekly to measure levels of salivary estriol in pregnant women at risk for premature birth. When a steep surge was detected, it indicated that labor was likely to occur in two to three weeks. When salivary estriol was low, labor in the following three weeks almost certainly would not occur.

Unfortunately, what seems like the perfect predictive test for prematurity has some limitations. One of them is that SalEst is more accurate in predicting when premature labor won't occur than when it will. This means that if your salivary estriol level is low, you almost certainly won't deliver soon—valuable information that may save some women from being treated with bed rest or anti-labor drugs unnecessarily. But if your salivary estriol level is high, although you have an increased chance of delivering in the next several weeks, your pregnancy could well go on for much longer. Also, to date, SalEst has been approved only for singleton pregnancies, because hormone levels in multiple pregnancies follow different, more complex patterns. Moreover, some medications that may be given in a high-risk pregnancy (such as steroids) can affect a woman's estriol levels and limit the validity of the test.

Another marker for a possible early delivery is a protein called fetal fibronectin. Fibronectin helps to keep the placenta and the membranes well attached to the uterine lining. If free levels of this protein inside the uterus rise, it may indicate that the placenta and the membranes are getting loose. Many obstetricians now use fetal fibronectin testing to help predict a preterm delivery. If on a simple swab of the vagina or cervix, the level of fibronectin is low, it's very unlikely that you'll deliver within the next two weeks.

Other tests look for inflammatory substances in a pregnant woman's body to signal that a premature birth may be approaching. That's because some of the substances the body naturally produces to help combat infection or repair damaged tissues can also cause uterine contractions, loosening of the cervix, and weakening of the membranes, making them more prone to rupture. (Up to 25% of women who deliver prematurely have low-grade vaginal infections, and any damage to the placenta or umbilical cord, even if minor, can lead to inflammation.) One sign of infection or inflammation in the uterus is a protein called interleukin 6: if it is found in high levels in a mother's blood and in her amniotic fluid (which would require an amniocentesis to detect), it indicates that she may have a uterine infection, which could lead to preterm labor and delivery. But more studies are needed before doctors know exactly how to use "IL-6" as a routine test.

Your obstetrician will decide what tests to use to monitor your pregnancy, and when. None of the new tests is a panacea, and experts warn that they are more effective in predicting which women won't deliver prematurely than they are at picking out all of the women who will. But awareness of new risk factors and more effective ways to detect them, combined with more traditional tools, such as your obstetrician's knowledge of your medical history, physical examinations, and tests of your baby's well-being, can give your doctor a better perspective into your future.

Diagnosing and Treating Preterm Labor

I've been feeling some tightening in my stomach. Should my doctor treat me for preterm labor?

There's always a mixture of science and art in the practice of medicine, but when it comes to treating preterm labor, the balance tilts solidly to art. Your obstetrician has to make a judgment call as to whether you are having "true" labor or "false" labor. Some women just have unusually active uteruses, well before real labor starts. It's not always easy to tell whether your contractions are the real McCoy—ones that will lead to cervical change and birth—or just harmless ones whose only consequence is to give you and your doctor a dose of anxiety. That means that if you're having contractions, but your cervix hasn't begun to change yet, you may not need anti-labor drugs at all. On the other hand, you may be in the very early stages of real labor, when treatment has the very best chance of succeeding.

If real preterm labor is suspected, a mother is generally sent to the hospital, the safest place to be in case she is about to deliver. There, her contractions are monitored, along with her baby's heartbeat, to make sure the baby is not sick or in distress. She is put on bed rest and given intravenous fluids while her doctor tries to determine whether there's a treatable problem, like dehydration or infection, that is causing the contractions. About half the time, if preterm labor is not accompanied by bleeding or ruptured membranes (if your water hasn't broken yet), fluids and bed rest alone are enough to stop it.

If bed rest and fluids are not enough, and you and baby are doing well otherwise, the doctor will probably prescribe anti-labor drugs (which in medical parlance are called tocolytics) to re-lax your uterus and halt the contractions. Most of the time, these drugs put a quick stop to preterm labor in women who don't have bleeding, infection, or whose labor isn't already far along (whose water hasn't broken, and whose cervix is open less than four centimeters).

Whether or not labor will return (even if you continue taking medications), and what will happen during the rest of your pregnancy, is unpredictable. Having an episode of preterm labor doesn't necessarily mean you'll end up having a premature birth. Very often, the labor passes, the medication is stopped, and your uterus is quiet and calm again. Sometimes, the doctors never know why the preterm labor came and went—whether it was an infection that flared up fleetingly, dehydration, or some other cause.

In other cases, preterm labor returns in a few days or at some later point in the pregnancy, and can result in a premature birth. If your preterm labor recurs while you are being weaned off the anti-labor medication, the first thing your doctor will do is reassess whether it is safe for you and your baby for the pregnancy to continue. If he thinks it is, he will restart anti-labor drugs, possibly switching you to one that can be taken orally, or that may have fewer side effects.

If this happens, you may be confused. Why do these medications seem to be working for you, when the studies say they only prolong pregnancy for a couple of days? That's a hard question for anyone to answer. It's possible that the drugs are making much less difference than it seems: that your contractions, scary as they are, are not the kind that would cause imminent delivery anyway, so your pregnancy would last just as long without the medication. It's also possible, since drugs can be more or less effective for different people, that they are helping your pregnancy more than average.

The two most commonly prescribed drugs to

inhibit labor are magnesium sulfate and terbutaline. Of the two, magnesium is thought to have fewer serious side effects. But it must be given intravenously, so it is rarely used long-term. Many, although by no means all, women feel horrendous while they're on it, with symptoms like nausea, hot flashes, headaches, palpitations, paranoia, muscle weakness, and visual disturbances, among others. When a woman remains on magnesium for more than a few days, the symptoms sometimes ease up or go away. Your doctors will keep a close eye out for potentially dangerous complications such as pulmonary edema (a buildup of fluid in the lungs) or abnormal heart rhythms. With careful monitoring, these occur rarely.

Are You in Preterm Labor?

Just because you are having contractions before term, it doesn't necessarily mean that you are in preterm labor. Contractions throughout pregnancy are normal and expected, and are considered "false" labor unless they occur frequently (usually defined as more than once every ten minutes). Generally, real labor is accompanied by the thinning and opening of your cervix.

What signs should you look for, to know if you are in preterm labor? As you read this list, keep in mind that many of these signs are present in perfectly normal pregnancies. You should call your doctor if their appearance represents a change for you:

❋ *Uterine contractions, painful or not, that occur more than four times an hour.* You may feel these as a tightening sensation in your belly. If you place your fingertips over your uterus when one is happening, it will feel firm. (If you think you are feeling some contractions, but they aren't that frequent yet, you can try drinking two or three large glasses of water and lying down for half an hour. Often, the contractions will gradually decrease in frequency.)
❋ *A dull ache or sharp pain in your lower back.*
❋ *Menstrual-like cramps.*
❋ *Upset stomach–like cramps, possibly with gas pains or diarrhea.*
❋ *Pressure in your pelvis.*
❋ *An increased or changed vaginal discharge.* (A blood-tinged discharge could mean the loss of the mucus plug that's like a stopper for the uterus. A greater than usual, clear leakage of fluid could be your water breaking.)

If you think you have any of these symptoms, or have any doubt, do not hesitate to call your doctor. Don't worry about being a pest. First of all, the people who worry about being pests rarely are. Also, you have obligations: to your doctor, who can't be with you all the time and counts on you to call with your concerns, and to your baby, whose well-being is at stake and who counts on you to represent him!

Terbutaline can be administered by injections, pills, or a tiny pump that is implanted under the pregnant woman's skin. It's common for women to start with shots, and then, if they'll be staying on terbutaline long-term, to be switched to pills or the pump, both of which can be used at home. Some women tolerate terbutaline very well. But in others, terbutaline is associated with some of the same, unpleasant side effects as magnesium sulfate. The most common symptoms are palpitations, nausea, headaches, jitteriness, fever, and hallucinations. Doctors must also watch out for dangerous complications, including pulmonary edema, abnormal heart rhythms, and high blood sugar. Since serious complications occur more frequently from terbutaline than from magnesium, terbutaline is generally not prescribed to women with high blood pressure, heart disease, diabetes, or hyperthyroidism, who are at particular risk.

After two or three weeks on terbutaline pills, a woman's uterus can become less sensitive to them, and contractions can start up again. A break of a few days (during which you may take a different anti-labor drug) is needed before terbutaline can be effective again.

Obstetricians have other anti-labor medications they can use, such as indomethacin, nifedipine, or atosiban. All work somewhat differently, but have the same effect of relaxing the muscles of the uterus. Because their advantages and disadvantages are less well known than magnesium's and terbutaline's, you should ask your doctor for the latest information available.

Drugs for Preterm Labor

I've been put on a drug to stop preterm labor, but I can't stand the awful way it makes me feel. Will it really make a difference?

No matter how stiff an upper lip you usually keep, the side effects from anti-labor medication can be hard to endure. Many women are lucky enough to be spared them, but others experience nausea, jitteriness, and other unpleasant symptoms that make them wonder whether the medication is really worth it.

For most women, anti-labor drugs make little difference in whether they deliver prematurely or not. Most studies suggest that the medications delay delivery for only two days, on average. But even a couple of days can be long enough to allow an expectant mother to get a course of prenatal steroids (see page 26), which can boost her preemie's maturity and give him the best chance of doing well. That alone can be a real benefit.

Because of their side effects, and the inconvenience and questionable value of staying on anti-labor medications for long periods of time, some obstetricians won't prescribe these drugs to pregnant women for more than a week or so. But others, who believe that they may be beneficial in some circumstances for certain women—especially those whose labor starts up again when the drugs are discontinued—may prescribe them for longer.

If the medication you're taking is making you feel terrible, you should certainly talk to your doctor about whether you need to stay on it. He may have good reasons to believe that in your case, the drug is more effective than average, and that its benefits outweigh its risks. He may be able to prescribe another medication that will work for you, which won't bother you so much. Or he may reconsider, and agree that given your discomfort, it makes more sense to wean you off the medication now.

Cerclage

My doctor is recommending a cerclage. What is it, and what will it do?

A cerclage is a minor surgical procedure, usually done in the hospital by an obstetrician, in which the cervix—the opening at the base of your uterus through which your baby emerges—is temporarily sewn shut. Obstetricians recommend a cerclage when they conclude that a woman has a weak (or, in medical language, "incompetent") cervix. (What a word! Whoever thought your cervix would get a performance rating?) This means that instead of staying tightly closed until labor begins, the cervix tends to open at an earlier stage of pregnancy. Once the cervix has opened, the membranes of the amniotic sac can bulge out into the vagina, where they can become infected or rupture, leading to a miscarriage or a preterm birth. If you have an incompetent cervix, a cerclage could help prolong your pregnancy to a point when your baby, even if born before term, has a good chance of being fine.

Most of the time, a cerclage is a short and safe procedure, and a woman is in and out within a few hours. First you'll be given local anesthesia or light sedation. Then, your obstetrician will reach through your vagina, and sew four or five stitches around your cervix in a circle (in French, *cercle*), pulling them tight and knotting them to seal your cervix shut. The stitches are generally removed in your doctor's office when a preterm birth is no longer feared (at about 37 weeks of gestation). If you go into labor or develop an infection, however, the cerclage will be taken out earlier, in the hospital.

After a cerclage, most women are told to reduce their activity, or to remain in bed. You'll be advised not to have sexual intercourse, so as

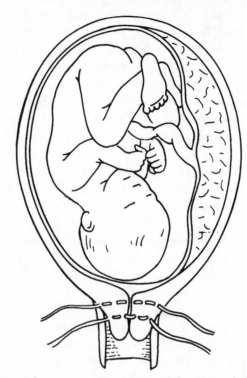

In a cerclage, sutures are sewn around the cervix to hold it closed.

to avoid stimulating the cervix and to reduce the risk of infection (which is higher than normal with a cerclage in place). Periodically, your obstetrician will examine you, to look for changes in your cervix and for any signs of infection.

You may be wondering why your cervix may be "incompetent." The most common cause is an injury from a previous obstetric or gynecological procedure. For example, if you've had any surgery on your cervix it could have caused incompetence, as could a second trimester abortion. First trimester abortions done before 1973, with dilation techniques that have since been discontinued, also could damage the cervix. If your cervix tore during a previous, difficult vaginal delivery, you may have been left with some cervical incompetence. Some women may have an incompetent cervix because they were exposed, in their own mothers' wombs, to DES, a medication given to pregnant women in the 1950s and '60s to avoid miscarriage, which sometimes caused malformations in the reproductive organs of their fetuses. Often, however, the reasons for an incompetent cervix are unknown.

Obstetricians don't have reliable statistics on how likely a cerclage is to help you, because the research isn't definitive. The good news is that nowadays, 80% to 90% of women with classic signs of cervical incompetence who get a cerclage deliver a baby who survives, compared to only 13% to 38% of similar women who were pregnant in the past, before cerclages were done.

If a cerclage is put in early (before 18 weeks), it rarely causes any problems. Occasionally, after a cerclage is removed, there is some scar tissue left in the cervix that prevents it from opening fully during labor, causing the cervix to tear during delivery, or requiring a C-section. And if you go into labor and your cervix opens before your cerclage is taken out, the stitches could tear your cervix. But these are complications that your obstetrician can usually manage well. What probably matters most to you now is to bring your baby closer to term. A cerclage may help you reach that crucial goal.

Diagnosing an Incompetent Cervix

My last baby was born way too early. Now I'm pregnant again and my doctor thinks a cerclage will help. Why didn't they do that the last time?

In most cases, doctors can't diagnose cervical incompetence in advance. Most women have your experience: they are found to have a weak cervix only after it has already opened too early. To help diagnose an incompetent cervix ahead of time, some obstetricians are now using ultrasound to detect changes (shortening and thinning) which occur in the inner part of the cervix shortly before it begins to open. But ultrasound testing, like most medical tests, is not 100% reliable. The diagnosis of cervical incompetence is further complicated by the fact that small amounts of cervical dilation don't necessarily lead to preterm birth, so it's not always clear if it's worth the risk of doing a cerclage. Possible, if rare, complications of a cerclage are injury to the cervix, scar tissue left in the cervix, infection, and premature rupture of the membranes.

Even with hindsight, cervical incompetence can be difficult to determine. Doctors generally suspect an incompetent cervix if your cervix opened painlessly, without any preceding signs of preterm labor or infection. But sometimes, an infection of the exposed membranes, with preterm labor, is the first noticeable sign that a woman's cervix has been open. And a pregnant woman can have uterine contractions or an infection without being aware of them—both of which can cause even a perfectly "competent" cervix to loosen and open up. Furthermore, many women who are diagnosed with cervical incompetence in one pregnancy won't have it again in another pregnancy. As a result, even with the best medical care, cerclages are given to some women who don't really need them, and are not given to all women who do.

Unfortunately, both a woman and her doctor may not know that her cervix is beginning to open. By the time they're aware of it, it's often too late to perform a cerclage. A cerclage is safe and effective only if you don't already have an infection or ruptured membranes (because the procedure could carry bacteria into your uterus, and make an infection more difficult to treat), if your cervix is not already dilated too much (there would be a high risk of damaging the exposed membranes of the amniotic sac, and infecting or rupturing them), and if you're not in labor (in which case it would be too risky, and not helpful anymore). The best time to do it is by 18 or 20 weeks of gestation, and before your cervix has opened. Most obstetricians, no matter what, would not perform a cerclage after 26 weeks of gestation, when the risks that the procedure itself could cause a preterm birth become very high.

So, there could be many possible reasons why you didn't get a cerclage in your last pregnancy. You can ask your doctor what factors were important in your particular case.

Hidden Infections and Preterm Birth

Do I really need to take medicine for an infection that doesn't bother me? If it isn't causing me any problems, how dangerous to my pregnancy could it be?

There's an increasing awareness that screening for and treating low-grade, often asymptomatic, infections in pregnant women may significantly reduce their risk of a preterm birth. It has long been known that some infections during pregnancy can cause a premature delivery, as well as congenital problems in the fetus. Substances that a mother's immune system produces as a reaction to infection can trigger changes in the uterus, cervix, and amniotic membranes that can lead to preterm labor. But obvious infections don't occur very often—certainly not frequently enough to explain why the membranes of the amniotic sac are found to be infected at delivery in up to one-half of all preterm births, and up to 80% of births before 30 weeks of gestation.

Of course, simply finding an infection at the time of delivery doesn't tell you whether it came before, and maybe caused, preterm labor, or whether it came afterward. (During labor, when the cervix opens and the membranes of the amniotic sac rupture, some natural barriers to infection are removed.) But an abundance of new data indicates that hidden infections in expectant mothers' genital and urinary tracts may play a much bigger role than was ever thought in causing preterm births.

In an effort to figure out how important hidden infections were in causing preterm births, one of medical researchers' first targets was urinary tract infections. Bacteria in the urine are more common during pregnancy, and are often present without the symptoms of burning, itching, or fever that make an infection apparent. Many studies have now shown that the risk of delivering prematurely is much lower if pregnant women with asymptomatic urinary tract infections are treated with antibiotics.

More recently, researchers pointed their finger at a hidden infection called bacterial vaginosis, or "BV." BV is caused by an overgrowth of common bacteria that normally live in the vagina. According to some new findings, BV may double some women's risk of delivering prematurely. It is silently present in about 10% of Caucasian women and about 25% of African-American women. It is not a sexually transmitted disease, although women who become sexually active at an early age are more prone to it, as are those who douche (douching can destroy the useful bacteria of the vagina, which help to keep other bacteria under control).

Luckily, BV is easy to diagnose (your doctor painlessly swabs your vagina with something like a Q-tip), and it can be treated effectively with oral antibiotics. Several studies have shown that treating BV in women at high risk (mainly those who had a previous, unexplained preterm birth) can lower their risk for another preterm delivery by up to 70%. But in women who haven't had an unexplained preterm birth, it's not clear that having BV is harmful, or that treating it will help. There's even a small chance that treating it could hurt—any time you take antibiotics, there's a small risk of an allergic reaction, or of developing an overgrowth of other bacteria that may be hard to treat. You can talk to your obstetrician about the pros and cons in your particular case.

Another hidden infection that is emerging as a possible cause of prematurity is gum disease. So don't be surprised if your dentist—and your obstetrician—tell you to floss to prevent prematurity, as well as cavities! If you've been diagnosed with gum disease, it is probably wise to get it treated by a dentist as soon as possible.

There are several other infections that can cause serious illness in a fetus, and occasionally lead to preterm birth, but which are sometimes so mild that a mother doesn't realize she has them. It will be your doctor's responsibility to decide if you need to be treated for any of these. Most obstetricians screen for sexually transmitted diseases like syphilis, gonorrhea, and chlamydia, and for viruses like hepatitis B, HIV, and rubella. Depending on your situation and exposures, your doctor may also add tests for other infections.

For most of these infections, prevention is the key: you'll be advised by your doctor to practice safe sex, not to eat raw or undercooked meat, fish, or shellfish, and not to touch dirty kitty litter (a great excuse to let your partner do that job!). You should try to stay away from anyone who's sick with something contagious. If you have Lyme disease in your area, try to follow even more carefully the precautions you already know: from late spring to early fall, whenever the temperature exceeds 40 degrees (when deer ticks are active), if you have to go near bushes or in the woods, wear light-colored clothes with a tight weave (to better spot ticks), socks over long pants, and long sleeves; keep long hair pulled back; spray tick repellent on your clothes (ask your obstetrician which product is safe for pregnant women); keep pets outside your house, or at least far from you, in a rug-free area that can be easily cleaned; and carefully check yourself for ticks every night. (If a tick is removed before it attaches to your skin, you will not become infected. If a tick is removed within 36 hours after it attaches to your skin, you have only a small chance of contracting Lyme disease: ask your doctor what to do next.)

Before your next pregnancy, if you haven't had rubella, mumps or chicken pox, you should get vaccinated for them. (These vaccines usually aren't given to women who are already pregnant, for fear they could harm the fetus.) You may have also heard about new vaccines for Lyme disease that are under investigation. It will be great news if these products are found to be safe and effective, but at this point it's too early to recommend them to a woman who is planning to get pregnant. Talk to your doctor about any recent developments, though.

If you had a preterm birth in the past, it may be tempting, but painful and probably useless, to go back and torture yourself about a hidden, undiscovered infection that may have been to blame for what happened. Even if you or your baby had signs of infection after delivery, there's no way to tell, in retrospect, if it was a cause or a consequence of your preterm labor. It is also impossible to know what would have happened if you had been diagnosed with an infection and treated with antibiotics during your pregnancy—

everything, or nothing, might have changed. Right now, if you can, try to focus on the present and future, putting your knowledge to good use, with the help of a trusted, expert obstetrician.

If Your Water Breaks

My water broke. Have we lost the battle?

Not necessarily. It's true that you may have to be in the hospital for a while, and it's likely that you'll deliver prematurely. But pregnancies often go on for some time after premature rupture of membranes (the medical term for water breaking), and it's quite possible that your baby will gain some additional, very valuable time in the womb.

It's understandable that you would feel scared at this point. There's something about the rush of fluid out of the womb that creates a feeling of great helplessness: there's nothing you can do to stop it while it happens, and nothing you can do to put it back. All you can do is wait and hope. One thing you should not do is blame yourself, or your partner, for what happened. We've known mothers who believed they brought it on by getting up from bed rest, and fathers who thought they were to blame for not carrying that last bag of groceries. In fact, nothing so simple has been found to be the cause of premature rupture of membranes.

Researchers don't have a full understanding of why some women's water breaks early, but most believe it's the culmination of a long-term process in which many medical factors combine. Women who smoke cigarettes are at increased risk, along with women who have had bleeding during the pregnancy, and those whose water broke before they went into labor in a previous pregnancy (at term or before). Uterine contractions, too much amniotic fluid, stress from the baby's growth, or the presence of more than one baby can all cause the membranes to weaken. Certain nutritional deficiencies may play a role. Experts suspect that infections (some without any symptoms) are often a key part of the story, with bacteria from a mother's genital tract climbing up through the cervix and irritating the membranes. Although it has been suspected that sexual intercourse might contribute to early rupture of membranes, studies have produced no clear evidence of that.

The first thing your doctor will want to do is to test the fluid that leaked out, to confirm that it was indeed amniotic fluid, rather than urine or vaginal secretions. Usually, when membranes rupture, there's a large gush of fluid, followed by a continuing trickle. In a few cases, though, women have some less dramatic dripping that goes on for a while. Once the doctor establishes that your water did break, he'll decide whether to deliver your baby right away or to wait.

Why shouldn't every pregnancy go on as long as possible? Because after membranes rupture, there are some real risks:

❋ *Infection.* The membranes that surround your baby act as a barrier to the bacteria that normally live in the vagina. When the membranes are broken, the bacteria can swim up into the uterus, infecting the mother, and possibly infecting the baby as well. A mother's infection can almost always be effectively treated, but for a fetus or newborn, an infection can be life-threatening, or cause long-term health and developmental problems. A premature baby who is born a little younger, but not infected, is often better off than an older preemie who is infected.

Fortunately, less than 20% of fetuses become infected after premature rupture of membranes, and usually not until after their mothers have symptoms themselves, like fever or abdominal pain. So your obstetrician may not feel that it's necessary to deliver your baby unless you or your baby shows signs of infection.

✳ *Inadequate growth of a fetus's lungs.* Called pulmonary hypoplasia, its causes aren't fully known, but it is thought to occur because without much amniotic fluid, the uterus presses tightly against the fetus and prevents the lungs from expanding well. Lung expansion is one of the signals that prompts a fetus's lungs to grow and develop. (It's one reason fetuses, in the womb, practice breathing movements). There may also be growth hormones in amniotic fluid that are no longer getting into the fetus's lungs. No matter how old a baby is at birth, if her lungs are too small, it will be difficult, or impossible, for her to breathe.

The risk that a baby's lungs won't grow large enough for her to survive outside the womb is greatest when a mother's water breaks early in the second trimester of pregnancy. The longer a baby is in the womb without much amniotic fluid, the greater the risk. The outlook is far better for a baby whose mother's water breaks after 26 weeks.

✳ *A greater risk that the umbilical cord could slip into a dangerous position.* This could cut off some oxygen and blood flow to the fetus.

✳ *A baby's movements can be constrained.* With little amniotic fluid to expand it, the uterus may press tightly against a fetus, constraining her movements. Lack of movement could cause her joints to become stiff and contracted, so that she can't bend or straighten some of them fully. Over time, these contractures may resolve, sometimes with the help of orthopedics or physical therapy.

You can see that these risks have to be balanced against the risks of your baby's prematurity, to come up with the right timing for delivery. In some situations, the decision is easy: as soon as there are obvious signs of infection or fetal distress, your baby will be delivered immediately. Before 32 to 34 weeks of gestation, in the absence of infection or fetal distress, most obstetricians believe that the risks of prematurity outweigh the risks of continuing the pregnancy. Most believe that the reverse is true once a baby reaches 34 weeks, when most preemies are practically as mature, if a bit smaller, than full-termers.

So how long can you expect your pregnancy to last? There's nothing more frustrating for parents to hear, but it is impossible to predict what nature will do in any, individual case. Occasionally, you're lucky, and the best possible outcome occurs: your membranes reseal within a few days, and amniotic fluid builds up again around your baby. No one knows why this sometimes happens, but when it does, the pregnancy can go on with nearly the same risks and benefits as if the membranes had never ruptured in the first place. Sometimes, the membranes partially reseal, leaving the door still open to infection, but providing the important advantage of an adequate amount of amniotic fluid around the fetus.

A majority of women give birth within a few days after their water breaks. But if labor doesn't occur within a few days, your pregnancy has a good chance of lasting considerably longer. Typically, pregnancies tend to last longer the earlier that membranes rupture. Some recent statistics from a small but heartening study reveal that women whose water broke between 14 and 19 weeks of gestation lasted a median of 72 days until delivery, while those between 20 and 25 weeks of gestation

If Your Water Breaks before Your Baby Has Reached Viability

Sometimes, a woman's water breaks very early, before the baby would be ready to survive if she were born. If this happens to you before, say, 23 weeks of gestation, your doctor may present you with an excruciating decision. He may ask whether you want to try to go on with the pregnancy, or think it would be better to go through with delivery immediately. Choosing delivery now means that you know your baby will not survive. Choosing to go on means that you are willing to accept the risks that your baby may not thrive in the environment she's in, even if the pregnancy lasts much longer. Many babies who are born after extremely early rupture of membranes have poor outcomes, dying shortly after delivery, or suffering from short-term or long-term health problems, or even lasting disabilities.

Don't hesitate to ask your doctor for his recommendation, and for all of the information you need, such as: what gestational age range your baby is likely to reach by the time she is born, what the outcomes are like for babies in her situation (how great her chances of survival and living a healthy and normal life will be), and how much intensive medical care she is likely to need. When you read about general outcome statistics for babies born at various gestational ages on page 49, keep in mind that your baby is facing additional hurdles, such as lung hypoplasia (see page 20), which can make her situation worse.

After weighing the facts, along with their deep feelings and beliefs, some parents conclude that the decision to deliver now, although incredibly painful, is the right one for them and their baby, given the risks ahead. Others want to try for more time. Either choice can be the right one for you and your family.

---

lasted a median of 12 days, and those between 26 and 28 weeks of gestation lasted a median of 10 days. Most women whose membranes rupture between 28 and 34 weeks of gestation, who were outside the scope of this study, give birth within a week.

Between now and delivery, you will most likely be kept in the hospital, where you and your baby can be monitored carefully, and taken care of if delivery occurs very quickly after labor starts. You will probably be kept on bed rest, partly to cut down on the amount of amniotic fluid that leaks out. Don't be alarmed, though, no matter what position you're in, if there is some continued leakage. Unless your membranes reseal, it's normal and unavoidable. Bed rest can also improve blood flow to the baby, which may help produce more amniotic fluid, and can lower the chance of the umbilical cord's falling into a dangerous position through the cervix. A few doctors occasionally use a technique called amnioinfusion (infusing fluid into the womb with a catheter), particularly to help a fetus tolerate labor, but the fluid tends to leak out so quickly that it doesn't seem to help with lung growth.

You will probably be given antibiotics to treat any infections you may have, and to prevent them in your baby. Antibiotics given after preterm rupture of membranes have been found to lengthen pregnancies and to give preemies a health advantage after birth. You may be given steroids (see page 26) to speed up your baby's maturation. You probably will not get anti-labor medications, which have not been proven to lengthen pregnancies after a woman's water breaks, and may mask signs of infection. You will need to abstain from sexual intercourse, which could introduce infection or bring on preterm labor.

To monitor for infection and fetal distress, your temperature and your baby's heartbeat will be checked several times a day. Your doctor may suggest an amniocentesis (taking a tiny bit of amniotic fluid out with a needle), if there's enough fluid left to do it safely. The fluid can be checked for infection, and can show how mature your baby's lungs are. You will probably get an ultrasound every few days, to observe your baby's breathing, heartbeat, and body movements, as well as to measure the amount of amniotic fluid.

One thing of which you can be sure: this period, when you have so little ability to predict or control the future, is going to be difficult for you and your partner. Taking one day at a time is the best strategy. Remember, every day you gain is valuable.

When Baby Needs to Be Delivered Early

My doctor says my baby isn't doing well in the womb, and he may decide to deliver him early. How does he know when the right time has come?

Few things are harder for an expectant mother than hearing that your baby would be better off being born prematurely than spending more time in your womb. Along with worrying about your baby's health and your own, you may feel inadequate, or betrayed by your own body. At a time when you should have been cheered by the tumbling presence of your baby inside you, instead you're undergoing checkups and tests—observing him with trepidation and alarm.

It may help you to know that you're far from alone in this difficult experience. Elective, preterm deliveries—done early for medical reasons—bring nearly one-quarter of all preemies into the world. The most common reason for an elective preterm delivery is preeclampsia (see page 8), which usually is done primarily to protect the health of the mother. But preeclampsia, and many other maternal medical conditions, also can adversely affect the health of a fetus. Sometimes, even when a mother is well, her uterus may not be the best environment for her baby.

These are the major reasons that an obstetrician might decide that the time has come—sooner than expected—when your baby would do better outside the womb:

* *His growth has become very poor.* If a baby isn't growing well in the womb, he may not be getting enough nutrients and oxygen, which can affect his long-term development. If your baby's growth is already slow, and it slows down even further or stops altogether, most obstetricians would decide that it's time to deliver him.
* *He has signs of fetal distress.* Fetal distress is a signal that a baby's supply of blood or oxygen is inadequate. It can be caused by problems with the placenta, anemia, an infection, or a severe illness of the mother or baby. Doctors recognize fetal distress when a baby moves a lot less, is unresponsive to stimulation, or has an abnormal heart rate. Obstetricians usually

decide to deliver a baby urgently in that case, because fetal distress usually means that conditions in the womb are dangerous enough to jeopardize your baby's life or health right now.

* *Congenital conditions.* Babies with congenital conditions may sometimes do better if they get prompt medical or surgical treatment. If so, your doctor may opt for an elective preterm delivery.

Your doctors will assess how your baby is doing in the womb using one or more of the tests described in the box "Checking on a Baby's Well-Being Before He Is Born." To decide whether he would be better off if he were delivered now and cared for in a newborn intensive care unit, they'll take into account your baby's gestational age and size (crucial elements affecting how he will do after birth), and weigh the risks he'll face if he's born prematurely against the risks he faces by staying inside the womb. If your baby is still very immature and small, your doctor probably won't recommend delivering him unless he's facing life-threatening dangers. As he gets older, the risks of prematurity lessen.

You should know that there's always a good deal of guesswork in a decision like this. Unless you're past 34 weeks, when the major hurdles of prematurity are behind your baby, there's hardly ever a definitive "right" time for an elective premature delivery. Doctors usually discuss with parents the pros and cons of an elective preterm delivery, and try hard, using the tools and experience they have, to make the right choice.

CHECKING ON A BABY'S WELL-BEING BEFORE HE IS BORN

There are various ways an obstetrician can "visit" a baby in his mother's womb, to find out how he's doing. Some are high-tech and may require a hospital visit. Others are simple ones you can do yourself at home. Depending on your particular medical situation, your obstetrician will decide when to monitor your baby's well-being, and which tests will be most helpful.

* *Kick counts.* This is the most basic kind of monitoring. It is based on the assumption that an active baby is a healthy baby. There are several different methods. A simple one is to lie down comfortably on your side once a day, and count how many times your baby kicks you. If you feel at least ten movements in two hours, that's good. (A fetus may be sleeping for 20 to 40 minutes, but then should wake up.) If you don't detect any movement, or your baby is moving much less than usual, you should immediately call your obstetrician. Some studies have shown that when expectant mothers do kick counts, they lower their risk of miscarriage or stillbirth.

* *Ultrasound.* Ultrasound uses sound waves to see inside your womb. An ultrasound scan is painless and completely safe for both you and your baby. Doctors use it to: estimate fetal weight and gestational age, and thereby determine if a baby is growing normally or not; check on how a baby's organs are developing; measure the amount of amniotic fluid (too

much or too little fluid can indicate a problem); make sure the cervix is staying closed; assess whether the placenta is properly attached to the uterus; evaluate a baby's position and movement patterns.

❋ *Fetal heart rate monitoring.* You'll be asked to lie down, and a belt with a probe that detects when your uterus contracts will be wrapped around your belly. At the same time, an ultrasound probe, also on your belly, will monitor your baby's heart rate. The probes will be connected to a machine that continuously records your contractions and your baby's heart rate on a long strip of paper. Your doctors will assess whether your baby's heart rate is normal, and how it responds to contractions. This kind of monitoring is done routinely during labor, to detect any signs of fetal distress. A heart rate that is too slow or unchanging is worrisome, possibly signaling that the fetus is not getting enough oxygen. A heart rate that is too fast can be a sign of infection.

❋ *Nonstress test.* A nonstress test is performed the same way as fetal heart rate monitoring, but the doctors will be specifically watching to see that your baby's heart rate speeds up periodically. The human heart normally speeds up in response to various bodily functions, especially movement—as when you dash to catch a bus, or when a fetus kicks—thereby assuring that the body gets more oxygen and blood flow when it needs it. When doctors see that a fetus's heart rate speeds up periodically, they know that your baby is active, that his neurologic connections are intact, and that his heart is able to respond appropriately. If your baby's heart rate accelerates four or more times within a 20-minute period, the nonstress test is "reactive," and your baby is probably doing fine. If not, your doctor will probably want to do other, more specific tests.

A nonstress test can last up to 40 minutes, because some babies may be peacefully sleeping and not move at all for some time. Some hospitals, to speed things up (and to spare you unnecessary worry) may try to wake up the little sleeper with a buzzing device, to get him finally to kick.

❋ *Contraction stress test.* This is also a kind of fetal heart rate monitoring. But unlike a nonstress test, which merely involves observing your baby, a stress test involves putting him in a stressful situation, to see how he reacts. That stressful experience is a uterine contraction, which has the power to temporarily decrease the blood flow through the placenta. If a baby is healthy, and everything is going well, he has a backup reserve of oxygen which allows him to sail through a contraction unscathed—after all, that's what he'll have to go through during labor. But if that reserve doesn't exist, because there's already a scarcity of oxygen, his heart rate will slow down. To stimulate uterine contractions, you may be given a medication called pitocin, a manmade form of oxytocin, which can make your uterus contract, or be asked to gently rub your nipple, because that stimulates your body to release oxytocin naturally. If you're having spontaneous contractions (which may or may not be a sign of preterm labor, depending on their regularity and intensity), you may not need any medication or stimulation. For a stress test to be accurate, you'll need to have at least three contractions within a 10-minute span, each one lasting at least 40 seconds. To achieve that, the test may last for up to two hours. Since uterine contractions can be the enemy for some mothers—those with preterm labor or vaginal bleeding, for example—a stress test may not be advisable for them. An excellent alternative to a stress test is a biophysical profile.

❋ *Biophysical profile.* This is a multifaceted exam in which your baby's behavior is observed with ultrasound for 30 minutes. The doctor will score your baby on five elements:

- *Breathing.* A healthy fetus will make breathing movements for at least 30 seconds.
- *Body movements.* A healthy fetus will move his body or limbs at least three times.
- *Tone.* A healthy fetus will have at least one episode of extending his limbs or trunk, and then returning to a flexed position (such as opening and closing his hand).
- *Heart rate acceleration.* A nonstress test should be reactive, or the examiner should see by ultrasound that your baby's heartbeat speeds up at least twice in 30 minutes, when he moves.
- *Amniotic fluid volume.* The amount of amniotic fluid around your baby should be normal.

If two or more of these elements are abnormal, it could indicate that your baby isn't getting enough oxygen or blood flow. (A simpler, "modified biophysical profile" consists of only two elements: the nonstress test and the amniotic fluid volume. Some doctors consider it almost as precise as a regular biophysical profile.)

❋ *Doppler studies.* Using ultrasound, doctors can measure the blood flow in the umbilical cord, and pick up problems in the circulation between a mother and her fetus. Doppler flow studies can be helpful in determining when the placenta is not functioning adequately. But because the results are not always accurate, they're not universally performed, and your doctor will have to use his judgment in interpreting them.

❋ *Percutaneous umbilical blood sampling (PUBS).*

This test involves taking a sample of your baby's blood from the umbilical cord. It is more risky than most other fetal diagnostic tests (because the cord could be damaged), and obstetricians do it only when they need very precise information about your baby that can be obtained in no other way. You will be given local anesthesia, and a long needle will be inserted in your belly. Your doctor will watch exactly where it's going with ultrasound, as she guides it through your uterus and into a blood vessel in the umbilical cord. PUBS may be used to evaluate your baby's blood counts, if there's reason to believe they may be abnormal, or to see if he has an infection or genetic problem that could explain why he's small for his gestational age. Normal results could confirm that your baby is doing well in your womb, perhaps allowing you to avoid an elective preterm delivery.

❋ *Amniocentesis.* You may already know that amniocentesis is offered to many women as a test for some birth defects (like Down syndrome). But amniocentesis—which involves taking a sample of amniotic fluid by passing a needle through your belly and into your uterus—has other useful applications, as well. In cases of preterm labor or premature rupture of the membranes, amniocentesis can detect a uterine infection sooner than maternal blood tests and other cultures. If your amniotic fluid were infected, it would probably convince the doctors to do an elective delivery. Moreover, the same amniotic fluid can be used to assess your baby's lung maturity. When a fetus's lungs have developed enough to breathe well on their own, certain substances are released into the amniotic fluid. If your baby will be delivered soon, and those substances aren't present, you'll probably be given steroids to speed up the maturation of your baby's lungs. If, instead, your baby's amniotic fluid says "lungs OK," your doctor may opt for an immediate delivery.

❋ *Tests to predict an imminent delivery.* Tests of hormones in your saliva, or a substance called fibronectin in your uterine and vaginal secretions, can be used to monitor whether your uterus is already preparing for labor (see page 10). If these tests are positive, it indicates that you may deliver your baby soon—within the next two weeks. Your doctor may use one or more of these tests to decide whether to treat you with steroids (to boost your baby's maturation in preparation for an early delivery), whether or not to keep you in the hospital or on the labor ward, or whether to go ahead with a delivery that may happen very soon anyway.

Baby's Fighting Spirit

My baby kicks a lot. Does that mean he is a fighter?

Some fetuses, with a constant stream of left hooks and right jabs, give their mothers the distinct impression that they have a future as heavyweight boxers. Others seem a lot more relaxed, moving more softly and fluidly, or, it sometimes seems, not that much at all.

There's no doubt that different fetuses have different movement patterns, but nobody knows whether they foretell who will be "fighters," those able to face down the challenges and hurdles of prematurity with particular vigor. First of all, strong children (physically and emotionally) come in many different packages: strong, silent types; feisty, impish types; or assertively physical types. In addition, at this point researchers don't even know whether movement patterns established in the womb persist into infancy and childhood. Plenty of parents are surprised to see their in utero prizefighter turn into an easy, calm baby—and vice versa. Many factors can affect fetal movements, including a mother's diet, mood, and activity level (when mothers are busier, they tend to concentrate less on their babies' movements and think they're moving less, even when they're not), the time of day (fetuses sleep sometimes, too), and the stage in pregnancy (as fetuses grow and have less room to move around, their movements tend to involve more wriggles and fewer kicks), along with the baby's own physical strength and character.

It's safe to say that whatever is going on in your belly now, you will be amazed by your tiny baby's spunk and spirit. Almost all parents of preemies are. In the nursery, you see one fighter after another after another. To adults, it is inspiring. To babies, it just seems to come naturally.

Steroids

My doctor is giving me a medication to make my baby's lungs mature more quickly, because she may be born any day now. How much difference will it make?

You've probably been told that every extra week, in fact every extra day, in the womb is valuable, allowing your baby's organs to mature just that much more, so they'll have a better chance of functioning well when the moment comes that she enters the world.

Are There Medications other than Steroids You Can Take to Help Your Baby?

Researchers are always on the lookout for medications that a mother can take before a premature birth, to help her baby mature faster or to prevent some of the complications of prematurity. Various drugs have been studied because they looked promising, but none other than steroids, as yet, have been proven effective.

For example, it was hoped that giving magnesium sulfate (a medication prescribed for preeclampsia and preterm labor) to mothers of preemies might help to prevent cerebral palsy. So far, research has come up with no solid evidence to support this. There's been speculation that phenobarbital and vitamin K, given to a mother before delivery, might reduce the risk of bleeding and damage in her premature infant's brain. As of now, the evidence isn't there, either, although a few obstetricians do prescribe these to their patients. Other possibilities have been investigated, and will continue to be, with the hope that one day, some will be successful.

Luckily, we live in an era when modern medicine can sometimes fill in for nature, at least partially, when nature isn't cooperating. Studies show that when a mother takes steroids at least twenty-four hours before delivery, her premature baby's lungs mature faster, giving them the equivalent of about an extra week in the womb.

Steroids are hormones that everyone's body produces, especially during periods of stress. These hormones surge, naturally, in pregnant women just before delivery, speeding up maturation of the fetus's organ systems—a kind of developmental boost just before they have to function independently.

Getting steroids can be incredibly valuable to a preemie. One of the most common illnesses in the intensive care nursery is respiratory distress syndrome, or RDS, which arises from lung immaturity. A baby with RDS is dependent on a ventilator or other breathing assistance, and at risk for other, potentially serious complications, until her lungs are able to breathe well on their own. The risk that a newborn will have RDS drops lower and lower with increased gestational age at birth. While virtually all preemies born before 26 weeks of gestational age have to deal with respiratory distress syndrome, only about a quarter of 30 to 34 weekers, with their more mature lungs, do. (If you want to know more about RDS, see page 101.)

When steroids are given before delivery to their mothers, newborn preemies between the ages of 28 weeks and 34 weeks of gestation have a dramatically reduced rate of RDS. For infants born before 28 weeks, it's not clear that the incidence of RDS is reduced, but the severity of the illness may be. Beyond 34 weeks, the risk of RDS is so low that a mother won't get steroids unless her fetus's lungs are known to be especially immature. Besides helping to prevent respiratory distress syndrome, steroids also speed up maturation of the brain and the intestines, lowering the rate of intraventricular hemorrhage (bleeding in the brain), and NEC (inflammation of the intestines), some of the most worrisome, potential health consequences of prematurity.

If your doctor is giving you a steroid called betamethasone, you'll get two shots, twenty-four hours apart, and if he's giving you one called dexamethasone, you'll get four shots, twelve hours apart. The maximum benefit comes when you get a complete course at least twenty-four hours before you give birth, although there's some benefit even if there is less than twenty-four hours before delivery. The effects last for seven days or more. If more than a week passes and you haven't yet given birth (which is good news!), you may be given another course. Most doctors would not give any more than that, however, because too many courses of prenatal steroids may adversely affect the long-term growth of a baby's brain, and possibly other organs, offsetting some of the future potential to help them in the short term.

What about other risks from the way that prenatal steroids are being used? Some mothers have medical conditions, such as diabetes, which steroids can worsen. Your obstetrician will judge whether taking steroids is safe for you. The fear that a course of steroids before delivery would increase a mother's risk of getting an infection, or have some negative short-term or long-term effects on her baby, has been extensively researched, including follow-up of preemies until they were twelve years old. Thankfully, studies haven't shown any adverse effects from one course of these extraordinarily valuable drugs.

MULTIPLES

Likelihood of Prematurity

I'm pregnant after an IVF cycle, and I'm having more than one! Am I likely to deliver prematurely?

You may know that if you're pregnant with more than one fetus, you have a higher chance of a preterm birth. That risk increases with the number of babies you're carrying. Most couples who undergo infertility treatments are told about that risk, but it's easy to be so focused on just getting pregnant that you put the possibility of having more than one baby into the back of your mind. Secretly, a couple might even hope for twins or triplets, to see their desire for a big family finally come true, all at once, while they have the chance.

But although a multiple gestation is sometimes an unavoidable consequence of infertility treatments, it's not usually a desirable one, especially when more than twins are involved. Multiple pregnancies have higher rates of miscarriage, stillbirth, and prematurity. A preterm delivery is much more likely for one simple reason: the amount of space in the womb. When the human uterus, which was not meant to carry more than one fetus, gets very distended, it tends to contract. That may be nature's way of trying to deliver a baby when it's well grown; but not surprisingly, with multiple fetuses the womb gets overcrowded and tends to contract before term. Also, because of the space and nutritional resources they have to share, multiples tend to be smaller than singletons after a certain

A Note If You Considered Multifetal Pregnancy Reduction

You may have been told by your obstetrician, early in your pregnancy, about the possibility of a multifetal pregnancy reduction. This procedure, in which one or more fetuses are aborted on purpose, is done to give the babies who will later develop a better chance to survive, so they can reach an age when they can be born without such very high risks of an early death and future disabilities.

Couples who were faced with this choice, no matter what decision they made, may feel comfortable that they did the right thing, or may be left with deep sorrow and excruciat-ing doubt. It's important to remember that, for this particular path, there is no absolutely right or wrong choice. Even the future cannot prove that your decision was good or bad, because not even time can tell you what would have happened if you had chosen differently. Try not to let your joy for the lives that are developing in your womb be shadowed by past choices or future statistics. Give yourself credit that whatever happens, you've done what was in your power, or what your conscience allowed, to best help your babies and your family.

gestational age. (You can see how much smaller on the growth chart, page 514.)

Women who are pregnant with multiples are more subject to pregnancy complications, like bleeding or high blood pressure, which also can lead to an early birth. To top it off, recent research suggests that women who had fertility treatments tend to give birth two to three weeks earlier than women who did not have fertility problems, when carrying the same number of babies. There may be a relationship between prematurity and infertility treatments, or prematurity and infertility itself.

Putting all of this together, a normal, singleton pregnancy lasts about 40 weeks, on average, while the average length of a twin gestation is about 36 to 37 weeks, and each additional fetus shortens it by about three and a half weeks. The likelihood of a preterm birth is only about 10% in a singleton pregnancy, but goes up to nearly 50% for a twin gestation, and nearly 90% for triplets and up.

There's a bright side to this, though. As you can read on page 51, the outcome for preemies born at 34 or more weeks of gestation, which would include most twins, is almost identical to that of babies born at term. Preemies born at 32 or 33 weeks, the average age for triplets, usually do very well. Plus, some studies suggest that multiples may be even better equipped than singletons to overcome some hurdles of prematurity—and that advantage increases with the number of babies in the womb. This means that a triplet may have a slightly better chance of survival than a twin born at the same gestational age and weight, and a twin may have a better chance than a singleton. Unfortunately, when a newborn is tiny and very immature, the small payoff of being a multiple may not improve his chances all that much. Still, it's something!

Twin to Twin Transfusion Syndrome

My doctor said my twins aren't doing well in my womb because they share a blood vessel. What problems will they have, and can anything be done to help?

Your doctor probably suspects a condition called twin to twin transfusion syndrome, which can affect the health and growth of identical twins during pregnancy. A twin to twin "transfusion" occurs when shared blood vessels in the placenta cause too much blood to circulate out of one twin and into the other.

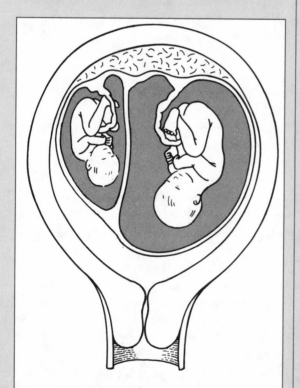

In twin to twin transfusion syndrome, one twin receives too much blood and is bigger, with more amniotic fluid. The other twin receives too little blood and is smaller, with less amniotic fluid.

To understand how this can happen, it's necessary to look at events occurring at the very beginning of life. A fertilized egg, in order to develop into a fetus, needs a placenta to supply it with vital amounts of oxygen and nutrients from the mother's blood, and to get rid of its waste. The placenta begins to form right out of the fertilized egg, the moment it attaches to the uterus, quickly growing into a net of fetal blood vessels connected to the fetus by the umbilical cord. Around the fetus, a sac of membranes—the amniotic sac—forms, and gradually fills with amniotic fluid, made mostly of fetal urine.

What about twins? Fraternal twins come from two different eggs, and always have two separate placentas and amniotic sacs. Identical twins come from the same egg, which splits sometime after fertilization, forming two fetuses. When that split happens very early after fertilization, before the placenta has developed, each identical twin will make its own placenta and amniotic sac. But when the split happens later, after the placenta has already formed, the twins will share the same placenta. Depending on whether the fertilized egg splits in two before or after the amniotic sac forms, each twin may make its own sac, or they may share one.

In a placenta shared by identical twins, there are almost always some blood vessels connected to both umbilical cords, which allow the circulation of a little blood from one twin to the other. As long as the blood vessels are small, and the amount of blood flowing from one to the other is minor, it's not a problem. But if the connection involves major blood vessels, a substantial amount of blood may flow from the first twin (the donor) into the other (the recipient).

The recipient twin gets more blood, with its oxygen and nutrients, so becomes bigger. But a lot of blood can be too much of a good thing, and bigger is not always stronger. The recipient twin can get overloaded with fluid, putting a strain on her heart to pump all that blood. When twin to twin transfusion syndrome is really severe, the recipient twin is at risk of dying in the womb or in early infancy of heart failure. The extra blood will also make her urinate a lot, filling her sac with excessive amounts of amniotic fluid (a condition called polyhydramnios, see page 35). Polyhydramnios is a main cause of spontaneous preterm labor.

The donor twin can also get into trouble. She gets less blood than she should, so lacks some oxygen and nutrients. This can restrict her growth, making her smaller than the other twin. She won't urinate as much, so there may be too little amniotic fluid in her sac (a condition called oligohydramnios, see page 35). Not having enough amniotic fluid increases the risk that the umbilical cord can get compressed in the uterus, leading to a dangerous interruption of blood flow to the fetus. In severe twin to twin transfusion syndrome, the donor twin is also at risk for heart failure, from profound anemia.

It's hard to generalize about the effects of this condition. If it's mild, both babies will probably do well, perhaps differing in size, or blood cell counts, but with few or no other consequences. If it's moderate, an early delivery and prematurity are its likely consequences. But if it's severe, the disturbances in blood flow can potentially damage the vital organs of both fetuses, leading to death, or to long-term disabilities if they survive.

Twin to twin transfusion syndrome is usually diagnosed by ultrasound, in the second trimester of pregnancy. Indicators are: a shared placenta, a difference in your twins' size by 20% or more, and too much fluid in the bigger twin's sac with too little fluid in the smaller twin's sac. Sometimes ultrasound measurements of fetal blood flow can pick up different circulation patterns in the twins, and show the blood vessels that are causing the problem.

Traditional treatments for twin to twin transfusion syndrome have not been very effective. Some obstetricians consider it useful to drain amniotic fluid from the sac of the receiving twin, because it has been suggested that this may sometimes slow down the passage of blood from one twin to the other. This procedure has to be repeated often, though, and other doctors don't think it works. Drugs may be given to the mother to help the babies' hearts, or to reduce their urine output (so the recipient twin won't make as much amniotic fluid), but they are not without risks. Once the obstetrician thinks that the babies' problems in the womb are worse than the possible complications of being born prematurely, an elective preterm delivery is commonly done.

A recent innovation—still experimental—is laser surgery on the placenta. This involves closing the blood vessels connecting one twin to the other while both babies are still in the womb, then going on with the pregnancy. So far, this procedure is only being done in a few hospitals in the United States and Europe. It carries a high risk of losing one or both twins, and there are some risks to the mother, but some doctors think it is promising.

One Twin Needs Early Delivery

One of my twins is having trouble in the womb, and the doctor says she'd benefit from an early delivery. But the other is doing fine, and could go to full-term. Whom should I put first?

The dilemma that arises when one of your babies is doing well during pregnancy, and the other is not, can be gut wrenching. While your womb is the best possible place for one of your twins, for the other it's dangerous, leading your doctor to believe that she would be better off being born prematurely, and cared for in an intensive care nursery. Doctors often want parents' input in deciding what's best: to deliver both twins now, before term, or both twins later—a decision that requires parents to help one of their babies at the expense of the other.

If you are faced with a painful decision like this, the first thing you need is information. It's important for you to understand, as clearly as possible, the risks and benefits of each course of action for each of your children. For your baby who is doing fine now and may abruptly become a preemie, you can read about a premature baby's prospects for survival and long-term health on page 49, and about the medical challenges she may face on page 84.

For your baby who is not doing well now, the best thing is to discuss her risks and prospects with your obstetrician, since she may have medical problems that make the statistics different for her than for the average baby, whether she stays in the womb or not.

Unfortunately, even when you've armed yourself with all of the information that's available, there is rarely an obvious "right" answer. If one choice is clearly better in balancing the welfare of both of your children, your obstetrician will direct you that way. Very rarely, the problem can be solved with a delayed interval birth (see page 66), in which one baby is delivered days or weeks before the other, but this requires that certain conditions be met, and is never a sure bet.

The only way that most parents can make a decision like this is to follow their values and their hearts. Some parents naturally want to protect their child who is most sick or vulnerable, and feel compelled to do whatever will help her. Others feel that it is their job as parents not to hurt their children who are thriving. So, for example, if one of their children is fine while the other will face daunting survival or developmental risks no matter what, they would not make a choice that would hurt their healthiest baby's chances. Some parents lean toward accepting the most natural course of events, believing that as long as the pregnancy would keep going on its own, they and the doctors should not intervene to stop it.

You will probably second-guess your decision many times over the coming months and years, no matter how things turn out. Just remember that the very nature and essence of a family is that several people are in it together. As parents, it's impossible for us to do what's best for every one of our children all of the time—much as we wish we could. We are forced to weigh everyone's needs, and to make decisions that are best for one member of the family in one situation, for another in another situation, always thinking about what's good for the family as a whole.

Take all the time you can to think and talk through your decision. Later, give yourself credit for trying to make the best choice for your family that you could, in an exceedingly difficult situation.

RISK FACTORS FOR PREMATURITY: ARE YOU AT RISK?

While you can learn from this list about some of the things that increase the odds of giving birth early, try not to use it to draw conclusions about your pregnancy or anyone else's you love. That would be a mistake, because in any pregnancy, the medical issues may be more complex than what you can read in here. Many women who have a risk factor on this list still give birth at or near full-term. Risk factors for prematurity may be weak or strong, and they often interact. Remember that only your doctor can adequately evaluate your own, individual case and make an accurate prognosis for your pregnancy and your baby.

SOME COMMON CAUSES OF PRETERM BIRTH

Obstetric history

* *Previous premature delivery.* This is one of the most important risks for a premature birth. If you've already had a premature baby, you have a 20% to 40% chance of seeing it happen again.
* *Previous second trimester abortion.* Women who have had a second trimester abortion have a higher risk for preterm birth, because that surgical procedure requires a wide dilation of the cervix, which can damage it and lead to cervical incompetence. A single, first trimester abortion doesn't increase the risk for delivering prematurely, but having several first trimester abortions may.

* *Becoming pregnant less than six months after a previous delivery.* Your body may not be fully recovered and prepared to handle another pregnancy so soon.
* *Infertility.* Women who have had a lot of trouble conceiving, including those who become pregnant while receiving treatment for infertility, have a higher incidence of preterm delivery, for reasons that are not yet clear.

Problems with the reproductive organs

* *Malformations of the uterus.* If you have fibroids, or a uterus with an abnormal shape, you have a higher risk for having a smaller than normal baby, and for delivering prematurely. That's because there may not be enough room in your womb for a baby to grow to full-term size. Many problems with the uterus can be corrected with surgery, after which you may have a much better chance of carrying a pregnancy to term.
* *Cervical incompetence.* Some women have what's called an "incompetent cervix": their cervix (the opening of the womb) tends to open too early in the pregnancy, causing premature birth. You can have an incompetent cervix for unknown reasons, as a result of previous gynecologic or obstetric procedures, or from exposure when you yourself were a fetus in your mother's womb to a medication called DES, which was given to women in the 1950s and '60s to prevent miscarriages. A simple surgical procedure called a cerclage

can be done during pregnancy, to try to keep your cervix closed until term (see page 15).

Obstetric complications during this pregnancy

❋ *Multiple gestation.* Twins have a 25% to 50% chance of being born before term, and that rate rises with each additional fetus. The main reason is purely mechanical: the uterus gets distended by all of the babies inside, and distention is a signal for it to contract. But some multiples are born prematurely for other reasons, such as high blood pressure or breathing difficulties in the mother, or because the fetuses aren't growing well in the womb (see page 28).

❋ *Bleeding in the second or third trimester of pregnancy.* The most common causes are two conditions of the placenta: placental abruption and placenta previa (see illustrations). Both are common causes of elective, preterm

delivery. They can be harmful to the mother, who can lose a lot of blood, and to the baby, because anything that interferes with good functioning of the placenta (which provides the fetus with oxygen and nutrients) can interfere with a baby's development.

Placental abruption means that a part of the placenta has detached from the wall of the uterus. When that happens, the detached part of the placenta is no longer able to get oxygen and nutrients from the mother's blood. The most common symptoms you would notice are vaginal bleeding and abdominal pain. If the area of abruption is large, it can be very dangerous, seriously disturbing the blood and oxygen supply to the fetus, and may require an emergency, preterm delivery. But if the area of abruption is small, and the rest of the placenta is working well, it won't make much difference for the growth and well-being of the fetus, and your pregnancy can continue. Ultrasound and

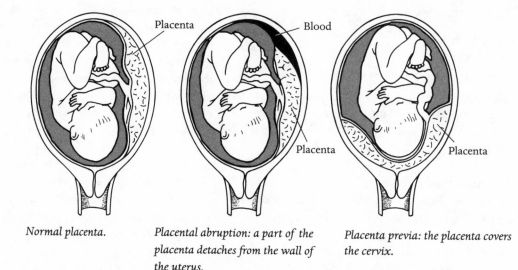

Normal placenta.

Placental abruption: a part of the placenta detaches from the wall of the uterus.

Placenta previa: the placenta covers the cervix.

Adapted with permission from *Planning for Pregnancy, Birth and Beyond,* 2nd ed. Washington, DC, © ACOG (American College of Obstetricians and Gynecologists) 1995

other tests of fetal well-being can usually assess the damage.

Placenta previa means that the placenta partly or completely covers the cervix, so that when your cervix dilates, or the fetus pushes against it during labor, it can tear and bleed. Bleeding may also occur as pregnancy advances, and the lower part of the uterus stretches. The usual reason for a premature delivery for a placenta previa is to prevent a serious maternal hemorrhage.

* *Polyhydramnios or oligohydramnios.* Polyhydramnios means there's too much amniotic fluid. The excess fluid can overly distend the uterus, leading to early contractions and preterm delivery. Since the fetus normally swallows large amounts of amniotic fluid, anything that impairs the fetus's ability to swallow (such as problems with his mouth, neck, or stomach, or neurologic conditions) can cause too much amniotic fluid to build up. A variety of other maternal and fetal conditions are associated with polyhydramnios, and your doctor will discuss any with you that apply. Sometimes, no reason for the extra fluid is found. If your case is severe, your doctor may drain some of the fluid out with a needle and syringe, in a procedure similar to an amniocentesis, to lower the immediate risk of preterm labor and delivery.

Oligohydramnios means there's too little amniotic fluid. This can be caused by premature rupture of the membranes (when your water breaks, most of the amniotic fluid leaks out), abnormalities of your baby's urinary system (because the amniotic fluid is mostly made of fetal urine), or a poorly functioning placenta (babies who get less blood flow through the placenta will urinate less). Often, oligohydramnios is accompanied by signs of fetal distress, because your baby is no longer protected by an intact, fluid-filled sac, or because the low fluid is a sign of inadequate blood flow to the fetus. Sometimes, a sufficient amount of amniotic fluid can be reestablished with bed rest, medical treatment, and time. Some doctors occasionally use a technique called "amnioinfusion" (directly infusing fluid into the womb with a catheter), particularly to help a fetus tolerate labor, but its advantages are still controversial. If your doctor thinks your baby will have a better chance of growing and developing outside of the womb, she may recommend an elective, preterm delivery.

* *Preeclampsia.* Preeclampsia is a disease that occurs only during pregnancy. If you have preeclampsia, your blood pressure will be high, you'll have protein in your urine, and your face and hands may swell (different from the annoying, although normal, swollen legs and feet that most pregnant women deal with). Preeclampsia causes blood vessels to tighten, including those going to the placenta, so it can decrease the amount of blood that goes to your fetus. Over time, this can impede his growth and development. If severe, preeclampsia can also cause life-threatening complications for you. It is the most common reason for an elective preterm delivery. Fortunately, preeclampsia always goes away within a few days after delivery (see page 8).

* *Fetal growth restriction.* If your baby is growing poorly, it usually means that he isn't getting enough nutrients and oxygen. If the problem is severe, it can cause damage to him, or even stillbirth. Your obstetrician may opt for an elective delivery to prevent these risks, or preterm labor and delivery may occur spontaneously.

Infection

Almost any severe infection in a pregnant woman can be a threat to both mother and fetus, and can lead to a preterm delivery. If you develop an infection, the odds are that you will still carry your pregnancy to term. However, there are some hidden infections that are believed to be responsible for a large number of preterm births. For example, research has linked bacteria that normally live in a woman's genitourinary tract to low-grade infection of the fetal membranes, placenta, and uterus; this infection causes inflammation that, over several weeks or months, can lead to preterm labor or premature rupture of the membranes (see page 17).

Chronic disease in the mother

If you have a chronic illness, you should discuss with your doctor how it might affect your pregnancy. Many illnesses, if not severe, don't cause substantial problems. But some chronic maternal diseases can disrupt the growth and development of the fetus, or can get worse in the mother during pregnancy because of the bodily changes that occur. Sometimes, a mother needs a medication that she stops taking while she's pregnant because it is dangerous to the developing baby. Her pregnancy may then be electively cut short, so she can safely take her medicine again. Probably the two most common chronic diseases that lead to premature birth are diabetes and high blood pressure.

❋ *Diabetes.* If you have diabetes, the amount of sugar in your blood (and therefore, the amount that passes into your fetus) can rise to high levels. Pregnancy makes diabetes worse, because a woman's body is programmed to allow her blood sugar levels to rise higher than usual, so her fetus can get enough fuel. You will be closely monitored with urine and blood tests, and counseled about how you should change your diet, exercise, and insulin injections, if needed. You'll also get ultrasounds, to check on the growth and well-being of your baby. Often, premature delivery in a mother with diabetes is elective, to avoid medical complications in the baby, and a difficult delivery at term. (A baby can grow too big from all that sugar.)

Gestational diabetes, which comes on during pregnancy, is usually discovered with a simple blood test done at about 28 weeks of gestation. It's more common in women over 30 who are overweight, have high blood pressure, or who have a family history of diabetes. If you find out that you have gestational diabetes, the good news is that you can probably control your blood sugar levels enough, simply by changing your diet, that they won't harm you or your baby. Gestational diabetes usually goes away after delivery, although women who have it are at higher risk of developing diabetes in the future.

❋ *High blood pressure.* High blood pressure can be an isolated problem, or it can go along with heart disease, kidney disease, or other medical conditions. High blood pressure can lead to prematurity because it can damage the placenta, or because continuing the pregnancy in the face of a severe underlying disease is harmful to the mother or to the fetus. Women who already have high blood pressure are at greater risk of developing preeclampsia during pregnancy, which often necessitates a premature delivery.

Abnormalities of the fetus

Approximately two to three babies out of a hundred are born with a major birth defect. Premature labor and delivery is common, often because these congenital conditions are associated with other risk factors, such as too much or too little amniotic fluid, poor fetal growth, a chronic maternal disease, or infection. Sometimes, though, the reason for preterm labor and delivery is unknown. If you find out that your baby has a serious abnormality, you and your doctor will make plans in advance for the best possible treatment for both you and your baby before, during, and after delivery.

Social and behavioral factors

Overall, women of lower socioeconomic status with less education are more likely to have premature babies. Because many social and behavioral risk factors go together, it's hard to evaluate their individual roles. Here are some of them:

* *Little or no prenatal care.* Women who are rarely seen by an obstetrician or midwife during pregnancy are more likely to deliver prematurely. However, attempts to make prenatal care more available have not been successful in reducing rates of prematurity.
* *Ethnicity.* African-American women have a higher rate of preterm birth than Hispanic and Caucasian women of the same socioeconomic level, for unknown reasons.
* *Smoking.* Cigarette smoking reduces blood flow to the placenta, and oxygen to the fetus. It is clearly connected to poor fetal growth, preterm rupture of membranes, and premature birth. Cigarette smoke and nicotine also increase the chance of placental abruption and placenta previa. The risk for your baby increases with the number of cigarettes you smoke. Ideally, you should quit smoking before you conceive, but it's never too late: even cutting back on cigarettes in the second half of your pregnancy can reduce your risk of having

a small for gestational age or premature baby.
* *Drug abuse.* Some street drugs, such as cocaine, marijuana, and amphetamines, are associated with preterm birth. Cocaine can cause placental abruption.
* *Sexual activity.* Studies have not found a clear link between sexual activity, orgasm, and prematurity. Still, most obstetricians will advise you to avoid sexual intercourse if you've had episodes of premature labor, rupture of membranes, or bleeding. That's because sex can cause some minor injury to your cervix, or spread infection into your uterus, and the resulting inflammation could cause a preterm birth.
* *Physical exertion.* Heavy labor or long work hours may be associated with preterm labor and delivery, although proof for that is indirect. There is no evidence that women who exercise moderately during pregnancy increase their odds of having a premature baby.
* *Low maternal weight.* Women who weigh less than 100 pounds at the start of pregnancy, or who gain too little weight during pregnancy, have an increased chance of delivering prematurely. Maternal malnutrition can also impair the fetus's growth. Your obstetrician will check on your weight gain throughout pregnancy, and if it isn't sufficient, will counsel you to eat more or better. Never take the initiative of adding vitamins, minerals, or supplements to your diet without your doctor's permission, though, because some supplements, especially in large quantities, can harm your baby. It's true what your mother told you: the best source of nutrients is a varied, balanced diet.
* *Age younger than 18 or older than 40 years.* If you're in one of these age groups, but don't have other risk factors for prematurity, your chance of having a premature baby is increased, but just by a small amount.

Part II

IN THE HOSPITAL

2

Welcome to the World

Your Baby's Delivery

▶ *Your baby's transition from the womb to the world.*
Preparing for, and understanding, a premature birth.

THE PARENTS' PERSPECTIVE   42

THE DOCTOR'S PERSPECTIVE   45

A DIFFERENT STORY FOR DIFFERENT
PREEMIES: *Survival and Long-Term*
Health   49

QUESTIONS AND ANSWERS

Moving Mother to Another Hospital   52
How a Maternal Transport Is Done   53
Father's Role When a Mother Is Moved   53
Meeting with Your Baby's Doctor   54
Why a C-Section?   56
How a C-Section Is Done   57
The Crowd in the Delivery Room   58

If Your Baby Needs Resuscitation   60
How Is a Baby Resuscitated?   61
Apgar Scores   62
Birth Weight Predictions   63
Bonding   64
Moving Baby to Another Hospital   65

MULTIPLES

Twins Delivered at Different Times   66
Who's A, Who's B?   68
Identical or Not?   69

IN DEPTH

Your Baby Is Small–for–Gestational Age:
    What Does It Mean?   70

The Parents' Perspective: Delivery

A premature delivery may occur unexpectedly, to parents who haven't had a chance to prepare for that life crisis. In other cases, a pregnancy is known to be at risk, and parents deal with uncertainty and fear for long weeks. Some parents cope by actively seeking more information. For others, denial works best.

Today is Thanksgiving and I'm in a hospital bed. My baby and I are doing great, she's moving a lot and kicking me more vigorously than ever. But my obstetrician decided to keep me in the hospital a little longer. "Just to be safe . . ." she said. Two days ago I began to bleed, so I came in and was rushed to a labor room. My contractions stopped, and since then, everything has been fine. Only I wish I could go home. It's so upsetting here. There are only curtains between beds, and little or no privacy. The woman to my left came in last night. She was in her first trimester, but they couldn't find her baby's heartbeat anymore. He was gone. I heard her story unwillingly, when she talked to a doctor before surgery. I was shocked: she and her husband didn't sound very upset. Maybe they didn't really want this baby. Or maybe they have exceptional self-control. I can't even think what I would be like in their shoes. In the bed across the aisle, there's a woman who cries a lot. She just gave birth to premature twins, and they are upstairs, in intensive care. "You don't know what I see there," she told me in tears, when we exchanged a few words. I tried to be nice to her, but I didn't want to hear what she was saying. My due date is in three months. Tomorrow, my baby and I are going home.

Obstetricians can prescribe bed rest and medications to expectant mothers, to try to prolong their pregnancies. But there are no simple instructions when it comes to taking care of older children, leaving jobs responsibly when you have to do so suddenly, and earlier than you had planned, and surviving the siege of worry and ominous waiting with one's psyche and relationships intact. Sometimes, an early delivery (though not as early as originally feared), is almost a deliverance.

Yesterday, Mark and Louise came over for lunch to celebrate my birthday. She'd been on and off bed rest for several weeks, and looked surprisingly round, in her long maternity dress, to have two more months to go. "I gained too much weight," she said, faking some shame. "Lawrence is going to be a big boy, like all the men in my family!" Mark, who's slight, joked about having to build up some muscles to be able to hold his son at birth. They seemed glad to join our family reunion, but looked weary and tense. It hasn't been easy for them. Yesterday was their first social outing—with the doctor's permission—in a long time. That's not how you should spend your pregnancy, poor Louise. She grew more tired and pale as the party went on, and they left after the cake. Then, that night, the phone rang. It was Mark, telling us that Lawrence had been born, at a mere four and a half pounds. Louise's water had broken, and labor this time could not be stopped. Mark found the strength to tease me over the phone: "We told you he was going to be a big boy!" He sounded worried, but, in some way, relieved. Lawrence was in an incubator, and breathing oxygen through a little tube, when we saw him today in the nursery. This little guy and I share a birthday, I realized. He'll do well, I know it.

"We have to deliver your baby." Depending on the medical circumstances, and the stage of gestation your baby has reached, this news may merely increase parents' anxiety, or plunge them into pure terror. Even if the doctors say encouraging words, some parents can't allow themselves to be hopeful. The fear of the unknown is just too overwhelming.

I don't want to see. I don't want to be awake. Put me to sleep and please, don't wake me up. I will not hear my baby crying, I know it. He'll be too exhausted, after this long run. His heart has been racing so fast in the last hours, like a little crazy horse, who's desperate to be freed. They say it's better for him to be born, even so early. Inside, I'm poisoning him. Outside, they can take care of him. I'm choking in my tears when they make me sit up, gently pushing my back from behind. "You'll feel a needle stick and some burning," a doctor says. The spinal anesthesia is quickly working, taking the pain out of my body, but not out of my head. Behind the drape, under the glaring lights, they're pushing and pulling strongly on a body that happens to be mine. "I'm giving you the kind of C-section that will allow you to deliver your next baby naturally," the obstetrician says. "But I'll never have another baby. I don't want another baby," I cry out, with no voice. How can he tell me that when my baby is fighting for his life? Seconds fly, voices overlap. "Oh . . . he's not so small after all . . ." "Did you hear him crying? Did you hear his voice?" This is my husband talking. No, I didn't. "This is your son, he's beautiful, you know?" somebody says, putting a little face, all bundled up in a blanket, really close to mine. But not close enough.

Premature babies are fragile, and the youngest of them need the kind of special care that only a few hospitals can provide. In order to get it, some of them have to travel right after delivery, leaving their shocked parents behind.

—Are you Mr. Wood? Hi, nice meeting you. I'm Alice Lewis, a transport nurse from St. Anne Metropolitan Hospital, where your twins are being transferred. My colleague, Donna, a neonatal nurse practitioner, is getting your babies ready for the ambulance trip. Do you know where our hospital is located?
—Yes, I've been there several times. My brother lives nearby.
—Oh, great, so you'll have some family to help you out. Will you be staying with him?
—I thought so. But now I'm concerned about leaving my wife. She's sick, with a very high fever.
—What does her doctor say?
—He says they're treating her with antibiotics, and that she should be better soon. Let's hope so . . .
—Does she know that the babies are being transferred?
—Not yet. She's only barely awake from the pain medicine, and can't handle any more bad news, I think . . .
—But moving them to St. Anne isn't bad news . . . It's a hassle, we know, having them 40 miles away, but you should think of it as a safety measure. This hospital doesn't have the expertise to treat preemies like your twins. Has your wife seen them yet?
—No, only some instant photos, but you could barely see the babies, with all the wires and tubes. She's too sick to get out of bed.
—If she can't come to the babies, the babies will come to her. Once we've put them in the transport isolette, we'll just make a stop upstairs to say good-bye to their mom, before leaving. Would you like to go up and tell her?

—Are you sure it's a good idea?
—Absolutely. Trust me.

Do preemies run in families? There's some evidence for that. Knowing what you may be in for, because you've had a preemie before, or because your sister had one, has both good and bad sides. You may live for months in apprehension, but you can take preventive steps, as well. You know the risks, but also know when it's safe, cautiously, to relax.

Stephanie and Tommy are fine. I'm a little shaken, but . . . so happy . . . Don't cry, Laura, everything is all right. Your sister was so good, I'm so proud of her . . . We were together, she had a natural delivery . . . and after all, the baby is only six weeks early . . . OK, OK, just kidding. You're right. We should have stayed in the city. But we needed some fresh air . . . and the doctor said we could go, so . . . Have you ever been up here? You should see the view from Stephanie's room. We have the whole valley at our feet . . . There was a helicopter ready to take Tommy to a city hospital. But he didn't need to go . . . exactly . . . he's already a mountaineer, like your father . . . Of course he's breathing on his own! I could hold him already. He's small, but beautiful. I can't wait to take Stephanie to see him . . . No, she hasn't yet, she can't move, the stitches they gave her are killing her . . . Breastfeeding? Yes, I think . . . Tomorrow we'll have a cellular phone, so you'll be able to talk to her. She has to begin pumping her breast milk right away. Of course I'll tell her. Listen, don't say that. How could it be your fault? Preemies run in your family? . . . Maybe . . . but to me . . . it's just that you and your sister . . . do all your things in a rush . . . Don't laugh, that's true! But this time you have to admit that Stephanie was much more patient than you were with your daughter. By the way, can I talk to my former micro-niece? Hi, Raphaelle! It's Uncle Ray. Did Mummy tell you that you have a little cousin?

The Doctor's Perspective: Delivery*

It's the moment you've been waiting for—although not quite long enough! Like all delivery days, the birth day of your child will be full of pain and joy, a remarkable, momentous occasion. But it will be different, too, as your baby will be met with more trepidation, and more technology, than the average full-term baby. No amount of advance information can predict exactly how your preemie will do when he's born. We're always ready to be surprised in the delivery room—by tiny babies who, remarkably, come out kicking and screaming, and by bigger babies who unexpectedly need more help to get going. One expectant mother asked her obstetrician, after an ultrasound, "How can you know so much about him, when he's in there, and you're out here?" Well, we do know a lot, from assessing you and your baby before delivery, and from having dealt with many other preemies of his age and size before; but until he's out here, too, there will always be an element of mystery. It all becomes real when your baby arrives.

PHYSICAL EXAM AND LABORATORY ASSESSMENT

In the delivery room, doctors initially focus on the basics—a baby's essential signs of life—leaving the rest of the physical exam until later. From the moment a preemie is born and delivered into our hands—as we carry her to the warming bed, dry her off, and clean out her nose and mouth—we're continually assessing her breathing, heartbeat, and circulation. We're hoping that she cries (that means she's vigorous, alert, and taking a deep breath—good, on all fronts). We're checking her color (pink means she's getting enough oxygen), watching to make sure that she continues to breathe regularly (many preemies don't, in which case we'll have to help her out). We're also making sure that her heartbeat is strong and regular, and that she doesn't have any life-threatening conditions we

need to treat immediately. Occasionally, in a baby born extremely prematurely, we're also assessing whether she appears mature enough to survive for longer than a few hours outside the womb, even with our best medical treatment. Based on your baby's vital signs and vigor, and how well she responds to medical treatment, we'll assign her Apgar scores (see page 62).

After I'm certain that a baby is breathing well (by herself or with our help), and has a normal heart rate, I do a quick physical exam, to make sure all her body parts are there and normally formed. We'll neatly cut her umbilical cord, examining that, too, to make sure the blood vessels that nourished her in the womb are normal. Then, we'll weigh her—in grams (the measure we use) and pounds (to tell you).

Your obstetrician will take some blood, painlessly, from your baby's umbilical cord after she's born, to check for such things as her blood type, whether she has certain infections (like

---

*"The Doctor's Perspective" describes how your doctor may be thinking about your preemie's condition, and what she may be considering as she makes medical decisions. All of the medical terms and conditions mentioned here are described in more detail elsewhere in this book. Check the index.

syphilis), and whether she was getting enough oxygen right before delivery. Other than that, and maybe measuring her oxygen level, we usually wait until a preemie is safely ensconced in the more controlled and closely monitored atmosphere of the nursery before getting x-rays and lab tests.

Don't worry if you're having more than one baby. Each of your preemies will get the same attentive care. As soon as each one is born, she'll be taken to her own warming bed, in the delivery room or in a special stabilization room for newly born babies, where she'll be evaluated and treated by her own, dedicated medical team.

COMMON ISSUES AND DECISIONS

Seeing and holding your baby: Given their early births, we don't expect that all preemies will come out rarin' to go. The reason a neonatologist (a doctor who specializes in the care of newborns) may be in the delivery room, along with the rest of the medical team, is to insure that your preemie's transition from the womb to the world is as quick, easy, and safe as possible. I know it can be agonizing to get only a quick glimpse of your baby, as we whisk her away out of your sight, and sometimes out of your earshot, too. We know that you want to be with her, and are wondering when she'll be back with you, and how long she'll be able to stay.

The answer depends on how young your preemie is, and how quickly we get her stabilized. (Some babies have to be resuscitated at delivery, as you can read more about on page 60.) The wait, usually twenty minutes or so, difficult as it may be for you, really is for your baby's welfare. Once your preemie is warm and dry, her

heart rate is normal, and she's breathing regularly (by herself or with our help), we no longer have to watch her quite so intensely, and can bring her back to you. If you have an older preemie who's doing well on her own, she can probably linger for a while in your arms—a joy for her and for you. But if she's younger than about 34 weeks of gestation, or needs help with her breathing, her stability is still fragile, so it's safer to take her quickly to the intensive care nursery. There, we'll continue to monitor and assess her, and give her any therapies, such as antibiotics or oxygen, that she may need. Above all, we'll make certain that she stays stable. It shouldn't be too long—usually about an hour—until she'll be ready for you to visit her there.

Babies at the edge of viability: Viability means the ability to survive. Some preemies are born so immature that they absolutely cannot survive, no matter what kind of medical treatment they get. Nowadays, that's the case for babies who are born at less than 23 weeks of gestation. Other preemies are far enough along in their development to survive, though they may need intensive care for some time. That's the case for most babies who are born at more than 25 weeks of gestation. Between those ages are preemies who are born at the edge of viability, where we aren't very good at predicting whether a baby is mature enough to survive.

It's rare for a neonatologist to believe that it's right to aggressively treat every newborn. Most, after giving the matter careful thought and weighing the outcome statistics for premature babies, resuscitate all preemies who are beyond the age or weight of viability, and do not treat preemies who are below it. For a baby born in between, though, at the edge of viability, your doctor will have to make difficult decisions about how much treatment to offer.

Because there are some real, unpredictable differences in how rapidly children develop, we usually don't know for sure how an individual preemie who is born at the edge of viability will do. In general, we know that a 23-weeker has a poor chance of surviving and being normal, while a 25-weeker has a much better outlook. But chronological age and physical maturity don't always go hand in hand. Other factors, too, may play a role in how mature a preemie is. For example, girls tend to mature faster than boys, African-American babies may have an advantage over Caucasians, and heavier babies usually do better.

It's occasionally obvious in the delivery room that a baby born at the edge of viability isn't mature enough to survive outside the womb. We may find that we can't get air into her lungs, or that her skin is so fragile that any touch injures her. More commonly, though, it takes longer before it's clear that a preemie is getting worse instead of better. This uncertainty about whether your baby has developed enough to be able to survive can be excruciating—for you and for us, because it makes it so hard to know what the best thing is to do.

I usually tell parents that we have three options. Although I may recommend one, based on what I know about your preemie's medical condition, I believe that any of these can be the most appropriate choice for you and your baby.

The first option is to do everything in our power to support your baby's life, even if that will take a great toll on her and you. I've met many parents who feel that there is nothing they wouldn't do to try to keep their baby alive. They want their child to live, whether or not she is very sick now, dies soon, or ends up with disabilities in the future. They'll love and cherish her no matter what.

The second option is not to provide intensive medical treatment, but to simply make your baby feel as warm, comfortable, and loved as possible in the brief time that she's alive. (Without intensive care, most babies this young will live for only a few hours, although some will live for several days.) Many parents feel that it is kinder and more loving not to extend their infant's life if it's only for a short time, will involve suffering and pain, and there's very little chance that their child can live a long, healthy, or happy life.

The third option lies somewhere in the middle: to start by giving your baby all possible medical treatment, but to reevaluate, and maybe stop, if things are not going well. That point may be reached as early as in the delivery room, or hours, days, or weeks later. Parents and doctors who choose to do things this way usually believe that their uncertainty about a baby's future will diminish over time. If you decide that this approach is the right one for you and your baby, let your baby's doctor know whether you want to play an active role in making the next decision—to stop treatment if necessary—or would rather trust her to make it for you.

Some hospitals and doctors won't feel comfortable with all of these options, and they won't all be appropriate in every situation. Each doctor will have her own, particular way of approaching you about this. But if you feel strongly about what you want done if your baby is born at the edge of viability, be sure to talk about it with your obstetrician and neonatologist before delivery, so that your wishes are heard and you know what your doctors are willing or able to do. Most will want you to be an active partner in making such a momentous decision, because it is you and your family who will be living with its reverberations for the rest of your lives.

FAMILY ISSUES

If we were lucky, we had a chance to introduce ourselves to you before your baby was born, to begin to prepare you (if that's really possible!) for the experience of having a premature baby. Some parents, though, will be meeting their baby's doctors for the first time at delivery. You may not even recognize us later, when we shed our masks and gowns. Try to excuse us if we don't say much to you in the delivery room. Most likely, we'll need to get down to work, and will have time to update you only briefly about how your preemie is doing, before taking him back to the nursery with us for further care. Most parents aren't in top shape for asking questions and taking in a lot of information in the delivery room, anyway. Mothers may be medicated or unable to see what is happening, and fathers' attention is often torn between their wife and their new baby. But be assured that you haven't missed any opportunities. We'll be talking a lot more, soon, including about what happened in the delivery room. It will just take place in a calmer place and time.

Few things lift my spirits more than being at a birth where a newborn is lovingly welcomed by his mother and father, with grandparents, aunts, uncles, and cousins all waiting outside the door. That's a lucky baby! But much as we value your presence at delivery, right after your preemie is born, we'll want you to hang back, to give us some time alone with him. That's so we can focus all of our concentration on observing his physical condition, and quickly providing any medical treatment he needs. I know that's a hard thing to ask you to do. Naturally, you'll be wondering what's going on, and you may be worried. But if we talk to you, we'll have to be less attentive to him. You may have to bite your tongue for a while, or miss out on some great photographs, but I promise you, it's a trade worth making.

I've seen parents of preemies react in all sorts of ways to their baby's birth. You may be thrilled and excited, with an unshakable faith in the future. You may be overwhelmed with doubt, afraid for your child. If your preemie's condition is really tenuous, you may be afraid for yourself, too, wondering how you're possibly going to handle what will happen next. Some parents are stunned and numb, going through all of the motions, but not feeling much of anything. But no matter how you're feeling now, your preemie's birth is a time for hope and faith, for deep looks inside to find sources of strength, for accepting things that you can't possibly change, and for figuring out what really matters. The Chinese philosopher Lao-tzu said, "A journey of a thousand miles must begin with a single step." Your journey is just starting, and like all new parents, your destination isn't clear. It's our job to help you on your way. Remember that all you have to do now is take that single step.

A Different Story for Different Preemies: Survival and Long-Term Health

We have mixed feelings about disclosing statistics on the survival and long-term health outcomes of premature babies. It is not easy for anyone to get this kind of information, let alone the already worried parents of a newborn preemie. And our own experience in the NICU has taught us that numbers are not only terrifying—they can be very misleading. For example: you read that 50% of preemies get a certain long-term health problem, and you conclude that your preemie has a 50% chance of getting it. Not true! No baby is "average," so the numbers that apply to preemies in general don't necessarily apply to yours. There are numerous different factors and symptoms that can transform a grim forecast for preemies as a whole, into a much more positive prospect for your baby.

So as you read the section below that applies to your baby, please keep two important caveats in mind. First, this part of the book is meant to help you develop balanced, realistic expectations—but not to make predictions about your baby. Even within each of the four gestational age groups, the range of medical outcomes for individual babies is very wide. Your baby is not a statistic, and the only guide you have to how he is doing is your baby himself. Spend time with him, look at him and how he's behaving, and, of course, ask the doctors about the results of their evaluations so far.

Second, the following statistics are merely estimates. Accurate projections for today's preemies are elusive, in part because neonatal intensive care is constantly improving. Ten years ago, babies born at 23 weeks of gestation did not survive at all—and all preemies receive better care today than ever before.

23–25 WEEKS OF GESTATION

Survival

Preemies this young, born at the very edge of viability, are the ones who benefit most from the recent advances in neonatal medical care. Ten years ago, babies born at 23 weeks of gestation did not survive. Babies born at 25 weeks survive today in greater numbers than ever before. But for the parents of these very, very premature babies, the numbers are still hard to hear: survival rates vary from about 20% for 23-weekers to about 65% for 25-weekers.

A baby's ability to live outside the womb depends on the maturity of his organs—whether his lungs can take in enough oxygen, his skin can hold in vital fluids, and his brain can withstand the perturbations of handling and medical treatment. The younger and smaller a preemie, the more defenseless he is. Every extra day in the womb can make a difference at this stage, and an extra week is a tremendous advantage. But gestational age is not everything. Other, individual factors can also influence a baby's maturity and prospects.

When can an extremely premature baby be considered safe? Doctors typically warn parents that it may take weeks or even months to know. But if your baby responds well to treatment during his first week, indicating that he is somewhat self-sufficient and resilient, his chances of eventually coming home with you improve dramatically.

Long-term health

Because their bodily systems are so immature, babies born at 23 to 25 weeks are at risk of developing long-term health problems. The earlier a baby is born, the greater that risk. But to quantify it—or predict what it is for a given, individual little baby—is not an easy task.

According to the best available estimates, about one-third of surviving babies in this age group will grow up normal. Another third will have mild or moderate disabilities, such as having respiratory difficulties requiring oxygen at home for a number of months, mild cerebral palsy that gives them weak or awkward control of some of their movements, vision problems that are correctable with glasses, hearing problems that are correctable with a hearing aid, or learning disabilities like hyperactivity or dyslexia. Finally, about one-third will suffer the heaviest consequences of their premature birth, such as having lasting, severe respiratory problems requiring chronic ventilator support, having severe cerebral palsy that calls for a wheelchair, or being blind, deaf, or mentally retarded.

It's impossible on the first day—and sometimes even for the first few months or years—to tell which preemies will be fine and which will be affected by one kind of disability or another. But not all babies are at equal risk. The main risk factors are very poor growth in the womb, brain damage (usually apparent on head ultrasounds before hospital discharge), and severe, chronic lung damage (called BPD, for bronchopulmonary dysplasia). And even with one of these conditions, some babies turn out just fine.

26–29 Weeks of Gestation

Survival

The increasingly high survival rates of babies born between 26 and 29 weeks of gestation leave room for great optimism. Your baby's odds of surviving vary with his gestational age—from about 75% for 26-weekers to 85% for 29-weekers.

Babies at greatest risk are those with severe infections (acquired in the womb or after birth), or whose lungs, brain, or intestines are particularly immature and have trouble withstanding the perturbations of intensive medical care. It can take weeks to know for sure that he is out of danger, but given the really good prospects, you should be prepared for that happy day when you'll take your baby home.

Long-term health

Many babies born at 26 to 29 weeks of gestation grow up perfectly healthy, but there is still a high risk of developing some sort of disability—usually, a mild or moderate one that will not prevent them from leading a happy and productive life. For this age group, the worst consequences of a premature birth are less likely.

Best available estimates—which do not take into account the most recent improvements in neonatal intensive care—indicate that about 40% of surviving 26- to 29-weekers will be normal. Another 40% will have mild or moderate disabilities, such as respiratory difficulties requiring oxygen at home for a number of months, mild cerebral palsy involving poor control of some movements, vision problems that necessitate glasses, hearing problems that necessitate a hearing aid, or learning disabilities like hyperactivity or dyslexia. About 20% will have a severe disability, perhaps requiring years of ventilator support for chronic respiratory disease, having severe cerebral palsy and needing a wheelchair, or being blind, deaf, or mentally retarded.

Being realistic is probably a good thing, but assuming the worst is not. Not all babies within this age group are at equal risk of developing a long-term disability. The closer to 29 weeks your baby was born, the smaller his risk. Even more important is whether your baby has certain risk factors: very poor growth in the womb, brain damage (which usually can be picked up on a head ultrasound before hospital discharge), or severe, chronic lung damage. If not, his chances of being normal are very high.

30–33 Weeks of Gestation

Survival
Today, with modern neonatal intensive care, the overwhelming majority of babies born between 30 and 33 weeks after conception survive—between 90% and 95%. In this age group, as with term babies, those whose lives are most at risk are those born with major abnormalities in their vital organs, such as their heart, kidneys, liver, or intestines.

So you should be ready to take your baby home with you—probably in six to eight weeks, just before his full-term due date.

Long-term health
Babies born at 30 to 33 weeks of gestation have very good odds of growing into perfectly healthy, thriving children, despite their early entry into the world.

According to best available estimates, fully 65% of preemies of this age will develop normally. Another 20% will have mild or moderate disabilities, such as needing oxygen at home for a few months to overcome their respiratory problems, having mild cerebral palsy, or having a common learning disability like dyslexia or hyperactivity. Unfortunately, about 15% of these babies still end up suffering from severe disabilities, perhaps needing chronic ventilator support to be able to breathe, having cerebral palsy so severe that they need a wheelchair, or being blind, deaf, or mentally retarded. These figures are scary, but be sure to keep them in context: even among full-term babies, about 5% have severe disabilities.

As in all gestational age groups, the earlier the birth, the higher the incidence of long-term problems. If your baby is 32 weeks or older, and does not have respiratory distress syndrome (RDS) or an infection, he will almost certainly be normal. But even younger and sicker babies within this group are at minimal risk, unless they had severe growth delay in the womb, or show signs of brain damage (usually apparent on a head ultrasound before hospital discharge) or have chronic lung damage. And even some preemies with these risk factors turn out just fine.

34+ Weeks of Gestation

Survival
Although preemies born at 34 to 36 weeks of gestation are less mature than term babies, the immaturity of their organ systems is so mild that, in this era of excellent neonatal care, they are about as likely to survive as if they had been born at term. In other words, you can feel safe. The greater than 95% survival rate for these older preemies is nearly identical to the survival rate for term babies.

Long-term health

After a preemie reaches 34 weeks of gestation, even if he has some acute medical problems initially (such as RDS, or difficulty starting to feed), he shouldn't be left with any long-term health problems stemming from his prematurity. So you can take heart: although no one can promise that his first few weeks will be problem-free, your preemie's overall prospects are as good as those of any full-term baby newly facing the world.

Questions and Answers

Moving Mother to Another Hospital

Why do they have to take me to a hospital far from home?

Your obstetrician is probably choosing to transfer you to a hospital where you and your baby, during and after the birth, can be taken care of by doctors and nurses specially trained to handle very premature labor and delivery. Only in some hospitals—those with a "level 3" nursery—can the smallest, youngest, and sickest newborns receive the highly specialized, intensive medical care they need. Following professional guidelines, hospital nurseries are classified according to the level of care they can provide to mothers and newborns:

❋ *Level 1* hospitals can assist mothers and babies through uncomplicated full-term, or slightly preterm (35 weeks of gestation or later) labor and delivery. The vast majority of community hospitals are in this category. Level 1 hospitals would be able to perform an emergency C-section or to resuscitate a baby at birth, however, if the need arose.

❋ *Level 2* hospitals can handle most high-risk labors and deliveries, and can take care of those premature babies who are bigger (usually those born at 32 weeks of gestation or more) and who don't have severe medical complications. Many level 2 hospitals have a neonatologist on staff, and a "special care" nursery for preemies.

❋ *Level 3* hospitals have a neonatal intensive care unit (NICU), and full-time obstetricians, neonatologists, neonatal nurses, and respiratory therapists, to assist mothers and babies with the most severe complications of pregnancy and prematurity. Most level 3 hospitals are located in cities, or affiliated with universities and medical schools. An expectant mother would normally be referred to a level 3 hospital if she had a serious obstetric, medical, or surgical complication, if there were a risk of premature delivery at less than 32 weeks of gestation, or if her fetus was diagnosed with a condition that was likely to require surgery or other complex medical care after birth.

Research has shown that very premature babies do better when they're born in a level 3 hospital. So ideally, as soon as a woman's obstetrician knows that she is at significant risk for very premature labor and delivery, he would refer her to a level 3 hospital in the region and prepare for her to be admitted there before she delivers. If an expectant mother is already hospitalized in a level 1 hospital, her obstetrician must decide whether it's best to keep treating her (and to deliver and stabilize her preemie) where she is, or to transport her to a level 2 or 3 hospital. He'll be weighing whether delivery is too imminent to attempt a transfer, since it's more dangerous for a preemie to be born in an ambulance or helicopter than in a level 1 hospital.

How a Maternal Transport Is Done

Most maternal transports to hospitals up to 100 miles away are by ambulance; a helicopter or airplane may be used for greater distances. The choice of transportation also will be influenced by:

❋ the urgency of medical treatment
❋ the availability of a helicopter or plane
❋ how close the helipad or airport is from both hospitals
❋ the weather (whether it's safe to fly)
❋ space constraints (whether a helicopter has ample room to carry an expectant mother as well as the equipment needed for her baby, in case the birth occurs during transport).

The medical team accompanying you will include two or more medical professionals (usually emergency medical technicians, nurses, respiratory therapists, or doctors) who can treat you if your condition suddenly worsens, deliver your baby if necessary, and stabilize the newborn until they reach their destination. Your baby's and your vital signs will be constantly monitored, and your conditions kept stable with fluids, medications, and portable medical equipment (including ventilators, oxygen tanks, and an incubator). Local anesthesia or sedation can be given if you should unexpectedly deliver. Before leaving, and while on their way if need be, the transport team will be in touch through mobile phone with the doctors at the receiving hospital, updating them on your condition, getting instructions about treatments, and making plans for your speedy admission.

Father's Role When a Mother Is Moved

My wife is being transferred to another hospital. What should I do?

The best thing you can do is to wait with your wife before she leaves, to comfort and reassure her on this sudden change of location, and to meet with the transport team when they arrive. Since your wife may not be able to move much (she may be in bed, attached to an IV line), you should help her pack the small bag she'll be allowed to carry on the ambulance or aircraft. Ask her what else she needs you to bring to her in the new hospital. Mothers in preterm labor or with complications of prematurity often rush to the closest hospital or emergency room without even a toothbrush or a change of underwear.

You or your wife will probably be asked to sign a written consent form for the transfer. Also, make sure you tell the transport team and your obstetrician how to reach you in an emergency. Be sure you write down: the name and telephone numbers of the hospital and ward your wife will be admitted to; the telephone number of the nursery; the names of the doctors who will be in charge of your wife and baby; and any other hospital rules or practical tips you'll need to know right away (like visiting hours, whether your other children can visit, where to park or stay overnight nearby).

Family members aren't allowed to ride in the ambulance—there's not enough room, and the situation could get too tense. But many fathers leave at the same time as their wife, so they can be with her soon after she gets to the other hospital. If you plan to drive, be careful. Remember that your wife is in good hands. (If the stress of the last weeks, days, or hours have taken a toll on your nerves and sleep, you might want to ask a friend or relative to drive you there, or take public transportation.)

Although you'll have to travel now, and probably for some time after your baby is born, take heart: once your preemie has gotten over the most serious complications of prematurity, he can be transferred back to your community hospital, to spend the last part of his hospitalization closer to home.

Meeting with Your Baby's Doctor

My obstetrician told me that the neonatologist is going to come meet with me, to answer my questions. Why is she coming, and what am I supposed to ask her?

A meeting with the neonatologist is often arranged for parents who are expected to have a premature baby. Having a premature newborn is quite a bit different than having a full-term one, and the neonatologist mainly wants to help you prepare for it, and get your questions answered. Since nobody learns about having a preemie in childbirth classes or from reading parenting books, she hopes to help you become a little more comfortable with what is going to happen after delivery. If you are having an especially small, young preemie, there's a second, important reason for the meeting: decisions may need to be made about your baby's medical treatment soon after birth, and the neonatologist wants to get you thinking about them.

If you have a sense of dread about this meeting, you're not alone. Many parents don't feel emotionally ready to deal with all of these issues in advance. They are still focusing their energies and hopes on trying to make it to term, and their anxieties about having a preemie may be just too painful to discuss.

Nonetheless, this meeting is important. It's the beginning of your relationship with your baby's doctor. Right now, she seems like part of the bad news you're getting, but she is going to be one of your baby's most important allies. There's even a good chance that the meeting will make you feel better, because you'll learn that your baby's prospects are better than you think, or because it uncovers and addresses some of your anxieties.

Neonatologists all have different styles, of course, and approach this meeting differently. Yours will probably cover some of the following topics—and if she omits any that concern you, feel free to ask about them:

✳ *Delivery.* What medical professionals will be there to take care of your baby? Will you be given your baby to hold, or will she be taken right away to the intensive care nursery? Will you hear your baby cry, and if not, what does that mean about her condition?

* *Your baby's outlook.* What are your baby's chances for survival? What are the chances that she will be normal in the long run, despite her early birth? What are the key medical hurdles that babies of her size and gestational age typically encounter? How will she be fed initially? When will she be able to breastfeed or bottle feed?

* *Spending time with your baby.* How soon can you or your partner visit your baby in the nursery? How soon can you hold her? What are the visiting policies—are any times off limits, are relatives allowed?

* *Keeping you informed and involved.* How will the staff of the nursery give you updates about your baby's health and progress? What kinds of medical decisions can parents participate in? (In intensive care nurseries, dozens of routine medical decisions are made around the clock, and parents, who often aren't there, are usually not consulted about them in advance. No matter what, your permission will be obtained before any major procedure is performed on your baby, unless it's an emergency and the staff can't reach you. But you should feel free to let the doctor know, now or later, if there are some other things you particularly want to know about before they happen—a blood transfusion or a new medication, for example. And even if you don't help to make every decision, you should expect to be kept informed about your baby's care.)

* *Homecoming.* How long is your baby likely to be in the hospital? If you're far from home, when might your baby be transferred back to your community hospital?

* *Breastfeeding.* What are the essential first steps in starting to breastfeed a preemie, and what supplies should you have ready in your hospital room?

* *In advance.* Can you or your partner get a tour of the neonatal intensive care nursery before your baby is born? Does your NICU have a handbook or other reading materials for parents?

* *Decisions for extremely premature babies.* Will the neonatologist be making decisions in the delivery room, or early on, about how much medical treatment your baby should be offered? (Doctors don't all agree, and neither do all well-meaning, loving parents, on whether it is good or bad for extremely premature babies to be resuscitated in the delivery room, and to be put through intensive medical treatment, if they have only a small chance of surviving and growing up healthy. To get help in understanding these decisions, you can read The Doctor's Perspective: Delivery on page 45.) What are the options? How will your wishes be taken into account? Can you meet with a hospital social worker or chaplain, separately or with your partner, to get help in sorting through your feelings, and working out any differences of opinion you may have? These are momentous, wrenching choices, which you and your partner both have to live with, and you don't have to feel that you need to give answers on the spot. Unless your baby's arrival is imminent, you should feel free to say that you need time to reflect on them.

One thing you cannot expect from this meeting is any definite answer as to how your own, precious baby is going to do. That is impossible to predict with certainty before she is born. But this is not your only chance for information. On

the contrary, it's just the beginning of your relationship with your baby's doctor. Most likely,
you will be traveling down a long road together,
and as questions or issues about your baby come
up along the way, you will have plenty of opportunity to talk about them in more depth.

Why a C-Section?

*I was dreaming of a natural childbirth, but
now my obstetrician is telling me a C-section
might be safer for my baby. Why?*

Your disappointment is understandable. Not
only has your pregnancy been cut short, now
you may have to miss the natural childbirth for
which you've been preparing. But at this point,
there's something more important at stake:
your baby's well-being. You should try to focus
on that, and keep in mind that a C-section, although unpleasant, can't beat the immense joy
of bringing your child into the world, no matter
how. For one thing, remember that as many
as one in five babies are born in this country by
C-section. Most of their mothers would probably tell you that they were utterly overwhelmed
by their baby's presence, and quickly made
peace with the fact that their birthing experience was different than they'd imagined.

You can be sure that your obstetrician has considered the pros and cons carefully. She is probably suggesting a C-section because it gives your
child the best chance of survival and a good outcome. A C-section is usually faster, and can be
less stressful and traumatic for a baby than a vaginal delivery. Your obstetrician will explain to you
why a C-section is indicated in your case. Here
are some of the most common scenarios:

❋ *There are signs of fetal distress.* Fetal distress is
usually diagnosed when a fetus's heart rate is

too fast, too slow, or too flat (meaning that it
doesn't respond to changes in his condition).
Whatever is causing the fetal distress—an infection, imperfect supply of blood or oxygen
from the placenta, or other illness or complication—a prompt cesarean birth allows a
baby to receive medical treatment sooner,
possibly preventing damage to his brain and
vital organs.

❋ *Labor hasn't begun, or isn't progressing normally.* Sometimes a pregnancy is purposely
cut short because of the mother's or baby's
health. Your obstetrician may elect to do a C-
section if prompt delivery is the goal, and
labor-inducing medications won't work fast
enough, or if she anticipates that a vaginal delivery is going to be difficult. Forceps and
"vacuum extractors" (devices that help pull a
baby out of the womb) increase the risk of
bleeding in the brain (what doctors call an intraventricular hemorrhage) in babies born
under 35 weeks of gestation.

❋ *Your baby is in a breech or other abnormal position.* Normally, babies are delivered head
first. Breech babies, who are head-up instead
of head-down in the womb, would be born
buttocks or feet first if delivered vaginally.
But coming into the world head last is considerably more dangerous, especially for
preemies. That's because an infant's head is
its largest part, and if it gets stuck inside after
the rest of the body has come out (because
the cervix hasn't yet opened wide enough to
let it through), the flow of oxygen and blood
through the umbilical cord can get cut off.
And if it becomes necessary to use forceps or
a vacuum extractor to help get the head out,
the preemie's delicate brain can be injured.
According to several studies, a vaginal delivery for preemies in breech position carries a
higher mortality risk, as well as a higher risk

How a C-Section Is Done

After making an incision in your skin and separating your abdominal muscles, your obstetrician will examine your uterus, check your baby's position, and decide what kind of incision she will make in the uterus to deliver him. The first choice is usually a horizontal ("transverse") incision in the lower, thinner part of the uterus (just above the pubic bone), because that segment bleeds less and heals with a stronger scar. The second choice is usually a vertical incision, again in the lower part of the uterus. These low incisions are preferred because they don't prevent a mother from delivering another baby vaginally in the future.

Sometimes, because of the position of the placenta or your baby, or if you're delivering earlier than about the 28th week of gestation, before the lower part of the uterus is well developed, your obstetrician will opt for a higher, vertical ("classical") incision in the uterus. That incision heals well, but the resulting scar is not as strong. As a result, there's a risk your uterus will rupture during labor in the future (a very dangerous complication, for a mother and a baby). Women who have had classical C-sections, therefore, are not able to deliver other babies vaginally. Still, that shouldn't prevent you from getting pregnant or carrying a future pregnancy to term. Since the position and shape of the scar on your skin doesn't necessarily correspond to the one made in your uterus, make sure to ask your obstetrician what kind of C-section she's performed. If it was a classical C-section, you can be sure that she chose it to make your baby's delivery as easy and gentle as possible.

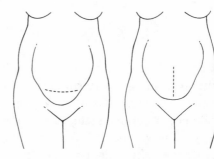

C-section: uterus with horizontal, or "transverse," incision.

C-section: uterus with vertical, or "classical," incision.

for brain damage, than a cesarean section. (An exception is twins, when the first twin can be delivered head first, and only the second twin is breech. In that case, the cervix may be sufficiently dilated by delivery of the first twin's head that the second one isn't in danger of getting stuck.)

* *You are having twins, or higher order multiples.* If your twins share the same sac of amniotic fluid, then a C-section is recommended to avoid possible tangling or mixing up of the two umbilical cords during delivery, with a risk of diminishing the blood flow to one twin, or cutting off the wrong cord. Triplets or more are delivered by C-section to give all of the babies the same chance for prompt medical attention.

* *There are other indications, such as a maternal illness, that make it unlikely a mother can tolerate going through labor, or pregnancy*

complications, or fetal birth defects that make a highly controlled delivery the safest option.

A cesarean section can be safely performed under either general anesthesia (which will "put you to sleep" for the procedure) or regional anesthesia (spinal or epidural, which will keep you conscious, but with little sensation of your body from your chest to your toes). Regional anesthesia offers you the great advantage of being awake during your baby's birth, and seeing him shortly after he's born. But it's slower than general anesthesia, so it won't be used if you have to deliver quickly and unexpectedly. You can discuss the choice of anesthesia with your obstetrician and the anesthesiologist. Since a C-section is surgery, you should also feel free to discuss your own health risks, and what to expect for yourself immediately after this delivery and in the future.

THE CROWD IN THE DELIVERY ROOM

Some births, when there are no complications and the pregnancy goes to term, are private affairs: an obstetrician or midwife coaching a woman and her partner in a secluded room as their baby gradually emerges. A premature birth, however, is usually a different story. If you give birth in a hospital, you can expect your preemie to be welcomed by a crowd of strangers, often in masks and gowns, all there to help your baby as she enters the world. Most parents look around the room and wonder: Who are these people? Why are they needed? Is this a bad sign for our baby? Don't worry. All their presence really means is that you and your newborn will get the best possible assistance.

Although every hospital and birth is somewhat different, here is a quick introduction to the typical members of that crowd in the delivery room:

✳ *If you are having a cesarean delivery,* more people will be present than for a vaginal one. In addition to your obstetrician and labor nurse, one or more anesthesiologists, several nurses to assist during the operation, and possibly an obstetrics resident, may all be involved in the delivery itself.

✳ *At every hospital birth,* whether premature or full-term, there is a medical professional who's designated to take care of the newborn infant. When it's a term baby, that may be your labor nurse or midwife. When it's a premature baby, either a pediatrician or a neonatal nurse practitioner will be called in, often with an extra nurse to assist, if it's a younger preemie who might need extra medical care.

✳ *When you give birth in a teaching hospital,* you can really get a crowd. Every teaching hospital has a pediatric team that is called to the delivery room whenever there is a premature birth. The team generally includes—at a minimum—a pediatric resident or neonatal nurse practitioner, and a pediatric nurse. It also may include a neonatologist and a respiratory therapist. In addition, the group may be joined by a pediatric intern, medical student and/or nurse in training, who can all help out and learn. If you're having multiples, you can expect even more company; most hospitals try to have a team for each baby.

A warning: it can be pretty scary to see some half a dozen people wearing surgical scrubs come running into the room when you're on the verge of giving birth. But it's rarely because of an unexpected emergency. Usually it's just the routine team, in a hurry to get their equipment set up before your baby makes her appearance.

The pediatric team's set-up activities should be finished a few minutes before the birth, and includes everything they need to welcome your baby into the world:

* A special, warming bed, which needs to be switched on a minute or two in advance. (Preemies don't maintain their body temperature as well as full-term babies, and this will keep your baby from getting cold.)
* Equipment that can help your baby breathe, if necessary.
* Warm blankets—one which is used to dry off the just-born baby, who comes out covered with amniotic fluid, and others to lay her on and wrap around her after she's been cleaned and dried off.

During or after the set-up, don't be surprised or alarmed if you hear the doctors and nurses chatting or joking quietly among themselves. Although you may be put off by their less than reverent attitude, you needn't worry: they're very well trained to do what they have to do, and know exactly when concentration is required.

After the obstetrician delivers your preemie and cuts her umbilical cord, he'll hand her to the pediatric team. While the obstetrician continues caring for you, the pediatric team will take care of your newborn, cleaning out her nose and mouth so she can breathe well, and making sure she's warm and dry. They'll also be continually assessing her condition. If your baby looks a little blue, or is breathing irregularly, as many younger preemies do at first, the doctor will decide to give her extra oxygen, by blowing some oxygen near her nose, or by pumping oxygen into her lungs with an oxygen bag and mask. She may perk up and become pinker, as she becomes accustomed to breathing on her own, or she may need more resuscitation. If that's the case, you can read about it on page 60. Once your baby is stable, the doctor or nurse will weigh her, dress her in a hat and a clean, warm blanket, and place her in an isolette (a closed, heated crib).

Most likely, you'll have a chance to see or hold your baby in the delivery room soon after she's born—and you'll be amazed by what a complete and tiny thing she is! But it may be only for a minute or so, if the doctors feel that she'll get cold or need immediate care. If the pediatric team is caring for your baby right in the delivery room, your partner can watch what they're doing—though it may be hard to get a good view, and he certainly should be sure not to elbow any of the doctors or nurses aside! In some hospitals, just-born preemies are taken immediately to separate stabilization rooms, where fathers may or may not be allowed.

Before you know it, your baby will be taken to the nursery, and the crowd in the delivery room will disappear, with just a nurse left to clean up and a doctor to jot down some notes about what went on. They all did their job of easing your baby's transition into the world.

If Your Baby Needs Resuscitation

I didn't hear my baby crying at birth, and they told me she had to be resuscitated. What does that mean?

Although the word *resuscitation* is terrifying to parents, it probably doesn't mean anything that you didn't know already: that your baby is a preemie, and preemies are not always ready to breathe on their own when they are born.

The conventional wisdom—that all newborns come into the world with a loud wail— is based on experience with full-term babies, not preemies. A newborn needs to be strong, vigorous, and breathing deeply in order to cry. The main reason that a preemie doesn't cry in the delivery room, or gives a weak, initial cry and then stops, is that below a certain age, most premature infants just don't have the strength or drive to breathe deeply. It's part of their immaturity.

For those same reasons, many preemies need to be resuscitated—meaning revived with extra oxygen or by being put on a ventilator, which gives them some deep breaths to supplement their own. Most of the time, the breathing problems that arise from prematurity are a combination of underdeveloped lungs (called respiratory distress syndrome, or RDS, a condition that is extremely common among preemies; you can read on page 101 about how many preemies with RDS get better within a few days, but some face a rougher road), weak muscles, and an immature breathing control center in the brain. In other words, immature respiration. Since that's usually the only problem, your newborn's prognosis is probably no different than before you entered the delivery room, knowing you were about to give birth to a preemie.

Occasionally, though, the problem is not just immaturity: something else is depressing a premature newborn's vital functions. If this is the case for your baby, it can, but doesn't necessarily, mean a worse prognosis. You'll need to discuss this with your obstetrician and neonatologist, because your baby's prospects will depend on what the other problem is.

Some things are quickly reversible. Say you were given magnesium sulfate just before delivery—to treat preeclampsia, or preterm labor. Magnesium passes to the baby through the placenta, and can cause respiratory depression. The more magnesium sulfate you were given, the more relaxed and limp your newborn may be; she may be barely breathing at all. Don't worry: the doctors will place her on a ventilator, which will breathe for her until the magnesium sulfate wears off (usually in a day or less). Then she should be fine, with no lasting short-term or long-term effects. Some other drugs, like general anesthesia or some pain medications, given to a mother for delivery, can affect the baby in a similar way. They, too, should wear off without causing any lasting consequences.

On the other hand, there are some times when a baby needs to be resuscitated for reasons that can be more serious. For example, infections can decrease a newborn's drive to breathe, and cause her heart to beat too slowly. If her vital signs are depressed because she is sick from an infection, her prognosis will depend on what kind of infection it is, and how soon the doctors are able to control it. Some infections are more likely than others to cause lasting damage to a baby's brain and other organs, and the longer an infection goes on, the more chance that it could be fatal. Children whose mothers had an infection of the membranes and amniotic fluid inside the uterus, called chorioamnionitis, have been found to have a somewhat higher incidence of cerebral palsy. When chorioamnionitis is de-

How Is a Baby Resuscitated?

Since premature newborns need to be resuscitated mainly because of breathing problems, doctors usually start by trying to stimulate the baby to breathe on her own (often just by rubbing her, and blowing oxygen near her nose), and then by giving her breaths. To give her breaths, they often use an oxygen bag and mask, placing the mask over the baby's nose and mouth, and pumping oxygen from the attached bag into her lungs. If, after a minute or two, the baby is still not pink, with a strong heartbeat and breathing regularly, the next step is for the doctors to "intubate" her. This means inserting a tube through her mouth or nose into her windpipe, to send air directly into her lungs. A preemie who is very young may be intubated immediately, since doctors know that these babies aren't yet ready to breathe on their own. After a baby is intubated, the tube can be connected to the oxygen bag, or to a mechanical breathing machine (a ventilator), that can continue to help breathe for her.

Most of the time, a preemie's heart will respond with healthy beats as soon as she is breathing well. Rarely, when this is not the case, the doctors will do chest compressions (CPR) or administer medications, to make the baby's heart beat stronger and faster.

Occasionally, other problems require treatment as part of the resuscitation. If there was a large placental abruption, for example, the baby may have lost a considerable amount of blood, and need intravenous fluid or a blood transfusion in the delivery room. Another example: if a small tear in a baby's lung has occurred, allowing air to escape around it and interfere with her breathing and heartbeat, the doctors may try to remove the free air with a needle or tube, through a small incision in her chest (see page 161). Your doctors will tell you about any of these unusual situations when they explain how your baby is doing, and what happened in the delivery room. Otherwise, you can assume that your preemie's resuscitation was a straightforward process of helping her to breathe better than she was ready to do just yet on her own.

tected during a pregnancy, an early delivery is often performed in the hope of catching it before the baby also becomes infected. Most babies whose mothers have chorioamnionitis, though, grow up with no long-term developmental problems.

There are situations in which resuscitation is necessary because the supply of blood and oxygen to the baby was disrupted before delivery. This could be due to various things, from very low maternal blood pressure, to a tear in the placenta (called a placental abruption), a knot or blood clot in the umbilical cord, or the umbilical cord lying in a position where it gets squeezed hard with the baby's movements in the womb during pregnancy, or with contractions during labor.

Most infants can withstand a short period of low blood flow and oxygen. (This often occurs intermittently during delivery, or for several minutes after birth.) These babies usually are fine. But when this kind of problem goes on for a longer time, either around the time of delivery, or earlier during the pregnancy, there can be damage to a baby's brain.

How would you know if your baby had a period of low blood flow or oxygen before delivery? A fetal heartbeat that is too slow or unresponsive (as seen on a fetal heart rate monitor), an excess of acid in the fetus's or newborn's blood (this can be measured before delivery by a test called a scalp pH, in which a tiny scratch is made on the fetus's scalp), passage of meconium—a baby's first stools—while she's still inside the womb (this only occurs in older preemies with more mature bowel function), low Apgar scores, or pulmonary hypertension (high blood pressure in the lungs) that persists after birth are some of the signs. The doctors will let you know if your baby shows any of these, and what that might mean for her.

If you are worried about the possibility of damage to your baby's brain from lack of blood flow or oxygen, you should know that signs of a recent, severe injury usually are apparent within the first week of life. A baby may have seizures, or be hyper-alert and jittery, or comatose. Or her other organs, such as her heart, kidneys, or liver may be damaged, leading the doctors to believe that her brain was injured, also. Babies who start recovering within a few days will most likely be fine. Occasionally, though, if the injury occurred earlier in gestation or was less severe, neurological problems may not show up until a baby is older.

Apgar Scores

Do preemies always get low Apgar scores? Our son's were only four and six, and we're very worried.

Preemies don't always get low Apgar scores, but they often do. The earlier a baby is born, the lower his Apgar scores are likely to be, simply because of his immaturity. Whereas in a full-term newborn, very low Apgar scores are likely to mean there's been some asphyxia (insufficient blood flow or oxygen before, during, or right after delivery), in a premature baby, low Apgars often have to be interpreted differently.

The Apgar score, developed by Dr. Virginia Apgar in the 1950s, is a tool to assess if a newborn infant needs resuscitation. It is comprised of five signs: a newborn's heart rate, respiration, reflex responses, muscle tone, and skin color. Each sign can receive from zero to two points, indicating a negative, mediocre, or optimal finding:

Sign:	0	1	2
Heart rate:	Absent	Slow	Normal
Respiration:	Absent	Irregular	Strong
Reflexes:	No response	Grimace	Cough/sneeze
Muscle tone:	Limp	Some flexion	Moving
Color:	Pale or blue	Body pink/extremities blue	All pink

A baby's first Apgar score is assigned at exactly one minute after birth (but if his heartbeat is slow or he's not breathing well, the doctors will begin to resuscitate him before then). Scoring is repeated at five minutes, and in some cases, again at 10, 15, and 20 minutes after birth, to check on a baby's improving or worsening condition. The highest score (rarely obtained by a preemie) is ten. A one-minute score less than six usually indicates that an infant needs to be resuscitated, and resuscitation will continue until the score is six or higher. Only if an infant's Apgar score remains lower than three for 15 minutes or longer does it carry a significantly higher risk for mortality and future disabilities.

The one- and five-minute Apgar scores are helpful in predicting a baby's long-term outcome only when they're combined with other information doctors gather about his vital functions and organs in the first few days of life. Moreover, Apgar score predictions are not as reliable for preemies as for term babies. That's because some findings that can be normal in a preemie, such as irregular respiration or low responsiveness, can take points off his Apgar score, but don't tell much about how he's really doing.

It is still too early to know what the future is going to bring for your baby, but in the next hours and days, you're going to find out much more detailed (and hopefully reassuring) information about him. In the meantime, you shouldn't focus on his Apgar scores, because for a preemie, things are much more complex than counting up to ten.

Birth Weight Predictions

They told me before delivery that my baby would weigh over two pounds, but he's a lot smaller than that. How could they have gotten that wrong?

Until a baby leaves his mother's womb and can be put on a scale, there's no way to measure exactly how much he weighs. Doctors can only make predictions, using different tools, knowing that a baby's actual birth weight can always be higher or lower than their estimate. In a small premature baby, weight can be overestimated more easily than in bigger babies. However, even an imperfect weight estimate can be very helpful in a high-risk pregnancy, to plan what kind of medical assistance a mother and her baby may need before, during, and right after delivery. For instance, when the dating of a pregnancy is unclear, estimated fetal weight can help determine a baby's gestational age. It can help assess how well a baby is growing in the womb, and lead to efforts to find out what's wrong, if growth is poor. It also can influence the choice between a vaginal delivery and a C-section.

The most common methods of estimating fetal weight are:

* *Carefully feeling the uterus.* With her own hands, and a good dose of clinical experience, an obstetrician can assess the size of the fetus in the uterus, and make an estimate of his weight.
* *Measuring the fetus by ultrasound.* The size of a fetus's head and abdomen, and the length of his femur (the long bone in the thigh), correlate with how much he weighs. An ultrasound is done to obtain these measurements, which are then used to calculate the fetus's weight.

If a pregnancy is close to term, doctors consider a clinical estimation as reliable as an ultrasound. But for premature, smaller babies, the ultrasound is more accurate.

No matter how skillful the doctor, the estimate of fetal weight is always, at best, a good approximation. That's because the fetus's size, or length, is used to estimate his weight, but babies of the same size may have different proportions of muscle and fat (fat weighs less than muscle), or heavier or lighter bones. Occasionally, a weight estimation is off because the baby is in a position in the uterus where his head size or femur length can't be accurately measured. (Factors such as low levels of amniotic fluid, or maternal overweight, which can lead to difficulty seeing subtle physical features well on a fetal ultrasound, don't usually affect estimations of fetal weight.)

It may seem unsatisfying, in this age of medical miracles, to learn that a series of educated guesses about a premature baby's condition is often all that doctors have in their hands before delivery. Still, that's usually all it takes to get ready to meet their little patient, and to make the choices necessary to take care of him in the best, possible way.

Bonding

My baby was rushed to the NICU as soon as he was born, rather than being placed on my chest. I'm so upset about the loss of bonding.

Your sense of loss is natural, and actually, a healthy sign that your bonding with your baby is already well under way. You only got a peek at your newborn, and then he was gone, leaving your arms painfully empty. Although right now, the stress and confusion around the birth of your preemie probably feels like it will affect your whole relationship with your newborn, you really don't have to fear that. Just because you couldn't have the picture-perfect experience of feeling him skin-to-skin on your belly after delivery, you aren't likely to be less attached to your baby, or he to you.

The theory that mothers go through a bonding period shortly after their infants' births, and if they miss that crucial window their relationship is forever flawed, has been widely criticized since it was first proposed in the 1970s. Goats or ducks may reject their offspring by instinct, if they're taken away right after birth, and then given back. But the growth of love and attachment between a parent and a child, although certainly cemented by physical contact, is primarily a psychological process. It can begin before birth, immediately after, or even months or years later (as adoptive parents and their children know well). It can amaze you with its immediate power, or slowly grow over time. The tempo and pattern of your relationship with your infant will depend on his temperament and maturity (preemies are not always as ready as full-term babies to be fully responsive to human contact and stimulation), your own needs, fears, personality, and cultural background, as well as the time you spend together and many other factors.

This doesn't mean that early contact between parents and their new babies has no value. Many studies have demonstrated that early contact can foster stronger parental involvement in their child's care later on. In fact, research on bonding has helped to humanize perinatal medical care, for instance allowing fathers to be present at delivery, and new mothers to keep their babies at their bedside in the hospital, unless a separation is necessary for medical reasons. In the neonatal intensive care unit, parents are now involved as soon as possible in the care of their fragile premature infants. But clearly, parents can love their babies desperately—and that love will be returned—even if they don't touch or see each other immediately after birth.

If your premature baby needs intensive medical care now, and you won't be able to hold him or take care of him for days, or even weeks, be assured that it won't be difficult to make up for the lost time. As soon as your baby can tolerate it, you can begin "kangaroo care" (see page 221), and feel your baby's naked skin on yours—that special, intimate experience you are now missing so much. We can promise you that by simply being at your preemie's side often throughout his hospitalization, talking to him, touching him, and holding him when you can, the bonding you're longing for will take place. Many parents of preemies think they are even closer to their child precisely because they went through the same painful, forced separation as you, and the whole experience of prematurity together. They say their love for their child turned out to be more intense and fulfilling than they ever imagined— even if that didn't happen in the baby's first minutes of life.

Moving Baby to Another Hospital

My baby is being transferred to another hospital. I'm terribly upset.

Even though you have understandable reasons to be anguished about it, your daughter's untimely travel and separation from you is in her best interest. The vast majority of hospitals around the country don't have the special expertise and equipment to treat infants who are very premature or have high-risk medical complications. If your baby was born at less than 32 weeks of gestation, or her doctors are worrying about some complication, there's no doubt that the benefits of being cared for by neonatologists, in a well-equipped neonatal intensive care unit (NICU), amply exceed the risks of being transported there. Thanks to the training and experience of the medical team who will ac-

company your baby, the therapies provided to preemies in the NICU can often begin during the transfer, and portable medical equipment allows even the tiniest baby to travel while receiving the critical care that's needed to keep her stable.

The transport team for your baby will probably be sent by the hospital to which she is going, and supervised, in person or by phone, by the neonatologist who'll be directing her care when she arrives. Most neonatal transport teams are composed of two or more experienced medical professionals who have worked in NICUs. They have special, additional training in transporting critically ill babies and performing emergency procedures on preemies.

The neonatal transport team will create a traveling, mini–intensive care nursery. Your baby will be warm and comfortable in a portable incubator—a battery-heated box that is resistant to shocks and is tightly attached to the vehicle for safety during transport. This incubator will enclose and protect her, and at the same time allow easy access to the members of the team, so they can monitor her condition and provide any medical care she may need during the trip. The transport team will take with them copies of your daughter's medical records, x-rays, and a note from her doctor summarizing the care she's received so far.

It's very important that both parents (or at least the father, if the mother is still too weak after delivery) see their baby before she leaves, to say good-bye until later, and to talk to the transport team. You will be asked to sign a written consent form agreeing to the transfer, and to leave numbers and addresses where you can be reached in an emergency. The transport team may also want to ask you some questions about the pregnancy or your family's medical history. They will talk to you about the medical assistance your baby will receive, and the logistics of the transfer. Be sure to write down the hospital your baby is going to, its address, the location and phone number of the nursery, the name of the doctor who will be in charge, ways to get there by car or public transportation, and information on parking and lodging in the area.

You won't be allowed to accompany your baby during the transfer. For safety reasons, nobody but the medical crew can ride in the ambulance or aircraft during a high-risk patient transport. However, if a mother needs to stay in the hospital for more than a few days, it may be possible to transfer her to the same hospital as her baby (although with a different transport team, in a separate ambulance), so the family doesn't remain apart for long. If you're in that situation, you can ask your obstetrician if it can be arranged.

Most likely, you will remain in the hospital where you delivered until you are discharged, and your partner will visit your baby in her new place first. Frequent phone calls, news, anecdotes, descriptions, and pictures will help you feel connected until you can see your baby. Her new doctors in the NICU will keep you updated on her condition, and you'll be encouraged to call and speak to the nurses taking care of her as often as you need. Be prepared to miss your baby a lot. But keep in mind that the best thing you can do for your daughter now is to get your stamina back. While you rest, you can read on page 92 about what an NICU is like, and about the specialists who are taking care of your baby. This forced separation will probably only last a few days. Soon you'll be able to walk through the doors of your baby's new hospital yourself, and be with her again.

MULTIPLES

Twins Delivered at Different Times

My doctor said that although it looks like one of my twins will be delivering early, she's going to try to give the other more time in the womb. How could that be possible?

It used to be only a twist of nature recorded by medical historians: quadruplets all born on different days, over a ten-day span; a boy born an amazing ninety-five days before his twin sister. But today, doctors are making it more common. Remember the Chukwu babies, the world's first set of octuplets to be born alive? Many people were too impressed by their sheer numbers to focus on the unusual circumstances of their births. The first baby, a girl, was born on De-

cember 8, 1998, while the other seven were delivered on December 20. Sadly, the smallest of the seven later-born babies did not survive. But the twelve extra days in their mother's womb must have helped at least some of the others.

You should know that what's called "delayed interval delivery" is still a rare and controversial practice in obstetrics. Normally, once one baby in a multiple gestation is born, the obstetrician makes sure to deliver the other babies right away. That's because the risks are substantial, primarily from serious infections that can quickly become life-threatening, for both the mother and the babies who remain in the womb.

In recent years, however, obstetricians have become more aware of the option to delay the other births, from case reports in medical journals and conferences. But there are no official records (a good guess would place the number of cases so far at only a few hundred), and delayed interval delivery has not been studied yet by medical researchers, so its relative risks and benefits are not known. It requires a lot of courage and motivation from expectant parents, and not all doctors are willing to chance it.

Among all multiple pregnancies at high risk for a premature delivery, only a few can take advantage of a delayed interval delivery. It's only possible when whatever threatens the continued gestation of one baby doesn't affect the others. Since your doctor believes you are a good candidate, it probably means that although the premature birth of one of your twins appears likely—perhaps because his amniotic fluid sac has ruptured, or he's already pushing through a slightly open cervix—you are healthy, and your other twin looks stable and secure in his own sac. The decision to attempt a delayed interval delivery is best considered before the birth of the first baby, so that a treatment plan can be made in advance, but your doctor won't know if it's really possible until you actually deliver.

Here are some of the necessary requirements:

* Each twin should have his or her own placenta and amniotic fluid sac (as all fraternal twins, but only some identical twins, do).
* Their gestational age should be in the range where even a few more days in the womb can greatly improve a premature baby's outcome, justifying the risks and efforts to prolong the pregnancy. That usually means that your babies are less than about 30 weeks of gestation.
* The first baby's delivery is vaginal, not by C-section.
* After your first baby's birth, your uterus stops contracting, and your cervix begins to close (meaning that your body will "cooperate," and continue the pregnancy).
* You are not bleeding heavily after delivery.

Your obstetrician will explain why it may be feasible in your case, and what her plan of intervention is, since a standard medical protocol for this procedure doesn't exist yet. Probably, you will be treated with antibiotics to try to prevent infections. Immediately after delivery, some doctors start intravenous medications to stop contractions, and/or perform a minor surgical procedure called a cerclage (see page 15), to keep the cervix closed. Others don't prescribe anti-labor drugs or do surgery on the cervix, preferring not to mask any signs of labor, which could indicate an infection. If a mother has chorioamnionitis—an infection of the amniotic fluid sac—most doctors would immediately deliver all of her babies. Some doctors, however, believe that aggressive antibiotic treatment could still make a delayed interval delivery possible.

If, after the first delivery, your condition stabilizes, and the baby still in your womb is doing well, you will probably be kept in the hospital on complete bed rest, under strict medical observation. Sometimes, an expectant mother is put on an inclined bed, with her feet higher than her head, to reduce pressure on the cervix. Eventually, after several weeks, if your pregnancy continues to proceed well, you may even be allowed to go home—although probably still on bed rest and taking medications—until the second delivery occurs. Despite the best medical care, though, nobody can predict whether, and for how long, your pregnancy can be sustained.

In the meantime, you'll have to cope with a very confusing and stressful situation: being new parents of a premature baby who may be in the hospital in an intensive care nursery, while still carrying on a demanding, high-risk pregnancy. Parents who face a delayed interval birth should be prepared for a time of great anxiety and tension, of strong, contrasting emotions. You will worry about the first twin you've delivered prematurely. If your baby is on a ventilator and can't be moved, and you are confined to bed, you may not be able to see him for several days or even weeks. At the same time, you'll be struggling to keep your stress to a minimum, to relax and be optimistic. You probably won't have much emotional energy to spare. Couples who have gone through this exceptional experience say they got through it by keeping hopeful, and by trying to take one day at a time.

Who's A, Who's B?

Throughout my pregnancy, my sons were triplets "A" and "B," and my daughter was triplet "C." But now in the NICU, it's changed—she's "B." What happened?

When you're having multiples, each fetus's growth and health is assessed and followed individually, to make sure each one is developing well. To do that, doctors have to keep each baby straight, so they label them with letters. "A" is always the one at the bottom of the uterus, "B" is the next one up, and so on. In a multiple gestation, as many letters as fetuses are used. For instance, the McCaughey septuplets, born in 1997, were known to their doctors, before delivery, as Babies A through G. Baby A, a boy, was given the nickname "Hercules," because he was at the bottom of an inverted pyramid of seven fetuses, with the weight of all of his siblings on top of him!

Sometimes, if there are more than two fetuses, doctors can't be sure exactly who's higher than whom. In that case, they may simply (sometimes randomly) decide to call the baby

on the bottom right "B," on the bottom left "C," and on the top "D," etc.

These alphabet letters are then reassigned at delivery, according to the babies' birth order. If it's a vaginal delivery, Baby "A" will remain "A," because being closest to the cervix, he will be born first. But when babies are delivered by C-section, occasionally the first baby to emerge from the womb isn't the one who was at the bottom. So the letters you knew your babies by before birth can get scrambled. That's what happened with your triplets. Your girl was born second, so she changed from Triplet "C" to Triplet "B," while one of your boys now has a blue sign on his bed saying Triplet "C" after his last name.

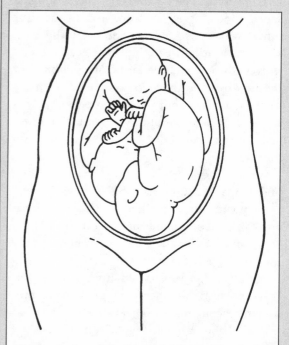

Triplets in the womb: doctors label the one at the bottom "A," the one in the middle "B," and the one at the top "C."

During a C-section of twins or triplets, the obstetrician is usually certain about which baby is coming out. With higher-order multiples, though, it's possible that matching the original letters to the babies won't be crystal clear at delivery. That can be confusing and upsetting for parents. During pregnancy, many parents attribute personality traits to their babies, using clues from their growth and behavior in the womb. Future parents of multiples may be even more apt to develop these impressions of their babies, because of differences they detect after seeing their size, favorite positions, and activity levels on ultrasounds. For instance, they may talk about their smaller girl, who moves around more and kicks vigorously, as the feisty one, with an active, outgoing personality, while thinking of their bigger boy, who is quieter, as a more contemplative, peaceful child. After delivery, if the letters get mixed up, it can feel like your babies are mixed up too.

Luckily, you needn't worry about any negative medical consequences. Any serious condition that was being followed before delivery should be readily identified in a baby soon after birth, so this "mix-up" shouldn't interfere with your babies' receiving good medical care.

Soon, even the doctors and the nurses will begin calling your babies by the names you've chosen for them, and those fickle, anonymous letters will become a thing of the past.

Identical or Not?

My obstetrician could not tell from the sonograms during pregnancy if my twins are identical. Now that they are born, can we finally know for sure?

As soon as parents learn they are expecting twins, their first question often is: Are they identical? All couples are eager to know if the additions to their family are two genetically identical individuals, or two siblings who by chance are spending their prenatal lives together.

Sometimes the answer is apparent even before the birth. If prenatal tests reveal two fetuses of the same sex, sharing the same amniotic fluid sac, then the twins are almost definitely monozygotic, or identical. Identical twins come from one fertilized egg that divided in two—so they carry the same genes. (At birth, the obstetrician can confirm this finding by looking at the placenta. If it has only one chorionic membrane, it means that only one sac formed around the fertilized egg; then, only after the sac had formed—surprise!—the egg split in two.)

On the other hand, if ultrasounds and other prenatal tests reveal that the fetuses are a boy and a girl, then they obviously don't share all of the same genes. They are dizygotic, or fraternal, twins. There's also a high likelihood that the twins are fraternal if they were conceived after treatments for infertility, because fertility drugs stimulate the ovaries and often cause release of more than one egg, and because more than one embryo is usually implanted during in vitro fertilization.

But sometimes the answer is more elusive. Say you learn that your twins are the same sex and are in two different sacs. Chances are they're fraternal, but you can't be sure; they could be identical twins who come from a fertilized egg that divided so soon after conception that each embryo went on to make its own sac. In these ambiguous cases, examining the placenta after birth doesn't help. But you can ask your babies' doctor to check their blood types. If they don't have the same blood type, they're not identical.

What if he still can't reach a definite conclusion? Looking at the babies themselves after birth may not tell you much. Even many parents of full-term twins find it a hard call, and preemies have slightly more immature facial features that can make many of them appear identical to inexperienced eyes. (Although it doesn't take long for parents to learn to identify their tiny offspring!) At that point, the only remaining option is genetic testing, in which blood is taken and the immunologic markers that are different in each person—except identical twins—are matched and compared. This is a complex and costly analysis that health plans don't cover, unless the information is needed for medical reasons, like organ transplantation. In very small babies, the amount of blood this testing requires is a significant loss, and your babies' doctor may advise against it for now. Don't worry; there's no rush except your own curiosity. The test can be done anytime—even when the twins are adults.

Is it worth it to get your babies tested? That's up to you. But most people find that the intense curiosity of the first few hours or days soon fades, as they are overtaken by the joy of watching their twins grow—and discovering, day by day, who they are going to be.

In Depth

YOUR BABY IS SMALL–FOR–GESTATIONAL AGE: WHAT DOES IT MEAN?

There's enough to absorb and understand when you're having a premature baby. On top of that, some parents are told that their baby is small for her gestational age. How could a tiny preemie be even smaller? Does it matter?

First, a definition. Of course, many infants—full-term or premature—are slightly smaller than average. But a full-term or premature infant is labeled small–for–gestational age, or SGA, if her weight falls below the tenth percentile on the standard growth curve for her age, meaning she weighs less than 90% of all infants her age. This means that your baby grew more slowly than usual in the womb, and it's important to know why. (You might also be told that your baby had intrauterine growth restriction, or IUGR, which is just another way of saying the same thing.) By contrast, an infant is considered appropriate–for–gestational age, or AGA, if her weight falls anywhere between the tenth and ninetieth percentiles for her age.

For example, a preemie who is born at 28 weeks of gestation is AGA if her weight ranges anywhere between 750 grams and 1500 grams. If her weight is less than 750 grams, she is SGA. You can check the chart on page 513 to see exactly where your baby falls.

Why do doctors make this distinction? Because in general, newborns who are small–for–gestational age have more health problems after delivery. Some, whose growth was severely restricted in the womb, are also at greater risk for long-term development problems. Whether and how your baby is affected is going to depend largely on what caused her growth to be restricted, and how long-lasting and severe the restriction was.

WHY SOME BABIES ARE SMALL-FOR-GESTATIONAL AGE

There are a wide variety of reasons that a fetus may not grow properly in the womb. Your obstetrician may already know, or be able to tell you soon, after doing some tests, if any of these most common causes seem likely:

* *Insufficiency of the placenta.* The fetus gets its supply of nutrients and oxygen through the placenta, so anything that disrupts an efficient flow of oxygen and nutrient-rich blood through the placenta will impede the fetus's growth. Placental insufficiency, as it is called, is often caused by an illness that affects the pregnant mother's circulation, such as preeclampsia, diabetes, or heart disease. It can also be due to any of a number of possible defects of the placenta itself, including a placental abruption (separation of part of the placenta from the wall of the uterus), a placenta that's poorly functioning because it is small and malformed, or one that has been damaged from inflammation, infection, or a lack of blood flow and oxygen. Placental insufficiency is often the reason that an obstetrician recommends an early delivery, if he thinks a baby will get better nourished, and face fewer health risks, in the nursery than in the womb.

* *Chromosomal or other congenital abnormalities.* Many different genetic and congenital anomalies, which may be discovered during the pregnancy (through amniocentesis or ultrasound, for example) or after birth are associated with fetal growth restriction.

* *Infection of the mother and fetus.* Common colds and flus rarely harm a fetus. But certain infections, which may be transmitted to the fetus if a mother gets them during the pregnancy, can affect the baby's growth and development, and cause other, serious problems. Some of the more common ones are rubella (which causes German measles), herpes, cytomegalovirus (called CMV), toxoplasmosis, and syphilis. In some cases, infections are discovered through cultures and blood tests done during pregnancy, and in other cases after the birth. (You can read more about congenital infections on page 183.)

* *Smoking, drugs, alcohol, and some medications.* Pregnant women who smoke, drink heavily, or use drugs such as cocaine, heroin, or amphetamines have a tendency to deliver small-for-gestational age babies. The same is true for mothers on certain medications, such as some anti-cancer and anti-seizure drugs. These substances can be toxic to the developing fetus and have direct, adverse effects on fetal growth, or they can cause growth restriction by interfering with the flow of blood and oxygen through the placenta.

* *Malnutrition.* Mothers who are poorly nourished and gain too little weight during pregnancy are also at risk for malnourished and poorly grown infants. That's because the fetus relies on the mother for the nutrients it needs to grow and develop well.

Being African-American, having multiples, and living at high altitude all increase the chance that one will have smaller babies. Studies also indicate that women who were small-for-gestational age themselves are at greater risk of having small-for-gestational age infants than their peers.

Of course, some newborns end up in the smallest ten percent for no reason other than normal variation in size. Remember that if you are small, your babies are more likely to be, too. In fact, some doctors prefer to use an alternative, stricter definition of SGA: that a baby is small–for–gestational age only if she falls below the third percentile on the growth curve, weighing less than a full 97% of babies her age. The rationale is that some, perfectly well nourished and healthy newborns (premature or full-term) will fall in the smallest ten percent, just due to the genetic luck of the draw—say their parents and grandparents are small—and the medical problems associated with being SGA won't apply to them. But babies in the smallest three percent are much more likely to have had some problem that significantly restricted their growth potential.

How Your Baby Will Look

Above all, your baby will look like a preemie, so the best description is in "Your Beautiful Newborn: A Portrait," on page 89. Only a few things in her appearance may differ because she is small for her gestational age. Some babies have so-called symmetric growth retardation, meaning all parts of their bodies were affected fairly equally. These babies are often described as looking "old" despite their little size, because they're short, skinny, and their heads are small. Usually, these babies' growth has been restricted since the early stages of pregnancy.

Alternatively, your baby may have "asymmetric" or "head-sparing" growth retardation. If that's the case, she'll still be scrawny, and maybe short, but her head will be normal in size for her age—disproportionately big for her small body. Usually, head-sparing means the baby's growth restriction was less severe, and occurred only in the later stages of pregnancy: there was at least enough nourishment for the brain to grow. One of the truly amazing aspects of fetal development is that when there are not enough nutrients to go around, the body knows to give preference to the brain, protecting it by giving it more than its fair share.

Sometimes, growth restriction is accompanied by very low levels of amniotic fluid. (That's because a fetus's urine is the main component of amniotic fluid, and when a fetus doesn't get enough blood flow, usually because of placental insufficiency, she doesn't urinate as much.) Without amniotic fluid to expand it, the uterus can press tightly around a fetus, constraining her movements. When a baby doesn't move around enough in the womb, her joints can become stiff and contracted. If this has occurred in your baby, you'll notice that she can't bend or straighten some of her joints as freely and fully as she should. Over time, and possibly with the help of orthopedics or physical therapy, these contractures often can resolve.

What Being SGA Means for Your Baby in the Short Term

Unfortunately, being small–for–gestational age does carry increased risks. The best way to think about it is that your preemie has two conditions to deal with, rather than one: prematurity and the problem that caused her growth restriction. This means that for SGA babies on average, the chances of survival are not quite as good as for appropriately grown preemies of the same gestational age. It also means that your baby may have a more complicated, and somewhat longer, hospital course than bigger babies of her age.

If the underlying problem is that your baby has an ongoing medical condition, such as a chromosomal or anatomic abnormality, or an infection, then that condition is likely to be the dominant factor determining her prognosis during her hospital stay. Of course, your baby's prematurity and size are going to count, too—but probably less than the other problem. Since there are a wide variety of congenital and genetic conditions that can affect a fetus's growth, ask your baby's doctor to go over your baby's specific problem, and its prognosis, with you.

If the underlying problem was solely pregnancy-related—placental insufficiency, with subsequent malnourishment of the fetus—then her prognosis will be determined by two things: how the lack of nutrients affected her before she was born, and what normal hurdles her prematurity brings.

There are certain health complications that affect many SGA babies in their early days and weeks of life. Your baby's doctors will look out for them, and manage them. Because many SGA newborns weren't getting quite as much oxygen as they needed from the placenta during pregnancy, more of these smaller babies have low Apgar scores, and need oxygen and breathing assistance right after they're born. (Be reassured that in preemies, a need for resuscitation at delivery is much more common and less grave than most parents think, as you can read on page 60.)

Many small–for–gestational age infants develop low blood sugar (hypoglycemia) during the first day or two; they have particularly high energy needs, but their own energy stores are low, after they used up every bit they could in the womb. This is a temporary problem. Hypoglycemia is only serious if it isn't recognized and treated promptly. Your baby's doctors and nurses will know to watch for it, so you don't have to worry. If she needs it, they'll give her extra calories, usually in the form of intravenous sugar water, or additional feedings of preemie formula, for several days until the problem resolves.

Small–for–gestational age infants also tend to have more feeding intolerance than usual. It takes longer to move them from intravenous feedings to full feedings of breast milk or formula. Once SGA babies do become adept at digestion, they often eat very large quantities for their tiny size, as if they are hungry and making up for lost time. Their parents like nothing better than seeing them eat like little pigs, as they deserve to do!

It won't be surprising if your baby is born with an excess of red blood cells, a condition called polycythemia. This happens when the body doesn't get quite enough oxygen over a long period of time—it responds by making more red blood cells, in a valiant attempt to deliver as much oxygen as possible to the organs and tissues. (Red blood cells transport oxygen throughout the body.) But an excess of red blood cells can be too much of a good thing, causing the blood to be too thick, and thereby making breathing harder, jaundice more severe, and blood sugar lower, among other problems. If your baby has this condition, the treatment is to thin out her blood, either by simply giving her extra fluid, or by taking out some of her blood and replacing it with another fluid. (This is called a partial exchange transfusion or a reduction transfusion.)

Another thing the doctors watch for—among all premature babies, but particularly among those with intrauterine growth restriction—is hypothermia (or in nonmedical language, getting cold). Babies who are SGA have a harder time holding in body heat because they have less body fat, and so less insulation. This is nothing to worry about, but may mean that your baby has to stay in an isolette a little longer than other babies of her gestational age.

Breathing is one of the main initial challenges for all premature babies. The younger they are, the more likely they are to have respiratory distress syndrome (RDS), and to develop chronic lung disease, which means they are dependent on supplemental oxygen, or other breathing assistance, for longer. Although it has long been thought that when a fetus is under stress in the womb (from malnutrition or any other cause), her lungs will respond by maturing faster, recent research seems to indicate that SGA preemies may actually have worse breathing problems—more severe respiratory distress syndrome and more chronic lung disease—than appropriately grown babies of their gestational age. It is not known why that may be the case, but it might have to do with a lack of protective nutrients, and/or some prenatal changes in lung structure from lower than normal oxygen levels. If your baby does have RDS, you can read about it on page 101.

One recent research study found that in a group of SGA babies who were extremely premature (born before 27 weeks of gestation), there was a higher incidence of an eye problem called retinopathy of prematurity, or ROP (see page 268). This association is new and not yet confirmed, but is certain to be researched further. In any case, if your baby is a very young preemie, she will be given an eye exam when she's closer to her due date, and old enough for any signs of ROP to appear.

All of this can sound pretty overwhelming, but remember that most babies won't have all of these complications, and most of them are highly treatable. While your baby's hospital course may be more complicated because of her small size, be assured that the nursery's tini-est babies can be a lot stronger and more resilient than you might think, and with good care, most do well.

WHAT BEING SGA MEANS FOR YOUR BABY IN THE LONG RUN

The long-term prognosis for a baby whose growth was restricted in the womb also depends heavily on what caused the problem in the first place. If your baby has a lasting condition like a genetic or anatomical abnormality, or had a congenital infection, you should ask her doctor to explain her prognosis, which will depend on the specifics of her case.

As a general rule of thumb, when it comes to long-term development, SGA preemies as a group face risks comparable to preemies who were born a few weeks younger and share their birth weights. In other words, a 30-weeker who is small–for–gestational age, and thus born at the weight of a typical 28-weeker, has similar long-term prospects to a typical 28-weeker.

What that means is that SGA babies have somewhat lower IQ scores, and a higher incidence of long-term neurological problems (such as cerebral palsy, seizures, blindness, or deafness) than appropriately grown preemies of their same gestational age. But in general, these IQ and neurological impairments go hand-in-hand in children who are SGA. In other words, if your child doesn't develop physical problems that are evident in the first couple of years of life, she is much less likely to have cognitive (thinking and learning) ones, either.

You shouldn't assume, here, that having a cognitive impairment means being mentally retarded. Although mental retardation is more common among SGA preemies than AGA preemies, milder deficits are even more frequent, with a loss of some of the intellectual ability a child might have had if her growth hadn't been restricted. Most SGA preemies are not intellectually "impaired" by any objective measure, but they may have slid down a few points—which could, perhaps, mean going from "superior" to "normal," or from "average" to "low average"—on the IQ scales. It is a loss, but a theoretical one that nobody, including you, is apt to notice. There is also some evidence that SGA babies may have more learning disabilities.

It's important to realize, however, that grouping all SGA babies together can be deceptive. Small–for–gestational age babies fall broadly into two groups: those whose lack of nourishment, or underlying reason for restricted growth, was relatively mild (usually causing asymmetrical, or "head-sparing" growth retardation), and those whose was relatively severe (causing symmetrical growth retardation).

The odds of being untouched by developmental problems are not as good for babies with symmetrical growth retardation. When the brain doesn't get enough oxygen and nourishment to grow normally before birth, or development is disordered because of a disease or genetic error, there is a high risk of lasting neurological impairments. When there is head-sparing, the brain may well have gotten the appropriate developmental signals, and enough nourishment to grow normally, or suffered only a mild injury from which it is still able to recover. Thus, if your baby has asymmetrical growth retardation with head-sparing, her chances of coming through with no long-term consequences are much better than those of SGA infants on average.

There is some new evidence that small-for-gestational age babies might have a higher likelihood of developing high blood pressure, diabetes, or heart disease as adults. But try not to worry too much now about this connection, given that it isn't fully proven, and that strategies to prevent cardiovascular diseases—through diet, exercise, and medications—are already very effective, and are likely to become even more successful in the years to come.

What about your child's size? She's tiny now, but will she always be? Small-for-gestational age babies, as a group, remain shorter and lighter than their peers, although many do catch up. Those who do often reach a normal weight and height for their adjusted age within the first six or eight months of life, the most critical period for catch-up growth.

As your baby grows, don't forget to put away her little newborn socks or hats. Keep them in a safe place: no matter how big your baby eventually grows, you can be sure that from time to time you'll want to pull out those mementos, to remind yourself of how tiny she once was, and how much you went through together.

3

The First Day

▶ *Entering the foreign world of the neonatal intensive care unit. Why it's the best place for your baby to be.*

THE PARENTS' PERSPECTIVE   77

THE DOCTOR'S PERSPECTIVE   80

A DIFFERENT STORY FOR DIFFERENT PREEMIES: *The Top Health Concerns*   84

QUESTIONS AND ANSWERS
Afraid to See Your Baby   88
The Extremely Premature Baby   89
Your Beautiful Newborn: A Portrait   89
Baby's Bed   91
The Cellophane Blanket   92
Through the Doors of the Neonatal Intensive Care Unit   92
Touching Your Baby   98
Baby's Twitches   98
Is Baby Sick or Healthy?   99
In Plain Language: What Is Respiratory Distress Syndrome?   101
Understanding the Doctors   105
Questions—Whom to Ask   105
Telephone Calls to the NICU: Do's and Don'ts   107

Is Baby on a Ventilator in Pain?   108
Pain in Preemies and Ways to Control It   109
Will Baby Become Addicted?   111
Baby Is Tied Down   112
Father Feels Faint   112
Difficult Start to Breastfeeding   112
Not Feeding Baby   113
Pumping Breast Milk   114
Blood Transfusion   116
Can You Be the Blood Donor?   116
Experimenting on Preemies   117
Any Alternative to the NICU?   118
Testing for Drugs   119
When Baby May Go Home   120

MULTIPLES
One Twin Doing Better   121
One Bigger Twin   122
Multiple Doctors   123

IN DEPTH
Breastfeeding or Formula Feeding Your Premature Baby: What Will Work Best for You   124

The Parents' Perspective: The First Day

When a preemie is born, his family's world freezes in expectation. At the beginning of the first day, little is clear and certain, most questions cannot be answered yet, and contradictory feelings come to the surface, in turmoil. Deep inside the parents' souls, a painful sense of separation arises.

The first hours of the first day of my daughter's life feel unbearably slow. In this limbo—a nowhere—we wait for the doctors to assess our baby's condition, to stabilize her vital signs, to come up with some news. The little creature they showed us after delivery, before rushing her to the NICU, was the baby I was carrying in my womb. Why is it already so difficult to remember her face? I know that my nurturing and nesting instincts must be put on hold, because medical care is now the top priority. By my hospital bed there's no bassinet, while women all around are nursing plump, full-term newborns. Instead of my baby, the nurse brings in an electric pump for breast milk. She says it is comforting to express your milk and freeze it for later, when your baby will start to be fed. If you intend to breastfeed, she says, you have to start pumping now. But along with my first milk, I express tears. Are they bitter tears or tears of joy? Visitors and flowers seem so inappropriate. There's a birth to celebrate, but where is the baby? Are we allowed to be joyful?

Sometimes the trauma of having been unwillingly separated from your premature newborn lingers in the subconscious, and can unveil itself later, as a mother recalls:

For some time after the premature birth of my son, I had a recurrent dream. I knew he was born, but I couldn't see him or even imagine him. I was standing at the edge of a crevice in front of a long, narrow, suspended bridge. All around, just a quiet, dark, empty space: I didn't fear any danger. The baby must be on the other side, I thought, I should go and find him. But I couldn't take a step onto the bridge because my foot wouldn't move. That didn't make me panic, or even worry, though: no baby was crying, after all. Meanwhile a voice inside me, the dreamer, was screaming aloud, to shake that woman who looked like me out of her crazy, incomprehensible stillness.

A father's reaction to the stress of a premature birth may be different from a mother's, perhaps to compensate for his partner's excessive pessimism or optimism. If they don't become too extreme, these differences are healthy, helping the couple to hold up in a time of crisis. There are plenty of good reasons to rejoice today: most preemies' stories have a happy ending, despite the difficult start. A new life together has begun.

My son was born tonight, eight weeks too early. "My son!" I've never said those words before. They make me think of the baseball games I'll take him to, the talks we'll have about manhood, the car I'll teach him to drive when he turns sixteen. I just wish my wife could feel happier tonight. The doctors say Max is healthy, just immature. And they say a three-pounder is a big preemie. My wife is so worried. Okay, I admit it, I'm a little worried, too. The doctors say it's still too soon to tell how everything will go. But our family, we're fighters. Max is our son, and I bet he's a tough little guy. Setbacks happen to everyone sooner or later—so, for Max it's a little sooner. I know he'll be fine. He's great! Hey, I wonder if I can find some tiny, preemie baseball caps and pass them out instead of cigars?

The nurses know how important it is to break the parents' solitude, on the first day, helping them to bond with newborns who don't seem real yet, because they cannot be held, cuddled, or breast-fed. But possessing just a symbol of the baby can create a strong sense of belonging.

A new mother is lying in her hospital bed, her husband at her side, after an emergency C-section. She is still drowsy and slightly nauseated. He looks pale and tense. A nurse comes by and places something in their hands: the first photos of their twins, a boy and a girl, who are now in the NICU. She kindly points out that the two babies look beautiful and not even too small, despite having been born ten weeks before term. But what the parents see are two rag dolls lying among tubes and tape, with snorkels coming out of their mouths, lips redder than wounds. Why is the nurse doing this to us, they think? Why this torture? It will take them time to realize what a great gift she has brought. It's the first link, a paper-thin, narrow bridge that connects them with their babies. When the nurse leaves, the parents cry together, and look again at the photographs. It is already less painful. And their children are just two floors above, in the NICU. All they need now from their parents is that they pull themselves together, and go up and meet them for the very first time.

Is it helpful to put an emotional journey such as giving birth to a premature baby into a rational perspective? Some psychologists have tried doing that, giving parents some additional tools for understanding their experience.

Worry, anguish, anger, terror, feeling cheated by life, guilt, loneliness, desire to escape. Just plain numbness. Joy, hope, excitement, trust, relief. And much more. There's a wide range of emotional reactions parents can experience after the premature birth of their children, from the first day of their lives through the many, later stages. Whatever you feel today may be influenced by the circumstances of your baby's delivery, by whether it was expected or not, by how early the birth was, by the medical condition of your baby, by your temperament, values, religious faith, personal history, and family relationships. It's hard, and maybe wrong, to generalize about what feelings are normal or to predict how your feelings will evolve. Some experts talk about a first stage of "denial," when you unintentionally refuse to realize what's going on. Something called "projection" is said to follow: blaming someone else or something else for what happened. Then there may be a stage of "detachment," when you pull away from your situation because it is too painful—before finally coming back to accept reality. Is all of that true? For some parents of preemies, it is. For some, only partially. Others may think it's just nonsense, psychobabble. Until they have done it, nobody really knows what it means to give birth to a child and to let him go off alone, in a high-tech medical world.

Your first meeting with your preemie in the NICU is going to be much different from the ideal picture described in ordinary pregnancy books. At least for today, before your baby's condition has stabilized, you'll have to forget about privacy, hugs, skin-to-skin contact, sucking at the breast. It's normal to be scared of what you may see and feel in the NICU: many parents are. But most of them feel relieved after having finally met their babies. Overcome by tenderness and desire to protect their tiny offspring, mothers and fathers pull themselves together, finding the energy to face this life challenge, and to overcome it.

During my twin daughters' first day of life I couldn't find the strength to go and see them in the NICU. My husband and sister had already been there several times, and had talked extensively to the doctors. I kept repeating to them, and to myself: I'm going to be a good mother, I just need more time to adjust and muster my strength. But I knew they must be worried about me, and I was, too. How am I going to survive all this? I thought. What if we lose our babies? What if something bad happens to them, and they end up severely disabled? I wasn't ready for all that, I wasn't. But as the hours of that long day passed, I felt something switching inside me. My maternal feelings were struggling with, and gradually overtaking, my fears. Whatever happened, my husband and I had each other, we would make it. My babies were downstairs, they needed me. That evening, when I went to see my beautiful daughters in the NICU, I was a better person. All that mattered was giving love and strength to my babies. It's as if inside me, the essence of mothering had been tested and revealed.

The Doctor's Perspective: The First Day*

We may have had a dramatic meeting at delivery, but now is the time when doctor and baby really get acquainted. I approach each new, tiny patient in the nursery with curiosity, excitement, hope, and trepidation—guessing at what I'll find, but not really knowing what's in store for either of us until I take a closer look and some time passes by. Even if you've had twins (or triplets, or more), each baby will be evaluated as a separate, distinct individual. Your babies may have been together in the womb, but just as their personalities may be different later, their medical and physical conditions may be very different now.

PHYSICAL EXAM AND LABORATORY ASSESSMENT

As soon as your baby reaches the nursery, we (the doctors and nurses) check her "vital signs"—her temperature, how fast she's breathing, her heart rate and blood pressure—and determine how much oxygen is getting into her blood. We want this information immediately, because significant problems with any of these would need to be attended to quickly. At the same time, we watch her intently for signs of health or distress. Is she moving (active and vigorous—a good sign) or limp (lethargic, exhausted, maybe sick)? Is she pink and resting comfortably, or blue and struggling to breathe? Most of the time, I'm relieved to find that she's acting just as we expect babies her age to act, and often I'm delighted that all looks so well.

Next, your baby gets a thorough physical examination, more extensive than the brief exam done in the delivery room. We'll scrutinize your baby from head to toes, asking and answering

questions as we go, aiming to be complete in noting what's normal or abnormal.

We evaluate her physical features: feel her head, including the fontanelles, or soft spots. Are they a normal size? Is her head swollen or molded, as commonly happens from moving through the birth canal? We need to know the size and shape of her head now to determine if it's growing normally later. We look at her eyes, ears, chin, and feel her palate—are they well formed? We press deeply into her belly. Is it soft and gently rounded, with normal sized liver, kidneys, and spleen? What is her skin like—clear and intact, or bruised, or thin? Thick, unbroken skin helps protect against infection and prevents her from losing important fluids. We look at her color to assess whether she might have lost or gained too much blood, as sometimes happens during delivery or between identical twins in the womb: Is she too pale, or too ruddy? We listen carefully to the sounds of her heart beating, and feel her pulse to make sure her blood is flowing well. We'll check that her joints move smoothly, and count her fingers and toes. This kind of exam is done

---

*"The Doctor's Perspective" describes how your doctor may be thinking about your preemie's condition, and what she may be considering as she makes medical decisions. All of the medical terms and conditions mentioned here are described in more detail elsewhere in this book. Check the index.

for all newborns, but, of course, my eye is drawn to details that are especially important for premature infants.

We also evaluate how well your baby is functioning. Is her breathing quiet, deep, and comfortable, or is it shallow and labored, a possible sign that her lungs are not quite mature yet? Is she responding appropriately to all of the stimulation and handling she's getting? I'm happy to see her resisting sometimes, or crying; it's a sign of neurological health if she's aware of what's going on and can respond vigorously.

If your preemie's breathing is labored, I'll probably get a chest x-ray to see if her lungs are open enough. And to help insure that all her organ systems are functioning well, we'll take blood to see that important substances like oxygen, carbon dioxide, salts, sugar, and blood cells are at normal levels. Over the course of this first day, and for as long as your baby remains in intensive care, we'll be doing these blood tests—as often as every few hours if your baby is very young or very sick—to make sure that her vital functions are in a safe range, and to treat them if they're not.

We don't expect everything to go perfectly right from the start, as babies make the difficult transition from life in the womb to life in the outside world. In fact, in the first few hours after birth, when mild functional abnormalities are common and usually transient, an infant is said to be "transitioning." For example, a little bit of grunting and hard breathing may resolve as soon as some extra fluid moves out of her lungs. (After all, your preemie has been "breathing" in amniotic fluid for quite a while.) A pale, mottled skin color could indicate insufficient blood flow; but more likely, your baby will turn a nice, even pink when her blood flow shifts from the routes it took when she was a fetus to patterns more suitable for a newborn. And extra acid in her blood that may have built up during labor and delivery is soon cleared, as her circulation improves. We'll decide what needs to be addressed immediately, and what can be watched for now and followed up on later.

Features that may seem strange and unusual to you may be commonplace for doctors who care for so many premature newborns, so sometimes I may not think to comment on something you're worried about. If you have questions, ASK! The answer will usually be less than earth-shaking, like "That bump is just the tip of her rib cage," or "I don't know what that rash is, but it doesn't mean anything, it will disappear soon." In most cases, you'll be reassured that your baby is just like other babies her age.

In addition to checking her physical features and general functioning, we'll also examine your baby to determine her gestational age (how many weeks have passed since she was conceived). To do so, we'll look at how thick her skin is, feel for the size of her breast buds and the stiffness of her ears, note how fully formed her genitals are and how mature her neurological functioning is. This method of calculating your baby's gestational age after she's born is called a Dubowitz or Ballard examination. It's less accurate than an ultrasound exam in the first trimester of pregnancy, or the dating of your pregnancy if you were certain about when she was conceived. But if the dating of your pregnancy is less exact, we may tell you that your baby appears to be a couple of weeks older or younger than you thought—and that can have an impact on her hospital course and outcome.

Although the first physical examination is the most extensive, it's just the first. Your baby will probably be examined several times today, and at least once a day for as long as she remains in a special care nursery. Her doctors (she may have more than one) and nurses will perform ongoing evaluations of her breathing and circulation, activity and muscle tone, and comfort or pain, in order to make sure she's doing well and to respond quickly to any problems.

COMMON ISSUES AND DECISIONS

Respiratory Distress Syndrome: It wouldn't be surprising if your premature baby had some breathing difficulties, since that's a natural consequence of having immature lungs. The breathing difficulty that occurs when a baby's lungs are immature is called respiratory distress syndrome, or RDS for short. Probably the most important decision her doctor will make on your baby's first day is whether or not she has RDS or some other problem (like pneumonia) that prevents her from breathing well, and what kind of treatments would best help her breathing.

If your baby has to suck her chest in deeply to pull in enough air, if she's grunting and her nostrils flare with effort, or even if she looks comfortable but our blood tests tell us that her lungs aren't taking in enough oxygen or getting rid of enough carbon dioxide, she may need the help of a breathing machine (called a ventilator) and a medication to help her lungs stay wide open (called surfactant). If your baby needs more than a little respiratory support—if she's on a ventilator, or on high amounts of oxygen—we'll monitor the oxygen and carbon dioxide in her blood fairly frequently (usually, every two to four hours). In that case, I'll probably decide to put a catheter into one of her arteries so we can take blood without hurting her each time. I'll probably also decide not to feed her yet, as that would be an added stress. So you can expect that she'll be nourished with intravenous fluids for now.

Pain: One of the things your baby's doctors and nurses will be monitoring on the first day—and throughout her stay in the nursery—is her comfort or pain. If she can get by without a breathing machine, then once the nurses and doctors are finished drawing blood and putting catheters in her veins or arteries, she'll probably be pretty comfortable in her warm bed in the nursery. The nurses can make a little nest around her body, or swaddle her in blankets, so she feels cozy and protected. We really don't know if being on a ventilator is actually painful for a baby, or if it's a mild discomfort that resolves quickly as the ventilator provides welcome breaths. We also don't know how much anxiety a baby feels from relying on a ventilator to breathe for her. Probably this differs from baby to baby, depending on her maturity and temperament, the general atmosphere in the nursery around her bed, how sick she is, and what kind of breathing support she's getting. (For example, some babies wriggle around and try to pull out prongs that blow air into their noses; others calmly tolerate nasal prongs, but don't like having a tube in their throats connecting them to the ventilator.)

Depending on how uncomfortable your baby seems, we'll decide whether or not she needs medicine to control pain, to calm her down, or even to stop her from moving and "fighting" against the ventilator. (If she fights too much, the ventilator's breaths can't get into her lungs, and her breathing gets even worse.) It can be hard to tell when premature babies are in pain—especially very young ones, whose normal behavior is most different from term babies—but clues that we use are agitation, excessive crying, and high heart rates and blood pressures. We only want to medicate your baby if she needs it. So we'll keep monitoring all those things, adjusting our care to make sure your baby is in as little pain as possible.

Infection: An infection in an expectant mother or her baby is probably the most common reason for a baby to be born prematurely, and infections often cause breathing difficulties in newborns that are indistinguishable from simple RDS. For that reason, we'll probably treat your preemie with intravenous antibiotics, especially if she needs help with her breathing. That decision is based on the philosophy "better safe than sorry"—infections are very dangerous (life-threatening if they remain untreated), and we usually can't know for sure whether she's infected until several days after she's born, and sometimes not even then.

Some signs that your baby may have an infection are: persistently low blood pressure, abnormally high or low numbers of blood cells, or an especially dense patch of lung on her chest x-ray. We'll be watching for those things, and take some blood for culture to see if any bacteria grow—a nearly certain sign of infection. Other cultures may be taken, too, such as a skin swab if she has suspicious blisters, or a spinal tap if her activity or movements are abnormal. Based on whether or not her cultures turn positive (bacteria grow) over the next couple of days, and on whether or not she has other signs of infection, we'll decide how long to continue the antibiotics. If it looks like she wasn't infected, the antibiotics will be stopped after two or three days of negative cultures. Otherwise, the antibiotics will be continued until the infection is cleared—usually one to three weeks.

FAMILY ISSUES

I may be meeting you and your family for the first time on the first day. I need to understand what you really care about, so that I can take your concerns into account when I tell you what's happening now, and what I think is in store for you and your baby later. I'll be trying to figure out (and you may be, too) your deeply felt values and concerns, as together we make treatment plans and decisions. You can help by talking about the desires and hopes that mean the most to you—what you most want for your baby and your family.

Don't be afraid that your wishes or worries are unacceptable or trivial. Any number or kind of things are significant for me to know.

You may feel that you want your baby to survive at all costs, or that it's most important that she not suffer with extreme handicaps; you may want to move to a hospital closer to home as soon as possible; you may want your twins to be kept together in the nursery; you may not want to make any decisions until Grandpa arrives; you may want to pray with a chaplain, even if things are going very well. You can't communicate (or even know) all these things at once, but the first day is a start. And although I won't always be able to make your wishes a reality, at least I'll know what to aim for.

Overall, for most families, and for those of us helping to take care of your baby, the first day is a time of uncertainty, waiting, and hope. It's often not clear immediately after delivery whether a premature baby's condition is going to improve or worsen. If your baby is an older preemie, and doing well, things will probably settle down quickly, and mild problems will disappear in a matter of hours or days. If your baby is younger or sicker, realize that the first day is a time to discover what treatments your baby needs and to get support systems (such as ventilator tubes and catheters for blood drawing, intravenous fluids, and medications) in place. Time is often needed before things become clearer.

A Different Story for Different Preemies: The Top Health Concerns

All parents of newborn preemies want to know whether their babies are going to be OK, and want to understand the health challenges they will face. To help you focus on appropriate concerns—and to avoid unnecessary worry about inappropriate ones—we've separated preemies into four gestational age groups. For each group, we tell you only about those serious health conditions that affect more than 5% or 10% of babies.

As you read the section that applies to your baby, please keep two important caveats in mind. First, this part of the book is meant to help you develop balanced, realistic expectations—but not to make predictions about your baby. The range of medical outcomes is very wide, even within a given gestational age group, and most preemies won't develop *all* of the serious problems listed here. Your baby is not a statistic, and could have other health concerns as well. The only reliable guide you have to how he is doing is your baby himself. Spend time with him, look at him and how he's behaving, and, of course, ask the doctors about the results of their evaluations so far.

Second, the statistics below are merely estimates. Accurate projections for today's preemies are elusive, in part because neonatal intensive care is constantly improving. Ten years ago, babies born at 23 weeks of gestation did not survive at all—today all preemies receive better care than ever before.

23–25 WEEKS OF GESTATION

Breathing: Nearly every baby born this soon needs the help of a ventilator. First of all, he is likely to have respiratory distress syndrome (RDS)—meaning his lungs are too immature for him to breathe effectively on his own (see page 101). If his lungs are extremely immature, even a ventilator may not be able to provide him with enough oxygen. But if his lungs are a little more developed, the ventilator can help breathe for him until he's ready to do it on his own. Chances are he'll come off the ventilator in several weeks, but if he continues to need some extra oxygen (which can be given through nasal prongs) up to 36 weeks after conception, it wouldn't be surprising. If, after 36 weeks, he still needs help breathing, it would indicate that he has some chronic lung damage, or bronchopulmonary dysplasia (BPD, see page 261). About 65% of babies who were born at 23 to 25 weeks of gestation develop BPD, but usually it resolves before age two.

A 23- to 25-week preemie also needs a ventilator because the breathing center in his brain isn't fully developed, so he'll sometimes forget to breathe. This is called apnea of prematurity (see page 218), and it gets milder over time, going away completely by about 38 weeks after conception. A baby doesn't have to stay on a ventilator until his apnea completely resolves—only until it's mild enough not to cause significant problems, usually by about 28 to 30 weeks.

PDA: In 40% to 50% of babies born at 23 to 25 weeks of gestation, the ductus arteriosus, a fetal blood vessel near the heart, which is supposed to close in the first few days after birth, remains open (see page 176). The problem with having a patent (meaning "open") ductus arteriosus, or PDA, is that too much blood flows through the lungs; this makes a preemie's RDS worse, increasing his risk for chronic lung damage, and puts a strain on his heart. If your baby has a PDA that doesn't seem to be causing him problems, his doctors may wait to see if it will close on its own. But if the PDA is interfering with your baby's breathing or heart function, his doctors will try to close it—first with medicine, which usually works, and then with surgery, if necessary. Approximately 10% of 23- to 25-weekers need to have an operation to close their PDA.

IVH/PVL: A baby's brain is very sensitive to changes in blood flow at this age, and it can bleed easily (see page 164). Bleeds, called intraventricular hemorrhages, don't cause any known problems if they are small (grades 1 or 2). Some 15% to 20% of babies born at 23 to 25 weeks have larger bleeds (grades 3 or 4). Some babies recover perfectly from these larger bleeds, too, but others develop long-term disabilities, such as cerebral palsy, mental retardation, or visual or hearing impairments, or don't survive. Nearly all IVHs occur within the first three days of life, so all young preemies get a routine head ultrasound—which can indicate whether there was an IVH and how big it was—sometime in the first week. A later ultrasound, done about six weeks after birth, gives more information on long-term prospects. It can show whether a baby has suffered any visible brain damage (called periventricular leukomalacia, or PVL) from insufficient blood flow to the brain, either because of a large IVH or for other reasons.

ROP: Nearly all babies born at 23 to 25 weeks of gestation develop some abnormal blood vessels in their eyes, known as retinopathy of prematurity (see page 268). In most babies, this problem resolves on its own without causing vision problems. In some, it results in nearsightedness or astigmatism that is correctable with glasses. A minority of these young preemies—about 15%—require surgery or other procedures to keep their retina from detaching, and about 5% become blind. Since ROP doesn't develop immediately, preemies get their eyes tested at about four to six weeks of age.

Infection: The more premature a baby is, the more susceptible he is to infections (see page 182). About half of all 23- to 25-week preemies develop one or more infections at some point during their hospital stay. An infection in a very young preemie can be severe, but with antibiotics and increased respiratory and nutritional support, the babies who get sick have about a 75% chance of surviving.

NEC: About 5% to 10% of 23- to 25-week preemies will develop an inflammation of their intestinal tract called necrotizing enterocolitis (see page 237). It usually doesn't occur until the second or third week of life, after feedings have begun, and it is one reason why doctors are so cautious about the amount of formula or breast milk they allow your preemie to eat. NEC can be mild—so mild as to cause only some feeding intolerance, and to make the diagnosis "suspected" rather than "definite" NEC. Or, it can be more severe, requiring several weeks of antibiotics and intravenous nutrition, and sometimes bowel surgery, to remove severely damaged areas of the intestine. On average, about 50% of babies with severe NEC undergo surgery. The majority of babies who have NEC survive (from 60% to 90%). Mortality is highest for the youngest preemies, but rates for successful treatment are continuing to improve.

26–29 WEEKS OF GESTATION

Breathing: Most preemies in this age group have respiratory distress syndrome (RDS), meaning their lungs are still too immature to breathe well on their own (see page 101). So, most 26- to 29-weekers get some help from a ventilator at first. Many come off the ventilator within a few weeks, but continue to need extra oxygen through nasal prongs until they're a little closer to term. If a baby needs oxygen beyond 36 weeks after conception, it would indicate he's got some chronic lung damage, or bronchopulmonary dysplasia (BPD, see page 261). About 50% of babies born at 26 to 29 weeks gestation develop BPD, but usually it resolves before age two.

Babies this age also have apnea of prematurity—because the breathing center in their brains isn't fully developed, they sometimes forget to breathe (see page 218). A ventilator is needed if the apnea is severe, but that rarely lasts more than a few weeks. Apnea gets milder over time and usually is gone altogether by 36 to 38 weeks after conception.

PDA: A fetal blood vessel near the heart, which is supposed to close within the first few days of life sometimes remains open in preemies (see page 176). Some 40% to 50% of babies born at 26 to 29 weeks of gestation have a patent (meaning "open") ductus arteriosus, or PDA. When there's a PDA, too much blood flows through the lungs, making a preemie's RDS worse, increasing his chance of developing chronic lung damage, and putting a strain on his heart. Some PDAs don't seem to be causing problems, and doctors may wait to see if these will close on their own. But when a PDA is interfering with your baby's breathing or heart function, his doctors will try to close it. Usually medicine works.

Surgery is done only if necessary—on about 10% of 26 to 29 weekers.

IVH/PVL: A baby's brain is sensitive to changes in blood flow at this age, and sudden changes can cause it to bleed (see page 164). Nearly all bleeds, or intraventricular hemorrhages, occur in the first three days of life, so a head ultrasound is routinely done during the first week. The ultrasound shows whether there was a bleed, and how big it was. Small IVHs (grades 1 or 2) are common and cause no known problems. Only about 5% to 10% of 26- to 29-weekers have larger bleeds (grades 3 or 4). Their prognosis is very hard to predict; some of these babies recover and are perfectly normal, while others develop long-term disabilities, such as cerebral palsy, mental retardation, or visual or hearing impairments, or do not survive. Waiting to find out can be agonizing, but another ultrasound done around six weeks after birth provides more information: whether the baby has lost brain tissue (called periventricular leukomalacia, or PVL), due to the IVH or other problems that caused insufficient blood flow to the brain. If there is no PVL and he didn't have a large IVH, his chances of having significant long-term neurological problems are very small.

Infection: Premature babies have immature immune systems, so they are susceptible to more frequent and severe infections than term newborns (see page 182). A baby born at 26 to 29 weeks of gestation has about a 30% chance of developing an infection while he is in the hospital. Antibiotics and increased respiratory and nutritional support help about 75% of these babies to recover and survive.

NEC: Among 26 to 29 weekers, approximately 5% to 10% develop necrotizing enterocolitis, an inflammation of the intestinal tract (see page 237). Doctors cannot predict which babies will get NEC, which generally occurs in the second or third week of life after feedings have begun, and it is one reason why preemies are introduced very slowly to formula or breast milk. In the mildest cases, NEC causes only feeding intolerance, and recovery is quick. In the worst cases, babies with NEC require a long course of antibiotics, several weeks of intravenous nutrition, and bowel surgery to remove parts of the damaged intestine. NEC leads to surgery in about half of the severe cases. Overall, survival rates after NEC vary from 60% to 90%, proportional to the baby's age and birth weight, so 26- to 29-weekers are not in the highest risk category. With today's increasingly successful therapies for NEC, a good outcome is the most likely one for your baby.

ROP: About 75% of 26- to 29-week preemies develop some abnormal blood vessels in their eyes, known as retinopathy of prematurity (see page 268), but this problem usually resolves without causing any vision problems. In some babies, it does cause nearsightedness or astigmatism that is correctable with glasses. A small group—about 7%—of 26- to 29-weekers have ROP that is serious enough to require surgery or other procedures to keep their retina from detaching. A very small fraction, 4%, become blind. All of these preemies will get their eyes tested at about four to six weeks of age, since ROP doesn't develop immediately.

30–33 Weeks of Gestation

Breathing: Many 30- to 33-week preemies have lungs mature enough to allow them to breathe well on their own, or with just a little help from some supplemental oxygen given through nasal prongs. Only about 25% have respiratory distress syndrome (RDS), a condition caused by immature lungs (see page 101). Even babies who have RDS and need the help of a ventilator usually come off it within a week. If they need extra oxygen for a few weeks after that, it wouldn't be surprising—after all, they weren't supposed to breathe room air until at least then! Only about 10% to 15% of babies born at 30 to 33 weeks develop chronic lung damage, or bronchopulmonary dysplasia (BPD, see page 261). Most of the time it's mild and resolves by age one or two.

PDA: The ductus arteriosus, a fetal blood vessel near the heart, which is supposed to close within the first few days after birth, stays open in 40% to 50% of 30 to 33 weekers, creating what's called a patent (meaning "open") ductus arteriosus, or PDA (see page 176). A PDA is much more likely to occur if your baby has respiratory distress syndrome, so the older your preemie, the less he is at risk. PDAs cause too much blood to flow through the lungs, making a baby's breathing problems worse and putting a strain on his heart. If your baby has a PDA that doesn't seem to be causing him problems, his doctors may wait to see if it will close on its own. But if the PDA is causing problems, his doctors will give him medication that will probably close it. If that doesn't work, they will do surgery, which is necessary for only about 10% of 30- to 33-week preemies.

Infection: A baby born at 30 to 33 weeks gestation has only a small—15%—chance of developing an infection during his hospital course (see page 182). With the help of antibiotics and increased respiratory and nutritional support, these preemies' chances of surviving an infection are high: greater than 75%.

34+ Weeks of Gestation

Great news: Your 34+ week preemie may seem tiny, but he is stronger than you think. His bodily systems are nearly as mature as those of a term baby, and any problems he has that are due to his prematurity (such as apnea, or difficulty feeding) should resolve within a week or two without consequences. (If your baby is one of the small minority of older preemies who encounter serious health problems, you can read about them elsewhere in this book.) So, you can think of your preemie just as you would any term newborn—give or take a few rolls of baby fat, they're essentially the same!

Questions and Answers

Afraid to See Your Baby

I haven't even seen my baby yet. The nurses have offered to take me from my room to the NICU, but I'm too afraid of what I'll find there.

Most parents of premature babies feel unprepared for, and scared of, the first sight of their baby in the intensive care nursery. Those feelings are nothing to be ashamed of; they're normal. After all, you've already been through a lot—preparing for a premature birth or being surprised by it, and possibly experiencing med-

ical problems of your own, or undergoing a C-section—a major operation. The next few weeks or months are going to be demanding, and if you feel you need an extra day to muster your strength, then you should certainly take it. Your baby is in good hands with the doctors; right now, that's the kind of care he needs most. There will be plenty of time and opportunity for bonding between mother and father and baby in the days to come.

Rather than getting overwhelmed by your fears, you can begin to prepare yourself for your first trip to the NICU.

❋ *Know what to expect.* If you already saw your baby in the delivery room, you know what he looks like. Parents of preemies are often shocked by how tiny their newborns are. Some are so small that they can fit within the palm of an adult hand.

But parents are also usually surprised by how fully formed their babies are. And love is blind. It's uncanny the way a preemie's parents soon start to find their baby the most graceful and beautiful in the world, and to view full-term newborns as ungainly giants.

Even if you saw your child in the delivery room, you probably got little more than a glance before he was whisked away by the doctors. So take a minute to read "Your Beautiful Newborn: A Portrait," on page 89. It describes some of the typical traits of premature babies, such as lanugo (a soft layer of hair covering some of his body), thinner than normal skin, and less-than-fully developed sexual organs, among others. It's good to know about these things in advance so they won't worry you.

Once your baby is settled in the intensive care nursery, he'll be attached to various wires, monitors, and machines. The first sight of them is disturbing; but again, once you understand why they're there, they're a lot easier to take. So reading "Through the Doors of the Neonatal Intensive Care Unit" on page 92 is another good thing to do before that first visit.

❋ *Ask for a photo and a description.* Someone close to you, or a helpful hospital social worker or nurse, can take a quick-developing photograph of your baby for you to look at, and can tell you about things the photo doesn't capture. There may be as much tubes and wires as baby in the picture, but that's not important—what matters is that you'll have a link to your infant. After you've looked at his picture, you may find that going to see him in person feels like less of a big step.

❋ *Knowing is more comforting than not knowing.* Keep in mind that for most parents, the first trip to see their baby in the NICU ends up being a great relief. They find that their baby's actual appearance is more comforting than the fantasy and fears that their minds had concocted. And being with their baby—seeing his tiny fingers and toes, caressing his soft skin, and in some cases looking into his little eyes or feeling his firm grasp around their adult finger—brings a rush of love that makes wires and tubes practically disappear.

Chances are that after a few seconds or minutes to adjust, you'll find your baby very beautiful—parents usually do. And remember, your preemie just needs some time before all those wires are history, and he looks like a typical, full-term newborn.

The Extremely Premature Baby

Extremely premature babies, born between, say, 22 and 25 weeks of gestation, look different than more mature preemies. As you might expect, they look more like fetuses: their eyes might still be fused shut; their skin and head, not yet covered with lanugo, might look translucent and be too delicate to touch; and their ears may be soft and folded where the cartilage hasn't thickened yet. Some parents don't find these babies of theirs beautiful—*yet.* By a few weeks later, the babies' looks change—their eyes are open and their skin is thicker—and so do their parents' feelings.

YOUR BEAUTIFUL NEWBORN: A PORTRAIT

Parents seeing their premature babies for the first time often have conflicting feelings. Pain and pleasure. Shock and a touch of relief. Most parents are shocked by how tiny their babies are—but impressed by their complete, perfectly formed little bodies. It's not unusual to see mothers and fathers staring in awe at a beautiful set of micro-sized eyelashes, fingers or toes, complete with all of the knuckles. Everything is already in place, just waiting to grow.

Obviously, though, preemies are not full-term babies, and you can't expect them to exactly resemble 40-weekers any more than you can expect 40-weekers to exactly resemble older, two- or three-month-old babies.

What are some of the differences you might notice?

✹ Preemies younger than 30 to 32 weeks have thin skin, lacking the layers of body fat that would have been put on during the final weeks of pregnancy. When skin is thin, the arteries and veins below it are easily visible, so the skin has a reddish-purple tint, regardless of the infant's ethnic background. (So don't be concerned that your baby was switched accidentally with someone else's! Babies born to African-American parents often look very similar in color to white babies at this stage. Natural pigmentation may not be obvious until around the eighth month of gestation.) Until those layers of fat appear and fill out the skin's folds, babies also tend to look a bit wrinkled. But their slender fingers and toes look unusually long and graceful.

✹ In extremely premature babies, the coarse, top layer of skin hasn't formed yet. So their skin can look smooth and shiny, and may be too fragile to caress and rub for the time being. (You can touch it gently.) This usually changes by the 26th week.

✹ The very youngest preemies don't have any body hair at all, and the hair on their head is just a fine fuzz. An older preemie, though, is covered by lanugo—soft, fuzzy, fetal hair—over much of her body. It is particularly heavy on the back, upper arms, and shoulders, and dark hair is more noticeable than light. Don't worry if your baby has more lanugo than the baby in the bed next to her; some preemies have more, some have less, but it always goes away. Even some full-term babies are born with some lanugo. Most preemies shed theirs by their due dates, or at the latest a few weeks after. It's not until approximately 36 weeks gestation that the hair on a preemie's head becomes thick and silky.

✹ A premature baby's eyes may still be fused shut if she is born before the 26th week. But around that time, they will open on their own—already framed by beautiful little eyelashes.

✹ Fingernails and toenails may look like tiny buds at first. By roughly your baby's due date, her nails will reach the ends of her fingers or toes, and you'll have to pull out the emery board or scissors.

✹ A preemie's ears have a little developing yet to do. Many parents get worried when they see one of their baby's ears doubled over, as if it's folded. Actually, that's a common sight in the NICU, and nothing to worry about. Before the 35th week or so, ears are very soft, without the firm cartilage that develops later. So an ear that gets folded (perhaps when a baby is laid down on her side) will stay that way, rather than springing back on its own. A mere touch from your gentle fingers can fix that.

✹ Breast nipples usually don't appear until the 34th week, although both boys and girls may already have hints of their areola—the circles of dark skin around where the nipples will be. Sexual organs are clearly differentiated even on extremely premature babies, but they aren't mature yet, as most parents quickly notice. A premature boy's testes have not descended yet from inside his body into his scrotum. Thus, his scrotum looks small and unusually smooth. A premature girl's outer labia, or vaginal tissues, are still small and spread widely apart, leaving the inner labia and clitoris looking large and fully exposed. This will change when the outer labia fill in with fat and come together. Some girls also have a little "tag," as the doctors call it, protruding from their vagina. Strange-looking? Yes. But don't worry; it will soon disappear. Both boys and girls will look just like full-term babies around their due date. In fact, neonatologists can often estimate a preemie's gestational age by looking at his or her genitalia.

❋ Whether a newborn is full-term or premature, it's hard to tell on the first day whether she has inherited your nose or Grandpa's chin. If your preemie is on a ventilator, it will be even harder, because parts of her face may be covered and stretched by tape that holds the equipment in place. When she finally comes off the ventilator, you'll see your baby's little face unobscured at last.

❋ A premature baby's posture and movements depend on how old she is at birth. Younger babies have less muscle tone. So while full-term newborns hold their arms and legs flexed and can curl themselves up into the fetal position, a very young preemie tends to lie flat on her back, with her arms and legs splayed out, frog-like.

❋ Before around 28 weeks, a premature baby doesn't move much. She'll sometimes curl her fingers into a fist, or stretch or flex an arm or leg—reminding you of those pokes your belly got while she was still inside you. A slightly older preemie, between 29 and 32 weeks of gestation, moves more often, but her movements are jittery and jerky. She can turn her head from one side to another to get comfortable, and she can grasp your finger (although not strongly enough to hold on if you try to pull her up to a sitting position).

❋ By around 35 weeks, a preemie has enough muscle tone to tuck herself into a fetal position, just like a full-term newborn. Although she startles more frequently than a full-term baby, her grasp is strong enough to keep hold of your fingers while you lift her, and her movements are more fluid and purposeful. Some babies are even coordinated enough to get their hands in their mouths and suck on them. Sounds easy? Many 40-weekers wish they could do it!

Baby's Bed

I thought preemies were put in incubators, but my baby is lying out in the open. Is this a good sign or a bad sign?

Probably neither. When premature babies are first born, they are usually put on an open bed—referred to in the intensive care nursery as a radiant warmer. This allows the doctors and nurses to have easy, free access to the baby in the early period when they are getting him stabilized and conducting tests to determine what kind of medical care he needs. While he is on the open bed, an overhead heater keeps him nice and warm. (Most preemies have very little fat tissue as insulation, and still can't regulate their internal body temperature on their own.)

Later on, the decision to put your baby in an isolette (a modern incubator), or to transfer him out of one to an open bed, is more meaningful. You can assume it's a good sign when your baby is moved into an isolette. It means his condition is stable, and he doesn't require frequent medical interventions. In an isolette, he can enjoy lying in a comfortable, warm little home, protected from drafts, dust, strange odors, and sources of infections. You or the nurse can even place a cover over it to give him some quiet, dark time.

Most preemies spend most of their hospital stay in an isolette. Unless your baby has to undergo surgery, goes back on the ventilator, or for some other reason needs frequent medical attention again, he'll probably stay in an isolette until he's almost ready to go home. Then, he'll move again to an open bed—but this time there won't be a heater overhead.

This move is a good sign, too: it means the doctors think your baby is ready to try maintaining his body temperature on his own. Intensive care nurseries typically wait until preemies are about 33 or 34 weeks old, and between three-and-a-half and four pounds before moving them out into the open air. Some babies do fine on their first try in the open air; others need to return to an isolette briefly and try again a day or two later. Every day that your baby gets older (and fatter), his ability to keep himself warm improves. Doctors and nurses can't tell for sure when a baby's ability to regulate his body temperature is mature without trying him out in the open, and sometimes they jump the gun a little. But at that point, chances are you'll be taking your baby home soon.

The Cellophane Blanket

The tiniest preemies—those with the least amount of body fat who weigh under, say, a pound and a half—are most susceptible to fluid and heat loss because they have the thinnest skin and greatest proportion of skin surface to body mass. Therefore, when they are on open beds, their beds may be wrapped in cellophane, a material that's very efficient at preventing too much fluid from evaporating and holding in the heat their bodies generate. To parents who aren't used to seeing it, the cellophane looks alarming, and maybe offensive. It's true, plastic is more appropriate to wrap snacks. But to the newborn, who cares if it's cellophane? It's a blankie!

THROUGH THE DOORS OF THE NEONATAL INTENSIVE CARE UNIT

When parents step through the doors of a neonatal intensive care unit for the first time, they often think: If my baby needs all that medical equipment attached to her, she must be very sick.

Thankfully, this impression is usually wrong. Most preemies are basically healthy. But they (and their organs and bodily functions) are immature and need a few more weeks or months to develop. In the meantime, your premature baby will get the extra help she needs from the medical staff and all of that high-tech machinery in the NICU. There are tubes that deliver nourishment to your baby until she is mature enough to eat on her own. There are machines called ventilators, which provide breaths to preemies who haven't mastered the art of breathing by themselves yet. There are doctors, called neonatologists, who are intimately familiar with the normal behavior of preemies—though it may not always look normal to you. And so on.

Believe it or not, in just a few days you'll become familiar with the gadgetry and the staff, and they won't seem so threatening. In fact, despite all of those tubes and wires your baby is entangled in, you'll soon be able to hold her in your arms, and even change her diaper. You'll come to know what the different beeping alarms emitted by your baby's monitors mean—and why you don't need to panic when you hear them.

To speed up your acquaintance with the NICU, here are some brief descriptions to browse through. First a quick tour of the equipment, then the staff.

WHAT IN THE WORLD ARE ALL THOSE MACHINES?

Your baby will not have all of these. On the other hand, if she has some equipment we haven't mentioned, just ask your baby's nurse what it is and what it's there for.

Your baby's bed
Most preemies spend the first few hours or days on a special, open bed under a device called a radiant warmer. The radiant warmer heats up the air around the baby and keeps her at a stable, healthy temperature. (Newborn preemies can't maintain their temperature on their own.) A sensor taped to the baby's skin (usually on her belly) monitors her body temperature and adjusts the heat accordingly.

Once a baby's vital signs have stabilized and she needs less constant medical attention, she'll be moved to a new home: a transparent Plexiglas box called an isolette. This is the newest model of what you probably know of as an incubator.

The isolette is fully enclosed, protecting your baby from sudden shifts in air temperature. Most of the simple things that the doctors or nurses now need to do for the baby can be done by inserting their hands through the round portholes on the isolette's sides, or on other models by partially sliding up the sides.

The isolette has a heating system, too. In some cases it is connected to a sensor on the baby's skin; the heating regulates itself according to the baby's temperature. In other cases, a fixed temperature is maintained inside the incubator.

The isolette's front wall can be unlatched and opened easily so that you or the nurses can take your baby out. Soon you will learn how to do this yourself for feedings, diaper changes, and to hold your baby.

Cardiorespiratory monitor
This machine is one of the most intrusive—but also one of the most important. Your preemie probably will be attached to it as long as she remains in the NICU. The cardiorespiratory monitor keeps constant track of her heart beat and breathing. It does this with three leads, or sensors, that stick on your baby's skin and attach with wires to the monitor. These leads—two on her chest and one on her leg or belly—count the number of breaths she is taking per minute and measure her pulse, or number of heart beats per minute. Both numbers are displayed prominently on the monitor's screen,

along with a graph of her breathing and heartbeat.

A preemie's pulse normally ranges from 120 to 160 beats per minute, and breathing from 30 to 60 breaths per minute. The monitor sounds a loud, beeping alarm if either one strays too far outside of the normal range. But very often a baby's own movements will displace the leads or cause false alarms—so try not to be terrified every time you hear the alarm go off. Nurses are trained to look at your baby, as well as the machine's readings, to see if something is actually wrong. If the baby is pink and healthy-looking, or wiggling around, they know it's a false alarm.

When there really is some irregularity, it may be an episode of bradycardia (a slow heartbeat) or apnea (a pause in breathing). See page 218 for what these episodes mean, and why they are common for preemies.

Blood pressure monitor

If you see a small, inflatable band wrapped around your baby's arm or leg, it is probably a blood pressure cuff (just a miniature version of the cuff used to measure blood pressure in adults). The nurses take the babies' blood pressure several times a day, using a machine that can pick up heart beats too soft to hear even through a stethoscope. Another way to measure blood pressure is through a catheter in an artery.

Pulse oximeter and carbon dioxide monitor

The amounts of oxygen and carbon dioxide in a baby's blood are important indicators of whether she needs help with her breathing. So your baby may have yet more monitors, to keep track of these.

Most preemies will have a pulse oximeter, at least initially. This is another machine that requires a sensor, or lead, attached to their skin.

(That's five leads so far—lots of wires!) This one, usually taped on the baby's hand or foot, measures the amount of oxygen circulating in her blood. The oximeter preferred by most NICUs these days relies on a special red light inside the sensor; the light shines through the baby's skin and indicates how much oxygen is being carried by the blood underneath. The monitor's screen displays the preemie's "oxygen saturation level," which can reach as high as 100%. Higher than 92% to 93% is considered normal; anything much lower will set off a beeping alarm.

In order for the pulse oximeter to measure the oxygen in your baby's blood accurately, it has to pick up her heart rate. So anything that interferes with that—like something as simple as the baby moving around—will set off a false alarm.

The most common kind of carbon dioxide monitor is called a transcutaneous (meaning across-the-skin) monitor. A tiny plastic cup sits on your baby's skin and warms the area underneath it; the machine measures how much car-

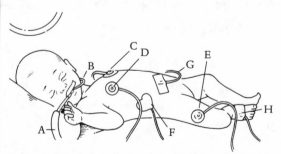

Tubes and leads attaching a premature baby to medical equipment. A: Breathing tube, connecting a baby to a ventilator (see page 95); B: Feeding tube (see page 95); C, D, E: Cardiorespiratory monitor leads, measuring heart rate and breathing (see page 93); F: Temperature probe (see page 93); G: Umbilical catheter, for fluid, medication, and drawing blood (see page 95); H: Pulse oximeter probe, measuring oxygen saturation (see page 94).

bon dioxide diffuses from small blood vessels into the warm skin. But don't be surprised if the warmth from the cup leaves a small, red mark on your baby's sensitive skin. The nurses or respiratory therapists will move the cup every few hours, before it causes a burn (and discomfort to the baby), and the red spots will fade within an hour or so.

These skin-based measurements aren't as accurate as measuring your baby's "blood gases" directly from a sample of her blood, but they can decrease the amount of blood the nurses have to take from your baby, and can give up-to-the-minute information on her breathing status.

Intravenous lines and other catheters

Intravenous lines, or IVs, as they're familiarly called, are common sights in all hospital patients, but it's still jarring to see them in the tiny hands, feet, arms, or legs of babies. Yet they're an essential part of your preemie's care. If you also notice a splint on your baby's arm or leg, don't worry: it's probably not because she broke something. Splints are used to keep lines from being accidentally knocked out of place.

IVs—tiny tubes called catheters, placed in veins to deliver liquids into the bloodstream—are used to sustain most premature babies during their first hours or days in the NICU, when they are not allowed to eat. If your baby is very premature, or if she is having breathing problems, she may be nourished intravenously for longer. Many babies also have a second IV line to give them antibiotics or other medications.

Because younger, newborn preemies, or those with breathing problems, need to have blood taken frequently to make sure their blood gases, blood sugar, and other substances are at healthy levels, they may have an additional line—this one running into an artery. Arterial lines can do double duty: they are used to

painlessly withdraw blood, and to continuously monitor a baby's blood pressure.

For reaching an artery or vein, newborns have one great spot that the rest of us don't: the umbilical cord, or belly button. Not only are umbilical catheters painless to put in (there are no nerves in the umbilical cord), but they go into major blood vessels. So an umbilical catheter can deliver high concentrations of nutrients or medications that would irritate more delicate, superficial veins.

As your baby gets older and healthier, one by one these lines will be taken out, until the happy day when she's free of them!

Feeding tubes

Preemies who are too young to breastfeed or drink from a bottle may get milk through a thin, soft tube that is inserted in their nose or mouth and goes down into their stomach. This method is called gavage feeding (see page 150). The gavage tube is very quick and easy to put in, and most preemies seem hardly to notice that it is there at all.

The ventilator and other breathing aids

The ventilator, also known as a respirator, is one of the most important machines in the NICU. Basically, it's a mechanical breathing machine. If your baby is not ready to breathe completely on her own yet, the ventilator will give her the extra breaths she needs until she's ready to take over.

When a baby is put on a ventilator, a small tube (called an endotracheal, or "ET" tube) is inserted through her mouth or nose into her windpipe, so that air can be sent directly to her lungs, and secured by tape to her face. The ET tube is attached to bigger tubes, which are attached to the ventilator—a box on legs that stands next to your baby's bed. The doctors set the machine to give the baby a certain number of breaths per minute, delivered with a certain amount of force per breath (enough pressure to keep the air sacs in the lungs open), and with a certain amount of oxygen (which can range from 21%—the amount of oxygen in normal, room air—to as high as 100%, or pure oxygen).

Don't assume that the ventilator is doing all of the breathing for your baby. It's far more common for the machine to be supplementing a baby's own, natural breathing. For example, the ventilator might give your baby 30 breaths a minute—while she takes another 30 of her own breaths in between. As she needs less and less help, the doctors will gradually decrease the settings on the ventilator. Finally, she will be extubated. (Some NICU language you're likely to hear: when a baby is put on a ventilator and the tube is put in, she is said to be intubated; when she is taken off the ventilator, she is said to be extubated.)

This is a big moment in more ways than one. While a baby is intubated, the tube blocks her vocal chords and you can't hear her cry. So, many parents now hear their baby cry for the first time since the delivery room. Let parents of full-term babies complain if their babies are "colicky"; for mothers and fathers of just-extubated preemies, those cries are precious, sweet sounds!

CPAP

If a baby doesn't need a lot of help from a ventilator, yet isn't quite ready to breathe completely on her own, she may be wearing prongs in her nose. The prongs are a way to give her something called CPAP. (Pronounced "SEE-pap," it's short for continuous positive airway pressure.) Translation: your baby takes every breath by herself, but a steady flow of air coming into her airway under pressure through the prongs, even when she exhales, holds the air sacs

open, and keeps them from collapsing after each breath.

Oxygen

Babies with the mildest form of respiratory problems—those who can breathe entirely on their own and just need some extra oxygen—may be given a set of smaller prongs, called a nasal cannula. Or they may get one of the bulkier pieces of equipment in the NICU: an oxygen hood. Don't be scared by the appearance of this clear plastic box, which fits around your baby's head. It may not look pretty to you, but with warm, moist air flowing into it, it can feel awfully cozy to a newborn.

THE PROFESSIONALS CARING FOR YOUR BABY

It's not just the machines that can seem overwhelming when you enter the NICU for the first time. It's also the staff: medical professionals everywhere, rushing around, all unfamiliar faces.

It's natural to feel anxiety about all of these people who are responsible for the health and comfort of your child. But be assured of one thing: the staff of a neonatal intensive care unit are exactly the people who should be taking care of your premature baby right now. They all have specific areas of expertise and specialized jobs to do—and they work as a team to provide complete care for the youngest and tiniest, and oldest and plumpest, preemies. Within a few days, you'll know who the key players are and what they do for your baby. After a week or so, if your baby is still in the hospital, you'll probably feel at home in the NICU—or if not quite at home, at least like part of the extended family.

But right now, you need some introductions. Keep in mind that not all NICUs are the same—here are some staff descriptions that usually apply.

Neonatologist

The doctor who is primarily responsible for making medical decisions for your baby is called a neonatologist. Neonatologists have highly specialized training—at least five years beyond medical school—in pediatrics and in newborn intensive care. The neonatologist examines and makes a treatment plan for every infant in his care every day, and supervises the rest of the medical staff in the nursery. You'll get to know your baby's neonatologist, as he keeps you informed and answers your questions.

Neonatal fellows and residents

In teaching hospitals, there are often neonatal fellows: physicians who are already trained in pediatrics and are currently doing further training in newborn intensive care (soon to be neonatologists). There are also residents: physicians who have completed medical school and are learning pediatrics. The neonatologist supervises the fellow, who supervises the residents. In most intensive care nurseries, at least one of these physicians or a nurse practitioner (see below) is in the unit 24 hours a day.

Neonatal nurse practitioner

A neonatal nurse practitioner is a neonatal nurse who has received advanced training so that she can perform many of the same tasks as a doctor. Neonatal nurse practitioners (or NNPs, as you might hear them called) prescribe medication, put in intravenous lines, and help decide on your baby's treatment plan, among other things. If you have a medical question and a neonatologist isn't around, try the nurse practitioner.

Bedside nurse

The nurse is a very important person to your baby; she is by her bedside 24 hours a day, feeding her, weighing her, changing her diaper, giving her the medications prescribed by the doctors, responding to her cries, and keeping a constant eye on her and the machines. Neonatal nurses have specialized training in newborn intensive care, too, and the doctors rely on their observations of how your baby is doing. You'll learn to rely on them, too, to teach you how to care for a premature baby, and to take your calls asking for progress reports, any time of the day or night.

Respiratory therapist

Many NICUs have respiratory therapists who are expert in handling the ventilators and other equipment that support your baby's breathing.

Social worker

Having a baby in an intensive care unit can be stressful, and social workers are there when you need them to help you cope. Social workers can offer counseling, and you can also consult them for practical tips, such as where to stay if you live far from the hospital, how to get financial help, and how to prepare for your baby's homecoming. For all of the other members of the NICU team, your baby is the patient, and her care is the primary concern. For the social worker, your well-being is the primary concern.

There are many other physicians and professionals who may care for your baby at one point or another. We'll introduce you to them at later points in the book. But in the meantime, if you meet someone and want to know what he's doing, feel free to ask.

Touching Your Baby

I want to touch my baby so badly, but I'm scared to. She looks so fragile, like I might hurt her.

Your baby may look breakable to you, but that's one thing you *don't* have to worry about. Just look at how the nurses and doctors move her around, and you'll understand. As long as she is 26 weeks of gestation or older, your little one is ready and eager for parental handling.

Premature babies born between 23 weeks and 25 weeks of gestation still have fragile skin, and although a gentle finger in her palm or a touch on her leg can help cement that irresistible physical connection between parent and child, it's best to let her skin mature and toughen before touching it much more than that. The nurses can let you know when her skin can take more handling. But if your baby is 26 weeks or older, far from being painful or harmful, your touch is likely to help her. Some studies show that consistent, gentle touching leads to better outcomes in premature babies—such as fewer episodes of apnea, faster weight gain, and earlier discharge from the hospital. And although no newborn appreciates vigorous rubbing, older preemies can benefit from (and usually love) a smooth massage, see page 250.

The only thing better than touching your premature baby is holding her. Although it seems scary before you've tried it, nothing could be more natural or enjoyable once you have. If your baby was just put on a ventilator today, has a chest tube because of a pneumothorax, or is medically unstable for other reasons, you may have to wait. But as soon as the nurse says your baby is ready, you need not hesitate. The nurse will help pick the baby up, hand her to you, and arrange things so you don't knock any intravenous lines or other equipment out of place.

All you have to do is support your baby's neck, be gentle—and relax. She'll be safe, and extremely happy, in her parents' arms. (And from then on, you'll be looking forward to holding her even closer to your body: ask your baby's doctor when you can start kangaroo care, described on page 221).

Baby's Twitches

My baby makes the strangest, jittery movements. I'm afraid there's something wrong with his nervous system.

Remember those twitches you used to feel inside your pregnant belly? Now you're getting a glimpse of what your baby was doing to cause those tickling sensations! You didn't worry then, and you needn't worry now. Your baby's nervous system is probably functioning just as it should at this stage—which is to say, immaturely.

A baby's motor activity follows a predictable pattern of development, as his nervous system and muscles mature. The earliest movements start just seven weeks after conception (though the mother doesn't feel them until later); complex movements, like putting his thumb in his mouth, or reaching and grasping the umbilical cord, can be seen by 24 weeks. Between 28 and 32 weeks, a preemie still has very little control, and his movements are expected to be uncoordinated and sudden, with lots of tremors and twitches. Sometimes you'll see jerky, flailing movements; other times you might see writhing or twisting.

Chances are you'll get so used to seeing these movements that you'll start thinking of them as normal (which they are!). But if you have any questions, ask your baby's nurses; they are trained to distinguish a preemie's normal movements from abnormal ones that could indicate a medical problem. They can also tell you if your baby's movements are unusually frantic or diffuse—a sign of stress that often can be alleviated by holding the baby's arms and legs close to his body, or swaddling him nice and tightly in a blanket.

Is Baby Sick or Healthy?

There's something really basic I don't understand. The doctors keep talking about things like lung disease. Is my premature baby sick, or just immature?

That's something that is confusing to many parents. The reason for the confusion is that a premature baby can fall into either category— and while the distinction may be clear to doctors, it isn't always obvious to parents.

Some preemies are perfectly healthy, just immature. They're developing normally, but outside the womb rather than inside the womb. But many newborn preemies (especially the younger ones) are sick or become sick at some point during their hospitalization, since being born early puts an infant at higher risk for certain illnesses.

How can you tell whether your baby is healthy or sick? Either way he'll have lots of wires and tubes attached to him, since even a healthy preemie has many bodily systems that are immature and not up to functioning on their own yet. Either way he'll be prone to breathing lapses that set off screeching alarms in the nursery.

Here's the way the experts look at it. Neonatologists define a preemie as sick if: 1) he has medical problems that are caused by something other than his simply having been born too soon (such as an infection or birth defect), or 2) he has medical problems that are typical for premature babies but are unusually severe (for example, he cannot breathe without a lot of support from a ventilator). The most frequent ailments making preemies sick on the first day are:

✸ *Lung disease, or respiratory distress syndrome.* It's very common for a preemie's immature lungs to cause breathing problems. This illness is called respiratory distress syndrome, or RDS for short. The earlier a preemie is born, the more likely he is to have it. If the breathing problems are moderate to severe, he may need the help of a ventilator.

✸ *Infection.* The most common cause of premature labor and delivery is an infection in the pregnant mother's birth canal or amniotic fluid around the time of delivery. These infections can be obvious, as when a mother feels sick, or they can be very subtle, showing up on lab tests only. If the germs spread to the fetus, he'll be born with an infection. Premature babies are especially susceptible to infection, because they have immature immune systems. And since their infection-fighting capacity is easily overwhelmed, instead of getting localized infections—say, in the ear or throat—they tend to get general infections, like sepsis (an infection of the blood) or meningitis (an infection of the fluid around the brain and spinal cord). Chances are, your preemie will be tested at birth to see if he has an infection.

✸ *Intraventricular hemorrhage (or IVH).* Some blood vessels in the brain are still fragile in a premature baby. The younger and smaller the baby, the more common it is for these blood vessels to rupture, usually within the first few days of life. Doctors don't worry about very mild intraventricular hemorrhages; not only are they asymptomatic, but they are believed to cause no long-term problems. But a baby with a more severe bleed—whether initially asymptomatic or not—would be considered sick, and would be watched carefully to see if complications develop.

* *Major birth defects.* Your baby's doctors will tell you if your baby has any physical abnormalities—noticeable ones or ones that affect his internal organs. These congenital (meaning existing before birth) problems can be caused by genetic or environmental factors—or by causes entirely unknown. Although fetuses with some congenital defects are more likely to be born early, the vast majority of preemies have no such abnormalities. Most major birth defects will be picked up by the doctor on the initial physical exam or within the first week of a baby's life, and nearly all will be apparent by the time a baby is a few months old.

On the other hand, there are many ways for a healthy preemie to be immature. Following are some examples of common problems that stem from a preemie's immaturity:

* *Fluid loss.* A full-term baby's skin is thicker and contains more insulating fat than a preemie's, enabling it to hold in heat and fluids. Some of the youngest, tiniest preemies lose a lot of water and can easily become dehydrated. Their beds may be wrapped in cellophane, which helps keep moisture from escaping. After birth, skin matures quickly; after four or five days, significant fluid loss is rarely a problem, and by two or three weeks, a premature infant's skin resembles a full-term baby's.

* *Inability to maintain body temperature.* With little fat for insulation, premature infants lose heat faster. Compounding the problem, preemies have more external surface area (from which to lose heat) compared to their total size than older, bigger babies. Plus, their brains aren't fully ready to regulate body temperature. So premature babies can't maintain their temperature on their own until about the 34th week of gestation. Instead, they are kept in special, heated environments: isolettes or radiant warming beds.

* *Apnea.* Because their respiratory and nervous systems are immature, premature babies have different breathing patterns than full-term babies. They breathe irregularly, and often stop breathing for brief periods. If a baby doesn't take a breath for 20 seconds or longer, or if his heart rate or color changes during the breathing lapse, then it's called apnea. Apnea is such a common problem among preemies that their version is called apnea of prematurity. As the nervous and respiratory systems mature, apnea of prematurity disappears—usually by 36 weeks after conception.

* *Inability to feed.* Whether you realize it or not, eating and digesting are incredibly complicated processes. The intestines and stomach of a very young preemie may not be ready to digest food. These babies are fed intravenously. When they can handle digestion, and would welcome some breast milk or formula, they still might not be ready to feed from a nipple; until around 32 to 34 weeks of gestation, the sucking-and-swallowing reflex is poorly coordinated. So, in the meantime, they are fed through a small tube that runs from their mouth or nose into their stomach.

Why do some premature babies get sick, while others don't? It's no easier to answer that question than to explain why some toddlers get more colds than others do, or why some adults develop arthritis before their friends. Risk factors, such as lower birth weight, exposure to certain bacteria, or genetic predisposition, are part of the equation. But they never tell the whole story. Indeed, among twins there's often one baby who is healthier than the other, although both came out of the same womb at the same time.

If your baby is sick, it's undoubtedly very hard on you, as well as on him. Illness can interfere with his eating and growing, and no parents can bear seeing their child uncomfortable. Just remember that preemies have lots of ups and downs on their way from birth day to going-home celebration—and most of them, initially healthy or sick, end up doing just fine.

IN PLAIN LANGUAGE: WHAT IS RESPIRATORY DISTRESS SYNDROME?

A premature baby's first—and often biggest—challenge couldn't be more basic: breathing. Mother Nature has programmed the lungs to be mature and fully functioning at around 35 to 36 weeks after conception. What happens if a baby is born before that? Some preemies are lucky; for a variety of reasons, their lungs happen to mature earlier, so although they are young, they are able to breathe successfully on their own. Other babies, whose lungs develop on or behind nature's usual schedule, develop respiratory distress syndrome, or RDS, the most common illness in the intensive care nursery. (You may also hear it called hyaline membrane disease.)

RDS can range from mild to very severe. If a baby's case is mild, it will be no more than a bump on the road toward his hospital discharge. If it is very severe, it can make that road a rough one. But neonatologists have excellent success treating RDS nowadays. More than 99% of babies with RDS survive. Those who don't tend to be the very youngest and smallest preemies, those born at less than 26 weeks of gestation.

Here's a simple description of RDS. In the tiny air sacs of the lungs, there's a foamy substance called surfactant. This substance—which is lacking in preemies with RDS—is crucial to the breathing process. When there's lots of it lining the air sacs (or alveoli, as they are called), the sacs remain open, and air slips easily in and out. When the air sacs don't have enough surfactant, they collapse between breaths. As a result, the lungs aren't as efficient at taking in oxygen or getting rid of carbon dioxide.

Picture the lungs as balloons. Blowing up a brand new, uninflated balloon is hard work, but once the balloon has expanded, adding air to it is easy. Similarly, a baby's first breath requires tremendous exertion, as he opens the air sacs for the first time. If the air sacs remain expanded, it's easy to inhale after that. But the air sacs of a baby with RDS collapse between breaths, and every subsequent breath is as difficult as the first one, like blowing up that balloon for the first time. So babies with RDS have to work very hard to breathe, and they can sometimes tire out if they don't get assistance with their breathing.

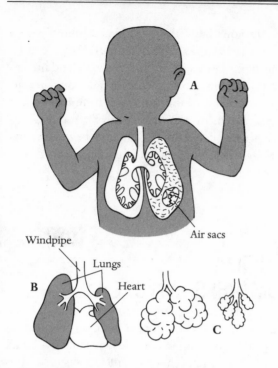

Windpipe

Lungs

Heart

B

A

Air sacs

C

A: Airways, lungs, and detail of air sacs in the lung.
B: On the left, a lung without RDS is fully inflated. On the right, a lung with RDS does not fully inflate.
C: On the left, air sacs with surfactant remain expanded; on the right, air sacs that lack surfactant collapse.

The earlier a baby is born, the more likely he is to develop RDS, and the more severe it is likely to be. Usually, surfactant starts appearing at around 24 weeks after conception and gradually builds up to its full level by 34 to 36 weeks. (Before 26 weeks, the alveoli themselves have barely developed, so nearly every baby born before 26 weeks has RDS.)

What makes some preemies in each age group luckier than others? As with all medical conditions that affect some people but not others, we have only partial explanations; the rest we chalk up to the mysteries of individual differences. Here are some factors that play a role:

* The bigger the baby, the lower his risk, in general. That's because size and maturity often go hand in hand.
* Boys are more likely to get RDS than girls, because their lungs mature more slowly.
* Caucasian babies may be more likely to get RDS than African-American babies, for the same reason.
* Preemies with diabetic mothers, and those with Rh blood-type incompatibilities, are especially susceptible, because the babies' lungs are slower to produce surfactant.
* If a preemie was under some stress in the womb, he is less likely to be susceptible to RDS. The body has a self-protective mechanism: when a fetus is under stress (for example, from episodes of preterm labor) it's as if his body knows he has to prepare for an early delivery, and his lung development accelerates.
* On the other hand, if the stress was extreme—say the mother had severe preeclampsia, or the baby became infected after his mother's membranes ruptured—then the baby is more vulnerable to RDS, because of disruption to his normal lung development and functioning.
* Babies whose mothers received steroid injections at least 24 hours before delivery are less vulnerable than those whose mothers didn't. Steroids (hormones which the body produces naturally in response to stress) speed up the maturation of the lungs, giving the baby the equivalent of about an extra week in the womb. For preemies born between 28 and 34 weeks of gestation, research shows that steroids reduce the incidence of RDS. For preemies born earlier, steroids may not reduce the incidence of RDS, but may reduce its severity.
* Preemies delivered by C-section, particularly if delivered electively, without labor, are at greater risk than those delivered vaginally.

That's because hormones produced during labor promote lung maturation, and uterine contractions may squeeze out some excess fluid that collects in a baby's lungs while he's in the womb.

DOES YOUR BABY HAVE RDS?

There's no single, easy test for RDS, like there are x-rays for broken bones. To make a diagnosis, the doctor assesses your baby's behavior as he breathes, the levels of oxygen and carbon dioxide in his blood, and the look of his lungs on chest x-ray—and then carefully monitors how all of these things change with time and treatment.

Because breathing is hard for him, a baby with RDS may suck in his ribs and chest deeply with each breath (these are called retractions) and grunt or moan as he exhales. His nostrils may flare, and he may breathe rapidly. Rather than a healthy pink, he may be dusky or bluish in color. And he may get tired: his breathing will become less regular, and he will have episodes of apnea, during which he stops breathing altogether.

On x-rays, his lungs will look partially collapsed, rather than fully expanded, with less air in them than usual. And in his blood, he'll have too little oxygen and too much carbon dioxide.

THE COURSE THAT RDS TAKES

Most babies who are going to get RDS show signs of it right away, in the delivery room or within a few hours after birth. Occasionally, a preemie will seem fine at first—only to have the symptoms slink up on him gradually. If your preemie has no symptoms of RDS after a day has gone by, you can relax. He doesn't have it.

RDS often gets worse for two or three days before it gets better. That's expected, and though it's normal for parents to worry, you should try not to. Around that time, your baby will start to produce more surfactant, and his lungs should gradually recover.

A baby with mild RDS, who needs just a little assistance from a ventilator, may be breathing entirely on his own within a few days. A baby with a very severe case (one who was born extremely early or who developed complications) will take much longer—days, weeks, or in rare cases months—to recover fully. If your baby is in this situation, try hard to take things day by day.

THE WONDERS OF MODERN TREATMENT

The only cure for RDS is time. Treatment focuses on buying babies the time they need, by providing breathing assistance, and by giving babies "replacement" surfactant until they can produce their own.

There are different levels of breathing assistance. If your baby has RDS, at a minimum he'll need extra oxygen. If that's all he needs, his RDS is mild. Either he'll be given a little set of nasal prongs called a nasal cannula, through which oxygen flows, or he'll be placed under a plastic oxygen hood. (You'll find descriptions of all of the respiratory equipment and how it works in Through the Doors of the Neonatal Intensive Care Unit, page 92.)

If your baby's illness is a little worse and he needs more help keeping his air sacs open, he'll get a slightly bulkier set of prongs, which deliver something called CPAP (pronounced "SEE-pap," it stands for continuous positive airway pressure). Your baby will take all of his own breaths, but a mixture of air and oxygen will flow steadily into his lungs, under pressure, and keep them from collapsing when he exhales.

If your baby has a moderate or severe case of RDS, it will be too tiring for him to take all of his own breaths. He'll be put on a ventilator that can do some breathing for him. The doctors will decide how to set the ventilator: how many extra breaths your baby needs to supplement his own natural ones; how much force, or "pressure," each breath should deliver to open the air sacs; and how much oxygen should be mixed in. As soon as your baby's condition stabilizes, the doctors will try to gradually reduce the settings. The goal is to have your baby do as much of his own breathing as possible, as quickly as possible.

There are certain, unfortunate things about ventilators. First of all, a baby has to be "intubated"—that is, an endotracheal (or ET) tube has to be inserted through his mouth or nose and down his windpipe (trachea) so the ventilator can send air into his lungs. Some babies don't mind this tube; others who seem uncomfortable are usually given sedatives or pain medication. Second, the ventilator can do some damage itself. Applying forceful pressure to a preemie's delicate lungs can cause small tears and scarring, and it takes a while for the lungs to return to normal. There is a further risk of secondary complications, described below. As frightening as these things are, they are a necessary (and for most babies, a small) price to pay for the life-saving help a ventilator provides.

One positive thing about intubation: it allows a baby to receive replacement surfactant. A dose of it is sent down the ET tube, and within several hours, it coats a baby's air sacs enough to significantly improve the RDS, increasing his chances of survival and making secondary complications less likely. Some neonatologists give surfactant within a few minutes after delivery to all babies who are likely to get RDS in hopes of preventing the disease—even though some of these babies won't need it. Others, who don't want to intubate any babies unnecessarily, wait until symptoms of RDS appear.

Don't be surprised if your baby has ups and downs, or if his progress is hard to predict; that's how RDS can go. Sometimes a baby on a ventilator can't handle a reduced setting on the first try, and then does fine with it a few hours later. Basically, if your baby's ventilator settings are gradually going down, or if he is graduating from the ventilator to CPAP or from CPAP to oxygen alone, you know he is getting better.

WILL YOUR BABY BE OK?

It's natural for a parent whose baby has RDS to worry, but it's worth developing a realistic understanding of the risks—so you know what you're up against, but don't suffer unnecessarily.

You already know that for all but the youngest and tiniest babies, the odds of surviving RDS are overwhelmingly good. Nonetheless, some babies—usually only those with severe RDS—may have to deal with some complications before they're discharged from the hospital, such as tears or bleeding in the lungs, or longer-term health problems, such as persistent breathing difficulties (known as bronchopulmonary dysplasia, or BPD), more frequent and severe respiratory infections in their first two years of life, and an increased likelihood of asthma. Fortunately, these complications affect only a small percentage of babies with RDS, and even the longer-term problems are usually successfully resolved before a child's second birthday. (Most are covered elsewhere in this book, but they're worth reading about only if they happen.)

What about long-term development? RDS by itself does not cause abnormal neurologic development. If your baby has a mild or moderate case of RDS, you shouldn't worry about resulting developmental problems. However, babies who are very sick with RDS are more likely to develop other medical conditions—such as an intraventricular hemorrhage or periventricular leukomalacia, retinopathy of prematurity, or severe BPD—that are associated with developmental problems. Again, please don't worry about these unless your baby gets them—because most babies never will.

If you possibly can, keep in mind that most babies recover just fine—and in just a few days or weeks, leave their RDS behind.

Understanding the Doctors

I feel really stupid when I talk to doctors. A lot of times I just don't understand what they're talking about, or I can't remember things they said a half hour later.

You may be surprised to hear it, but the same thing happens to the vast majority of preemies' parents—even to those who are physicians themselves!

When a baby is born prematurely, his family is hurtled into a complex world of medical terms and devices that are familiar only to specialists. Parents want to understand what is happening, but emotional turmoil makes it difficult for them to concentrate—especially on explanations that they dread may contain some bad news. They sit quietly and listen to the doctor's words, but with so much going on in their minds and hearts, they can scarcely remember the words a few minutes later.

It's important to realize that the doctors understand this well, so they expect you to ask the same questions as many times as you need to. Some doctors will always be warm and reassuring, while others may seem impatient—but that has to do with differences in their temperament, not with the appropriateness of your behavior.

If you think you're dealing with a doctor who is a poor communicator, don't hesitate to rely on the nurses in the NICU. They're very knowledgeable and can be great translators of medical jargon for parents.

Questions—Whom to Ask

I'm confused. I have questions about my baby, but I don't know which questions I'm supposed to ask the doctors, and which I should ask the nurses.

On your baby's first day of life, the neonatologist taking care of her will probably talk with you at length, giving you a detailed picture of her health status so far, and describing future developments you can reasonably expect at this point. Throughout your baby's hospitalization, the attending neonatologist will keep you informed of your baby's condition on a regular basis, and will discuss significant new medical issues with you as they arise.

When you're with the doctors, ask any questions that come to mind. Some parents hold back, afraid that their questions are inappropriate, or trivial. Every question is appropriate—and those you don't ask will end up making you feel frustrated or worried. Don't be inhibited by the fact that you don't know the appropriate medical terms. Few parents do.

What if you have questions at other times? Here are some rules of thumb. The neonatologist is the one who determines what procedures and medications your baby receives and when.

Ask the doctor if:

❋ You want to understand what a medical test means.

❋ You want help in putting medical findings into perspective—whether the results are good or bad, serious or not serious.

❋ You are wondering why a particular treatment was chosen.

❋ You would like an overview of how your baby is doing overall, and what the implications are for her long-term health.

Your baby's nurse's eyes and ears are always focused on your baby—while the doctors usually check on each baby only intermittently throughout the day. It is from the nurses that the doctors get much of their information on your baby's breathing, feeding, sleeping, and crying patterns, daily weight gain, temperature, and signs of stress or well-being. All of this information is available to you also; just ask.

Ask the nurse if:

❋ You would like an update on how your baby is doing and what has happened since your last visit to the NICU.

❋ You want to learn how to touch, handle, feed, and bathe your baby—either early in your baby's hospital stay, so you can be involved as much as possible with your baby in the hospital, or later, to ease the transition from hospital to home.

❋ You want help interpreting your baby's signals—what she looks like when she's content, mildly stressed and in the process of soothing herself, or highly stressed (see page 203).

❋ You would like to do kangaroo care (see page 221).

❋ You need assistance in your first breastfeeding attempts—you can ask her questions about pumping, storing, and transporting breast milk (see page 222).

❋ You want her to help you understand the doctor's words if they weren't completely clear to you, or you just want to hear them again.

What if you have a question and you're still confused about who to ask? Don't worry. There's no wrong question to ask anybody. Everyone in the NICU is committed to helping you and your baby, and if they can't answer your question, they'll find someone who will.

Telephone Calls to the NICU: Do's and Don'ts

1. *DO* ask if there are any restrictions on when you can call. In many NICUs, phone calls from parents are welcomed by the neonatal nurses 24 hours a day, and during the doctors' shifts (when they are not busy seeing patients), they are also available to talk to parents on the phone, with or without an appointment. This accommodating policy is intended to allow parents of preemies to stay constantly in touch with how their babies are doing.

2. *DON'T* be afraid of calling your baby's nurse for an update, even when you have nothing specific to ask. The nurses realize that parents want to feel connected even when they cannot visit—and the staff of the NICU encourages that. Talking to parents, on the telephone as well as in person, is an important part of the nurses' job. In fact, you'll find that they are experienced at it. They understand the anxiety that parents feel as they dial the NICU's number, fearful of hearing bad news. They know how to start the conversation with reassuring words, and to be forthcoming about your baby's condition.

3. *DON'T* be afraid of calling too often. There's almost no such thing. It's common for parents to check on their babies once or twice a day, by telephone or in person. Unless you're calling more than once per nurse's shift (in many NICUs, about eight hours) about a baby who is stable and doing well, or your phone calls last more than five or ten minutes, no reasonable nurse is going to find it inappropriate. If your baby is sick, everyone will understand if you want to call more often. As a general rule, it will help if you show that you're considerate of the NICU staff's time, and realize that they have other obligations, also. If you know a call is going to take a long time, schedule it with the doctor or nurse in advance, or ask them to call you back when they're free to talk.

4. *DON'T* encourage grandparents, aunts and uncles, or close friends to call. Information on babies is given only to parents, not to other callers, and requests for special permission are usually denied. The reasoning: talking to too many people can cause confusion and misconceptions; parents should decide what they want to tell others; and nurses and doctors should save their precious time for moms and dads, who need all of the attention and support possible during their painful separation from their babies in the NICU. Repeating information isn't a good use of their time, when they'd otherwise be with the babies. If you really want Grandma to hear something about your baby directly from the nurse or doctor, you could ask one of them to call her. But do this only if you feel it's very important, and don't do it more than once or twice.

Is Baby on a Ventilator in Pain?

My baby is on a ventilator, and with that tube going down her throat she must be in pain. Are they giving her pain medication?

How best to recognize and control pain is still a controversial issue in neonatology (see page 109). There's a huge difference in practice among NICUs, so only the doctors and nurses taking care of your baby can give you a straight answer on their approach.

But it's pretty safe to assume that if your baby is on a ventilator, she's either not bothered by it much or she's been sedated to help her relax, so she doesn't "fight" the machine and resist letting its breaths into her lungs.

Although an endotracheal tube (the tube that goes down your baby's windpipe, connecting her to the ventilator) is a distressing sight to all parents, sometimes it's the parents who suffer more than their babies. Being on a ventilator is often not as uncomfortable as it appears. Many preemies tolerate it well, showing hardly any signs of pain or agitation. Others need just a little medication in the beginning to help them get accustomed to it.

It's true that there are some preemies who don't like the ventilator at all—they gag, become agitated, or continue to fight it. Most NICUs give pain medication or sedatives to these babies, to help them relax and ensure that every vent breath is as effective as possible. Calming the babies is also a precaution against a complication called a pneumothorax—a tear in the lung that can occur if a baby exhales against an incoming breath from the ventilator. The medication is usually administered as needed—typically, every few hours as long as the baby shows signs of agitation. Babies are also sedated when the ventilator is working at very high pressure settings. Because high pressure can be damaging to a baby's lungs, it's important for the vent to do its work of breathing as efficiently as possible.

Although it surprises many parents, some babies find nasal prongs delivering CPAP (short for continuous positive airway pressure, see page 96) more objectionable than the ventilator. (Try asking a friend to blow forcefully up your nose, and you'll see why!) A preemie who persistently tries to pull the prongs out of her nostrils may be sedated—though more lightly, because she has to initiate all of her own breaths on CPAP, and most sedatives slow down the natural drive to breathe.

Doctors and nurses are trained to keep a constant watch for signs of discomfort in each little patient. But if you think you notice that your baby is uncomfortable, *don't hesitate:* speak up. Maybe something more can be done—and if not, at least you'll know the reason why.

PAIN IN PREEMIES AND WAYS TO CONTROL IT

Parents in the intensive care nursery, watching their babies undergoing all kinds of medical procedures, are often in agony over a big question: How much pain is their baby feeling? And another question soon follows: What consequences will this early pain and stress have on his psychological development?

HOW PREEMIES SHOW THEY ARE IN PAIN

Before the 1970s, the medical community assumed that premature infants, who still have immature nervous systems, were unable to perceive intense pain. As recently as the mid-1980s, anesthesia was not routinely used when newborns underwent surgery, because doctors feared that its risks outweighed its benefits—and believed that infants would have no memory of the pain later, anyway.

Thankfully, these beliefs have been overturned. Widely accepted studies have shown that preemies as young as 24 weeks of gestation already have a strong physical response to pain. It's true, preemies cannot speak up and ask for relief. They may not be strong enough to kick the doctor away when he pricks their foot. But preemies do signal that they're in pain. When a preemie is in pain, his breathing and heart rate may change, his blood pressure may rise, and the oxygen level in his blood may drop. He may become agitated, move jerkily, stiffen his body, arch his back, and become flushed—or he may become drowsy and lethargic, lose his muscle tone, and turn pale.

Preemies can show the same behavioral changes when they're simply upset and irritable. But based on the medical context and their experience, doctors and nurses usually can judge when pain is the problem and step in to relieve it. Alleviating discomfort is doubly important, because research has shown that pain and other stress can impede a premature baby's recovery, growth, and development. Of particular concern is the effect that stress might have on the development of the brain, at a very vulnerable time. The brain grows at an especially fast pace between 30 weeks of gestation and 3 months postnatal age—just at the time when most preemies are hospitalized.

Researchers still know very little about the emotional experience of pain in a prematurely born baby—that is, the memory of pain, the fear of it, or what lingering effects it may have. We don't know, and probably never will know, what preemies remember of their time in the NICU.

MEDICATIONS TO TREAT PAIN AND STRESS IN PREEMIES

Both analgesics (drugs that relieve pain), and sedatives (drugs that calm and relax), are given to preemies. The need for them often overlaps. For example, sometimes calming a baby with a sedative makes it easier, and therefore less painful, to perform a medical procedure;

sometimes alleviating pain makes a baby's agitation go away.

Pain management varies a lot from one NICU to the next. Here's a quick run-through of the most commonly used medications and their effects:

* *Opiate narcotics,* such as morphine, fentanyl, and methadone, are among the most effective and commonly used drugs. They both relieve pain and are sedating.
* *Sedatives,* such as Valium and its relatives (like Versed and Ativan), barbiturates (like Nembutal or phenobarbitol), and chloral hydrate are commonly used to calm babies down, but don't provide pain control.
* *Non-steroidal anti-inflammatory drugs (NSAIDs)* like Tylenol, Motrin, and Indocin, are used for mild or moderate pain. They have no sedative effects.

EMLA, a local anesthetic cream, is painless to apply, causes loss of sensation in the skin within an hour or two after its application, and can be used for drawing blood, inserting IVs, and other, minor medical procedures. But EMLA is a relatively new drug and is not widely used in NICUs yet because there are still concerns about its safety: preemies have thinner skin that might absorb too much of the cream's chemical agent.

WHY TREATING PAIN CAN BE A DILEMMA

Experts still disagree on when and how to control pain in preemies. Everyone gives preemies anesthesia for major surgical procedures in the operating room, but routine procedures in the NICU, from intubation to insertion of IV lines, may or may not be performed with pain medication.

Before accusing neonatologists of being callous, consider the dilemma they face: All analgesics and sedatives have side effects that can be dangerous to preemies. Many of these drugs diminish the drive to breathe. Other common side effects include decreased heart rate, decreased blood pressure, injury to the kidney or liver, and drowsiness that can interfere with learning and development. So there's a balance to aim for when a preemie confronts pain: that point where the benefits of relief outweigh its risks.

NON-MEDICAL WAYS TO TREAT PREEMIES' DISCOMFORT

By observing preemies in intensive care nurseries, and using concepts from child psychology and common sense, neonatal doctors and nurses have identified a number of effective, non-medical measures that soothe preemies. They can be very helpful in relieving pain and helping babies relax, so it's worth trying them:

* Decreasing the levels of light, noise, handling, and other stimulation;
* Giving your baby a pacifier dipped in sugar water, or sugar water in a bottle (this has been shown to control mild to moderate pain);
* Doing something repetitive and rhythmic, like rocking your baby, or singing to him softly;
* Applying firm touch and gentle pressure, for instance placing an open hand on your baby's back, or holding him against your body;
* Containing him by swaddling him tightly in a

blanket, or positioning him in the fetal position, with arms and legs flexed close to his body.

If you watch your preemie carefully, you'll begin to learn how he expresses pain and agi-

tation. Ask the nurses to help you interpret behavioral or physical changes that you notice. Always ask whether your baby can be given more relief, if you think he needs it. Soon you'll be able to take over some of the tasks of comforting your baby yourself.

Will Baby Become Addicted?

If my baby gets too much morphine, could she get addicted?

Not really. It's important to clarify what addiction means: it refers to a physical and psychological craving for a drug—because of its euphoric or calming effects—that produces an irresistible drug-seeking drive. Several studies have shown that adults who are given drugs in the hospital to control pain don't get addicted in the psychological sense, and never develop that compulsive drive. In other words, once their pain goes away, they have no further desire for the drugs.

On the other hand, pain medications and sedatives can cause tolerance and withdrawal, indicating physical dependence on the drug. Tolerance means that higher doses of the drug are needed to get the same effects. Withdrawal refers to a wide range of negative symptoms that may occur when the drug is suddenly suspended. Tolerance and withdrawal are predictable side effects of many pain medications and sedatives (such as morphine, fentanyl, methadone, benzodiazepines, and barbiturates).

Neonatologists are well aware of these side effects, and usually take some measures to minimize them, such as:

* starting babies on low doses of pain medication, and increasing the amounts gradually, only as needed;
* attempting non-medical methods of pain control, as well (see page 110);
* prescribing sedatives along with analgesics, to decrease any anxiety that may be contributing to the baby's agitation and pain;
* decreasing the dose slowly when it's time to wean the baby from pain medication.

Few preemies—usually only those who have been on high doses of an opiate, or some sedatives, for more than a week or two—ever need enough pain medication to cause withdrawal symptoms. Nonetheless, neonatologists are very used to handling this. They wean babies from the drug slowly, watching for signs of discomfort and using all possible measures to help calm the babies. If weaning is taking a very long time (it usually doesn't), they can switch the baby to an oral drug like methadone or oral morphine. But usually a preemie needs the drug for only a few days after painful events have passed. And once a baby is off the drug, she's off.

Clinical trials have proven that controlling pain can hasten and enhance a patient's recovery. Unfortunately, in today's society where illegal drugs are a scourge, the use of the same substances to relieve pain is often surrounded by suspicion. Several studies over the last decade have found an unjustified underuse of morphine and other opiates in hospitals around the country. Only in recent years, after long campaigning by pain experts, are more adequate tools being employed to relieve the unnecessary suffering of patients of all ages.

So don't worry about drug addiction. When pain medication makes your baby feel good, you can feel good, too.

Baby Is Tied Down

They tied my baby down! Isn't that cruel?

Sometimes a preemie is restrained for a brief time, when the doctors or nurses are doing a procedure, and movement could cause pain or potential danger to the baby. For example, restraint is often used when a baby needs a catheter placed in an artery or in his umbilical cord. It's considered a preferable alternative to extremely heavy sedation or medication-induced paralysis, and is generally used with light sedation, to make the baby feel comfortable and ease his anxiety.

Restraining a preemie usually involves taping or tying down one or more of his arms or legs, or holding his head or torso in a particular position with a cloth that is pinned to his bed sheet. It looks cruel to an adult, but doesn't seem to bother preemies much. The youngest preemies—under about 30 weeks of gestational age—don't seem to mind restraint at all, while older preemies very quickly (usually in less than a minute) stop fighting and relax easily.

Father Feels Faint

As the father, I'm supposed to be the strong one, but I feel like I'm going to faint in the NICU. What's wrong with me?

Nothing at all. Because of the stereotypes in our culture, most fathers feel a sense of responsibility to be the strong one in the family, and to support their wives as well as their children. It's a common sight in the NICU: parents standing by their baby's bedside, the mother weeping, and the father patting her on the shoulder to comfort her. How many of these fathers, even the most stalwart ones, feel like weeping, too?

Even the strongest fathers may be unprepared for the way they feel when a premature baby enters the family. Nothing in life can prepare them for walking into a neonatal intensive care unit, where infants not much bigger than the palms of their hands lie splayed out and defiled by needles and tubes. It's not uncommon for fathers and mothers to faint in the NICU. (Don't worry, the nurses are used to it by now!) Those who don't faint often have other physical symptoms. They feel woozy or nauseated, or their skin gets clammy. Or they just feel overwhelmed. Not only are all of these responses normal, but they come from a wonderful source: the tremendous depth of emotion, and protective instinct, that parents feel for their children and all of the babies there.

Studies of how couples have reacted to a premature baby's birth show that there were fewer divorces and marital problems among those who openly expressed their feelings of anxiety, depression, and frustration. So don't feel you are weak if you accept help from your spouse, other family members, and friends.

Difficult Start to Breastfeeding

My doctor said my preemie was old enough to begin breastfeeding right away, but we're on the third feeding, and it doesn't seem to be going well.

Keep in mind that nobody should expect the first tries to be real feedings—just a tender, intimate way for mother and baby to get acquainted and stimulate the mother's breasts.

All newborns, and particularly premature infants, tend to be sleepy and not very interested in nursing during their first days of life. Also, since breast milk has not come in yet, babies generally lose up to 10% of their weight in this period. In a preemie who starts out with an already meager body weight, this initial loss can cause anxiety to parents, but it is completely normal and expected. Your baby will regain the weight as soon as she begins to feed more efficiently. If the doctors are concerned about her intake of fluid or nutrients, they can supplement the breastfeedings with gavage feedings of breast milk or formula.

You can be sure that the nurses and doctors want to help you and your baby in your breastfeeding efforts. Don't hesitate to ask whether your baby is doing what they'd anticipate at this stage, or if there seems to be a problem. Most likely, you'll be reassured. If, however, breastfeeding really isn't going well, even for a newly born preemie, and doesn't improve over the next few days, the nurses may elicit the help of a lactation counselor. (You should feel free to suggest that yourself, too.) Many hospitals have such breastfeeding experts on their staff, or can recommend someone locally. Chances are, though, your preemie is acting just as she should—like a tired, normal, not-all-that-hungry, newborn baby.

Not Feeding Baby

They are not giving my baby any food yet. Won't that starve him and make him feel weaker, at a time when he needs all the strength he can get?

What could be more natural than a parent concerned that his child isn't eating enough? But it's not something you need to worry about right now. Remember that a mother's breast milk doesn't really come in for a day or two, so all breastfed babies don't eat much of anything on their first day, either—and we do still believe that mother nature knows best!

Most preemies born at less than 34 weeks of gestation remain NPO, as doctors put it—meaning nothing *per os* (Latin for "by mouth")—for at least one day, until it's clear that they're medically stable enough to handle being fed. But although you can't see it, your baby is getting some nutrients today. On his first day of life, a preemie usually receives nutrients he can easily metabolize: a clear intravenous fluid made up of water and sugar. As long as his blood sugar level doesn't get too low—and the nurses will watch that closely—he'll have all the calories he needs right now. (He won't get enough calories to grow today, but that's not the primary medical concern.) In fact, introducing food could jeopardize the doctor's efforts to stabilize him. If the food puts too much stress on his immature digestive system, for example, his belly could swell, impinging on the volume of his lungs and interfering with his breathing.

In a day or two, if your baby is still not being fed orally, he'll advance to something called parenteral nutrition, which means nutrition that does not go through the mouth or digestive system. Parenteral feedings are administered through an umbilical catheter or IV line, delivering a wholesome mixture of nutrients directly into his bloodstream. Parenteral nutrition typically consists of sugar and protein, vitamins (which give the fluid its yellow color), minerals, and salts dissolved in water. Parenteral fat, called intralipid (a thick, white fluid), is usually given, as well. The doctors will gradually increase the number of calories in the parenteral nutrition over several days, so your baby will soon get enough to grow on.

Most premature babies are off parenteral nutrition and on to complete feedings of formula or breast milk within a few days or weeks. As soon as their medical condition stabilizes, oral feedings are gradually introduced, and the amount of parenteral nutrition reduced. So get ready to help feed your baby; see "How Your Baby is Fed: A Journey from Parenteral Nutrition, to Gavage Feedings, to Breast or Bottle" on page 149.

Pumping Breast Milk

I've tried to use the electric pump to express my milk, but it really hurts me. Is there any other system I could try?

First of all, if no one has done it already, give yourself a pat on the back just for trying it. Your breast milk (and particularly the first days' colostrum, which is especially rich in antibodies and nutrients), is top-choice for your premature baby, as its health benefits are still unparalleled by modern formulas. (You can read more about whether to breastfeed or bottle feed a preemie on page 124.) Unfortunately, starting to breastfeed is a hassle since your baby cannot nurse from your breast yet. So you do have to learn how to use an electric pump to express your milk and store it for later, when it can be fed to him through a tube or bottle.

To every mother, the first pumping sessions are unpleasant. But to some women—whether because of differences in anatomy, aversion to machines, or other personal reasons—the first sessions may feel unbearable. Besides the physical discomfort you might experience, there's a lot of psychological suffering involved. This is a time when you fully start to taste the frustration of not being able to take care of your baby yourself, as you expected during your pregnancy. But expressing your milk is something only you can do for your baby now, something that may even help lessen some of the risks of a premature birth. So if you want to try to overcome the obstacles to breastfeeding a premature baby, it's certainly worthwhile.

Remember that it's hardly ever easy to start nursing, even with a full-term baby. The first few breastfeeding attempts are often frustrating and painful, because of Mom's and baby's inexperience. It's normal to feel an achy, biting sensation in the areola (the dark circle around your nipple) during breastfeeding when your newborn is still learning how to latch on. Nipples get sore and irritated, even if sucked by your own offspring's mouth. So how could it feel anything but miserable to have your breast squeezed in a plastic funnel, your nipple pulled by a sudden, mechanical force? Nevertheless, an electric pump is the best way to build your milk supply, because (believe it or not) its suction most closely resembles your baby's. And there are things you can do to make it less painful and upsetting. (Other kinds of tips are in "Practical Advice for Pumping and Storing Breast Milk," page 222.)

* *Try to relax.* Try draping warm washcloths on your breast and massaging the nipple and areola before pumping. Listening to your favorite music while you pump may help soothe your nerves. If you have visitors, don't hesitate to kindly send them away. During your first pumping attempts, you need to be alone—or even better, helped and comforted by your partner or someone else you feel particularly close to.

❋ *Get comfortable.* Sit—or lie—comfortably. If you had a vaginal delivery, and you had an episiotomy (a small incision between the vagina and rectum to facilitate the birth), you may prefer to lie in bed, positioning the electric pump at your side. (Hospital pumps are often placed on a stand with wheels for this reason.) If you had a C-section, you may want to wait a day or two before starting to pump—until you feel better and are able to walk a few steps.

❋ *Pump often.* Once you start, pump consistently: at least once every three hours during the day, about 10 minutes at each breast. You don't need to wake at night, unless your breasts are uncomfortably full, but make sure you do pump right before going to bed, and first thing in the morning. Night pumpings can start a few days before your baby comes home from the hospital, to get your body accustomed to your baby's night feeding schedule.

❋ *Start slowly—and stop if it hurts.* Start with the lowest level of suction and gradually increase it to a comfortable level. If you feel any pain, stop the machine immediately and reposition the funnel on your nipple until the pumping becomes more bearable. If the entire nipple and surrounding areola are well centered and covered completely by the funnel, pumping should not hurt much, and you should gradually get used to it. After a few sessions, you'll become familiar with the machine, and you'll get the level of suction right from the beginning. If your nipples get sore or irritated, try rubbing a little purified lanolin on them, but make sure to wash it off before pumping again. (Too much ointment left on your nipples can affect the suction power of the machine.)

❋ *Don't expect too much.* Even though an electric pump is great at helping to establish a new mother's milk supply, some women never develop a good "let-down reflex" with it. For them, mechanically expressing their milk will always take a little longer. The let-down reflex is an involuntary reflex that forces the milk down from the breast's ducts into pools behind the areola. It is initiated by hormones that are stimulated by the presence of the baby, his crying, or by the simple expectation of nursing him. No wonder that a machine can't always trigger it! (Some other mothers, on the other hand, have no let-down problem even with the pump, and can get a large quantity of milk from each breast in a short time.)

❋ *Remember it isn't forever.* The first two weeks are a crucial time to become accustomed to the electric pump and establish your milk supply. (If your milk doesn't start to flow right away, your baby might be fed special formula for preemies in the meantime; this doesn't influence his ability to digest or assimilate breast milk later.) After your milk supply is established, you can take more liberties and try other methods to express your milk. For mothers who have to go back to work, there are lighter, portable, electric pumps that can be carried easily. Occasionally, you can even use a smaller, hand-held pump, or even simple, low-tech, manual expression. But keep in mind that these methods, which may come in handy when you're traveling or at work, cannot completely empty your breasts. So whenever you can, try to continue using a hospital-quality, electric pump—at least until your baby comes home and is breastfeeding well. At that point, while happily nursing your baby in your arms, you will feel very proud of what you've accomplished—and deservedly so.

Blood Transfusion

They told me my baby might need a blood transfusion. Can I refuse? I'm terrified that he'll get AIDS.

Your situation is very common. During their first days of life, many preemies, especially while on ventilators or receiving intravenous nutrition, have blood drawn frequently to monitor their blood chemistries. All of these draws deplete the number of circulating blood cells. Because a premature baby's bone marrow, which is responsible for making more blood cells, is still immature, it usually can't replace them fast enough. As a result, he develops anemia (a low number of red blood cells). Red blood cells deliver oxygen throughout the body, so without enough of them, a baby's tissues won't get the oxygen they need to function and grow. If anemia isn't treated soon enough, it can be dangerous, but fortunately, one or more blood transfusions can easily solve this problem .

You really shouldn't worry about the safety of the blood your baby will get. The Red Cross has built up a special pool of donors whose blood type is O negative (meaning it's safe to give to nearly all premature babies) and CMV negative (meaning it doesn't carry cytomegalovirus, a virus that causes only mild, flu-like symptoms in a healthy child or adult but can be dangerous to anybody who doesn't have a fully functioning immune system, such as a preemie). The combination of O negative, CMV negative blood is rare, and the Red Cross saves this blood to give to newborn infants.

Because these donors have blood that is unusual and precious, they are called on to give it more often. Thus, they end up being screened for infection more frequently than other blood donors. Data from all of this testing show that the people in this pool are less likely to have HIV (the AIDS virus), Hepatitis B, or Hepatitis C than even the thoroughly screened pool of donors that the Red Cross uses for other blood donations.

While no blood donation can be considered 100 percent safe, the chances of getting an infection from a transfusion are very low. In the U.S. overall, the chance of getting infected with HIV is 2 per million units of blood transfused; with Hepatitis B, it is 5 per million units; and with Hepatitis C it is 3 per ten thousand units. (In babies, Hepatitis C usually causes mild liver disease, which in some cases can become chronic.)

But remember, even these numbers don't take into consideration the extra safety provided by the O negative, CMV negative blood donors. And premature babies, depending on their body weight, usually get only 10 to 25 milliliters of blood with each transfusion—a small fraction of a full unit, which contains 250 milliliters. So the already small risk may be even lower for a preemie.

It's scary to think about putting your baby at any risk, even if it's small. But if your preemie needs a transfusion, take comfort in the fact that the safety of the blood supply for premature babies is greater today than ever before. And remember that when your baby needs more blood to fight his anemia and stabilize his health, getting a transfusion is less risky than not getting one.

Can You Be the Blood Donor?

My friend had a premature baby, and they let her donate blood to her son. But the doctors won't let me do it for my daughter. Shouldn't that be my choice, since my daughter has my blood type?

It's natural that you'd prefer for your baby to get your blood, because you feel it's the best and healthiest she could get. Nevertheless, some hospitals don't allow directed donation of blood from relatives, preferring to rely on a special group of blood donors identified by the Red Cross (see page 116). This blood pool, which is O negative and CMV negative (free of cytomegalovirus, which is dangerous to premature babies) has proven safer for preemies than blood from people close to them (even parents), who are well-meaning, but not always aware of their own risks for infection.

There's also a timing issue. It takes four to five days to screen and process the blood from a new donor, and your baby might need her transfusion sooner than that. Once she has one transfusion, the hospital will want to continue using blood from the same donor, if possible, for any future transfusions, because exposing her to blood from an additional donor (even a parent) actually increases her risk of infection.

Incidentally, there's another reason that a father's blood, in particular, might be less preferable than the blood of a well-chosen stranger. Research has shown that blood cells from fathers and paternal relatives sometimes don't circulate as long within a baby's body. So using her father's blood means your baby could need more frequent transfusions.

Many hospitals do allow directed blood donations, because they're requested so often by parents. In that case, if you still want to donate your blood, go ahead. You can be sure that all precautions will be taken to make your blood a safe gift from you to your baby.

Experimenting on Preemies

Are they going to experiment on my baby?

While you were pregnant, you probably envisioned your newborn baby's doctor as a warm, pleasant pediatrician. You may have imagined proudly standing by as your baby received her first exam in a colorful office, with Dr. Seuss books in the waiting room. But now she is off by herself in a high-tech, intensive care unit where the doctors and nurses are strangers. You have only the foggiest idea what they're doing to your baby—and little control over it.

Many parents get nervous under such circumstances. You're not the first to wonder if your baby might be treated with experimental therapies without your even knowing about it.

Let us reassure you: your baby cannot be used as a subject in a research study without your permission. The federal government imposes strict guidelines on medical research. Investigators must provide research subjects (or their parents, in the case of children) with information on all of the significant risks and potential benefits of the study, and must obtain their signed consent. Moreover, most hospitals have review boards that monitor all research protocols and ensure that the interests of research subjects are protected and the government guidelines strictly followed.

If your baby is in a teaching hospital (a hospital affiliated with a medical school), there are sure to be some research projects going on there, and you may be asked whether you want your baby to participate in one or more of them. Don't reject the idea out of hand; there are some studies you might want your baby to be part of. (Say, for example, a promising, new drug is being tested for an illness that has no good, existing therapies.) But do ask for lots of information—you can request written information and ask your family doctor or other people you trust for help making a decision—and feel perfectly free to say no. Researchers are used to being turned down—it happens all the time—and your baby won't be treated any differently because of it.

Even with all those assurances, though, there is a grain of truth to your concern. Neonatology is one of the youngest and fastest-changing fields of medicine. Innovations have dramatically improved the outcomes of premature and ill newborns over the last twenty years. So not only will your baby benefit from past innovations, but the innovations are still continuing today.

There's a fine line between innovative treatment—using promising, new therapies when your baby needs them, but before all of the potential benefits and risks are thoroughly known—and experimentation. It can take years to know how effective a new therapy is, and decades before all of the long-term effects are discovered. Most neonatologists feel that if they waited that long to use new treatments, they wouldn't be helping babies to the best of their abilities now. Even treatments that have been well-tested in older babies could be considered innovative when performed on 23-weekers, since these very young preemies have only been surviving—and doctors have only been treating them—for a few years now.

There are some critics who say that neonatologists, in their desire to help babies, are too quick to rush new, unproven techniques into the intensive care nursery. Others say it wouldn't be right not to use a therapy that could work. It's an important ethical question. What can you, as a parent, do if you're concerned about this? Talk openly with your baby's doctors, and tell them that you want to be kept informed. Listen carefully to them (remember that they have years of training and experience), and ask them to explain the rationale for their choices of treatment. But also trust your own instincts as a parent, and don't hesitate to speak up. In short, try to establish a partnership in decision-making.

Most neonatologists are not gathering data or trying to advance themselves or their field; they're simply trying to do what's best for your baby. An open relationship of mutual trust is crucial for your preemie's best care.

Any Alternative to the NICU?

I don't like taking medications, and I don't trust doctors very much. Isn't there a less invasive, more natural way to take care of a preemie? Isn't it true that preemies did very well decades ago, before NICUs existed?

While some parents of preemies find great comfort in the existence of NICUs and neonatologists—specialists in the latest medical techniques for taking care of premature babies—others, like you, react differently.

Maybe you longed to have a natural delivery at home, with your partner and a trusted midwife. Maybe you wanted to welcome your child into the world while gently floating in water. Maybe you planned to breastfeed your baby within minutes after delivery, holding him on your belly, as your companion cut the umbilical cord. And then came a very different premature birth.

Those tubes and wires attached to your baby, the people in hospital uniforms, and the sights and sounds in the NICU, may be horrifying to you. You ask yourself: Isn't this is a perfect example of excessive medical intervention?

Here is a fact that may reassure you: intensive-care spots are so precious that they are given only to babies who really need them as a potential life-saving measure. Once your preemie's medical condition stabilizes, he will go to a so-called "step-down" unit—an intermediate care nursery (in the same hospital or elsewhere), where premature babies can grow in quiet isolettes or cribs, with much less medical attention, before they are sent home.

It's true that some preemies survived, decades or even centuries ago, before the era of isolettes and antibiotics, artificial surfactants and ventilators, but only a small fraction of the number who survive and thrive today. In fact, one of the spurs for the development and spread of neonatal intensive care units in the United States was the death of President Kennedy's 34-week-old premature son in 1963 from respiratory distress syndrome—a baby who surely would have survived in a modern NICU today. The survival rate of extremely premature babies, those weighing less than about two pounds, has tripled since the late 1970s, without an increased rate of major developmental problems.

As long as your baby is in an NICU, your options are limited. You could try to transfer him to a different hospital, if you find one that's more compatible, but most insurance companies won't pay for an expensive ambulance transfer for this reason. You can't take your baby home if it is seen as threatening his life or health. (Parents have the legal right to withhold consent for medical treatment for their baby. But if a doctor feels that parents are preventing their child from being treated to a point that constitutes medical neglect, the doctor can appeal to a judge, who will decide whether the parents' choices are reasonable or not, and, if not, can appoint a temporary legal guardian to take over medical decision-making.)

Nonetheless, you certainly can discuss with your baby's neonatologist whether there are less invasive, alternative therapies available. You'll be interested to know that there are experts in the U.S. and abroad who are pushing to make neonatal intensive care units more hu-

manized. They generally do not reject the tremendous advances in neonatal medicine of the last few decades, but they do believe that babies could benefit if the technological environment were made more natural and soothing. They advocate things like regular light and dark cycles, lower noise levels, keeping babies in a more flexed, "fetal" position, and the healing power of parents' touch. They are studying whether preemies have better developmental outcomes when treated with individualized, less disruptive care.

If you want your baby to get the benefit of some of these Developmental Care techniques, you can learn more about them on page 198. As a start, ask your baby's nurses if they can lower the lights, try to keep things quiet around your baby's bed, and hold him whenever he is fed. (But remember that sometimes even these seemingly easy changes may be impossible in a busy intensive care nursery.) Also ask your baby's doctor when you can start doing kangaroo care and infant massage.

While you can't change the high-tech environment of the NICU into an intimate home nursery, you can see to it that your preemie gets a lot of loving care. And that, along with the latest advances in medical treatment, may be the best combination he can get.

Testing for Drugs

They are collecting my baby's urine to test it for drugs, to find out why she was born so early. I'm not a drug abuser and I'm deeply offended.

Nobody is trying to accuse you of anything unjustly, or to violate your privacy. At most hospitals, it's the policy to screen for maternal drug use whenever the pregnancy or baby has certain characteristics. In other words, if specified criteria are met, your baby will be tested no matter who you are, what you look like, or what you do for a living. The idea is to benefit all children in the hospital's community, without discriminating against anyone by guessing who would or wouldn't use drugs. So don't take this as a personal affront.

The specific criteria for drug testing vary from hospital to hospital. Many hospitals require drug screening when a baby is born prematurely due to a placental abruption, because cocaine use can cause abruptions. (Many other things can, too.) Other reasons for testing may include: a baby who is inexplicably small for his gestational age; a baby who has symptoms that could indicate drug withdrawal (such as marked irritability, seizures, tremulousness, or diarrhea); a baby who has an unexplained neurological complication (such as a stroke that occurred before birth); a baby with a major birth defect; a mother who has a history of drug use or sexually transmitted disease; a mother who received no prenatal care; or even a premature birth that cannot be explained otherwise.

The drugs that are tested for are those most commonly abused—usually amphetamines, Valium, cocaine, marijuana, heroin, and PCP—but nearly any drug could be included. Many hospitals inform the mother before doing a drug test, although obtaining the mother's consent may not be legally necessary. In other hospitals, parents sometimes discover that a test is being done by noticing a little plastic bag taped to their baby's groin, collecting his urine. The newborn's feces, or meconium, can also be analyzed. Results from this test usually take longer to come back—sometimes one to three weeks, compared to a day or so for urine analysis. Analysis of meconium can reveal drugs used anytime in the last months of pregnancy, whereas urine testing only detects drugs that a mother used within several days of delivery.

In most cases, the mother didn't use drugs and the test results are negative. What if they are positive? The mother is informed privately, usually by a social worker or physician. Not all drug use during pregnancy harms the fetus, but it can still have significant implications for a family. At the least, discussion or counseling can determine whether drug use is a serious problem—and a mother who is addicted to drugs may be able to get help before her baby is discharged from the NICU, and she has to cope with the responsibilities of caring for a preemie at home.

When Baby May Go Home

Now that I've seen my baby, I feel so much more hopeful. She looks healthy to me. Maybe she'll be coming home soon, after all.

If your parental instinct makes you feel optimistic, that's a great sign. As time goes by, you'll probably notice that even the doctors give your judgment high regard. They've got the high-powered diagnostic tools, but nobody is more attuned to how a baby is feeling than Mom or Dad.

On the other hand, your preemie is only one day old now, and even if she's doing well, it may be a long time before you can take her home. She needs time to develop in the nursery just as she would have developed inside the womb. And since life outside the womb is not what mother nature planned for her, she'll probably experience some ups and downs before reaching her due date.

This warning is not meant to scare you, only to give you realistic expectations. The earlier your baby was born, the longer she's likely to have to stay in the hospital. Most premature babies go home about two to four weeks before their due date, because that is when they've matured enough to be safe and thrive outside a hospital. Requirements for discharge vary somewhat among doctors and hospitals, but in general, a baby is not considered ready to go home until she:

* weighs at least 1,800 grams,
* is gaining weight at a rate of 15–30 grams per day,
* is able to maintain her body temperature in an open bassinet,
* has had no significant apneas or bradycardias for at least five to eight days, and
* is able to take all of her feedings from a bottle or breast.

Some babies who take longer to convalesce, such as those who undergo surgery or need breathing aids for several months, may have to stay in the hospital even beyond their due date.

A piece of advice? Try to live this monumental experience day by day. If you focus too much on taking your baby home, the hospital stay may feel even longer than the few weeks it generally lasts. You also may miss many moments of happiness with your developing baby along the way.

MULTIPLES

One Twin Doing Better

One of my twins was put on a ventilator, but the other wasn't. Why would one be doing better than the other, when they both came out of the same womb at the same time?

So soon after delivery, it's natural to think of your twins as two little peas in a pod. And in a way they are: they shared the same uterus during pregnancy, and they were born at exactly the same gestational age. That usually puts them in the same medical ballpark, but it doesn't mean they have identical medical conditions or prognoses.

To make sense of it, you have to consider all of the possible differences between them. Individual characteristics vary: if your twins are fraternal, they're as different genetically as any two siblings are. Boys tend to mature less quickly than girls (anyone who thinks back to early adolescence won't be surprised by that!), so if you have a boy and a girl, your son's lungs are likely to be less developed than your daughter's. Stress tends to make the lungs of a fetus mature faster; so if one of your twins was subjected to more stress in the womb, he may be more likely than his sibling to be able to breathe on his own. If one twin's membranes ruptured and he developed an infection, the illness makes him less likely to be able to breathe without a ventilator. Sometimes the twins' dissimilar medical conditions relate to their different sizes: if one twin got more blood flow and nutrients through the placenta, he will be the bigger baby, and bigger babies tend to do better medically. On the other hand, his smaller sibling may be the one doing better, because stress made him mature faster.

You can see that it's impossible for anyone to

predict how all of these factors will balance out. The two things that are entirely clear are: (1) different people develop differently, and that process starts as early as when they're fetuses in the womb; and (2) this is not the last time you'll marvel at how your twins have turned into two very different individuals.

One Bigger Twin

One of my twin daughters is much bigger than her sister. Does that mean my smaller baby is going to have a lot more health problems?

Although it's natural for parents to be anxious about their smaller baby, some difference in weight is almost universal among twins. Unless your twins are truly discordant (meaning differing in weight by 20% or more), their different sizes don't usually indicate that your smaller baby is more apt to have health problems. A baby's weight is just one factor to be considered, together with other, often more important ones. (See page 121 for why one twin may do better than another.)

To make general predictions about a preemie's health and development, doctors determine whether her weight is in a range that's normal for her gestational age. A preemie whose weight falls between the tenth and ninetieth percentiles for her age is considered "appropriate for gestational age," or AGA. For example, twins born at 30 weeks of gestation are AGA if their weight ranges anywhere from 1,000 grams to about 1,750 grams. If your smaller twin's weight is within this AGA range (see chart, page 513), you shouldn't be particularly worried; any unpredictable turns she takes probably will be due more to her prematurity, or to factors other than her smaller size.

If your baby's birth weight falls under the tenth percentile (meaning that she weighs less than 90% of the babies her age), then she's "small for gestational age," or SGA (see page 70). SGA babies do tend to have more health problems after delivery, including low blood sugar and feeding difficulties. If the growth restriction is severe, there is also a higher risk for developmental problems in the future. Your baby's doctor can help you determine your twin's particular health risks, depending on why and how severely her growth was restricted in the womb.

When fraternal twins have very discordant birth weights, one twin is usually normally grown, and the other is SGA. This usually occurs because of insufficient blood flow to one fetus, perhaps due to a twisted, small, or unfavorably attached umbilical cord, or an imperfectly developed placenta. Other possible causes of restricted growth in one twin are an infection in one sac, or a birth defect that affects the normal development of that fetus. In all of these cases, the smaller twin would be at higher risk of health problems.

If identical twins are discordantly grown, it can mean that during pregnancy there was a passage of blood from one fetus to the other, because of shared placental blood vessels. This is called twin to twin transfusion syndrome (TTTS, see page 30). It is usually diagnosed during pregnancy, but may not be picked up until after the twins are born.

In twin to twin transfusion syndrome, too little blood flows from the placenta into one fetus, and too much into the other, causing one twin to be small for her gestational age, and the other large. When twin to twin transfusion syndrome is mild, there may be no serious effects. On the other hand, if it's a significant, long-standing problem, then the twin with insufficient blood flow can become severely anemic, deprived of oxygen and nutrients, and her growth and development can be slowed. The extra blood going to the other twin will accelerate her growth, but it can also lead to complications such as fluid overload, which can wear down her heart, an overproduction of amniotic fluid, which can induce preterm labor, and an excess of blood cells, which can cause problems with breathing, low blood sugar, jaundice, and long-term development. Sometimes, babies with twin to twin transfusion syndrome will have their abnormal blood counts treated at birth—the smaller twin may be given more red blood cells to correct her anemia; the larger twin may have some blood removed. If your twin daughters' different weights have been attributed to twin to twin transfusion syndrome, it's hard to predict whether the smaller or the bigger baby will do better, because both can be at risk for complications.

Your babies' doctors may not have all the answers ready for you immediately after delivery, but they should come up with more information shortly. Soon they'll be able to tell you if your twins' different sizes are a relevant issue, or just a natural occurrence of no consequence.

Multiple Doctors

I just delivered triplets. Today my husband talked to three different doctors, but he liked one of them more than the others. Why can't we just have that doctor for all of our babies?

While you thought you'd have to get "three of everything" for your triplets, you never imagined that included doctors! But there's a reason that many attending neonatologists assign twins, triplets, and other multiples to different doctors. The thinking is that each doctor will treat the baby he's taking care of as a separate individual—rather than as "one of the triplets"—and give him the full amount of attention that any single baby would get.

Of course, the flip side is that this policy is somewhat harder on the parents—whether because they have a preference for one of the doctors, or because they feel that having three doctors to get to know, and three phone calls to make when they want updates, isn't easy. If you feel strongly that three doctors is two more than you can handle, you should explain this to the attending physician in the NICU and ask if there's any flexibility in the assignments. Sometimes there is.

BREASTFEEDING OR FORMULA FEEDING YOUR PREMATURE BABY: WHAT WILL WORK BEST FOR YOU

The trauma and wonder are still so fresh, a few hours after your baby's premature delivery, that you should be spared any additional decisions or worry. But there's an issue you have to face soon: making up your mind whether you want to breastfeed your preemie. In only a few days it may be too late, so if you decide to try, you must take action soon.

Chances are, you need more information. Maybe you already have an opinion on breastfeeding, or maybe you don't: after all, your pregnancy ended sooner than you planned, you may not have had enough time to think about it. But even experienced mothers who breastfed an older child and intended to do it again don't know much about nursing a preemie. Some new moms who want to nurse their preemies, but who don't get the right advice on how to go about it, may miss that opportunity, and deeply regret it. Others may find themselves in the awkward situation of feeling forced to breastfeed, by nurses or doctors who strongly believe in the importance of mother's milk for premature babies, and whose advice sounds more like an order. "You must give your milk to your premature daughter, she needs it more than a full-term baby," is a typical comment, certainly well-intended but inappropriately phrased.

Women who, earlier in their pregnancy, had already decided not to breastfeed, may now want to reconsider their choice, carefully weighing the pros and cons. So, first of all, you should know the facts.

CAN A PREEMIE BE BREASTFED?

Yes, it is possible to breastfeed a premature baby. However, if he was born before the 34th week of gestation, because of his immaturity or other medical conditions, he probably won't be ready to nurse at your breast immediately. But you can start to express your milk with a breast pump and bring it to the nursery, where it will be frozen and stored for your baby. When the doctors say he's ready to eat, usually within a week or two, he still may not be able to breastfeed well enough to get all of his nourishment that way. But even when your baby can't nurse, he can be given your breast milk through a thin tube going from his nose or mouth to his stomach (a method called gavage feeding). As he grows, he'll be put to your breast, to practice his nursing skills. Then, when he's finally mature enough to coordinate sucking with breathing and swallowing (usually at around 34 weeks after conception), he will step up to bottle feed or breastfeed fully, a piece of cake for a full-term newborn, but a truly big accomplishment for a preemie. (See "How Your Baby Is Fed: A Journey from Parenteral Nutrition, to Gavage Feedings, to Breast or Bottle," page 149.)

ADVANTAGES OF BREASTFEEDING A PREMATURE BABY

Mother's milk is universally accepted as the best food for normal, full-term newborns. For preemies, though, the matter is more problematic, because of the huge task they have to accomplish: replicating the fast growth and development they would have experienced in their last weeks in the womb. During pregnancy, the mother would have provided all of the necessary nutrition through the umbilical cord; now, the baby has to strive to do it by himself, through his still immature digestive system.

Nevertheless, recent studies indicate that milk from a preemie's mother may be particularly well-suited to his special needs. Nature seems to know what a preemie needs most, and is smart enough to program his mother's breast to produce it. And the acknowledged benefits of breast milk over formula may be especially advantageous for preemies:

❋ *Human milk is easier to digest than formula because of its protein, fat, and carbohydrate composition.* To a preemie, this means a lot. Digestion stimulates the development of his immature gastrointestinal system, and the sooner his gastrointestinal system matures, the sooner he'll be free of intravenous lines to give him fluids and nutrition.

❋ *The proteins and fats in breast milk differ slightly in composition from those in formula.* Breast milk proteins are more quickly and completely metabolized than the proteins in formula, leaving fewer of certain amino acids that are potentially damaging to a preemie's developing organs. The fats found in breast milk are also better assimilated than the fats in formula. This may be important for optimal brain development, as the particular kinds of fatty acids found in breast milk are found in brain cells, as well as in other organs.

(According to some researchers, these connections between nutrition and brain development may explain why, in several controlled studies, premature children who were breastfed in their first weeks of life had higher IQs and developmental scores than entirely formula-fed preterm infants. Not everybody agrees on this, though, because many factors other than feeding may have affected the study babies' outcomes.)

❋ *The milk of a mother who gives birth prematurely is different from breast milk expressed after a full-term birth.* It contains higher concentrations of nitrogen, sodium, chloride, magnesium, and iron—substances that preemies need more of.

❋ *Preterm human milk is richer in infection-fighting components than full-term milk.* The well-known ability of breast milk to provide protection from disease is even more precious to premature infants, who are less able than term babies to fight infections. Some studies have found that preemies fed at least some human milk, compared to those fed only commercial formula, have lower rates of infection. In particular, there seems to be a lower risk of necrotizing enterocolitis (NEC, see page 237), a disease of the intestine which is one of the possible complications of prematurity.

❋ *Breast milk can be particularly beneficial to a preemie if a mother has been having skin-to-skin contact with him (kangaroo care, see page 221).* Spending time in the nursery, and holding her baby close, allows the mother to develop antibodies against the specific germs present in her baby's environment, and to pass those infection-fighting antibodies along to him in her breast milk.

❋ *Breastfeeding helps to create strong bonding and attachment.* Parents can feel frustrated or useless because their preemie is hospitalized and cared for by the medical staff. Expressing milk is a special, exclusive gift from the mother to her baby: a promise of a future, happier time together.

WHY FORMULA CAN BE AN EXCELLENT CHOICE, TOO

Nonetheless, not all experts agree on the superiority of breast milk for premature babies, for several reasons:

❋ *Some preemies who are fed only their mother's milk grow more slowly than formula-fed preemies.* After a few weeks of life, most preemies need more calories than mother's milk can provide. Breast milk has insufficient quantities of calcium and phosphorus for growing preemies—minerals needed to develop healthy, strong bones—and is relatively deficient in some other important nutrients, such as iron, zinc, copper, and magnesium. Formulas designed for preterm infants have higher quantities of these substances than human milk. (Most breastfed preemies are given iron and multivitamin supplements, and special products called human milk fortifiers, to make up for any shortages in breast milk.)

❋ *Some of the shortages of breast milk are exacerbated by the fact that, at least initially, the baby is not taking it from the breast.* Expressing breast milk, storing it, freezing it, thawing it, and giving it to the baby through feeding de-

vices can diminish important components. Fats can remain attached to tubes and syringes. Exposure to bright light can affect its vitamin content.

❋ *Breastfeeding is not advised if you are taking a medication that may be harmful to your baby when passed on to him in your milk.* Your doctor can tell you what's safe and what's not. (Some mothers express and discard their milk while they're taking medication, then resume breastfeeding when the risk of harm is past.) It is also not wise to breastfeed if you use drugs like cocaine or heroin, or if you drink large amounts of alcohol.

❋ *You should not breastfeed if you are HIV positive.* Most other infections will not be transmitted to your baby through your milk, but be sure to check with your doctor if you're sick.

❋ *Today's new, nutrient-enriched "preterm" formulas made expressly for preemies have been shown to promote much better growth and neurological development than standard infant formulas.* So you can rest assured that preterm formula is a very good alternative to breast milk. Its mineral, protein, and caloric content is tailored to a premature baby's needs, and does not vary over time, as breast milk does, depending on the mother's nutritional status or stress load.

❋ *Even if breastfeeding promotes cognitive development, some researchers suggest that the later intelligence of a child is more influenced by his family's educational level and social environment.* To evaluate the specific role of breastfeeding is particularly difficult, because today's mothers who nurse tend to be better educated and belong to a higher social class. If you give your preemie lots of love and stimulation, you are probably "feeding" him what is most crucial to his development.

WHY BREASTFEEDING A PREEMIE MAY BE A HASSLE

Even for mothers who are prepared to breast-feed, a number of factors can make breastfeeding a premature baby who is in the hospital a particularly difficult enterprise.

❋ *The process of expressing milk through a bulky and noisy electric pump is not pleasant, and initially can be painful.* In order to give your breasts the right stimulation, you have to start soon after delivery—if possible within 24 hours, when the hormones that stimulate lactation are at their peak. The pumping should be frequent and consistent, every two to three hours during the day, to build up an adequate milk supply.

❋ *It's important not to miss a pumping session in the early days, even if you are exhausted, stressed out, and maybe even sick after delivery.* If you are taking antibiotics or other medications, your milk may not be stored—but your lactation will be started.

❋ *The more premature your baby is, the longer you'll have to go on expressing your milk—for several weeks and maybe months.* You'll have to rent or buy a pump to use at home, store your milk, and get organized to carry it to the NICU. Figure on pumping even after your baby starts to latch onto your breast, because initially his sucking may not be strong enough to keep your milk supply going.

❋ *If you have premature twins, breastfeeding them is obviously more demanding, although definitely possible.* (You can read more about breastfeeding twins on page 290.)

Remember: Even if you do everything you can, you may not produce enough milk for your baby, and may need to supplement his nutrition with an increasing number of bottles. In that case, you shouldn't feel disappointed, but rather congratulate yourself on what you've accomplished. Studies have shown that the benefits of breast milk are preserved with partial breastfeeding: for instance, when the baby is given his mother's milk in the day and formula at night. You can justifiably see your "glass" of milk for your baby as more than half full!

SO WHAT DO I DO? SOME HINTS TO HELP YOU DECIDE

Considering all the patience and time it takes, most mothers who succeed in giving their preemies at least some of their milk are very proud of it. But should all mothers feel compelled to breastfeed their preemies even if they don't want to, or cannot do so for practical reasons? Should they risk their own well-being or health by discontinuing useful medications, in order to be able to nurse? Of course not.

The best solution is one that benefits both mother and child, and doesn't create a conflict in this intimate and precious relationship. So, for example, a mother might try to breastfeed during the first several weeks, to give her baby some infection-fighting antibodies. But she might supplement her milk with formula to assure that while her baby gets sufficient nutrition, she doesn't overtax herself.

A practical approach to keep in mind if you're not sure of what you want to do on the first day: You could start to pump, to at least give your baby the colostrum (the first, thick, yellow milk expressed after delivery, which is particularly rich in nutrients and infection-fighting antibodies). Then in a week or so, you can make a final decision about whether to continue expressing your milk. If you decide not to continue, slowing down gradually will allow your lactation to taper off, and then stop, without causing pain or engorgement in your breasts.

Buying yourself some time by starting to pump on the first day will allow you to ask more questions of the doctors and nurses who are taking care of you and your baby. If you are on medication, you should ask your doctor to advise you on possible options that would allow you to breastfeed. If you want to breastfeed your premature twins, or triplets, you should try to talk to another mother who did it, to find out if it could work for you, too.

It's also important that you discuss the issue with your partner and perhaps with other people you love and trust—so, whatever you decide, you'll be surrounded by understanding and support. But don't let anybody press you into a decision you're unhappy with. In the end, whether to breastfeed your preemie or not is your choice. Everybody should respect it.

The First Week

▶ *A time of crucial test results and waiting. Understanding
that things sometimes get worse before they get better.*

THE PARENTS' PERSPECTIVE   130

THE DOCTOR'S PERSPECTIVE   133

A DIFFERENT STORY FOR DIFFERENT
   PREEMIES: *What Your Baby Is Doing
   and Sensing*   138

QUESTIONS AND ANSWERS
   Birth Announcements   142
   A Desire for Privacy   143
   Holding Baby on a Ventilator   144
   Sores from Tape   145
   Why So Many IVs?   146
   What Kinds of IVs Are Those?   147
   Discolored Toes from Umbilical Catheter 148
   *How Your Baby Is Fed: A Journey from
     Parenteral Nutrition, to Gavage
     Feedings, to Breast or Bottle*   149
   Breast Milk Banks   153
   If You Want to Be a Breast Milk Donor 154
   Attention Paid to Diapers   154
   *Getting Acquainted With: Jaundice
     and Bilirubin*   155
   Nurses' Response to Alarms   158
   Afraid to Leave Baby   160
   Air Leak   161
   *High-Frequency Ventilators and How
     They Might Help*   163
   *In Plain Language: What Is an
     Intraventricular Hemorrhage?*   164

Seizures   170
High Blood Pressure in Baby's Lungs   171
X-Rays   172
Suctioning Baby   173
Bleeding in Lungs   175
In Plain Language: What Is a PDA?   176
Low Blood Pressure   179
Diagnosing Pneumonia   180
Catching Infections from Other Babies   181
*In Plain Language: Infections in
   Preemies*   182
Handwashing   184
Siblings' Visits   185
*Getting to Know a New Brother or Sister
   in the Hospital*   186
Making an Isolette Feel Like Home   188
Parents Asked to Leave   191
When to Circumcise   192
Medical Costs   192
Coping Emotionally   193

MULTIPLES
   Babies in Different Hospitals   196
   Keeping Twins Near Each Other   197

IN DEPTH
   *Ways to Make a Baby Feel Loved in the
     NICU: Developmental Care*   198

The Parents' Perspective: The First Week

The first week of a young preemie's life is a time of stress and upheaval for his family. Joyful excitement and anxiety often go hand in hand, one prevailing over the other depending on the baby's condition. Even if their baby is doing well, some mothers and fathers find it difficult to release their tension, and aren't yet ready to deal with relatives and friends who want to meet the new baby, or to know more about him. The happy events that all new parents take pleasure from may feel a little strange and out of place in an NICU. But they occur anyway, bringing relief and warming everybody's heart.

"Go ahead, your baby is stable now," the doctor told us. Steven was born a week ago, 11 weeks before term, at the bouncy—somebody said—birth weight of 3 pounds 2 ounces. We have been very worried for him, and still are, but today we're getting ready for something a bit vain: Steven's first photo session in the NICU. We owe my parents some pictures of him, since we asked them not to visit until he leaves the hospital. For the occasion, I'm making Steven wear some fine newborn clothes: an embroidered shirt, a matching blue knit cap. Under the supervision of Steven's nurse, I open one side of the isolette, carefully put a little hand and arm through one sleeve, then the other. Trying not to knock off any of the wires connecting Steven to the monitors, I turn him on one side, and button the back. The shirt covers all of him, past his toes. The cap is so large it comes down to his mouth. "Wait, don't take pictures yet," I tell my husband, who looks amused. At this moment, I find Steven funny too, my little elf who hides under a tiny cap. Let's take it off, my baby, you're so precious without it. It's the final proof of how small you are. With no giant clothes, and no adult hands in the picture, nobody will be able to figure out your size.

Adjusting to a premature birth means having to face a lot of emotional and practical problems at the same time. Daily engagements may seem impossible to reconcile with the need to stay at your baby's side. Most painful to deal with are the demands of older children who feel left out, creating in their parents a sense of inadequacy.

A father in the corridor outside an NICU, talking on a pay phone.
—Hi Sidney, honey, it's Dad . . .
—. . . Mom can't talk to you right now. She's with Nicholas. They took him out of his crib, the special one with glass walls all around, and now she's holding him in a rocking chair. Yes, like the one in your bedroom, where we read books. She gave him all your hugs and kisses. Yes, she did.
—Oh, he loved it. I think I saw him smiling.
—No, we can't take Nicholas home tonight. I told you why. He's very small because he came out of mummy's tummy too early. That's why he has to stay in the hospital, where tiny babies grow bigger and stronger before they go home . . .

—. . . *No, sweetie, don't cry. . . . You'll meet your baby brother in a few days! The doctor said we can push Nicholas's crib into a little room, where you and Mom and I can visit with him for a while. Isn't that great?*

—*Yes, you can bring him your new Beanie Baby . . .*

—*When is Nicholas's birthday? Next year, in March. He will be one then, and you will be four and a half. A big sister!*

—*Of course you can help him blow out his candle. We'll have a birthday party with cookies, cupcakes, and all of our friends. OK?*

—. . . *That's a wonderful plan, baby. We're missing you so much, Mom and I.*

—. . . *Sweet dreams, Sidney. I'll tell Nicholas you love him. Be nice to Grandma.*

During the first week, most likely you finally will be allowed to spend some quiet time with your premature baby: holding her, looking at her, silently talking to her. This longed-for intimacy can release powerful, sometimes overwhelming emotions. But it can also make you feel an incredibly lucid sense of purpose. The bond between you and your baby, stronger than you ever imagined, is created.

Forgive me, daughter, for delivering you so soon. I'm holding you in my lap, a bundle of clothes, tubes and wires, a snorting machine pushing air into your lungs. Are you really sleeping? Do you feel my love? Do you feel pain? Can I take over some of it? They tell me you're so strong, so determined to live, that I'm starting to believe it. One day, I know, we'll laugh and play together. Then guilt comes back to stop the good fantasies. To remind me that my body betrayed you when you were still needy. Still not able to open your eyes, feed at my breast, breathe air. It wasn't my fault, but who cares, it's now you who has to pay. My baby, forgive my weakness, my sickness, my haste. Give me a second chance. From now on I promise, I'll be strong and patient. I'll hold you against my skin. I'll enclose you in my arms. I'll make you a new womb in the world outside. Take all the time you need to learn to breathe and grow. Then, when you're ready, I'll take you home.

Anxiety and hope, worry and relief, melancholy and happiness. The combination of contrasting feelings can be so draining that some parents of premature babies unplug their emotional connection to their problems, in an unconscious attempt to maintain their stability. As a result, they may act unnaturally cool or detached. If these signals are misread, they can create frustration and misunderstandings in family relationships.

How could Paula ask me to take her shopping today? She only came back from the hospital three days ago, after an emergency C-section. Her placenta tore, and our twins, Laura and Ben, were born. At 33 weeks gestation. Now they're doing well, the doctors say, but still . . . They have tubes, wires, needles everywhere, they forget to breathe several times a day. And all my wife can think about is furnishing their nursery. "Don't you realize they won't be home for several weeks?" I tell Paula, upset. But it may take time to get the cribs she wants, and a certain brand of double stroller. I finally agree to take her to the biggest baby store in New Jersey. When we're finished with the furniture, it's almost four o'clock. "Time to call the NICU," I say. Paula looks up at me, and says: "Come on, they were doing fine this morning, why should we bother the nurses?" I choke back angry words, and head out of the store. Paula reaches me in the parking lot a few minutes later. "No apneas this afternoon. They started feeding them my milk," she informs me. And then she says, in a softer tone: "You know why I never call the NICU? Because I'm way too scared." I'm driving back home now, and I can't see Paula's face. She's turned to the other side, leaning against the seat. Maybe she's asleep. Or maybe she wants to hide some tears in her eyes.

Calling the nursery, going to the nursery, spending time in the nursery. Meeting doctors and nurses, talking to them, trying to understand what they say. Delivery was only a week ago, but parents of premature babies don't have any time to relax and recover. No wonder they all, mothers and fathers, look and are exhausted. But they must keep going, and they do. Where does their energy come from?

Holding my baby for the first time, I am happy, truly happy, for the first time since his premature birth. He looks up at me to study my face. I look down at him to study his. He was crying in his bed, but as soon as the nurse handed him to me, he became calm and content. He seems at home in my arms. My arms ARE his home. I shield his eyes from the bright, overhead lights, protecting my baby for the first time.

The Doctor's Perspective: The First Week*

During our first week together, your baby and I will become very familiar. I'm learning some important things about her that help guide her treatment, like whether she's basically sick or well, how gingerly I need to handle her (making small, gradual changes in her treatment, or moving forward in leaps and bounds), and, if I've been able to spend time with her parents or grandparents, what special place she holds within her family. Just as with any new acquaintance, there can be lots of surprises, too. Preemies, in particular, have a reputation in medical circles for unpredictability! With that in mind, though, by the end of the first week, I have a good idea about how quickly she's improving, and often whether it's going to be a long haul or not.

PHYSICAL EXAM AND LABORATORY ASSESSMENT

As long as your baby remains in intensive care, she'll be examined several times a day, by doctors and nurses, so we can respond quickly to changes in her condition. We'll be gauging how effectively your baby is breathing, listening with our stethoscopes to how much air moves in and out as she inhales and exhales, and watching how far her chest expands with each breath. If she's on a ventilator, we'll compare the effectiveness of her own breaths with those the vent is giving her—a clue as to how much extra "oomph" the vent is providing.

We'll also be assessing her circulation. Good circulation is vital, because blood carries oxygen and nutrients to all her tissues, and helps remove waste products. We'll be concerned if her skin looks mottled or saggy, if her urine output or blood pressure is low, her heart rate is too high, or if she's losing too much weight. She may need more fluid or a blood transfusion if she's "dry." If her heart is having some difficulty pumping blood, she may need medicine to help it function better.

We'll watch your baby closely to make sure that she's as comfortable as possible. Depending on how well she's adjusting to her strange, new environment, and how quickly she's recovering and shedding herself of encumbering equipment, her needs for pain control will change. It's a good sign if she's responsive without being too irritable.

A baby on a ventilator or receiving IV fluids will get periodic chest x-rays and blood tests. A chest x-ray shows that the ventilator is expanding her lungs well, the endotracheal tube is correctly positioned—not so high that it could slip out of her windpipe, not so low that it could scrape against her airway or block off part of her lung—and that fluid isn't accumulating in her lungs. We'll be checking the amounts of oxygen and carbon dioxide in her blood to assess her breathing, and whether she needs more or

---

*"The Doctor's Perspective" describes how your doctor may be thinking about your preemie's condition and what she may be considering as she makes medical decisions. All of the medical terms and conditions mentioned here are described in more detail elsewhere in this book. Check the index.

less help from the ventilator. Her blood will also be checked for calcium and electrolytes (or "lytes" for short, as you'll hear us say)—substances that are crucial for the normal functioning of all her organs. The amount of calcium and electrolytes in her blood must be kept within a narrow range, and we usually do that by adjusting the composition of the fluid we give her. If we don't have to do much tinkering with the fluids, it means that her kidneys, liver, and other organs are functioning well. She'll get other blood tests to count her blood cells; if her blood counts are too low, she may have an infection, or may need a transfusion.

As your baby's feedings progress and she comes off IV fluids, she won't need so many blood tests. Her digestive system can maintain tighter control over the composition of her body fluid than when we put IV fluid directly into her bloodstream—the intestines know to hold onto some substances and get rid of others. And when she comes off the ventilator, we won't need to check blood gases as often. As time goes on, we'll trust her body more to keep her stable and healthy on its own, with progressively less help from us and our high-tech equipment.

Some older preemies, those without respiratory problems who aren't getting intravenous fluids, won't need intensive monitoring and treatment for long. These "feeders and growers," as we affectionately call them, may graduate in a few hours or days to a step-down unit, where exams and lab tests are done less frequently. Other preemies will remain in the NICU for their first week of life or longer, receiving intensive medical attention until they've matured enough to do without it.

COMMON ISSUES AND DECISIONS

Respiratory Distress Syndrome: If your baby has RDS (see page 101), we'll carefully follow the course of her illness, watching for signs of recovery. Maybe she'll be one of the lucky ones who breezes through the first day or two, weaning rapidly off the ventilator without blood pressure problems or significant lab abnormalities. Then, unless she's one of the tiniest preemies (say, 25 weeks or under) whose future course is so hard to predict, I won't worry too much about her. In my mind, she becomes a "well preemie," who will, of course, need close attention and careful handling—particularly as her feeding progresses. But her risk for serious medical complications will fall precipitously, and I'll breathe a sigh of relief.

For babies who have a more difficult time with RDS—requiring high levels of respiratory support, stalling on their weaning from the ventilator, or having a lot of instability, with blood pressure problems and other laboratory abnormalities—something else may be complicating the picture. We'll investigate, with blood counts and cultures, whether she has an infection, and make sure it's treated with the right antibiotics at the right doses. We'll wonder about a PDA (a fetal blood vessel that hasn't closed as it should; see page 176) or an intraventricular hemorrhage (bleeding in the brain; see page 164), and ask for ultrasounds of her heart and head. We're always hoping that the amount of assistance she needs from the ventilator isn't damaging her lungs, and watching for evidence of lung injury—primarily air leaks (caused by small tears in the lung; you can see them on an x-ray). If she has an air leak, or if the vent settings are very high, I'll probably decide to switch her to a different kind of ventilator—an oscillating ventilator—which may be gentler on her lungs.

Except in the very youngest preemies (those born at the edge of viability) it's rare that a baby's RDS can't be adequately treated. Overall, our goal is to correct serious problems now, and to prevent her from developing chronic lung or brain damage. I want things to get better quickly, partly because I know that the more rapidly the RDS resolves, the less likely it is that she'll have such complications from it later, but also because doctors, like parents, can't wait for their tiny charges to get well. Luckily, patience is something that we learn with time and experience, and I remind myself that a few more days or weeks on a ventilator can mean nothing about a baby's final outcome—even babies with far more than their share of complications and setbacks often turn out just fine.

Apnea: Apnea of prematurity—pauses in a preemie's breathing that last more than 20 seconds—makes its appearance in the first week of life (see page 218). We'll be deciding whether to put your baby on apnea medication (usually aminophylline, a relative of caffeine); and as with every medical decision, we'll weigh the benefits of treatment with its risks. The main benefit is that apnea medicine can reduce the number of breathing pauses she has and make them milder, so she's easier to rouse to start breathing again. The risks are overdosage, which can occur because other medicines or changes in a baby's medical condition can affect her metabolism of the drug; and, possibly, a longer hospitalization, because I'll need to know that all of the medicine is out of her system and she's breathing well on her own before I'll be comfortable sending her home. It takes five to seven days for the last dose of medicine to be cleared from her body. So I don't want to use it unnecessarily.

Nonetheless, since apnea is ubiquitous in very young preemies, and in them it won't go away anytime soon, if your baby is younger than 30 weeks of gestation, I'll start her on apnea medicine just before she comes off the ventilator. If she's older, I'd wait to see if she really needs it before starting medication. (Some older preemies don't.) If your preemie is close to being discharged (say she was born at 33 weeks of gestation, and just needs a week or two in the nursery to get good at nipple feeding), I might tolerate a few, mild episodes of apnea a day without starting medication, as long as they resolve easily with a little stimulation. (Don't worry—we won't discharge her until about a week after her last apneic episode.)

Patent Ductus Arteriosus: All babies are born with a patent ductus arteriosus (PDA), a blood vessel close to the heart and the lungs, which is open in the womb but is supposed to close in the first few days of life. If a PDA doesn't close, it can cause breathing problems, particularly in preemies. We can often tell from physical exams or chest x-rays if a baby has a persistent PDA—she may have a heart murmur, bounding pulses, low blood pressure, apnea and bradycardia, and extra fluid in her heart and lung. An echocardiogram is a more certain test, and I'll ask for one to be done if, for example, I suspect that a PDA is hampering her recovery from RDS.

If she does have a PDA, we'll usually try to close it by treating her with a medication called indomethacin. If the medication doesn't work the first time, it can be tried again. But if a baby still has an open ductus after two courses of medication and still needs assistance with her breathing, I'll recommend surgery to close the PDA. This isn't always an easy decision (particularly if the PDA is small), because I'm not always sure that it's behind the baby's breathing difficulties.

But a PDA can cause fluid to build up in the lungs, impede the strong pumping of the heart, and interfere with good blood flow to the brain and intestines—all of which could cause problems, now or later. I try to convey to parents when I am uncertain, but usually I believe it's better to close that PDA—and although no one wants their baby to go through an operation, it usually ends up being a benefit.

Intraventricular Hemorrhage: Although an IVH (short for intraventricular hemorrhage, meaning bleeding in the brain; see page 164), is a possibility in any baby born under about 32 to 34 weeks of gestation, and preemies at risk will get a "routine" head ultrasound within about a week of age to check for it, we don't really worry much about an IVH in all of them. I do worry about an IVH when a baby is less than 26 weeks of gestation, or having trouble with severe RDS (air leaks, blood pressure problems, anemia, or too much acid in her blood). In the smallest and most unstable babies, I might want to see a head ultrasound sooner, say within the first three days after birth. Most of the time my fears are allayed—there's no bleeding, or just a small amount. If there's a large intraventricular hemorrhage, there is usually no medical treatment for it in the first week of life, but I will watch its progress carefully, hoping that it resolves without causing further problems.

However, in a very few babies—usually those who are younger than 26 weeks of gestation or whose respiratory problems are exceedingly severe and life-threatening—the added problem of a large intraventricular hemorrhage may cause me to believe that a baby's prognosis for survival, or for a life without debilitating handicaps, is now very grim. In those few cases, I would meet with the parents and discuss frankly the option that we have of discontinuing medical treatment. Since some babies with very severe RDS and large intraventricular hemorrhages will not survive no matter what we do, this option can be a way of not prolonging suffering. In babies who might survive, but with extraordinary difficulties and after much pain, it's a way of acknowledging that there are some things that are not worth going through, when a baby's ultimate fate is so uncertain or dire. For most babies, these issues never come close to arising. But if such an agonizing decision becomes necessary, we'll work together to come to the best solution for your baby.

Feeding: We have to decide when your baby is ready to start eating, and how quickly to advance her from small, partial feedings to "full feeds," as we call them. Most preemies begin feeds sometime in the first week. Because intestinal function isn't fully mature in babies younger than about 34 weeks, and because food is a stress (it requires energy to digest, and diverts some blood flow to the intestines), your baby won't be ready until her breathing and circulation are stable enough that she's getting more than enough oxygen and blood flow throughout her body. For me, this usually means that she's not on medications to keep her blood pressure up, nor on extremely high ventilator settings. Even if your baby is relatively stable, there are other reasons we may decide not to feed her temporarily. For example, I won't feed her if she's on medication to close a PDA, because both the medicine and the PDA can interfere with intestinal blood flow. Some doctors won't feed babies if they have an umbilical artery catheter in place, for the same reason. You can read about feeding on page 149 for more information, and, of course, ask your baby's own doctor what factors she's weighing in making the decision for your baby.

Anemia: If your baby is very young (say, less than 30 weeks), on a ventilator for more than a couple of days, or has a severe infection, chances are she'll become anemic during the first week of life. That's because the many blood tests needed to monitor her condition also deplete her body of red blood cells. Anemia can cause problems because red blood cells deliver oxygen to all her tissues; if she's anemic, she may not get all the oxygen she needs. We'll decide whether or not to transfuse your baby, trying to judge what level of anemia she can tolerate. (We don't want to transfuse her unnecessarily, even though nowadays the risk of infection from a blood transfusion is very low.) If she's on a ventilator or showing signs of circulatory problems, I'd transfuse her sooner, thinking that she could use the additional oxygen-carrying capacity. If she's more stable, and I know that we'll be taking less blood from her in the future, I might wait to see if her body can catch up and make enough red blood cells on its own.

FAMILY ISSUES

I hope that you're delighting in your new baby, despite her early arrival and (for now) maybe less than perfect health. Even if you are, it's natural to feel frightened, angry, and tensely vigilant, as well. It's easy to feel displaced by all of us (the doctors, nurses, respiratory therapists, etc.) who seem to know so much more about your baby—and how to help and care for her—than you do. Sometimes it may feel like this isn't your baby, but ours, and you'll think that

we believe that, too. We don't—we know that we're the professionals, not her parents, and that there's so much we can't possibly do for her that you can.

Although our first priority is meeting her medical needs, we also want to meet your needs, in part so you'll be strong and knowledgeable enough to care for her now and later, in ways that only parents can. She needs love, affection, support, and attention—things that call for parents, not doctors. You can help us by getting to know us, and letting us know you. It's okay to ask questions over and over. If we forget to explain something, or don't explain it in a way you understand, ask again. I promise we won't be offended. No doctor means to be obtuse; it's just that sometimes it's hard to know what information you want to hear and how you need to hear it. And you may be surprised that all the information you may dread getting can also help you overcome your fear. The more you learn, the more comfortable you'll become. The initial shock of "this is my baby?!" will evolve into familiarity and togetherness as you learn what she's like and what to expect of her.

Try to trust that we're not purposely hiding things from you. If you ask us whether your baby is going to be OK and we tell you we can't answer, it's not because we're keeping a secret from you. There are many things we honestly don't know; and although we can tell you about some good or bad signs, we're often far from certain about what the future holds.

Finally, try not to judge the staff too harshly. You'd be amazed at how varied different parents' needs are. So, please forgive us our lapses, let us know how to do better, and realize that we're in this together—trying to do what's best for your baby.

A Different Story for Different Preemies: What Your Baby Is Doing and Sensing

Among all of the great joys of parenting, one of the most moving is the first interactions with your newborn baby. You see your baby's eyes opening and calmly scanning the features of your face. You sense his little hand grasping strongly at your finger. You realize that, at the sound of your voice, his head is turning toward you. And right away you know that all the love and attention you'll give him from then on is going to be returned, magnified.

Parents of preemies are often deprived of these experiences—but only at first, when medical care is the top priority, and the baby's senses and behavior are still immature. Then, over the next days and weeks, the same joy unfolds slowly and gradually.

During gestation, the sensory organs mature and gradually switch on: first touch, then smell, then the vestibular sense (the sense of balance and position of one's body in space), taste, hearing, and, last of all, vision. A baby's behavior at birth depends partly on how developed his senses are, because the senses are connected to all of the functions directed by the brain and nervous system—moving, eating, paying attention, and so on. Full-term babies are already good at eating, communicating their needs, getting love and attention, and understanding what's going on around them—in other words, at taking the star role in the family. But even they have a lot of growing to do, in more ways than simply adding inches and pounds. Their brains, nerves, and muscles continue to mature during infancy and childhood, to allow them to blossom into self-sufficient young adults. Your preemie's developmental expedition is the same—you are simply watching it a few steps earlier than usual.

To help you understand what your baby is doing and sensing, we've separated preemies into four gestational age groups below. As you read the section that applies to your baby, please keep one important caveat in mind. The range of normal development is very wide; few babies are on an exactly average schedule. If you're worried that some aspect of your baby's behavior seems out of sync with his gestational age, ask the doctor. Chances are he'll reassure you that everything is fine.

As your baby grows and jumps from one gestational age group to another, you can come back to this section and read about his new developmental stage. In the meantime, enjoy him!

23–25 WEEKS OF GESTATION

Preemies at this age, the youngest of all, sleep almost all of the time. They never wake up fully, with eyes open and alert to everything around them, but they do reach a drowsy state from time to time, when they are more responsive to external stimulation like sound and touch.

Your preemie's sense of touch is well developed already. He knows when he's being handled—in ways he likes or dislikes—and you'll learn to recognize clues as to which is which (see page 203). At this age, his skin is very thin and fragile, so you may have to wait a week or two until you can caress him. But as soon as the nurses give the OK, you can start touching him in gentle ways that let him know you are there.

It's very likely that your 23- to 25-weeker can hear your familiar voice, which he knows well from before birth. (Studies of 25-week preemies show that they react to sounds. Studies haven't focused on younger babies yet, but the auditory organs are fully formed by about 20 weeks.) Your baby can't hear extremely soft sounds yet—nothing under 40 decibels, similar to a normal speech tone. So you can't whisper little nothings in his ear, but you can say them. (Don't speak too loudly; sounds get amplified inside an isolette, and preemies like only small amounts of stimulation.)

Preemies of this age already have a sense of taste, but their gustatory experience has been limited to swallowing amniotic fluid in the womb. Further ability to discriminate tastes will come later, with more experience.

Similarly, 23- to 25-weekers have the ability to smell, but had little opportunity to practice when they were in the womb. Studies have shown that newborns already know and prefer two smells: if given the choice, they will choose to suck at a breast moistened with amniotic fluid; and if one of their mother's breasts is washed and the other is left unwashed, they will choose to suck on their mother's natural, unwashed skin. It won't be long before they learn to recognize both Mom and Dad's unique body scents.

At this age, many preemies' eyelids are still fused, tightly or loosely, like a newborn kitten's; they'll open any time now. In just two or three weeks, your baby will begin to see light and darkness, his first exposure to the visual world.

Your baby doesn't have any muscle tone, and can't flex his limbs yet, which explains his completely flat posture. But his arms and legs aren't motionless; they flutter slightly, as if they were still floating in amniotic fluid. Because nerves and muscles are still immature, his movements are very uncoordinated, with a trembling or jerky quality. They increase or decrease depending on whether he is in lighter or deeper sleep.

26–29 WEEKS OF GESTATION

Babies of this age still sleep most of the time, but their sleep is becoming more regular, with quieter periods, in which body movements almost stop, alternating with more active sleep. Slumber is necessary for your baby's nervous system to mature, and the gradual appearance of a rhythmical cycle means that this development is taking place. Sometime between 28 and 30 weeks, preemies start having periods of REM sleep (Rapid Eye Movement, when eyes flutter incessantly beneath closed lids). This kind of sleep is crucially important for learning and memory. For brief moments, they can arouse to a drowsy, partially awake state, though not long enough to focus much attention on their loving parents staring at them beside their beds.

Your baby's senses of touch, hearing, and smell are already functioning at this point. (See section on 23- to 25-weekers, above.) But since nerve cells involved in the sensory and motor systems develop at different times, senses and movements are still not well coordinated. This means your baby may not react in ways that are easy for you to notice and understand. For instance, he may not startle at a loud, sudden noise, but show his distress in some other way, or just not react at all.

Studies have shown that preemies' brains start responding to visual stimulation around the 25th week. When your baby opens his eyes, he probably perceives blotches of light and darkness, but he's not able to focus on any object or to distinguish patterns yet. Here's an NICU tip: Your baby will find it easier to open his eyes if you shade them from the bright, overhead lights. You can use your hand—or create a tiny, homemade visor for him by folding a disposable washcloth and tucking it into the front of his hat. (True, it's not much of a fashion statement, but it works!) If your baby's eyes don't stay centered or work together well, don't be alarmed; most full-term newborns have the same problem until they're a few months old.

Most of your baby's movements are still quite flimsy and uncoordinated. Don't worry, that's perfectly normal for a baby who was only supposed to be giving you little kicks from inside your uterus. When not flapping or twisting, his arms and legs lie flat at his sides. By about 29 weeks, your baby starts to flex his thighs at the hip, and his legs begin to show a little more muscle tone. This means that normal muscle and nerve cell development is occurring in the legs and gradually moving up to the arms and trunk: more coordinated movements are just a few weeks away. One thing your baby is coordinated enough to do even by around 28 weeks: he can curl his fingers toward his palm, and softly grasp your finger. What an unforgettable moment! His grasp will get stronger over time.

Another important developmental milestone comes at about 28 weeks: preemies begin to suck. Their sucking is feeble at first, and still not coordinated with swallowing, so they aren't ready to breastfeed or bottle feed yet. But they can suck on a tiny pacifier or the tip of your pinky. Try it when your baby seems agitated, and you'll see that this first "non-nutritive" sucking can help him relax and can even soothe mild pain.

Preemies of this age don't like too much stimulation. More than one thing going on at a time can be too much for them. Your baby already loves being held close to you, and loves when you talk or sing to him soothingly, but he may not like being held and talked to at the same time. In fact, don't be surprised if even your touch sometimes seems stressful to your baby. His quick development over the next few weeks will allow him to enjoy your loving interactions much more. In the meantime, you can try so-called vestibular stimulation, such as holding him while rocking in a rocking chair. Studies have found that rocking motions can decrease apnea, improve weight gain, promote sleep, and increase alertness in preemies. And what about soothing parents' nerves? That's certainly an extra boon.

30–33 Weeks of Gestation

Although they are still seven to ten weeks from term, these premature babies can already sense a lot of the world around them, and can begin to interact with it. Their sleep is now cycling regularly between active stages and quieter ones. Although they can't reach a deep sleep yet, quieter sleep stages, which facilitate growth and restorative processes in the body, are getting longer. Along with a more mature type of sleep, a 30- to 33-weeker has a more mature type of wakefulness. If your baby is medically stable, he can probably remain awake and alert for a few minutes at a time, focusing his attention on the world around him. All of his sensory and motor functions get involved in this new, huge feat, and every new experience provides stimulation that helps him develop further.

It helps that the motor system is getting more efficient. By 31 weeks, a baby shows a fair amount of muscle tone and can flex his legs; as a result, his movements are more coordinated, with less twisting and writhing, and his posture starts looking more like the flexed position of a term newborn. He can even turn his head to the side (although he doesn't have the strength to lift it up yet). What independence! This new ability allows him to locate an image he wants to focus on, or to find the source of a sound or smell.

And there are plenty of interesting sights, sounds, and smells in your baby's world now. Vision takes a big leap forward at this age and preemies start taking the time to scan the world around them. At 30 weeks they can fix on a simple pattern, like black lines on a white background, if it is placed at a distance of eight to ten inches from their eyes. (Full-term babies are also very nearsighted, until about three months of age.) Research indicates that as early as 31 or 32 weeks, babies already show visual preferences, focusing on one pattern longer than another. Most likely, your face will soon become your baby's favorite visual object. Don't worry if he seems cross-eyed or his eyes sometimes wander, though. Babies' eye muscles don't become perfectly coordinated for several months longer.

Studies show that 32-weekers can differentiate among odors they like and don't like. Newborns already have a preference for breasts that smell of their mothers' natural, unwashed skin or of amniotic fluid. They'll soon learn to recognize Mom and Dad's unique body scents.

The hearing of your 30- to 33-weeker is improving, too, although whispers are still out of reach; until 34 weeks, the hearing threshold remains about 40 decibels. (See section on 23- to 25-weekers, above.) In just a few weeks he'll be able to hear the same soft sounds that full-term newborns can.

Preemies of this age begin to show some of the built-in behaviors, called "automatic reflexes," which allow a newborn to fulfill his basic needs. At 32 weeks, a baby's sucking becomes stronger and better coordinated with swallowing. At the same time, the rooting reflex appears: if touched near the mouth a baby turns his head in that direction, in search of a nipple to latch on to. These new abilities are exciting signs that your baby will soon start his first feedings at the breast or bottle.

Parenting preemies of this age can be very fulfilling, as they open up to their external environment—and start showing signs that you are what brings them most pleasure and comfort. But now that they're better at paying attention, they're also more apt to feel stressed and overstimulated. Try to address your baby one sense at a time, and not for too long. You'll start to learn from his reactions whether he likes the stimulation, or if you should step back (see page 203). You can just talk or sing to him, or just gently stroke him, or just let his eyes gaze for a while at your face. If he ends up falling asleep in your arms, with a look of peace and contentment on his face, you'll know you made one, special preemie very happy.

34+ WEEKS OF GESTATION

Babies born four to six weeks before term may need intensive medical care, and may have the skinnier appearance of preemies, but their neurological development is quite advanced. Their senses of touch, hearing, smell, taste, and sight are almost as fully developed as those of a full-term baby. So once their breathing and vital signs are stable and they've made it through the jarring transition of the first few hours of life, they are pretty adept at organizing their behavior in the new world outside the womb, and interacting with the audience they find there.

These older premature babies still sleep about 18 to 20 hours a day, a few hours more than full-term newborns, who sleep 16 or 17 hours a day. To arouse them completely can be difficult, so at feeding time you'll often see nurses using little wake-up tricks like flicking the baby's feet, or gently sweeping his face with a damp cloth. It's a good sign that your baby is a deep sleeper. At 36 weeks comes the first appearance of really deep, quiet sleep, which is crucial for growth and development of the body and brain.

All of the automatic reflexes are now at least partly in place. Most babies can coordinate sucking with swallowing and breathing. Their grasp is so strong that they can be pulled upward as they hold on to adult fingers. And their Moro (or "startle") reflex—they throw out their arms and legs and arch their backs when they are startled by a sudden noise or fear of falling—is strong enough to startle their parents! (But don't try to test this or other reflexes on your own; if you don't know the correct method to use, you may scare or even hurt your baby. If you want to see how developed your baby's reflexes are, you can ask a doctor to demonstrate, when he has some time.)

Your baby's movements are still less coordinated than those of a term newborn, since muscle cells are still developing, along with nerves and the motor cortex of the brain. But they are becoming smoother day by day. At 34 weeks a preemie's posture may still be a little frog-like, with unflexed arms, but by 36 weeks all four limbs are flexed. When you sit your 36-weeker on your lap, with his head hanging down on his chest, he can briefly straighten his neck and hold up his head. This achievement, which allows him to see so much more of the world, may last for less than a second. But it is a big step for a preemie, and you should be proud of him. In the next few weeks, you'll see his neck muscles slowly become much stronger.

All in all, you've got a baby with abilities that will allow you to have a lot of pleasant experiences together, even if it's in an NICU or step-down unit. He can express his needs, likes, and dislikes. You can console him with the sound of your familiar voice, which he knows well from before birth, by caressing him, or by holding him and gently patting his back. But even though he thrives on your presence and enjoys play and stimulation, don't forget that your baby was supposed to spend these last few weeks quietly growing in the womb. He also needs lots of time when he is left alone to sleep peacefully. Learn to read any signs of stress he may express (see page 000), and if possible, avoid taking him to that point. Too much of a good thing—even displays of endearment—can be overwhelming for a little creature like yours.

Questions and Answers

Birth Announcements

My husband wants to send out birth announcements, but how can we? We're not going to send out a joyous announcement that our baby was born under 3 pounds.

Who decreed that a birth announcement should have the baby's weight listed on it? No one! In fact, it's a tradition that many people ignore, even for full-term babies. They include their baby's name and date of arrival—the important things for their friends to know. That's what you should feel free to do, too.

Please don't misunderstand us: Your baby's birthweight is nothing to be ashamed of. In time, you'll probably end up discussing it, and your hospital experiences, with all of your close friends. But at the moment, it may still feel private to you—like an intimate detail of your baby's medical history. You may even feel that it might cast your precious newborn in a negative light to people who've never had experience with a premature baby. (To those of us who have had premature babies, your baby's birthweight is more apt to be seen as a badge of honor, evoking admiration for the beautiful, little thing. What energetic, gutsy fighters those one-, two-, three-, and four-pounders are!)

We do urge you to send those announcements out. You don't have to do it this week, or next; you're awfully busy right now, and your first priority is caring for your baby. Birth announcements are typically mailed out anywhere from a few days to a few months after the arrival. But if you let this birth go publicly unacknowledged, you may regret it. The birth didn't go as you had hoped, but as things get back to normal, you will want to feel that you gave your child the celebration and honor that she deserved.

A Desire for Privacy

When parents are dealing with the shock and stress that accompanies the birth of a premature newborn, it's not uncommon for them to isolate themselves in a self-protective cocoon. They may not want phone calls or visits, even from close friends. If you've reacted this way, try not to feel guilty, or to worry about your friends. Don't hesitate to tell anybody that you would rather be left alone. It's better to let them know that you need some time to yourself now, than to be evasive or short with them when they visit or call. When you finally emerge and are ready to deal with the rest of your life again, you'll be able to explain to them why you reacted this way—and close friends will understand.

Why do you need this distance right now? Partly because it is easiest to cope with the tremendous fears and obligations of a premature birth by focusing on only one thing: what is happening in the nursery. Anything else seems like a distraction that saps the emotional and physical energy you are trying desperately to preserve. Partly because you may feel that no one else could possibly understand what you are going through. Maybe because you want your friends to see your tiny baby as perfect—as you do—and don't think they'd be able to see beyond the tubes and wires and medical crises right now. Also because this wasn't how it was supposed to be—and all of the social rituals that go on after a birth make that fact too painfully obvious.

The most sensitive of your friends are probably letting you know that they're thinking of you, eager to help in whatever way they can, and that when you're ready, they'll still be there.

Holding Baby on a Ventilator

The nurses say I can hold my baby, and I really want to. But he's still on a ventilator, and I'm afraid of knocking the tube out. Shouldn't I wait until he's off the vent?

Of course you're nervous about holding your baby for the first time—any honest parent of a preemie would tell you that they felt anxiety, too. Some parents, like you, are particularly concerned about the ventilator tube. Others, whose babies are not on the vent, worry about dislodging intravenous catheters, getting wires tangled, knocking leads out of place, and, of course, hurting their tiny, fragile-looking babies themselves. What pregnancy book or class prepares you for an experience like *this*?

But we can assure you of two things. First, if the nurses tell you that it's OK to hold your baby, they aren't saying it lightly. Remember that their first concern is always your baby's welfare. They have the experience to judge which babies are stable enough to safely spend some time out of bed, with their parents, and which babies need to lie quietly, without disturbances (even from loved ones), to conserve all of their energy for recovery.

Second, despite all of the medical accessories, as soon as you've done it once, having your baby in your arms will feel like the most natural thing in the world.

So let's consider the risks. You're right that accidental extubation (the ventilator tube getting dislodged) can, and does, occasionally happen. But according to a recent study, the most common cause of extubation is regular care and handling by the nurses. The second most common is movement by the babies themselves. Third is loosening or wetting of the tape that holds the tube in place. The fourth, least frequent cause of accidental extubation is the holding of babies by parents.

Parents tend to be extremely careful—and it's clear from your concern that you will be, too. Also, the nurse will make things easy for you. Once you're sitting down, she'll place your baby in your arms. She'll show you how to hold him; try to keep him in the position that she recommends. She'll stay near you at first, and check frequently to see if your baby shows any signs of unusual stress, such as breathing difficulties or back arching. (When he is first moved from his bed to your arms, he will undoubtedly show some signs of stress—a normal period of adjustment. But these should calm down after a few minutes, as he gets comfortable. If they continue, your preemie is probably just overstimulated. The nurse will suggest that he go back into his bed for some quiet sleep, and you can try again later.)

The nurse will also be there in case your baby's tube does come out while you're holding him. If that happens, alarms will go off, scaring you mightily. But the NICU staff will be ready to reintubate him almost immediately. The few minutes that he must breathe on his own are unlikely to harm him. Remember that he isn't relying on the ventilator for all, or even most, of his breaths; if he were, the nurse would most likely consider it too risky for you to hold him. And if he does run into breathing trouble, the nurse can help him breathe, temporarily, as well as a ventilator can, simply by using an oxygen bag and mask.

What about intravenous lines? They're really pretty stable—secured with lots of tape, and often with supporting cotton, gauze, bandages, and even little covers. Just try not to move the IV catheter or pull the connecting tubing too tightly. If you think that's happened, let the nurse know, and she can check on the IV. And don't worry too much—a little knock or tension is unlikely to dislodge an IV line.

As for wires and leads, there's hardly a parent who doesn't tangle them up or knock them off at some point while holding their baby. (If it makes you feel any better, the doctors do, too, as they turn the baby this way and that during physical exams.) But it doesn't matter. An alarm will sound, the nurse will see that your baby is fine but his wires or leads need fixing, and she'll do it. End of problem!

Although there are risks to holding your baby, there are benefits that override them. You will introduce your baby to something he greatly deserves: the feeling of being loved. You will teach him that all touch is not clinical and hurtful; it can be tender and sweet. And then there's something that you greatly deserve: resting your baby's little body against yours will confirm your feelings of parenthood. Our advice to you: Don't put these precious things off any longer than you have to.

Sores from Tape

My baby has sores on his belly where the nurses put tape on him. Will he have scars from them? Couldn't they be more careful?

Your baby's sores will probably heal completely without scarring—one of the benefits of having newborn skin that regenerates beautifully. Even preemies with deep skin injuries usually end up with scars that are pale and barely visible. Luckily, the most serious skin injuries are rare today, because of careful nursing techniques and gentle adhesives made especially for preemies.

Unfortunately, there's no way to avoid using adhesive tape in an NICU. Nearly all intensive care equipment must be held fast to a preemie's skin, so he doesn't accidentally dislodge it. All adhesives can cause skin irritation and breakdown, and while tape or probes and leads (which come with their own adhesive pads) can be periodically changed and moved, even that's not as simple as it sounds, because removing them can itself damage the skin of a premature baby.

The problem arises because preemies have immature and delicate skin. For the youngest babies, under 27 weeks of gestation, superficial skin injuries are inevitable even when the nurses are extremely careful. Simple handling can cause abrasions or bruises. These babies can also develop pressure sores easily, so they may be placed on waterbeds, gelled or furry mattresses, or thick foam pads.

Even preemies who are older are more susceptible to skin injuries than bigger children or grown-ups, because the layers of their skin are not as strongly anchored to each other. Recent studies have shown that changes in the normal functioning of the skin can be detected after ten consecutive removals of adhesive tape in adults, but after only one removal of adhesive tape in a premature infant.

But here's the good news: we've come a long way in preventing skin injuries in the NICU. When removing tape or a lead from a preemie's skin, a careful nurse may gently lift an edge, then rub the remaining adhesive away with cotton soaked in warm water or alcohol. Mineral oil or an emollient can help, but only if there's no need to reapply adhesive on the same area of skin. (Special solvents that dissolve adhesives aren't used because of their toxicity to preemies.)

Recently, some new, safe, adhesive gels have been developed that help protect preemies' skin from injury. You'll see that many of your baby's probes and leads are attached to his skin with what looks like clear gelatin: this gummy, sticky cushion keeps the skin under it moist, and is much more preemie-friendly than traditional adhesives. And barriers made of pectin (a natural gel extracted from plants) can be used beneath regular adhesive tape, easing its removal.

Even with special care and these new products, some preemies will still get skin sores. But these superficial injuries usually heal quickly. If this happens to your baby, try not to feel outraged. Nobody can be blamed for giving your baby the intensive care he needs to heal and grow. Once he comes home with you, his tender skin will get the soft, loving touch that it deserves.

Why So Many IVs?

Why does my baby need so many IVs? It breaks my heart to see the poor thing with all of those needles sticking into her.

Of course it's painful, seeing your tiny baby stuck with so many needles, not only in his little hands and feet, but maybe in his umbilical cord, or scalp, too. Your immediate reaction probably is: Take the extra ones out! One IV is enough! But as you might expect, the various lines haven't been put in arbitrarily. There's a good reason for each of them. Here are the main ones:

✻ More than one IV line is necessary if your baby is getting intravenous substances that are incompatible, meaning they must not go through the same catheter. A blood transfusion, for instance, shouldn't be contaminated by nutritional fluids or medications.

✻ Say your baby is getting fed through a central line (like an umbilical catheter), but he also needs medications every few hours. The nurses may prefer not to open the central line for the medications, since every time you "break" a line, its sterility is compromised, and the risk of an infection rises. So the medications may be given through a separate, peripheral IV.

✻ One of those catheters may not be an IV, or intravenous, line—it may go into an artery. While intravenous lines are used for delivering substances like fluids and medications to the baby, arterial lines are used for drawing blood and measuring blood pressure.

What do the lines feel like to your baby? Think about when you've had an IV in your hand. After an initial puncture, it wasn't painful anymore. You just had to remember to keep your hand still. When the IV was taken out, there was a bruise and some adhesive left behind, but a few days later, every trace of the IV had disappeared.

Your preemie's IVs are no different—except for the fact that managing them is more of a hassle for nurses, who cannot talk a baby into keeping his arm or leg still. This is why IVs in little hands or feet often require the whole limb to be taped onto a big, clumsy board. All parents hate to see their preemie loaded with such a bulky swaddle, but it is necessary to keep him from flexing his joints and dislodging or kinking the catheter.

One by one, your baby's lines will be taken out, as he grows older and more stable. And then, one great day, you'll arrive and find that your baby is completely catheter-free.

WHAT KINDS OF IVS ARE THOSE?

Some of the catheters that you see in your baby may be IVs, or intravenous lines, and others may be arterial lines—going into arteries instead of veins. You wouldn't believe how different each kind of line is, with its own, special advantages and uses:

❋ Some IVs go into small peripheral veins—superficial blood vessels, usually in the arms and legs. These are used to give your baby medicines, fluid, and some nutrients. To precisely control the amount of fluid getting into your baby's bloodstream, these catheters may be attached to machines called infusion pumps, which provide a continuous stream of fluid. Alternatively, an IV may be used intermittently—say, for a medicine given twice a day—and capped off between doses. Peripheral IVs have to be moved occasionally; tiny veins with catheters in them can get damaged or inflamed after a few days. So you might find your baby with an intravenous needle in her hand one day, her foot the next. (If a baby has IVs for a long time, it might even become necessary to have one in his scalp at some point. Doctors try not to use scalp IVs too often, simply because parents find them disturbing. See page 274.)

❋ Other IVs, called central lines, are placed in large veins in the arms, legs, or neck, and passed into bigger, deeper blood vessels near the heart. The two most commonly used central lines are *percucaths,* which neonatologists or nurse practitioners usually insert right in the NICU, and *broviacs,* which are usually inserted by surgeons in the operating room.

There are two great things about central lines. One is that they can deliver highly concentrated nutrition or medications that would be irritating to smaller veins. The other is that they can be left in place for weeks or months, and can be used if a baby will need intravenous nutrition or medicines for a long period of time.

❋ An arterial line goes into an artery instead of a vein. Arterial lines are used for measuring blood pressure, and for drawing blood for frequent blood tests. Doctors use them to keep an eye on levels of crucial substances like oxygen, carbon dioxide, and calcium. Arterial lines may be placed in wrists or feet, but the most common kind in preemies goes into the baby's umbilical cord, or belly button. It's called a UAC, or umbilical arterial catheter. A UAC is painless to put in, since there are no nerves in the umbilical cord, and can do triple duty. Not only can it be used for drawing blood and monitoring blood pressure, like other arterial lines, but it can be used to deliver fluids and nutrition, too. And since it's a central line (going into a large blood vessel), it can deliver very high concentrations of nutrients, so it's often used for feeding babies on total parenteral nutrition. But nothing's perfect. A UAC can't be used for more than a week or two; after that, it has to be taken out to prevent blood clots or infection. If a baby needs longer-term parenteral nutrition, this line would probably be replaced with a percucath or a broviac.

❋ Your baby's umbilical cord has a large vein, too. A UVC, or umbilical venous catheter, is a central line that can also provide doctors with some key information: whether the baby has enough, or too much, fluid circulating in his body. The usual ways of telling, like measuring urine output, don't work well for very little babies, who tend to lose a lot of fluids from their skin. Measuring pressure through the UVC is more reliable. A UVC can't be used for long, though. Like a UAC, it needs to be removed within a week or so, to avoid clotting and infection.

Discolored Toes from Umbilical Catheter

My daughter's toes turned bluish-black, and the doctor said it was because of a blood clot in her umbilical catheter. How could they have let this happen? Is it serious?

It's an alarming sight, but not one you should have to worry about for long. Your daughter's nurse will watch to make sure that the blood flow in her foot is good, and that her toes gradually return to normal over the next hour or so. If she has any doubts, or if your daughter's toes stay bluish-black, the doctor will remove the umbilical catheter, which should solve the problem.

This complication of an umbilical artery catheter is so common that doctors and nurses even have a nickname for it: *cath toes*. Cath toes occur when tiny blood clots form around the tip of the catheter, then break off and travel down to the toes. Most NICUs put heparin, an anticoagulant, into babies' UAC fluids, to help prevent large blood clots from forming around the catheter. But despite the heparin, tiny blood clots are almost inevitable. Your baby's natural anticoagulants will work over the next few hours to get rid of the clot.

Small clots, like your daughter's, rarely cause any lasting trouble. Very rarely, a clot does not resolve on its own, but grows bigger and obstructs a large blood vessel, seriously impeding blood flow to an organ or extremity. In that case, doctors would treat the clot with medication to help break it down. If medication didn't work, they might try surgery to remove the clot. Above all, they would give the body's own clot-dissolving mechanisms time to do their work.

Even when there's a rare, more serious clot, treatment to dissolve or remove the clot is usually effective. Very, very occasionally, a baby's toes or leg is irreparably damaged and has to be amputated, but this doesn't happen unless blood flow is completely disrupted for hours or days.

If only your daughter could put on a pair of socks to help you forget about this passing flaw—but the nurses need to monitor how her toes are doing. Before you know it, her little toes should be perfect again.

HOW YOUR BABY IS FED: A JOURNEY FROM PARENTERAL NUTRITION, TO GAVAGE FEEDINGS, TO BREAST OR BOTTLE

There's nothing more natural than putting a newborn to his mother's breast right after birth, or bringing the first bottle of formula to his eager mouth. Yet feedings, which most parents of full-term babies take for granted, can be a real hurdle for a preemie. Older premature babies, who are born after 32 or 33 weeks of gestation and are healthy, may be ready to breastfeed or drink from a nipple within a matter of days. But if your baby is younger or sicker, it will take longer for him to get to that point.

Why can't a young preemie just go ahead and eat? Because, although a fetus's intestinal tract is fully formed by 20 weeks, some important functions don't mature until later. For example, peristalsis—contractions of the intestines that propel food through them—doesn't start working well until about 28 or 30 weeks, and preemies don't yet produce sufficient amounts of some important digestive enzymes. And it's not on nature's agenda for preemies to feed by mouth before 32 to 34 weeks, when they develop the ability to coordinate sucking, swallowing, and breathing. Before a preemie masters this coordination, he could choke on his milk, or it might just dribble out of his mouth as he breathes.

A young preemie's feeding journey usually proceeds through three steps:

❋ *Parenteral nutrition,* meaning that it bypasses the baby's digestive system and goes directly into his bloodstream, through an IV or other catheter;

❋ *Gavage feedings,* in which a baby is fed breast milk or formula through a tube that goes from his mouth or nose into his stomach;

❋ *Drinking from a nipple*—breastfeeding and/or bottle feeding.

This progression allows a baby to be fed according to his developmental stage and medical condition. Keep in mind, though, that the passage from one leg of a preemie's feeding journey to the next is never clear-cut. Parenteral nutrition usually overlaps with gavage, and gavage usually overlaps with bottle or breastfeeding, to allow the baby some time to get used to each new, more demanding step. Probably there will be ups and downs, too, and you may get frustrated at times. But you'll also get joy from watching your baby's progress, and from many intimate moments along the way. Feeding your baby, and watching him grow, is one of the most basic pleasures of parenting—for parents of full-term and premature newborns alike.

THE FIRST STEP: PARENTERAL NUTRITION

It is normal for preemies, as for all newborns, not to eat much, and to lose some weight, right after birth. But since premature babies have fewer body stores of fats and other nutrients, they need nourishment soon. The first nourishment for many preemies comes from IV fluids, usually sugar in water. This progresses in a few days to a more nourishing solution containing protein, vitamins, minerals, and other nutrients. Called TPN for total parenteral nutrition, this solution can contain all of the fluids, calories, and nourishment your baby needs to live and grow, or it can be used to supplement his feedings by mouth. Preemies usually get intravenous nutrition for several days to several weeks after birth.

While your baby is on TPN, his doctors will be on the lookout for some possible complications, such as infection from the IV catheter, skin injury if some solution leaks out of the vein, too-high levels of glucose or fat in the blood (this is only a problem if it goes on for a long time), and liver damage (in the vast majority of babies, the liver heals after TPN is stopped).

Chances are that your baby will not have any of these problems. But they explain why, despite its many benefits, the NICU's little patients are kept on TPN only as long as they absolutely need it.

THE SECOND STEP: GAVAGE FEEDINGS OF BREAST MILK OR FORMULA

It is a truly big accomplishment for a preemie: the first gavage feeding of a few drops of formula or breast milk.

Although a baby may not be ready to drink from a nipple yet, putting nutrients in his intestinal tract will stimulate it to grow and mature faster. So very young babies, even while they're sustained primarily by parenteral nutrition, can be fed small amounts of formula or breast milk by tube, or gavage. (Gavage is a French word meaning "cram" or "stuff," giving you some sense of what's in store for your preemie!)

Gavage feeding involves a very small, soft tube going through your baby's mouth or nose, down to his stomach. An OG tube (which goes through the mouth and stands for oro-gastric) is generally preferred because babies breathe through their noses. An NG tube (which goes through the nose and stands for naso-gastric) is good for some older preemies who have a strong gag reflex, and for those who are already nippling or breastfeeding, but need extra calories through gavage.

Inserting a gavage tube through a baby's mouth or nose is a painless procedure that usually doesn't bother preemies at all. The nurse slides the gavage tube down the back of the baby's throat, down his esophagus, and into his stomach. She secures the tube in place by taping it under his nostril, or beside his mouth. The whole thing takes a matter of seconds, so if the tube seems to bother the baby—which is rarely the case—it can be taken out and put in again for each feeding. (It is usually left in, since removing the tape can irritate a preemie's delicate skin, and there are a few babies who gag or have bradycardia while the tube is being placed.)

When it's mealtime, the nurse connects a plastic syringe to the baby's gavage tube, pours in the right amount of breast milk or formula, gives the plunger one gentle push, and lets the liquid flow down into the tube by gravity. (Sucking on a tiny pacifier, while he's being gavage fed, can help a preemie rehearse for the next step on his feeding journey, nipple feeding.) Alternatively, the nurse may connect the syringe to a pump, so the milk can be dripped into your preemie's stomach very slowly.

The first gavage feeding may be just a few drops of water, diluted formula, or breast milk. If your baby tolerates it (meaning he doesn't vomit and the milk moves well through his intestines), the amount of milk or formula he gets with each feeding will be gradually increased, until he no longer needs intravenous nutrition.

The nurse may offer—if she doesn't, make sure to ask—to let you feed your baby by holding him and the syringe full of milk. It can feel impersonal at first, but once you see how satisfied and peaceful your baby gets as he's fed in your loving arms, you'll probably change your mind. Many parents remember gavage feedings as some of the most moving moments of their NICU experience.

FEEDING INTOLERANCE, AND WAYS TO OVERCOME IT

Feeding may not always go smoothly. Some feeding intolerance is expected in preemies until their digestion matures, and although it may warrant a pause, it's rarely a cause for alarm. During this delicate stage of the feeding journey, your baby will be watched carefully for any of the following signs:

* *An incomplete emptying of the stomach.* Before starting a feeding, the nurse may use the syringe to gently pull out and evaluate the contents of your baby's stomach, and then return them to avoid the loss of any precious nutrients. If the aspirate is too large or contains bile, the doctor may consider the possibility of an infection, obstruction of the intestine, or necrotizing enterocolitis (NEC). NEC is the biggest concern when a preemie starts gavage feedings. Most of the time, though, more fluid than normal in a preemie's stomach just means that her immature intestines are moving slowly, and need more time to completely digest their food.

* *A tense or tender abdomen, or blood in the stools.* These can also be a sign of infection or NEC. They may be investigated with an x-ray of the baby's intestine.

* *Vomiting.* This could indicate an infection or intestinal obstruction, but usually reflects less serious problems, such as overstimulation, or reflux. So don't be alarmed if your preemie occasionally vomits—every baby does. The doctors will see if the problem goes away when, for example, your baby is fed more slowly or is placed on his stomach.

* *A bloated but soft abdomen.* This can be a sign of gas, constipation, or poor movement by the immature intestines. Full-term newborns usually have their first stool within the first 24 or 48 hours, but preemies may take a week or longer. A sliver of a glycerin suppository (a gentle laxative) might help relieve your baby's gas and help him stool. There are also medications that can improve intestinal movement.

* *Diarrhea.* This can indicate incomplete digestion, usually because the feedings contain too many calories for the baby's immature intestines to digest, or because of lactase (an enzyme needed to digest milk) deficiency. The remedy is to temporarily change the composition of the feedings. Infection is another possible cause, but less likely.

* *More frequent episodes of apnea (a pause in breathing) and bradycardia (slow heart rate).* These may be brought on by the gavage tube itself, if it slips out of the stomach back into the esophagus. Removing the tube between feedings might solve the problem. Doctors will also consider causes like reflux or infection.

* *Excess gas.* Some babies who are on nasal CPAP have feeding intolerance because their stomachs fill up with gas. Some of this pressure can be relieved by placing a second

gavage tube in the baby's stomach, just to let the gas come out.

Changing any of the elements of a preemie's feeding schedule may improve his digestion, but it's a matter of trial and error. Your baby's doctor may adjust any of the following:

* the quantity of milk—going back to the amount previously tolerated by the baby;
* the interval between feedings—raising it from three to four hours, for example, or changing to continuous, pump feedings;
* the strength of breast milk or formula—diluting it with more water, or discontinuing fortifiers or supplements;
* the type of formula—changing it to a soy formula for babies who can't digest cow's milk, or a predigested formula for babies with especially immature digestion;
* where the gavage tube is placed—bypassing the stomach, by placing feedings directly into the intestine, if reflux is a severe problem, or if stomach distention on CPAP persists.

Often a change that seems tiny to you will be all that your baby needs.

GRADUATING TO THE BOTTLE OR BREAST

It's a great moment for all parents of very premature babies. Your preemie has reached the age of 32 to 34 weeks, when he can probably coordinate sucking, swallowing, and breathing all at the same time. He has already proven that he can suck vigorously on a tiny pacifier or the tip of your finger. His vital signs are stable, he's off the ventilator, and on less than 40% oxygen.

He has been tolerating and gaining weight on his gavage feedings. All of these encouraging signs lead the doctors and nurses to one conclusion: this preemie is ready to start "nippling"—drinking from a bottle or breast. If you are breastfeeding, your preemie may begin even earlier, at 28 to 30 weeks, as recent studies have shown that a preemie may be able to nurse at the breast before he can drink from a bottle.

At first your baby may barely latch onto your breast, or swallow only a teaspoon or two of formula or milk, and he may not be strong enough to drink from a bottle or your breast at every feeding. This new task, nippling, can be so difficult and tiring for a small preemie that he uses up more calories than he's taking in. Therefore, babies who have just graduated to bottle or breastfeeding may do it only once or twice a day at first, learning how to nipple while getting the rest of their feedings from gavage. But your baby's feeding skills will improve gradually over time, until he's eating perfectly well on his own. In the meantime, the nurses will be happy to help you participate in your baby's feeding efforts, by scheduling his daily bottle feedings during your visits to the NICU, or by assisting you during your first breastfeeding attempts.

Sometimes, a baby may need some minor, extra help, like switching to a different kind of nipple (there is a special preemie nipple that is softer and easier to suck), or, having his supplemental oxygen, if he's on it, increased during feedings. Even if your baby was born after 33 weeks of gestation, his immaturity can make bottle or breastfeeding hard for him temporarily.

Occasionally, preemies who have been sick for a longer time have a harder time adjusting to the breast or bottle. Endotracheal tubes, suction catheters, and tape on their faces can result in an unpleasant sensation in or around babies' mouths, which can disturb the natural association of mouth, sucking, hunger relief, and pleasure. Due to the hard experience of their first months of life in the NICU, these infants may become "disorganized feeders," who refuse to nipple feed. Time and extreme patience by parents or caregivers is the answer, and it nearly always works. In the rare cases when it doesn't,

introducing the baby directly to feeding with a cup and spoon is usually successful.

Your baby will reach the end of his journey when he has replaced all gavage feedings with bottle or breastfeedings, can complete each "meal" in less than 20 or 30 minutes, and is gaining weight steadily. While you hold him snugly in your arms, just think of the long way your preemie has come, getting stronger and very well fed.

Breast Milk Banks

I'm not going to breastfeed. But I've heard that breast milk is best for my baby, and there are banks I can get breast milk from.

Yes, it is true that some mothers who have plenty of breast milk, more than their own babies can take, generously donate it to breast milk banks. These are non-profit organizations that collect breast milk, guarantee its safety, store it, and ship it to babies who need it. Among the donors are some lactating mothers of preemies. Their breast milk, which is different from full-term milk (see page 125), is reserved for other preemies, who can particularly benefit from it.

Donor milk from a breast milk bank can be an excellent choice for your premature baby. Breast milk is easier to digest than formula, so it is less of a strain on a preemie's immature intestines, and contains substances not found in formula that may improve a baby's health and development. Donor mothers are screened in the same way that blood donors are, to look for infections, illness, ingestion of dangerous substances, and risky behaviors. The potential donor's physician and her baby's physician are questioned, as well. After the breast milk is collected, it is pasteurized, then screened for bacte-

rial infection. So you can feel confident that it is safe. And despite the fact that the pasteurization process destroys some of the infection-fighting qualities of breast milk, some remain.

If you are not going to breastfeed your preemie, but want to give him donor breast milk, tell your baby's doctor. Some hospitals have standing arrangements with a milk bank, and automatically use donor milk as a first choice for preemies who are not being breastfed, after obtaining their parents' permission. Other nurseries use formula first, but can help you to get in touch with the closest breast milk bank yourself. To prepare you, here are some possible obstacles you may find in your way:

* *Sometimes the supply of preterm donor breast milk runs low.* When only a limited amount is available, it is rationed to preemies who need it the most, usually those who are extremely premature, or have feeding complications.
* *Most banks will provide breast milk to you while your baby is in the hospital.* But after your baby is discharged home, you may have to show a doctor's prescription for breast milk, or a certificate stating that you cannot breastfeed your baby yourself.
* *Donor breast milk is expensive.* It costs about $2.50 per ounce, and sometimes shipping is

extra. The price arises entirely from the high cost of running a safe, efficient bank. Some health insurance plans will pay for donor breast milk, but they may require a certificate of medical need.

Some mothers ask if they can feed their baby breast milk donated by friends or relatives. Most breast milk banks will screen and process milk for "directed" donation (from a particular donor, to a particular baby). You will probably need to contact the nearest milk bank yourself (see appendix, page 522) to make arrangements for a directed donation. Hospitals either don't allow, or strongly discourage, private donations of breast milk that don't go through a bank: first, because donors and milk cannot be rigorously screened, as a bank would do; and second, because preemies don't thrive as well on term milk, and most private donors are mothers of full-term babies. But in some cases, you might be allowed to do this after signing a release, and assuming full responsibility for any possible consequences to your baby.

Pasteurized, preterm breast milk from a bank can be the next best feeding choice for a premature baby, after his mother's own. If you can afford the expense, and are willing to go through some bureaucracy, you may want to give it a try.

Attention Paid to Diapers

Why are the nurses always examining our son's bowel movements and weighing his wet diapers?

Every NICU's golden rule is to closely monitor all preemies' vital signs and bodily functions, even those you may take for granted. For instance, most full-term babies pass their first stools, the peculiarly black meconium, within

---

If You Want to Be a Breast Milk Donor

If you are interested in donating your breast milk, you can be sure it will be a valuable gift to a premature baby who needs it. You or your doctor should contact the nearest breast milk bank. The bank will send you a cooler, packing instructions, and a Federal Express call number for picking up your milk and shipping it back to the bank. They will also explain their screening procedure to you. Donors are not paid—except in unspoken appreciation from those who receive their milk.

---

24 hours of birth. But a premature baby may not have his first bowel movement for several days: the earlier a baby is born, the longer the wait, because of the immaturity of his intestines. No wonder the nurses will proudly announce to you when that natural event has finally taken place for your baby!

Your baby's diapers will get a lot of attention, because they contain such useful clues and information. In addition to a visual exam, the nurses may perform tests on your baby's stools to evaluate how well he's absorbing the nutrients in his feedings or to check for hidden blood. They will register the time, amount, and appearance of each stool in your baby's medical chart. If your baby has diarrhea (watery, frequent bowel movements), it may be due to incomplete absorption of his feedings—possibly because the caloric density is too high for his immature intestines, or because he has an intolerance to lactose. Both problems can be treated by changing what he eats. Diarrhea could also be a sign of an infection.

On the other hand, constipation, in a tiny preemie, may cause enough abdominal distention to compromise his breathing! If your baby is constipated, the nurse may give him a suppository to encourage a bowel movement.

A little invisible blood in a preemie's stool is usually nothing to worry about; it's common, and often results from minor irritation of the stomach from a baby's feeding tube. (The nurse knows the blood is there because it shows up as a blue color on a guaiac test. Pronounced "GWY-ak," this painless test is done at your baby's bedside, and involves the nurse putting a tiny bit of stool on a special card, then dripping a chemical on it and watching for color change.) Small streaks of visible blood might come from a tiny cut around his rectum, or a particularly bad diaper rash. If there's a lot of bleeding, though, or it lasts, it might be a signal of more severe inflammation, maybe due to reflux or necrotizing enterocolitis. Doctors would want to treat these conditions early, to prevent progression of the illness.

Most of the time, the color of a bowel move-ment isn't significant (including the "green" stools that surprise many parents), but in the rare cases that stools are pale gray or white, they may indicate that a baby is not passing bile appropriately.

Wet diapers get plenty of attention, too. Your baby's urine is monitored by weighing his diapers, as you noticed, and by periodically performing dipstick tests. (A plastic stick painted with chemicals is dipped into urine. It changes color if the urine contains certain substances, including blood, sugar, protein, and acid). Dipstick tests may be done to check for mild metabolic disturbances (like whether a baby is fully utilizing the glucose he's given) or infection, and to verify the overall functioning of the urinary system. The quantity and concentration of a baby's urine helps indicate the baby's level of hydration (whether he has the right amount of fluid in his system), and the effectiveness of some medications he may be taking.

When you start changing your preemie's diaper, make sure that you leave it aside for the nurses, and don't drop it by mistake in the wastebasket. Remember: what may look like a common, dirty diaper is actually a valuable piece of information about your preemie's health.

GETTING ACQUAINTED WITH:
JAUNDICE AND BILIRUBIN

Most people know what jaundice is: a yellowish tinge of the skin. But it's less well known what jaundice comes from: a yellow substance called bilirubin that the body makes naturally all the time, as it breaks down used red blood cells. The reason so many newborns have jaundice is that they aren't good at getting rid of bilirubin yet, so it builds up. It's the liver's job to convert bilirubin into a form that can be passed out of the body, in the stools, but it can take a few days after birth for the liver to switch this process on. A preemie's immature liver can take longer—a week or two. Plus, newborns produce a lot more bilirubin than older babies, since their red blood cells have shorter lives.

When doctors see jaundice in a newborn, full-term or premature, they usually don't get worried. The jaundice is usually a result of immaturity, not illness, and small increases in bilirubin aren't harmful. Furthermore, there is a very effective treatment, phototherapy, to keep the bilirubin level from getting too high. If it does, it can cause brain damage—but your baby's doctor will treat her jaundice well before it gets to that point.

WHICH BABIES GET JAUNDICED

All preemies, but especially the youngest and smallest ones, are apt to become jaundiced, because their livers and intestines are more immature than term babies. Their livers aren't as quick to start converting bilirubin into a disposable form, and they have fewer bowel movements to eliminate it (especially if they aren't being fed at first). Babies who have a lot of skin bruising from a difficult delivery, those who are born with unusually high numbers of red blood cells, or who have intraventricular hemorrhages will be watched especially carefully, because they'll produce lots of bilirubin as those used red blood cells are broken down. Infants whose mothers are diabetic, or have a different blood type, and babies who have respiratory distress syndrome, infections, or who suffered some birth asphyxia are also more likely to become jaundiced.

DIAGNOSIS: OBSERVATION AND BLOOD TESTS

Compared to many other medical conditions, jaundice is easy to diagnose. As bilirubin levels rise, a baby's skin turns progressively more yellowish-orange, starting at her head and continuing on down toward her toes. Depending on your baby's color, and how much of her body is jaundiced, the doctor can guess at her bilirubin level. If he wants a precise measurement, he can measure the exact level in her blood.

If your baby's bilirubin level is high for her age and size, or if it is rising quickly, her doctor will check out a number of possibilities, including whether something has caused more breakdown of red blood cells than usual (for example, an incompatibility with her mother's blood), whether bilirubin is not getting passed out as feces quickly enough (depending on the reason, something as simple as a little suppository, or starting feedings, may solve the problem), or whether the problem is actually a different sort of jaundice due to liver damage (direct hyperbilirubinemia, see page 242). Most of the time, though, there's no cause other than your baby's natural, to-be-expected immaturity.

THE COURSE THAT JAUNDICE TAKES

Normal jaundice in preemies usually follows a typical pattern, becoming visible 36 to 48 hours after birth. Bilirubin levels increase gradually, peak after five to seven days, then decrease gradually to minimal levels over the following week or two.

HOW JAUNDICE IS TREATED

Enter any NICU, and you'll see bright blue, green, or white lights called bililights, shining on naked babies wearing eye shields, as if they were in a tanning salon. Phototherapy originated after some nurses in England noticed that babies near windows were less jaundiced than other newborns in the nursery. Like the sunlight streaming through those windows, the light waves from bililights change bilirubin into substances that can be eliminated easily from a baby's body—like the liver does, when it is mature. Phototherapy is extremely safe. A very few babies may have some temporary side effects—diarrhea and skin rashes, in particular—but they go away when the lights do. During phototherapy, eye covers protect your baby's retinas from damage, and her reproductive organs are kept covered, too, by her diaper—although these precautions may not even be necessary. (When you're around, the lights can be turned off for a while, and your baby's eye covers removed, to allow you and your baby to look into each other's eyes.)

Most preemies remain under bililights for a few days or a week. If your baby is already eating breast milk and her bilirubin level is very high, she may be taken off it and given formula for a day or two, because breast milk can raise bilirubin levels. (Don't forget to keep pumping in the meantime.)

When your baby's bilirubin drops to a low level, the doctors will turn off the phototherapy. Often, the bilirubin level will rebound higher again for a day or two after phototherapy has stopped, and the lights may be restarted. This isn't a setback, it just means your baby wasn't quite ready to come off the phototherapy. Chances are, the lights will be turned off again a few days later, and her bilirubin level will continue to fall.

In rare cases, a baby's bilirubin will continue to climb, and her doctor may feel that the next therapeutic step is necessary: an exchange transfusion. In an exchange transfusion, the baby's blood, with its circulating bilirubin, is drawn out through a catheter, and replaced with fresh blood from a donor. Exchange transfusions are hardly ever necessary in preemies, because phototherapy works so well.

SHOULD YOU BE WORRIED?

Not unless your doctor tells you to be—and he probably won't. Up to 60% of full-term babies and 80% of preemies develop jaundice within the first few days of their lives. At low levels, there are no lasting effects of jaundice. (In fact, a little jaundice may even be good, protecting the body against tissue damage caused by natural toxins called "free radicals.") At high levels, bilirubin can pass to the brain and cause brain damage, or even death. The exact level at which brain injury will occur varies, depending on many interrelated factors having to do with a baby's age, size, and medical condition, among other things. You can ask your baby's doctor what level he would consider harmful for your child, but realize that the number he gives you is more of an educated guess than a certainty. Fortunately, thanks to the widespread use of phototherapy, many NICUs haven't seen a case of serious brain damage in years.

So if your baby has jaundice, be glad she's bathing comfortably under those lights, and don't worry.

Nurses' Response to Alarms

I jump when one of the alarms goes off in the NICU, but I swear that the nurses act downright blasé. When I'm not there, they might not respond in time to save my daughter!

What can be more terrifying than the sudden beep-beep-beep of your baby's alarms? If you're like most parents, you feel a rush of panic, and your eyes fly to the machine next to your baby's bed, to see which of her vital signs is in a danger zone. A flashing light tells you that she has stopped breathing, or her heart has slowed, or she is losing oxygen. You're on the verge of screaming for an army of medical reinforcements. And what does your baby's nurse do? She saunters over, and with a mere glance at your baby and the monitor, turns off the alarm and walks away again. Perhaps, noticing your look of panic, she also reminds you: "Look at your baby, not the machine."

To you, the nurse may seem overly casual, but chances are she's not—she's just experienced. Parents tend to think of the monitors attached to their baby as precise instruments, but they're actually subject to false alarms and unnecessary scares for any number of reasons:

❋ Your baby squirms around, or the nurse moves her, causing one of the wires to the cardiorespiratory monitor to come loose, or one of the leads on your baby's chest to slide out of place or fall off. Since the leads are held on with very mild adhesive, this happens frequently. The result is that the monitor can't detect your baby's chest movements, and thinks she's having apnea (a pause in breathing). Or it can't detect her pulse, and thinks she's having a "brady" (short for bradycardia, a slow heart rate).

❋ Squirming also often causes the oxygen monitor to alarm—either the sensor comes loose, or it's just unable to pick up your baby's pulse until she settles down. This machine needs an accurate reading of a baby's pulse to figure out whether there's enough oxygen in her blood; if it gets a low reading of her pulse, it thinks her oxygen saturation level is falling (she is "desatting"). It's easy to tell if the sensor isn't picking up your baby's pulse: If the cardiorespiratory monitor shows a heart rate of, say, 160, but the oxygen monitor shows a heart rate of 80, or if the red line that represents your baby's pulse is gyrating wildly (heart rates don't gyrate like that), you've got a false alarm for sure.

❋ All preemies do something called "periodic breathing." They may take a few, deep breaths, and then pause for five or ten seconds before taking another one. It's not apnea unless the pause lasts at least twenty seconds or is accompanied by a change in heart rate or skin color. But the cardiorespiratory monitor, because of the way it's programmed to calculate numbers of breaths, can sometimes misinterpret periodic breathing as longer, apnea spells.

❋ Sometimes preemies have what's called shallow breathing—they pull their chests in slightly, rather than deeply. If the lead can't feel these subtle chest movements, the monitor will think your baby isn't breathing.

Your baby's looks are far more reliable than the machines. The nurses know—and you should learn, too—that when an alarm goes off, you shouldn't stare at the scary numbers on the monitor's screen (which is everybody's instinct). Instead, look over at your baby. If your baby is in distress, she'll show it. If her chest is moving in and out, and her nostrils are gently flaring, she's breathing—even if the monitor says she isn't. If she's nice and pink, she has plenty of oxygen.

Even when they have real apnea, a real brady, or real desatting, preemies often recover quickly on their own, without getting into trouble. Unless they're already showing signs of poor oxygenation or blood flow (we'll explain the signs in a minute), there can be good reasons for the nurse to wait and see what happens, rather than rushing to intervene:

* It's important for the doctors and nurses to know if your baby can recover on her own. This is an important piece of clinical evidence that will influence whether she needs further treatment (such as medication, supplemental oxygen, or other breathing assistance), and when she can be discharged.

* Whenever possible, your baby should be left alone, and allowed to sleep undisturbed. It's far better not to bother her than to wake her, if the episode is going to resolve on its own, anyway.

* Sometimes it's the monitor that needs intervention, not the baby. As preemies get older, their normal heart rate slows down, especially when they're in deep sleep. So if your maturing baby starts setting off lots of alarms with no signs of distress, it simply may mean that it's time to reset her cardiorespiratory monitor to sound an alarm at a lower heart rate than before. Also, there are some babies who just breathe faster, or have faster heart rates, than others. If the doctors are convinced these babies are healthy, they'll simply reset the monitor accordingly.

* Some preemies are particularly sensitive to stimulation. They get so easily stressed out that even loud noises, being handled, or their own movements can trigger apnea or desatting. When these babies are feeling overwhelmed, the last thing they need is more touching and handling. They really want to be left alone, and once the stimulation subsides, they recover. (You can read about how to make your baby's environment more peaceful on page 200.)

What are the signs that your baby may really be in trouble? Her lips will soon turn bluish-gray if she isn't breathing, or if her heart is pumping too slowly to send enough oxygen to the skin. After a little while longer, she may become limp, and her skin will become bluish-gray, too. This color change is called cyanosis. If the nurse sees it, you can be sure she will intervene to help your baby. (A bluish color of the hands and feet alone, in the first few days of life, is different; it is normal for newborns and goes away on its own.)

If your baby needs a reminder to breathe, the nurse's first step may be to touch her gently: a tickle or tap on a preemie's foot is often enough. If she needs a little more rousing than that, the nurse can rub her arm, leg, or back slightly more vigorously. If that's still not enough, the nurse will provide the baby with oxygen. In an intensive care nursery, every baby has the necessary equipment right beside her bed. The nurse can blow oxygen from a tube near her face, or place a mask over her nose and mouth and gently pump some oxygen into her lungs. (Since the oxygen comes out of a bag, this is called "bagging" the baby—a terrible name, if you ask us!) As soon as the baby is pink again and her pulse is back up, she's fine.

What does it mean that your baby is having apnea and bradys? Probably nothing more than that she's an official, card-carrying preemie. As long as the episodes are usually mild, they're probably just a normal consequence of her immaturity and will go away by about the 36th to 38th week of gestation. It's the parents who suffer from these alarms the most. For more information, see Getting Acquainted with Apnea and Bradycardia on page 218.

Afraid to Leave Baby

I'm afraid to leave my baby's side. What if there's an emergency and I'm not there?

That's a fear you share with many parents whose babies are in an intensive care nursery. But there are a few things that should reassure you. First, if your baby's doctor and nurse say she's stable, it's very unlikely that an emergency will occur suddenly. Just like older babies, preemies usually provide their doctors and parents with a warning that something is wrong, by getting sick and unstable first.

Second, in the rare event that an unexpected emergency does occur—say a baby needs to have an urgent medical procedure performed, or CPR—an intensive care nursery is set up to handle it. Although the incident may signal that there's an underlying problem, it would be very rare for a baby's health to deteriorate so rapidly that you wouldn't have time to receive a phone call, and come in to be with her after the emergency intervention, when she needs you.

If your baby is unstable, you can ask her doctor if there's any immediate danger—he can almost always tell you. Many illnesses that preemies get have an acute period, then gradually resolve. For example, when a baby has NEC (necrotizing enterocolitis, see page 237), there is often a span of a few days when the need for emergency surgery could suddenly arise. The initial days after a baby gets an infection are usually the worst. And babies can be very sick for one or two days after they have a major surgical procedure. If the doctor thinks your baby is in a very unstable or dangerous period, you would probably want to stay in or near the hospital, to reach your baby quickly if anything were to happen. After those few days of greatest uncertainty pass, the likelihood of a sudden emergency will largely pass, too— and you should try not to worry. This even applies to extremely premature babies whose parents fear they won't survive: after the first three or four days of life, they are out of the most dangerous period, and their chances of surviving go way up.

Some parents whose babies are sick find they just can't shake the fear that their baby will die while they are away from the nursery. If this is what's worrying you, we can assure you: it almost never happens. Doctors can tell when a baby's condition is becoming very serious, early enough to reach the parents so they can return to the nursery. If your baby's doctor has told you that there is some immediate danger, you can decide to stay in the nursery, in a hotel close to the hospital, or, if your hospital has one, in a special room where parents can sleep.

Some parents find it comforting to buy or rent an automatic pager, or to carry a cellular phone—others find it heightens their anxiety. The most crucial thing is to tell your baby's doctor and nurse that it's important to you to be with your baby if something happens, and to give them every phone number they may need to reach you. That way, the doctor will know to call you sooner rather than later, so you'll have plenty of time to get to your baby's side. You may have some false alarms—thankfully! But when the phone isn't ringing, you can relax a bit, knowing that everything remains all right.

Air Leak

We just got a terrible phone call from our baby's doctor. He said our son, who's on a ventilator, had a "setback"—an air leak. I don't even understand what that means, let alone how worried we should be.

The first reaction a parent has after hearing about an unexpected complication is fear. That's understandable; like you, most parents have never heard of an air leak before. It will help you to understand what one is, why it happens, and why the doctor can't tell you yet whether your baby's air leak is merely a temporary setback from which he'll recover in a few days, or one that will affect his health for a longer time.

When we breathe, air goes into our nose or mouth, down our windpipe, and into the many, small airways and air sacs of our lungs. An air leak occurs when one of these tiny airways or sacs tears, leaking air into places where it's not supposed to be. There are different kinds of air leaks, depending on where the air goes.

A **pneumothorax** occurs when air leaks into the space between the baby's lungs and chest wall. Some pneumothoraces are so small that they don't cause any significant problems, and don't need treatment. Roughly one out of every hundred newborns has an insignificant pneumothorax. If a pneumothorax is large, though, or if a baby's respiratory function is marginal, as it is in many preemies, a pneumothorax can cause the baby's condition to deteriorate suddenly. The oxygen level in his blood drops, his blood pressure sinks, and his heart rate falls. The doctor can quickly check for a pneumothorax by shining a bright, transilluminating light on the baby's chest: the light shines through the chest wall, and pockets of air outside of the baby's

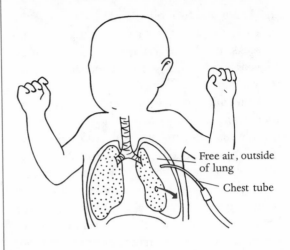

Air from a small tear in the lung (see arrow) leaks into the space between the lung and the chest wall. A chest tube can draw the air out, until the lung heals.

lungs show up as luminous patches. If necessary, a chest x-ray confirms the diagnosis.

A serious pneumothorax must be treated. The tear itself will heal on its own, the same way any minor cut would. But the air trapped between the lung and the chest wall must be removed, because the large pocket of air will press on the lung, causing it to collapse. The doctor may try simply sucking the air out with a needle and syringe. But if more air continues to collect, a minor surgical procedure is required. Right at the baby's bedside, the doctor makes a little incision in the baby's chest, and inserts a plastic tube into the space between the lung and chest wall. With continuous suction, the tube will draw out the air that has collected, and prevent more from reaccumulating.

Once the chest tube is working, your baby's condition will stabilize and the emergency is over. The tube usually has to stay there for several days—until the tear in the lung heals. Then the doctor will turn off the suction or close the tube off, and watch to make sure that no more air leaks out. If it doesn't, the tube can be removed, leaving just a tiny bandage on your baby's chest.

A preemie who has just one, isolated pneumothorax has a very good chance of healing up quickly and being just fine. One risk which doctors always watch for is an intraventricular hemorrhage: the rapid changes in blood pressure accompanying the pneumothorax can cause some of the delicate blood vessels in a preemie's brain to rupture. Your baby's doctor may ask for a head ultrasound, or may wait to see whether any symptoms of an intraventricular hemorrhage appear over the next few days. (If your baby does have an IVH, the doctor will tell you whether it was mild or severe, and you can read about what it means for your baby on page 164.) Most of the time, a baby's lung heals with no IVH. Once he is weaned from the ventilator, a recurrence of an air leak is extremely unlikely, and you can celebrate the fact that this incident is completely behind you.

For some babies, recovery goes less smoothly. A pneumothorax is one indication that a baby's lungs are being damaged by the ventilator, so a baby on a ventilator who has had one pneumothorax has a higher chance of getting a second one, especially if he has pulmonary interstitial emphysema (described below). Doctors can't predict which path your baby will take, but they can tell you that once he has been weaned to low ventilator settings, the risk of any further air leaks is low—and you can feel more confident that he's on his way to recovery.

Pulmonary interstitial emphysema is also a sign that a baby's lungs are being damaged by the ventilator, but in this case the damage is not just in an isolated area of the lung. It's more diffuse. Many airways and sacs develop tiny tears,

and air leaks out of them, into the small spaces in the tissues of the lung. Pulmonary interstitial emphysema is more difficult to treat than a pneumothorax. The leaked air cannot be drawn out with a tube, so the baby is simply supported on a ventilator, waiting for his lungs to gradually heal, and the leaked air to get reabsorbed. Babies with PIE, as you might hear this condition called, are often placed on lower ventilator pressures, and allowed to have lower oxygen saturations, so as to minimize the lung damage caused by the ventilator. They may also be switched to a relatively new kind of ventilator, a high-frequency ventilator, that may be gentler on the lungs (see page 163).

Babies who develop PIE often have severe respiratory problems, and need to be on higher than average ventilator settings for longer periods. As a result, many babies with PIE develop bronchopulmonary dysplasia, or chronic lung disease. Try not to get too discouraged after reading this: not all babies do, and some get mild cases that resolve before they're a couple of years old. Your baby's doctor can help you understand how your baby is faring now, and what she expects to happen in the future. If it becomes necessary, you can read about BPD on page 261.

Why some babies get air leaks and others don't is one of the toughest questions to answer. The best we can do is to explain why some babies are more susceptible than others—but you may never know why your little one, in particular, was one of the fewer than 20% of premature babies with RDS to develop one.

Premature babies who are on ventilators at high settings are more susceptible to air leaks; the high pressures and levels of oxygen that are so beneficial to them also do gradual damage to their lungs. Babies with more immature lungs sustain more damage, as do those who "fight"

High-Frequency Ventilators and How They Might Help

Today's premature babies who have air leaks, or who require high levels of respiratory support, have a resource that preemies of past generations did not have: high-frequency ventilators, the newest innovation in ventilator design. The main advantage of high-frequency ventilators is that they are probably gentler on the lungs. While conventional ventilators use high pressures to deliver breaths, and maintain a relatively normal pattern of inhalation and exhalation, high-frequency ventilators provide tiny quantities of air at rapid rates using lower peak pressures, and keep the lungs continuously inflated. It's strange to see your baby being ventilated this way—not being given conventional, deep, in-and-out breaths, but being jiggled as if she were getting a vibrating massage. But some studies have shown that babies on high-frequency ventilators have a lower incidence of air leaks and chronic lung disease, because these machines do less damage to their lungs.

Why shouldn't every premature baby who needs a ventilator be given the benefit of a gentler-on-the-lungs approach? Because there may be risks associated with high-frequency ventilators, too. For instance, babies on the new vents need more sedation (to keep them from breathing too much on their own, which would interfere with this ventilator's special process) and may have lower blood pressure. Some studies—though not all—have shown a slightly higher incidence of intraventricular hemorrhage and periventricular leukomalacia (PVL, see page 285). Also, a high-frequency ventilator may not work as well as a conventional one if a baby has a lot of mucus plugs or needs frequent suctioning.

Given the benefits and unknowns, different doctors make different judgments about when to put a baby on a high-frequency ventilator. Some will start out with it. Some will switch a baby who has had a pneumothorax to a high-frequency ventilator, while others will wait to see if it's an isolated incident, or if it recurs. High-frequency ventilation is often tried for babies who are not improving on conventional ventilators, or who have complications like pulmonary interstitial emphysema (PIE), persistent pulmonary hypertension, pneumonia, or a pulmonary hemorrhage.

If your baby is on a high-frequency ventilator, you'll see his body shaking with the vibrations. It's nothing to worry about. In fact, adults who have been on such ventilators describe it as soothing. We shouldn't be surprised: haven't people been paying for vibrating beds and massages for a long time?

against the ventilator (exhaling against the vent's incoming breaths). Babies whose lungs are smaller than normal (for example, some who are born weeks after their mother's water broke), or those with pneumonia, are also more prone to air leaks. On the other hand, preemies who are given surfactant soon after birth are less likely to have air leaks. (Since surfactant works so well in improving a newborn preemie's lungs, some parents wonder why it isn't given again if their babies have air leaks. Studies have shown no benefit when surfactant was given after the first few days of life, or after the first few doses—probably because by then, a preemie's lung problems are no longer caused by inadequate amounts of surfactant.)

It is heartbreaking for many parents, seeing their babies with a chest tube, to wonder whether they are uncomfortable or in pain. We have some advice for you: Don't wonder silently. It's too hard on you, and doesn't help your baby. Instead, talk to your baby's doctor, and ask what is being done to keep your baby comfortable. The practice of pain control still varies widely among NICUs, as explained on page 109. Most likely, although your baby may have felt some pain when the air leak occurred—neonatologists really don't know—he's resting comfortably now. Most NICUs give pain medication before putting a chest tube in, and if the baby seems at all agitated later, while the chest tube is in place, most doctors will give him more pain reliever or a sedative. Nevertheless, if you suspect that your baby is uncomfortable, don't hesitate to say so. You may influence the doctor to give your baby more relief, or, alternatively, will hear why he doesn't think it's needed—which may set your anxious mind at rest.

IN PLAIN LANGUAGE: WHAT IS AN INTRAVENTRICULAR HEMORRHAGE?

Since a premature baby's brain is still at an early stage of development, it is not quite ready to withstand all of the stress of living outside of the womb. Some tiny blood vessels in an inner part of preemies' brains are especially fragile, and vulnerable to changes in blood flow. If they rupture, bleeding occurs in or near the ventricles, which are fluid-filled chambers located within the brain. This is why doctors call this event an intraventricular ("intra" means inside), or sometimes periventricular ("peri" means near), hemorrhage. (You'll also hear the abbreviations IVH or PVH.)

An intraventricular hemorrhage is an often inescapable consequence of a premature birth. Fortunately, in most cases the bleeding is mild, and completely benign. Concern for a baby's health arises, however, when the bleeding is large and widespread, because in the worst scenario it can lead to permanent brain injury, or even to death.

When doctors find out that a baby had a moderate or severe intraventricular hemorrhage, they will inform his family about the possible negative consequences. From personal experience, we know that this is heartbreaking news. But after the initial, unavoidable shock, you should try to remember that a preemie's brain, which is still developing, has tremendous resilience, and how he is doing now counts for a lot. If he is stable, without significant respiratory complications or other abnormal symptoms, he has a good chance of overcoming a serious intraventricular hemorrhage—and being developmentally untouched by it.

WHY SOME BABIES HAVE AN IVH AND OTHERS DON'T

As with many complications of prematurity, the younger, smaller, and sicker a baby is at birth, the more likely he is to develop an intraventricular hemorrhage. Today, a baby with a birth weight less than 1,000 grams has a 50% to 60% chance of developing an IVH, while the risk for older and bigger babies, weighing between 1,000 grams and 1,500 grams at birth, is only 10% to 20%.

Abrupt changes or disturbances in blood flow or blood pressure to the brain can cause an IVH. The trauma of birth itself—labor and delivery—is a risk factor in a premature baby. Mechanical ventilation is another cause of IVH, particularly when the baby is breathing out of synchrony with the ventilator. Even common medical procedures, like suctioning or being weighed, can overstimulate a preemie and increase the risk of a bleed.

Premature babies who were treated before delivery with steroids are less likely to have an IVH. (Steroids speed up the maturation of the brain, as well as other organs.) Treating preemies after delivery with a medication called indomethacin may also help to prevent IVHs, possibly by altering blood flow patterns. The use of synchronized ventilation and heavy sedation may be helpful, although this has not been demonstrated conclusively. And Developmental Care advocates are trying to prove that an individualized, gentler treatment regimen (see page 198) can lower rates of IVH.

DIAGNOSIS: THE HEAD ULTRASOUND

Ninety percent of all IVHs take place during the first three days of a preemie's life and fully 97% take place within the first seven days. So if your baby doesn't have an IVH at one week of age, you can relax; he is unlikely ever to have one.

Premature babies who are at risk for bleeding in the brain, usually those born before 32 weeks of gestation or weighing less than 1,500 grams, are routinely given a head ultrasound in the first three to ten days of life, or as soon as doctors suspect an IVH might have occurred. The ultrasound scan, or sonogram, is a completely harmless test that allows doctors to look into a tiny baby's head without disturbing him. It doesn't involve radiation like an x-ray, but uses sound waves to record images on videotape. A technician brings the ultrasound machine to the baby's isolette or bed, squirts some gel and places a transducer on the soft spot at the top of the baby's head (where his skull is still open), and carefully scans the area. The whole thing takes only about fifteen minutes, and the resulting pictures of the brain are detailed and precise. Later, the videotape is analyzed, usually by a pediatric radiologist, neurologist, or neonatologist.

HOW INTRAVENTRICULAR HEMORRHAGES ARE CLASSIFIED

The brain, with its complex organization of different structures, may be the least familiar of all organs of the human body to those who are not physicians. The illustration shows, in cross-section, where IVHs occur.

IVHs usually begin with the rupture of

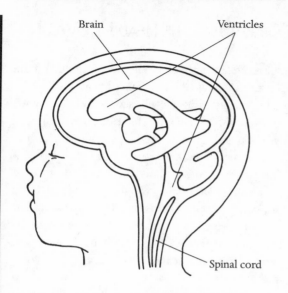

Brain

Ventricles

Spinal cord

The cerebrospinal fluid, circulating around the brain, is collected in chambers called ventricles and flows down, into and around the spinal cord. The germinal matrix lies along the ventricles.

delicate blood vessels in the germinal matrix, a primitive and fragile region of the brain along the ventricles, which is very active during the development of the brain. The germinal matrix gets smaller as the fetus matures, disappearing by approximately 32 to 34 weeks of gestation: that's why IVHs rarely occur in older preemies.

The germinal matrix is located along the lining of the ventricles—a series of connected chambers that are filled with cerebrospinal fluid. This fluid, which functions as a cushion for the brain and spinal cord, circulates around the brain, is collected by the ventricles, and flows down into the spinal canal. Cerebrospinal fluid is constantly being produced and reabsorbed—if not enough fluid is reabsorbed, it can build up to dangerous levels.

Intraventricular hemorrhages are given a grade, depending on their location and size:

* *MILD—Grade 1.* This is also called a periventricular hemorrhage, because it doesn't get into the ventricles. The mildest type of bleeding, it begins and remains in the germinal matrix.
* *MILD—Grade 2.* From the germinal matrix, some blood ruptures into the ventricles, but it doesn't cause the ventricles to enlarge.
* *MODERATE—Grade 3.* A substantial amount of blood pours into the ventricles, causing them to swell.
* *SEVERE—Grade 4.* A hemorrhage outside the ventricles, in the substance (usually the white matter) of the brain. Babies with grade 4 bleeds have bleeding from other blood vessels in the brain, in addition to germinal matrix bleeding.

Among all babies who are found to have an IVH, 40% will have a grade 1, 30% will have a grade 2, 20% will have a grade 3, and 10% will have a grade 4.

AFTER A MILD IVH

If your baby had only a mild intraventricular hemorrhage (grade 1 or 2), you really don't have to worry. There's very little risk of short-term complications, and the odds of your baby growing up normal are just as high as those of other preemies without bleeds. In a week or so, doctors will want to check whether the hemorrhage has gotten bigger, because about 20% do enlarge. But even if this happens, there's only a small risk that your baby's good prognosis will change. So take heart and don't focus on the next head ultrasound. Most likely, he'll have just one or two more, and you'll soon forget all about intraventricular hemorrhages.

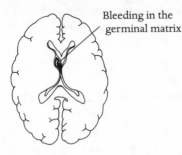

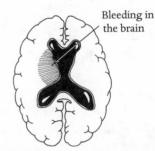

MILD—Grade 1. The mildest bleeding, it stays within the germinal matrix and doesn't reach the ventricles.

MILD—Grade 2. Some blood enters the ventricles without enlarging them.

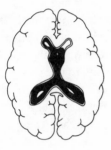

MODERATE—Grade 3. A lot of blood in the ventricles makes them swell.

SEVERE—Grade 4. The hemorrhage occurs beyond the ventricles, in the substance of the brain.

Adapted with permission from Rozmus C: Periventricular-intraventricular hemorrhage in the newborn, *MCN* 17(2):79, Lippincott-Raven Publishers, Philadelphia, PA 1992

AFTER A MODERATE OR SEVERE IVH: SHORT-TERM OUTCOME

Most babies with moderate bleeds will be fine in the short run. They will not have abnormal neurological symptoms, and their general health won't worsen significantly. This is great news, because it gives hope for a positive outcome.

But an IVH of grade 3 can carry some immediate risk for babies, and the danger increases with an IVH of grade 4. Babies with moderate to severe bleeds may have a sudden worsening of breathing, a drop in heart rate or blood pressure,

and seizures or abnormal posturing. These symptoms of brain swelling and inflammation are most commonly mild and transient, but they can sometimes lead, within minutes to days, to death. The risk that this will happen is 10% after a grade 3 IVH, and 50% after a grade 4.

Many preemies need one or more blood transfusions after a moderate or large intraventricular hemorrhage. If the doctor suspects an infection in or around the baby's brain may have been responsible for the bleeding or for any of his symptoms, she may start antibiotics or do a lumbar puncture (also called a spinal tap). In this procedure, a needle is carefully inserted between two vertebrae (back bones) in the lower, or lumbar, segment of the baby's spine. The needle withdraws a sample of the cerebrospinal fluid, which is sent for biochemical analysis and culture.

After a grade 3 or 4 IVH, your baby's head circumference will be measured every day: a simple but crucial test to watch for progressive hydrocephalus (an excess of cerebrospinal fluid in the ventricles).

HYDROCEPHALUS: THE MOST COMMON COMPLICATION OF A GRADE 3 OR 4 IVH

The word *hydrocephalus* comes from Latin, meaning "water in the head." Twenty per cent of babies with a grade 3 IVH, and 65% to 100% (depending on the location of the hemorrhage) of surviving babies with a grade 4 IVH, will suffer from persistent hydrocephalus.

This complication is the result of a hydraulic problem created by a severe bleed. Blood clots and scar tissue can plug the normal drainage of cerebrospinal fluid out of the ventricles, disrupting its flow and reabsorption. If too much fluid accumulates inside the ventricles, they can swell. When an adult gets hydrocephalus, perhaps from a head injury, the resulting very high pressure on the brain can give him an instant headache, make him vomit, or possibly even make him go into a coma. If the pressure is not rapidly relieved by removal of fluid from the ventricles in an emergency procedure, irreversible brain injury or death can result.

Fortunately, babies have a natural defense system against hydrocephalus. Their tender skull bones are not yet fused together. So the swelling of the ventricles makes the whole head expand, enlarging its circumference. Much of the pressure on the brain is relieved.

What to do if your baby has hydrocephalus

If your baby's head seems to be growing too fast, he will probably get frequent head ultrasounds to check the size of his ventricles. Sometimes their swelling will stabilize in a couple of weeks, and no intervention or surgery will be needed.

If your baby's head keeps enlarging, he will be watched closely for signs of excessive pressure on his brain: sleepiness, inability to nipple feed, increasing episodes of apnea and bradycardia, and hypertension. If these occur, it is important to act quickly to prevent brain damage. Today, the only effective way to treat hydrocephalus is with neurosurgery (see page 316). Medications that decrease the production of cerebrospinal fluid don't work well and can have serious side effects, but are sometimes used temporarily if surgery must be delayed. Immediate relief of pressure inside the ventricles can also be obtained by taking fluid out of the spinal canal with a spinal tap, or out of the ventricles directly, with a ventricular tap (a needle is inserted through the soft spot in a baby's skull and carefully advanced into the ventricle, where some cerebrospinal fluid is withdrawn). But the effect of these taps is very transient, and they are usually used only as a temporizing measure, until surgery can be performed.

Some babies, despite their expanding head size, continue to do fine—sleeping, eating, and growing as before. They may need surgery eventually, but not necessarily right away; they can grow a little older and stronger before going to the operating room. In the meantime, some NICUs attempt to avoid neurosurgery altogether by doing a series of spinal taps, often one or two a week for two to three weeks, hoping that as the blood clot in the ventricle shrinks, cerebrospinal fluid drainage will improve.

You should discuss with your neonatologist and neurosurgeon what chance your baby has of avoiding an operation, and what the risks are of postponing surgery. If they tell you that your baby can wait, trust them and try to relax. It is normal for you to be very scared, but don't stop giving your baby all of the cuddling he needs from you. Remember that if his head is growing, it means he is defending himself well. Don't give up on kangaroo care, if you are doing it, or on your breastfeeding attempts. Some parents become so obsessed by the daily rite of the head circumference measurement that they end up losing sight of everything else. Remember that your baby can grow up normal, despite the hydrocephalus. Between early detection and today's excellent surgical techniques, babies have a better chance than ever before of overcoming this condition.

WHAT YOU CAN EXPECT IN THE LONG RUN

The long-term outcome of premature babies who had an intraventricular hemorrhage depends on the extent of the injury caused by the lack of blood flow and oxygen to the brain around the time of the bleed, and from its complications. Although bleeding can be detected on the first head ultrasound, the kind of damage most closely associated with long-term problems takes several weeks to show up on a head ultrasound (see periventricular leukomacia on page 285). Some forms of brain damage are invisible on a head ultrasound, but between the ultrasound findings, and observations of a preemie's neurological behavior and develop-

ment, doctors can generally make some reasonable predictions of what his family can expect before he is discharged from the hospital.

Statistics on long-term developmental outcomes after IVH vary a lot. Approximately 65% of preemies who had a grade 3 IVH and 25% of preemies who had a grade 4 IVH were found normal in follow-up studies. Consequences of a moderate or severe IVH can range from mild developmental problems, like low-grade cerebral palsy, or partial sight, hearing, or speech impairment, to serious handicaps, like severe cerebral palsy, mental retardation, blindness, or deafness.

Why do some preemies who survive a grade 3 or 4 intraventricular hemorrhage grow up completely normal, while others don't? It probably has to do with the size and location of the bleed (a smaller hemorrhage, or one that affects just one side of the brain, is easier to recover from), whether the insult that caused the bleeding also injured other parts of the brain, and a variety of factors (many, as yet, undefined) that influence the resilience and plasticity of the brain.

Some studies have shown an improvement over time in children who were found neurologically impaired at an early age: encouraging news, testifying to the brain's self-repairing ability. On the other hand, some learning disabilities may become apparent only at school age.

It is very important for parents to understand that the results of research studies represent just the average outcome of large groups of babies. They don't take into consideration what really counts for you: your baby's unique medical course, how he is doing now, and the attention and stimulation he'll be getting in his early months and years to give him the best possible start in life. These are the factors that make your baby's future different—and possibly better—than average.

Seizures

The doctors say they can't tell for sure if my son is having seizures. I don't understand this. I've seen someone have a seizure, and there's nothing subtle about it.

You're right that when an adult has a seizure, it's usually an unmistakable event. But seizures in a premature infant can be so subtle that they're easy to miss, by parents or trained observers. Once you know how a seizure works, it's easy to understand why.

A seizure occurs when there are abnormal electrical discharges in the brain. Picture it as a kind of short circuit of the brain's normal nerve signals, due to a brain injury or irritant. In an adult, these abnormal signals usually lead to an obvious seizure, but in a preemie, whose behavior and nerve connections in the brain are still immature, the same disturbances show up in less obvious ways. Usually seizures cause a slight variation of normal preemie behavior.

There might be one or more of the following:

* twitching of the arms or legs;
* fluttering of the eyelids;
* sustained opening of the eyes, with a fixed gaze;
* trembling of the mouth, sucking motions, or drooling;
* rhythmic movements of the arms or legs (called "swimming," "rowing," or "pedaling");
* stiffening or arching of the back, or of the arms or legs;
* a spell of apnea.

But different from a seizure, a preemie's normal jittery movements can be stopped—by restraining the baby's arms and legs, or placing a calming hand on the baby—while seizure activity cannot.

If the doctor suspects that your baby is having seizures, he will probably ask for an EEG. This is a painless test for your baby, in which electrodes attached to little pads are placed on his head, to record the electrical activity in his brain.

Sometimes an EEG is definitive: some abnormal brainwave patterns are clearly recognizable as seizures. But even EEGs can leave the doctors unsure. Other irregularities may be seizures, or may simply result from medications a baby is taking, stress, illness, or the very fact that he is a preemie, with a brain that behaves in immature ways. Ideally, your baby's EEG will be read by a pediatric neurologist who has experience with premature babies. A normal EEG is a very good sign, but it doesn't tell you that an episode that occurred before the EEG was performed was definitely not a seizure. The doctors may also want a CT scan or MRI of your baby's brain—detailed pictures that should reveal any swelling, bleeding, or structural abnormality that might be causing seizures.

There are a few common causes of seizures in premature babies. One is a severe intraventricular hemorrhage, which most often leads to just one or two transient seizures at the time of the bleed—although occasionally, scarring in the brain causes the seizures to continue. Babies with severe birth asphyxia can have seizures beginning several hours after birth. Another common cause is infection—especially meningitis, an infection around the brain. With meningitis, seizures may continue if there is lasting damage to the brain, but otherwise don't recur. Metabolic problems—levels of glucose, sodium, calcium, and other substances that are too high or low—are another major cause of seizures. When the metabolic imbalances are fixed, the seizures stop. But some premature babies' seizures remain a mystery: no cause is ever found.

You may be wondering: why don't the doctors treat my baby for seizures just in case, whether they're sure or not? Because as usual, there are pros and cons to treatment. On the one hand, it makes sense to treat seizures, since some of them may be harmful. During a seizure, the brain uses up a lot of oxygen and glucose, so it may not get enough of those crucial substances. While one brief episode probably causes no trouble, a long, sustained seizure could cause damage to some of the brain's cells. And if the seizures are accompanied by apnea, a baby may need to be put on a ventilator.

On the other hand, the most common treatment for seizures—a medication called phenobarbital—works by sedating the brain. Phenobarb, as you'll hear the NICU staff call it, is usually effective in controlling seizures. The concern is that it may turn the brain down in bad ways as well as good, interfering with a baby's learning. In long-term studies of premature babies, those who were on phenobarbital for long periods tended to do less well developmentally than their peers. Thus, many doctors don't treat babies who have had a single seizure, since it might be an isolated incident that won't recur. When babies have had more than one seizure, though, most doctors agree on treating them.

Here's an important thing that's often misunderstood: one or two seizures in a preemie is not the same as epilepsy, which is an ongoing seizure disorder. Most premature babies with seizures have a temporary problem, and will never develop epilepsy. So treatment doesn't have to last long.

Most of the time, coming off medication involves some trial and error—the doctors try taking the baby off as soon as they think the seizures won't recur, and watch to see how he does. If the problem is metabolic, as soon as it's fixed the baby can come off medication. If the seizure occurred with an intraventricular hemorrhage or meningitis, many neurologists would keep the baby on medication for several months. If there's an underlying brain abnormality, or a scar from a severe IVH, treatment would probably continue longer.

How a preemie who had seizures will do in the future depends on the underlying problem that caused them. Lasting brain injuries may be associated with developmental problems that range from mild to severe. Your baby's development will be monitored closely after his discharge from the NICU, to detect any problems early and help insure that he reaches his maximum potential. But many seizures have temporary causes, and babies leave them behind, with no signs of long-term neurological damage.

Since the doctors aren't even sure that your baby is having seizures, you should definitely try not to imagine the worst. He may have no problem at all, or one that needs attention, but with treatment will soon pass, never to return.

High Blood Pressure in Baby's Lungs

The doctor says my baby is needing higher vent settings than he expected, because of high blood pressure in her lungs. Why would she have that?

Sometimes the blood pressure in a baby's lungs doesn't fall as it should when she starts breathing at birth, but instead stays very high. This condition is called persistent pulmonary hypertension, and it can be clearly diagnosed with an echocardiogram. Neonatologists usually suspect it when a baby's oxygen levels are lower or more erratic than they expected.

Persistent pulmonary hypertension may be caused by severe respiratory distress syndrome, or pneumonia, or even by a baby having had recurrent episodes of fetal distress. It is much more common in term babies and older preemies, because only lungs that are relatively mature can sustain very high blood pressures.

Why are your baby's vent settings high? Because the high blood pressure in her lungs creates a tremendous obstacle to the incoming blood pumped by the heart, blocking it from flowing into her lungs. In essence, your baby's blood continues to circulate in its fetal route, partly bypassing her lungs, just like before birth. When blood doesn't get into the lungs, it can't pick up oxygen, so her oxygen saturations fall. The illustration on page 177, showing how the blood circulates in a fetus, may help you understand what's going on. As long as your baby's blood is still flowing in its fetal route, a fetal blood vessel that normally closes at birth (called the ductus arteriosus) thinks it is supposed to stay open, and does. Much of her blood bypasses her lungs by going through the patent—meaning open—ductus arteriosus (or PDA).

Although serious, pulmonary hypertension usually resolves in four or five days. The first treatment is more oxygen. Some babies will need to be put on a ventilator to improve their oxygenation. If a baby is already on a ventilator, the settings may be raised, as happened to your baby. Her doctors may decide to use various medications to try to lower the pressure in her lungs, and to help her heart beat more strongly.

Once the hypertension is gone, your baby's breathing should improve. Babies who had pulmonary hypertension are at a somewhat higher risk of developing chronic lung damage, due to the extra time they spent on high ventilator settings—but it's very possible that this will never become an issue for your daughter.

You might think that closing the PDA would solve the respiratory problem, but it won't. Some blood would still bypass the lungs through a small hole in the heart called the foramen ovale. Furthermore, the baby's heart would get so overworked from pumping blood into the lungs against high pressure, with no release, that it would give out. This is far worse than just waiting until the pulmonary hypertension resolves.

Most of the time, once the pulmonary hypertension resolves, the PDA closes on its own. If it doesn't, you can read about PDAs on page 176.

X-Rays

They are always x-raying my baby. I'm afraid she's going to be sterile or get cancer.

In our society, we all hear so much about health risks. That's helpful when it causes us to avoid serious, unnecessary risks—like when we stop smoking, or strap our kids into car seats. But when it causes us to worry about insignificant or unavoidable risks, it's doing a lot more harm than good.

No one needs groundless worry less than an already stressed parent of a preemie, so let us alleviate your anxiety: the chances that the x-rays will cause health problems for your baby are absolutely minuscule.

While no amount of radiation is truly "safe"—the less the better—there is a natural, background level of radiation that we're all exposed to in daily life, from sources like the sun, cosmic rays, the soil, and natural elements. Consider the amount of radiation (which is measured in units called rads) that your newborn gets from a chest x-ray, compared to the amount of radiation people get from other sources:

* Natural, background level of radiation at sea level: .08 rads per year
* Exposure of professional jet pilot and flight crews (from natural sources at high altitude): 1 rad per year
* U.S. government's permitted exposure for workers: 5 rads per year
* Radiotherapy done for curative, medical reasons: 7,000 rads per week
* Chest x-ray of a newborn: .004 rads.

In other words, only after your newborn gets 20 chest x-rays does he even reach the natural level of radiation we're all exposed to. (Some tests, such as CT scans, performed on preemies much less frequently than chest x-rays, have a higher radiation level. Ultrasound, on the other hand, involves no radiation at all.) Experts have calculated that it would take more than 2,000 chest x-rays for there to be any increase in your baby's cancer risk. Obviously, the dangers of withholding diagnostic x-rays from ill preemies would be far greater.

To guard against risk to a preemie's reproductive organs and genes, some nurseries used to shield a baby's genital area when other parts of his body were being x-rayed. This precaution isn't necessary anymore, though, so shields are hardly ever used. Today's x-ray technology is very good at reducing "scatter," meaning that the beam focuses on the precise area the doctors want to look at; if they're x-raying your baby's chest, hardly any radiation will reach her head or her toes. Essentially none will reach other babies in neighboring beds.

Why, then, do nurses often scurry from the room before the x-ray machine goes on? Partly from habit, left over from past years when x-ray machines did scatter more. And because unlike your baby, who will be leaving the nursery, the nurses may be around for thousands of x-rays a year over a period of twenty years or more. Interestingly, one study indicates that they still don't have to worry: the nurses in one intensive care nursery wore radiation badges (to calculate the amount of radiation they received). After one year, the badges found that the nurses' radiation exposure was no greater than the natural, background level of radiation that anyone else is exposed to.

So don't worry about your baby's x-rays. So far, there have been no reports of any premature babies who have been worse off because of x-rays—and many have been far better off because of them.

Suctioning Baby

Do the nurses have to suction my baby so often? He seems to hate it, and he always does worse while he's being suctioned and for a while afterward.

It is true that most preemies don't like to be suctioned. They may fight it, cough or gag, or respond with one of their special stress signals, like apnea or bradycardia, or a temporary loss of muscle tone. Their reaction is painful for parents to witness, but understandable. Who wouldn't hate getting a catheter put down their throat, to have their secretions sucked out?

Of one thing you can be certain, though: the nurses wouldn't suction your baby if he didn't need it. This unpleasant procedure is meant to clear your baby's airways and provide him with the pulmonary hygiene that he cannot achieve yet without help. Babies do seem to appreciate it afterward: once it's over and they settle down, many breathe more easily and quietly, have better oxygen saturations, and seem calmer than they were before.

Just consider this. A preemie has a tiny airway, more than four times smaller than that of an adult, so it can easily get clogged by mucus and other debris, such as cells the body naturally sheds, bacteria, or particles the baby breathes in. Preemies with respiratory distress syndrome, bronchopulmonary dysplasia, or respiratory infections, in particular, produce copious secretions. Older babies and adults can effortlessly clear their throats and airways with a cough, but a preemie's cough is still too weak. Moreover, when you're always lying down and not moving much, as preemies are, secretions tend to accumulate in the lungs, creating a risk of dangerous infections like pneumonia.

Pulmonary hygiene is especially useful to babies who are on ventilators. The vent's artificial airway prevents most self-cleansing activities, like sweeping mucus into the back of the throat, and coughing. The presence of the endotracheal tube itself increases secretions in the airways. So it is vitally important to suction the tube to keep it from getting obstructed.

Preemies on ventilators get their endotracheal tube suctioned with a catheter connected to a suction machine, usually every three to six hours, or when a change in their condition signals a need for it. Usually they're temporarily disconnected from the ventilator, and ventilated with an oxygen bag during suctioning. Babies who are breathing on their own may get suctioned with a bulb inserted in their nostrils, or with a catheter, connected to a suction machine, that goes down their throat. The goal is to remove secretions and stimulate coughing.

Even with regular suctioning, a plug of mucus might at some point block a baby's airway or endotracheal tube, stopping air flow and setting off all of his alarms. Nurses and doctors call this a plug episode, and they are always ready to react with quick, emergency suctioning (or by replacing the tube, if it is thoroughly clogged). If the preemie's parents are present, they will surely feel panic and terror. But as soon as the mucus plug is removed, and air flows through the tube and baby's lungs again, the crisis is over. So if this happens to your baby, try to remember that the NICU staff knows exactly how to handle such an unpleasant event.

Sometimes, mucus plugs block off branches of small airways deeper in the baby's lungs. When this happens, his breathing may not be affected as dramatically. But his blood gases and oxygenation will worsen, and a chest x-ray may show patches of collapsed lung where air can't get past the plug. Chest physiotherapy (or "chest PT") may help clear out these kinds of plugs. Because its effectiveness is controversial, some nurseries use chest PT, and others don't.

Chest physiotherapy involves percussion or vibration: the nurse gently taps or vibrates a small area of the preemie's chest or back, to loosen the mucus in the underlying part of the lungs. (Good pulmonary hygiene also involves changing a preemie's position every two or three hours: sometimes lying him on his back, sometimes on his stomach and both sides. Varying positions, with gravity, allows the secretions to move from different parts of the outer lungs into the central airways, where they can be expelled more easily.) Then comes suctioning.

During suctioning, the nurses are always careful to watch for your baby's stress signals; if they can, they'll stop and give him a rest if he's very uncomfortable. (Babies on vents might be sedated or given pain medication.) As soon as the few minutes of discomfort are over, your baby gets a great pleasure: breathing some very clear, deep sighs of relief!

Bleeding in Lungs

I saw blood coming out of my baby's ET tube, and it scared me to death. The nurse tried to explain what was happening, but I was too shocked to understand. How serious is this, and what does it mean?

When a premature baby is on a ventilator, it's not uncommon to notice some streaks of blood in his mucus when he's being suctioned. Both the endotracheal tube and the suctioning procedure can bruise the inner lining of the airways, causing them to bleed slightly. This may be an upsetting sight, but it's nothing to worry about if it only happens occasionally. If the nurse thinks it was caused by suctioning too deeply, she may try to advance the suction tube less far down next time.

Sometimes, a copious amount of blood mixed with secretions can come up a baby's ET tube, or leak from his mouth if he's not intubated. This is a visible sign of what doctors call a pulmonary hemorrhage. It comes from deeper in the lungs than the other, lesser bleeding that results from injury to the upper airways, and is thought to be the result of overly high blood pressure in the small vessels of the lungs (the capillaries), which causes an increase of fluids (water and blood) in the surrounding tissues. Eventually, this excessive buildup of fluids can damage the delicate lung tissues of a preemie, bursting through them into the air sacs and the airways.

If it happens to your baby while you're visiting him, it's understandable that you'd be very scared. But you should try not to panic or despair. Although it usually requires medical intervention, this complication is most often treatable, and usually less serious than it may look to a shocked parent. Some babies, due to their compromised respiration and the loss of blood and fluid, appear very pale, limp, and sick. Other babies will keep on doing surprisingly well, during and after the pulmonary hemorrhage.

Pulmonary hemorrhages are more likely to occur in extremely premature babies with severe respiratory distress syndrome. Most at risk are preemies who also have a patent ductus arteriosus. The reason is that a PDA allows too much blood to flow into the lungs, leading to increased blood pressure in the lungs, and fluid buildup. Other complications can also increase a baby's chance of developing a pulmonary hemorrhage, such as having suffered from a severe lack of oxygen at birth, having an infection, or a blood clotting disorder. Being on a ventilator, an otherwise beneficial medical treatment, increases the likelihood of bleeding, because it can damage a baby's lung tissues. Also, surfactant therapy, although effective in treating RDS, can predispose a baby to a pulmonary hemorrhage.

A pulmonary hemorrhage usually needs immediate treatment:

* The first priority is to help the baby's breathing, keeping his lungs well inflated. If he is on a ventilator, the machine will probably be adjusted to higher settings to improve his oxygenation. (A restless baby, who fights" against the machine, may need to be sedated.)
* The baby may be given fluid, blood, or special medications to improve blood clotting or heart function.
* If a PDA is identified as the cause of the pulmonary hemorrhage, it will most likely be treated (see page 176). Most doctors wait to give indomethacin (the usual treatment) until the bleeding has stopped, because indomethacin can interfere with blood

clotting. If the medication doesn't work, the ductus can be closed surgically.

When your baby's vital signs have stabilized, the crisis is over and you should try to relax.

Your baby will have to be gradually weaned from his higher vent settings, as his lungs heal. But a pulmonary hemorrhage, as scary as it is, is something from which most preemies recover.

IN PLAIN LANGUAGE: WHAT IS A PDA?

PDA stands for patent (which means open) ductus arteriosus (which means arterial canal in Latin). A PDA is not an anatomical flaw. It is simply a blood vessel near the heart and lungs that was a normal, necessary part of your preemie's circulation when he was a fetus. It's meant to close within a few days after birth, then disappear. But in many premature babies the PDA lingers, making it more difficult for the baby to recover from complications like respiratory distress syndrome. In that case, the PDA is treated—with medications or, more rarely, with surgery. Some 40% to 50% of all preemies under 34 weeks of gestation have a PDA, but only about 10% of preemies with a PDA will end up needing surgery.

A BIG CHANGE, FROM THE WOMB TO THE WORLD

When a baby is born, he has to leave his sheltered environment in the womb and start breathing on his own. That pivotal first breath triggers a big change in the baby's lungs—opening them up and filling them with air. As a fetus, he got oxygen from the placenta. But after birth, the baby's blood circulation must switch to a new route: the blood must travel to the lungs to pick up oxygen. This re-routing of blood flow, among other events, involves closure of the PDA.

As the picture on page 177 shows, the ductus arteriosus is a small blood vessel connecting the pulmonary artery (the main blood vessel going from the heart to the lungs) and the aorta (the biggest artery, carrying blood from the heart to the rest of the body). Before birth, the ductus is open, so most of the blood flowing from the heart into the pulmonary artery goes through it and bypasses the fetus's lungs (which are not used yet for breathing). The blood goes into the aorta, where it flows back to the placenta to get oxygen. When breathing starts at birth, and the lungs expand with air, blood flow to them increases. A sudden rise in the blood oxygen level, among other signals, gives the PDA the message that it's time to close.

The first phase of closure generally occurs within a baby's first few days of life. The ductus tightens and shrinks, so no blood flows through it. In the second phase, which occurs over the next several weeks to months, the PDA is replaced by scar tissue, becoming just a thread.

In some preemies, the PDA doesn't close spontaneously. In others, it tightens and closes

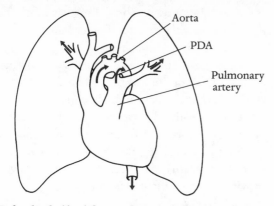

Before birth: blood flowing from the heart through the pulmonary artery is diverted into the aorta through the PDA, bypassing the lungs (not yet used for breathing).

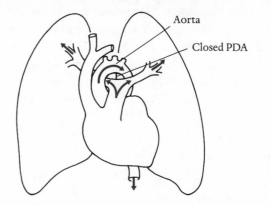

After birth, with a closed PDA: normal circulation.

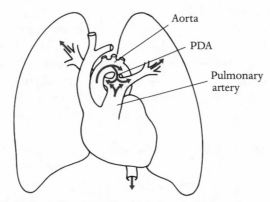

After birth, with a PDA: blood can flow back through the PDA from the aorta into the pulmonary artery, burdening the lungs with too much blood.

briefly, but re-opens before scarring takes place, and blood begins flowing through it again.

What If the PDA Remains Open?

After delivery, when a baby begins breathing, the blood flow shifts direction through the PDA: now it goes from the aorta to the pulmonary artery, adding to the blood that the lungs are get-

ting. If the PDA is starting to shrink, allowing just a little blood to go through, the baby may not be disturbed by it at all. On the other hand, if the ductus is still large and open wide, it may burden the lungs with too much blood, making it harder for the baby to breathe, and overloading the heart with work to pump extra blood to compensate for the PDA. A large PDA can lead to complications like pulmonary edema (a buildup of fluid in the lungs), chronic lung disease, necrotizing enterocolitis (a bowel dis-order—a PDA can cause decreased blood flow to the intestine), and congestive heart failure. (This latter, scary term isn't an irrevocable ver-dict, but a treatable, if still serious, condition, in which the heart shows signs of not being able to pump all the blood that the body needs.)

How a PDA Is Suspected, and Diagnosed

A PDA is generally diagnosed by a baby's neona-tologist, in consultation with a pediatric cardi-ologist. There are several clues that raise suspicions of a PDA:

* A murmur on a chest exam—but sometimes a PDA is completely silent
* An increase in the baby's heart rate, or bounding pulses in his arms, legs, or chest
* Low blood pressure
* Widening of the blood pressure interval (for instance from 60/40 to 70/20)
* Worsening of a baby's breathing problems.

This last possibility can be a real disappoint-ment, arising just when a preemie with RDS should be rapidly weaning from a ventilator or supplemental oxygen. Why does the weaning become so difficult? For several days after birth, while a preemie is still suffering from RDS and receiving respiratory assistance, the pressure in his lungs remains high. The high pressure in the lungs blocks some of the blood flow from the PDA (just as a clogged drain won't let much wa-ter through), so the lungs don't get overloaded with blood. But after a few days, and as the baby recovers from RDS, his lungs expand and the pressure in them falls. Like a drain opening up,

the blood then flows into the lungs through the PDA, stressing them, and often causing a recur-rence of respiratory problems.

The diagnosis of a PDA can be suspected from a chest x-ray, but the way to confirm it is with an echocardiogram: a completely benign, painless test that uses sound waves to get a clear picture of the structure and function of your baby's heart and surrounding blood vessels. An echocardiogram can be performed without even moving a preemie from his isolette.

How a PDA Is Treated

If your baby has a PDA but, thankfully, no symp-toms, he may not need any intervention. The doctors will monitor him carefully, to catch signs of any possible complication early. The PDA may close by itself, and you'll soon forget about it, and its pretentious Latin name!

Other medical problems, such as anemia and infection, might worsen a PDA, or prevent its natural closure. Doctors are aware of these con-ditions, and will try to correct them.

But if your baby's PDA looks like it's delaying his recovery from RDS, or causing other com-plications, doctors will want to act quickly. They will most likely prescribe indomethacin (also known as indocin), a drug that can cause the PDA to shrink and close. Indomethacin is given intravenously, usually as three doses over a cou-ple of days. Your baby will be closely monitored for fluid retention and poor blood clotting—in-domethacin's major side effects. Most of the time, babies do fine with this medicine, and the PDA closes. Indomethacin, unfortunately, is much less effective after the first two weeks of a baby's life, although doctors may still decide to give it a try.

When indomethacin is not a good option, because the preemie is already too old (what an irony, for a premature baby!), the doctors think he can't tolerate its side effects, or his PDA is causing such problems that the doctors believe it should be closed immediately, the remaining option is surgery (see page 311). To parents, the idea of surgery on their little baby can be really unbearable. Some parents mistakenly think that an operation to close a PDA is heart surgery. But a PDA ligation doesn't touch the heart muscle at all. In fact, in many hospitals the operation is performed by general surgeons, not by cardiac surgeons. The risks involved are very small if it is performed by an expert surgical team.

Most important of all, once a persistent PDA has been closed, your baby's lungs and heart can recover and heal—often perfectly normally.

Low Blood Pressure

I've always heard that high blood pressure is a problem, but why are the doctors and nurses so concerned about low blood pressure in my baby?

All premature babies normally have lower blood pressure than full-term babies. That is not a problem. But because of their immaturity, their regulatory systems to keep blood pressure stable are not as effective. These systems are crucial to prevent sudden increases or decreases in blood pressure that can damage all vital organs.

If blood pressure falls under a certain level (doctors call this hypotension), some parts of the body will not receive enough blood, and that region's cells may be damaged. (The brain is particularly vulnerable in preemies, in part because of their susceptibility to intraventricular hemorrhage with changes in blood flow.) Thankfully, most of the time hypotension can be controlled and reversed, without causing any harm. In rare cases when a baby's hypotension is extremely severe despite treatment, the doctors may talk to his parents about the possibility of withdrawing life support, because of irreparable damage to the brain, heart, kidneys, or intestines.

Low blood pressure may signal that a newborn is dehydrated or anemic, and needs more fluid or blood, or that his heart is not pumping as strongly as it should. Very young preemies easily become dehydrated, because their skin and kidneys don't hold in fluids well. They can become anemic when their blood is frequently withdrawn for lab tests. Heart malfunction can occur because of metabolic disturbances (like abnormal levels of acid, electrolytes, and calcium in the blood), as a result of birth asphyxia (signaled by severe fetal distress during labor), or because of severe respiratory distress syndrome, or pulmonary hypertension. A PDA and infection are common causes of hypotension in preemies, because they can cause fluid shifts and mild heart failure. A sudden collapse of blood pressure can also be a sign of an acute complication, such as an air leak (see page 161).

All premature babies have their blood pressure checked frequently. The youngest and frailest are monitored constantly through an arterial catheter, to allow for immediate intervention if their blood pressure becomes dangerously low.

There are several ways to sustain and stabilize a preemie's blood pressure, if it falters. It may help to increase the volume of circulating blood, by giving fluid or a transfusion. Medications, such as dopamine and dobutamine, can be used to improve the blood-pumping ability of the heart. Hydrocortisone, a hormone that is part of the natural blood pressure regulatory system, may be given. Correcting metabolic abnormalities or an air leak will improve blood pressure quickly. And hypotension generally resolves as RDS, a PDA, or an infection get better.

The good news is that treatment for hypotension is usually effective, and lasting damage prevented.

Diagnosing Pneumonia

They don't know if my baby has pneumonia. Shouldn't they be able to tell?

It's disappointing, especially for parents trying to safeguard the health of their children, to be reminded that medicine is not an exact science. To make a diagnosis, both clinical evidence and experience—the so-called "clinical eye" of a good physician—are needed. But that detective process isn't always quick and smooth, and some questions may never be answered with certainty.

Pneumonia—an infection deep in the lung that impedes a baby's respiration—is particularly hard to verify in premature babies. Why? Because the symptoms of pneumonia can be the same as those of RDS, excess lung fluid (from a PDA, for example), an area of collapsed lung due to a plug of mucus, or inflammation caused by the ventilator. In each case, a preemie will breathe faster and harder than normal, and have lower oxygen levels in his blood. Even an x-ray of the baby's lungs cannot reliably distinguish pneumonia from many other, common respiratory problems in preemies.

What makes pneumonia even trickier is that it may be caused by different infectious agents: bacteria, viruses, or fungi, which can infect a preemie before birth, during delivery, or in the NICU. Depending on what kind of pneumonia is suspected, the doctors may perform different tests and cultures of a baby's respiratory secretions, nose, throat, eyes, blood, urine, or other tissues. But culture results can take up to several days for bacteria, and several weeks for viruses and fungi. And even then, a culture can be falsely negative if the infected tissue wasn't sampled (perhaps because it's too deep in the lung to reach), and falsely positive if it turns up simply harmless organisms from the upper airway that live in every baby's nose and throat.

Eventually, with patience and repeated tests, pneumonia and its cause can often be ascertained. But it may not be necessary or wise to pursue a definitive diagnosis. The most reliable cultures are obtained from deep in the lung, where the infection would be, but these may involve invasive tests, even a lung biopsy, that carry some risk. And it may be too dangerous to wait that long. As soon as doctors suspect pneumonia in a preemie, they'll give him a course of broad-spectrum antibiotics, to try to stop an infection before it gets worse. Usually, that does the trick. If not, they'll probably search further. If a guilty microorganism is found, your baby will get the appropriate antibiotic for as long as it is needed to eradicate the infection.

Besides antibiotics, a premature baby with pneumonia will get all sorts of supportive care in an NICU. He will often receive respiratory assistance, with extra oxygen or a ventilator, and his fluid intake and breathing will be watched closely. Everything will be done to help his lungs recover. This scary complication is, unfortunately, quite frequent among preemies; but they have an excellent chance of overcoming it.

Catching Infections from Other Babies

The baby in the isolette next to my son's has been diagnosed with an infection. Is my son going to get it?

Nurseries know all too well that good fences make good neighbors. All hospital nurseries take precautions to prevent the transmission of infections. They follow guidelines issued by the Centers for Disease Control and Prevention, and many American hospitals have infection control departments that formulate policies based on their own circumstances and special needs. So, you should feel reassured: if there were a significant risk that your baby's neighbor could spread his infection to other little patients, he would have been moved to an isolation room until he was no longer contagious.

Infections are spread in nurseries by two main routes. The first is by contact with an infected person's skin, stool, urine, saliva, or blood. The second is by breathing in droplets that are shed when the infected person coughs or sneezes. To prevent the spread of infection, the NICU medical staff follows standard rules such as washing their hands before touching a baby, changing gloves between patients, and carefully handling and disposing of every instrument or object that has come in contact with blood, body fluids, or broken skin.

The transmission of most infections that preemies get—such as diarrhea, urinary tract infections, skin and wound infections, and most kinds of sepsis, pneumonia, and meningitis—can be prevented just by observing these precautions. Preemies who have infections such as these don't need to be quarantined.

Infections spread by respiratory droplets include colds and flu, and some kinds of pneumonia. In order to infect another person the infectious agents must come in contact with his eyes, nose, or mouth. But, in most cases, droplets containing these microorganisms can be propelled in the air only a very short distance, and the germs have a short life span. So they can't reach babies in the next bed or isolette, which, by regulation, are spaced a certain distance apart. Nurses, however, can pick up these kinds of infection from babies. And sick staff and family members can infect babies with whom they're in very close contact. So, nurses, doctors, and relatives who get close to babies with respiratory infections, or who have colds themselves, will wear a hospital mask.

Infants who have infectious diseases that are more highly contagious, or that are resistant to conventional antibiotics, will be put in isolation rooms, or in an area of the nursery separated by screens or curtains until the danger of spreading the infection is past. Often, babies who are contagious are cared for by only a few members of the nursing staff, who then don't come in contact with unexposed babies. In that way, spread of the infection is limited.

Of course, no system is perfect, and there are occasional outbreaks of infection, or inadvertent exposure of the babies in the nursery to a disease like chicken pox. When outbreaks occur, hospitals often do some detective work to pinpoint the source, if possible, and do everything possible to interrupt the transmission. Babies who were exposed, but not yet infected, may be treated with preventive medications or vaccines, and sometimes quarantined until it's clear that they're not contagious.

It's natural for parents, who want to do everything to protect their preemie, to become nervous about what their baby is being exposed to in the nursery. But thanks to all of the precautions, most infections that preemies get they don't catch from their neighbors.

IN PLAIN LANGUAGE: INFECTIONS IN PREEMIES

Babies get infected by coming in contact with a potentially dangerous germ, or microorganism. The usual infectious microorganisms in preemies are bacteria, viruses, or fungi. Many of these live harmlessly (either temporarily or permanently) on a baby's skin, in her intestines and airways, or elsewhere in her body. But, sometimes, a microorganism overcomes a preemie's first-line defenses. It starts to reproduce very quickly, spreads to a place it shouldn't, and an infection results. If the infection remains small and contained (a superficial skin wound, for instance), it may resolve with only a local antibiotic, or no treatment at all. But other infections can be more serious, and damage vital organs like the lungs (pneumonia), liver (hepatitis), kidneys (urinary tract infection), or brain (meningitis). These infections require more extensive therapy. Most serious of all is when the bloodstream is invaded by many microorganisms. In that case, vital functions like body temperature, respiration, heart rate, and blood pressure can become unstable. Doctors call this *sepsis*. Luckily, thanks to antibiotic therapies and attentive supportive care, the majority of infected preemies recover well.

The most immature preemies, and those in intensive care the longest, are most at risk of infection. Premature babies are particularly vulnerable to infections for several reasons:

* Their immune systems are immature and don't fight off infections well;
* Life-saving intensive care techniques like intubation, catheterization, surgery, and treat-ment with medications like steroids increase a baby's risk for infection;
* The stress of being born early, and some of the medical complications of prematurity, afford opportunities for microorganisms to flourish;
* All hospitalized patients—including preemies—are exposed to germs that may be particularly virulent or resistant to conventional antibiotics.

DIAGNOSIS AND TREATMENT

The symptoms of infection in preemies are very non-specific, and can be confused with normal difficulties that preemies often have. Apnea and other breathing problems, low blood pressure, high or low blood sugar, anemia, abnormal blood cell counts, jaundice, feeding problems, even seizures and temperature instability—all may indicate an infection . . . or not. Your baby's doctor will probably suspect infection if there's been a sudden worsening of her condition, or if several new signs or symptoms show up at once.

The usual diagnostic workup for infection in preemies includes:

* Obtaining cultures of blood, urine, and often spinal fluid and other potentially infected sites, such as a baby's skin, eyes, or respiratory tract;
* X-rays of her chest and abdomen to look for signs of inflammation;

✺ Lab tests to make sure that an infected baby's organs are functioning appropriately, and that important substances like blood gases and calcium remain at normal levels. These tests of organ function are also used to gauge the severity of the infection.

Since early treatment is often crucial to reverse a preemie's symptoms, the doctor will probably start a course of broad-spectrum antibiotics while the infection is merely suspected, but not proven. When the cause is finally found (culture results may take several days to weeks), a more specific antibiotic may be used. Other therapies, such as transfusions, treatment of seizures, and support of breathing and blood pressure will be used if your baby needs them. If the infection hasn't cleared after a few days, and your baby has a central line (see page 275), the doctors may remove it, for fear that it may be harboring the infection.

Sometimes, frustratingly, no guilty culprit is found to be the organism behind your baby's worsening condition—leaving parents and doctors with lingering questions as to whether a preemie's symptoms were due to infection or not. You can read more about why this happens on page 180.

INFECTIONS PREEMIES MAY GET IN THE NICU

Most of the infections that preemies get while they're in the hospital are caused by their own body's microorganisms that get out of hand. But despite careful, preventive measures, preemies may also get infected by other patients, the medical staff, or visitors (see page 181).

INFECTIONS PREEMIES MAY GET AT BIRTH

Some preemies get infected around the time of birth. These so-called early-onset infections are usually caused by bacteria in the mother's birth canal (which may or may not infect the mother, too). They can be transmitted to the baby during, or just before, labor and delivery. Bacterial infections are a major cause of premature birth, and can provoke early delivery without infecting the baby. But when they do, a preemie can have life-threatening pneumonia, sepsis, or meningitis.

You may have been tested or treated during pregnancy or labor for the most notorious of these organisms—group B strep. If you were treated for group B strep, your baby's infection most likely was prevented. If your obstetrician suspected that you had chorioamnionitis (an infection of the membranes and amniotic fluid that often leads to premature delivery), she may have cultured your amniotic fluid, placenta, urine, and genital tract, and treated you with broad-spectrum antibiotics. Treatment of chorioamnionitis certainly helps to prevent spread of the infection to the baby, but it isn't always successful.

INFECTIONS PREEMIES MAY HAVE GOTTEN EARLIER IN PREGNANCY

Sometimes, an illness that a mother gets during pregnancy is transmitted to her fetus. Most common colds and flus don't harm the baby. But some infections, including syphilis and various viruses, such as HIV, rubella (which causes German measles), herpes, and others, can. The most serious of these so-called congenital infections result in miscarriages, premature delivery, birth defects, and problems with growth and development.

Babies who have congenital infections are often small for their gestational age. They can be severely ill with pneumonia, hepatitis, meningitis, and all the other signs of sepsis, or not show any symptoms. Some babies with congenital infections never develop symptoms, although they may remain contagious for months. Others have problems that show up later, such as difficulties with vision, hearing, motor skills, or learning.

The diagnosis of a congenital infection is usually made with cultures or other blood tests. Sometimes the infection is suspected because of findings on a baby's first physical exam (for example, a large liver or spleen, or a rash on her skin), initial lab abnormalities such as low blood cell counts, or the presence of calcified areas in her liver or brain that show up on x-rays or a head ultrasound.

Effective treatments are available for some of these congenital infections (for example, syphilis or toxoplasmosis), but not for all. If your baby has a congenital infection, her doctor will explain what further tests he'd recommend. He'll also discuss with you what can be done, and how to insure her best possible future growth and development.

PARENTS, PREEMIES, AND INFECTIONS

An infection is a truly scary event in a young preemie's life. If a mother or father is convinced that they were the cause of her illness, they may feel devastated. But try to remember that most of the time, no one really was to blame, and feeling guilty or assigning responsibility is a waste of your precious energy. Your baby needs you to stand strong at her side now, while she's going through this big trial, to help her feel comfortable, recover, and grow.

Handwashing

I'm really concerned about hygiene in the NICU. I always wash my hands before going in, but I've seen other people, including doctors and nurses, who don't seem as careful.

You're absolutely right to be careful. Simple handwashing with an antiseptic soap, before handling a premature baby, is the most effective way to control the spread of infection in a neonatal intensive care unit. All parents and visitors who come to the nursery to see their pree-

mies should wash their hands to get rid of the extra load of bacteria they may have picked up from sources of contamination, such as the knob of a public restroom door, or a bus seat.

What about their shoes, their clothes, their hair? Interestingly, several studies have shown that requiring visitors to cover their clothing with a clean hospital gown, or preventing family members from touching preemies, does not lower the rate of infection. Nor does prohibiting visitors in the NICU, even if the visitors include young children. You should, of course, avoid going to the nursery if you're sick with a cold or flu. And if you've been in contact with somebody who has a contagious illness, like an older child with measles or chicken pox, be sure to let the doctor or charge nurse know before you visit. They'll want to make sure that you're immune to that illness; if not, you could inadvertently expose the babies to it, even if you don't have any symptoms.

The medical staff is well aware of the risk of infection in premature babies, and the necessary strategies to control it. Handwashing between patients is mandatory in all NICUs. If the doctor or nurse expects to come in contact with blood, body fluids, skin sores, or mucous membranes—like when they put in an IV, or suction a baby's endotracheal tube—they will also wear gloves. Procedures that involve entering deep body spaces, like spinal taps or placing central lines, are performed under sterile conditions. And if a doctor or nurse must work in the nursery despite having a cold, they'll wear a mask over their nose and mouth, to prevent spreading any infectious droplets.

Visitors in hospital nurseries (who are mostly, like you, the parents of little patients), generally react in a responsible way, trying to comply with precautions to control infections. But people get ill at unpredictable times, and can forget about doing things. Thus, if you look around you in a neonatal intensive care unit, you may see somebody sneezing and blowing his nose. Or a mother, coming back from pumping breastmilk, who forgets to wash her hands before touching her baby. Should she wash her hands again? Probably, yes. But should you be outraged, or scared, by what may look to you like unforgivable carelessness? Certainly not. That sneeze may be an innocent allergy, and that mother may have washed her hands in the breast pumping room. There may even be times when it's more important for a nurse to assist a

baby rapidly, rather than stopping to wash her hands before coming to his aid.

Some well-meaning parents take the hygiene issue so seriously that it becomes a bit of an obsession, leading them to scrutinize the behavior of every visitor and all of the nurses and doctors. But good hygiene shouldn't be confused with sterility. An NICU can't and shouldn't be a sterile ward, because babies need to feel the comforting, healing touch of human skin on their bodies in order to grow and develop normally. And premature babies need to be exposed to the microorganisms that are part of our normal environment, in order to develop antibodies and strengthen their immune defenses against them.

If you happen to notice, in your preemie's nursery, a person who consistently violates common sense rules of hygiene, you should point this out to someone on the medical staff. But don't let an exaggerated fear of infection ruin your pleasure in being with your baby, holding him close to your skin, and putting the tip of your finger in his mouth to feel how strong his sucking has become. Those are things your preemie needs, too, to develop happily and healthily.

Siblings' Visits

My older daughter is begging to visit her new brother in the hospital. Will we be endangering our baby's health by exposing him to his sister's germs, or hurting our daughter emotionally by letting her see the baby connected to tubes and wires?

Sometimes young children, who aren't yet burdened by second thoughts and responsibilities, seem to know by instinct what the right thing is to do. This appears to be the case with your daughter. Her requests raise a very important point. Her baby brother was born, and she needs to get acquainted with him as soon as possible, for her sake and everybody else's in the family.

Your worries are understandable. Families find themselves torn between their desire to take their older children to the NICU, and their concern over damage it might do—exposing the older siblings to the shocking sight of the new baby looking tiny and sick, in a scary hospital environment, and exposing the preemie to any infectious illnesses an older child might be carrying. Some parents end up deferring a hospital meeting indefinitely, but that can be a mistake.

If your NICU allows sibling visits, as most do, you should take advantage of that opportunity. Sometimes, the "visit" may only consist of taking a brief peek at the new baby through a glass wall. But limited as that may seem, it will be remembered by your child as a significant experience. Besides visits, there are other useful things parents can do (see below) to help create a bond between their kids at home and the new baby in the hospital. That's a precious gift you are giving them.

GETTING TO KNOW A NEW BROTHER OR SISTER IN THE HOSPITAL

Everybody knows what a child goes through when a little brother or sister is born in the most normal, happy circumstances: feelings of joy and pride are mixed with a painful sense of being "dethroned" by the new arrival, with whom the parents' love and attention must now be shared.

No wonder a premature birth makes things so much harder for the kids, since it takes away all the goodies, leaving only the negative consequences. There's no adorable, new baby at home to be proud of. The adults' anxiety about the infant's health, topped by lots of organizational problems, can make older children feel excluded and abandoned. When mothers and fathers spend long hours in the hospital, they often rely on unusual childcare arrangements with relatives or caretakers, sometimes even sending the children away from home, or leaving them with unfamiliar people. In the first days and weeks of a preemie's life, the parents have to deal first with their own grief and disappointment, for the loss of a normal delivery and healthy, full-term newborn. So they may not be available, practically or emotionally, to comfort their children, whose reactions and needs can sometimes be overlooked.

HOW TO PICK UP YOUR CHILDREN'S SIGNALS OF DISTRESS

There are kids who hide their stress well, and others who don't. Their age will partly determine their behavior. Preschoolers can regress to habits like bedwetting and thumb sucking; eating or sleeping problems; irritability, disobedience, excessive clinginess, or demands for attention. Older children can demonstrate inattentiveness at school, or indifference toward their parents and the new baby. Some children are afraid they may have caused the premature birth with some kind of bad behavior. They may also fear that they could catch the baby's illness and have to go to the hospital, too. So they may need a lot of reassurance.

A simple explanation that the baby needs to get bigger before coming home is usually enough for children who are two or three years old, while older children may benefit from a brief description of why the baby was born so early, and what his main medical problems are. Of course, children vary in maturity, and you are the best judge of what your kids can understand and handle.

Whatever behavioral changes you may notice, or distress you may suspect in your kids since your preemie was born, the good news is that psychological research shows that most of these problems can be alleviated by taking the siblings to meet the new baby. Some children cannot grasp that the baby really exists unless they get to see him in person. Or they have fantasies of deformities or other problems that are far worse than the reality. Some experts also talk about the importance of "sharing the burden" of a family crisis: a visit to the hospitalized baby can make a child feel closer to the parents, and helpful to them. All of these benefits can be felt by children and adults immediately, and in the long run.

WHY MOST NICUs ALLOW CHILDREN TO VISIT

In last two decades, several studies have also disputed the fears that accepting young visitors will bring infections, noise, and disruption into hospital nurseries. Sibling visitation does not increase the rate of infection in an NICU, provided that the children wash their hands, and are screened for contagious illnesses by their parents and the hospital staff. Sometimes, placing a screen or curtain around an infant's bed during a visit can give a family enough privacy and peace of mind to talk to an older child, without disturbing other patients.

Considering the benefits of sibling visitation, and the few risks involved, most NICUs now allow it. So you shouldn't be shy about inquiring about your nursery's policy, or asking the staff to help you organize the visit. Most likely, you'll find doctors and nurses surprisingly helpful and supportive.

HOW TO MAKE THINGS WORK

A successful visit to the new baby in the hospital should be prepared for, if possible. You can show your older children pictures, describe how preemies look, and explain why they may need help breathing and eating, before they catch up and become like other infants. Your older children can send in advance, or bring to the baby, a small, meaningful object of their choice: a toy, a music box, a drawing, a picture. During the visit, you should display this present inside or near your preemie's bed, pointing out that it will keep the baby company, reminding him of his brother or sister. If the nurses give permission, tell your children to gently touch the baby and talk to him. Overall, try to focus on their reactions, and answer all of their questions.

Don't be offended by apparently indifferent or cold behavior: that may be your child's way of protecting her feelings, or expressing her anxiety about the baby.

ESTABLISHING A LIFE-LONG RELATIONSHIP

Even after a single, quick visit to the nursery, it will be easier to tell the older children about the baby, mentioning people or things that they may remember from their visit. Some kids will want to talk a lot about their experience, and others won't, at least for a while.

If your older daughter is in school, you should inform the teachers of the premature birth, and her visit to the hospital. They can create opportunities for your daughter to express her feelings about the new baby, and to make drawings, notes, and presents to be sent to the NICU. All of these messages should be acknowledged and praised, to make her feel good and important.

You can make up thank-you's sent by the baby to his big sister. New snapshots, reports about how the baby is doing (for instance, his weight gain or feeding improvements) especially addressed to the sibling by doctors and nurses, and anything else you do to keep the kids interested and involved will ease the strain that the hospitalization of a premature baby can cause the whole family.

With your help, your older children will be able to stand strong at your side, while your preemie heals and grows in the hospital. Patience and sensitivity will bear fruit for a long time, especially when the baby comes home. His brothers and sisters will have learned how to love him already. And you will know you gave all of your children your best support.

Making an Isolette Feel Like Home

We can't bear the idea that our tiny baby is all alone in the hospital. A friend suggested that we decorate her isolette, and make a recording of our voices that the nurses can play when we're not there.

For months, you've been imagining bringing your baby home to a cozy bassinet in your home. When you weren't holding her, she'd have been surrounded by soft blankets, teddy bears, and musical mobiles that would convey how precious and loved you wanted her to feel.

Parents like you, with nurturing spirits, feel heartbroken at the thought of their babies lying alone in the NICU, even though they know it's temporarily the best place for them to be. Like your friend, many wonder: Why not try to create a little of that personal, warm touch in the intensive care unit?

We have two reactions. One: it's a wonderful idea, and you should certainly do it. Two: it needs to be executed with care.

The reason is that although preemies need their parents and signs of love, they are easily stressed out by stimulation—and stressing your baby is just the opposite of what you're trying to accomplish. As your preemie gets older, she'll be able to handle increasing amounts of stimulation without getting overwhelmed. Often, very premature and sick infants can tolerate just one kind of sensory activity at a time—whether it's being talked to, being touched, or being faced with something to look at. Though it comes as a surprise to parents at first, the things that we intend to be pleasant, positive stimulation can be just as stressful for these babies as negative stimulation.

So, the best way to start is with a few, carefully chosen things for your baby's home away from home; you can plan to "redecorate" and introduce new elements later, as you get to know her better and she gets closer to term. The following guidelines incorporate some views of experts in the young, evolving field of Developmental Care (see page 198), who have studied premature babies' reactions to different kinds of stimulation:

❋ *An isolette cover.* No premature baby wants to be constantly confronted by the bright fluorescent lights of the intensive care nursery. So one of the best things you can give your baby is an isolette cover, made of thick fabric, to shield her from the light. Opinions differ as to whether you should keep it on your baby's isolette all the time, or only at night (see page 200).

Some nurseries give isolette covers automatically to every baby, others give them to parents who ask (so do!), and others don't have them at all. If your nursery doesn't, you can buy one from various suppliers (see appendix, page 528)—or easier yet, just bring a blanket or quilt from home, drape it over your baby's isolette, and fold the sides up so the nurses can see your baby and reach the isolette's doors. Make sure the fabric is thick enough to keep the light out (it will also help absorb some of the loud hospital noises), and choose one whose colors and patterns aren't too bold. It could even be dark, as the womb is; don't worry, your baby will still get more than enough stimulation if you or the nurses

interact with her during the day, or when you notice that she's awake.

❋ *Works of art: family photos, pictures, and mobiles.* What does a baby want to look at when she's awake? What's appropriate for a newborn at one gestational age can be very inappropriate for another. For example, those striking, black-and-white designs that are believed to be appealing to full-term babies can be overwhelming to a preemie. In fact, experts are wary of any fixed image in an isolette. If it's stressful, and a preemie can't move away from it, she has to use up her valuable energy to tune it out. What about faces? They are a preemie's favorite thing to look at, especially her parents' faces, or her own in a mirror. But even these may be better when introduced intermittently—when you or a caregiver is there and can pay attention to when your preemie wants more stimulation, and when she's had enough and needs a rest.

❋ *The special sound of your voice.* Preemies are drawn to the familiar voices of their parents. And researchers have noted distinct differences between the genuinely loving intonations of a mother's or father's speech, and those of a well-intended, but nonparental caregiver. On the other hand, just as preemies need to be protected from bright lights, they also need to be sheltered from sounds, which tend to bombard them in the NICU. Many parents assume that an isolette muffles noises, but the opposite is true: loud sounds reverberate inside it. Noise has been associated with physiological signs of stress in premature babies, who were still supposed to be hearing only their mother's heartbeat and the soft, muted sounds of the womb.

So should you put a tape recording of your voices, talking and singing, in your baby's isolette or not? That depends. If you have good rapport with your baby's nurses, and can count on them to observe and make sure that the tape is comforting your baby rather than disturbing her, by all means do it. However, if you notice that your baby is particularly sensitive to noise, or if you think that the nurses may just play your tape indiscriminately, over and over again, then your baby may be better off without it.

❋ *Mommy's scent.* Here's something wonderful you can do for preemies of all ages, since even the youngest preemies recognize the smell of their mother. By introducing your scent into the isolette, you can give your baby precious continuity at a time when she is experiencing so many new, different things. It's simple to do. Just take a small cloth and keep it tucked against your body for a while—perhaps overnight. Keep it against you while you're in the hospital, holding your baby. Then, when you go home, leave the cloth behind with her. (Just be sure to tell the nurses why it's there, so they don't mistakenly remove it.) You can do this again with a clean cloth each day, or as often as you like.

❋ *Teddy bears and other stuffed companions.* The truth is, your baby probably won't even notice a teddy bear you put in her isolette. But it can still be an important addition, because it can help you and others. Just like a stuffed animal on the shelf of a full-term baby at home, one in an isolette makes a statement: this baby counts. And it will help the NICU staff look at your preemie as a real *baby*, not just a clinical case: a child who is cherished and given special, carefully chosen things of her own.

Actually, some stuffed animals—like long snakes—can be extremely comfortable for a preemie to lie against, also. A soft, stuffed snake curled around your baby can help her feel contained and tucked in—a feeling that's very soothing to a preemie, and is one of the best ways to alleviate her stress. You can also rest the snake behind your baby to help her stay in a side-lying position. At other times, it may be something that her little hands can grasp and hold. Some parents are partial to beanie babies, which seem a perfect size to be a support and friend to a preemie.

❋ *Beautiful baby clothes.* There's something very special about dressing your baby. Like seeing a teddy bear keeping a preemie company in her isolette, seeing a preemie in real baby clothes can warm any parent's or nurse's heart. When babies are still on radiant warming beds, they're kept undressed so the NICU staff can quickly see any small change in their condition. They also have to be naked when they're under phototherapy lamps for jaundice, so the light can reach their bare skin. But at all other times, clothing is fine. Just make sure that what you choose fits loosely, is made of a soft fabric, that you wash it once in a gentle soap before putting it on your baby, and that it's not too expensive, since clothes occasionally (though not often) get lost in the nursery. Little hats and pairs of socks are great, and so are other outfits if they open easily in front, so your baby can be examined and have her diapers changed.

Don't worry if your baby's clothes are a little big at first; that's part of the charm, and will eventually become one of your fond memories. Preemie clothes are sold by the Gap, some national chains and department stores, and specialized retailers (we've listed a few of these for you in the appendix, page 528).

Even though these guidelines are worth considering carefully, if there's one thing that all parents learn, it's that no two little individuals are alike. Your preemie, no matter how tiny, already has her own distinct personality, with her own likes and dislikes. Her personal preferences are far more important than any general guidelines—and as you spend time with her, you'll have the intimate joy of beginning to discover and respond to them.

Parents Asked to Leave

Sometimes when I'm visiting my baby, the nurses ask me to leave for a little while. One time it was change of shift, and another time they said there was a procedure I shouldn't watch. What's so secret that I can't be there?

When you're asked to leave your preemie's bedside, it's natural to feel upset. If a nurse or doctor is going to do a procedure, like drawing blood or doing a spinal tap, you may be anxious about the pain your baby will suffer while you're not there to comfort him. If the doctors are making rounds, you may feel entitled to hear, firsthand, how your baby is doing. If it's a change of nursing shift, you may not understand how your presence could interfere. And above all, why should you lose some of the precious time you could be spending with your baby, instead of waiting idly in the corridor or family room?

There are some good reasons—and some debatable ones. Many nurseries require all visitors to leave the room for privacy reasons while the doctors make rounds. (All medical information is considered confidential.) In teaching hospitals, it also helps residents and medical students express themselves freely and feel more at ease. Privacy is also a concern during the change of nursing shift, since the nurses have to pass on detailed information about each patient.

When there's a procedure to perform, either on your baby or a baby nearby, the medical staff may be concerned about your emotional reaction (don't take this personally; the rules apply to all parents alike), or that your presence could make them feel nervous, interfering with their ability to complete the procedure quickly and smoothly.

It may be that they shouldn't be so worried. A recently published study looked at whether it made a difference when parents were allowed to be present while doctors or nurses performed simple medical procedures on their children in an emergency room. The researchers evaluated the amount of pain felt by the child (as signaled by his behavior and the intensity of his cry); the successful performance of the procedure; and the anxiety level of parents, doctors, and nurses.

One of the findings may be reassuring to parents who are not allowed to stay with their babies: the parents' presence didn't make a difference in reducing their children's pain. On the other hand, the performance of the medical staff wasn't impaired by the parents' presence, and there was one major benefit: a much lower anxiety level in mothers and fathers who stay. "We should encourage parents who want to be present to stay during procedures," the study's authors concluded.

Some parents will gratefully exit, so as not to witness their baby in pain, while others will be reluctant to leave, feeling that even if they can't take the pain away, they can offer their baby something very important: the assurance that his parents are there, to comfort him. Since it's only fair to take into account both the parents' instincts and the medical staff's nerves, some flexibility is often built into these rules in NICUs. If you feel strongly that you want to stay with your baby during a procedure, be sure to convey that to the staff; they may be able to accommodate you.

When to Circumcise

We want to have our son circumcised, but the doctor is telling us to wait. It seems like he just doesn't understand how important it is to us.

The doctor may seem insensitive to your wishes, but he's actually just trying to be extremely sensitive to your son's health. Any kind of stress—and that certainly includes even a relatively minor surgical procedure like circumcision—can be destabilizing to a newborn preemie, causing changes in breathing, heart rate, and other vital functions that could be troublesome. The procedure itself will be safer later, too: the smaller the area the doctor has to work with, the more difficult the surgery is to perform. For both reasons, all elective surgery is usually postponed until premature newborns get bigger and stronger, and their medical condition is stable.

In most nurseries, circumcision is done a few days before a baby boy is discharged from the hospital. Although that may not be as soon as you'd hoped, you can bet your son will be circumcised by the time he's lying on your changing table at home.

Medical Costs

We have no idea how much all of this intensive medical care is going to cost, or whether we can afford it.

In the midst of your other worries, at some point, naturally, it crosses your mind: Are we going to be able to afford all of this? The answer is almost certainly yes. Your baby will be able to stay in the hospital as long as she needs to, getting the care she deserves—and it is unlikely to bankrupt you.

To be sure, you may get some steep bills. As you might guess, intensive care hospitalization is extremely expensive—to give you some idea, a bed in many neonatal intensive care units now costs between $1,000 and $2,000 a day, and there are extra fees for certain tests and medical specialists on top of that. (Your hospital might charge more or less than this, and rates change every year.) When your baby leaves intensive care and graduates into an intermediate care unit, the daily cost will go down, but it still won't be cheap.

Here's why the situation is not as dire as it sounds. First of all, if either you or your spouse is covered by insurance, the chances are that your baby is, too. (You should notify your insurance carrier immediately of your baby's birth. Many plans give you 30 days after delivery to include a baby in your coverage.) Many insurance plans pick up 80% to 100% of the hospital and medical costs.

If you do not have insurance, you may be eligible for Medicaid. The social worker at your baby's hospital should be able to give you information on it, and help get you enrolled in the program. Medicaid generally picks up the entire cost of the baby's hospitalization. (Or, if you are insured, Medicaid will pick up whatever costs your insurance company doesn't, as long as your baby is in the hospital for at least 30 days.) The social worker can also tell you about, or help contact, any other government programs or private charities that may be willing to help out. Some help families while their babies are in the hospital, others provide support for those whose babies have continuing medical needs once they get home.

If the amount that's left for you to pay—either the deductible and co-pay, if you're insured, or more, if you're not—is still overwhelming to you, most hospitals will be willing to work out a payment plan. Many hospitals will agree to spread payments out over a number of years. Some will also make agreements on a case-by-case basis to reduce or forgive charges that aren't covered by insurance.

Since the social worker can be your best ally and guide to managing the financial end of this experience, don't hesitate to contact her. She'll be glad to help alleviate your anxiety about these practical matters, so you can concentrate on your baby.

Coping Emotionally

I need help! I'm feeling so emotionally overwhelmed.

Don't think for a second that you're the only one. Most parents who deliver a very premature baby are confused and emotionally overwhelmed for weeks or months. It's not strange at all, considering the mounds of new, often frightening information you're getting, the utterly different world of the NICU you find yourself a part of, and the disruption of your life that any birth—but especially a premature birth—entails. Not only are your feelings normal, they're healthy. Acting as if nothing traumatic or stressful had happened would indicate that you're trying to shield yourself from reality. The best way to heal is to do what you've done already: acknowledge your emotions and need for help. This is a necessary step, and there are others you can take, too, so that you and your little one can move on with your lives together.

Most likely, there's a bright future ahead for you and your baby, and his premature birth is a temporary crisis. But at this moment things are hard. Nobody prepares themselves for a newborn who needs intensive medical attention and isn't at home in his bassinet. Certainly, all mothers and fathers go through an initial period of adaptation to a new baby and the new responsibilities that come with him, and some of what you're feeling may be just that. But a premature birth adds on much more:

* *worry*—and for parents with sick babies, perhaps even terror—about whether your baby will come through this OK;
* *regret* that you can't enjoy the intimacy with your newborn you longed for;
* *uneasiness* with having to deal with doctors and nurses to whom you're completely entrusting your baby's well-being;
* *guilt* that you let your baby, and perhaps your partner, down;
* *confusion* as to why it happened;
* *sadness* that your baby is being deprived of a normal life's beginning;
* *anger* that it happened, undeservedly, to you;
* *shock* that your baby and family are the actors in this weird, unexpected drama;
* *helplessness* at not being able to turn back the clock and make it all come out different.

The list of upsetting feelings can be so long—those above are just some of them. But when at least part of your emotional burden is spelled out, it may feel less heavy.

Ultimately, it is time that will help you heal and get back to normal. But there are things you can do to make this difficult time feel more manageable. Since you may not be ready to talk to anyone right now, you should first try to talk to yourself. A good way might be to keep a diary. If it seems silly to you, hold on. Jotting down some notes every night, after visiting your baby or calling the NICU, could help you put into words—and balance—your greatest hopes and worst fears. (And, believe it or not, you are going to want to remember many of the details of this experience, which will always be one of the most important of your life.) Some parents who are good at drawing find relief in sketching their impressions. If writing or drawing doesn't feel right, you could try to confide your inner thoughts to a tape recorder.

Since you have no privacy at the NICU, and probably feel self-conscious about expressing your reactions and feelings there, you should let your emotions unravel at home. Spend some private time listening to your favorite music. If tears come, give yourself permission to cry freely. Shedding tears, sobbing, or even kicking a chair or punching a pillow to get rid of some anger, can be very liberating.

Don't feel that you're being disloyal to your baby, yourself, or, if you're religious, to God, by not being hopeful and optimistic all the time. Recognizing and acknowledging fear and dread—and for many people, praying for strength—may be the most helpful way to handle these painful emotions. Unexpressed, they can fester, and undermine the joyful, comforting feelings that being with your baby will also arouse.

While you're beginning to explore your emotions, if you have a spouse or partner, remember that there's probably at least one other person who wants and needs to share all of this with you. Chances are, there's no one closer to what you're experiencing than the other parent of your baby. In fact, studies have shown that both mothers and fathers of premature or ill newborns find each other to be their best source of support and help during the first two weeks their babies spend in an NICU. To cultivate that mutual support, it's important to share with your partner the details of your baby's daily events, and your reactions to even the tiniest triumphs and setbacks. Without that fine-tuning, there's a risk of building up misunderstandings that in the future may cause you pain. Even if

your partner cannot express his or her emotions now, you should make the effort to keep your feelings open. The love you both nurture for your infant can give you the strength to overcome a crisis that could be tough on even the happiest couple—and perhaps to emerge with an even stronger relationship.

If you don't have a partner, probably there are other people with whom you're intimate, who can share your baby's daily ups and downs with you, and to whom you can express your deepest feelings. Whether it's your mother, father, sister, or best friend, they most likely want to help in any way they can. If they hang back, it may be that they're afraid of intruding in case you don't want them to. In fact, they may be feeling some of the same emotions you are—but don't feel they have permission to say so.

Even if you aren't ready to reach out to a lot of friends and family members, it can help to choose at least one or two people to talk to freely and involve as much as you can. Invite them to come visit your baby, and give them a tour of the NICU. You'll be helping someone close to you by letting them help you, and you won't have to carry this tremendous burden alone.

If you ever feel like you are sinking into a quagmire of despair (some days may be like that), you should remember one thing: all of your children—your preemie in the hospital, your older kids at home—are counting on you to be a strong, supportive parent. Just acknowledging their presence, and their need for you to be there, can give you the extra strength to overcome the most difficult moments.

Self-help methods are often the first steps mothers and fathers take to cope with the stress of having a premature child. There may come a time, however, when you want to talk to somebody who is an expert in helping families in your situation.

✳ *A social worker* connected with your NICU is the right person to talk to about any practical problems that concern you, such as the cost of your baby's medical care, health insurance issues, and transportation and accommodations (which can be extremely costly if you live far from the hospital). Social workers are also trained (and usually have a great deal of experience) in dealing with parents who are grieving and fearful about this unexpected outcome of their pregnancy, and can help you express and understand your emotions.

✳ *A therapist* can do more long-term counseling than the hospital social worker. She can also treat postpartum depression, which may be exacerbated by having a baby in the hospital. Look for one with experience and expertise in counseling families—particularly parents and their children—through medical crises.

✳ *A hospital chaplain* (a minister, rabbi, or priest who visits and counsels families and patients in the hospital), or your own religious advisor, can discuss with you all of the spiritual issues related to your experience, and in particular the meaning of this experience for your baby and family. Don't exclude the possibility of talking to a hospital chaplain of a faith that is not yours, but whose compassion, knowledge of the issues that illness raises in a family, and willingness to address ethical questions and profound concerns may help you find some of the peace of mind that you're looking for.

✳ *Support groups* usually consist of parents of babies now in the hospital, or "graduate" parents who make themselves available for talking and listening to mothers and fathers of hospitalized premature babies. Current parents can share your joys, fears, and uncertainty, and make you feel less isolated. Graduate parents can give you the insight of somebody who's "been there" in an NICU. They can explain things to you in plain, understandable, nonmedical language. Most of all, as living proofs, they'll comfort you that there's a happy life coming after the NICU. You, too, can look forward to that.

Be assured that in a brief time, you'll feel much more in control. You will never forget what you're going through now, but you can learn how to accept and make sense of what happened. This upsetting period, in the beginning of your baby's life, can also be an occasion for personal growth, as an individual and as a couple. Many people feel they come out of it as better, more mature people, and as more understanding parents.

MULTIPLES

Babies in Different Hospitals

One of our twins is in a hospital near home, but the other one was taken to a bigger hospital an hour away. I don't know how we're going to handle the logistics.

You always knew that having twins was going to double the rewards *and* trouble of parenting. But who could know you'd have to take care of twins in two different cities at the same time! If you have enough time in your day to travel back and forth between hospitals, you can, of course, spend some morning hours with one twin and afternoon or evening hours with the other. But many parents find it too difficult to juggle daily, double hospital visits with their other obligations.

The first thing to do is to allow yourself to accept that it's OK for you not to see both of your twins every single day. Whatever attention and intimacy they get from you in these early weeks is plenty to help them recover and grow, so long as it's gentle, sensitive, and loving when you're together. Even skipping a few days is not going to change that.

Here are some other possible solutions to your problem:

* Split up the visits with your spouse or partner, each of you spending some time each day with one of your babies, but alternating daily, or every few days, so you both get to spend some time with each.
* Along with your partner, spend one day, or every few days, with one baby, and the next day, or few days, with the other. This will give

you and your partner some time together—which can be important in maintaining your relationship.
* Ask a grandparent, aunt, or close friend to step in and help you, by visiting one of your preemies when you can't.
* Try to have your other twin transferred to the larger hospital, too. Particularly if you have significant transportation problems, and if your twins are expected to remain in separate hospitals for several weeks or more, you may want to investigate this possibility. Stumbling blocks you may encounter might include lack of an available bed for your relatively well baby, and the expense of transporting your twin if your insurance doesn't pay for "non-medical" moves.
* Visit your sicker baby more often, for now. You may even want to consider staying at a motel near the distant hospital for a few days, while your sicker twin is most unstable. Remember that responding to one of your twin's needs is not playing favorites—it will even out over time, and there will be plenty of times in the future when you'll be doing the same for your other twin.

Fortunately, this logistical hardship doesn't usually last for more than a few weeks. Your sicker baby should soon catch up with his sibling, and be able to join him in the same hospital. You may still find it difficult to divide your time between your babies! But leaving behind worries about transportation, traffic jams, parking places, and travel expenses can only make things easier.

Keeping Twins Near Each Other

They've put our twin daughters in different rooms in the NICU. I don't want them to be separated.

Most nurseries try their best to put multiples near each other, since it's easier, and nicer, for their families. But it isn't always possible when the babies first arrive in the nursery. They may have to be separated initially if one sibling is sicker than the other, since some nurseries have designated areas or rooms for babies who need the most acute care. (The training of the nurses who work there, the nurse-to-baby ratio, and the equipment and layout may all be different.) Even if that's not an issue, it may not be possible to give siblings the same nurse, and they may have nurses who are stationed far apart from each other. (Nursing assignments are carefully juggled so that no nurse is too overloaded to provide good care to all of her patients.) Sometimes, twins are separated at first simply because there aren't two free bed spaces next to each other when they arrive.

Some parents feel more strongly about this issue than others, so you should certainly mention to the nurses that it's important to you. Most likely, they'll arrange for your twins to be close together as soon as possible.

Some parents want their twins to be not just in neighboring beds, but in the same bed or isolette, so they can feel each other's presence like they did in the womb. In some Scandinavian countries, "cobedding" multiples has been a fairly common practice in NICUs for many years. In the U.S., the practice of cobedding is controversial. Although some nurseries are willing to try it, there is hardly any research on whether there are benefits or risks—and many medical professionals have concerns.

While parents think about the importance to their babies of remaining close, neonatologists are aware that closeness can increase the risk of a doctor, nurse, or technician mixing the babies up, compromising their treatment. While parents feel that their babies would thrive on continued physical contact with each other, neonatologists have always tried to prevent contact among babies in the NICU, to minimize the chance that they'll pass serious infections from one to another. Premature babies also need to be kept from getting too hot or too cold, and may need different amounts of heat in their isolettes. Advocates of cobedding say they've observed that the warmer twin tends to radiate heat to the colder twin, so their temperature becomes more in sync. But right now, temperature control is still an unmeasured risk.

Once studies are done on the benefits and risks of cobedding, it will become more apparent whether it's better to keep newborn, preemie twins together or apart. Certainly, to parents of multiples, it seems natural that their babies, who have been lifelong companions, would be a much-needed comfort to each other in a new, harsh world. And there have been a few inspiring stories of premature twins who were struggling—with apnea and bradycardia, or poor oxygen saturation—until they were put in the same bed, where they snuggled into each other, and quickly became more stable.

If you and your doctors agree to try cobedding, keep in mind that precautions need to be taken. For your babies' safety, if either has an infection, is on a ventilator, or has an umbilical catheter or chest tube, they will probably have to wait.

In Depth

WAYS TO MAKE A BABY FEEL LOVED IN THE NICU: DEVELOPMENTAL CARE

Dear Mommy and Daddy,
I know I came out sooner than you expected, and
I understand that you had to put me in the
hospital nursery until I mature and grow. But
I'm still your little baby, and I wish you could do
something to make me feel a little better here.
Can't you think of something?

Love you, Your New Arrival

How do you place a newborn infant in an impersonal, machine-filled hospital environment, subject her to frequently painful, though necessary, medical procedures, and still give her the feeling of being loved? That's a tough question, and parents of premature babies worry about it tremendously—as they should. But most write it off as an impossible task—which they shouldn't.

There *are* things you can do. Many of them are being studied by proponents of a fairly new field spanning neonatology and psychology, called Developmental Care. These researchers are trying to amass evidence that paying attention to a preemie's signals (how she tells us what makes her feel good and what is upsetting to her)—as any good parent would try to do with a baby at home—can influence the baby's health while she's in the hospital, and affect her long-term outcome.

The idea of Developmental Care is to provide preemies, as much as is possible, with appropriate amounts and kinds of stimulation—as nature intended in the womb—while protecting them from things that make them feel overloaded and stressed. Whether it's something obviously unpleasant, like a loud noise, or something seemingly innocent, like a vivid mobile or a painless touch, the immature nervous systems of preemies aren't adept yet at screening out sensory input, and get easily overloaded. All of us have physiological reactions to stress, adults included. A preemie usually will make one or more characteristic movements, like startling, back arching, or flailing her arms and legs. As she feels increasingly out of control, the stress may lead to changes in her breathing, heart rate, or blood pressure that can quickly become medically destabilizing.

As scientists learn more about the impact of early life experiences on the wiring of the brain, many also wonder whether taking preemies out of the womb and placing them in the starkly different environment of the NICU, at a time when the brain is developing so rapidly, may actually alter the architecture of their brains.

One thing researchers have noticed is that as premature babies grow into toddlers and school-age children, they have a higher incidence of subtle problems like learning disabilities, attention deficit disorder, excitability, and language and speech problems than other children. There could be many reasons for this, including prenatal conditions and problems in the home environment.

But consider what is happening in brain formation while many premature babies are in the NICU. During the second and third trimesters of pregnancy, the brain's billions of neurons migrate through the cortex to specific locations. Once migrated, they develop interconnections, or synapses. There are too many synapses for all to survive, so they get gradually pruned down over the next weeks, months, and years. It is thought that those connections that get strengthened through stimulation and life experiences will be preserved, while those that aren't used will wither away. If you believe (as most scientists do) that mother nature knows best, and the womb is the optimal environment for a fetus, you can't help but wonder about the impact of those early days in the technological environment of the NICU.

Your baby's hospital nursery may have started incorporating a little of the developmental approach in their caregiving. But many neonatologists still question its value, especially for critically ill newborns. One reason is that developmental guidelines often conflict with traditional, medical practices in intensive care nurseries. For example, traditional intensive care medicine involves examining babies and gathering vital information, like their temperature and blood pressure, periodically on a set schedule, and when certain physicians are available. That often requires bright lighting and waking the babies up. Developmental Care urges that the nursery staff let babies sleep undisturbed for long periods of time, in darkness and quiet. This can involve very real medical trade-offs for a baby.

Another reason for resistance is that Developmental Care, being a relatively young field, still rests on a limited amount of research. And although the results of much of the early research are dramatic enough to make everyone sit up and take notice, more trials will need to be done before the results are considered proven.

DEVELOPMENTAL CARE: THE RESEARCH FINDINGS

Thus far, the research findings on Developmental Care have been extremely provocative, but not conclusive. Several studies have found that premature babies who were cared for with the developmental approach spent shorter periods on ventilators, made a quicker transition to bottle or breastfeeding, and had shorter hospital stays. One study even found that babies who received Developmental Care suffered from fewer pneumothoraces and intraventricular hemorrhages, and less severe chronic lung disease. At two weeks of age, and again at nine months of age, these babies tested better on developmental measures like self-regulation, motor skills, complexity of play, and task persistence. Preliminary results on a group of children who received Developmental Care when they were in the NICU indicate that they scored higher than their counterparts at three and seven years of age on several, important cognitive and behavioral measures.

But critics have pointed out some flaws in these studies that raise doubts about the dramatic findings. In fact, one other recent study failed to find any significant developmental advantages, at least in the measures it looked at, in two year olds who had received Developmental Care.

Thus, it's still too early for doctors and scientists to conclude whether Developmental Care can change a preemie's medical or long-term outcome.

Although the science may be inconclusive, from a parent's perspective, you could view Developmental Care differently: as a way of expressing love. Unfortunately, as long as she's in the NICU, you can't shield your newborn baby from experiencing some unpleasant and painful things. You can't offer the sheltered cosseting you wanted to give her at home. But you can help her realize that she isn't alone, and her feelings aren't ignored; someone is by her side, looking out for her, responding to her signals, and soothing her. Your parental intuition will tell you whether this makes your baby feel better. That in itself is enough. If there are long-term benefits, so much the better.

SOME BASIC PRINCIPLES OF DEVELOPMENTAL CARE

One of the primary goals of the developmental approach is to soften the discrepancy between what a baby experiences in the womb, and what she experiences after unexpectedly arriving in the loud, bright, bustling intensive care nursery. In practice, that translates into some basic principles, such as the following:

Lower the lights and reduce the noise. How do you make an NICU more like a womb? As a start, you dim the lights. In many intensive care nurseries, intense fluorescent lights are shining from the ceilings twenty-four hours a day. Bright light can be arousing, contributing to sensory overload, and can cause oxygen desaturation, rapid heart rate, and lost calories in some babies. Moreover, when bright light shines in their eyes all the time, it is harder for preemies to come to an alert state when they're awake, and to experience regular, daily cycles of waking and sleeping—both of which are considered important for a baby's development.

Developmental Care guidelines include, for younger preemies:

* keeping overhead lights dim
* adding bedside lighting for use when an individual baby needs care
* covering isolettes with thick blankets or special isolette covers to shut out light;

And, for older preemies who will go home soon:

* introducing day-night cycles, with the lights brighter during the day than at night.

You should know that keeping young preemies in darkness at all times is one aspect of the Developmental Care program that has aroused some disagreement. Some specialists in brain development argue that daytime light is actually a powerful, positive influence on a preemie's development (as long as the lights are at comfortable, not glaring levels). They say that what's important is day-night cycling, because in the womb, everything from the mother's blood pressure to her heart rate and body temperature creates a day-night rhythm for the fetus. By this way of thinking, dim lights and isolette covers are actually disadvantageous to a baby during the day, and should be used only at night.

You can see that Developmental Care is a young field that's still evolving. Until each aspect of the program is studied rigorously, parents will have to come to some of their own conclusions.

However, many elements of the developmental approach are not contentious. Take sound, for example. It's easy for adults, who are more adept at tuning sounds out, to underestimate the amount of noise that bombards a baby in the NICU. Normal adult conversation typically measures between 45 and 55 decibels, an industrial factory around 80 decibels, and a lawnmower around 100 decibels. A preemie in an intensive care unit is surrounded by a continuous noise level between 50 and 86 decibels—and has to deal with frequent, sudden sounds that are much louder. Although an isolette may look like a quiet haven, measured sound levels inside them are the same as, or higher than, the sound levels outside. The seemingly minor act of placing a bottle on top of an isolette measures 108 decibels, closing one of the isolette's cabinets measures 95 decibels, and shutting one of the isolette's portholes measures 111 decibels.

In a preemie, who isn't a good self-regulator, loud sounds lead to a state of arousal that interferes with sleep, depletes energy, and wastes calories. Sudden noises can be associated with oxygen desaturation, startles, crying, and changes in pressure within the brain (which may increase the risk of an intraventricular hemorrhage).

So, Developmental Care's commonsense guidelines include:

* speaking softly
* avoiding loud radios in the nursery
* keeping traffic to a minimum around each isolette
* shutting isolette cabinets and portholes gently, and
* avoiding tapping fingers or placing bottles on an isolette.

An isolette cover will help with noise, as well as light, so you should certainly ask for one, or bring one in yourself, to give your baby a more peaceful night.

Many parents wonder if they should make a tape recording of their voices to put in their baby's isolette. This can be good for some babies in some situations; but for very young or easily agitated babies, the sweetest sound may be the sound of silence (see page 189).

Be sensitive with handling. Over time, your baby's nervous system will mature and become less fragile. For now, she needs especially sensitive handling, to help her remain as calm as possible.

One problem Developmental Care tries to rectify is that despite preemies' tremendous need for sleep, they are rarely allowed to sleep uninterrupted. One study reported that some preemies in the NICU were handled as often as 132 times in a typical twenty-four-hour period. While preemies at home may be held, touched, or caressed just as often, it's not normally done in a way that interrupts their quiet sleep. A basic principle of Developmental Care is to cluster caregiving procedures (feeding, diapering, having blood pressure taken, being given medication, for example), so a baby can get undisturbed sleep for long periods in between. Unless medically imperative, these caregiving activities are not done on a schedule determined by the clock. The nurse watches to see when a baby awakens from quiet sleep on her own, and then goes over for some social and medical interaction.

Preemies are particularly vulnerable to stress during transitions: for example, at the start of any caregiving cluster, when a nurse shifts from the first activity to a second one, and when she finishes her tasks and leaves a baby alone. Too often, caregiving tasks in an intensive care nursery are done impersonally and quickly, without taking the baby's needs for soothing into account. One researcher documented that nurses spent an average of 45 to 85 seconds near a preemie's isolette after completing their tasks, although babies would initiate signs of distress for up to five minutes after the caregiving activities—often, after the nurse had left.

Using Developmental Care, nurses prepare a baby for an intervention, and help her recover from it afterward. The nurse approaches a preemie calmly, talking to her soothingly before any activity begins, and while it is taking place. All the while, the nurse watches to make sure the baby is doing well, and stops to give her a rest when she seems to need it. Parents are also encouraged to be part of all caregiving (even painful events like drawing blood), since their intuition will tell them when their baby needs soothing.

Afterward, the nurse stays at the bedside until she's sure the baby is calm and comfortable again. After a bath or gavage feeding, the parents or nurse are encouraged to hold the baby for an extended period, letting her feel their arms around her as she drifts peacefully and contentedly back to sleep.

Provide comfort measures, and help the baby to calm herself. While a full-term baby is mature enough to take in various kinds of stimulation and stay calm (tuning out stimuli that's becoming disturbing to her), a premature baby is less able to shut out stimuli, or to calm herself down after being disturbed. She tends to become overloaded and is easily stressed out. Besides being unpleasant and scary for a preemie, this can be medically precarious, causing physiological responses like changes in heart rate or breathing.

Developmental Care suggests that all caregivers try to employ some simple methods that are exceedingly effective in keeping preemies calm:

✸ When lying down, preemies like to be on their stomachs best. It makes them feel in control of their movements—in contrast to lying on their backs with their arms and legs splayed out (think of a baby animal who doesn't like his tummy exposed). Side-lying is fine, too, but to give that same feeling of control, supports (such as rolled up blankets) should be placed around them.

✸ Preemies get a feeling of control and security by being contained within boundaries. There are many ways of doing this: wrapping a preemie within a blanket (though not swaddling her too tightly, since she should be able to move, as she did in the womb); placing a nest of blanket rolls around her (depending on what an individual baby seems to like, they could be placed at her sides, above her head as a headrest, and below her feet so she can brace against them when she feels stress); and, the most natural and parentally rewarding of all, holding her in one's own arms, with her arms and legs firmly but gently contained and her neck supported. (Don't stroke her, which is arousing. Holding her still will comfort her most.)

✸ Even if your baby has to stay on her warming bed, you can give her that feeling of containment by making what one Developmental Care pioneer calls a "hand womb" around her: with one hand, give her your finger to grasp, and place your other arm against her back, cupping her head in your hand. Whenever she wants to move, let her, and help her with containment again as she settles down.

✸ Sucking, which even a four-and-a-half-month-old fetus can do, is incredibly soothing to a preemie. Studies have reported that sucking on a pacifier—for example, during gavage feedings, painful procedures, or whenever a baby needs calming—can improve oxygenation, decrease crying, and keep blood pressure more stable. You can ask at your baby's nursery for little pacifiers that you or the nurses can offer to your baby. If you want, you can order one that Developmental Care experts especially like, because rather than being shaped like a breast nipple, it's shaped like a finger, which fetuses suck on in the womb (for ordering information, see appendix, page 528). Even if you don't like pacifiers, keep in mind that you can always stop using them later, when your baby comes home. The much-needed soothing they provide is what's most important for your baby right now.

Follow each baby's cues. This is one of the most important, core ideas behind Developmental Care. According to the underlying theory, a premature baby is engaged in a valiant struggle to adapt the unexpected hospital environment to her needs. She is actively trying to regulate the amount and kind of stimulation she gets, in order to avoid sensory overload and to continue down the normal developmental path she was embarked on in the womb. If we want to help her, we need to follow her lead, by simply following her cues.

Preemies have different needs: each is at a different stage of development, has a different degree of medical stability, and her own, distinctive personality. In order to stimulate your baby in the right ways and at the right times for her, you have to "listen" to her signals, which will tell you when she's overwhelmed and needs comforting or quiet.

Of course, a baby's signals are expressed nonverbally, through behavior. Developmental Care experts recommend that parents and nursery staff learn to recognize these, and try to respond to them. By doing so, you may be helping your baby's long-term development, and you'll certainly be helping her feel more competent and cared for. (Please keep in mind that this is not a complete list, and some of these signals may have a different meaning for your baby. If so, you'll discover this as you spend time with her.)

Signals often meaning "I feel content." When you see these, you can assume that your baby is comfortable and likes whatever sensory input she's getting. Keep it up!

* Relaxed arms, legs, and facial expression
* Smooth movements
* Looking around
* Alert and cooing or almost smiling

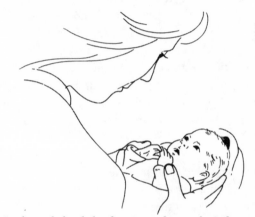

A calm and alert baby, focusing on her mother's face.

Adapted with permission of Children's Hospital Oakland, CA

Signals often meaning "I am soothing myself." These signals indicate that your baby is feeling slightly overloaded, but is able to help herself. It's good to encourage this kind of self-regulation.

* Sucking on fingers or hands, or searching for them (you can help her find them)
* Clasping hands together
* Grasping something
* Tucking into corners of the isolette or other boundaries

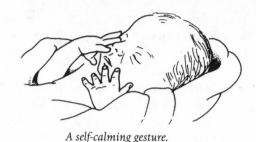

A self-calming gesture.

Signals often meaning "I feel stressed, please help." When you see these, your baby needs some kind of change or rest. Try limiting the stimulation she's getting, and soothing her with some of the comfort techniques described above. Remember that preemies often can take only one kind of stimulation at a time—for example, being held or being talked to, but not both. And don't take it personally that even the most pleasant stimulation, such as the sight of a parent's face, can be overwhelming to a preemie at times.

* Yawning
* Frowning or grimacing
* Flailing arms or legs, spreading fingers apart
* Crying and fussing
* Staring or glassy-eyed alertness
* Averting gaze or suddenly falling asleep
* Arching back and neck

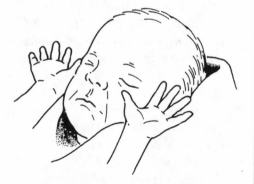

Finger splaying, a possible sign of stress.

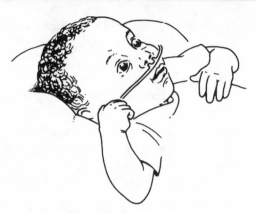

A hyperalert baby with a wide-eyed, staring gaze.

Adapted with permission of Children's Hospital Oakland, CA

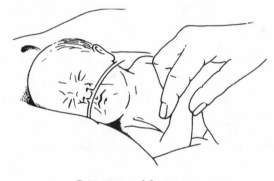

Grimacing and frowning.

Adapted with permission of Children's Hospital Oakland, CA

Encourage immersion of parents in their preemie's care. There is one more principle that is particularly important for you and your newborn. Developmental theorists believe that nature has adapted babies to need two other environments, besides the womb, to support their development: parents' bodies, and a family group. Developmental Care aims to get back that parental nurturing, and to safeguard the relationship of parent and child.

In their first weeks or months, many preemies don't get the so-called "on-parent body phase" that full-term newborns bask in at home.

A pivotal part of Developmental Care is called kangaroo care, in which a preemie is held against her parent's naked chest, skin-to-skin. One Developmental Care theorist calls this the "mother bed"—although fathers do it, too! We can say from personal experience that there's nothing more satisfying than taking your preemie from her solitary isolette, placing her on your warm chest, and falling asleep together in peace and contentment. You can read about how to do kangaroo care on page 221.

In nurseries that practice Developmental Care, the area around a baby's isolette is designed to be a home away from home for baby and family. (Actually, some ardent developmentalists won't even use the word "isolette," with its connotation of a baby being isolated. They prefer "incubator.") There is a comfortable chair by every bed, and a folder or mailbox that the nurses use to leave notes for parents, and vice versa. The baby's siblings are often invited to decorate it. Parents are encouraged to bring some of the warmth of a home nursery by personalizing their preemie's isolette. (Before you do this, we suggest you take a look at some considerations on page 188.)

Parents are also encouraged to stay in the nursery twenty-four hours a day. Of course, in our society most parents have jobs, older children, or other obligations that make such long hours impossible. And mothers or fathers should not get so tired or stressed that they can't take care of themselves, physically and psychologically. If you want, you can build shifts for your baby by calling on a small, consistent group of grandparents, aunts, or close friends.

You can also ask whether your hospital has volunteers who act as "cuddlers," tenderly holding the baby they're assigned to for an hour or so a day.

Your preemie isn't the only one who will benefit if you immerse yourselves in her care. You will, too. After the loss involved in a premature birth, it's tremendously affirming to start caring for your baby, and to realize that your relationship may actually be stronger and deeper because it started earlier than you expected.

Of course, developmentally appropriate care counts here, too. Don't expect to play and kid around with your baby yet. Parents learn not to be offended if their preemie wants just small, rather than bold, demonstrations of love from them. In fact, one of their most important parental roles at this point is shielding their tiny babies from stimulation, not offering it.

This is just a sampling of some of the important facets of the developmental approach to care. What if you like the sound of Developmental Care, but your baby's nursery doesn't practice it? Don't be discouraged. Adopting any little piece of this approach may help your baby, and you, too. Remember, it will be a while before all of the individual pieces of Developmental Care are separately studied, anyway. So find the things that seem most important to you, and that you can do or can convince the staff to do, and focus on how much they may help your baby. Don't let anyone make you feel pushy or odd. You aren't. You are your baby's protector—nothing more, nothing less—trying your best to help her.

Settling Down in the Hospital

▶ *Making the NICU the best possible home-away-from-home for you and your baby.*

THE PARENTS' PERSPECTIVE   208

THE DOCTOR'S PERSPECTIVE   212

QUESTIONS AND ANSWERS

Getting Acquainted With: Apnea and
    Bradycardia   218

Kangaroo Care   221

Practical Advice for Pumping and
    Storing Breast Milk   222

Breastfeeding a Preemie   226

Nipple Confusion   228

Milk Supply   229

The Possibility of Later-Onset Lactation   230

Bottle Feeding Tips   232

Baby Not Gaining Enough Weight   234

A Preemie's Caloric Needs   236

In Plain Language: What Is Necrotizing
    Enterocolitis?   237

Fractures   241

Another Kind of Jaundice   242

Baby's Positioning and SIDS   243

Why Is My Baby's Chest Indented?   243

Getting Acquainted With: Reflux   244

Skin Care   246

Tiny Babies at Risk for Big Diaper Rashes   247

Hernia   248

Hydrocele: A Related Condition   250

Preemie Massage   250

How Much Time to Spend with Baby   252

Whether to Go Back to Work   254

Parents Feeling Depressed   255

Baby Still on a Ventilator   257

Steroids   258

Bronchoscopy: A Peek inside Your
    Baby's Lungs   260

In Plain Language: What Is BPD?   261

ET Tube Accidentally Pulled Out   265

Hoarse Voice   266

High Blood Pressure 266
Eye Exam 267
In Plain Language: What Is Retinopathy
    of Prematurity? 268
Hearing Exam 272
Antibiotics 274
Scalp IV 274
Central Lines 275
Anemia 276
Heart Murmur 277
Abnormal Thyroid Test 278
False Alarms on Newborn Screens 279
Relations with Nurses 279
Changing Doctors 282
He Says "Potato," She Says "Potahto" 283
Cysts in the Brain 284

In Plain Language: What Is PVL? 285
Moving to Intermediate Care 287
Transfer to a Hospital Closer to Home 288
Vaccinations 289

MULTIPLES

Breastfeeding Twins 290
Breastfeeding Triplets? 293
The Same Tests for All? 293
How to Divide Your Time 294
Feeling Inadequate because of
    Famous Multiples 295

IN DEPTH

The Father of a Preemie 296

The Parents' Perspective:
Settling Down in the Hospital

It sounds like a contradiction in terms. But, yes, premature babies and their families do settle down in the hospital nursery. To the compelling rhythm of their daily weight gain, the bigger babies—the "feeders and growers"—are marching toward going home soon. Experience makes the medical gadgetry less intrusive and disturbing to parents of the preemies who still need to be carefully watched. Parents discover how to get closer to their babies, despite the high-tech, impersonal ambience.

My baby girl, Chloe, was born at 27 weeks, under two pounds. When she was just a week old, and still being given oxygen, a nurse asked me if I wanted to "kangaroo" her. Blurred images of Australian marsupials with a pouch came to mind. How could that relate to us? Well, I found out. The nurse got a screen to give me privacy, and told me to unbutton my shirt. Then she had me sit on a rocking chair, and handed me Chloe, with only her diaper and a wool hat on. "Put her against your naked skin, and hold her upright, her head between your breasts," the nurse said. "I'll cover her back with this blanket. She'll sleep peacefully, listening to your heartbeat." So we sat there together for more than an hour. And we have been doing it every day for the last three weeks. For me, it's heaven. I long for it so much that every day I wake up and rush to the hospital. Chloe seems to thrive on it, too: the nurses say she looks so peaceful, and she's never had an apnea in my arms. Now she's learning how to nipple, and steadily putting on weight. Maybe it doesn't have to do with kangaroo care. But I like to think she's getting better partly because of me. I feel like I'm breathing my life into her, when I hold her so close. We have a private nest in the middle of the hospital nursery.

After the frantic quality of the first days, time in the hospital relaxes into a more reassuring routine, which can last just a few days, or many weeks for the babies who still have a lot of maturing to do. In the process, the parents learn a lot about prematurity, and keep busy, doing things for and with their babies. Their behavior is controlled, but underneath, anxiety still looms. It may take only a spark to ignite it again. ◦

"There's still a few minutes to go before the 9 o'clock feeding," I tell myself with relief, while I wait for the elevator. Every tile under my feet looks familiar, I'm a veteran NICU father by now. It's been a month since our twin boys Simon and Zachary were born, eleven weeks before term, and I've come to visit them every single day. We've had an intense time here, with setbacks and improvements. Simon got pneumonia and went back on a ventilator. He's off the vent now, but still smaller than his brother. "Zac has such an appetite," I mumble with a smile, preparing to see him awake and eager for his bottle. How strange, he's not here, I must have taken a wrong turn. But I know the baby girl on the left: this is the right spot. While looking at the empty space where my son's isolette has always been, I'm starting to feel

dizzy. Now something must have happened to Zac. I'm rushing to the nursing station, ready to shout "Where is my baby!?" when one of the doctors approaches me. "Are you happy that Zachary graduated to the step-down unit?" she asks. "Your wife was so excited about it on the phone. And it probably won't be long before Simon joins his brother." What is she talking about? The step-down unit. Where preemies go when they don't need as many doctors around. The good news came this morning, minutes after I left the house. I never imagined! I'm still breathless, but I can feel my tension deflating, like air from a punctured tire. Let's go see how Zac is doing in his new place. Or should I first visit Simon, and hold him for a while? Gee, when you have twins, you really have to juggle.

Social relationships are not always easy to resume after the premature birth of a child. A birth is supposed to be a happy event. But when a newborn has to stay in the hospital for weeks, people often don't know the appropriate way to react. Perceiving that awkwardness, parents ask themselves: How much do I have to tell about my baby? Is there a correct formula I should know?

"You look painfully thin, my dear! I can't believe you just had a baby!" My wife is embarrassed, and I'm annoyed that she has to respond to that comment for what seems like the hundredth time. "I didn't have much time to put on weight, since my pregnancy lasted barely six months," she utters, startling the older woman. "But our daughter Emily is doing great," I step in, trying to rescue my wife. "Would you like a drink?" It is true that Emily is much better now. But her fight to survive in her first few days has taken a heavy toll on us. While I lead my wife to our table, holding her hand, I can feel how nervous she is. This wedding party is our first social engagement since Emily's birth, almost two months ago. "What kills me is that I have to tell our story over and over again," my wife says. "But you don't have to!" I object. "Why do you assume that everyone knew your due date? Besides, people don't know anything about premature babies, so they can't understand what you're talking about." Somebody is approaching us: it's Mary, my second cousin, with a tall, handsome boy at her side. "I just wanted to introduce you to my nephew Matthew. He was a preemie. And look at him now!" she says. Mary is eager to know all about Emily; she's nice and engaging. So I have to start recalling, beginning from day one: the delivery. My wife, sipping a drink, nods and gives me glances of approval. This time it's my turn to be the storyteller.

Some parents manage to deal with impossibly rigid schedules, trying to reconcile their daily chores with caring for their baby in the hospital. But in striving for perfection, they may overlook something important. And come to realize that flexibility is the key.

I've always been very organized. So, when our third child, Phil, was born a month and a half ago at 28 weeks of gestation, it didn't take me long to work out a daily schedule to accommodate visits to him in the hospital, with taking care of my two older sons, who are in school, and my other million engagements. I don't have a minute to spare! But it is such a joy to watch Phil's progress. I get to stay with him for two feedings. At noon he nipples from a bottle (that I give him!), while the three o'clock feeding comes quickly through gavage, to keep him from getting too tired. Then I have to put him right away in his bed and kiss him good-bye: it's time for me to go. Today, though, things went differently. A nurse I hadn't met before was assigned to Phil. When she saw me standing up right after the gavage, she asked: "Are you going already? Your baby just ate, can't you hold him for a little longer?" "I'm afraid that's not possible . . ." I began to say. But then I looked at Phil, well-fed and fully asleep in my lap, a satisfied expression on his round little face. To him, a meal is a meal, coming from a bottle or a tube in his stomach. The good part is getting full and relaxed and napping in the cocoon of my arms. How could I be so blind and interrupt this moment of bliss? That was it. I blew my schedule. I was late to pick up my kids. We had fast food instead of a healthy meal. I'm afraid we'll have to get accustomed to a little disruption, from now on.

Most parents spend a rather isolated time in the hospital nursery, even though they're surrounded by other families, nurses, and doctors. They are too focused on their babies to be able to develop other relationships. Even if they would like to reach out, they may not have the time or sheer energy to do it. Others are luckier.

Here she comes, Liz, silent and swift, a figure in black slacks and a crisp white shirt. Her eyes are pointed on her son's isolette, to make sure nothing has changed since she left him yesterday. I know her anxiety, because it's also mine. "He's awake, he's been kicking the air for a while," I whisper, and she gratefully smiles back in return. Liz is my friend here in the step-down unit, where our premature sons are now out of danger, but still learning the basics of being a newborn. When she's not here, I check on her son from a distance, without intruding, and I know she does the same with mine. What makes me feel we're friends? Lots of smiles, silent words, understanding nods at each other, while we're holding our babies in our rocking chairs: like stranded sailors waving at each other from nearby islands, the sound of the waves covering their voices. Every morning we forecast our future from our babies' last numbers. "How many apneas?" "How much weight did he gain yesterday?" We had a few longer conversations in the corridor, rushing back from pumping our breast milk: both eager to talk, but also wary of losing too much time chatting. Precious minutes belonging to our babies. Who will go home first? Let's make sure we exchange phone numbers. I had an image, a fantasy of our sons playing together one day, but I'm not telling her. We must live in the moment. These are things we can only say with our eyes.

Once they've settled down in the hospital with their premature babies, some parents finally allow themselves to take a break. For others, it's hard to accept that they may need it. But taking a short leave from the NICU, at least one or two days without visiting, is a fundamental sign of healing, a necessary step in the slow process of returning to normality. Things can be seen with more clarity, often with a more ample—and appropriate—dose of optimism, from a distance.

On this early summer morning, everything is too bright on the little beach facing the bay: the lush green all around, a deep smell of honeysuckle, the sunshine on the water, as still as my heart is. I haven't been really outdoors for many weeks now, since our baby was born prematurely. I've grown accustomed to the features of his world, the hospital nursery: gray and white colors, Plexiglas and steel, plastic, metal, and coarse bleached cotton. Last night he fed at my breast, without getting too tired. Then he fell asleep in my arms, lulled by the rocking motion of the chair, and by my whispers of gratitude and love. "You should leave," said the nurse, "we have plenty of your milk to give him, for tonight and tomorrow. And don't worry. He's breastfeeding so well, he won't forget how to do it." My husband and I had a deal. A single day at the beach, far away from the hospital. I'm a city person who functions well surrounded by concrete. But I had forgotten how beautiful it could be, out here. Inside, I'm really quiet. And empty: I miss our baby. But I know at last that the tempest is behind us. Soon we'll be able to take our baby into this brightly colored world.

The Doctor's Perspective:
Settling Down in the Hospital*

Some babies and families never settle down in the hospital. They're grown and on their way home long before the nursery becomes a familiar setting. Others stay longer and eventually become—though it's hard to believe that now—kind of comfortable here. You have your routine, and you know ours. We form an enclave, the staff and the long-term parents: waiting, sharing a knowledge and togetherness in this strange, intense environment.

PHYSICAL EXAM AND LABORATORY ASSESSMENT

We'll continue to watch your baby's breathing, circulation, and activity level, and tailor our medical support to her changing needs. Sometimes, new conditions will develop—a new heart murmur, for example, is commonly heard, or a hernia appears. We'll investigate and handle these if they arise. Although these new problems often provoke a lot of anxiety in parents (even the slightest problem, after all you've been through, can trigger fears of catastrophe), doctors know that they're rarely life-threatening, and simply part of the routine ups-and-downs of a growing premature baby. As time goes by, we'll be able to give you more information about what your preemie's future medical condition will be, and how that might affect your family.

After the first week or two of life, another parameter of health and development comes to the forefront—how well your baby is growing. Doctors are particularly interested in growth, because as preemies grow, they can make healthy tissue to replace what may have been damaged earlier—lungs, brain, intestine, or whatever. Her new and more mature tissues can function in ever-more-sophisticated ways, so her body will become more adept at regulating its vital functions itself. As she grows and matures, she'll need our medical help less and less, and eventually she'll graduate from our hands to yours.

We'll monitor your preemie's growth by weighing her daily and measuring her head circumference weekly. (Babies who are more than several months old may be weighed less frequently, because small daily fluctuations become relatively less important. Babies with large intraventricular hemorrhages will have their head circumferences measured more frequently, to evaluate changes in ventricular size, as well as brain growth.) Because a baby's length changes too slowly to be a good reflection of her immediate nutritional status, and is hard to measure accurately, we won't be following her length closely. We may also check her nutritional status with lab tests that measure the pro-

---

*"The Doctor's Perspective" describes how your doctor may be thinking about your preemie's condition, and what she may be considering as she makes medical decisions. All of the medical terms and conditions mentioned here are described in more detail elsewhere in this book. Check the index.

tein and minerals she has available to make muscle and bone, some vitamin levels, and her red blood cell count to see if she's becoming anemic. These tests are particularly important in babies who are fed with TPN, and may need further nutritional supplementation.

Nearly all babies lose weight in the first ten days or so of life—from fluid shifts, and until the mother's milk supply and baby's feeding behavior are well established. Doctors also don't expect babies who are acutely ill to grow well—they're using all the calories we can give them to fight their illness. But after that, while your baby is convalescing, we'd like to see her gain 15 to 30 grams a day. (Thirty grams is an ounce, so that's about a third of a pound a week.) If she's gaining faster than that, we might worry that she's retaining fluid, rather than actually growing. If she's gaining slower, we'll probably try to increase her calories, or cut down on her energy expenditure—maybe by limiting the number of meals she takes by mouth (sucking requires a lot more energy than being gavage-fed), or by keeping her in an isolette a while longer, so she doesn't have to generate so much of her own heat.

If your preemie was born at less than about 30 weeks of gestation, I'll be contacting an ophthalmologist when she's approximately a month old to examine her eyes. He'll do a detailed examination of her retina to see if she's developed any signs of retinopathy of prematurity (ROP, see page 268). As a neonatologist, I don't have the expertise to do this kind of an exam, so I'll be relying on the ophthalmologist to tell me the results, determine how frequently your baby should get follow-up eye exams, and choose any appropriate therapy. I wouldn't be surprised if she has some mild ROP, as that's extremely common in the youngest preemies, and doesn't require any treatment. But if her retinopathy is more severe, I'll consider chang-

ing some aspects of her basic care that could affect the progression of ROP—perhaps raising or lowering her oxygen level, for instance—and may try to keep her in a medical center where she has easy access to a pediatric ophthalmologist.

All preemies will also get a hearing test before they're discharged (see page 272). We usually wait until a preemie is approximately 32 weeks of age post-conception (and try to do it after a good meal!), because the test is more accurate in older babies who are quiet and relaxed. If the test is abnormal the first time, I don't worry much—there are a lot of falsely abnormal screening tests. We'll just repeat it in a week or two. Often, the second test will show us that the baby's hearing is normal.

COMMON ISSUES AND DECISIONS

Breathing: For babies with respiratory problems who are in the hospital a long time, the weeks they spend on the ventilator or on oxygen can seem interminable to their parents, and apnea of prematurity may seem to go on forever. In reality, your baby's time frame may be absolutely typical of babies her age and size. That's one of the things I'll be evaluating—whether she's showing the usual breathing immaturities (in which case, time and nurturing will be almost all she needs), or if her respiratory patterns indicate we should be looking for other diagnoses, or escalating our therapy.

I'll be assessing whether or not she's developing chronic lung disease (BPD, see page 261), based on how normal her lungs look on chest x-rays, and how comfortable and independent her breathing is becoming. Officially, a diagnosis of BPD can't be made unless a baby has required supplemental oxygen for at least a month, but doctors often know sooner if a baby has some lung damage. Babies with very mild BPD may just need some oxygen for support until they recover on their own. Others may do better on medications such as diuretics to get rid of excess fluid, or bronchodilators to open up their airways (especially if they wheeze or sound "tight"). Babies who seem to be "stuck" on the ventilator may improve with a temporary course of steroids, weaning to lower settings that are less damaging to their lungs, or even coming off the ventilator altogether. Since nearly all of these treatments have some side effects, I may want to give a baby a brief trial of a therapy to see how well she responds, before making it a regular part of her regimen. Even if I decide that your baby does have some chronic lung disease, this is by no means a sentence of doom. Only preemies with the most severe lung damage have long-lasting, serious problems. I look at a baby with mild or moderate BPD as apt to be with me longer, requiring some more attention and care, but with a bright and open future. And I hope her parents see that, too.

Even if your baby is on medication for apnea, such as caffeine or theophylline, she's probably still having some A's and B's (apnea and bradycardia)—most preemies do. I don't worry about apnea of prematurity if most of a preemie's bradycardias are mild, her apneas usually resolve with just some mild stimulation, and she's averaging fewer than 10 or 12 episodes a day. But if your baby's apnea is worse than that, I'll consider whether something else may be exacerbating it. If she has frequent wet burps or worsening apnea and bradycardia after feedings, for example, I'll suspect that gastroesophageal reflux (see page 244) may be contributing to her apnea. I might try some therapies for reflux— maybe thickening her feeds with rice cereal, or

prescribing a medication like reglan, to help her stomach empty faster. If her apnea has worsened suddenly, I'll worry that it may be due to an infection, and may check for that with blood tests, cultures for viruses and bacteria, and a chest x-ray. Some babies need more oxygen, and have more apnea, when they're anemic, so I may see if giving her a blood transfusion helps. And if the pattern of her breathing indicates that she's very sensitive to noise, light, and handling, we'll try to do what we can to ameliorate some of the overstimulation of the nursery.

Feeding: Another developmental process that can seem interminable to parents, particularly if their preemie is having difficulty with it, is "working up on feeds." This is the feeding journey that ends when your baby's intestines can digest all the food she needs to thrive, and her brain is giving her all the right signals to take it in. This sometimes long process can be nearly as frustrating to doctors and nurses as it is to you, but we've learned from experience that great patience pays off. There comes a time for most babies, when they reach some more advanced level of maturity, when the problems—whether diarrhea, bloating, reflux, or poor nippling— just, seemingly miraculously, resolve. In the meantime, we'll be adjusting the content of your baby's feeds, their timing, and the amount she's getting, deciding when to challenge her with more nutrition, and when to back down. The reason we don't just push on with more and more feeds, regardless, is our concern that she could develop NEC (see page 237) or an aspiration pneumonia if feedings are advanced recklessly. The reason we don't stop pushing her feedings at all, is that as long as she needs TPN she's tied to IVs, blood tests, and the hospital; and parenteral nutrition simply can't nourish her as well as her own gastrointestinal tract was meant to do. So it's a balancing act—one of the many that we do with preemies until they take over their own vital functions.

Anemia: All preemies become gradually anemic (see page 276 for reasons why), with their red blood cell count dropping to its lowest point at about two months after birth, then slowly rising again to normal. Many preemies show no symptoms, not seeming to mind being anemic. Based on whether your baby has symptoms, and whether her blood counts are likely to drop further (which might happen, for example, if she's less than six weeks old, getting a lot of blood tests, or has severe BPD), I'll decide whether or not to correct her anemia with a blood transfusion, or with a medication called erythropoietin.

If your baby is active and growing well, isn't needing increased respiratory support or having worse apnea, and doesn't have an excessively fast heart rate, I may decide that she's tolerating her anemia just fine. But if she has symptoms, or if I think she's going to need more blood before her body can make enough on its own, then I have to choose between giving her a transfusion or starting her on erythropoietin. As usual, there are risks and benefits to weigh. A blood transfusion works immediately, but it carries a small risk of infection, and can postpone the time when your baby's own body takes over the job of making lots of new red blood cells. Erythropoietin involves shots three times a week, takes a couple of weeks to work, and has to be given with oral iron supplements.

If your baby needs blood soon, or isn't tolerating her feedings (so she can't take oral iron), I'd probably opt for the transfusion. I might also choose the transfusion if she's gotten blood in the past, and I know that the blood she'd get now would come from the same donor as before. (This could happen if your hospital has a policy to "dedicate" a donor's blood pack to a specific baby, giving that donor's blood only to her until it runs out.) In that case, the transfusion carries no extra risk of infection. But if I think she might continue to need more blood even after the dedicated blood pack has run out, she can wait a little while for her anemia to be corrected, and she can take oral iron, I'd probably begin her on erythropoietin. That way, she'll need fewer transfusions in the long run.

Infection: Most preemies who are in the hospital for more than a few weeks will end up getting evaluated for an infection (although far fewer of them will actually have one), including blood tests, urine tests, maybe a chest x-ray and spinal tap, cultures of other areas that may be infected, and some antibiotic treatment. I wish we could be more discriminating about who gets evaluated, eliminating some of those false alarms that make trouble for preemies and basket cases of their parents! Unfortunately, we're not very good at determining who does and doesn't need to be treated for an infection, because the symptoms are often the same as those that all preemies may show intermittently—for instance, apnea, a temporary need for more respiratory support, feeding intolerance, or mild metabolic abnormalities. Preemies have immature immune systems and don't fight infections well. So, we're often loathe to just wait and see whether a baby's symptoms develop into anything serious or not, for fear that severe complications might occur while we wait. Occasionally, the diagnostic tests are inconclusive, and your baby's doctor has to decide, based on his experience and knowledge of your baby, whether her symptoms were truly due to an infection or not. Most of the time, if your baby does have an infection, treatment works, and she'll recover from it completely.

Timing of back-transfer: If your baby is in a hospital far from home, there will come a time when she no longer needs state-of-the-art neonatal care. She'll be able to return to a hospital closer to home, where she can grow and mature until she's ready to go home with you. I'd consider a baby ready for such a "back-transfer," as we call it, only when she's stable, and no longer needs complicated reevaluations or changes in therapy. This is a time for celebration—a graduation as momentous as high school! Many parents are anxious about this transition, scared that their baby won't be cared for as well in a local hospital. But you can be sure that doctors and nurses take the responsibility for their little charges very seriously, and would never transfer her to a hospital that couldn't adequately take care of her. Some hospitals can handle more complex patients than others. For example, some nurseries accept preemies on oxygen (knowing that they can evaluate any problems and wean a baby to room air safely), while others do not. The medical staff planning your baby's back-transfer are aware of what kinds of patients your community hospital can handle. And your baby's doctor will discuss her medical condition with the physician and nurses there, so that the important information is passed on.

There are a lot of benefits to moving to a hospital closer to home. It's true that you'll be leaving a place and people you've become familiar with, and perhaps attached to. But this is a move closer to normality. You won't have to travel so far to see your baby, so you can spend more time with her, with your family or friends, and on daily tasks. You'll be able to relax in the knowledge that your baby has reached a comfortable level of stability. Your baby may be calmer—there's usually less hustle and bustle. Her own pediatrician or family doctor can start getting to know her, by taking care of her medical needs in his own hospital. And your baby's former intensive care bed can be made available to another sick baby who may desperately need it.

FAMILY ISSUES

Let's talk about some of the temptations that parents who have babies in the hospital for a long time may fall into. There are some that I think are counter-productive and best avoided whenever possible.

It's tempting to compare the progress that your baby is making with other babies in the nursery, particularly if you're making friends with other parents. Don't. There are always unique features that make your baby's path different from any others'. Some babies tend to take little gradual steps forward, while others seem stuck for a while, but then surprise everyone with a great leap of progress. Every baby can have a triumph or a setback, and it takes longer to get over some kinds of medical conditions than others. It's no better or worse to have trouble with breathing than digestion—or anything else. Try not to compare yourself to other parents, either. Parents are people with individual needs and temperaments, who will cope differently at various times in their baby's hospitalization. Remember that there is no such thing as "the" experience of having a premature baby. There is just your experience . . . and yours . . . and yours.

Try to avoid the temptation to see a lack of visible progress as failure. Your baby's doctor will tell you if medical treatment really isn't working, and you should certainly take that seriously. But usually, it's just that growth and development take time. Your baby's schedule of maturation is directing the time frame of his recovery much more than the doctors are. The doctor will periodically try to move things forward. If your baby doesn't tolerate, say, an extubation from the ventilator, or a feeding increase, it's not a setback. It probably just means we've moved too fast. Patience is a virtue for all parents—but especially for parents of preemies!

If you're in the hospital long enough, and learn the medical jargon, you'll be tempted to judge how your baby is doing by focusing on numbers—the amount of oxygen she's getting, her vent settings, her oxygen saturations, how many apneas she's had, her blood counts, etc. It's not surprising that this happens—numbers are objective measures in plain view, and the doctors and nurses use them to monitor your baby's condition and help plan her treatment.

But numbers can be misleading. The experience that doctors and nurses have with thousands of babies allows them to put these pieces of information in context, while parents can be sent into a tailspin by normal up-and-down variations. Some abnormal numbers indicate true improvement or worsening, but others are just ebbs and flows around a plateau, or even false readings. Some dips and spikes are unimportant for one baby and crucial for another.

Although it can be very informative for parents to ask doctors and nurses to interpret the significance of what they're measuring, it's not helpful for you to focus too much on the changing, or unchanging, numbers—what is helpful is for you to gather the kind of knowledge that parents are best at, like how peaceful or content or interactive your baby is, and what

makes him feel good or bad. The involvement he needs from you is a tender touch and loving voice, not more measurements and spinning dials.

And finally, you may take your time at the hospital to extremes—either putting everything else in your life on hold, or feeling like there's no point in coming to the hospital because there's nothing you can do. It's tempting to relegate everything else to secondary importance until this momentous time has passed. And, for a while, everything else will be less important. But then other responsibilities, pleasures, and bonds should reassert their rightful place. Despite the difficulties, you should try to maintain some of your normal daily activities. Leave the hospital for a while—and don't feel guilty about it. You can be a better parent if you're more balanced and refreshed. Try not to let important relationships languish. It's not just your baby who needs you, but your spouse, or partner, or other children—and they can support parts of you that are vital for your own strength and health. By bolstering yourself, you can bring to your baby's world the strength and depth that will enrich your time together, now and in the future.

On the other hand, it may be tempting to stay away from the nursery to escape sad conversations and feelings of loss, or to avoid meetings with strangers and the discomfort of a harsh environment. You absolutely do need breaks and time away—but don't ever think that your presence doesn't count. Even if you feel powerless, you can do something great—give your baby a mommy or daddy, to touch him in a way that none of the nurses or doctors do, to whisper to him that you love him and are there with him, to show him he's not alone. That's what you'll be doing the rest of his life; you might as well start settling into it now.

Questions and Answers

GETTING ACQUAINTED WITH:
APNEA AND BRADYCARDIA

It will be a few years before your preemie learns the ABC's. But she may be quite familiar already with A's and B's—of the NICU variety.

The expression *A's and B's* is shorthand for episodes of apnea (a pause in breathing) and bradycardia (a slow heart rate), two of the most common problems of premature babies. These episodes frighten parents, and keep nurses busy attending to all of the beeping alarms. But doctors only worry about them if they're unusually severe, or if they appear to be a sign of some underlying illness. Most of the time, that's not the case—all they mean is that your preemie's control of her breathing is immature. It's not that surprising when you consider that she wasn't supposed to be breathing air yet at all.

It's normal for preemies to do something called periodic breathing; they take some deep breaths and then pause for five or ten seconds before taking the next one. Only when a pause lasts for at least 20 seconds, or is accompanied by a slow heart rate or change in the baby's skin color, is it considered apnea. Bradycardia—or a "brady"—which in most cases is a result of apnea—is defined as the slowing of a baby's heart rate from its usual range of 120 to 160 beats per minute to a rate of less than 100 beats per minute. (A preemie's heart beats about twice as fast as a typical adult's.)

WHAT CAUSES APNEA IN PREMATURE BABIES?

The complex physiological system that regulates everyone's breathing and heart rate is not yet fully developed in preemies. Sometimes, the immature respiratory center in your preemie's brain may forget to send a signal to breathe—and breathing movements stop. Other times, her brain may remember to send the signal to breathe, and her chest will move as it should, but the muscles that are supposed to keep her upper airway open become lax—so airflow to the lungs stops.

The failure to send the signal to breathe can be brought on by deep sleep, or strangely enough, a lack of oxygen. Sedative medications can make it worse. And if a baby breathes quickly for a while, her body may overcompensate with an overly long pause for a few moments afterward.

Apnea may be triggered by stress—resulting from common procedures, like suctioning mucus from the baby's airways, or from a change in temperature, as when she's placed on a cold scale to be weighed. Sheer fatigue can cause it. Apnea can even happen in response to a seemingly normal action like feeding, having a bowel movement, stretching, or excessive bending of the neck.

WHO GETS APNEA OF PREMATURITY?

A lot of preemies: eighty percent of those born before 30 weeks of gestation, one third of those born between 30 and 34 weeks, and 7% of those born at 34 to 35 weeks.

To make things more complicated, apnea and bradycardia can occur as a symptom of other illnesses, including respiratory distress syndrome (RDS, see page 101), intraventricular hemorrhage (see page 164), seizures, infection, anemia, gastroesophageal reflux (see page 244), necrotizing enterocolitis (see page 237), or a patent ductus arteriosus (see page 176). If your baby's A's and B's follow an unusual pattern—starting with severe incidents on the very first day of life, starting very suddenly later on, or growing increasingly severe—then her doctor will investigate the possibility of an underlying medical condition, which will need to be treated for the apnea to disappear. But this is less common than simple apnea of prematurity alone.

HOW APNEA OF PREMATURITY IS TREATED

Sometimes, if it's very mild, apnea of prematurity isn't treated at all. When a baby's apnea or bradycardia alarm goes off, her nurse will watch to make sure that she starts breathing again on her own. If she doesn't, the nurse will stimulate her with a gentle tap or rub, which will usually do the trick.

Some babies have more frequent or severe episodes of apnea, when they need more vigorous stimulation or extra oxygen. Once the baby is pink and breathing again, she'll be fine, but her doctor will probably want to treat her with medication to help prevent such episodes from recurring. Very young preemies, who are more prone to apnea, are often put on medication early, even before they have severe episodes of apnea, as a preventive measure.

There are two common medications for apnea: caffeine and a drug called theophylline (or aminophylline), which babies metabolize into caffeine. Although it's a startling thought—your newborn being given a double espresso, hold the cup—caffeine is very effective at stimulating respiration, which is just what your baby needs. (Once her apnea of prematurity goes away, the medication will be stopped, and she'll lose her caffeine privileges until you give her the OK later on.)

There are also other ways to make apnea and bradys less frequent. One is to reduce their triggers, such as sudden changes in temperature and overstimulation. Studies have shown that premature babies have less apnea when they lie prone, on their stomachs; that's one reason you'll see most preemies sleeping peacefully on their stomachs in the NICU. (This concerns some parents who are aware that a prone sleeping position increases the risk of sudden infant death syndrome in full-term newborns. See page 243.)

Pulsating or rotating beds may reduce apnea, and are used in some NICUs. To avoid too much neck flexion and obstruction of babies' airways, nurses may place small rolls under their necks and shoulders. You'll learn to make sure that your baby's chin doesn't fall forward when you are feeding or just holding her in your arms. Ask your baby's nurse to show you how.

If your baby is not responding to these measures, or has severe apnea as a result of an illness, she may be put on a ventilator temporarily, until the serious episodes have subsided.

THE COURSE THAT APNEA OF PREMATURITY TAKES

Apnea of prematurity tends to take a very predictable course. It usually starts within the first few days of life. Some babies have two or three episodes a day, and some have a dozen—but over time, as their bodies mature, their apnea gets milder. It almost always disappears by two to four weeks before their due date.

If you're wondering whether your baby's apnea really will disappear soon, we can tell you this: Many parents have the same doubts, and almost all of them are pleasantly surprised when their baby's apnea goes away on schedule. Chances are you'll be pleasantly surprised, too. But if your preemie turns out to be one of the few who need more time, don't worry. She may just stay a week or two longer in the hospital. Or, if she's otherwise ready to leave, she could be sent home with some medication or a monitor, so her apnea doesn't stand in the way of her homecoming.

A PARENT'S CONCERNS

Several concerns are foremost in a mother's or father's mind when their baby has apnea. One is: could one of these episodes be life-threatening? If your baby has simple apnea of prematurity, the odds of her having a life-threatening episode are minuscule. She has monitors to alert the nurses when her vital signs are weakening. The monitors are set high, to give the nurses plenty of time to respond before your baby is in distress. They know just how to stimulate her, or even resuscitate her, if it's necessary.

Another frequently expressed concern is whether A's and B's can cause long-term damage. Mild or occasional apnea or bradycardia, even when followed by desatting (oxygen desaturation), is believed to pose no danger; babies can safely tolerate low amounts of oxygen for short periods of time. But if apnea is more severe, with frequent, deep desats, a baby's risk of developing retinopathy of prematurity (ROP, page 268) or pulmonary hypertension (page 171) does increase. Whenever a premature baby's heart rate drops below 50 or 60 for more than a few seconds, blood flow to her organs may be inadequate, increasing her risk of NEC (page 237) and other organ damage. A's and B's may also be harmful to babies who are recovering from surgery and need good oxygen and blood flow to their wounds. But as long as the baby's oxygen levels and heart rate rise again quickly, and the deep A's and B's are infrequent, there's little chance of a problem.

Finally, parents often wonder whether apnea of prematurity will increase their baby's risk of sudden infant death syndrome. This isn't something you need to worry about. Apnea of prematurity is not related to SIDS. It goes away as your baby matures, and when it is gone, it is completely and totally behind you.

Kangaroo Care

I've read about kangaroo care, and my instinct tells me it's the right thing to do. But nobody in my unit does it, and I don't know how to get started.

If your baby had been born at term as expected, holding her is something you wouldn't have given much thought to. It would have been the most natural thing in the world.

For most full-term babies, much of early infancy is spent snuggled against their parents' bodies—feeding in their mothers' arms, falling asleep on their fathers' chests, and being held close up against them throughout the day, crooked inside an elbow, a baby-carrier, or a sling.

But when your baby is born prematurely, you don't have many opportunities to do what comes naturally. Maybe that explains the appeal and benefits of kangaroo care, which means nothing more than holding your naked preemie (usually clad in just a diaper) against your own, naked, warm chest. With a blanket draped over your baby's back to keep him warm, you can sit that way for hours at a time, quiet or talking, still or rocking, and, at times of greatest peacefulness, even falling asleep together.

What are the medical and long-term effects of kangaroo care? The truth is we don't yet know. Some experts believe that we will eventually learn that skin-to-skin holding enhances a preemie's long-term development, by offering something that all babies are biologically programmed to expect: parental nurturing and physical contact during infancy. Other experts disagree that any long-term effects will ever be revealed, and recommend skin-to-skin holding simply because it is a way to make a preemie happier, to smooth out the wrinkles in her day.

(It's common for parents to say that kangaroo care has a profound impact on them, also, giving them the feeling that they're being the kind of parent to their baby that nature intended.) Still others believe that nakedness is nice, but that extended physical contact with you, clothed or not, is what's important. So, if you're uncomfortable doing skin-to-skin holding in the nursery, perhaps for modesty or privacy reasons, and would rather hold your baby clothed, that's fine, too. Your baby will love it.

By the way, real kangaroos really do know something about prematurity. The baby kangaroos they have about once a year are born only partially developed, so they hop into their mother's warm pouch, and continue their development there for months. The human version of kangaroo care originated twenty years ago out of a crisis at a hospital in Bogota, Colombia. Its intensive care nursery was so poorly equipped, and had such a high infection rate, that it started a new program, discharging even the tiniest premature babies within hours or days after birth, to be held and cared for by their mothers at home, kangaroo-style. In the first few years, the number of neonatal deaths significantly decreased, as did the number of abandoned infants.

Since then, the practice of kangaroo care, done voluntarily by mothers and fathers in the intensive care nursery, has spread around the world. Research studies have consistently shown that up against the heat of their parents' bodies, these preemies maintain their body temperature as well as, or better than, in an incubator. Some studies have also suggested that while being held skin-to-skin, preemies were apt to cry less, and to have less apnea, higher levels of oxygen saturation, and more restful sleep. Babies held skin-to-skin during breastfeeding were more likely to be nursing one month after hospital discharge than those who were fed wearing more than a diaper, and their mothers had more stable milk production. The researchers speculated that skin-to-skin contact helped stimulate lactation.

Kangaroo care is so easy and natural that you'll be an expert after your first try. Here's how to get started:

* Ask the doctor or nurse if your baby is stable enough for kangaroo care. Practices vary: some nurseries prefer that a baby be breathing on her own, or with just supplemental oxygen, while others encourage it even for babies on ventilators.
* Wear a shirt that opens in front. If you don't have one, just ask the nurse for a hospital gown, and put it on without any other clothing on your chest.
* Find a comfortable chair. Some nurseries now have special recliners for kangaroo care, but a regular rocking chair is great, too. If you don't see one near your baby's bed, don't hesitate to ask where you can find one.
* Ask a nurse to place your baby comfortably on your chest. First, you or the nurse should undress your baby, down to her diaper. Then, open your shirt or gown (if you want

privacy, ask if your nursery has a portable screen—most do), and have the nurse place your baby upright on your chest, between your breasts, with her cheek resting comfortably on your skin. Help her get into a comfortable position if she squirms a little. Cover the baby's back with your shirt or gown, and with a light blanket. The nurse will periodically take your baby's temperature, to make sure she stays warm enough. If she gets too warm from the heat your body gives her, you can remove the blanket.
* Now . . . relax! There's nothing more important than that. You can try talking or singing to your baby for a while, letting her enjoy the pleasurable sound of your voice, and then letting her rest while you rock, recline, read a book, or fall asleep yourself. You can stay together as long as you like and the nurse agrees. Some parents and babies do kangaroo care for just a half hour a day, while others stretch it out as long as possible—to four or five hours or longer. Once you get started, you'll probably understand why. These are precious moments for a parent and child.

PRACTICAL ADVICE FOR PUMPING AND STORING BREAST MILK

So, you've started expressing your milk, and you want to breastfeed your preemie. There are many things you will learn by yourself during this highly rewarding experience, no matter if you breastfeed for a short time, or for many months to come. Here is some practical guidance to lead you through the challenging, early stages of your preemie's nursing. After that, his feeding behavior will become no different from that of a baby born at full-term.

EXPRESSING YOUR MILK

These days, most mothers who breastfeed eventually learn to express their milk for one reason or another, often because they're working, shopping, or traveling without their baby. But as a mother of a premature baby, you'll become a true expert on breast pumps and expressing your milk from the very start.

In the first days: The milk production system in your breast develops during the very first months of pregnancy, prompted by hormones. Even if your baby was born extremely prematurely, just at the limit of viability, you'll be ready to breastfeed him. A remarkable sign that mother nature is looking out for you and your preemie is the fact that your milk will be different from that of a mother who delivers at term: it is perfectly tailored to the nutritional needs of a premature baby.

For lactation to get started, your breast must get a signal from the hormone prolactin, which is normally stimulated by a baby's sucking. The hungrier a newborn is, the longer and stronger his sucking, the more stimulation he gives to the nipple, and the more milk his mother's breast will make. It is a finely tuned supply-and-demand system that allows the breast to make exactly as much milk as a baby needs, and no more. But if your preemie is not ready to nurse yet, you have to rely on the artificial stimulation of an electric breast pump, which provides the closest approximation to a baby's sucking.

Mothers of preemies who begin using a hospital-quality, electric breast pump within hours after delivery have the best chance of producing enough milk to satisfy their babies' growing needs. With a pump, mothers can express their milk and store it, so it can be fed to their preemies later, through a gavage tube, until their babies become mature enough to suck at the breast. The first attempts to express milk with an electric pump can be unpleasant or occasionally painful, depending on the sensitivity of your nipples, but most mothers quickly get used to it or find that a breastfeeding expert can help identify and solve the problem. You can find suggestions to make the initial experience easier on page 114.

In the hospital: In your room on the maternity floor, or in your baby's nursery, you'll have access to a hospital-quality electric pump. Most nurseries have a quiet, secluded pumping room, giving mothers the privacy they need. Every time you want to express breast milk, you'll be given a new kit of sterilized equipment (tubing, funnel, collecting container, lid), and some sterilized containers for your milk (disposable bottles or special plastic bags). Don't be shy about asking the nurses for help or advice. On the maternity floor or in the NICU, helping you express breast milk for your premature baby is an important part of a nurse's job. Some hospitals even have lactation specialists dedicated to teaching mothers and babies how to breastfeed.

At home: Soon after delivery, find out where you can rent a high quality electric pump to use at home (common brands are Egnell and Medela). Pharmacies near the hospital or medical supply companies often rent them: ask your nurse about it, or contact a breastfeeding specialist. (You can get a referral through La Leche League—a nonprofit organization that advocates breastfeeding—at [800] LA-LECHE.) Since your baby was born prematurely, the cost of the rental may be covered by your health insurance.

You'll have to buy a personal kit of collecting

equipment (tubing, funnel, etc.), to use with a rented pump, which you should wash and sterilize before each use. Just bring a pot of water to a boil, put in all of the pieces, and boil them for 10 to 12 minutes. Remove them from the water, and let everything dry on a clean cloth.

How soon and how often you should pump:
You should start pumping as soon as possible after delivery, ideally within two to three hours and with a double pumping set-up. Pumping should be frequent, at least every three hours while you're awake, for at least six to eight daily milk expressions. You shouldn't go for more than six hours without pumping—including at night. (If you prepare all of the equipment before going to bed, you can set your alarm for an early morning pumping session, then go back to sleep for a few more hours.) A few days before your baby comes home, some experts recommend that you get ready by waking up during the night and pumping every two to four hours, as often as you would breastfeed him.

You'll need to keep your breast pump throughout your baby's hospitalization, and probably for another two or three weeks after he comes home. It can take a while for a preemie to become an efficient breastfeeder and completely empty your breast at each feeding. You should continue, for some time, to pump for a few minutes after breastfeeding, to supplement his efforts and keep your milk supply going. You'll be able to stop pumping when you find that there's no milk left in your breast after your baby has finished nursing.

If you plan to travel or go back to work soon, you may want to rent or buy a lighter, portable electric pump. It won't empty your breasts quite as completely as a hospital-quality pump, but it has one big advantage: when it's packed up it looks like a briefcase, and many working mothers bring them to their offices with no one the wiser! When your milk supply is well-established, you'll occasionally be able to use other, less powerful pumps—battery operated or manual ones that every pharmacy carries—or simply breast massage (see below).

How to get started:
When you handle breast milk, good hygiene is a must. Wash your hands before touching your breast or the collecting equipment. In the hospital, the collecting units are for individual use only, so make sure you open a new package, and discard it when you're through. At home, make sure everything is clean and sterilized. Connect the tubing to the pump, to the collecting cup for your milk, and to the funnel you'll be applying to your breast. The first time, you may want to ask a nurse to show you how.

The best way to express your milk is to use a double kit that allows you to pump from both breasts at the same time. Although it may feel awkward in the beginning, you'll find that it's convenient and saves time (something parents of preemies never have enough of). Most important, double pumping can stimulate your breasts to produce more milk; that's why mothers of twins who breastfeed both babies simultaneously are often able to produce enough milk for both of them. (If you're a mother of multiples, you'll find more breastfeeding advice on page 290.)

Position the funnel on your breast: it should completely cover your nipple and areola (the darker skin around the nipple), and not pinch or hurt you. Before turning on the pump, adjust its suction to the lowest level. Then, as you pump, gradually increase the suction to a comfortable level. (Any discomfort that you feel during your first few pumping attempts should subside. If it doesn't, or if you feel sharp pain, even during your first sessions, ask your nurse or a breastfeeding consultant to help you figure out what is causing it. For a referral, call La Leche League, see page 522.) Through the transparent funnel, check to make sure that your milk is trickling into the container. If the spray stops, switch off the pump and reposition the funnel on your nipple. Often, with some adjustment, your milk will start to flow again.

In the first few days, you should pump each breast for about ten minutes. Most milk is "let down," or released, in the first five minutes; the additional pumping will stimulate your breast to produce more. Later, you can gradually increase the time you pump each breast up to 15 to 20 minutes, to completely empty your breasts every time.

Why you might not get much at the beginning: It can take a few days for your milk to come in, so don't worry if you get very little in the beginning. You may only express a few drops, but they are precious. Your first milk, called colostrum, is yellow and very thick. Colostrum is important to feed to a preemie, because it is particularly rich in proteins and antibodies. Transitional milk, which comes in about a week after delivery, is also rich in proteins, but contains more water than colostrum. Mature breast milk, which resembles skim milk in its thin, bluish appearance, has more calories and fats than earlier milk, and generally takes one to two weeks to develop.

GETTING THE MILK FROM YOU TO YOUR BABY

Bacteria can easily flourish in breast milk, so you should be very careful how you collect and store it.

Collecting your milk: When you're pumping in the hospital, you can detach the container holding your milk, close it with a lid, and bring it directly to the nursery. At home, you'll have to pour the milk from the collecting container into a disposable, sterile bottle or bag. Your baby's nursery may give you some, or you can buy them at a pharmacy. They are made of a special kind of plastic—polypropylene—that doesn't change the infection-fighting properties of breast milk. Remember not to use other, nonsterile plastic cups or food bags, or your milk will have to be discarded. In order to reduce the risk of contamination, you also shouldn't mix milk from different pumping sessions in the same container.

Breast milk bags have special seals to keep the milk from spilling. You can get familiar with them by filling one bag with water, closing it with the clip included in the kit, and learning how to roll the edge of the bag around the seal. (You'll find instructions that are generally easy to follow.) Every breast milk container must be labeled with your baby's name, hospital identification number, and the date and time you collected it: it is your responsibility to do so. Some nurseries will provide you with pre-stamped labels (to which you will add the date and time of collection), and won't accept handwritten ones. Ask your nurse about your hospital's policy.

Storing and preserving your milk: Ideally, breast milk is fed to a preemie fresh, right after pumping. If you're in your hospital room, waiting for somebody to pick up your container of milk and take it to the nursery, place it in a pan with water and ice, to prevent the growth of bacteria.

Breast milk can be safely stored in the refrigerator for 24 to 48 hours, or in the freezer for much longer. Before feeding it to a baby, frozen milk can be thawed by putting the container in a room temperature water bath. (High temperatures or microwaving can deprive breast milk of important components.) Freezing and thawing will lower the nutritional and infection-fighting qualities of breast milk slightly, but it's still the best choice for your baby, when fresh is not available.

Some hospital nurseries use the amount of breast milk from one container for one feeding, and discard the excess to prevent contamination. Other nurseries don't automatically discard thawed breast milk, but will pour out what they need for one feeding, and keep the rest in the refrigerator for up to twenty-four hours. You should learn what your hospital's policy is, and how much milk your baby is taking at each feeding, so you can fill each bag accordingly (with just a little more than what is needed), and not waste any.

Transporting breast milk from home to the hospital:
If you'll be taking your milk to the hospital within twenty-four hours of pumping, keep it in the refrigerator, then carry it to the hospital packed in ice. If you're storing breast milk for longer, freeze it immediately after it's pumped, and bring it to the nursery packed in ice. Make sure it stays frozen until you give it to the nurse to put in the nursery freezer. Since there is limited space for each baby, you may be asked to store your extra milk in your home freezer, and bring it only when your baby's supply is running low.

When your baby begins feeding, your colostrum will be given to him first. After that, your frozen milk is generally used as a backup for your fresh milk. The oldest milk is used first: that's why it's important to properly label each container. Because fresh milk is somewhat higher in nutrients and antibodies, many mothers try to bring some from home every time they visit, then pump more in the nursery before they leave. You should also check before each visit that there's enough breast milk left for times you're not around, and bring more if it's needed. But don't feel bad if your baby is occasionally fed formula when there's no breast milk left or you didn't make it to the hospital on time: the advantages of breastfeeding are preserved with partial breastfeeding.

Breastfeeding a Preemie

When will my baby, who was born very premature, be able to nurse from my breast?

Though it may be hard for you to imagine now, in just a few weeks your young preemie probably will begin his breastfeeding "lessons." In the past, breastfeeding was considered too tiring and stressful for preemies, because babies have to suck more forcefully to get milk from the breast than from a bottle. Preemies were usually allowed to nurse only after they first learned how to nipple from a bottle without distress.

In the last few years, that approach has changed. New evidence is showing that many preemies can begin breastfeeding several weeks earlier than they can safely drink from a bottle (as early as 28 to 30 weeks, compared to 32 to 34 weeks). Some recent studies have found less oxygen desaturation, less bradycardia, warmer skin temperatures, and better coordination of sucking and breathing when preemies nursed than when they drank from a bottle at the same age.

The reason is simple. A baby can regulate the milk flow from the breast with his sucking bursts; when he pauses to breathe, milk stops flowing. A bottle with an artificial nipple, though, delivers milk partly through gravity, so in order not to choke or gag, a baby has to learn how to stop the milk flow with his tongue or by clenching his jaws, while swallowing and breathing in the meantime. It's a complex technique that requires more mature coordination.

Your baby will have to wait until he is off a ventilator, but he can start breastfeeding even if he's still getting supplemental oxygen through a nasal cannula, provided that he's breathing at relatively normal rates. (Babies who are breathing faster than 70 to 80 times a minute don't have enough time between breaths to suck and swallow safely.) A nurse will stay close by, to make sure your baby's oxygen saturation remains high before, during, and after his first breastfeeding tries.

Even if breastfeeding is easier than bottle feeding, the path to peaceful nursing in their mothers' arms can still be laborious for preemies who are born at an early gestational age. The following methods can be useful to help a young preemie:

* *Introducing the smell and taste of breast milk.* To help a young preemie develop a sucking reflex, you can introduce him to your milk earlier than he's able to drink it. With his doctor's permission, a few times a day you can put a drop of milk on your baby's lips. He will love its smell and taste, and later, he'll associate those pleasurable sensations with his feedings.

* *Nutritive and non-nutritive sucking.* A baby born very prematurely, who has had an endotracheal tube in his mouth and been fed with parenteral nutrition or by gavage for more than a month or so, may have difficulty associating sucking with the pleasant feeling of getting his hunger satiated. To prepare him, it can be helpful to let him suck while he's being gavage fed—either by giving him a tiny pacifier, or better yet, letting him suck at your breast. (Since your baby is not ready to swallow yet, you should pump first.)

* *Kangaroo care.* This is the perfect preparation for breastfeeding for a very young baby. When the doctor thinks he's stable enough, even if he's still on a ventilator, your preemie can learn to recognize your smell and feel the pleasant contact of your warm skin on his. If he's not on a ventilator, he may start to lick and nuzzle your nipple, and perhaps begin practicing sucking. (Since this stimulation may induce a strong let-down reflex with a sudden pouring of milk from your nipple, which may be dangerous for a baby who cannot yet coordinate breathing and swallowing, it's safer to pump and empty your breast before kangarooing.) Gradually, as your baby matures, he will start to latch on and actually breastfeed. Kangaroo care can also help preemies keep warm during their early breastfeeding sessions. Kangaroo care is very easy to do (you can read about it on page 221).

* *Breastfeeding positions.* It's best to start out with the cradle position. Sit comfortably in a chair, and cradle your baby in one arm, holding him diagonally on your body, tummy-to-tummy. The side of his head should rest in the curve of your elbow, his mouth on your nipple, so he doesn't have to turn or bend his neck while he's feeding. (It's more difficult for him to swallow when his head is turned on one side.) This is also the most natural way to begin breastfeeding while doing kangaroo care.

✴ *Helping your baby latch on.* Sometimes a small baby can't latch on to his mother's nipple, because it's too large for his mouth. If this happens, you can help your preemie by shaping your nipple between your thumb and first two fingers. Nipple shields that can make it easier for a baby to latch on are not advised for preemies, because they require a stronger suck to make the milk flow and they lessen breast stimulation, possibly reducing the supply of milk.

✴ *Frequency of breastfeeding.* To avoid exhaustion and excessive energy expenditure, young preemies are usually introduced to breastfeeding progressively. You can start with one session a day, moving on to alternating gavage and breastfeeding, and finally to breastfeeding every time.

✴ *Getting help with breastfeeding.* Even if your baby is not on supplemental oxygen, you'll need the assistance of a nurse in your first breastfeeding sessions, to make sure your baby doesn't show any sign of distress, like color changes, bradycardia, oxygen desaturation, or a drop in temperature. Another major concern for any first-time mother is whether her baby is actually feeding. With more experience, you'll learn to feel when your let-down reflex occurs, but in the beginning, the nurse will check to see if your baby's sucking pattern has changed (indicating he's getting milk) and if he's swallowing. Sometimes, your let-down reflex can be too strong for your inexperienced preemie, who may choke on too much milk; the nurse will help you not to panic, and will show you how to handle the situation. Your baby's nurses or a lactation specialist, if your hospital has one, will work with you and your preemie to develop comfortable and effective ways to nurse. Soon,

you and your baby will be left alone, to breastfeed in quiet.

✴ *Assessing whether your baby is getting enough milk.* Every breastfeeding mother worries about this, but especially mothers of preemies. Try not to worry: you can be sure that your baby's doctor and nurses will be watching him carefully. Your preemie's behavior (whether he's fussy or satisfied), how many wet diapers he has, and his daily weight gain will make it clear whether he's taking in enough milk. Your baby may even be weighed before and after a breastfeeding session to determine just how much milk he took in; but the results of this method aren't always accurate, and most of the time, it's not necessary.

Nipple Confusion

Will my baby have nipple confusion if the nurses give her bottles when I'm not in the nursery to breastfeed?

A premature baby—even an older one, born at around 34 weeks of gestation or more, who can be put at her mother's breast soon after birth if her condition is stable—won't be discharged from the hospital until she's steadily gaining weight, and taking all of her feedings herself, from the bottle or breast. Since a baby has to eat every few hours, there will be feedings at night and other times when her mom is not around. Some doctors and nurses, afraid of creating "nipple confusion" (between a bottle's artificial nipple and the breast) will avoid a giving bottle to a preemie who has just started to breastfeed, and will feed her by gavage, instead, when her mother is not there. Others, however, think it's more important for a baby to practice feeding on her own, and believe that if nipple confusion occurs at all, it is minor and fleeting.

If you feel strongly one way or the other, let the nurses know how you prefer your baby to be fed in your absence. Finger-feeding is one compromise. It involves feeding a baby through a gavage tube taped to a caretaker's little finger, which the infant sucks together with the tube. This method avoids any nipple confusion, while giving a baby the satisfaction of sucking while being fed. Since finger-feeding is more time-consuming than giving a bottle, the nurses may not always be able to do it. But when the father is visiting the nursery, doing kangaroo care together with finger-feeding can be the closest approximation to breastfeeding a dad can have.

You may want to keep in mind that if you opt to forgo bottle feeding in favor of gavage when you're not there, you may be asked to room-in with your baby for 24 to 48 hours in the nursery before she goes home. That's so the medical staff can observe your baby when you nurse her exclusively, to be sure she continues to grow well, and doesn't get tired from the extra effort, taking in all the nourishment she needs on her own.

Milk Supply

Every time I pump in the nursery I get frustrated, seeing how much milk some mothers can express. My milk supply, instead, seems to be getting less and less.

When beginning breastfeeding, some mothers have to surmount more hurdles than others. One of the most disappointing—and one that can turn into a real obsession—is a mother's realization that her milk supply is diminishing or insufficient.

But a mother of a preemie who is expressing her milk should be prepared for this—it frequently happens, and it's not her fault. An electric pump can't equal a nursing baby in stimulating a mother's breast. True, some women are able to express large quantities of milk without extraordinary effort. Seeing them in the pumping room, mothers with a scarcer milk supply can feel inadequate. But they really shouldn't. The stress and emotional turmoil following a premature birth are unfortunate companions for a mother who chooses to nurse. Breastfeeding a baby is a highly emotional experience: in fact, for many women, a good let-down reflex appears only after their baby starts to nurse at their breasts.

Thus, some mothers—especially those who have been exclusively pumping for several weeks—find that, despite the time and energy they have put into pumping, their milk supply doesn't increase as fast as their infant's demands. For most women who pump, there is a lactation cycle, which can last days or months, during which their milk supply first increases, then plateaus, then diminishes to zero. Sometimes the cycle can be restarted, and sometimes not. Here are some useful tips to reinforce a dwindling milk supply:

❋ *Drink more, eat well, get more rest.* Keep a bottle of water handy for before and after you pump, and remember to drink at least six to eight big glasses of water, milk, or other liquids (excluding caffeinated drinks) a day. Breastfeeding also requires adding about 600 calories to your normal diet. Allow yourself to nap frequently, and try to get as much help as you can with your older children and family chores. Your preemie in the hospital needs you to visit him, but it is equally important that you go home, relax, and rest.

❋ *Don't smoke.* If you're a smoker, you're surely

The Possibility of Later-Onset Lactation

Not all mothers are ready to start pumping within a few hours of their preemie's birth, as breastfeeding experts suggest. Sometimes mothers are sick themselves. Often they are worried about their babies, and so distraught that expressing their milk may seem completely out of place. To avoid painful engorgement of their breasts, they may decide to take medications to counteract their milk production. But when the initial crisis is over and their preemie's condition has stabilized, they may regret that they haven't started their lactation.

Hope is not lost, though. Breast tissue and mammary glands don't immediately switch back to their pre-pregnancy state. Hormones that bring back menstruation and inhibit the ability to breastfeed take a while to return. The window during which lactation can be reinstated varies from a few days to a few weeks, even when a mother has taken medications to stop her milk production. So you may still be in time.

The best way to find out if you can achieve later-onset lactation is to get in touch with your obstetrician and a breastfeeding expert. (For a referral, call La Leche, see page 522.) The methods they suggest will probably be a combination of those advised to increase a diminishing milk supply (see page 229):

* frequent pumping and breast massage
* diet
* rest
* increased fluid intake
* medications.

Milk production cannot be guaranteed, and even if you get your breasts going, it may be for just a short time. But if you want to try, it's certainly worth the trouble.

---

tired of hearing people tell you not to smoke. But if you can stop while you're breastfeeding, it may have a significant effect on your milk supply. Research has shown that the amount of milk produced by mothers of premature babies who smoked was substantially less than the amount produced by those who didn't.

* *Massage your breasts before pumping.* Start by placing warm washcloths on your breasts, for relaxation, and then take a few minutes to massage your nipples and the surrounding areolas in a circular motion, using increasing pressure. Massage can help your milk flow more easily through the ducts and relieve engorgement. Tactile stimulation can also increase the release of the hormone prolactin in your bloodstream, and possibly boost your milk production.

* *Do kangaroo care.* Skin-to-skin contact with your baby can increase a mother's milk supply.

* *Look at your baby's picture, listen to his voice, smell his scent.* When you're at home, a picture of your baby, a tape recording of his voice, or his odor on a recently worn T-shirt

or gown can put you in the right mood to sit down, relax, and express your milk. Just hearing an infant crying (not necessarily your own!), or stroking your face with his clothing, can stimulate the let-down reflex in many mothers. Remember, though, if these mementos of your baby make you feel very sad and emotional, pumping may be more difficult rather than easier.

✳ *Pump more often.* Sometimes pumping every two hours or so for a few days can help increase your milk supply. According to breast-feeding experts, the key is to pump more frequently, not for a longer time: if you do it 10 or 12 times a day, 10 minutes per breast will be enough. If you're not double pumping yet, you should try it.

✳ *Have your pump checked.* More often than you think, electric pumps (even of the same brand) can differ in sucking strength, or may need to be adjusted. If you notice that your breast yields more milk with the pump you're using in the hospital than the one at home, send your home pump back to the pharmacy or supplier, and ask for it to be replaced.

✳ *Inquire about traditional medicines and herbal remedies.* There are several medications (metoclopramide, oxytocin, reserpine, phenothiazine, estrogen) that your obstetrician can prescribe to stimulate your milk production. Since babies can be sensitive to drugs in mother's milk, your doctor may need to consult with your preemie's neonatologist. There are also several herbal preparations (Brewer's yeast, fenugreek, herbal tea mixtures), sold in health food stores, which may increase a mother's milk supply; but you should never take them before asking your baby's doctor. Some of these remedies contain essential oils, such as fennel or anise, that

can appear in your breast milk and cause your baby to have feeding difficulties, vomiting, or lethargy. A premature baby is at greater risk for complications from these substances than a full-term newborn.

✳ *Consider a Supplemental Nursing System (SNS).* This low-tech, effective device can increase your milk production when your baby is trying to latch on, but not yet good at sucking from your nipple. It consists of a bag or bottle filled with your expressed breast milk or formula, which you hang around your neck with a cord (see illustration). Attached to the bag is a thin tube that is taped to your breast, the tip placed against your nipple. The goal is to have your baby suck your nipple and the tube at the same time; he'll get milk at the right flow and volume, learning that he can

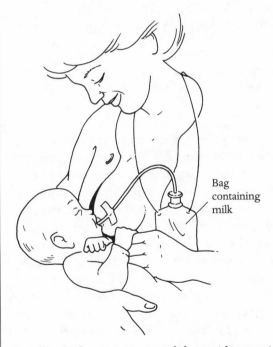

Bag containing milk

A supplemental nursing system can help nourish a preemie, while at the same time stimulating a mother's lactation.

get nutrition and satisfy his hunger through your breast. While your baby practices the art of breastfeeding, your breast will be stimulated by his sucking, possibly increasing your milk production. There are two brands of SNS sold in pharmacies: Lact-Aid Startrainer Nursing System, and Medela Supplemental Nursing System.

Keep a positive attitude, hoping for the best, because worrying is only going to diminish your milk. If these tips don't work, don't feel guilty, and be grateful that your preemie can thrive on today's special formulas. You should feel happy that you've given at least some of your breast milk to your baby. In that sense, your breastfeeding experience is a success, regardless of its length.

Bottle Feeding Tips

I'm so excited. My baby just graduated from gavage feedings to nippling from a bottle. The nurses want me to try to do it, but I don't know how.

No wonder you're excited and happy. Being ready to eat from a bottle is a major step forward in your baby's physical and psychological development. You'll enjoy a new time of closeness and tender interaction, when you can give your baby nourishment, and he can thrive on the pleasure of actively taking it in. But as natural as it is for a newborn, the act of feeding—whether from a bottle or a breast—still has to be learned. Not only must your preemie be developmentally ready to coordinate sucking with breathing and swallowing, but he has to master the bottle feeding technique: how to control and stop the flow of milk from the nipple, by clenching his

jaws and pushing with his tongue, so he can safely swallow and breathe while he eats.

Here are some useful tips that can help you guide your preemie through some initial difficulties of bottle feeding:

* *Position.* During his first nippling attempts, a preemie should be protected from formula flowing too rapidly into his mouth. To slow it down, sit your baby in your lap almost upright, supporting his back, shoulders, and neck with one hand, while the other holds the bottle. It may seem more comfortable for the baby to recline in your lap, but gravity can make the formula flow out too fast. This will increase his chances of gagging, choking, or having a brady while he eats.

* *Nipple.* Ask the nurse to help you choose an easy, soft nipple made especially for preemies—but not one that's too soft, because the milk could flow too fast from it, increasing a baby's anxiety. Some babies are very sensitive to the length of a nipple, which can stimulate their gag reflex. So, try the shortest kind first.

* *Sucking.* You can stimulate him to suck by pressing the nipple down on his tongue and gently pulling it from his mouth at a rate of about once a second (the normal sucking rhythm). If your baby isn't able to suck forcefully, gently pressing on his cheeks and pulling them forward to purse his lips more may improve the strength of his sucking (see illustration). For babies who are irritable or having trouble focusing on taking the nipple, this trick sometimes works: holding his hand and pressing the center of his palm will elicit a reflex that causes him to turn forward and open his mouth.

* *Chin.* If your baby is sucking but doesn't seem to be swallowing well, try pushing up

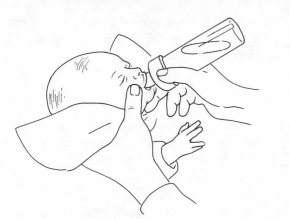

The thumb and fingers of the adult's left hand are pressing gently on the baby's cheeks to pull them forward and purse his lips, helping him to suck. The middle finger of the right hand, under the bottle, is gently pushing under the baby's chin, to stimulate swallowing.

under his chin. This gentle pressure will move his tongue against his palate, helping him to complete the natural act of swallowing.

✳ *Swaddling.* Some preemies nipple better if they're swaddled, with their arms and legs contained by a blanket, to limit their upsetting startles. Others tend to fall asleep if they're too warm, so they should be left unswaddled (or even partly undressed).

✳ *Tickling.* To stimulate a sleepy baby to continue nippling, you can tickle the sole of his foot, or gently squeeze his toes.

✳ *Talking.* To keep him awake, or to encourage or soothe an agitated baby, you can softly sing or talk while you're feeding him, encouraging him to suck and swallow: he can do it!

✳ *Time.* A premature baby who just started to nipple can be a very slow feeder. But each feeding should not last longer than about 20 or 30 minutes, or he could expend so much energy that he actually loses calories. (Try sucking on a bottle yourself for a few minutes, and see how much work it is!) This is why some preemies are initially limited to just one or two nipple feeds a day. By alternating gavage with bottle feedings, they can avoid getting too tired or cold, at the expense of their growth.

✳ *A mealtime routine.* If your baby is still getting some gavage feedings, it may help to pair behaviors like sucking and holding with them. During gavage feedings, giving a baby a pacifier, holding him on your lap, and even placing a drop of milk on his tongue can help him associate these things with the pleasant feeling of having his hunger satisfied.

✳ *Burping.* Not all newborns need to burp at every feeding, and preemies are no different. But you should give your baby the opportunity—with a brief pause in the middle of a feeding (or after every two to three ounces of formula), and again when he's finished, unless he's peacefully asleep. Also, if you notice that your baby is restless or agitated when he's nippling, try burping him. You'll immediately find out if some extra air in his stomach was bothering him.

Burping techniques are the same for breastfed and bottle fed preemies, although an infant who drinks from a bottle may need to burp more often. Hold him upright against your shoulder, facing toward you, and gently pat or just rub his back. Or, try the burping technique that many nurses use: sit him upright in your lap, facing away from you, head leaning slightly forward, with his chest, neck, and chin supported with one of your hands (leaving the other hand free to pat his back). Or, lie him on your lap, belly down, with his head resting on one of your thighs, his

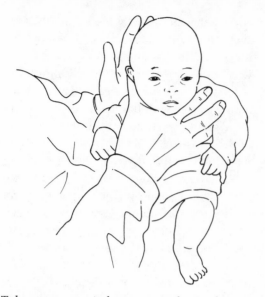

To burp your preemie the way nurses do it, sit him in your lap, support his chest, neck, and chin with one hand, and pat his back with the other.

stomach on the other. Try these out to see what works best for your baby and you.

❋ *Afterglow.* The moments after your baby has fed can be some of the most intimate and loving that you'll share together. Try to arrange your schedule so you don't have to rush off after a feeding. Hold your baby tenderly, letting him see you or feel your warm closeness as he gradually drifts back to sleep. For him, there can be no greater joy.

Day by day, even feeding by feeding, you'll see your baby progress, gradually taking less time and more formula at each session. There may be occasional setbacks: some spitting up or episodes of feeding intolerance (all preemies go through that), some more gavage feedings to save precious energy, possibly some adjustments in what he's eating, to ensure his best possible growth. But you'll have lots of rewards.

Feeding is finally becoming a total pleasure for your baby, as it will become a great source of satisfaction for you.

Baby Not Gaining Enough Weight

My baby isn't gaining weight as fast as the doctors think she should. They tell me not to worry, but are adding things to her formula. Should I be concerned?

How to help a premature infant grow well outside of her mother's womb is one of the biggest issues in neonatal medicine. It's easy to understand why. Good growth is a sign of good nutrition, and good nutrition is crucial for a preemie's recovery and well-being in the short run, as well as for her life-long health and development. But because most preemies take a while to begin feeding properly, and don't all grow at the same pace, doctors have to figure out each little patient's nutritional needs, and adjust her diet to meet them.

In your daughter's case, the doctor is probably supplementing her formula with extra nutrients based on his knowledge of your baby's health and medical conditions, blood tests, previous growth rate, and activity level. It's commonly done, and no cause for worry. There are many reasons why a baby might need more calories. Preemies who are using a lot of energy drinking from a bottle or breast, rather than being gavage fed; who have to keep up their body temperature because they're outside an isolette; who breathe faster and harder than other babies; who are fighting a medical complication, such as an infection, or are recovering from surgery; or who are just particularly lively, may all need more calories to sustain and speed their growth. You can ask the doctor to explain what your baby is being given, and why.

Parents of preemies are always eager for the results of the daily weighing. But the scale doesn't tell the whole story. Babies may gain or lose mere water weight (usually due to changes in fluid intake, medications like diuretics, or conditions affecting the kidneys, heart, or lungs). Being weighed on one scale or another in the nursery can deceptively change a baby's weight. And a preemie's weight may change dramatically when medical equipment such as IVs and arm boards are put on or taken off—or even when she has a large bowel movement.

Real growth is sustained over time, and is most accurately reflected in increases in a baby's length and head circumference. In the hospital nursery, head circumference is measured at least once a week. A normal, steady increase indicates that the baby's brain is growing, as it should. Body length, which changes more slowly, is measured less frequently—every few months or so.

Good nutrition is not only a matter of the total number of calories. To detect particular nutritional shortages, doctors check blood tests. For instance, one reason for poor growth is a deficiency of sodium or bicarbonate, which can be wasted by a preemie's immature kidneys. Low levels of calcium and phosphorus, together with high alkaline phosphatase, can indicate a shortage of minerals needed to make strong bones (see page 241). Scarcities of protein, salts, and iron may also cause slow growth. Many of these problems can be corrected by changing or supplementing a baby's nutrition.

There are several ways a preemie's diet may be supplemented:

✷ *Breast milk can be supplemented with human milk fortifier.* Proteins are the body's main building blocks. According to experts, the best kind of proteins are those contained in breast milk, which are slightly different from those in formula. Although breast milk from a mother who has delivered prematurely has more protein than milk from a mother of a term baby, it still isn't sufficient for the tremendous growth requirements of a very small baby.

To make up for that, and for other nutritional shortages, human milk fortifier is added. It contains extra calories (in the form of protein, fat, and carbohydrate), as well as calcium, phosphorus, sodium, iron, copper, zinc, and vitamins. When a preemie is tolerating her fortified feedings fully, even more iron and vitamins are given. The resulting diet is the best nutrition available for a small preemie, giving her the advantages of breast milk (which helps her fight infections and is better digested and tolerated than formula), together with the extra nutrients she needs for bone mineralization and growth.

✷ *Breast milk can also be supplemented by alternating it with preterm formula.* Called partial breastfeeding, this is usually done when a mother doesn't have enough breast milk for all of her baby's feedings. It is an excellent way to feed a preemie.

✷ *For babies who are not being breastfed, preterm infant formula can be supplemented with multivitamins.* These special formulas have been designed to be as similar as possible to breast milk, without its shortages. The proteins, carbohydrates, and fats of preterm formulas are more easily digested by a preemie's immature digestive system than those in formulas for full-term babies. They also contain higher concentrations of salts, vitamins, and minerals.

Unless a baby on preterm formula is eating large quantities, she may still need multivitamin supplements to meet the recommended daily requirements. These are the vitamins that are particularly important for preemies: folic acid (a B vitamin), which helps combat anemia; vitamin D, which helps prevent rickets; vitamin K, which helps prevent hemorrhages; and vitamins A, C, and E (all antioxidants), which help prevent the tissue damage that is involved in many complications of prematurity, including bronchopulmonary dysplasia, retinopathy of prematurity, and intraventricular hemorrhage. These vitamins, together with minerals like iron, can be considered a premature baby's best nutritional allies. Doctors usually supplement them automatically, without monitoring blood levels.

Some preemies need even more calories than standard, preterm formula or fortified breast milk provides. One solution is simply to increase the amount of food they're given. Or, for babies whose water intake must be restricted (because of their medical conditions), it is possible to create a very concentrated feeding, containing up to 30 calories per ounce. This is usually done by adding special carbohydrates and fats to preterm formula or breast milk. Because concentrated formula is more difficult to digest, and some babies don't tolerate it initially, doctors usually increase the caloric content of a baby's feedings gradually, over a week or so.

Some babies don't tolerate even unfortified breast milk or regular preterm formula. This may be because they've had NEC (see page 237), or another serious intestinal problem that has left them with difficulty digesting and absorbing nutrients. Or they may be allergic to the proteins in cow's milk (which are the base of most infant formulas) or have difficulty digesting lactose, the sugar in milk. Both allergy to cow's milk protein and lactose-intolerance tend to run

---

A Preemie's Caloric Needs

Ideally, a premature baby should grow as much as she would have in the womb: about 15 to 30 grams a day. To grow that well, most preemies need to get about 120 calories a day for each 1,000 grams of their current body weight; they need about 70 calories so as not to lose weight. But babies' energy requirements can vary a lot, and may be higher or lower.

Most preterm formulas contain 24 calories per ounce, transitional formulas for older preemies usually contain 22 calories, and formulas for term babies contain 20 calories. Breast milk has about 20 calories per ounce, but when it's fed to preterm babies in the hospital nursery, it is usually supplemented up to 24 calories with milk fortifiers (see page 235).

Knowing that, you can make a rough calculation of how much milk your baby should get. Let's say she weighs 1,000 grams. Her daily caloric requirement is about 120 calories. If she's eating 24-calorie (that's 24 calories per ounce) formula or breast milk, she should take 5 ounces of milk a day.

in families. (Babies with these problems usually do well with breast milk, but not formula.)

Thanks to the many modified formulas available today—lactose-free, protein-free, soy-based, or "elemental" (meaning predigested)—babies with most kinds of feeding intolerance can be nourished successfully. Since these formulas lack some of the nutrients in preterm formula, however, preemies on nonstandard formulas may need further nutritional supplementation.

There are some other, common conditions in preemies that often require dietary supplements to insure good growth. Preemies on diuretics lose a lot of essential salts in their urine, so many of them will be given supplements of potassium, sodium, and chloride. Very young preemies, or those with kidney problems, have a tendency to build up too much acid in their blood, so they may be given supplements to neutralize the acid. And babies with reflux (see page 244) often have rice cereal added to their milk, to help their feedings stay down.

Many parents might be thinking now that to be able to feed their preemie, they should get a Ph.D. in biochemistry. But be reassured: most feeding supplements are given just for a few weeks, and most infants don't need them once they're discharged from the hospital. Some special diets—like soy formula, or thickening milk with rice cereal—may continue for a long time, but they are easy to deal with at home.

For now, trust the creativity of your baby's doctor, who will try new regimens until the right menu is found: the one allowing a baby to eat, digest, fight her illnesses, and grow. What other chef has such a challenging, but rewarding task?

IN PLAIN LANGUAGE: WHAT IS NECROTIZING ENTEROCOLITIS?

If premature births could be effectively prevented, very few babies would suffer from NEC. Necrotizing enterocolitis is an intestinal disease of the newborn, which almost exclusively affects preemies. Even in hospital nurseries, NEC is not common: only about 5% of premature babies get it. (The younger they are, the higher their risk, as for many other scourges of prematurity.)

Still, since NEC is dangerous, and not easy to diagnose, parents of preemies often hear it mentioned as a possible complication. Many cases end up being only "a NEC scare" with a happy ending, to everyone's relief. But if your baby is, in fact, diagnosed with NEC, you shouldn't panic. Although serious, this illness can be overcome in the majority of cases with medical treatment, or, if necessary, with surgery. It is a trial, but it can be endured.

WHY NEC CAN BE SO SERIOUS

NEC is an inflammation that damages the lining of the intestine. It may affect only a small portion, or large areas, of either the small intestine or the colon (large intestine), and when severe, it can cause the bowel to tear, or "perforate." NEC is sometimes accompanied by an infection of the gastrointestinal tract or bloodstream, but even without an infection, all of the baby's vital systems can become unbalanced, posing a serious threat to his life. Luckily, the vast majority of babies with NEC survive the illness.

THE UNCERTAIN ORIGIN OF NEC

Medical researchers still don't know for sure what causes NEC. In addition to an immature gastrointestinal tract, three factors have been blamed: an injury to the intestinal tissues caused by a lack of oxygen or blood flow; an intestinal infection; or the presence of undigested residuals of milk, lingering in the bowel. These elements are often involved in the disease. But NEC can develop even without them.

WHAT'S THE ROLE OF INFECTION?

An intestinal infection is not necessarily a cause of NEC, but more likely its consequence. Most often, the bacteria involved in NEC are just those normally living in the gut, that can overgrow and invade damaged intestinal tissue, contributing to its inflammation and destruction. Some cases of NEC in hospital nurseries do happen in clusters—possibly indicating that they are linked to an infectious strain of bacteria or viruses—but if another preemie in your baby's nursery has NEC, you shouldn't get anxious. Finding a culprit that all of the affected babies in a nursery share is unlikely, and contagion is relatively rare.

Infections in other organs, or sepsis (an infec-

tion in the bloodstream), can sometimes precipitate NEC, as can other serious complications that cause stress to a preemie's vital functions, by interfering with oxygen and blood flow to the gut.

ORAL FEEDINGS: RISKY OR BENEFICIAL?

Milk residuals, fermented by bacteria, are one source of the intestinal gas that can seep inside a damaged intestinal wall and collect in pockets. Gas in the bowel wall, called pneumatosis, is a sign of full-blown NEC, detectable by x-ray. But babies who have never been fed can also get NEC, and the long-standing practice of withholding oral feedings in preemies, to try to prevent this illness, has been abandoned. Neonatologists today believe that preemies should be cautiously introduced to tiny quantities of milk as soon as possible, because the process of digestion itself can stimulate the stomach and intestine to mature faster. Some studies have also suggested that breast milk may have protective qualities against NEC.

Nevertheless, doctors will not feed a baby if they believe his gastrointestinal tract is compromised, since putting food in a damaged gut has been shown to increase the risk of NEC. Babies who may be at higher risk for NEC because of a compromised intestinal tract include preemies with poor intestinal blood flow (perhaps due to a PDA or, some believe, an umbilical catheter), or those with decreased oxygenation (because of a difficult delivery, severe RDS, profound apnea and bradycardias, or other reasons). Until the doctor thinks a baby's gut has healed, he'll be nourished with intravenous nutrition.

NEC AND PREMATURITY

Despite the extensive studies done on NEC in the last 30 years, its initial triggers remain uncertain. The only clear risk factor is immaturity of the intestines. Steroids given before delivery, which make a preemie's lungs mature faster, are helpful in preventing NEC, too.

The earlier a baby is born, the longer the time before he is no longer at risk for getting NEC. While NEC is apparent within an average of six days in an infant born at 34 or more weeks, the average age of onset for babies born at 30 weeks is twenty days, and it is even later for younger preemies. It can seem to come out of the blue, particularly if a preemie, who may have gone through a hard time in his first week, is now feeding and growing, and seemingly doing well.

HOW NEC DEVELOPS, AND HOW IT SHOWS UP

NEC can be puzzling when it comes to diagnosis, too. Its early signs can be mild, and can mimic those of a respiratory problem, a PDA, or an infection: more frequent apnea and bradys, lethargy, temperature instability, a change in blood sugar levels. Other signs may point to a problem with digestion, but are often the same as those caused simply by feeding intolerance due to prematurity (see page 151): vomiting, the presence of milk residuals in the stomach, a slightly distended belly, diarrhea, or invisible blood in stools, picked up on what is called a guaiac (pronounced "GWY-ak") test.

But babies who are developing NEC can worsen quickly. They may have an acute respiratory crisis, with severe apnea and bradycardia, pass visibly bloody stools and develop a very distended and tender abdomen, and show signs of sepsis, with lethargy and low blood pressure. Advanced NEC can occur suddenly, also, with no early warning.

An x-ray can confirm a diagnosis of NEC, but its findings are not always definitive. So NEC is usually diagnosed using a combination of x-ray findings, observation of the baby, and blood tests (which in NEC may show low levels of sodium, white blood cells and platelets, and too much acid in the blood). Once a diagnosis of NEC is made, x-rays may be repeated as often as every six hours, to detect a possible perforation of the bowel as early as possible.

HOW NEC IS TREATED

Doctors are always on the alert for the first signs and symptoms of NEC, because early intervention is the key to giving your baby the best chance to fight this illness, and recover from it well. When they suspect NEC, doctors give a baby's bowel a rest by stopping his feedings and inserting a tube in his stomach (passing through the nose or mouth), to remove extra gas and secretions. They also take an x-ray of his abdomen, do blood cultures to detect infection, monitor all of his vital signs for the slightest deterioration, and start a course of broad-spectrum antibiotics. The nurse will measure the circumference of the baby's belly frequently, to monitor how well the intestines are passing gas and emptying.

Antibiotics are usually continued for one to two weeks, to treat infection and stop the progression of the illness. If the baby's condition worsens, he may need to be put on a ventilator. His blood pressure will be sustained with fluids and medication if needed, and possibly blood transfusions. Babies with NEC generally will have a surgical consultation. But the majority do not end up needing surgery.

A baby with NEC will be fed intravenously, with parenteral nutrition, for a while, until his intestines heal. When his gastrointestinal function has returned to normal, and the pockets of gas in the bowel wall have been gone for five days or more, he can gradually resume oral feedings. His feedings will be advanced, slowly and cautiously, until he no longer needs intravenous nutrition.

When medical therapy alone is successful, the complete course of NEC usually lasts between ten and twenty one days, from its first onset to full recovery. The critical stage of the illness is often over much sooner, though, and many babies are stable after a couple of days. Your baby's doctor can tell you when the crisis stage is past, so you can relax.

If despite all therapies, the infant's condition deteriorates, or if x-rays reveal perforation of the bowel or areas of damaged intestines that aren't recovering, an operation has to be performed. The goal of surgery is to remove any torn or dead bowel, and to clean any local sources of infection. If your baby needs NEC surgery, you can read about it on page 313.

AFTER NEC, IN THE SHORT AND LONG RUN

Most of the time, once a premature baby heals from NEC, there are no further flare-ups or serious difficulties. But occasionally, the healing process leaves scars in his belly or intestines that cause complications later. The most common result of scarring is a stricture, or narrowing of a small area of the bowel. A stricture, if it's mild,

may be completely silent and unnoticeable. If it's tighter, it can cause cramps, abdominal distention, vomiting, constipation, or intermittent bleeding. The most serious risk after NEC is a complete intestinal obstruction, which can lead to a severe infection or intestinal perforation. Strictures and other obstructions can be diagnosed with special x-rays using dye (either swallowed or given as an enema) to outline the shape of the intestines. This is a common follow-up test for infants who have feeding difficulties after NEC.

The other serious, long-term consequence of NEC is called short bowel syndrome. Be assured that it occurs only rarely, when very extensive portions of the intestine are damaged and must be removed. The loss of large amounts of the intestine leads to a lack of digestive capacity, with malabsorption of nutrients, undernutrition, and frequent infections. Infants with short bowel syndrome usually need to integrate their scarce oral feedings with parenteral nutrition for months or years, and their growth and development are often compromised. But some infants with short bowel syndrome do better than others (usually, the ones who have a longer length of intestine left). If a child with short bowel syndrome can grow over time, the remaining intestinal tract may extend and adapt, making it possible for many of these children to make the transition from parenteral nutrition to oral feedings.

Preventing long-lasting growth delays is crucial to ensuring normal intellectual development in preemies. Medicine is becoming better at avoiding malnutrition during and after NEC with parenteral nutrition and appropriate vitamin and mineral supplements. That, together with the wonderful ability of the human bowel to regenerate itself, gives your baby the best opportunity ever to grow, after NEC, into a happy and normal child.

Fractures

My baby has a rib fracture. How do I know the nurses haven't been handling him too roughly?

Parents often marvel at the ease with which nurses handle their tiny patients—deftly turning them without catching floppy arms and legs on the bedding, or dislodging tubes and lines. Preemies are less fragile than they seem, and a nurse's experience makes it very unlikely that she'll ever hurt a baby. So something else has to be blamed.

A rib fracture is usually discovered by chance on a chest x-ray. It can occur if a preemie's bones have become soft because of insufficient vitamins and minerals in his diet. Since ribs are the thinnest bones of the body, they're usually the first to weaken, and can be fractured inadvertently by a movement that would normally be safe.

When severe, this nutritional deficiency is called rickets, and it results in less dense, slightly bowed, bones. Thankfully, even if a preemie has rickets, once his nutrition improves he should recover from it completely, with strong, straight bones and no long-term consequences.

Doctors are often able to catch a nutritional shortage soon, and correct a baby's diet accordingly. One way they assess a preemie's nutrition is through blood tests. Among the warning signs are abnormal levels of minerals and other substances in his blood, such as calcium, phosphorus, and something called alkaline phosphatase, a measure of bone growth or loss. Rickets can be reversed with dietary supplements such as calcium, phosphorus, and vitamin D. These substances can be given by mouth, or added in greater quantities to your preemie's intravenous nutrition.

The most effective way to prevent bone demineralization is to feed a baby, and leave intravenous nutrition behind, as soon as possible, because nutrients are best absorbed through the intestine. A deficiency of vitamins and minerals usually occurs only when preemies need to be fed for more than a few weeks with total intravenous nutrition. Preemies who are restricted in the number of calories they're given, and are on medications that cause them to lose too much calcium and sodium, are at particular risk. Also, babies who spend many weeks inside a hospital nursery often lack vitamin D (an essential factor for incorporating calcium into bone), which is normally made by the skin when it's exposed to sunlight.

Since breast milk is poor in vitamin D, and has less sodium and minerals than a rapidly growing preemie needs, most preemies fed breast milk will have liquid or powdered milk fortifier added to their gavage feedings, and will be given multivitamins. (By the time a preemie is nursing fully at the breast, he usually doesn't need these supplements anymore.) A preemie who is fully bottle fed with a commercial preterm formula, and who digests it well, will receive high enough concentrations of vitamins and minerals to make healthy bones, without the addition of fortifiers.

The good news for your baby is that his rib fracture should heal quickly, without bothering him too much. Rib fractures don't need casts or splints; you'll just have to be especially careful for a couple of weeks when you move or hold him. Since rickets can almost always be successfully overcome, you can think of your son's accident in the nursery as a helpful warning, leading him to get the right nutrition, so he'll grow up with strong, healthy bones.

Another Kind of Jaundice

My baby is jaundiced, but she's not being treated with phototherapy like before. The doctor says this is a different kind of jaundice. What does he mean?

There's another form of jaundice that's different from the kind that nearly all newborns get in their first week of life. Notice that your baby's skin color is slightly different than when she was jaundiced before: rather than the yellowish-orange of regular, newborn jaundice, now she's more of a yellowish-green. It's not most people's favorite color, but luckily, it's not often a long-lasting problem.

As you can read on page 155, jaundice is caused by a buildup of bilirubin (a yellow substance produced when red blood cells are broken down, as they naturally are in everybody). The initial underlying problem for infants, especially preemies, is that the liver is too immature, at first, to convert bilirubin into a disposable form which can be excreted in the stools. The phototherapy lights help by temporarily taking over the liver's job, and converting the bilirubin into a form that the body can excrete.

In your daughter's case, though, there's more going on than plain immaturity. She has what's called direct or conjugated hyperbilirubinemia (another name for jaundice), meaning that her liver has done its mature job of converting the bilirubin into a disposable form, but despite that, something—a different problem in the liver, or elsewhere—is holding up her body from getting rid of it.

If your daughter is still being fed with total parenteral nutrition, or TPN (the intravenous solution that preemies get until they are ready to digest breast milk or formula), then it's a good bet that that's the reason for her jaundice. TPN, over time, can damage the liver, and according to some estimates, roughly a third of newborns who are on it for more than a couple of weeks develop some liver complications. But fortunately, damage from TPN in preemies is almost always reversible: once a baby comes off TPN, the liver gradually recovers, moving the bilirubin better into the intestines, from which it is excreted, and the baby's jaundice gradually goes away. In the meantime, your baby's doctor may give her some medication to speed the flow of bile out of her liver, or if her jaundice is mild, and she's expected to come off TPN soon, they may simply wait. Direct hyperbilirubinemia doesn't seem to make babies uncomfortable (it can cause itching in adults), and won't cause other medical problems unless it goes on for a long time—months or more.

The doctors may do some blood and x-ray tests to rule out other, possible reasons for her jaundice that are less common. For example, direct hyperbilirubinemia is sometimes found in babies who had a congenital infection that damaged their liver. It can be a sign of a urinary tract infection, or a metabolic problem, or hypothyroidism. Occasionally, a preemie who had the intestinal disease called NEC gets scarring that can partially block the flow of bile into her intestines. Your baby's doctor will tell you about any further tests and treatments they would recommend if she appears to have any of these problems.

But if your baby's tests come back normal, her doctors will probably attribute her problem just to TPN. Their aim, then, will be to get her off TPN as soon as possible. (Even if your baby didn't have jaundice, her doctors would usually try hard to do that.) As soon as she can take in enough nourishment with regular feedings, the

TPN will be discontinued. Within a week or two afterward, you should notice that her jaundice is getting better, and within a few months, it should be gone.

Baby's Positioning and SIDS

Why do the nurses put my baby down on her stomach, when that's been proven to increase the chances of SIDS?

It's not just the nurses in your baby's unit who think many preemies should be placed on their stomachs, but also the American Academy of Pediatrics. This is the same organization that has made a very strong point of recommending that healthy, full-term babies be put to sleep on their backs or sides, to reduce the risk of Sudden Infant Death Syndrome (SIDS).

The American Academy of Pediatrics guidelines say: "For premature infants with respiratory distress, for infants with symptoms of gastroesophageal reflux [spitting up—see page 244], or with certain upper airway anomalies, and perhaps for some others, prone may well be the position of choice." Prone means tummy-down.

There are good reasons for this. When preemies are on their stomachs, they're able to breathe more easily, so their oxygen levels increase, and they have less apnea. Preemies also sleep better on their stomachs, with more "quiet sleep," which is an important sign of maturation and brain development. Moreover, lying on their backs too much can create certain postural problems later on. (For example, when young preemies lie on their backs, they tend to have their legs splayed out in a frog-like position, simply because they don't have the muscle tone to adopt other positions. So, as older infants and toddlers, they're more likely to have problems with turned out hips, or ankles and feet.) Above all, preemies seem to like being on their stomachs—it lowers their stress levels, which conserves their precious energy and keeps them more stable.

Of course, while premature babies are in intensive care, they are being constantly observed and monitored, so any problems with their vital signs would be noticed and responded to immediately. Once your preemie is healthy and mature enough to go home, it's different: unless her doctor tells you otherwise, she'd be better off sleeping on her back, to reduce the risk of SIDS.

Why Is My Baby's Chest Indented?

One reason preemies breathe better on their stomachs is that the support from the bed keeps their chests from sucking in too deeply, so their lungs stay inflated better. Preemies have very flexible chest walls, because they don't have firm cartilage yet. So when they inhale, particularly if they're breathing hard, their chests may suck in deeply, caving in at the middle. Some parents even worry that their babies have strange, permanently indented chests. They don't; it's just temporary!

GETTING ACQUAINTED WITH:
REFLUX

As any parent knows, being a baby means spitting up now and then, after a good meal of breast milk or formula. But some babies spit up or throw up more than usual, and they are said to have gastroesophageal reflux—or reflux, for short.

Most of the time when full-term babies have reflux, it doesn't cause problems, so their parents don't do much about it, except for spending a lot of money on laundry detergent! But preemies are more likely to have other symptoms accompanying their reflux, so treatment can become important. Happily, with treatment and time (for babies' upper intestinal tracts to mature and get better coordinated), reflux is almost always a temporary problem—not one of the more serious, threatening complications of prematurity.

WHAT IS REFLUX?

The best way to understand reflux is to picture what is supposed to happen when we swallow food. First it travels down the long tube that connects our mouths to our stomachs, called the esophagus. At the bottom of the esophagus, there's a little "gate" that opens to let food pass into the stomach: a muscle called the lower esophageal sphincter. After the sphincter lets the food go through, it closes again so the food can't go back up.

Your stomach is like a blender: it mashes up the food and mixes it with acid. When the blend-ing is finished, another "gate," a muscle at the bottom of the stomach, opens and lets the food move on to the small intestine.

What if babies have reflux? They swallow their food, and it travels normally down their esophagus and into the stomach. But while their stomachs are churning away, the lower esophageal sphincter opens, letting some of the food escape back up the esophagus. Sometimes, but not always, it even goes all the way out of the mouth.

WHEN IS REFLUX A PROBLEM?

As we mentioned, all babies (and, in fact, all adults, too) have some reflux. Research shows that healthy infants have about 24 episodes of reflux in 24 hours. Half of them spit up two or more feedings a day in their first few months of life. (Only 1% are still vomiting by the time they're a year old.)

Reflux is only characterized as problematic when someone has too much of it, or it causes other complications. Adults complain when they have reflux that's bad enough to cause heartburn: a burning sensation after eating, as food that's already mixed with stomach acid gushes back into their esophagus and irritates it.

Perhaps babies feel the same sort of discomfort, but they can't pipe up and say so. When they have reflux, they may show other signs that alert doctors that there's a problem.

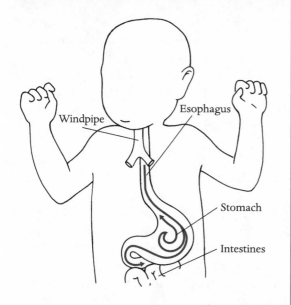

With GE reflux, food from the stomach can escape back up into the esophagus, reach the throat, and sometimes enter the windpipe.

These can include: frequent vomiting; apnea, bradys, or oxygen desaturation during or after meals; and aspiration pneumonia, caused by inhaling regurgitated milk or formula into the lungs. A baby's esophagus can become irritated enough to cause some bleeding, or pain during feeding. One consequence of reflux for a preemie can be slower weight gain, since frequent spitting up, or refusal to eat, can deprive a baby of precious calories.

Preemies with BPD (see page 261), especially, have trouble with reflux, because they're more prone to oxygen desaturations, need more calories to grow, and their harder breathing can make reflux more severe.

DIAGNOSING REFLUX IN PREEMIES

If your baby's doctor suspects that reflux may be causing her problems, he may want to confirm it with a test called a pH probe. A small tube will be placed through your baby's nose and down into her esophagus. The tip of the tube has a sensor that can detect acid—so it knows when there is reflux from the stomach. It is usually left in place for twenty-four hours, recording all episodes of reflux on a computer. The test tells doctors whether an unusual amount of reflux occurred, and whether the timing of reflux episodes corresponded to your baby's apnea or other symptoms.

If the pH probe indicates that your baby has moderate to severe reflux, or maybe even if she is just vomiting a lot, her doctor may also request a special x-ray called a barium swallow or upper GI study. She'll be fed a liquid (barium or some other dye that shows up on x-rays) which the doctors will watch as it travels down her esophagus, through her stomach, and into her small intestine. They want to make sure she doesn't have any blockages, kinks, or narrowings in her stomach or upper intestinal tract that might be causing the reflux.

TREATMENT OF REFLUX IN PREEMIES

If there's no anatomic abnormality, reflux will almost always eventually go away on its own. Nevertheless, your baby needs some relief from its symptoms, if they're causing her problems.

If her reflux is mild, her doctor and nurses may first try some simple adjustments: feeding her smaller amounts more frequently; burping her more often during feedings; feeding her continuously using a pump; waiting longer between feedings; making sure she is lying stomach-down or on her side during and after meals (on her back, it is easier for refluxed food to get into her airway or lungs, causing choking or breathing problems); raising the head of her bed; or thickening her milk or formula with rice cereal.

Some medicines that help apnea of prematurity (theophylline, aminophylline, and caffeine) can make reflux worse. So if the doctor thinks your baby's apnea of prematurity is mild, he may try stopping those medicines, to see if her reflux improves.

If these measures don't work, your baby may be given medication for her reflux. Two kinds are commonly used. One kind (such products as reglan and cisapride) improves the mobility of the stomach and intestine, so food spends less time in the stomach, making a quicker getaway down into the small intestine. The other (usually Zantac) reduces the production of stomach acid, so when reflux does occur, it's less irritating to the esophagus.

If medication doesn't help, and a baby's symptoms are severe, doctors may try passing her feeding tube beyond her stomach into her intestine, so the food can't reflux up the esophagus so easily.

Finally, if these temporizing measures fail, and complications from the reflux are serious, surgery will be considered. This is rare, so don't expend energy worrying about it unless it happens. There's more on the operation for reflux, called a fundoplication, on page 319.

HOW LONG WILL REFLUX BE A PROBLEM?

Just as the rest of your preemie's movements and bodily systems are pretty uncoordinated right now, so is her upper gastrointestinal tract. Her reflux will probably get a lot better by around six months of age, and disappear by age one or two.

It's possible that your baby will have a slightly longer hospital stay because of her reflux, and will need to keep taking medication after she goes home. Some babies with reflux go home with a cardiorespiratory monitor, so their parents and caregivers will be aware of any apnea or bradys they have because of it. Fortunately, most preemies with reflux tend to eat, grow, and thrive as well as their peers.

There are some suggestions for dealing with reflux at home on page 358. They may be helpful at first, but chances are you won't need them for long.

Skin Care

My baby has such delicate skin, and to bathe her they're using plain old Dove soap! Couldn't they come up with something better for preemies?

When it comes to skin care, a minimalist approach fits premature babies best: the fewer and simpler products that are used, the better. That's because a young preemie's skin is so thin and sensitive that it can be hurt by rough handling or rubbing, and will absorb many of the substances that are put on it. Exposure to chemicals (including perfumes) at this very early age can cause irritation, and may contribute to future development of skin allergies. So most NICUs opt for a sparing use of the most common baby soaps (like Baby Magic) or adult soaps with a neutral pH and no perfumes or dyes (like Dove or Neutrogena) to bathe the babies. Some nurseries have tried special antimicrobial or disinfectant soaps to fight skin infections. However, these products contain chemicals that can build up to toxic levels if preemies absorb too much through their skin. The goal is to maintain good hygiene with a minimum of intervention.

Since using any soap can irritate a preemie's

Tiny Babies at Risk for Big Diaper Rashes

What infant doesn't get a diaper rash at least once? Well, preemies get them, too. Commonly, a diaper rash progresses from simple skin irritation to a mild skin infection. A diaper rash caused by yeast or bacteria can spread quickly and look scary: a bright red chafing, with pustules, that may extend from the diaper area up his belly or down his thighs. Sometimes a baby will have a yeast infection in his mouth at the same time.

Because a baby's skin is easily irritated by exposure to urine and stool, preemies' bottoms are cleaned at diaper changes. Wet washcloths with water only are used. Avoiding soaps and pre-packaged baby wipes, which can deplete a baby's skin of its natural acid barrier, and keeping the diaper area as dry as possible are the best preventive measures.

When a rash or irritation develops, a baby's skin should be protected and allowed to heal by applying a thick layer of barrier cream (such as the common, white ointments for the diaper area). At each diaper change, the baby should be cleaned without removing the whole layer of cream, and more should be added on, generously. A yeast infection can be treated with an antifungal cream or powder that's applied several times a day, before the barrier cream. If a baby has thrush (white spots in his mouth caused by a yeast infection), he'll be given an antifungal liquid to take orally. If you're breastfeeding, the doctor may also give you some antifungal cream to rub on your nipples between feedings. Steroid creams, which calm inflammation and are sometimes used to treat diaper rashes in older babies, can be dangerous if used too much on preemies, so are generally avoided.

If a rash is really severe, with bleeding, the nurses may decide it's worth the extra mess to let a baby go without diapers at all for a while. That way, moisture isn't trapped in the diaper, and urine and stool don't stay on the skin to irritate it. They may even put your baby's bottom in the air, under a heating lamp, to thoroughly dry his skin. But don't worry; although a bad diaper rash looks awful, with proper care and attention it will go completely away.

skin, bathing isn't usually done more often than two or three times a week. The tiniest preemies, born under 26 weeks of gestation, may get just a sponge bath in plain water at body temperature, with no soap at all. Bigger preemies have the fun of getting dipped in a basin of warm, soapy water.

Washing can also aggravate the dryness of a preemie's skin, which, because of the immaturity of its sweat glands, is short of water and natural oils. When skin is dry, simple contact with clothes or bedding can cause irritation and injury, and lesions can be quickly invaded by germs. Recent studies on premature babies have indicated that dehydration and skin lesions can be partly prevented by applying an oil-in-water moisturizing lotion, with no dyes or perfumes. You can ask your baby's neonatologist if he believes in the benefits of skin moisturizers; and perhaps get permission to give your baby this pleasant daily treat yourself, with your gentlest touch.

Hernia

I thought men got hernias from lifting things that were too heavy. Why in the world does my preemie have one?

Hernias are very common in premature babies—not surprisingly, if you consider how they occur. An inguinal (meaning in the groin area) hernia forms when a loop of intestine—or sometimes, in girls, an ovary—slides down into the groin from the abdomen, through a canal that's open in the fetus, but normally closes during the last few weeks of gestation. Because premature babies are usually born when that canal is still open, or only partially closed, a rise in pressure inside their abdomen, from crying,

straining to have a bowel movement, or just breathing hard, can cause a hernia. On average, 15 in 100 preemies develop a hernia, compared to only one in 100 term infants, and the likelihood increases the younger and smaller a preemie was when he was born.

An inguinal hernia usually shows up as a swelling in the groin, extending down into the scrotum in boys, and into the labia in girls. It may be only on one side, or on both. It will get bigger and smaller at times, depending on whether your baby is crying or calm, for instance, and the size of the intestine in it changes. It may even disappear temporarily, but once a hernia forms, it won't go away completely unless it is repaired surgically.

Your baby's doctors and nurses will watch his hernia closely, to make sure it remains soft and pliable. If the intestine goes back and forth from his groin (where you can see it) to his abdomen (where you can't), by itself or when you gently press on it, that's a good sign.

But if the hernia becomes hard, purple, or the loop of the intestine can't be pressed back into his abdomen, a baby's doctors will worry that the intestine is trapped, or incarcerated. An incarcerated hernia is an emergency, because it can quickly lead to some dangerous complications. One is a decrease in blood flow to that part of intestine or any other organs in the hernia sac, such as the testicle or the ovary, which could permanently damage them. An intestinal obstruction or life-threatening infection can also occur.

To avoid the risk of incarceration, your baby will need surgery fairly soon. But you shouldn't worry too much about that. A hernia repair is a very straightforward and safe procedure (see page 324). Since so many preemies get hernias, it is the most common surgery performed on

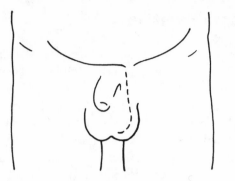

A canal between the abdomen and the groin normally closes in the last weeks of gestation.

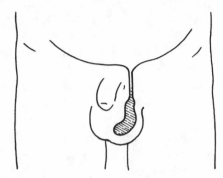

Hydrocele: a narrow passage remains open, allowing fluid to seep from the abdomen into the groin.

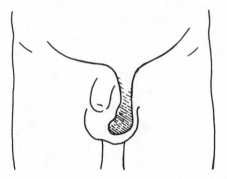

Hernia: a large canal remains open, allowing a loop of intestine to slide down into the groin.

small babies. And such frequent practice makes for excellent surgical results.

Most premature infants who have a hernia are operated on just before they are discharged from the hospital nursery, when they are bigger and stronger. But an incarcerated hernia requires urgent surgery—within 24 to 48 hours if a baby hasn't developed complications from it and the surgeon is finally able, perhaps with the help of some light sedation, to reduce the hernia—or right away, if there are complications and the hernia remains trapped. After one episode of incarceration, there is a high risk that it will happen again, until the hernia is repaired.

Fortunately, only a very few premature babies develop complications from an inguinal hernia. For most, it is just another small bump—literally—along the road to their recovery.

Hydrocele: A Related Condition

Hydrocele means water *(hydro)* in a cavity *(cele)*. It is a collection of fluid in the scrotum, around one or both testicles, making a boy's scrotum look swollen or asymmetric. A hydrocele forms the same way a hernia does: fluid seeps into the scrotum from the abdomen, through a canal that's open in the fetus, but that normally closes in the last trimester of pregnancy. If the canal remains wide open, then loops of intestine can slide from the abdomen into the scrotum, creating an inguinal hernia. If just a narrow passage remains open, loops of intestine can't pass through, but fluid can, creating a hydrocele.

Doctors can distinguish a hydrocele from a hernia by its shape, or by shining a light on the scrotum and noting that the clear fluid inside makes it translucent. Unlike hernias, hydroceles usually can't be "reduced" meaning the fluid can't be pushed back into the abdomen).

In most baby boys, hydroceles resolve on their own in the first 6 to 18 months of life. If your son has a hydrocele and it is getting smaller or staying the same size, it probably won't need to be repaired. Chances are that the canal between his abdomen and scrotum has closed, and his body will gradually absorb the fluid that's left over. But if a hydrocele grows in size, or periodically gets bigger or smaller, especially after a boy is 18 months old, it means that there's still a connection between his abdomen and scrotum which, at that late date, is unlikely to close by itself. Doctors then worry that a small channel might enlarge over time, causing a true hernia to develop (see page 248).

The surgical procedure to repair a hydrocele—the same as for a hernia—is extremely safe. Most children with hydroceles have their surgery as outpatients when they're about two years old, and are ready to go home just a few hours afterward.

Preemie Massage

Someone told me that massage is supposed to be beneficial to preemies. Isn't that kind of flaky—and maybe even dangerous for a fragile preemie?

It's a funny thing: Even people who love having an occasional massage themselves, who find it relaxes them when they're feeling tense, think it's odd for a baby to have one.

Premature babies, however, don't seem to agree at all. In fact, research studies have consistently suggested that preemies appreciate a good massage as much as their parents do. In one clinical trial, a group of healthy premature babies in an intermediate care nursery got 15-minute massages three times a day for ten days. They gained almost 50% more weight than the babies who didn't—even though they ate the same amount. The massaged group was also more alert and active, and was discharged six days earlier from the hospital, on average.

The underlying mechanism explaining why

massage may help premature babies is not yet known. But there are certain things we do know. We know that preemies, born too early, separated from their parents, and subjected to the noises, lights, and interventions of the nursery, can be under great stress. We also know that nature has wired all parents with an instinctive urge to calm their babies using touch. Without ever having to be told, new parents stroke and pat their babies to soothe and comfort them. And we know that touch is the first sense to develop in a fetus—and therefore the sense that is most fundamental in a newborn preemie. Since a preemie's eyesight and hearing aren't yet fully developed, touch is an important element of how he experiences the world. Doctors have known for a long time that infants and children who aren't held, touched, played with, and fondly attended to can have stunted growth, regardless of how much they eat. There's even a name for this: psychosocial failure to thrive. Some related research in animals and humans suggests it may have to do with the ability of touch and physical activity to increase levels of some growth-stimulating hormones.

So, it's crucial that your preemie get plenty of loving touch. It can come in many different forms: simply cradling him in your arms; holding him skin-to-skin against your bare chest (see page 221); or, if he is not yet stable enough to be picked up, letting him grasp one of your fingers as you wrap your other arm behind his head and back.

Although you don't have to massage your baby for him to benefit from your touch, if you want to try it, and your baby's doctor agrees, by all means do. Just remember that preemie massage has little to do with the vigorous kind of manipulation that adults occasionally enjoy; it's better described as an organized touch technique. Please read the following tips before you begin, to make sure your massages are safe, pleasurable, and most likely to benefit your baby:

❋ Don't start massaging your baby until you get an OK from your baby's doctor. While massage is perfectly safe for older, medically stable preemies, it may not be for young or sick ones. Since a young preemie's skin is fragile, and massage hasn't been thoroughly studied yet at young ages, we'd recommend that you wait until your baby is at least 30 weeks of gestational age before starting. If your hospital nursery has an intermediate care unit, you may also have to wait until your baby gets there before he's ready. But be patient. The babies in the research trial mentioned above weren't massaged until they were an average of 31 weeks of gestational age, and off oxygen and IV feedings.

❋ Ask the doctor whether your baby's leads, attached to the cardiorespiratory monitor, need to stay on during the massage. The doctor will consider how stable your baby is, and how long the massage will last, in deciding whether it's safe or not.

❋ Now to get started. Choose a time for the massage when your baby isn't likely to be hungry, but not just after he's eaten—perhaps an hour or so after feeding time.

❋ You can take all of your baby's clothes off for the massage, if he is going to be staying in his isolette. Some people even take the diaper off, but be prepared for things to get a bit messy if you do! It's very common for a baby to urinate as his muscles relax during a massage. If he's in an open bassinet, you could ask the doctor if it's OK for him to wear only a hat during the massage, or you could massage him under a loose shirt or gown.

❋ Wash your hands thoroughly before beginning the massage, and then warm them by rubbing them together vigorously. To protect your baby's delicate skin, make sure your nails are short, and that you aren't wearing any dangling or protruding jewelry on your hands or wrists.

❋ Your hands may glide smoothly even without any massage oil or lubricant. But if you would like to use one, ask the doctor whether it would be OK on your preemie's immature skin, and whether he suggests oil or moisturizing lotion. You'll need to avoid any product that contains perfumes or dyes (see page 246).

❋ Place your hands on your baby and talk to him for a moment, to let him know you're there, before you start massaging. Once you start massaging, don't talk too much, in case it's too much stimulation for your baby. Let him focus on your touch.

❋ For the massage itself, use a gentle but firm touch, rather than a light, stroking one. Preemies don't respond well to a light, stroking touch, apparently because it feels like a tickle to them, and isn't soothing. Apply moderate pressure, but try not to pull on the skin.

❋ You can try a routine similar to the one used in research studies. For the first five minutes, with your baby lying tummy-down in his isolette, put your hands through the portholes, and stroke him, starting at the top of his head, and moving down to his neck, shoulders, back, waist, legs, feet, arms, and hands. Then, turn him over, so he's lying on his back. For the next five minutes, flex his arms and legs very gently, holding each flex for about ten seconds. Finally, turn him back over for another, five-minute stroking period similar to the first.

❋ If your baby starts to cry or show signs of stress during the massage, stop and comfort him. You might try placing your hands gently but firmly over him, without moving them

for a minute or so. Once he seems calm and comfortable, you can keep going. But if he again becomes unhappy, you should stop the massage. He knows best when he's had enough, and maybe he wants to be left alone right now. (Don't we all sometimes feel that way?) You can try it again some other time.

❋ After you've finished massaging your baby, you might want to hold him snugly for a while, perhaps rocking him, so both of you can enjoy the pleasure and intimacy of the moment.

How Much Time to Spend with Baby

I'm really torn about how much time my husband and I should spend with our daughter in the hospital. We both have jobs and an older son to take care of.

In all the research on premature babies, there's none that can offer a simple answer to the question: how much time should parents spend in the NICU?

Yet in the real world, away from the research lab, even the most devoted parents of preemies grapple with this question, explicitly or implicitly, every day their baby is in the hospital. Some, like you, must strike a balance among conflicting obligations, while others live far from the hospital, and others just wonder how hard to push themselves against the natural limits of physical and emotional fatigue.

Most parents have an intuitive sense that their preemies need them, in those stressful, difficult days, weeks, or months in the hospital—and they're right. There is plenty of evidence that being held, touched, and talked to by an affectionate caregiver are all important spurs to any infant's emotional and cognitive development. It is known that some babies and children who are deprived of loving care for a long period of time can suffer from a disorder called failure to thrive: they don't grow normally, no matter how much they eat. And some children develop what psychologists call attachment disorder: having lacked the early experience of being comforted by one or a few, special caregivers, these children never develop the capacity to form trusting, affectionate relationships, or to be able to comfort themselves.

So it's critical that your baby get plenty of love as she grows. But "plenty" doesn't mean that unless you envelop her in your presence twenty-four hours a day while she's in the hospital, she will be emotionally scarred. Remember that most preemies are hospitalized for a transient period of only a few weeks or months. And they're still at a stage of development when nature didn't intend them to be attuned to receiving affectionate touches and loving words at all, while they were in the womb.

For advice, we spoke to some professionals who think about these kinds of issues, and almost all delivered essentially the same message: Do all you can to maximize your time with your baby, but don't feel guilty or worry about the times you can't be there.

One expert in the field of Developmental Care, which studies the impact of the NICU experience on premature babies, says this: Your baby benefits from the time that you give. If you are free and can be with her all the time, and you're enjoying it, do it. (Just take care of yourself, you'll get tired.) If it's a real struggle for you to be there six hours a day, but you can be there for four hours, do that. If you can only get there for one hour a day, your baby will enjoy that hour. At the end of one to two years, will you be able to tell the difference? Probably not.

One reason, he explains, is that the normal attachment process between baby and parent takes place throughout the first year or two of life. When a preemie is hospitalized for less than a few months, any disruption in the process is fleeting, and can easily be mended once the baby gets home.

A similar response comes from a psychologist who does research on attachment problems among adopted children who spent the first months or years of their lives in orphanages. He explains that babies seem to be particularly sensitive to the existence, or absence, of a loving caregiver between the ages of six months and a year. At this point, some who have never had a consistent, nurturing caregiver show the first signs of emotional and cognitive delays. When deprived of loving stimulation only before six months of age, though, babies seem to recover completely. In fact, he suggests that if you get a limited leave from your work, and have the choice of taking it while your preemie is in the hospital or after she gets home, you should strongly consider waiting.

A few other pieces of advice:

❋ *Using your time in the hospital well is as important as how much time you spend there.* A Developmental Care researcher recalls two mothers, one who lived far from the hospital and could only visit her preemie on weekends, but lavished devoted attention on her baby while she was there, and the other who came daily, but always with some girlfriends to whom she paid more attention than her baby. The first baby showed no signs of attachment problems later, while the second one did.

❋ *Time your visits so you're with your preemie for as many feedings as possible.* These are times when you can really interact, whether you simply give your baby the feel of your arms around her while she is gavaged, or you give her a bottle or your breast. Hold your baby as much as possible while you're with her.

❋ *If you are concerned that you and your partner can't visit your baby enough, enlist help.* A grandparent, aunt, uncle, godmother, or even a close friend whom you trust to be sensitive and responsive to your baby, can help provide her with the human warmth she needs until she gets home. Since it's best for your baby to become familiar with the people caring for her, there shouldn't be more than a few, and they should be able to visit her consistently.

❋ *If you are spending a lot of your time at the hospital, take some breaks.* These aren't just for your sake, but for your preemie's, too. You aren't hurting her, you're renewing your energy so you can be a better parent.

❋ *Whatever you do, don't feel guilty.* You're doing the best you can. Preemies have intuition, too, and your baby knows that.

Whether to Go Back to Work

I always took for granted that I could be a mother and a working woman, but that was before having a premature baby. I don't know if I should go back to work as planned.

For some mothers, the choice is clear: they need to keep working for financial reasons, or want to because their career is so important to them. For other mothers, deciding whether to stay at home with their baby or go back to work can be agonizingly difficult. It's not just mothers of premature babies who have these feelings. Leaving your newborn, even if she's big and healthy, is a difficult choice, no matter how much you cherish your career.

Having a preemie, though, does involve some special considerations. When a preemie leaves the hospital, she may still be more difficult to care for than a term newborn (for instance, she may be fussier, see page 373, or on a cardiorespiratory monitor for weeks or months, see page 385). That makes it harder for her parents to entrust her to a baby-sitter, or to find daycare that can accommodate her needs. Some parents, who have to deal with the consequences of a medical complication, find their choices drastically limited. For instance, daycare is not advisable in the first year for a baby with a VP shunt or BPD, because she's at a higher risk for infections (see page 366).

While it's impossible to give you advice about such a decision, which depends on your child's and family's specific circumstances, and your personal priorities, there are some things you may want to consider:

❋ You may be eligible for a leave of absence from your job, with the assurance that you can return to work after your leave is over. The Family and Medical Leave Act requires employers with 50 or more employees to give up to 12 weeks of unpaid leave related to pregnancy problems or childbirth. You are eligible if you have been working for your employer for 12 months, and have worked at least 1,250 hours during the last year.

❋ To ease the financial sting, you may also be eligible for disability payments for the first few weeks that you aren't working after your baby is born—ask your employer. Under state-run disability programs (only a few states have them), new mothers typically collect disability pay for six weeks after a vaginal delivery, and eight weeks after a C-section.

❋ If you will be taking just a temporary leave of

absence from your job, you may find it more satisfying for you and your baby to postpone your leave until your baby comes home from the hospital. Although it is hard to return to work when your baby is still in the hospital nursery, so small and fragile, you can be sure that she's well cared for there by her doctors and nurses. Moreover, young preemies who are still at an earlier stage of development don't need much stimulation (see page 198). Taking time off when your baby is discharged, instead, will give you more leeway to get her home schedule well organized and settled, and to find the best kind of child care for her before you go back to work. By the time she's home, your baby will be even more responsive, and ready to get well acquainted with you.

❋ For the complicated mechanism of a working mom's schedule to run smoothly, few surprises or extra burdens can disrupt her daily routine. Can you anticipate, because of your baby's medical needs or the psychological consequences of a long hospitalization, that there will be more than the average number of "bumps in the road"? Consider how able and willing your partner is to pitch in when an unforeseen situation arises with your baby's health, and determine how flexible your schedule needs to be.

❋ Remember that there are many good recipes for a happy family life and career, and that what works well for another woman may not be best for you. It may help ease your mind to know that researchers have been unable to establish whether children who are in daycare or at home with a baby-sitter are better or worse off than those who are at home with their mothers. Good quality child care—no matter who gives it—is what's most important.

Parents Feeling Depressed

Now that I'm home from the hospital, I spend hours just sitting next to our daughter's empty bassinet, crying. Is this postpartum depression?

The "baby blues" can hit any mother a few days after delivery. Many new mothers cry by their baby's bassinet, as you do, even when the baby is in it!

Some 80% of new mothers—and new fathers to a lesser degree—suffer from the blues in the first couple of weeks after their baby's birth. In addition to floods of tears, the baby blues can make you feel anxious, fatigued, unable to concentrate, and easily irritated. In mothers, this is partly due to hormonal changes. But stress also plays an important role, as parents realize the full extent of their new responsibilities, and make adjustments to settle into their parental roles. Sleepless nights don't help, either.

Most cultures recognize that some emotional and practical upheaval will occur after delivery, and try to provide for that. British midwives talk about the "ten-day weepies." In China, new mothers are never left alone in the first month, and families are constantly helped in their daily chores. In the United States, it's traditional for grandparents to visit for extended periods of time after a baby is born.

For parents of preemies, the huge stress of having a premature baby heightens and complicates the normal reactions after birth. Several studies have found that in the month after delivery, parents of preemies are significantly more depressed and anxious than parents of term babies. One study found that 85% of mothers and 65% of fathers of extremely premature babies experienced "crisis" reactions in the week after delivery, consisting of disbelief, anger, guilt, sadness, and sometimes, uncontrollable crying. An early delivery itself is so scary that even many parents of healthy preemies react with shock and anxiety. No wonder. While a preemie is in the hospital nursery, his parents suffer from worry about him, being separated from him, fear of what the future might bring, and the difficult struggle to adapt to an unfamiliar and intimidating environment.

Normally, the baby blues are transient, beginning to disappear after a couple of weeks. Although you may continue to feel worried and stressed during your baby's hospitalization (riding what many parents have described as "the rollercoaster" of a preemie's first weeks), your feelings of crisis should soon subside. Mothers of premature infants begin to regain their emotional balance in the first weeks and months after birth, and by the end of the baby's first year, their levels of psychological distress, on average, have been found to be similar to those of mothers of term babies. (When premature children are at high risk for long-term health problems, their mothers, understandably, are more likely to report moderate symptoms of depression and anxiety for longer. But by the end of the child's third year of life, almost all mothers have adapted well to their situation, showing a strong attachment to their children, and satisfaction with their parenting experience.)

But while the baby blues come and go, and most parents of preemies find that they're gradually adjusting to their situation, some mothers go on to develop a real, postpartum depression. The risk factors for postpartum depression are a family history of postpartum depression, severe premenstrual syndrome (PMS), or a previous psychiatric illness. It can evolve from the baby blues, or strike at any time in the first year. Because stress also plays a large role in its development, fathers can get postpartum depression, too.

A deep sense of anxiety or depressed mood that persists longer than a few weeks, and is severe and debilitating, is what distinguishes a significant postpartum depression from normal baby blues. Feelings of helplessness or hopelessness, loss of self-esteem with guilt and self-accusation, poor appetite, and an inability to sleep, even when you should be tired, are some of the common symptoms of depression. In addition, postpartum depression may be signaled by reactions such as:

* extreme irritability, with explosions of hostility and anger;
* feeling confused, with a progressive inability to organize even easy things (like writing a shopping list);
* unnatural agitation and excitement;
* violent thoughts or actions directed toward yourself, your family, or your baby;
* recurring suicidal thoughts.

In some parents, the depression passes on its own in a few months; in others, if untreated, the changes in personality and behavior can last for years.

What can you do if you think you may be experiencing a postpartum depression? First of all, you should accept that any emotional reactions you're having are a normal consequence of what you're going through, and not feel guilty or shameful about them. Second, you should try to talk about your discomfort to the people who love you (your partner, your family, your friends). Many people find solace by seeking out religious counselors—hospital chaplains, or their priest or rabbi—who can offer some spiritual guidance. After about a month, or sooner if your symptoms are severe, you should try to talk to a mental health professional (a psychiatrist, psychologist, or social worker), who can counsel you and make sure you get antidepressant medications or hormonal supplements, if you need them.

Here's something encouraging for you to know. While parents of preemies suffer more from stress reactions during their baby's hospitalization, by about a month after their baby has come home, parents of preemies actually handle day-to-day stress and overwork better than parents of term infants of the same age. This may be because they adjust faster to the reality of their baby's needs (perhaps having imagined them to be harder than they actually are), while parents of term infants find their newborns need more care and attention than they'd anticipated. Also, despite the pain of separation, a preemie's stay in the hospital has one positive effect: mothers have more time to recover physically, and have usually recouped their strength by the time their babies come home.

So, take heart: parents of preemies do regain their emotional balance, exactly as other new parents do, just a little more slowly sometimes, depending on their children's health. In fact, although it may seem like small consolation now, once your baby comes home, this painful experience is likely to make you appreciate him, and the happiness he brings you, even more.

Baby Still on a Ventilator

My daughter is still on a ventilator, and even though the doctor tells me that she's making good progress, there have been several times when he lowered her vent settings and then had to raise them again. The way it's going, I'm afraid she'll never be able to breathe on her own.

It practically never happens that babies need ventilators for the rest of their lives, and it's rare for a preemie to be on a ventilator for longer than a few months. Especially since your baby's doctor feels she is making good progress (and even that wouldn't be necessary), there's no reason to believe that she'll be any different. So you shouldn't worry about that.

That's the rational answer. On an emotional level, we can empathize with your fear. Every parent waits for that moment when their baby is free of the ventilator tube, reassuring her parents that she can accomplish the vital act of breathing independently. No matter how long your baby has been on a ventilator, it can be extremely frustrating, even agonizing, when the doctor is trying to wean her off, and it's not going smoothly.

You should certainly talk to your baby's doctor, and tell him about your anxieties. Most parents have a few fears that the doctors aren't even aware of—and often can dispel quite quickly. In this case, they will probably tell you that weaning from the ventilator often involves taking two steps forward, and one step back. There are times when it might involve taking one step forward and one step back, or unfortunately, even two steps back. One thing that's true in all cases: it always takes longer than parents want.

If your baby seems to be having trouble coming off the ventilator, there could be many reasons why. Your baby's doctor can tell you whether any of the following, common reasons apply to her:

❋ *Simple prematurity.* Some babies who are very young and small just need more time. The reason is that a very tiny baby's chest wall and respiratory muscles are still weak. When she takes a breath, her chest wall may suck in deeply, pushing much of the air out of her lungs. Without enough air left in them, her lungs can't remain wide open. Many babies have to reach a weight of 1,000 grams or so before they overcome this problem. Very young babies also may need a few weeks for their respiratory drive to mature, if apnea is keeping them on the vent.

✳ *Lung damage.* Unfortunately, those valuable lifesavers—ventilators and extra oxygen—are double-edged swords. At high levels, they also cause some lung damage themselves. Babies who develop lung damage from the ventilator and oxygen need time to heal. Once your baby's oxygen and vent settings are not so high, the healing will outstrip any injury they're causing. (In general, oxygen concentration is considered high when it's more than 60%. It's more complicated to determine what counts as high vent settings, since that varies with the size and age of the baby. You can ask your baby's doctor to help you understand how much respiratory support your baby is getting.) Sometimes the doctor can push the weaning from the vent along by giving a baby steroids; but since steroids have side effects, no one wants to use them unless it's necessary. If the doctor tells you your baby has BPD (lung damage that persists for more than a month or so), you can read about it on page 261—but many preemies' lungs will heal before then.

✳ *A new wrinkle in the baby's health.* Sometimes just when a baby is breathing better, and her ventilator settings are steadily going down, something happens to weaken her medical condition—an infection, a PDA, surgery, aspiration of some vomit, or some other complication. In that case, the doctors must fix the problem—and start the weaning process again.

We know it's easier said than done, but the most important advice we have for you is to try to be patient. Weaning a baby from a ventilator is really a matter of trial and error; doctors don't have an exact way to tell when a baby's lungs are ready to function on their own. It's not really a setback when your baby's ventilator settings are lowered and raised again—it's just that the doctor was guessing that your baby was ready, and it turned out to be a little too early. She'll come off the vent in her own good time . . . showing us parents once again that children will determine their own schedule, thank-you!

Steroids

My baby is having trouble coming off the ventilator, and the doctor wants to give him steroids. Wouldn't that be dangerous for a small baby?

Like you, many people think of steroids as powerful drugs with serious side effects. The truth is, you're right. But no drug is without its risks, so it's always a matter of weighing the risks and the benefits. We'll tell you a little about both, so you'll have an idea of the kinds of things your baby's doctor is taking into consideration.

What steroids do is dampen the immune response, thereby cutting down on inflammation—the body's reaction to any injury, germ, or irritant. This can be a big boon to a preemie on a ventilator. Since the ventilator always causes some injury to the lungs, it's really common for the lungs to get inflamed. Same with the trachea and vocal cords, which are irritated by the presence of a foreign piece of hardware, the endotracheal tube. They may swell, secrete a lot of mucus, and, over time, become scarred.

This inflammation in the lungs and airways

makes it harder for a baby to breathe, sometimes keeping him dependent on the ventilator even after his lungs have matured. That's why steroids often work quickly and dramatically: a baby's need for oxygen may go way down within a day or two after starting steroids, and he just starts weaning himself from the vent.

Doctors (and parents, of course) would like babies to come off the vent as soon as possible, not just to avoid any lung damage the machine might cause, but also because of the uncomfortable or undesirable things that go along with being on a ventilator, like suctioning or sedation. Some doctors are so convinced of the tremendous value of steroids that they advocate putting preemies with respiratory distress syndrome on them right away, soon after birth. And some doctors will give steroids to all preemies just before they're extubated, to minimize the chance that they'll land right back on the vent, due to swelling in their airway.

OK. What about the risks? The major one is that a baby's immune response will be suppressed so much that he'll be more prone to getting infections. Babies on steroids also often have a jump in blood sugar or blood pressure. Doctors will watch carefully for these things, to catch and treat them before they become serious problems. There's also a chance that a baby on steroids will grow more slowly, although the long-term effect of that is not yet clear. And recently, some studies have pointed to steroids as a possible factor in some of the potentially serious developmental problems (both motor and cognitive) that preemies may have later.

If the doctor thinks your baby is not benefiting from the steroids, he'll stop them within a matter of days. If your baby does get a lot better on steroids, the question will be when to take him off. The doctor may stop them after a few days, pleased that they helped lower the ventilator pressures and oxygen to safer levels, or he may wait until your baby is weaned off the vent, or continue them for as long as six weeks (which some research recommends). A shorter course of steroids will cut down on side effects, but may not provide as many benefits.

If side effects are a particular concern (as they are, say, in babies with severe BPD who might benefit from being on steroids for many weeks), steroids can be inhaled, rather than taken intravenously or orally. The hope is that they'll suppress inflammation in a baby's lungs without affecting the rest of his body. But steroids given this way aren't as powerful, and may not get deep enough into the lungs to work well.

You can see that a decision to treat a preemie with steroids isn't taken lightly. By talking it over with your baby's doctor, you will probably be reassured that he has thought through carefully what's best for your baby.

Bronchoscopy: A Peek inside Your Baby's Lungs

Say your baby is really having trouble weaning off the ventilator—not just by your measure, since all parents get understandably anxious, and think a normal time frame for weaning is way too long. If your baby has come off and gone back on the vent three or four times, has already tried steroids, the doctor is hearing sounds that could indicate obstruction of the upper airways, or some areas of his lungs aren't clearing up on x-rays and the reasons aren't apparent, then it's time to find out why things aren't going according to plan. One way to do it is with a procedure called a bronchoscopy. A long tube or "scope," with a fiberoptic viewer on it, is passed through the vocal cords, down the trachea, and into the bronchi (the large airways of the lungs). The specialist who does the procedure simply looks around, to see what's going on that might make breathing more difficult. She'll probably also take cultures of lung fluid and samples of the cells in the airways.

Some of the things your baby's doctor might be wondering: Is there scar tissue from the endotracheal tube, or some other mass or cyst, that's causing an obstruction? Is there a condition called malacia in which the baby's airways are soft and collapsing, and need time for the cartilage to stiffen up and remain open like in older babies? Is there an infection that's so deep in the lungs it didn't get cultured through normal sampling? Is there inflammation from reflux, caused by aspiration of milk or formula?

A bronchoscopy can often answer those questions, and provide information needed to guide future treatment. There are two kinds of bronchoscopies: flexible and rigid. A flexible bronchoscopy, usually done by a pulmonologist (a lung doctor), is often first choice, because it can be done right in the nursery, with the baby sedated but awake. If the baby's endotracheal tube is big enough, he may not even need to be extubated; the bronchoscope will be passed right through it. One of the reasons this technique is preferred is that the pulmonologist can see the baby's airways at work as he breathes, and can tell whether or not there's malacia.

If the endotracheal tube is too small for the scope to fit through, and the baby isn't stable enough to be extubated during the procedure, then a rigid bronchoscopy is done. This procedure is usually performed by a surgeon in an operating room, with the baby under general anesthesia (which you can read more about on page 308), so he can be ventilated and kept physiologically stable for its duration. Although the doctor won't be able to diagnose malacia (since the baby's airways aren't moving while he's under general anesthesia), as with a flexible bronchoscope, she can look deep inside the airways, see any inflammation or obstruction, and get brushings of cells to culture. And if an obstruction is found, the surgeon is sometimes able to remove it right then and there.

A bronchoscopy, which usually takes about 30 to 60 minutes, probably isn't comfortable for a baby, but it isn't painful. And when the scope sheds light on your baby's lungs, it also sheds valuable light on what steps to take next in his treatment.

IN PLAIN LANGUAGE: WHAT IS BPD?

When a premature baby who had respiratory distress syndrome at birth is still on a ventilator several weeks later, doctors usually suspect he has BPD, or bronchopulmonary dysplasia. This means that the very life-saving assistance he's required—supplemental oxygen and mechanical ventilation—has damaged his delicate lungs and impaired their natural healing process. BPD is a catch-22: a baby is dependent on respiratory assistance, but this assistance is exactly what prevents his lungs from recovering.

The medical answer to this dilemma is a slow process of gradual weaning from respiratory aids, with good nutrition, medications, and a lot of care and attention to help the baby's lungs grow and heal.

Thankfully, many cases of BPD resolve in just a few more weeks. But it can take longer. Some babies go home on supplemental oxygen. Parents should know, though, that the most severe forms of BPD are rare. The majority of premature babies recover from it, in time, without serious long-term consequences.

WHAT BABIES ARE AT RISK FOR BPD

Without neonatal intensive care, BPD wouldn't even exist. It's a mixed blessing: BPD occurs because preemies who are born too young to breathe on their own are now surviving.

Besides immature lungs, any other medical condition that causes preemies to require mechanical ventilation and supplemental oxygen at high levels, or for longer than a few days (such as pneumonia, prolonged apnea, a PDA, or necrotizing enterocolitis), increases their risk of developing BPD.

Therapies that can speed up the development of the lungs and make RDS less serious (such as steroids administered before a premature delivery, surfactant, and good intravenous nutrition) have helped lower the risk of BPD in preemies born weighing more than 1,000 grams. Doctors have also become better at limiting damage to the lungs, by carefully monitoring concentrations of oxygen, and minimizing the pressures of the ventilator. But the high risk of BPD in the youngest infants (around 50% for those weighing from 600 to 1,000 grams at birth) is the price they pay for a very good chance of surviving RDS and the other complications of prematurity. It's a reason for worrying, but also for rejoicing.

WHAT CAN HAPPEN IN A PREEMIE'S LUNGS

Initially, RDS injures a preemie's lungs, by causing inflammation. The inflammation makes breathing difficult, so oxygen and a ventilator must be used to support the baby's respiration. Meanwhile, lung cells near the injury try to repair the damage, by quickly multiplying and differentiating. But the healing process is disturbed by the force of the ventilator and the extra oxygen the baby is getting. (A preemie's fragile tissues aren't able to withstand strong pressures from the ventilator, as it pushes air into the lungs. And oxygen is particularly toxic to the immature lungs of preemies, because they're deficient in the natural "anti-oxidants" that protect the body from the damaging effects of oxygen's free radicals.)

As the new lung cells become injured, the lung tissue they make isn't normally formed. This is how BPD develops. That's also why it's called "dysplasia," meaning abnormal tissue growth.

How and When BPD Is Diagnosed

If, after the first week of life, a preemie's need for respiratory support is increasing instead of going down, he may be developing BPD. The diagnosis is confirmed if a chest x-ray shows scarring in his lungs, and he's still on oxygen by four weeks after birth, or by 36 weeks after conception. (The latter criteria—oxygen at 36 weeks after conception—is more accurate for babies born at less than 30 weeks gestation, and is better at predicting which babies will go on to have long-term respiratory problems.) Babies with BPD tend to breathe faster and harder than normal. They may wheeze and become short of breath from too much fluid seeping into their lungs, or from a tightening of their airways, similar to asthma.

What Preemies Need to Overcome BPD

For their lungs to heal, preemies with BPD need attentive, supportive care in the hospital nursery:

* **Pulmonary hygiene.** Chest physiotherapy and suctioning can help prevent obstruction of a baby's airways by mucus and secretions, and keep small areas of his lungs from collapsing.
* **Medications.** Bronchodilators and steroids can open the airways and reduce inflammation in the lungs.
* **Treatment of exacerbating conditions**
  * Closing a PDA (see page 176) can help decrease excess fluid in the lungs.
  * Treating pneumonia and other infections can reduce reliance on a ventilator or oxygen.
  * Preventing reflux can decrease airway tightening and lung inflammation.
  * Correcting anemia can improve the blood's ability to deliver oxygen throughout the body.
  * Treating high blood pressure can ease some of the heart's workload, improving blood flow and oxygen.
* **Developmental Care.** Preemies with BPD are often very sensitive to overstimulation, and are easily stressed by bright lights, noises, and touch. Reducing overstimulation and stress by following some of the guidelines of Developmental Care on page 200 can be especially helpful for babies with BPD, because stress can lead to oxygen desaturation, airway tightening, and higher blood pressure in the lungs—all of which can worsen BPD.
* **Fluid management.** It's common for fluid to build up in the lungs of preemies with BPD, which can interfere with their breathing. So doctors may restrict the amount of fluid a preemie gets intravenously or in his feedings. They may also prescribe diuretics (medications that increase urination) to decrease the fluid in his lungs, and ease weaning from oxygen or the ventilator.
* **Nutrition.** Preemies with BPD need to eat

more than other babies, because they use up more energy breathing, and the extra calories and nutrients are crucial for building healthy, new lung tissue. Good nutrition is sometimes difficult to achieve, though. If a baby's fluid intake needs to be restricted, his breast milk or formula may be densely concentrated, making it harder to digest. Parenteral nutrition, delivered intravenously, is a good solution for a while, but it's not as wholesome as breast milk or formula. And starting to nipple feed may be difficult and frustrating, because a baby who has been on a ventilator for a long time may associate touch around his mouth with the negative sensations of the endotracheal tube. (Some older preemies with BPD may actually do better feeding with a cup and spoon.) For all of these reasons, preemies with BPD tend to be smaller than other premature babies, and they may continue to get tube feedings to bolster the calories they take in themselves. But as they recover from BPD, they can experience remarkable catch-up growth.

How BPD Is Treated: A Slow Phasing-Out of Assisted Respiration

It's a patient process of trial and error, whose goal is to keep a preemie stable, while slowly weaning him from the ventilator and oxygen. The doctor finds the right pace for reducing respiratory support by closely monitoring blood gases, oxygen levels, and the baby's comfort. The time frame will vary, depending on the severity of a baby's lung injuries. It most often takes several weeks, but can stretch to months.

Rarely, a baby with BPD will need supplemental oxygen for several years.

Most preemies with BPD are able to inflate their lungs by themselves before they can maintain good oxygenation, so they come off the ventilator first, and oxygen later. Some are treated with CPAP (see page 96) for a while, to help keep their airways open as they make the transition from the ventilator to breathing on their own.

Since intubated babies can't feed by mouth, and must be kept relatively motionless so they don't accidentally dislodge the endotracheal tube, prolonged intubation threatens a preemie's ability to grow and develop normally. There is a surgical procedure called a tracheostomy, in which a tube is inserted into the trachea, that will allow a baby to move more freely, engage his environment, and use his mouth, tongue, and face to express himself. You can read more about it on page 323. A tracheostomy is usually considered if a baby has been intubated for three months or more. It doesn't prevent a baby from eventually coming off a vent.

Fortunately, most babies with BPD get well quickly enough to go home shortly after their due date, breathing completely on their own. But even babies who are still on oxygen may be able to go home with their families. (There's more about going home on oxygen on page 350.) By the end of their second year of life, and often well before then, nearly all babies with BPD leave supplemental oxygen behind.

To get to that happy ending, a few families have to go through very hard times in the hospital. Parenting a baby with BPD in the NICU can be difficult, and you may think you're losing control of the situation. Please don't be scared: you're going to overcome these moments. But you may feel better if you know that certain patterns of behavior are typical for babies with BPD, and they'll be outgrown as their breathing improves.

Babies with the most severe BPD—a small number—may become so agitated by their struggles to breathe that they become oversensitive and react negatively to even the gentlest stimulation. Their parents' attempts to soothe and console them (even simple holding) may stress them more. Some severely affected babies will have episodes of frantic restlessness, followed by periods of exhaustion. Depleted of energy, they may become lethargic, sleeping a lot, or appearing depressed and unresponsive, even in their mothers' or fathers' presence. There's nothing more frustrating for a parent than being unable to comfort or interact with your child. It's normal to feel devastated, resigned and angry, because you can't seem to make any difference in your child's life. But the answer is not to disconnect from your baby: just imagine that you've been put on hold for a while, by some disturbances on the line. Try to remain strong, go often to see him in the hospital, stand by him. Slowly, you'll notice a two-way communication developing. You'll see that your love will be acknowledged by your baby, and amplified.

HOW BABIES DO AFTER BPD, IN THE LONG RUN

Despite the fact that babies who get BPD are often the youngest and sickest preemies, almost 80% of them survive and recover. A baby's prognosis will vary a lot, depending on whether his BPD is mild or severe.

Preemies with mild BPD are often fine by the time they go home.

For those with more severe BPD, families should keep in mind that even if the first year or two of life is very difficult, things are likely to improve. Preemies with BPD are more likely to get respiratory viruses and ear infections in their infancy. Respiratory infections may become serious, and a baby might need to be rehospitalized. Parents should be aware of this possibility, and seek medical attention if their baby starts to have more difficulty breathing. Preemies who had BPD are also susceptible to wheezing and asthma, and shouldn't be exposed to cigarette smoke, or other airborne irritants, such as chemicals in home cleansers. (On page 338, you'll find some guidelines for caring for your baby at home.)

A long-term consequence of BPD can be smaller lung capacity, with less ability to exercise strenuously. But this usually doesn't prevent a child from running, playing, and living a normal, active life.

BPD is frequently accompanied by other complications of prematurity. It can prolong a baby's hospital course and slow his weight gain, body and brain growth at a crucial time. Although 80% of preemies with BPD develop normally, about 20% show some developmental delay at three years of age. BPD seems to increase the risk of motor problems and cerebral palsy (having uncoordinated or abnormal movements) and, to a lesser degree, mental problems (including retardation or learning difficulties), although mental problems are more closely related to whether a child, in addition to BPD, had an intraventricular hemorrhage or periventricular leukomalacia. Also, cognitive ability is greatly influenced by environmental factors (such as the parents' educational level, socioeconomic status, and attentiveness to the child). This means that parents who provide a nurturing and stimulating environment can improve their baby's chance of growing up mentally normal and sound.

To be the best parent of a child who is recovering from BPD, you'll need to acknowledge the huge emotional load you carry: the trauma of a premature birth, prolonged anxiety from a long and complicated hospitalization, and worry about what the future may bring. Practical, as well as emotional, problems may add to your distress, making it extremely difficult to resume a normal lifestyle. But family life is exactly what your child will need to grow and develop to his best potential. Just keep in mind that getting any help you may need, emotional or physical, will put your baby's interests on top, too.

ET Tube Accidentally Pulled Out

My baby is always trying to pull out his ventilator tube, and yesterday he finally succeeded. Is there any possibility he's going to hurt himself?

Very little. You'd be surprised how common it is for babies to pull out their own endotracheal, or ET, tubes, or for the tubes to slip out accidentally. Accidental extubations (the technical term for removal of the tube from the windpipe) can happen simply because the tape near the baby's mouth that holds the tube in place gets wet from saliva, and comes loose. Or, in some of the younger babies, just because the windpipe is tiny, and there's a very small distance between the right and the wrong position. Bigger, stronger babies who are able to pull on the tube when it's bothering them—a mature act of coordination for a preemie!—are the ones who are most likely to extubate themselves.

Although there are some risks from accidental extubations, and the NICU staff tries hard to prevent them, the chance that they'll cause a significant problem is very small. In an intensive care unit, nurses are always within a few steps of every bed. If there is a decline in the baby's heart rate or oxygen levels, an alarm will sound, and within seconds, a nurse will start giving him oxygen. (An oxygen bag and mask are usually kept at every bedside for this purpose.) This will nearly always keep the baby breathing fine until his tube is reinserted. The reinsertion itself is sometimes accompanied by complications like bradycardia, but that rarely lasts more than a few seconds—not long enough to be damaging.

If your baby was eating, his feedings may be stopped for a few hours, as he resettles himself. A chest x-ray may be taken to make sure that the tube is back in the right position. The worst part of the episode, usually, is that it's slightly uncomfortable (though not painful) for the baby when his tube is put back in. Some babies may develop hoarseness, or swelling around their vocal cords, from repeated intubations. These are almost always temporary.

If this happens to your baby more than a few times, his doctor may try inserting the endotracheal tube through his nose rather than his mouth. This can only be done on bigger preemies (the nostrils of littler ones are too small for the tube), and the procedure is a little harder and slower to do, but it's more stable. The doctor may also consider restraining a baby's movements, prescribing sedatives, or using measures such as swaddling, nesting, and cutting down on light, sounds, touch, and other exciting stimuli (since a calm baby is less likely to extubate himself).

Every once in awhile, some good comes from an unplanned extubation. The doctors may discover that your baby can breathe on his own better than they expected, so he may be allowed to stay off the ventilator. And babies who are re-intubated get the benefit of a cleaner, and sometimes larger, endotracheal tube, which may provide better airflow, sooner than the doctors might have troubled them to make the switch otherwise.

By the way, some neonatal nurses claim they can tell a lot about a preemie's personality from the start, and they'd say you've got a feisty little guy on your hands. Over the next few months and years, you'll find out if they're right!

Hoarse Voice

I was so eager to hear my baby's voice, but now that she's off the ventilator, she sounds as hoarse as Louis Armstrong.

Imagine that great American jazz musician and your teensy preemie having something in common! Actually, it's typical for babies who have been on ventilators to have hoarse or weak cries when they come off; their vocal cords get slightly irritated and swollen by the endotracheal tube, and it usually takes several days for them to return to normal. Preemies who have been intubated for a long time (several weeks or more) may not recover their full, vocal powers for a couple of weeks. So just relax and wait for your baby to demonstrate her first full-volume, clear cries. Eventually, you may look back wistfully on this brief period when her fussing was still easy on your ears.

High Blood Pressure

My baby has high blood pressure. Why would a little baby have that, and how serious is it?

Most people associate high blood pressure with middle-aged men and women who are getting a little chubby around the middle. But this condition affects skinny preemies, too—only for different reasons. The good thing about high blood pressure in preemies is that doctors can usually figure out the cause, and eliminating the cause usually solves the problem.

First, you should know that what counts as high blood pressure in a preemie is very different from what counts as high blood pressure in an adult, so don't be surprised if the numbers sound low to you. In fact, the numbers that are considered normal change as a preemie gets older, and your baby's doctor may have to look at a chart to determine whether your preemie's readings are elevated for her age and size.

The most likely reason your baby has high blood pressure, or hypertension, is that she's having a side effect to a medication she's taking, like steroids. The solution may be to take her off steroids—or sometimes, just lowering the dose does the trick. If the doctor thinks it's best for your baby to remain on steroids, he may give her medicine (common antihypertensives for preemies are enalapril or hydralazine) to treat the high blood pressure, which will go away once your baby's course of steroids ends.

Another, fairly common reason for high blood pressure in a baby in the NICU is agitation or discomfort. Most often, the hypertension will go away when the baby calms down; in that case, the doctors won't even count the high blood pressure readings as significant. If they persist, though, it may be that she needs more pain medication—or, if she's being tapered off a pain medication she's received for a long time, that her dose shouldn't be lowered quite as rapidly.

Sometimes, high blood pressure occurs in babies who have had umbilical arterial catheters, because a small blood clot forms in the artery leading to the kidney. This is treated by removing the catheter, if it's still in place, and giving the baby medication to treat the high blood pressure while her body takes care of eliminating the clot all by itself. (It usually takes a few weeks for a clot to resolve on its own. Additional therapy to remove it is rarely necessary.) Hydrocephalus (see page 168) that is severe enough to require a shunt can cause high blood pressure, but once the shunt is in place, the problem should disappear. And babies who have severe BPD may get high blood pressure. In this case, the hypertension lasts longer, but it can be treated with medication. As the BPD gets better, it should gradually go away.

Serious, persistent causes of hypertension are rare in preemies. So try not to be too concerned. Chances are your baby's blood pressure will soon be back down, and you won't have to worry about it again until she's middle-aged and chubby around the middle.

Eye Exam

My baby's going to have her eye test tomorrow, and I couldn't be more anxious about it. I know vision problems are very common among preemies.

Many people associate prematurity with vision problems. Even though it's true that this is a possible complication of a premature birth, it's probably less common than you think.

The eye condition that affects premature babies is called retinopathy of prematurity, or ROP for short. It's explained in detail on page 268, but you don't need to read that unless your baby's eye exam tomorrow reveals that she has it.

Here's all you need to know right now. These days, most preemies do not get ROP, or if they do, it's usually mild and goes away completely on its own. There was a tragic epidemic of ROP among premature babies in the 1950s, which is probably why the problem became so well known. But that was a long time ago, and was caused by giving preemies excessive amounts of oxygen—a practice that has long since been abandoned. Now that neonatologists know that high levels of oxygen can cause damage to a preemie's retina, babies are given only as much oxygen as they need.

The eye exam, done by an ophthalmologist at your baby's bedside, will be quick and painless. Your baby's eyelids will be held open with a clip (which looks a lot worse than it feels), because that's the safest and most accurate way to do the exam. Some babies don't seem to mind, while others make it clear that they don't like having their eyelids held open, or having someone shine a bright light at them. After it's over, the drops used to dilate your baby's eyes will make her very sensitive to light, so she may be more comfortable if you keep her isolette covered with a blanket for a few hours afterward. The ophthalmologist can tell your baby's doctor the results immediately.

If your baby was born after 28 weeks of gestation, the chances of her having ROP are small. Even among younger, sicker babies, who are at greatest risk of developing ROP, the vast majority end up with normal vision. So try to put this particular problem out of your mind for now. The chances are you're worrying unnecessarily.

IN PLAIN LANGUAGE:
WHAT IS RETINOPATHY OF PREMATURITY?

Once a premature baby's eyes open—usually by 26 weeks of gestation—she can see, though very fuzzily. Over the next several weeks, she'll gradually become able to focus on objects around her, and eventually you'll notice her staring with fascination at your beloved face, or even looking around and enjoying the sights. Her visual abilities will mature as she does. So it should come as no surprise that inside, her eyes are still developing, too.

Beginning at around 16 weeks of gestation, the retina (the lining inside the back of the eye) starts to develop a network of blood vessels. This intricate web initially forms in the center of the retina, at the very back of the eye. Gradually the blood vessels spread to cover the retina's surface, moving toward the front of the eye. By around the time of a full-term birth, their growth is complete.

These blood vessels, which supply the retina with oxygen, sometimes don't grow as planned after a premature birth. They are supposed to spread from areas of high oxygen (in other words, where they are already), into areas of low oxygen (where they haven't formed yet). But once the baby is born, the signals directing blood vessel growth can become confused. Extra oxygen that a baby may be getting (even oxygen from the air), episodes of low oxygen (because of RDS or apnea, for example), and numerous, other, unexpected things, may send errant signals and cause abnormal, new blood vessels to grow. These abnormal vessels can block out light, and damage the retina by pulling on it, possibly even causing the retina to detach from the wall of the eye.

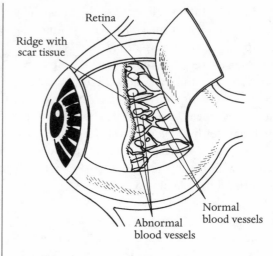

In ROP, new abnormal blood vessels grow at the edge of the normal blood vessels supplying the retina and can form a ridge of scar tissue that may pull on the retina and damage it.

Adapted with permission from *Understanding Retinopathy of Prematurity.* IRIS Medical Instruments, Inc., a subsidiary of IRIDEX Corporation 1996

The possibility of vision problems arouses great fear, and most parents feel terrified and distraught when doctors diagnose ROP in their baby. But the wonderful fact is that most cases of ROP—roughly 90%, by some estimates—cure themselves spontaneously. Within a few months, the abnormal blood vessels regress and disappear, usually leaving the baby with normal vision. An additional group of babies will need treatment, but can avoid serious damage with its help. Thankfully, today it is rare for a baby to lose her vision.

WHY SOME BABIES GET ROP AND OTHERS DON'T

Most premature babies never develop ROP. As usual, it's the youngest, smallest, and sickest preemies who are at greatest risk. ROP is so uncommon among babies born after 32 weeks of gestation that many hospitals don't even bother to give these preemies routine eye exams.

Preemies born at less than 28 weeks of gestation are the ones who are mainly at risk. Roughly 15% of babies with a birth weight between 1,250 and 1,500 grams, 35% of those with a birth weight between 1,000 and 1,250 grams, 50% of those with a birth weight between 750 and 1,000 grams, and 80% of those with a birth weight between 500 and 750 grams, develop some ROP. While these numbers sound high, remember that the vast majority of these babies will outgrow the condition, with no harm done, by the time they're three or four months past their due date.

Doctors still don't know the exact cause of retinopathy of prematurity. They learned the hard way, from an ROP epidemic in the 1950s, that supplemental oxygen is one major factor. At that time, premature babies were often given oxygen whether or not they had breathing problems, and after a while it became apparent that those who were given high concentrations of oxygen were developing ROP in especially large numbers. More recent research suggests that preemies who have a lot of swings in their blood oxygen levels—from very low to high—are particularly prone to ROP. Today, doctors are able to measure oxygen levels in the blood more precisely, and babies get only as much oxygen as they need. The risk of ROP is kept as low as possible, without harming the baby's medical stability.

Although some research has suggested that bright or fluorescent lights in the NICU may contribute to the development of retinopathy of prematurity, reducing light exposure in clinical trials (in one large study, by having preemies wear goggles for at least their first month of life) doesn't seem to decrease the incidence of ROP.

Other possible risk factors that need further study include: intraventricular hemorrhage; apnea; anemia; blood transfusions; infection; use of medications such as indomethacin or steroids; respiratory distress syndrome; high levels of carbon dioxide in the blood; seizures; vitamin deficiency; chronic, inadequate oxygen during pregnancy; and intrauterine growth retardation. It's not clear yet whether these factors have an independent impact on ROP, or whether they're just another indication that smaller, sicker babies are at greater risk.

Twins, triplets, or other multiples are no more likely to develop ROP than single babies born at the same gestational age and weight. Boys and girls seem to be at equal risk, but black babies are at less risk than babies from other racial groups. Some research indicates that preemies who receive surfactant after birth are less apt to develop ROP. There's also some evidence, although it's not considered conclusive, that treatment of vitamin E deficiency may be helpful.

DIAGNOSIS: THE EYE EXAM

Most NICUs have regular screening programs for ROP: all babies who fall under a certain gestational age or birth weight get routine eye exams before they leave the hospital. The timing varies, but the first test is usually scheduled about four to six weeks after delivery.

The eye test is easily administered right in the NICU. Your baby will be given eye drops to enlarge her pupils, so the back of her eye will be more visible. An ophthalmologist will look all the way into the back of your baby's eyes, using a medical instrument called an indirect ophthalmoscope, to see whether her retina's blood vessels are growing normally. The doctor will be able to tell right away if your baby's eyes are fine. She may get follow-up exams every few weeks, until her eyes' blood vessels have finished growing.

How ROP Is Classified

When ROP occurs, it is usually in both eyes, but it may be more severe in one eye than the other. If your baby's ophthalmologist does see some sign of retinopathy on the exam, he'll describe it, using four criteria:

❋ *The stage of the ROP* conveys how mild or severe your baby's condition is. This is probably the key measurement to become familiar with. Although retinopathy of prematurity is a progressive disease—it starts at stage 1 and may keep going through Stage 4 or 5—it doesn't always progress. It may stop at any earlier stage and disappear entirely.

> *MILD—Stage 1.* When ROP is only stage 1, the eye doctor sees a white demarcation line separating the normally developed retina near the back of the eye from the undeveloped retina in front.
> *MILD—Stage 2.* The demarcation line has been replaced by a ridge of tissue.
> *MODERATE—Stage 3.* The ridge has gotten bigger, with some new, abnormal blood vessels and scar tissue forming on it and extending toward the back of the eye.

Treatment is often considered at this stage, to keep the ROP from progressing further.
> *SEVERE—Stage 4.* The scar tissue has pulled on the retina, and caused it to partially detach. Since the detachment is not complete, it may or may not seriously affect the baby's vision. Surgery to reattach the retina is usually recommended.
> *SEVERE—Stage 5.* The scar tissue has pulled hard enough to completely detach the retina. This allows no useful vision. Corrective surgery to reattach the retina can sometimes help.

❋ *The location of the ROP* conveys where it is in the eye. Zone III (where the blood vessels form last, around the edges of the retina) is of least concern, followed by Zone II (the middle section), followed by Zone I (where the vessels first start to form, and where most vision occurs).

❋ *The extent of the ROP* describes how large an area is involved. It's measured in the number of hours on an imaginary clock. If you picture the eye as the clock, and there is retinopathy between, say, 12:00 and 4:00, then the extent of the baby's ROP is 4 clock hours.

❋ *The presence of "plus disease"* means that the abnormal blood vessels are especially large, twisting and inflamed. It indicates that the ROP is expected to progress rapidly.

Doctors can convey a lot about a baby's ROP using this shorthand classification. For example, ROP that is Stage 3, Zone 1 with Plus disease is severe enough to require treatment, while ROP that is Stage 1 Zone 3 will almost always disappear on its own.

Every baby with ROP must have frequent, follow-up exams until the retinopathy disappears.

Even if your baby has already been discharged from the hospital, it's extremely important not to miss these follow-up appointments, since early treatment can make all the difference for your baby's eyesight.

MODERN TOOLS TO FIGHT ROP: LASER THERAPY AND CRYOTHERAPY

Since most cases of ROP cure themselves spontaneously, the need for treatment will probably never arise for your baby. Most ophthalmologists recommend treatment only if a baby's ROP reaches at least stage 3, in zones 1 or 2.

We're very lucky today. Forty years ago, no treatment for ROP was available. Then a procedure called cryotherapy was developed: a little probe is placed on the outside of the eye to freeze the retina and make the abnormal blood vessels disappear, so normal ones will grow in their place. In a large research trial, cryotherapy cut the risk that moderately severe ROP would progress to retinal detachment in half, from 43% to 21%, and two-thirds of the treated eyes developed no serious vision problems.

If your baby has cryotherapy, she'll get local or general anesthesia during the procedure, and pain medication for a few days afterward. Her eyes will be very swollen and red for a week or so. Try not to worry about this; although it's very upsetting for a parent to see, it's absolutely expected. Your baby may also be given medicines or cold compresses to help reduce the swelling.

Today, most babies have the benefit of receiving an even more modern treatment: laser therapy. Laser therapy appears to be at least as effective as cryotherapy, and far less uncomfortable for the baby. It works in a similar way: the abnormal retinal tissue is destroyed, arresting the growth of abnormal blood vessels and scar tissue.

Laser therapy can be done right in the nursery. With the same instrument the ophthalmologist uses to examine your baby's eyes, he can deliver a laser beam into her eye. Since the beam goes directly to the retina, there's less inflammation and risk of damage to the rest of the eye. The procedure is also less painful than cryotherapy, so lower doses of anesthetic and pain medication can be used, and fewer babies need to be on a ventilator after it's over.

Laser therapy sounds very new and high-tech, but it's been used for over two decades to treat eye disorders in adults. Some parents get scared by it, but be assured that your baby is getting the best, most modern treatment available.

IF YOUR BABY NEEDS SURGERY

In a few babies, the retinopathy of prematurity keeps progressing, even after laser therapy or cryotherapy. If it reaches stage 4 or 5, the eye doctor generally recommends surgery to reattach the retina. There are two surgical options, and they are discussed on page 321.

With surgery, too, early treatment is key to the best possible outcome for your baby. So please forgive the repetition, but once your baby is diagnosed with ROP, don't miss those follow-up exams.

WHAT YOU CAN EXPECT IN THE LONG RUN

The long-term effect of ROP on a baby's vision depends on whether the illness caused permanent injury to the eye.

The body's response to mild ROP is a testament to self-healing: If the ROP regresses and disappears without treatment, the eye most often grows and develops normally. Thus, babies who had stage 1, 2, and 3 retinopathy of prematurity that didn't require treatment usually have normal vision, or can see well with glasses. By the time your baby is six to twelve months old, if no serious problem has been identified, you'll be able to relax—there probably won't be one.

Babies who had stage 3 retinopathy of prematurity that did require treatment can also have good vision, although most will need glasses for various degrees of nearsightedness.

In fewer than 10% of all cases, ROP reaches stage 4 or 5, involving partial or complete detachment of the retina. If the retina is only partially detached, and depending on where the detachment is, there's a chance that a baby will have useful, or even good, vision after surgery. After complete detachment of the retina, some vision may be recovered through surgery, but it's likely that the baby will be legally blind in that eye.

In general, babies who had retinopathy of prematurity are more likely to be nearsighted than other preemies. Strabismus (crossed eyes) and amblyopia (a lazy eye) are also more common among premature babies who had ROP. Since both problems are usually treatable—with muscle surgery for strabismus, and eye patches for amblyopia—all premature babies who had ROP are followed carefully during their first few years of life.

In a very small number of cases, complications may show up later. Glaucoma or late-onset retinal detachment have been reported in a few teenagers or young adults who had ROP as babies. (Luckily, the prognosis is far better than when retinal detachments occur in infants.) For this reason, all children who had ROP should continue to have retinal exams annually throughout adolescence and young adulthood.

Retinopathy of prematurity has long been one of the most feared complications of a premature birth. But just remember, even if your baby develops it, the odds that she will emerge with good vision are extremely high.

Hearing Exam

My baby failed his first hearing test, and we're devastated, but the doctor says there's a good chance his hearing will be normal. How could that be?

It's definitely too soon for you to worry. You can't imagine how many false scares there are on preemies' first hearing tests—lots of them. Parents are understandably terrified by the results, only to find out later that their baby has perfectly normal hearing.

The hearing tests done on newborns are actually hearing "screens," designed to be overly inclusive, so they don't miss any babies with hearing problems. It's only if a baby has difficulty with a later, more definitive hearing test that he'll be diagnosed with a true hearing impairment—far fewer than the number who fail the newborn screens.

Here are some of the reasons that a preemie may falsely "fail" his hearing screen:

✳ The room may have been too noisy;
✳ Ear wax (or, if the test was performed within

a few days after delivery, amniotic fluid or vernix) may have been blocking the ear canal;

✸ The baby may have been crying, fussy, or wiggly;

✸ The baby may have had an ear infection or some other medical problem, like jaundice, that temporarily affected his hearing;

✸ The baby may have an immature, narrow ear canal that is too small for accurate testing;

✸ The baby's brain may still be immature (not a surprise, in a preemie!).

If you notice that your baby startles in response to sudden, loud noises, and sometimes seems to be listening to the sound of your voice, then a hearing problem is unlikely. Even if you don't notice these things, that's not necessarily a bad sign. Because preemies have a lower hearing threshold, what may seem like a loud sound to you may not be for your baby. And even if he is disturbed by a noise, his reaction might not be immediately clear to you, because preemies don't always react to sounds the same way full-term babies do. For instance, instead of startling, he may lose muscle tone, or close his eyes.

In any case, your baby will get his hearing tested again in a few days or weeks, either in the nursery if he's still in the hospital, or as an outpatient if he's gone home. If he passes, you can relax. But even if his screen is abnormal a second time, he may still be just fine. He'll be scheduled for a definitive hearing test when he's around three months of age, and you'll know more then.

A preemie's hearing screen, usually done right in the nursery in his own bed, only takes about 15 minutes, doesn't hurt at all, and is harmless. It involves giving him a set of earphones, and placing a few little electrodes attached to pads on his head, with paste to hold them on. Alternatively, a small probe may be placed in his ear. Then, clicking sounds are delivered into his ears, and the baby's brain waves are recorded. The recording is either interpreted by a computer or reviewed by an audiologist (a specialist in hearing problems), who compares it to a normal pattern.

Some hospitals give hearing exams to all babies before they're discharged. Others test only those who have certain risk factors for hearing problems, such as:

✸ birth weight under 1,500 grams

✸ occurrence of an intraventricular hemorrhage

✸ the presence of a viral infection at birth

✸ meningitis

✸ extended use of certain medications

✸ very high bilirubin levels that required an exchange transfusion

✸ extreme lack of oxygen around the time of birth

✸ abnormalities of the head or neck.

While these factors increase a preemie's risk, it's still only about two out of one hundred premature babies who will have a significant hearing impairment.

When a baby does turn out to have a hearing problem, you can be sure it will be followed carefully, since early detection and treatment is a tremendous advantage. At the appropriate time (which may not be until three to six months corrected age; see page 446), the baby may get a hearing aid, and he and his family may start working with a communications specialist. But try not to think about all of that yet, since it's still unlikely you'll ever have to.

Antibiotics

I always try to avoid antibiotics when I get a cold or the flu, and now my daughter has been put on them for two weeks. I wonder about the consequences.

Your attitude toward antibiotics is wise. As you probably know, these medications can cause the emergence of resistant organisms (meaning germs that have become "accustomed" to antibiotics, and are therefore difficult, or impossible, to fight). It is a problem that involves our society as a whole. Doctors are well aware of the risk, and don't prescribe antibiotics lightly.

On the other hand, antibiotics are the cornerstone of treatment for infections. Preemies, in particular, have immature infection-fighting abilities, and need the extra help that medicine provides. Your daughter's two-week treatment may seem very long to you, but her doctors must believe it is needed to completely eradicate the infection.

In an individual patient, antibiotics don't generally breed resistant organisms unless the same medication is taken repeatedly over extended periods of time. While your preemie is in the hospital, any germ she's infected with will be tested to see which antibiotics are effective against it. If it's resistant to some, the doctors will be aware of that, and choose others.

Most antibiotics are used very safely in preemies. Their side effects are generally well-known (most commonly, changes in kidney or liver function, loss of salts and minerals, changes in blood counts, or hearing problems). Doctors can monitor your baby for these effects, and stop the medication or decrease its dosage if complications develop, or if safe blood levels are exceeded. With close monitoring, it's rare for any long-term damage from antibiotic treatment to occur.

Antibiotics may also temporarily alter the kinds of organisms that live peacefully within a baby's body. Since these organisms help with digestion, and fight off other germs, some babies on antibiotics will get diarrhea, or other infections. Allergies to antibiotics are practically never seen in preemies, so you don't need to worry about that. New therapies, such as intravenous infusion of antibodies like immunoglobulins, or treatments that stimulate a baby to make more infection-fighting white blood cells, are under investigation today. But until their benefits are clearly proven, antibiotics will remain the primary, life saving weapons to fight premature babies' infections.

Let's rejoice that they exist, and still work well.

Scalp IV

This morning I had the worst surprise. I found my baby with an IV in her head. It looks awful, and I'm afraid it will injure her brain.

It looks like medical aggression of the worst kind. Not satisfied with having pierced your daughter's feet, ankles, hands, and arms already, the doctors have stuck in yet another needle—this time in her scalp. Looking at it, your heart sinks, and you think, this time they've gone too far. You don't understand why they would do such a seemingly dangerous thing to your baby.

Well. Some medical procedures look painful and invasive, but in reality are quite benign. A scalp IV line belongs in that category. As you already know, intravenous catheters are required to deliver the fluids, nutrients, or medications that your baby needs to recover and thrive. The

Central Lines

A "central line" is a catheter that lies in a large, deep blood vessel close to the heart. Central lines are used if a premature baby might need an IV for more than a few weeks (for instance, if he's not expected to be able to eat for a while, or if long-term antibiotics are required for an infection), if he needs medications that would be irritating to smaller blood vessels, or simply because there aren't many suitable peripheral veins left in which to place catheters. Because large, deep veins aren't as fragile as superficial ones, central lines can usually be left in place for as long as they're needed (think how many needle sticks this will save your baby), and more concentrated substances can be delivered through them.

The two most common central lines are *percucaths* and *broviacs*. Percucaths are tiny, flexible catheters that are usually inserted in the NICU by a neonatologist or nurse practitioner. The pain medications and sedatives given in the NICU are adequate to keep a baby comfortable and still throughout percucath placement. Broviacs are somewhat larger and stiffer, with a cuff to hold them in place under the skin. Broviac insertion is a more complex procedure, requiring minor surgery.

Surgeons may also be asked to help place a central (or even a peripheral) IV line in the NICU using a "cut down" technique, which involves making a small incision in the skin so that a vein can be seen and held, as a catheter is placed directly into it.

All central lines are foreign objects that dwell deep inside the body, so they carry a higher risk of serious infection than peripheral IVs. (If your baby happens to get a line infection, the doctors will treat him with antibiotics, and may remove the catheter.) But balancing this risk are their enormous benefits: they are essential tools to help your baby heal and grow.

---

simplest and safest IVs to use are those in the small veins lying close to the surface of the skin. If your preemie has been in the hospital for a while, the superficial veins in her arms and legs may have housed quite a few catheters, and need a chance to rest and recover from any inflammation.

There's another place left that has safe, superficial veins, though: the scalp. A scalp IV is usually easy to insert, and, like all IVs, painless for the baby once it's in. It has the advantages of being readily visible for the nurses to check, and

less likely to be knocked out than a catheter in a hand or foot. Since the catheter runs very superficially just under the skin, it doesn't pose any risk for the brain, which is securely protected by the thick bones of the skull, and several layers of tough membranes.

Despite their many advantages, scalp IVs are somewhat lacking in the "looks" department! The doctor or nurse may have shaved off a patch of your baby's hair where the catheter was inserted, and he may now be wearing cotton pads and an eccentric-looking little cap to keep the IV from being dislodged. Soon you may find it cute (some doctors and nurses swear they do), but the main reason most nurseries use scalp IVs only when necessary is the initial reaction of shock they're greeted with by most parents. Just remember that the IV is temporary, and under your baby's future hair, there will be no evidence that it was ever there.

Anemia

My baby's doctor wants to give her shots three times a week so she won't get anemic. Is that worth it? Will it work?

Your baby's doctor is probably talking about giving her erythropoietin (EPO), a hormone that stimulates the production of red blood cells. All infants become anemic (develop a shortage of red blood cells) during their first two to three months of life, because natural secretion of EPO temporarily falls—causing a slow-down in the creation of new red blood cells. A newborn will become gradually more anemic, until her red blood cells reach a low enough level to switch back on the secretion of erythropoietin.

It's a natural cycle that doesn't cause any problems in most full-term newborns and a lot of preemies. Your baby's doctor will monitor her hemoglobin (the substance in red blood cells that carries oxygen) and hematocrit (the concentration of red blood cells in her blood), to make sure they don't fall too low—and that she starts producing new red blood cells when she should.

But the natural cycle is more pronounced and lasts longer in preemies (especially younger ones, with birth weights under 1,500 or so grams). That's because small preemies grow very rapidly, and need to make a lot more blood

to keep up with their increasing body size. At the same time, their red blood cells are depleted by frequent blood draws, and their levels of erythropoietin are lower than in term babies. In fact, this early anemia is so universal in preemies that it has been dubbed "anemia of prematurity."

In some premature infants, the anemia becomes serious enough to affect their medical condition. Since red blood cells transport the oxygen that the body's organs and tissues need to function and grow, anemia can prolong a baby's reliance on supplemental oxygen. It can aggravate cardiac problems if the heart works too hard trying to deliver the little oxygen that's available. Very anemic preemies also tend to be more lethargic, eat less and gain less weight, and may have more apnea. Sick babies are most likely to have trouble when they're anemic.

In the past, blood transfusions were the only answer. Even today, a premature baby who develops acute anemia and is sick will need one or more blood transfusions, the only effective, fast-acting treatment. But thanks to genetic engineering, babies like yours now have the option of getting laboratory-produced erythropoietin, to try to prevent severe anemia of prematurity in advance.

The medication is given to a baby three times a week, intravenously or as a shot, for about six weeks, or until she reaches 36 weeks of gestation. EPO takes about two weeks to work, and has been shown to reduce the need for future blood transfusions. While it's painful to think of your little baby getting shots, this particular shot doesn't hurt much at all, and a lot of people think it's a price worth paying. Because the drug has been available for only a few years, long-term studies haven't been done, but so far there are no known, serious risks or side effects.

Since production of red blood cells requires iron, a preemie who goes on EPO also needs to take iron supplements, which are usually given orally. Since iron can upset the stomach, it can make feeding intolerance worse, so babies don't start on EPO until they are stable and tolerating most of their breast milk or formula feedings. Some babies who take iron have dark green or black stools. Don't be scared: the color might be weird, but it's harmless.

Heart Murmur

The doctor told me they just discovered my baby has a heart murmur. Not something serious again! How could they not have found it before?

Your baby is in good company. It's not uncommon for preemies to have a heart murmur suddenly appear at a few weeks of age, and it usually indicates something that's harmless, or merely needs to be followed for a while. Heart murmurs that arise from serious problems usually show up within the first week of life. If your baby happens to have had an echocardiogram (perhaps because the doctors were checking to see if she had a PDA), and you already know that her heart is normally formed, there is even less reason to worry.

Anything new that comes up at this point, just when you were beginning to feel more optimistic that your baby was out of the woods, can feel like a terrible blow. But the majority of the time, a late-appearing heart murmur in a preemie is due to something called peripheral pulmonic stenosis (PPS). That's a fancy name for nothing of consequence; it means that the blood flow through some small and sharply bent blood vessels to the lungs is turbulent, causing a swishing sound. Doctors don't know why it suddenly appears in some premature babies who are a few weeks old, but they just grow out of it, and it doesn't cause any problems.

Other possible reasons for the murmur are less common. One is a PDA (a fetal blood vessel that failed to close) that the doctors haven't noticed before, either because it hasn't caused any symptoms, or didn't show up on an earlier echocardiogram. (A PDA can partially close, and then reopen. There's a full description of PDAs on page 176.)

If a PDA is the cause of your baby's murmur, it may, in a sense, be good news. If your baby is doing well, the PDA isn't affecting her much, so the doctors may not even treat it. They'll probably just watch to see if it closes by itself, or if it causes any problems in the future. On the other hand, if your baby is still on a ventilator, the doctors may have found a reason why. A PDA can make it more difficult for a preemie to recover from respiratory distress syndrome; so after it's fixed, your baby could get better. And you might have the red flag raised by the murmur to thank.

Other possible causes of a late heart murmur are a little hole in the heart, which often closes on its own, or a tight valve or blood vessel, which is almost always noticed earlier if it's a serious problem. For either of these, it's the same situation as for a PDA: if your baby is doing well, she probably won't even be treated. If she's been having difficulties, this discovery may be the key to her treatment and recovery.

Finally, the murmur could be caused by other, usually innocent things (for example, anemia, or just the way your baby's heart is positioned in her chest), or something the doctors may never discover, because it won't cause your baby any problems. Consider it the special sound of your preemie's heart.

Abnormal Thyroid Test

The health department said my baby's newborn thyroid test was abnormal. The doctors are checking it again. Is that serious?

Most probably, your baby's abnormal test is just a temporary consequence of her immaturity, and nothing is really wrong with her thyroid. Transiently low thyroid levels are extremely common among preemies—occurring in all 23- to 25-weekers, 40% of 26- to 27-weekers, 33% of 28- to 29-weekers, and 17% of 30- to 31-weekers. When a baby reaches about 34 weeks of gestation, thyroid levels normalize spontaneously, without treatment. Chances are, there's no need for you to worry.

Nevertheless, your baby's doctors will do another screening, to make sure that she doesn't have true hypothyroidism, which is more severe and long-lasting. Since adequate levels of thyroid hormone are important for the development of the brain, as well as the skin, blood, bone and other tissues, a baby who is diagnosed with true hypothyroidism will be given thyroid hormone replacement therapy immediately to prevent delays in her neurological development and her growth. The sooner the medication is given, the better it works.

To promote early diagnosis and prevent the worst consequence of a lack of thyroid hormone—mental retardation—a mass population screening was started in 1975, administered by the each state's health department. Today, all newborns get a routine blood test for hypothyroidism within their first week of life in a program that, like immunizations, is considered one of the most successful efforts of preventive medicine. It has allowed thousands of kids to grow up completely normal, by detecting their hypothyroidism early enough.

Early blood screening is particularly important for preemies, because many symptoms of hypothyroidism—such as an inability to keep up body temperature, poor feeding, constipation, prolonged jaundice, puffiness, and lethargy—are subtle, and easily confused with common conditions of prematurity. If it turns out that your baby has a true inability to make sufficient amounts of thyroid hormone, due to congenital problems of the thyroid gland or the organs that regulate it, the disorder can be easily treated with hormone replacement therapy (in liquid or pill form), once it's diagnosed. But this problem is very rare, occurring in only 1 in 3,000 to 4,000 births.

The transiently low readings that are commonly found in premature babies are caused by factors that soon disappear. The most common, not surprisingly, is simple immaturity. The hypothalamus—the part of the brain that regulates the secretion of many hormones—operates at a lower level until it is fully mature. Sickness in a premature baby—whether RDS, lack of oxygen, infection, or hypoglycemia—can also cause an abnormal thyroid reading. These preemies aren't really hypothyroid, and their "disorder" disappears by itself without treatment, in a few weeks, as they recover from their other medical problems.

There are other, less likely causes for a preemie to be hypothyroid. If a pregnant woman has a thyroid disorder, her illness, or the medication she's taking to treat it, can pass to her fetus during pregnancy. Its effects may linger for a while, show up as an abnormality of a newborn's thyroid screen, and then go away. Iodine, found in antiseptics in many hospital nurseries, can alter the functioning of the thyroid gland. When these antiseptics, like betadine, are used on the umbilical cord, or to disinfect the skin prior to blood drawing or surgery, a preemie's immature skin can absorb too much iodine. But doctors are very aware of this risk, and use iodine-containing products sparingly in preemies.

It's hard not to feel threatened by any irregu-

lar test your baby may have, since fear of a life-long, chronic condition always arises. For premature infants, though, it is much more likely that your anxiety will be as fleeting as your baby's abnormal thyroid test.

False Alarms on Newborn Screens

Just like all newborns, your baby will be screened automatically for various medical conditions, such as hypothyroidism, PKU (phenylketonuria), sickle cell anemia, galactosemia, and others. (The diseases screened for will vary by state.) Each test is potentially beneficial, but for a newborn preemie, it's also another opportunity for a false result. What causes inaccuracies in these tests? Here are some of the more common reasons:

❋ Intravenous feedings, with total parenteral nutrition, can falsely elevate some substances in the blood;

❋ Not feeding the baby at all may mask some metabolism problems;

❋ Steroids given to the mother before the birth can temporarily alter the newborn's hormone levels;

❋ Stress the baby experiences after birth can temporarily alter hormone levels;

❋ Blood transfusions can mask genetic problems or blood diseases;

❋ Minor errors, like collecting too much or too little blood for the test, collecting it too soon after birth, or even allowing the screen to sit for a few days in a hot mailbox, can affect the test's accuracy;

❋ Plain old immaturity, something every preemie has, can make almost any level abnormal.

The solution is to repeat these tests when a preemie is older, healthier, eating, and/or several months after his last blood transfusion. Doctors are aware of this, and will do it automatically, if the original screening conditions weren't optimal, or if an abnormal level is obtained.

Relations with Nurses

My mood in the NICU can be so influenced by who my baby's nurse is that day. Some I like, but there is one I just can't stand.

Relationships with neonatal nurses are emotionally charged for many parents of preemies,

and often result in strong attachments and equally strong dislikes. At such a demanding time, when you're so anxious about your baby, you need to feel comfortable with all of the medical staff. But normal differences in human temperament always make some relationships easier than others. And in this case, things are complicated by the fact that parents and nurses have not chosen each other, yet find themselves joined by—and sometimes at odds over—weighty concerns about the needs and well-being of the same baby.

Parents are particularly vulnerable after their child's premature birth. Just when they're struggling to understand what the early birth means for them and their child, they find that an NICU nurse has taken over their parental duties and pleasures. This is a real hot button for parents of preemies: problems in fulfilling their parental role has been consistently identified in clinical studies as a major source of parents' stress in the neonatal intensive care unit.

Parents feel incompetent and frustrated because they are unable to make their baby feel better, disturbed by being separated from their baby, and afraid of interacting with a baby who appears so fragile. Each of these powerful feelings runs headlong into the nurse-parent relationship. Who's attending to the premature baby's needs instead of his parents? The nurse. Who spends all day with the baby? The nurse. Who grants permission to touch, hold, change, bathe, and feed their baby? The nurse, of course. It's natural that parents would become jealous, bitter, or passively resigned, and gradually develop a sense of impotence.

This is especially likely to happen to parents of preemies who have to stay in the hospital nursery for several months. Sometimes the nurses who are regularly assigned to these babies become very attached to them, expressing their affection with kisses, coos, playfulness, and holding. Nurses who spend so much time with a baby can feel that they know his moods, needs, and ways of responding better than his parents do. While parents may be happy to see how much love and attention their preemie gets, which can only be good for the baby's development, they may resent how much of their parental role and author-

ity has been taken over by the NICU staff. Not surprisingly, these feelings can engender conflict between parents and nurses.

Most nurses are aware that parents might be jealous of them—but feel like they're in a bind themselves. Some parents like the nurses to touch their children like they are their own, others don't. What's the answer?

Psychologists talk about a need for "role negotiation" in the nurse-parent relationship. They mean that parents and nurses should try to understand their own responsibilities, concerns, and feelings toward the baby, and what they each expect from the other. Ideally, this should be a work in progress throughout a preemie's hospitalization, as the nurses gradually help parents take over what is rightfully theirs: responsibility for their baby's care. As part of this, it is crucial that they develop trust in each other's competence.

Unfortunately, for some parents, organizational obstacles may obstruct the process, as they have to deal with the sometimes dozens of different nurses who are assigned to take care of their baby. Thankfully, most nurseries can provide some continuity in assignments, so parents can get to know at least several familiar faces and styles. But when a preemie moves to another unit in the hospital, or is transferred to a hospital closer to home, his family has another complete change in the nursing staff to face, and new relationships to develop. Of course, some tensions and insecurities—on the part of nurses or parents—may arise and need to be worked out.

Even though neonatal nursing training gives tremendous importance to empathy, communication skills, and methods to help provide parents with practical and emotional support, anyone who works in an NICU tends to lose their sensitivity about what premature babies look like to their parents, with their shockingly small size, tubes everywhere, and strange skin colors. So nurses have to remind themselves to acknowledge parents' difficulties, help them express their concerns, and be reassuring whenever possible.

Most parents, at the beginning, need to be encouraged by the staff to become more involved with their babies. Some parents assume a completely passive role, expecting the nurses to provide their child with everything he needs: touch, holding, attention, and stimulation, as well as medical care. Feeling uncomfortable in the NICU, and uneasy about what to do, some parents show up only for infrequent, quick visits—not spending enough time with their preemie to get to know him and understand his needs. As a result, the nurses, who can be very protective of the babies in their care, might become openly critical of a family's behavior, leading to antagonism.

Mutual understanding may help to avoid conflict. The nurse needs to know that passive, even absent parents are rarely uninvolved or uncaring, but may be scared, intimidated by the intensive care environment, or simply unaware of their babies' problems and needs. As a parent, trying to be open about your anxieties, and about what your uncertain role as a parent of a hospitalized preemie involves, may smooth your relationship with the nurses, and help you find ways to participate in your baby's care.

Other mothers and fathers ask for responsibilities, and take them, with or without permission. Outspoken parents may want things done to their children only "their way," stimulating struggles and competition between them and the medical staff. Nurses feel that these parents are apt to judge everything they do in a critical light, taking them to task if, say, they're a few minutes late in giving a medication or a feeding.

The nurses may have to be understanding, realizing that difficult, controlling parents are often trying to establish their parental role in the only way they consider effective in the foreign environment of the hospital nursery. If this sounds like you, try to relax your vigilance. Keep in mind that there are different nursing styles, and that most little slips in schedule, and varied ways of doing things, won't harm your baby in the least. Sometimes, a nurse won't be able to accommodate your request because of nursery rules and protocols (usually adopted for the safety of the babies—to cut down on errors, and allow the unit to run smoothly). Moreover, because nurses often have tight, busy schedules, there are constraints on the amount of time they can spend with each baby. You may end up having to settle for competence and consideration, and give up a little bit on the absolutely "ideal" nursing situation that you envision.

Different kinds of parents may be easier or harder for particular nurses to deal with. Of course, there will inevitably be times when, because of a nurse's temperament and needs, inexperience, tiredness, or momentary distraction—or your own stress—a situation or relationship will be handled poorly or misjudged.

Parents' positive experiences with the NICU staff outnumber negative ones, by far. According to research, the majority of families find neonatal nurses to be: their best allies; a more compassionate, reliable, and understandable source of information than the doctors; and a major source of support in the experience of parenting a hospitalized preemie.

One of us will never forget how a motherly NICU nurse taught her to bottle feed her baby, with unmatchable patience. Another nurse encouraged her to bathe her baby, in a basin no bigger than a man's shoe. If such a tiny, sick baby could be bathed by his mother's inexperienced, trembling hands, it surely meant that better times could be expected. And they did come.

Memories like these are hard to forget, for parents and nurses alike. True friendship often develops, keeping nurses, parents, and preemies in touch for years after discharge. In the NICU, we heard nurses proudly telling anecdotes about the wonderful, happy outcomes of former preemies they had been following from infancy through adolescence.

On the other hand, in one study, 15% of parents interviewed in the NICU reported difficult relationships with the staff. Interestingly, families tend to recall more problems with the staff's behavior, communication, and caregiving several years after discharge. Psychologists speculate that this could be due to the fact that when their babies are still dependent on the NICU staff, parents may not feel at ease acknowledging or discussing these issues.

There are times when you may conclude that you don't trust a nurse's professional skills, or don't find her compassionate enough, or feel that she unfairly doesn't trust you or like you very much. Perhaps she has an uncanny ability to come up with comments that make you feel bad. This happened to a mother we know. Getting to the nursery and finding that a particular nurse was assigned to her baby became so disturbing to her that several times she considered talking to a supervisor. Every day she expected that nurse to say something unpleasant— mainly, insensitive comments about her baby— which punctually happened. She was surprised and disturbed by the intensity of her emotional reactions, which interfered with the pleasure of being with her baby. Eventually, she decided not to do anything about it, mainly because she was afraid of damaging the quality of her son's care.

That's one thing you don't need to worry about, though: your baby won't be neglected or abused because of anything you say. Neonatal nurses and doctors tend to keep their feelings about parents very separate from their feelings about the babies. In fact, if you've been labeled a troublemaker, you can even take comfort in knowing that many nurses are most protective of the babies whose parents they see as not acting "appropriately."

If you're concerned about a serious offense (a lack of professional skills, for instance, noncompliance with principles of hygiene, or gross insolence, etc.), you should definitely express your complaints about a nurse to the nursing supervisor or attending physician. But most often, what upsets parents is something subtler, or personal, and may be hard to spell out. Mentioning what's bothering you can still be helpful. Somebody who has seen lots of such situations can help you better understand a nurse's behavior, and perhaps make sense of what's happening. There probably won't be changes in your baby's nursing assignments, since organizing the nurses' day and night shifts in a busy nursery is too daunting a task to let parental preferences become a factor. But if what you report about a nurse is a recurring pattern, it could lead to better awareness by the supervisors about their staff, and maybe some constructive changes.

Trying to understand other people's feelings and motivations, and being open about one's own, usually improves human relationships in the nursery, as elsewhere. You can try that. And later, when you're in a calmer frame of mind, take a moment to revive the images of your baby's nurses. There will be those who loved your baby, and who deserve to be remembered.

Changing Doctors

Do the doctors have to change so often? Just when we start to feel comfortable with one, we have to move on to another.

It's hard when the doctor you've come to trust, whom you've counted on to help you and your baby make it through this difficult experience, is leaving. Naturally, you feel like you're being deserted. Of course, you question the merits of a system that rotates doctors in and out of the nursery, rather than allowing them to establish lasting, close relationships with babies and their families from birth until hospital discharge.

It's true that the system has some disadvantages—especially the hard transition it means for you. But its advantages are very real, also, even if they're less immediately apparent. In an intensive care nursery, the days of the attending physicians are long, and often the nights are, too. The work is not just physically, but emotionally, draining: most doctors truly care about their patients, especially the ones they've worked with a long time and have come to know well. Although they will never take your baby's ups and downs as hard as you do, they can't help but find sad conversations with parents, and their inability to prevent inevitable difficulties for some babies, to be wrenching experiences. Working in such an intense environment, after more than a few weeks it's unavoidable that a doctor's energy would start to flag, and his judgment perhaps suffer. To prevent this from happening—to keep every doctor's standard of performance high—it's considered vital that all neonatologists take frequent breaks, and come back to the nursery fresh.

If you're in a teaching hospital, your doctor may also have to rotate out of the nursery because these institutions (which typically offer state-of-the-art medical care) expect their doctors to do medical research as well as take care of patients. It's not easy on you, but it's part of the doctor's job, and is intended to benefit the patients and families who receive neonatal care over the long-run.

When you have moments of frustration after

He Says "Potato," She Says "Potahto"

A confusing thing can happen when your baby's doctor changes: the old doctor and the new doctor may give you different interpretations of the same medical "fact." One may tell you that a certain test result indicates a problem, while the other says the result is normal and nothing to worry about. One doctor may recommend a treatment that the other says is probably useless. One may be very concerned that your baby is behaving this way or that, while the other shrugs his shoulders and acts uninterested.

When you try to figure out who's right and who's wrong, you'll usually learn something else instead: that medical diagnoses and treatment plans are rarely black and white. Two equally competent doctors can differ in their interpretations and advice. Disconcerting? Yes, highly. But one way to think about this is that it's an opportunity to discover more about your baby, and the many aspects of her condition. If you want to learn more, ask the doctor to explain what's black and white, and what's gray. And don't hesitate to tell the doctor about your own parental instincts and observations. Chances are you'll develop a good working partnership.

a changeover, as you probably will (like when you realize that the new doctor doesn't know something you think is important about your baby, and you feel like shouting: "How could you not know that about my child?!"), here's one other, hidden advantage of the rotating system to keep in mind: a fresh pair of eyes and point of view can go a long way. Every doctor, even your favorite one, can get settled into a certain medical routine and way of thinking for each patient. A new doctor's willingness to say: "Why don't we try this?" may turn the tide for a baby who is having problems, or enable a healthy baby to do just a little better than she already is.

Cysts in the Brain

The doctor said our baby has some little cysts in her brain, and could have some brain damage. What does this mean for her and us?

When the blood flow and oxygen supply become insufficient in an area of the brain, some of its tissue may be damaged. This can happen to a preemie before birth (because of a pregnancy complication), around the time of delivery (especially if there is some fetal distress during labor and a baby has to be resuscitated), or after birth (because of many medical problems of prematurity). A few weeks after the damage occurs, the resulting brain injury may show up on a head ultrasound as some tiny cysts—a scarred area—or eventually as just some extra fluid where the injured brain tissue had been.

Like most abnormal features on a baby's head ultrasound, brain cysts are worrisome findings, leading doctors to provide close follow-up for a preemie and her family. They indicate some brain damage, and carry the possibility of motor or cognitive impairments in the future. It's the kind of news that can shake a parent deeply. But nobody at this stage can predict just what will happen to your baby. And despite the uncertainty that you'll have to live with for some time, there are reasons to keep your hopes high.

Cysts in some areas of the brain may have no future effects. For instance, some small, single cysts (called choroid cysts or subarachnoid cysts) inside the ventricles are usually insignificant, reflecting mild bleeds that are resolving, or other processes, which shouldn't cause any problems. Cysts in more "important" areas, most commonly near the ventricles (called PVL, short for periventricular leukomalacia; see page 285), are more ominous, but even they may not impede normal development. Also, a single head ultrasound is not always conclusive. Several head ultrasounds, or possibly another kind of study, such as a head CT or MRI scan, if the cysts are in an unusual place, may be needed to confirm the diagnosis and better identify the site and extent of a brain injury. Sometimes, a suspected injury turns out to be only a bad scare.

You've probably been told that you may not know for several years or more how this will affect your daughter. That's true, but how your daughter is doing now, and in the near future, are important, too. Premature babies who suffered from serious brain damage usually show signs of it in their first months of life; the most common are weakness and lack of tone in their legs and trunk. If your baby still looks fine on a developmental evaluation at a year of age, there's a good chance that she will have only mild consequences from her brain injury, if any at all. Following your baby closely, in the future, will enable doctors to pick up problems early, and to manage them with appropriate, expert intervention. Most of the time, impairments resulting from brain damage in a preemie don't interfere with a rich and fulfilling life.

IN PLAIN LANGUAGE: WHAT IS PVL?

A head ultrasound is performed during the first week of life on almost every preemie born at less than 32 to 34 weeks of gestation, to find out if there's been any bleeding in an inner part of the brain. (You can read about intraventricular hemorrhages, or IVHs, as they're called, on page 164). That first head ultrasound, though, usually can't detect if a baby's brain tissue has suffered permanent damage. Another ultrasound, done several weeks later, is more definitive, because it takes from two to six weeks for small cysts—spots where brain tissue has been injured—to develop and become visible. Later, they may fuse together, forming areas of calcification or scarring. These cysts are called PVL (periventricular leukomalacia) if they occur in the white matter of the brain, near the ventricles. PVL is the most common brain injury seen in premature babies.

Is There a Cure for PVL?

No treatment can regenerate damaged brain tissue. But a newborn's brain is still developing. If the damage isn't extensive—if it involves only a small area, or is present on just one side of the brain—then other parts of the brain may be able to take over the function of the injured tissue.

What Babies Are at Risk for a Brain Injury?

Long-term studies of premature babies have found an average rate of PVL of about 5%. The rate is inversely related to birth weight and gestational age; so, as usual, smaller and younger preemies are more at risk. Other factors may also play a role:

* Some infections that a mother may get during pregnancy (such as toxoplasmosis, German measles, herpes, cytomegalovirus, and others) can cross the placenta and damage the fetus's brain.
* Identical twins with discordant growth are more likely to develop PVL.
* An extended period of time when the fetus got less blood or oxygen than she needed (say, from a knot in the umbilical cord, or a severe illness in the mother), can result in brain injury.
* An infection of the amniotic fluid, detachment of the placenta, or other complications around the time of delivery are risk factors for PVL.
* Resuscitation at delivery, with more than ten minutes passing before a baby's heartbeat and breathing recover, suggests a significant lack of oxygen and blood flow.
* Various complications of prematurity, such as persistent low blood pressure, moderate to severe RDS, infection, very severe episodes of apnea and bradycardia, a persistent PDA, or BPD requiring prolonged mechanical ventilation, can increase the risk of PVL.
* A grade III or grade IV intraventricular hemorrhage raises the likelihood of PVL, because it is accompanied by a lack of blood flow and oxygen in nearby areas of the brain. Swelling of the ventricles from hydrocephalus after an IVH (see page 168) can also damage the white

matter around the ventricles. But even a moderate to severe IVH with hydrocephalus does not always lead to PVL.

How PVL Is Diagnosed

PVL is an x-ray diagnosis, which may or may not be reflected in a baby's neurological examination or behavior. It is usually picked up on a head ultrasound performed when a preemie is several weeks old, or before he's discharged from the hospital. Early PVL may be subtle and difficult to recognize, looking just like a slightly bright area around the ventricles. It may disappear (perhaps indicating minor damage, or recovery, or a mistaken diagnosis), or may, in a matter of a few weeks, develop into cystic areas. When cysts develop, the diagnosis of PVL is confirmed. PVL is mild if it involves just one or two tiny cysts in one small area of the brain. Severe PVL involves bundles of larger cysts, or cysts on both sides of the brain.

A premature baby with PVL may show neurological signs in the first days and weeks, like seizures or weakness in the trunk and legs, but often there are no very early symptoms. Developmental delays usually appear by several months of age, most often involving poor muscle control and tone (such as an inability to hold up her head), stiffness in her legs or arms, or decreased interaction with her environment. If a premature baby is absolutely normal at hospital discharge, it is less likely that she will develop a serious, disabling impairment. So her parents should take heart.

What You Can Expect in the Long Run

When extensive PVL has been diagnosed and confirmed by brain imaging, there's a high risk of a later developmental deficit. But if the PVL is mild, the outcome is much better. Overall, about 75% of babies with PVL will have some disability, which can range from mild to severe.

Cerebral palsy, a condition in which a person has difficulty controlling her voluntary movements, is the most frequent consequence of PVL. The legs are most commonly affected in preemies, because the nerves controlling leg movements pass closest to the ventricles. When PVL is more extensive, the nerves controlling the arms, or even the face, may be involved. There are many degrees of cerebral palsy, from very mild and non-disabling (which may be hardly noticeable in a child) to more moderate (in which a child may need braces to walk) or severe (in which a child may be in a wheelchair, and have difficulty talking or eating). A small lesion in the brain will most likely result in only a mild impairment.

Cognitive delays are less common results of PVL than movement disorders. About 45% of children with PVL have normal intelligence, and 15% are classified as "low-normal." The 40% diagnosed with mental retardation may be anywhere from mildly to severely affected. Mental retardation is most likely in those preemies whose head ultrasounds show enlarged ventricles with global loss of brain tissue. Several studies have found that special educational programs, and early individual intervention, may reduce the risk of mental retardation in some children (see page 442). Among children with normal intelligence who have PVL, there's a higher risk of learning disabilities at school age. If detected soon, these can be treated very successfully.

Less commonly, some children with PVL will have seizure disorders. Much rarer consequences of PVL are visual impairments or deafness.

The data and statistics available today can be devastating for families to find out. How can a parent make sense of them without withering? First of all, by remembering that clinical studies present the average outcomes of large groups of children. They cannot reflect the individual, unique clinical and developmental profile of your baby, which may be much better than average.

Another positive way to read these results is to focus on the full half of the glass: many of the children who have been diagnosed with a brain injury will have normal intelligence, or a mild motor impairment that does not prevent them from leading full lives. And since the long-term follow-up studies reflect outcomes of former preemies who are already in school, there's a chance that the outcomes of babies born now, like yours, could be even better, because of the constant improvement of neonatal intensive care and developmental interventions.

Finally, knowing about risks means empowering yourself. You can put yourself in the best position to help your child, since there's so much that can be done to assist her. The amazing ability of a child to compensate for problems, together with her parents' good faith and strength, make the most formidable team.

Moving to Intermediate Care

My baby was just moved to the intermediate care nursery. Everyone assumed I'd be happy about it, but to tell you the truth it makes me nervous. Is he going to get all of the attention he needs?

Be reassured that your baby is going to be exactly where he needs to be now: in a less hectic, calmer place, where he can feed and grow peacefully, and where you'll also find yourself more at home. Most parents find the intermediate nursery far more pleasant and comfortable than the NICU. In the step-down unit, you and your son will be able to enjoy more of each other, without the distractions of so many doctors and nurses rushing around you, removed from the tension that fills the air during an emergency or when a newborn first arrives in the NICU.

If you feel nervous about your preemie's new accommodations, that's understandable. You've been through a crisis, and you're still emotionally vulnerable. The change of environment can exacerbate fears and anxieties that were calmed while your baby was watched so closely in intensive care. You may feel abandoned by the NICU nurses or doctors, and miss their guidance and company, if they don't rotate through the step-down unit. After all, they were so involved with your baby that some of them even seemed like part of your extended family.

But your baby will still have doctors who do rounds and check on him frequently, as before. True, there are fewer nurses per baby in an intermediate care nursery, but their number is designed to guarantee appropriate, individual attention and care for each baby. The quality of medical assistance is the same as in intensive care. Don't worry: the nurses can jump to provide emergency, stabilizing treatment if they have to. But you're going to see it only if your baby needs it, which is something that, day by day, will become less and less likely. You should really be thrilled about that! And shortly, you will be.

The intermediate nurses' focus is tailored to your preemie's ever-developing needs, which are somewhat different now. The nurses will help him with feeding, assist him in regulating his body temperature and movements, and help train you to recognize his signals and take over some important caregiving tasks. In fact, the intermediate unit is where many babies start to enjoy many new pleasures—such as kangaroo care, periods of quiet time, and infant massage—that they may not have been ready for before. With the change in focus from medical priorities to developmental ones, you'll be able to see your baby much more as a normal baby, rather than as a sick one. And that's wonderful.

In a matter of days, you're going to feel more comfortable in the intermediate care nursery. Try to picture this change of location in the hospital as a step toward another transition you'll soon be making: going home with your baby. Take the step-down unit as a useful rehearsal. Here, you can savor the idea of being alone with your baby, but with the support and reassurance you may still need at your fingertips.

Transfer to a Hospital Closer to Home

They just told us that our baby is ready to go back to the hospital where he was born. How could he possibly be strong enough to travel 30 miles?

It's natural for you to feel anxious, both about the travel and the adequacy of care in a smaller, community hospital nursery. But what the doc-

tors are telling you is that your little tyke is now stronger than you think. After all you've been through, it's going to take a while before you can believe it. But your baby has made it through the most arduous part of his journey, during which he needed state-of-the-art neonatal care. He's now medically stable, less vulnerable, and ready to take on some new experiences, including a trip that will bring him closer to the arms of his loving family.

The most important thing to realize is that your baby's doctors would never let him go on a trip, or to a nursery, that wasn't safe. Your baby will probably travel in an ambulance that's like a mobile intensive care unit, with his isolette, monitors, and, if he needs them, oxygen, intravenous equipment, and drugs. He will be accompanied by at least one specialist in neonatal care, usually a neonatal nurse, who can provide emergency medical care if need be. (If you want to travel with your son, too, you can ask his doctor. The answer will depend on the hospital's policies, and whether there is enough room in the ambulance.)

Your baby's doctors will know what kind of patients his new hospital nursery can give good care to. Feel free to ask them to go over this with you. For instance, if your baby needs follow-up eye exams for retinopathy of prematurity, ask if there's a specialist to do them. You can also make an appointment to tour the nursery and meet the staff who'll be taking care of your baby. Ask specific questions to get reassurance on the following points: Are they able to provide care for the conditions your baby has? Have they done it before? Under what circumstances would your baby be sent back to his current hospital?

Most parents can't really relax until their baby has been in the new nursery for a few days, and they've witnessed themselves that all of his needs are being met. Just as parents of older children often lose sight of how much their kids have grown, because they see them every day, it often takes a move like this for parents of a preemie to realize just how far their baby has come.

If your baby was born at the hospital he's moved to, he'll probably be greeted with open arms by the doctors or nurses who helped care for him the day he was born. If he wasn't born there, he'll still be received warmly by a staff who feel he's part of their community, and are eager to care for him.

Many parents underestimate the advantages of being in a smaller, quieter nursery that's near home. Your preemie will probably see more of you, and maybe his siblings or grandparents, since it won't take as long to reach him. His pediatrician can start establishing a relationship with him, and help you get familiar with any local specialists or support services you may need. The nursery itself will probably be a lot calmer than you're used to, and that's good: it means more, precious quiet time for your baby, and more individual attention from the nurses for him and you.

Every now and then, a baby will lose weight for a few days after back-transport (as the move to a hospital closer to home is called), or need a little more supplemental oxygen, or tolerate his feedings less well. It doesn't mean that the new nursery isn't taking good care of him. It just means your baby needs some time to get settled into his new home.

If none of this eases your fears, and you believe your son is better off staying where he is, it may help to raise your concerns with his doctor. The hospital can't move your baby without your permission, and you may convince the doctor of the wisdom of keeping him a little longer. But most likely, the doctor will try to convince you of the many good reasons for the move to take place, including your baby's own needs and the need to open intensive care beds for sicker babies, as your son once was. Just remember that the doctor cares about your baby's well-being, too, and whatever other factors she's balancing, she's not going to do something that would hurt him.

You may also need to check with your insurance company. (The social worker can help you with this.) Some insurance plans, particularly HMOs, will not pay for continued care in your baby's current nursery, once he is ready to move. That doesn't mean you have to move, but it does mean that if you choose not to, you could be responsible for the remainder of the hospital bill.

After the move, your baby may still remain under the comforting, watchful eye of his current doctors, if your NICU has a follow-up clinic. Many clinics see their NICU "graduates" every few months, for a few years. Even if there's no clinic, you can call your baby's old doctor if you're worried about something important. Neonatologists tend to be caring and protective of the babies they've cared for, so even when you move, you don't have to say a final good-bye.

Vaccinations

My older son got his first vaccinations when he was two months old. Is a preemie scheduled according to his birth date or his due date?

This is one time when you don't have to pull out that mental calculator and start figuring out your baby's corrected age. The American Academy of Pediatrics generally recommends that preemies receive immunizations on the same schedule following their birth dates as full-term babies, no matter how early they were born.

That means your baby would get his first series of immunizations two months after birth: the DTP (diphtheria, tetanus, and pertussis, which is another word for whooping cough) vaccine, polio vaccine, and Hemophilus influenzae b (Hib) vaccine. (Hemophilus influenzae b bacteria can cause various kinds of serious infections, such as meningitis.)

That's the rule, but there are exceptions. If your baby is sick when he's due to be immunized, the doctor may decide to postpone the series until he's well (as a pediatrician might do for a full-term baby). If your baby was treated at some point with immunoglobulin, perhaps because he had an infection, his vaccinations will be postponed for a few months, because his body's response to vaccines will be dulled for a while. Finally, his first Hepatitis B vaccine, which is usually given to term newborns in their first day or two of life, will be given to him only after he's reached 2,000 grams in weight, when the vaccine is more likely to be effective.

For a long time, neonatologists and pediatricians were concerned about giving immunizations to preemies who were still very young and small. For one thing, they wondered whether preemies' immune systems were mature enough for the vaccines to produce adequate, lasting levels of immunity. There's been a lot of research on this, and those doubts have largely been dispelled. The other concern was that the stress of immunizations might trigger a temporary increase in apnea. That's still unresolved, but as long as your baby is in the hospital, on cardiorespiratory monitors, there's no reason to worry. That's what the monitors are there for. They'll keep your baby safe, while the vaccines do their work to keep him safe, too.

MULTIPLES

Breastfeeding Twins

The nurses convinced me to pump breast milk for my twins. It's OK now, while the nurses are tube feeding them, but isn't it going to be too hard for me to breastfeed two babies?

According to many mothers who have successfully breastfed premature twins (you can get in touch with some of them through La Leche League, see page 522), it may not be an easy or tidy business in the beginning. But if you can just hold fast, after the first, demanding weeks, double nursing will deliver double the rewards, for you and your babies. Maybe we can help with some of your concerns, and explain why breastfeeding twins may be the best choice for many mothers:

* *Quality.* The benefits of breast milk for premature babies are still unparalleled, even by the latest preterm formulas. A diet of human milk (see page 125) is the best your twins can get.
* *Quantity.* A mother's breasts can make enough milk to allow healthy twins (or even triplets) to grow and thrive during their first months of life. Nature manages this feat by the simple mechanism of supply and demand: there's no more powerful stimulation

for plentiful production of breast milk than twins nursing, even more so when they're sucking at the same time, one at each breast. (That's why now, while your twins are still gavage fed, you should try to express your milk by double pumping. There are more tips for establishing and boosting your milk supply on page 229.)

❋ *Time and money.* Time is something very precious to mothers of twins. Nursing twins, especially simultaneously, takes a lot less time than washing bottles, preparing formula, and then feeding each baby, one after the other, many times a day. You'll also save money: about $2,000 a year, the average cost of formula for two babies.

❋ *Partial breastfeeding if your milk supply is low.* If you have enough breast milk to feed both babies, that's great. If not, dividing the available milk between babies, and supplementing it with formula (an excellent option called "partial breastfeeding"), will provide both of them with the benefits of nursing.

On the other hand, you can discuss with the doctors the possibility of continuing to provide breast milk for only one of your babies for a while. Since breast milk is easier to digest than preterm formula, and it provides more protection against infections, you may decide to give breast milk to only your smaller, sicker twin, if your supply is limited. Although it's a tough decision that you probably don't want to make, it's still better than stopping breastfeeding altogether. And for now—until your milk supply increases, or indefinitely—your other, stronger twin should thrive easily and well on formula.

Try not to feel guilty if you end up feeding your stronger twin formula. Remember that providing breast milk is not the only or best way to show parental love. Kangaroo care can be an excellent substitute for the intimate contact of breastfeeding, making both of your babies feel you're utterly there for them—and it may even stimulate your breasts to produce more milk.

❋ *Beginning to breastfeed.* It is never easy to start nursing in the NICU. Chances are you've got a couple of sleepy preemies who are still learning to coordinate sucking, breathing, and swallowing, or who have been feeding from a bottle already and may need just a little time to sort out any "nipple confusion" they might encounter. Add on a disturbing lack of privacy, time, and help, since not all of the medical staff may be equally supportive of your nursing efforts, and some justified stress, and the list of difficulties is complete.

One strategy some mothers suggest is to introduce the breast to one baby before the other, to avoid getting too frustrated with two inexpert babies at the same time. This may happen quite naturally in the hospital nursery, if one of your preemies is ready to begin nursing before the other. (One twin may have been healthier, or simply matured a little faster.) After nursing, you would pump milk for the other twin. At the next feeding, you would start with the pumping, then continue with breastfeeding the baby who's learning to nurse, so that over the course of the day, both twins will get some of the fore-milk and some of the hind-milk. (The breast milk that comes out first has different nutritional qualities than the milk that comes out last.)

By the time the other twin is ready to be introduced to the art of nursing, the first twin will probably have become sufficiently acquainted with it that you feel more confident. (You're likely to be more confident in your baby's ability to breastfeed after just a few feeding "lessons.")

❋ *Breastfeeding twins simultaneously.* When both babies nurse well, it can be done, and mothers talk about it as an exhilarating, tender experience. It's not easy to be discreet, though. Since you have both arms full of babies, you can't easily juggle things around to shield yourself from people's eyes. So this is something you may want to try first where you have some privacy.

There are many benefits to simultaneously breastfeeding twins—like being less sleep deprived. (Some mothers suggest keeping one baby latched on to a breast in bed at night, with the other sleeping in a bassinet nearby, and switching them during the night.) Nursing your twins together will halve the total feeding time, which in a day can add up to several precious hours.

❋ *Breastfeeding twins one at a time.* If you find simultaneous breastfeeding a little weird, don't force it on yourself. To avoid the emergency situation of both babies waking up at the same time and screaming to be fed, you can wake one of them a little early, and nurse him first. In time, you'll know which of your babies is calmer and can wait for a few minutes, entertaining himself.

❋ *An obstacle.* The most frequent obstacle, for both simultaneous and one-at-a-time breastfeeding, is having to deal with one good breastfeeder and one slower, less efficient one. You may not immediately notice any difference in your babies' sucking patterns: you may just assume that when they stop nursing, they are both satisfied. But one twin may not be satiated, just tired, or needing to be burped, and should be kept at the breast for longer. The imbalance may show up after a few days, with one twin's slower growth. To fix that, you may want to offer this baby longer nursing sessions, and give him occasional, extra bottles of breast milk that you've pumped after your breastfeeding sessions. This hind-milk (which comes out after a few minutes) is richer in calories. It should help your smaller baby to catch up on his growth.

Lots of practical and emotional help (from friends and family, and particularly from an understanding partner or spouse) can make an enormous difference in a mother's experience of breastfeeding twins. Eventually, the turmoil and confusion of the first weeks will shape up into a reassuring routine, pleasurable and relaxing, as well as efficient.

Nonetheless, successful breastfeeding doesn't depend only on your goodwill. So if you have to give up your plans to breastfeed, please don't torment yourself. What's most satisfying is watching your twins grow, no matter how you feed them.

A mother nursing her twins together.

Breastfeeding Triplets?

Yes, it is possible to nurse an entire family of babies! Nevertheless, it is a very demanding enterprise, requiring a mother who can count on a lot of help and support, self-confidence, a good dose of stubbornness and total dedication. Be prepared, for the first few months, to just eat, drink, and sleep in your time off from breastfeeding your premature triplets. The problems you will face are mainly those already mentioned for twins, but with a bonus baby on top. In fact, although simultaneously nursing two babies can be very helpful to you, too, it is never the end of the story.

La Leche League (see page 522) or support groups for parents of multiples (see page 532) can put you in touch with mothers who have successfully nursed triplets. All of their personal testimonies stress the importance of having around-the-clock help at the beginning: someone who can assist you during the day and at night, who can bring you the babies, make sure they're all fed (overlooking one is easier than you think!), change them, put them back to sleep, and help provide you with the healthy food your body needs to feed a trio of newborns.

In time, things are likely to become more organized and easier to manage, but you'll still need a lot of assistance with the babies as well as for any older children you may have, and with household chores. So, although one mother can breastfeed triplets, it may take a village to help her do it!

The Same Tests for All?

They just discovered that one of our triplets had a PDA that may be causing his apnea. Now I want them to do echocardiograms on my other babies, too.

For parents of twins or triplets, anxieties about one baby often expand to include the others, even if the others are doing just fine. Why? Because it's natural to assume that, sharing genes as siblings do, and having been born prematurely at the same time, your babies are likely to have the same medical conditions. But that's not true for many complications of prematurity, including a PDA, an intraventricular hemorrhage, or NEC, among others.

Although getting echocardiograms on each of your triplets seems logical to you now (and may help ease your anxiety), they're probably not needed. A PDA is not a congenital defect (meaning something you can inherit with your genes, or caused by an event that happened during pregnancy), but something all babies are born with (see page 176). The reason why this blood vessel quickly closes, as it should, in some premature babies and not in others, has to do with many unpredictable events. Just because it has been found in one of your triplets, the other two babies don't have a higher probability of having it. There are certain symptoms—such as a heart murmur, low blood pressure, or frequent apneic spells—that raise the suspicion of a PDA before an echocardiogram definitely confirms it. To perform this test on babies who have no signs or symptoms would put your baby through a procedure she doesn't need, as well as being an unwise investment of medical resources.

Many parents feel exactly like you do: when one of their twins or triplets is diagnosed with a new medical condition, they fear the others have it, too, and want them all tested. But it's best to let the doctors decide when diagnostic tests are indicated, based on their medical information and experience in caring for lots of preemies. It may be hard for you right now, but try to limit your apprehension to the one baby who has the problem. Your premature triplets, who may sometimes seem to you like one great, big, complex source of joy and worry, are actually three different individuals, with their own specific inclinations. Soon you'll discover more about each one that will shape their personalities in your mind: the cuddly one, the one who spends more time awake, the one who holds on to your finger most strongly. Soon, when each one's individual problems of prematurity fade away, you will be left discerning these delectable clues about each of them, telling you who is who.

How to Divide Your Time

Who needs me more, our smaller and sicker twin, who is still on a ventilator, or our healthier baby who really seems to love being held?

That's a tough one—and it's the kind of dilemma you'll soon get used to. For years beyond your babies' hospitalization, you're going to be juggling and balancing your children's different needs, trying not to feel guilty for shortchanging one or the other, and wishing you could split yourself into two equal pieces.

Unfortunately, that isn't possible, and right now you have two babies who both need you. So you do have to make some choices. While we can't make that easy by giving you a definitive answer, we can offer you some advice that may help:

❋ *Don't keep your distance from your sick twin.* Many parents hold back emotionally when they have a newborn preemie who's sick. They may be afraid of falling in love with their baby, and then losing him. They may be having trouble adjusting to the shock of having a baby who isn't the perfectly healthy newborn they always imagined. They may be trying to shield themselves from the pain they feel when they're with their baby and see him struggling. All of these feelings are normal, but they don't last. When they're gone, and pure love has taken their place, you won't want to be left with regrets that you weren't there for your baby when he needed you.

❋ *Keep in mind that even though your sick twin seems less responsive, he still benefits from being with you.* Your baby needs to be in an intensive care nursery to get well, but being in that environment isn't easy for him. A sick baby needs a lot of quiet rest, and gets easily overloaded by stimulation, so the bright lights, loud noises, and medical rather than loving touches can be very stressful for him. His parents can soothe him better than anyone else. If the nurses say your baby is stable enough to pick up, you can hold him in your arms, or even skin-to-skin against your warm chest. (See kangaroo care, page 221.) If he's not ready to be held yet, you can soothe him in other ways: by letting him grasp your little finger; by making a "hand womb" around his body (see page 202); by massaging him if his skin is not too fragile (make sure to ask the nurses first, and see page 250); and by talking and singing to him in the voice he recognizes so well from his days inside the womb. Until he's older and more stable, try just one form of interaction at a time.

✳ *Don't assume your healthier twin is less needy because she's stronger.* With your sicker baby, who needs a lot of peace and quiet, a little time with you goes a long way. If your healthier twin thrives on being held, it may mean that she can benefit from longer periods of interaction and more stimulation (using all of the same techniques mentioned above). If you decide that's the case, and give your healthy baby more time right now, don't feel guilty. The important thing is to follow your intuition and give each baby what's right for now, even if it's lopsided. You have years ahead of you to even things out.

✳ *Stretch the amount of time you have by setting priorities.* For the moment, it's appropriate to neglect your housework, your errands, and your friends (they'll understand). Let others do the cooking, or eat pizza and takeout food. If possible, ask your partner to spend time with the babies in the hospital, too. And remember that somebody close to you—a grandparent, uncle, aunt, or friend—might be happy to accompany you to the nursery, providing you with an extra pair of loving arms to hold one of your babies, or to take turns visiting them when you can't. Don't feel guilty asking for this special kind of help. Just make sure that the person you choose has time to visit the hospital consistently, so they and your babies can get intimately acquainted and thrive on each other's presence.

✳ *Don't think that there's a magic formula—a "right" amount of time—for a parent to spend with a preemie each day.* There isn't, as long as you visit both of your babies consistently, and try to respond to their different needs, trusting your instincts and feelings day by day. More than quantity, the quality of your presence is important. Preemies, like all babies, know when their parents love them. That's what counts.

Feeling Inadequate because of Famous Multiples

Thinking about the famous septuplets and octuplets we've read about in magazines makes me feel so inadequate. How could those babies have sailed through, while I only have twins, and one of them is struggling for his life?

While the good fortune of the recently born sets of supertwins, at least during their early hospital days, is reason for rejoicing, the tragic underside of all of the media attention is that it leaves you and many other people, who've had more normal experiences, with a sense of failure or guilt. You didn't "fail" at your pregnancy and birth any more than you've "failed" to win the lottery.

If there's one thing that parents learn, it's that every pregnancy, and every child (preemie or not), runs its different course. Having healthy, newborn septuplets—or even twins—is not something that can be achieved by simply following a recipe of a healthy lifestyle with a dollop of positive thinking. Remember that the press loves to tell modern fairy tales. Despite all of the endearing stories about how many diapers a mother of septuplets has to change, or about the number of volunteer helpers willing to back her up, any experienced parent knows that the fun facts hide a lot of agony, exhaustion, and doubt.

The truth about being pregnant with multiples, as you know from personal experience, is that it is much riskier than pregnancy with a single fetus. Pregnancy with a single baby lasts 40 weeks, on average. But nearly half of all twin births are premature. As a result, the number of twins who do not survive until hospital discharge is five to ten times higher than singletons. Triplets are born at 33½ weeks, on average, and quadruplets at 31 weeks. Higher order multiples are so rare that there are no reliable statistics—and in many cases, they are miscarried before birth, or are born too small and weak to survive.

These sad counterpoints are so well known to doctors that some professional groups, like the American Society for Reproductive Medicine and the New York State Task Force on Life and the Law, have proposed medical guidelines for infertility treatments, in an effort to decrease the number of multiple births. Their goal—conception of single babies, or no more than twins—is based on an expectation not of patients with unusual outcomes, but of many more patients like you.

The other truth about preterm multiples is that whether they are darlings of the media or not, they face the same, painful beginnings, and the same medical and developmental risks, as any other preemie. This is something that some supertwins and their parents, unfortunately, have to live with over the years, well after they've disappeared from the front pages.

Glossing over all of this does no service to parents like you, who are struggling with heartache and fears. Neither does it help couples who face tough, personal choices concerning whether to undergo more cautious infertility treatments, or to reduce pregnancies with high-order multiples—and who need accurate, rather than rose-colored depictions, to help make these choices wisely.

So, you shouldn't feel at all inadequate, just because you aren't a fictitious image of a super-parent. You are your twins' own, loving parent, and that is just what they need.

THE FATHER OF A PREEMIE

Every father, of course, has his own personal way of coping with an event as stressful as a premature birth. But fathers of preemies have some things in common: pain and a sense of loss, because the birth and your newborn baby weren't what you had planned and dreamed; concern that your wife or partner needs emotional and practical help, as does your newborn in the hospital and any older children you may have at home; tension from the need to balance competing demands from different parts of your life; and a strong desire to handle this family crisis as well as possible. What's the best way to support your family, and meet your own needs and responsibilities? What should you expect of yourself? Do you have a special role, as a father of a preemie?

TYPICAL EMOTIONAL REACTIONS

The premature birth of a baby is experienced by most parents as a fearful and dangerous event, and like any powerful threat, it sets off a "fight or flight" response. This is a reaction that humans share with animals, essential to survival. In this state of alarm, all energies are completely focused on overcoming or fleeing from the danger, and feelings of fatigue, pain, or anguish may not sink in. If you exhibited almost superhuman strength in the rushed beginning of your baby's life—going without sleep for many hours; shuttling between hospital, home, and work; dealing with countless decisions and arrangements— it's because the fight or flight response was keeping you going. Because men are often raised to keep their emotions in check, the shocking moment of a premature delivery and the following hours or days of emergency may be, paradoxically, the easiest to handle for a father.

Later, though, as the initial emergency subsides, and you begin to realize the full extent of what's happened, strong emotions may surface. Psychologists interviewing fathers and mothers after premature deliveries have documented high levels of anxiety, grief, and fear, in addition to positive emotions like amazement, hope, and love. So, if you feel overwhelmed with anxiety and contradictory emotions, that's to be expected.

Luckily, the anxiety generally resolves as the baby recovers and grows. But many parents of preemies have said that for the rest of their lives, they have occasional flashbacks of panic, brought on by something as simple as a cold their baby catches, or a beeping smoke detector that sounds like the monitor alarms in the NICU. Things that once seemed very important often become less so. So don't expect to be the same person you were before. Having a child, and especially a premature child, is a life-changing experience.

WHAT KINDS OF REACTIONS TO EXPECT OR AVOID

First, don't minimize the intensity of the experience you and your family are going through, especially if your preemie is sick and you don't know what the future holds. By acknowledging the wrenching emotions it brings, you're not being weak. Just the opposite. Terror, grief, frustrating feelings of impotence, bitterness, and rage are frequent reactions to the trauma of a premature birth. The positive emotions that parents often feel can be overwhelming, as well. Love can be frightening, too, when it's very strong.

A common response to fear and anxiety is to avoid the situation that's generating the disturbing emotions. One typical escape for many fathers is work. Considering all the time you may have taken off during your baby's first difficult days, your responsibilities may indeed be calling you back to the workplace. But it's important to ask yourself: is there some leeway? Do you really need to stay there for such long hours now? Remember that this is one of the most critical periods of your and your partner's lives. After it's over, you won't want to be left with regrets—or your partner to be left with resentments—that can linger and grow.

Another way that people protect themselves from too much hurt is through "anticipatory grief." They shield themselves from strong feelings of loss in the future, by relinquishing attachment in the present. For parents of premature babies, this may take the form of avoidance—not visiting the hospital nursery, taking little interest in the details of your preemie's day, being overly pessimistic about his progress, not wanting to see photographs of him, even avoiding giving your baby a name. Anticipatory grief is adaptive, in that it helps lessen future pain. But it does so at the expense of emotional engagement with your child. Just remember: if you repress love in self-defense, you risk losing it altogether.

Another reason some fathers of preemies work excessively long hours, or don't visit the nursery much, is that they feel out of place there, and are convinced that their presence isn't really needed. It may be because the mother is already spending so much time at the hospital, and the father believes his talents and expertise lie elsewhere. The hospital, with its sometimes opaque ways of doing things and rigid assertion of authority, can also be unsettling, especially for those fathers whose role in the family is to take charge and manage events. Most men in our society have been raised to think that the appropriate response to situations that are getting out of control is to take action.

This, unfortunately, flies in the face of the situation a father finds himself in with his preemie. Given how utterly unresponsive it is to any interventions you can come up with, it's easy to end up feeling incompetent and to retreat, or to become aggressive and hostile, just to assert some control. But if you have been feeling frustrated by your inability to make a difference in your preemie's well being, just know that your assumption is probably wrong. Some research has found that a father's presence in the hospital nursery can improve his premature infant's growth, health, and long-term development (see Fathering a premature baby, below).

Finally, because this premature birth has completely disrupted your life, you should expect to have feelings that you may be ashamed of: most commonly, jealousy and anger directed at your wife, your baby, or the doctors and nurses. You may even regret that your baby has survived.

It may help to know that many fathers and mothers have these thoughts. It's natural to feel angry and resentful when your world has been turned upside down. Acknowledging your negative feelings, at least to yourself, or better yet, talking about them with your partner, a close friend, or even a counselor, can be a relief, and allow warmer feelings to surface. With time, your parental instinct and love for your preemie should overtake the rancor or bitterness you may feel, making them slowly, but surely, disappear.

HOW TO SUSTAIN YOUR RELATIONSHIP, YOUR PARTNER, YOUR KIDS

Avoiding a couples crisis

Studies have shown that a child's serious illness is one of the most disruptive experiences a couple can go through. Although both mothers and fathers are apt to feel the same strong emotions, they may feel them at different times, and may rely on different coping mechanisms, which can create stress and put a couple off-balance. For long months, parents may not have much time for each other. Perhaps because of the stark contrast with pre-baby times, sometimes couples who were the closest can feel the most painfully distant.

When both partners are exhausted, physically and emotionally, resentments don't get talked out right away, as they ideally should. Small misunderstandings can lag on, and grow into big problems, increasing the risk of separation or divorce. Being aware of the danger can help prevent you from minimizing signals of distress, so you can recognize and respond to them before they grow deep roots. If your partner accuses you of being emotionally distant from her or the baby, or if she just seems upset with you, try to analyze the reasons for your behavior and, if you can, confide your underlying worries to her. Tell her how much you care for her and the baby. You'll feel better—more of a team.

While for some couples, a premature birth can destroy a relationship, for others it makes the relationship stronger. One study found that in the majority of cases, fathers and mothers of premature babies were each other's most vital source of support, sharing the special kind of love that parents have for their child.

Making your wife or partner feel supported and understood

To help make sense of your wife's or partner's reactions, you should realize that they, too, may be complicated by several factors. First of all, she may perceive the events surrounding the premature birth as a failure of her maternal abilities. She may blame herself for something specific that happened during the pregnancy, or simply because she failed to carry the baby to term. Because a mother is socially and hormonally "programmed" to take complete charge of her newborn after birth, being separated from her infant can also make her feel especially deprived and helpless. For that reason, mothers tend to feel more jealous of nurses than fathers do, and have more problems working out their roles with them.

Your partner may be physically debilitated after the delivery, particularly if it was an emergency, or she was ill. Her weariness, sometimes worsened by postpartum depression, can last for weeks after the baby's birth. When a mother is sick, or in a different hospital from the baby, it may be the father who sees the baby more frequently, and is "ahead" of the mother in bonding with their newborn. If your wife or partner doesn't seem as interested in your preemie's medical details or progress, don't be taken aback. When she gets to spend more time with the baby, it won't take long for her to reach your greater level of involvement.

There are other reasons a preemie's father may feel his partner is simply on the wrong wavelength. He may be puzzled by her concern with seemingly tiny details: a nurse's cold behavior, a relative's insensitive words, or minor, practical problems. If you feel that your wife is missing the point of what really counts right now, try to temper your disapproval with attempts to understand what might underlie her reactions. They could be her way of coping with unbearable fears. Or her guilt may lead her to interpret things as slights or personal attacks.

Most of all, try to reassure her that she's in no way responsible for the premature birth of your baby. "If I had stayed in bed . . ."; "If I hadn't exercised . . ."; "If I had told the doctor about those first contractions . . ." can haunt mothers of preemies for a long time. Let her express her guilt, fears, and regrets, and then patiently reassure her, as many times as needed, that it wasn't her fault. If you make an effort to empathize with your wife's feelings, she's more likely to be understanding of your own reactions, which can be as difficult to read for her, as hers are for you.

Helping your other kids

Take the time to focus on your older children. As you can imagine, they are going to miss their parents a lot, during their premature sibling's hospitalization. A toddler may not understand why you're gone so much, and may interpret your preoccupation with the new baby as abandonment or rejection of her, particularly if she thinks her new little sister's or brother's difficulties magically resulted from her own misbehavior or feelings of jealousy. If your children are old enough to appreciate what happened, it's easy for them to feel deeply insecure about this unexpected turn of events, scared that something bad could happen to them or you, too. Putting your older children very high on your list of priorities can help redress some of their insecurity and need for attention. In "Getting to know a new brother or sister in the hospital," on page 186, you'll find some tips on how to help your children cope.

Other things you can do

* *Get someone to help with chores, errands, child care.* Since both you and your partner are vulnerable and distressed, dealing with mundane responsibilities may take more effort than you can muster. Calling on relatives and friends for practical help, even hiring someone temporarily, can preserve some of your precious energies and allow you to focus on top-priority items, like visiting your baby, dealing with medical issues, keeping up at work, and supporting your wife and older children.

* *Be your partner's eyes and ears.* Right after delivery, when your partner isn't able to move around much yet, you can be a bridge between her and the NICU, making sure she gets all of the available information, and telling her all about your baby. Take pictures, take notes, tell her where your baby is, who's taking care of him, and what he's going through. Deciding to "spare" her worrisome news may be a way for you to control your own fear, but is not a good idea, because it

breaks down the lines of communication and understanding between you.

* *Spend time with your baby.* Whether your partner spends a lot of time at your preemie's bedside or not, the more you visit your baby, the more comfortable you'll feel that you're involved in and knowledgeable about his care. Learning how to hold, feed, and comfort your baby in the hospital can make you a better father and a more helpful husband or companion. Other fathers have said that learning how to care for their baby in the hospital helped them overcome feelings of powerlessness, and bolstered their courage to carry on through this difficult time.

* *Keep contributing, and also keep your sense of humor when the baby comes home.* The pressures on you and your partner will change, but they won't diminish for some time. Premature children often require more patience and nurturing than full-term babies, even after they're discharged from the hospital. They may be more irritable, and their daily rhythms more erratic. As even parents of full-term newborns learn, feeding, diapering, and soothing are going to be your main preoccupations in the next weeks and months. So, forget about regular family meals, uninterrupted sleep, and the rest of your daily routine, and be prepared to hone your survival skills. Contributing to family chores, and joking about, rather than criticizing, your chronic lack of clean socks or that millionth pizza dinner, will be greatly appreciated by your wife and kids.

* *Expect a temporary change in your love life.* The most likely victim of your frantic schedule is your intimate relationship with your partner. All parents go through a transition, a temporary change in their sex life when a baby is born. But a premature birth can disrupt a couple's intimacy for much longer. Accord-

ing to psychologists, it's helpful to accept the idea that for a while you may not be the lovers you had been. When you feel romantic, your wife or partner may not be interested, and the other way around. Don't let this disharmony loom over you without acknowledging it, because it can lead to resentments. Take the pressure off having sexual intercourse, and try to express love in other ways. If you don't force it, passion will come back.

FATHERING A PREMATURE BABY

Studies done in the 1970s and 1980s showed that a father's involvement is important for his children's optimal development. More recently, some interesting psychological research has focused on fathers of premature babies, in particular. (If you are the male central figure in your preemie's life, even if you're not his biological father, everything here is relevant for you, too.)

The concrete power of a father's love
If your wife spends a lot of time in the hospital nursery, you may think your baby doesn't need you much right now. This is not true. One study found that premature babies who were visited more often by their fathers in the hospital recovered and grew faster—gaining more weight, leaving the hospital earlier, and showing better social development in their second year. Even when things like the frequency of mothers' visits, how small or sick the babies were, and the socioeconomic conditions of the families were taken into consideration, the frequency of fathers' visits remained a significant factor in their preemie's recovery.

Visiting may bring some other benefits, too.

The more frequently fathers went to see their preemies in the nursery, the more likely they were to be nurturing parents, involved in caregiving, talking to, and playing with their baby, at the time of hospital discharge and at eight months of age. Fathers who visited more often were also less likely to view their preemies as difficult children at 18 months of age. One explanation for these findings, in addition to any possible differences in attitudes or temperament that fathers and babies started out with, has to do with parental bonding: having frequent contact with a newborn increases a parent's motivation and emotional involvement. So, if you visit your baby as often as you can in the hospital, in the future you may take more joy in fathering him.

What fathers do in the NICU
Various studies have noted that fathers' behavior in the hospital nursery tends to be different from mothers'. For instance, fathers tend to touch their preemies less, if they're younger than 28 weeks of gestation. They may start doing kangaroo care later than mothers, and seldom gaze at, speak to, or fondle their babies while they're holding them. This may have to do with deep-seated differences in parenting behavior between fathers and mothers, but it may also be because of insecurity in handling a newborn—especially a fragile and seemingly vulnerable preemie.

Given the evidence that a father's presence can be comforting and healing, the challenge is to not be self-conscious about people around you. Remember that your preemie finds your arms and your voice especially soothing and beneficial.

Fathers and preemies, back home
Although patient and dedicated nurturing may not be considered a traditional male virtue,

fathers of preemies beat that stereotype. Research has shown that fathers of preemies tend to be more involved than fathers of full-term infants, devoting a larger share of their time to the care of their offspring at one, five, and 18 months. Several studies have also found that fathers of premature babies were actually more responsive to their infants than fathers of term babies—and that their preemies rose to the occasion by becoming as responsive as the term babies were. (Interestingly, fathers of premature infants tended to be more appropriately responsive to their babies than preterm mothers were. Mothers, who possibly had more preconceived notions about what mother-infant interactions should be like, were more likely to be either overactive and intrusive, possibly to make up for a less responsive baby, or to be less interactive and understimulating, maybe because of lower expectations about the infant's capabilities.)

Fathers show a distinctive style of interaction with their children, mainly dedicated to play—a more vigorous, arousing, and stimulating play than mothers tend to engage in. One study on nearly 1,000 preemies from ethnically diverse families found that a large majority of fathers played with their premature child every day, even when they didn't live in the same house. This held true at one, two, and three years of age; and the sicker a baby was at birth, the more highly involved in his care his father tended to be. There is evidence that both preterm and term children, especially from disadvantaged groups, thrive on this, having better social and cognitive outcomes than toddlers whose fathers are uninvolved.

Researchers can't pinpoint exactly what aspect of paternal involvement is most beneficial for a baby. But based on a landmark experiment done in 1988, which showed that baby rats who were more frequently and vigorously touched grew up smarter, some have suggested that the high levels of physical stimulation provided by fathers during play might be the key to their children's improvements in cognitive development.

It's also difficult to assess the influence that an involved father has indirectly, by giving love and support to his child's mother. But any experienced parent would say that this counts for a lot. In general, a father's impact is broad and deep—for all of his children. But maybe, for a preemie, even more.

If Your Baby Needs Surgery

▶ *Guiding parents through an event that is usually scarier than it needs to be.*

INTRODUCTION   304

QUESTIONS AND ANSWERS
Too Small for Surgery?   304
Who Is in Charge?   305
Your Preemie Needs Surgery: Decisions
    and Precautions   306
Avoiding Pain and Discomfort   308

KINDS OF SURGERY A PREEMIE
MAY NEED   310
Surgery to Close a PDA   311

Surgery to Treat NEC   313
Surgery to Place a Broviac Catheter or
    Other Central Venous Line   315
Surgery to Treat Hydrocephalus   316
Surgery to Treat GE Reflux   319
Surgery to Treat ROP   321
Tracheostomy   323
Surgery to Repair a Hernia   324

Introduction: If Your Baby Needs Surgery

The idea of surgery is scary to almost everyone, and especially to the parents of a small and frail preemie. Partly, that comes from fear of the unknown: the mystery of the operating room, where a surgeon can look and reach inside the human body. In fact, most people feel relieved when they are told what a surgical procedure actually involves, because the reality is often more reassuring than what they imagined. You still will worry until you see your infant fully recovered, but knowing more about his surgery may make you feel a little better.

There are some important things you need to know if your preemie needs surgery. You should ask the neonatologist or surgeon to explain clearly your baby's medical condition, why surgery would help, and what its risks are. Ask how much experience the anesthesiologist and surgeon have doing this kind of surgery. You may also want to ask whether your baby is likely to be in any pain, and what will be done to soothe it. Some of the information in this chapter may help answer your questions. But because the technical complexity of surgery, anesthesia, and recovery can vary greatly depending on your baby's situation, you should rely mostly on his doctors to explain exactly what's going on with your child.

Questions and Answers

Too Small for Surgery?

My baby is so small. How could he withstand surgery?

Everyone's heart is touched by a premature baby who has to undergo surgery, at a time when he would not even have been born. As if it weren't difficult enough to see him so tiny, struggling to make it outside the womb! If it's your premature baby who needs surgery, it can feel like the worst news you could get. But in reality, it isn't, as you'll soon realize.

True, it is challenging to operate on a human being who weighs only a few pounds, and may also be sick. But pediatric surgeons and anesthesiologists have had years of special training, taking care of newborns and preemies like yours. A pediatric anesthesiologist is familiar with the ways that a preemie reacts to anesthetic drugs and to the stress of surgery, and knows what doses and combinations of therapies to use, to see him safely through the operation. There are dozens of surgical subspecialties in pediatrics, so if your premature baby is having a shunt placed for hydrocephalus, for example, he'll be operated on by a pediatric neurosurgeon, while if he's having kidney or bladder surgery, a pediatric urologist will take care of him. That precise specialization allows your baby's surgeon to develop very finely honed expertise and experience.

Today, surgery is often performed on tiny preemies, some weighing less than two pounds. Most of these operations are extremely safe and successful, with survival rates approaching 100% for many of them. Unless your surgeon tells you otherwise, you have every reason to be optimistic. Although it's stressful, you should try to look upon the surgery as a turning point in your preemie's life, toward a better, healthier future.

For a preemie's surgery to be as safe as possible, it is important for it to be done in a hospital with a neonatal intensive care unit. Good teamwork among the NICU staff, anesthesiologist, and surgeon is essential to ensure that a baby gets the best care, particularly in the delicate time right after surgery, as anesthesia is wearing off and a baby's body is adjusting to the stress of the operation. If your preemie has to be transferred into a NICU, you may find it distressing, and the intensity of the environment may add to your anxiety for your child. But most likely, it won't be for long. Most babies who were relatively healthy before surgery bounce back very soon, usually in a matter of days.

Most parents, understandably, would like to avoid surgery for their child, if they could. Although the desire to protect your baby may make you feel defensive right now, you should try not to perceive the doctors as antagonists. If you tell them that you would like more time to think things over, and there is no immediate need to operate on your baby, they will almost certainly comply. They know this is your child. No doctor or surgeon wants to take him to the operating room unless there's a clear benefit for him, and until you, although worried, have also become convinced of that.

Who Is in Charge?

My baby needs surgery. Who is in charge now, the neonatologist or the surgeon?

When a premature baby needs surgery, his already worried and bewildered parents may have to deal with another stressful change: the sudden appearance of new faces around his iso-lette, as the surgeon, and maybe some surgical nurses and residents, come to the nursery to meet their new little patient. Most of them will make sure to introduce themselves and talk to you. But since families are not always in the hospital, the surgical team may have seen your baby several times in your absence, and then come back as old acquaintances, while you're still puzzled about who they are.

Most likely, after some initial unease with your baby's surgeon, you'll become more comfortable, and develop a trusting relationship with him. But many parents have problems understanding who is in charge. Is it the neonatologist, the surgeon, or both? Who makes the decisions? Whom should you talk to? You'll be dealing with two sets of doctors, who will sometimes focus on different things, and who may not always think alike.

Most of the time, your confusion can be solved by asking the neonatologist you know by now to explain your baby's situation, and to tell you clearly who's in charge of what. In general, the surgeon is in charge of the surgical procedure, deciding exactly when it will be done, how to prepare your baby for it, and how to take care of the incision and any equipment he puts in (like a VP shunt or a gastrostomy tube) afterward. Other than that, responsibilities may be assigned differently. In some hospitals, the neonatologist always remains in charge of a premature baby. In others, the neonatologist and the surgeon share equal responsibility until your baby has recovered from the operation and the surgeon signs off. So, for a while they'll collaborate on such medical decisions as when feedings will resume, when sedation can be lightened, and what lab studies to order. Finally, in other hospitals the surgeon temporarily takes over the care of a baby, with the neonatologist becoming his consultant for medical decisions.

Usually, events lead quickly and smoothly to your baby's surgery, and to your great relief as he recovers well. Sometimes, though, a baby's situation is more complex, and there is controversy about his need for surgery, or how his medical problems should be handled during his convalescence. Parents may then hear somewhat different messages from the surgeon and the neonatologist. If that happens to you, try not to get upset, and don't be afraid to lift your hand and question them. One solution is to ask to meet with both doctors together, the neonatologist and the surgeon, to figure out what's best. Everybody can benefit from that meeting, but most of all, you will gain a better understanding of what's going on with your baby, and that's the most important thing.

YOUR PREEMIE NEEDS SURGERY: DECISIONS AND PRECAUTIONS

When your premature baby needs surgery, you may find yourself under a lot of pressure, in addition to being worried and upset. It would be helpful if you could stop the clock, to discuss the matter more thoroughly with your family, talk again to your baby's doctors and to other physicians, and get more information before giving your consent to the operation. Even if your baby's surgery is not an emergency, most likely you'll feel that time is going too fast.

The questions below cover the essential information and support you should receive before your baby's surgery. If you are missing any of it, don't be shy about bringing your questions or needs to the attention of your baby's doctors. On the other hand, if you have all of this information and support, you can be assured that you and your doctors have done what you could to make the best decision for your baby.

1. *Do you know why your baby needs surgery, what the benefits and risks of the procedure are, how urgent it is, and what's involved in her recovery? In other words, do you feel you know enough to give "informed" consent for the operation?*

All surgeries are invasive procedures, carrying benefits and risks. The doctors should explain clearly what your baby is going to gain from the operation, how soon it needs to be done, and what her convalescence will entail. Only your doctors can tell you exactly what you can expect for your baby, but most of the time, the prospects for preemies who undergo surgery are very good.

Sometimes, surgery for a preemie is an emergency, needing to be done immediately to avert serious injury or death. But more commonly, you'll be told that your preemie's operation should be done soon, but not necessarily right away. For instance, if your baby needs a PDA ligation (see page 311) she is likely to be sick and fragile, and her doctors to believe that she'll do better after the operation. But she is probably not so unstable that you can't take a day or two to think it over. Some surgeries, like hernia repairs, are even less pressing. They need to be done eventually, but are often postponed for several weeks until a preemie is bigger, stronger, and better equipped to withstand the stress of surgery. Some procedures are elective, meaning that they are not absolutely necessary. For instance, a tracheostomy or a gastrostomy may be done to enhance a baby's life and development, or to make caring for him easier. They can sometimes be put off for a long time, or even not done at all, so you can take as much time as you need to learn about the pros and cons.

2. *Do most doctors agree on the best treatment for your baby? If there are alternatives to surgery, do you know their risks and benefits, and what would happen to your baby if surgery weren't done?*

Don't be afraid to ask your doctors whether all doctors would agree that surgery is the best way to treat your baby's condition. It is their duty to inform you about the risks and benefits of other possible treatments, and of not doing anything at all, even if they are convinced that surgery is the best way to go. Some families feel that if there is time, they would like to consult another specialist or surgeon for a second opinion, but they may be afraid of offending their doctor. You shouldn't worry about that. Physicians don't tend to take a request for a second opinion personally. In fact, if they're facing difficult dilemmas and having to make hard decisions on how to best treat your baby, they may be relieved to share that responsibility with a colleague.

3. *Were you and your partner given enough time to reflect, have family discussions, and reach a considered decision about your baby's surgery? Are your values and feelings being taken into consideration by your baby's doctors? Has the medical staff been supportive?*

You should not feel pressured to make quick decisions, unless it's unavoidable because of your baby's medical situation. Even when there isn't time for much reflection, the doctors should give you as much time as possible, even if it is just a few minutes alone to talk things over. Before surgery, if your baby's medical condition allows, you should be able to spend time with her, take her picture, have your family visit her. After surgery, just being told that everything went well may not be enough to reassure a preemie's anguished parents. You should be told clearly, and in detail, what you need to know about the procedure and her expected recovery. Try to accept different personality traits and communication styles as part of the variety of human nature: some doctors and nurses will just be more patient and understanding, forthcoming and supportive than others. Still, your needs, as much as possible, should be accommodated by the nursery staff, to sustain you psychologically, and to make you a stronger, more informed advocate for your baby.

4. *Do the doctors and nurses know how to reach you shortly before, during, and after the surgery?*

Sometimes, the surgeon or neonatologist needs to talk to parents urgently about changes in their baby's medical condition, or to get consent for additional procedures. For a day or so before and after your baby's surgery, when you're not in the hospital nursery, it will be important to let the medical staff know how to get in touch with you. Also, because the exact starting time and duration of most operations aren't known in advance, you should let the nursery staff know if you want to be notified when your baby goes to the operating room, and when she returns. This may not be done automatically.

Although it may be impossible for you to believe right now, the memory of your baby's surgery will become less painful in the future. You'll always feel grateful, though, to the doctors and nurses who were most supportive, and gave you the information you needed to make the best decisions.

Avoiding Pain and Discomfort

My baby has to have an operation. I can't bear to think what he'll be going through, and that he'll be in pain.

It should comfort you to know that shielding your baby from pain, during and after a surgical procedure, is a primary goal for the doctors and nurses taking care of him. Your baby's anesthesiologist, surgeon, neonatologist, and nurse will be watching to make sure he's as comfortable as possible.

To keep a preemie stable and pain-free during surgery requires the special skills and experience of a pediatric anesthesiologist. You will probably meet your baby's anesthesiologist a day or two before his operation. She'll explain what will be done to keep your baby from feeling pain, and tell you what to expect after the surgery. Both will depend, to some degree, on your baby's medical condition, the surgery that he's having, and the preferences and expertise of his doctors. Don't hesitate to ask about these or anything else regarding your baby, if you have questions.

✳ *Before your preemie goes to the operating room,* the anesthesiologist will examine her new little patient and review his medical history. She'll want to be aware of anything that would influence the choice of anesthesia and be prepared for any problems that your baby could have in the operating room. The anesthesiologist, working with the surgeon, will order any special medications that have to be given right before surgery (for instance, a baby may be given antibiotics to reduce the risk of infection from surgery, or caffeine to reduce the risk of post-operative

apnea), and will give instructions on his feedings.

Although fasting is required before having surgery, to avoid the risk of aspirating food from the stomach into the lungs, premature babies don't have to fast for as long as older children or adults, so your baby won't have time to get very hungry. Preemies are allowed to have their last feeding of formula six hours before surgery, or of breast milk (which is easier to digest than formula) four hours before, and they can take clear fluids (like sugar water) up to two hours before surgery.

Right before the procedure, the anesthesiologist and a nurse will come to the nursery to personally escort your baby, in an isolette, to the operating room, where he'll be delivered into the expert hands of the surgical team.

✳ *The operating room will be specifically prepared* to host a tiny preemie. To keep him warm during surgery, the room temperature will be raised—making it tropical for the team of adults working in there! He'll be kept covered as much as possible during the procedure, with a cap, blankets, or even plastic wrap, which is great for keeping preemies warm. His intravenous fluids can be heated, too, to avoid lowering his body temperature.

✳ *Most major surgical procedures in premature babies are performed under general anesthesia,* meaning that your baby will be "put to sleep" for the operation. He won't be able to move or feel any pain during the procedure, and he'll have no memory of it afterward. He also won't be able to breathe on his own until the anesthesia wears off, so he'll need to be on a ventilator. Your baby will be given his anesthetic in liquid form through his IV, if he already has one in place, or as a gas that he breathes through a face mask (it takes only a few seconds to work). After your baby is asleep, when it won't hurt him, the anesthesiologist will put in any catheters and tubes that may be needed for the procedure.

While it's wonderful to know that your baby will be sleeping peacefully, and feel no discomfort through the whole operation, general anesthesia always carries some risk of complications. The main ones are heart rate and blood pressure abnormalities, and in the worst cases, death. Although small, that risk is higher for a young preemie than for a term newborn, because of the immaturity of his organs.

For some short surgeries that involve body areas below the waist (such as hernia repair or circumcision), the anesthesiologist may use regional, instead of general, anesthesia. This involves injecting local anesthetics into the spinal canal *(spinal anesthesia)*, or around large nerves near the spine which carry pain sensations from the areas where the surgeon is working *(caudal* or *epidural anesthesia,* similar to what many women receive during labor). The effect of both is to block pain sensations from traveling up to the brain.

Regional anesthesia can be difficult to administer to a preemie, but it has several benefits. Since it numbs only a specific region of your baby's body, his respiratory muscles and the breathing center in his brain aren't affected. That means he should still be able to breathe on his own, and may avoid having to be put on a ventilator. An additional advantage is that an epidural catheter can be left in place, and local anesthetics continually administered through it, to provide uninter-

rupted pain control for several days after surgery. Preemies who receive regional anesthesia also have lower rates of post-operative apnea (see below).

Some babies who receive regional anesthesia don't need any sedation beyond a pacifier soaked in sugar water, which they quietly and contentedly suck throughout the procedure. Often, though, in order to perform the spinal or epidural block, it is necessary to give a baby extra sedation, so he will be sleeping.

In some cases, a preemie may receive a combination of regional and general anesthetics. This allows lower doses of general anesthesia to be used, reducing the risk of complications.

❋ *In the delicate post-operative time,* every preemie needs very attentive care. When the operation is finished, your baby will remain in the operating room, or be taken to a nearby recovery room, where he will be observed closely to make sure that he remains stable as the anesthesia begins to wear off. Then, your baby will be prepared for the trip back to the NICU. Some of the catheters, lines, and monitors that were used during the surgery will be detached, or switched to portable medical equipment. When your baby is all set, the surgeon, anesthesiologist, and a nurse will accompany him back to the NICU. They won't leave until they've given the neonatologist and your baby's bedside nurse the information they'll need to take care of him after his surgery: details about what went on in the operating room, and any special instructions regarding your baby's post-operative care. While a baby is recovering from surgery, there will always be teamwork among the surgeon, the anesthesiologist, and your baby's neonatologist, but the exact assignment of responsibilities may differ from hospital to hospital.

After surgery, you should be prepared to see your baby in the newborn intensive care unit, even if he was in a step-down unit before the operation. That doesn't mean the operation didn't go well. Preemies generally need to stay in an NICU and be monitored after a surgical procedure because of the risk of post-operative apnea (an overly long pause in breathing), which is a complication of general anesthesia in all newborns, especially preemies. The risk of apnea is greatly increased for 24 to 48 hours after anesthesia.

Your baby may also be attached to a ventilator, not breathing on his own, for what seems like long hours, or perhaps even days, after surgery. That's because a premature baby's immature liver and kidneys take some time to clear the anesthetics out of his body, so he may not wake up or breathe for a while, especially if he's given more pain medication in the NICU. Usually, babies who didn't have previous breathing problems are off a ventilator within hours or a few days after their surgery. But babies who had respiratory problems before the surgery, and whose lungs are not completely normal yet, may have a harder time, and take longer to come off the ventilator afterward.

Post-operative pain in preemies can be treated very effectively, so you shouldn't worry about that. You can read all about pain control on page 109; the same principles will apply to your baby's care after his surgery. Your baby's doctors will probably use narcotics like morphine or fentanyl to keep him comfortable. Those drugs will make him sleepy, and probably further prolong his stay on the ventilator, but they're excellent at preventing pain and suffering. Other medications, like Tylenol or Motrin, which won't sedate him or suppress his breathing, are helpful after several days, when your baby's pain is milder.

After your baby's surgery, you can help to make sure that he receives any comfort and care that can make him feel better. Sometimes, parents are the best judges of how their baby is doing. Don't hesitate to ask what pain medications he's getting, and what other relief measures have been taken. You should feel free to call a nurse or doctor if you notice that your baby is agitated; they may want to give him more pain medicine. When you see that your baby is conscious enough to be aware of your presence, try to give him a gentle signal. Touch his hand and tell him, softly, that Mommy and Daddy are there, patiently waiting for him to get well. And when your baby is more awake and a little better, ask the nurse if he can suck on a pacifier, be swaddled, or held in your arms.

KINDS OF SURGERY A PREEMIE MAY NEED

On the following pages, you can find some basic information about the most common surgical procedures performed on premature babies, along with their usual indications, outcomes, complications, and recovery. To get the full picture for your baby, you will need to talk to his surgeon and neonatologist. This brief overview is designed to help you know what to ask your baby's doctors, and to understand what their answers mean.

Some preemies need surgery in their first weeks of life because of a congenital condition— a problem that was present before birth. If that's the case for your baby, his surgeon and neonatologist will discuss his specific medical problems and future prospects with you, as well as the risks and benefits of the operation. The operations that we discuss below are not for such congenital problems, but are, instead, specifically for complications of prematurity.

There are some risks that are common to all surgeries—mainly infection, bleeding, damage to nearby tissues, and complications from general anesthesia. You should also know that operations are not always successful, either because the surgeon can't accomplish what he set out to do, or because the procedure doesn't end up benefiting the patient as it was hoped, or because the problem recurs and surgery needs to be redone. These risks vary from procedure to procedure, and from patient to patient, and you should ask your baby's surgeon about them. He can tell you what he's planning to do to try to prevent complications, and what could be done to treat your baby if they occur.

Most of the problems of prematurity that lead to surgery have been described in other chapters. It's a good idea to go back and read about your baby's underlying condition again, as some information in there might help you to better understand his surgical treatment.

It will be hard for you to feel at peace until your child comes out of the operating room, and you hear the surgeon and the anesthesiologist saying that everything went well. But in the meantime, try to be optimistic. Most of the time, preemies sail through their operations with flying colors.

SURGERY TO CLOSE A PDA

Why it may be needed

If a premature baby has a large PDA (patent ductus arteriosus, see page 176) causing breathing problems or some heart failure, and if it cannot be closed with medication (either because the medication hasn't worked, or because something about a baby's condition makes his doctors believe that using medication is not advisable), his doctors will recommend that the PDA be closed surgically. The operation is called a PDA ligation. Among those patients who need it are some of the smallest and youngest patients in the NICU.

How a PDA ligation is performed

A PDA ligation isn't heart surgery—in fact, your baby's heart won't be touched at all. The operation is performed under general anesthesia, with your baby on a ventilator. To reach the PDA, the surgeon will make a small, horizontal incision on the left side of your baby's back. He'll lift up your baby's lung to find the patent ductus, then close it tightly with a tiny clip, which will stay on permanently. Alternatively, some surgeons sew the ductus closed first, then cut it.

Outcome and possible complications

A PDA ligation is a safe operation with a mortality rate close to zero. It is nearly always successful in closing the ductus.

Although complications are uncommon, they do sometimes occur. Rarely, during a PDA ligation, a major blood vessel, several of which lie close to the ductus, is nicked. If that happens, while the surgeon immediately repairs the blood vessel, the anesthesiologist will give your baby a blood transfusion, to replace the blood he's lost, and make sure that everything is done

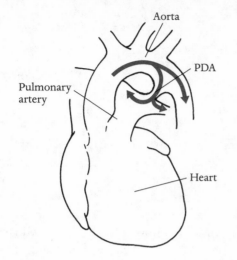

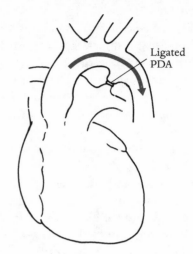

With a PDA, blood can flow back from the aorta into the pulmonary artery, overloading the heart and the lungs.

A PDA ligation closes the ductus, reestablishing normal circulation.

to keep his breathing, heart beat, and blood pressure stable. Another possible complication of a PDA ligation is a small tear in a lung, called a pneumothorax. This will heal naturally on its own in a few days. The most likely long-term complication of a PDA ligation is accidental damage to one of the nerves that passes near the ductus. Nerves near the ductus control such things as the vocal cords and the movement of the diaphragm. An injury to one of them could temporarily (for several weeks or months) or permanently give a baby a hoarse voice, increase his risk for accidentally aspirating food into his lungs (because his vocal cords may not close tightly when he swallows, allowing food to go down the "wrong pipe"), or make it more difficult for him to take deep breaths. Often, these problems can be improved with further surgery.

Recovery and healing

Due to a combination of general anesthesia and the pain medication your baby will get after surgery, it will take a while for him to wake up and breathe on his own. Usually, a baby's breathing improves gradually, beginning about eight to twelve hours after the operation, with continued improvement over the next several days. Some babies, though, are sicker for a couple of days after surgery, as their lungs and heart recover from the added stress of the operation.

How much your baby ultimately improves—for example, whether closing his PDA allows him to come off the ventilator or not—will depend on how much the PDA was contributing to his medical problems. Often, it's impossible to know this in advance: doctors are sometimes surprised by how completely a preemie's lungs recover once his PDA is closed. Unfortunately, they are occasionally equally surprised by how little difference closing a baby's PDA can make. Most of the time, a preemie's lungs get steadily better after his PDA is closed.

If your baby was taking breast milk or formula before the operation, he will probably resume his feedings in several days. His stitches will be absorbed by his body, so they won't need to be taken out. The remaining scar on your baby's back will eventually look like a thin, light line.

Surgery to Treat NEC

Why it may be needed

If a baby with NEC (necrotizing enterocolitis, see page 237), does not begin to get better within a couple of days of starting medical treatment, it can mean that parts of her intestine have torn or died. Once that happens, the damaged areas need to be surgically removed in order for the infection and inflammation to subside, allowing the remainder of her bowel to rest and heal.

How NEC surgery is performed

NEC surgery is performed under general anesthesia. The surgeon makes an incision just above or below a baby's belly button, going from one side of her belly to the other. He thoroughly cleans her abdomen and drains any abscesses, then carefully examines the whole length of her bowel, from the stomach to the rectum, looking for holes and signs of damage. The surgeon's main goal is to remove any areas of intestine that are torn or irreparably damaged, while still preserving as much bowel as possible, allowing your baby to absorb enough nutrients from her feedings later.

Sometimes, it won't be obvious at the time of the operation whether an area of intestine can recover or not. In that case, the surgeon may leave it in, hoping it will heal. But if your baby's condition isn't steadily improving after 24 to 48 hours, he'll probably check on her

bowel again with a second operation, called a "re-exploration," or "second look."

Occasionally, if a baby has just an isolated hole in one part of her intestine, and the rest of her bowel looks healthy, the surgeon may immediately reconnect her intestine. But most of the time, it is safer, and recovery after NEC is faster and more complete, if the intestine is not rejoined immediately. Instead, the surgeon brings the two open ends of the bowel out through a small incision in your baby's belly. That procedure is called an enterostomy, or "ostomy" for short (see illustration).

To be told that your baby has been given an ostomy is shocking news. But be assured that it is only temporary. Usually in about six to eight weeks, your baby's intestine can be reconnected safely, and tucked back inside where it belongs. In the meantime, having an ostomy allows the lower tract of her intestine to rest and heal, because food and stool won't be passing through it. Until her bowel is reconnected, your baby's stools will come out of the end of the higher intestinal tract, into a special bag taped to her belly. (The ostomy bag is usually completely covered by a baby's diaper, invisible to anyone who isn't changing her.)

Many babies will have their ostomy closed when they are still in the hospital nursery. In the meantime, parents usually can learn, by watching the nurses, how to clean and protect the delicate skin around the ostomy, while changing the bag. If your baby is discharged earlier, when she still has an ostomy, you can be sure that you'll be instructed carefully and thoroughly on how to take care of her at home.

The surgery to reconnect your baby's bowel (called an enterostomy closure, or "take down"), is a simple procedure from which babies recover very rapidly—usually in a few days or less (much quicker than from NEC surgery). Most of the

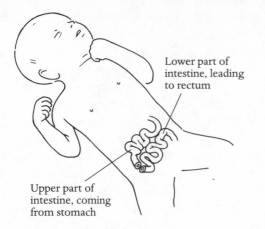

Lower part of
intestine, leading
to rectum

Upper part of
intestine, coming
from stomach

After the area of intestine damaged by NEC has been re-
moved, the two open ends may not be rejoined immediately,
to promote healing.

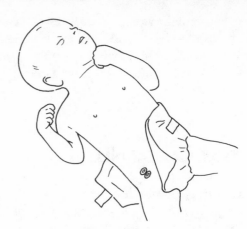

The two open ends of the intestine are brought out through
the skin of the belly, forming an enterostomy.

time, the surgeon can go in through the previous incision, so your baby won't have additional scars.

A different procedure for some babies

Sometimes, if a baby with NEC is extremely premature and sick, her doctors may believe that the stress of surgery would be too much for her. In that case, her surgeon may do an initial, simpler procedure called peritoneal drainage. It can be performed in her bed in the NICU, under local anesthesia.

The surgeon will make a small incision on each side of your baby's belly, and insert a soft tube, called a "drain," that goes into your baby's abdomen and comes out through her skin. The tube allows gas, infected fluid, and stool to drain out, lowering the pressure in your baby's belly, and helping the inflammation to ease. Most babies, once they're more stable, will still undergo definitive surgery for their NEC. But a few babies treated with peritoneal drainage recover completely, and don't need further surgery.

Outcome and possible complications

Surgery to treat NEC is very effective in stopping the disease. The overall survival rate after NEC surgery is about 70%. (That figure reflects the average outcome of large numbers of babies, including those who are extremely premature and very ill. Bigger babies, especially those who weigh more than 1,000 grams, and those who aren't as sick, tend to do even better.)

How quickly your own baby recovers after NEC surgery, and how well she'll do in the long run, will depend on how advanced her illness was before the operation, and the amount of healthy bowel she has left. Right after surgery, your baby's doctors will be able to make more precise predictions about her outcome. Babies who lose more than half of their intestine are at risk for a condition called "short-bowel syndrome," and may need intravenous nutrition for a very long time. (If you are told that your preemie may have short-bowel syndrome, you can read a little more about it on page 240, and your doctors will explain what you can expect for your child.) Most babies will have an adequate amount of intestine left, and once they fully recover from their NEC, will be able to eat and grow normally.

The most common short-term complications of NEC surgery are infection and bleeding, especially if some of your baby's fragile bowel develops new tears in it. Some babies with enterostomies don't grow well temporarily, and have metabolic disturbances, because their upper intestinal tract is too short to absorb enough nutrients. These problems usually resolve when their bowel is reconnected. About 20% of babies will develop an intestinal stricture—a narrowing of the bowel due to scar tissue—after NEC surgery. A stricture usually shows up as feeding intolerance or a bowel obstruction, and can be diagnosed by x-ray, using a special dye. Intestinal strictures are easily removed surgically, with a much simpler operation than your baby's original NEC surgery.

Recovery and healing

A preemie who has just had NEC surgery is usually very sick. You can expect that your baby will be on a ventilator for several days or more after the operation, as she slowly recovers from her illness and the surgery. Your baby's doctors and nurses may notice the happy signs that she's getting better sooner than you do, because her laboratory values will improve, and she'll need less intensive medical support, before she begins to look visibly better.

You should be prepared for your baby to have a lot of swelling all over her body, which will get worse for a couple of days, but then should gradually get better over about a week or so. She will continue to receive antibiotics until any infection is adequately treated (usually about two weeks), and won't be given anything to eat except intravenous nutrition until her intestines have begun to heal. The doctors will be watching for the return of her bowel function, which will be heralded by her passing stool (the nurses will proudly display it to you in her ostomy bag or diaper!), and a clearing of the bile that is being drained out of her stomach.

When the doctors think your baby is ready to eat again, they will reintroduce feedings very slowly and cautiously, using small volumes of a "predigested" formula or diluted breast milk. Most infants after NEC surgery don't absorb nutrients well, because it takes time for their intestines to fully recover, and because many will have ostomies, so they will be using only part of their intestines for a while. Your baby's feedings will be gradually advanced as she shows that she can tolerate them.

In general, you should be prepared for some fits and starts on the road to full feedings. But despite the terrifying experience of undergoing NEC surgery, unless your preemie has other lingering complications of prematurity, her long-term outlook is good.

SURGERY TO PLACE A BROVIAC CATHETER OR OTHER CENTRAL VENOUS LINE

Why it may be needed

Premature babies who need intravenous nutrition or medications for more than a couple of weeks may benefit from having a Broviac catheter or other central venous line. (Broviac is the brand most commonly used, but there are many other, equally good ones.) This is simply an intravenous catheter that is designed to be surgically inserted in a central (meaning major) blood vessel, and used long-term. These catheters have the advantage of being stable and less likely to be dislodged, and are painless and convenient to use. Moreover, substances like high-calorie intravenous nutrition and some antibiotics, which could damage smaller and more fragile blood vessels, can be infused through them.

How surgery to place a central venous catheter is performed

Insertion of a Broviac or other central venous catheter is a minor surgical procedure. It can be performed in the operating room under general anesthesia, or at a baby's bedside in the NICU. If it's done at her bedside, your baby will be immobilized, using medication or soft restraints, and will be given medicine that calms her and prevents pain. The surgeon will locate a large vein, generally in your baby's chest or neck, although her legs may be used, too. He'll make a small incision, and put a soft plastic catheter into her vein, then carefully thread it forward so that its tip is in the correct position, in a very large blood vessel near her heart, or in the upper chamber of the heart itself. A soft cuff on the Broviac will be stitched under your baby's skin, where the catheter comes out, to hold it securely in place.

Outcome and possible complications

Surgery to place a central venous catheter is usually very safe, even in small and sick preemies. A chest x-ray will be done immediately after the procedure, to confirm that the tip of the Broviac is in the right place, and make sure that no accidental tears were made in the lung nearby. The main, possible complications for a baby from having a central venous line, both of which usually can be adequately treated, are infection (if the infection can't be cleared with antibiotics, the line would have to be removed), and formation of blood clots in the catheter, which could block the line, or possibly travel to other spots in the body, and cause some damage.

Recovery and healing

Recovery is usually very rapid. Often by the time your baby is back in the NICU, or fully awake, she's back to her old self—with just a new bandage and a different kind of IV line to show for her surgical experience. Most babies aren't bothered by the soft catheter, and after awhile, most parents barely notice it's there. Best of all, your baby will be spared the pain of frequent needle sticks to put in new IVs. When she doesn't need a central line anymore, the catheter can be removed in just a few minutes at your baby's bedside. Eventually, she'll have only a small scar.

SURGERY TO TREAT HYDROCEPHALUS

Why it may be needed

When a baby has hydrocephalus (see page 168), the buildup of fluid inside her skull can put pressure on her brain, and eventually damage it. If your baby's doctors find that her hydrocephalus is getting worse instead of better over time, or if it is putting enough pressure on her brain to cause problems with her breathing or heart rate, they will want to drain off some of the excess fluid to relieve the pressure. The most effective long-term treatment for hydrocephalus is a VP (short for ventriculo-peritoneal) shunt. A VP shunt is a small plastic tube, inserted surgically, which carries excess fluid from the ventricles in the brain, where it builds up, to the inside of the abdomen (or peritoneum), where it can be reabsorbed.

Most of the time, in preemies, a VP shunt insertion is not an emergency. That's because their open skull bones can diffuse the increasing pressure by simply letting their heads expand. Surgery to place a VP shunt can often be postponed for several days or even weeks, until the doctors are certain that it's necessary, and a preemie is big and strong enough for a shunt to be inserted safely.

How a VP shunt insertion is performed

A VP shunt insertion, in the hands of an experienced pediatric neurosurgeon, is a simple and safe procedure. It affects only a very small area of the brain, and carries almost no risk of damaging your baby's brain functions. It is always done under general anesthesia, with your baby on a ventilator. The operation usually lasts an hour or two.

There are several types of shunts: your neurosurgeon will choose the one he thinks is best suited for your baby. The upper end of the shunt is placed into one of your baby's ventricles, by passing it through a small, crescent-shaped incision on the top or side of her scalp, then through a tiny hole in her skull. The surgeon then takes the rest of the shunt tubing, and tunnels it just underneath her skin—passing behind one ear, down the side of her neck and chest, to reach her belly. There, the surgeon makes a very small incision below her ribs, so that he can insert the lower end of the shunt through the tissues of her belly, into her abdomen. He'll coil some extra tubing inside, too, to make sure the lower tip of the VP shunt stays in her abdomen (where it needs to be for the fluid coming from the ventricles to be absorbed), as long as possible, as she grows.

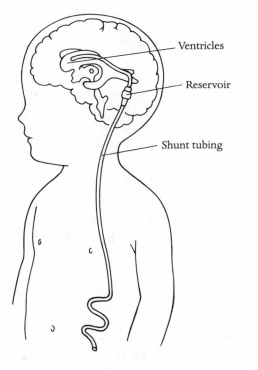

Ventricles

Reservoir

Shunt tubing

The upper end of a VP shunt, placed inside one of the ventricles, drains out the cerebrospinal fluid and carries it through long tubing into the abdomen, where it is reabsorbed.

An important component of a VP shunt is the reservoir, or bubble. You'll notice it as a small bump underneath your baby's scalp, near her incision. The reservoir contains a valve, which controls the amount of cerebrospinal fluid that flows through the shunt, and ensures that it doesn't drain too quickly or too slowly. The valve can also be used by the neurosurgeon to assess the functioning of the VP shunt.

Other surgical treatments for hydrocephalus

Hydrocephalus in preemies is most often a consequence of an intraventricular hemorrhage, and is due to blood clots or scarring that obstruct the flow or the reabsorption of cerebrospinal

Adapted with permission of author Elizabeth Ahmann and illustrator Teresa Ahmann from *Home Care for the High Risk Infant: A Family-Centered Approach*, 2nd ed., Figure 18-2, p. 271; Aspen Publishers (1996, Gaithersburg, MD)

fluid. Some preemies are too small or too sick when they develop hydrocephalus to have a VP shunt placed, or the surgeon may want to wait for a few weeks, until there's less blood and protein in the ventricles, to see if a baby's hydrocephalus will resolve.

Temporary drainage of fluid to relieve hydrocephalus can be done with a simpler procedure, called a ventriculostomy. There are various techniques, which involve either placing a tube in your baby's ventricle and draining the excess cerebrospinal fluid into a plastic bag, or inserting a small reservoir, or "tapping chamber," under her skin, where the fluid can easily be withdrawn by the doctor with a needle and syringe.

Sometimes, temporary drainage is all it takes, and a preemie never needs a VP shunt. But if permanent treatment for your baby's hydrocephalus is needed, the neurosurgeon can easily close her ventriculostomy later, when she is bigger and stronger, and put in a VP shunt.

Outcome and possible complications

A VP shunt is nearly always successful in treating a preemie's hydrocephalus when it is put in. Shunt malfunctions, leading to a recurrence of hydrocephalus, and shunt infections, are the most common complications after VP shunt insertion. A shunt malfunction can occur soon after surgery if the tubing becomes blocked by blood cells and debris from the hemorrhage that caused the hydrocephalus, or if the tip lodges in the tissue or wall of the ventricle. A shunt malfunction can also occur months or years later, if the tubing breaks, or if a child gets so tall that the lower tip is no longer in her abdomen. A malfunctioning shunt requires another surgery (called a shunt revision) to change or fix the system.

Most shunt infections occur around the time of surgery: 70% of them within two months of the VP shunt insertion. Infections are serious because they can affect the brain, and because they can lead to a shunt malfunction if bacteria and other inflammatory debris obstruct the tube. If a shunt infection can't be cleared within a few days by antibiotics alone, the shunt will have to be removed surgically (bacteria can hide in the tubing, where antibiotics can't reach them). After the infection is successfully treated, your child will have a second surgery to put in a new VP shunt.

Most neurosurgeons will not place a VP shunt in a preemie who weighs less than 1,200 to 1,500 grams. Complications are more common in the smallest babies, because their delicate tissues don't stand up as well to surgical manipulation, their skin is thin and easily irritated by the shunt tubing, and their immune systems aren't as strong in fighting off infections.

Your baby's long-term developmental outcome will depend more on other factors than on factors related to his surgery. The overall statistics are that 50% of preemies with VP shunts who don't have visible brain injuries on their head ultrasounds are normal. Only a small group of infants less than 1,250 grams have good outcomes, unfortunately. Some of the considerations are the grade and extent of the intraventricular hemorrhage that caused his hydrocephalus, the presence of visible brain injuries on his head ultrasound (see page 284), the timing of the VP shunt insertion (waiting too long can be dangerous), episodes of shunt infection or malfunction (which sometimes, but not always, can worsen a child's neurological development), his size at surgery, whether he has additional medical problems, and how he has developed so far. You should keep in mind that many preemies who need a VP shunt have normal intellectual development. If they have a long-term developmental problem, it is more likely to affect their fine and gross motor skills, and the impact can be severe or mild.

Recovery and healing

Your baby will come back from the operating room to the NICU, probably still asleep and on a ventilator. He will be given antibiotics to prevent infections, and medications to keep him from feeling pain. Don't be scared if his head looks strange, with a patch of hair shaved off and sunken fontanels, because that's normal and just temporary. You'll probably see its shape change a lot in the next weeks and months. Very soon, the bump of the reservoir and the tubing under his skin, which may seem prominent to you initially, will become less visible, as your baby puts on some weight and his hair grows. By the time he's a toddler, his shunt will be practically invisible.

Most likely, your child will need his VP shunt for the rest of his life. A very few children eventually outgrow the need for a shunt, as their ability to drain or reabsorb cerebrospinal fluid improves. But since removing a shunt requires an operation, which is much more dangerous than leaving the shunt in, doctors don't test for that, and don't plan on electively removing a VP shunt.

Many preemies recover quickly after a VP shunt insertion, and in two or three days are markedly more stable, alert, and active than before their surgery. Seven to ten days after the surgery, your baby's stitches will be taken out. Many preemies, by that time, are already out of the intensive care unit, and doing great.

SURGERY TO TREAT GE REFLUX

Why it may be needed

Usually, medical treatment and other measures are effective in keeping GE (gastroesophageal) reflux under control (see page 244). But for babies who have the most severe, persistent reflux, surgery may be the best route. Serious GE

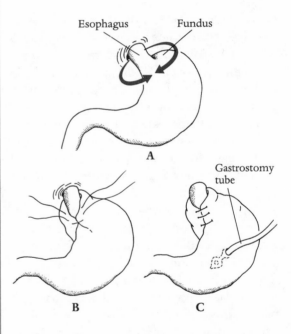

A: The fundus, the rounded upper part of the stomach, is wrapped around the esophagus.

B: A valve is created by securing the fundus with sutures.

C: A gastrostomy tube can be placed in the stomach, to help recovery and feeding.

Adapted with permission from Schatzlein MH: Gastroesophageal Reflux In Infants and Children, *Archives of Surgery* 114:505–510, © American Medical Association 1979

reflux can trigger potentially life-threatening episodes of apnea, bradycardia, and wheezing. A baby who spits up food in her airways can suffer from recurrent pneumonias, and the chronic inflammation in her lungs can make her breathing worsen over time. The acid from her stomach can also irritate the lining of her esophagus, causing pain, bleeding, and anemia, and feeding problems. And if a child vomits a lot, it can cut down on her food intake, impairing her growth.

How surgery for GE reflux is performed

The surgical procedure to treat GE reflux is called a fundoplication. There are different techniques, the most common of which is a Nissen fundoplication. It is usually performed under general anesthesia, with your baby on a ventilator.

The surgeon makes an incision in your baby's belly, over her stomach. He then wraps the round upper lobe of the stomach (the fundus) around her esophagus, and secures it with sutures (see illustration). As a result, a valve is created. Food can go down her esophagus and into her stomach while your baby eats and her stomach is relaxed. But after a meal, when the pressure inside her stomach increases as it grinds up food and propels it into the intestine, the part of the stomach wrapped around the esophagus pinches the esophagus shut and prevents food from backing up, keeping it in the stomach and intestines where it safely belongs.

Most babies who get a fundoplication will also have a gastrostomy tube (or "g-tube") placed in their stomach as part of the procedure (see illustration). Keep in mind that a g-tube is usually only a temporary measure, to help a baby recover from surgery and to make sure she is feeding and growing well afterward. After a fundoplication, the g-tube will help relieve gas pressure inside your baby's stomach, since as long as the fundoplication is working, she won't be able to vomit, and while there's still some swelling and the wrap is tight, she won't be able to burp. After several days, the g-tube can also be used for feeding, until your baby is ready to take in as much food or milk as she needs, by mouth.

A simpler procedure: placing a g-tube alone

Some older preemies, who have feeding difficulties and can't get enough nutrition by mouth to grow well, may need a temporary gastrostomy tube even without a fundoplication. In that case, the procedure to insert a g-tube is much simpler; it involves only a very small incision in your baby's stomach, and can sometimes even be done under local anesthesia in the NICU. (If an older preemie who has been discharged home needs to have a g-tube placed, he may not even be hospitalized at the time of surgery, and can go home right after it.) Although most parents are initially upset by the idea of a g-tube, once they see how their child's growth is boosted by it, they feel better about it.

Outcome and possible complications

GE reflux is successfully treated by a fundoplication in the vast majority (about 90%) of babies who don't have other abnormalities. How much your baby's overall condition improves after surgery—for example, whether she stops wheezing or having apnea—depends on how much the GE reflux was contributing to her medical problems. Most of the time, you'll see some immediate improvement, followed by more gradual progress over the next several weeks to months.

Like all surgical procedures, a fundoplication carries some risks. The chance that your baby will die from the operation is very low, one to two percent, and is actually not related directly to the surgery, but to other problems that some babies with reflux have. Any patient who has had abdominal surgery can develop a bowel obstruction sometime in the future, from scar tissue blocking the intestine. Complications specific to a fundoplication are gas bloat syndrome—an excessive accumulation of gas in the stomach, which can last for several weeks after surgery, but usually improves on its own; poor feeding for a while, possibly because a tightly wrapped stomach can make eating uncomfortable; leaking and irritation around the g-tube; and a loosening of the wrap over time, so that symptoms of GE reflux return. Children who have neurological impairments are more likely to have complications from the procedure, including a recurrence of GE reflux requiring a second operation later. Fortunately, the majority of babies won't have any of these complications.

Recovery and healing

Most preemies stay on a ventilator for at least several days after a fundoplication. To keep your baby comfortable, the nurses will be giving her pain relief medication, and will drain gas and fluid out of her stomach through the gastrostomy tube. After a couple of days, the doctors will try closing the g-tube, to see if she can pass stomach secretions and gas through her bowel on her own. If she can, then they'll begin putting some milk in her stomach, through the g-tube, gradually increasing the amount at each feeding. When she seems ready and willing, she'll be offered some food by mouth, too. Some babies who were eating well before surgery are back up to their full feedings within a week or so. Others, especially those who weren't nippling on their own before, can take several weeks or longer before they get the hang of eating by themselves.

Your baby's gastrostomy tube will probably be left in for a few months, until she is growing well, with no signs of gas bloat or the need to supplement her nutrition with tube feedings. As a result, your preemie may be discharged from the hospital with the tube still in place. Don't worry: you'll be instructed on how to take care of it, and what to do if the tube is accidentally dislodged. After a few weeks, most g-tubes can be replaced with a gastrostomy "button": a small valve that sticks out of your baby's stomach just a little bit beyond her skin. It's better looking than a g-tube, and much more comfortable for her to wear and you to care for.

When the time comes to close your child's gastrostomy, the surgeons can do it with a minor procedure, from which she should recover very rapidly. Your child will have a couple of scars on her belly—but she'll get great relief in return.

SURGERY TO TREAT ROP

Why surgery for ROP may be needed

The first line of treatment for ROP—laser therapy or cryotherapy (see page 271)—can greatly lower the risk that a baby's retina will pull away (or "detach") from the wall of her eye and result in a severe loss of vision. But if, despite treatment, your baby's retina does detach, there are some surgical procedures that may help restore some of her sight. They are called *scleral buckling* and *vitrectomy,* and each is a way of repairing a retinal detachment.

How a scleral buckle is performed

A scleral buckle is called that because the procedure involves placing a band of silicone, like a belt, around the sclera (the white of the eye). While your baby is under general anesthesia, the ophthalmologist puts the band of silicone in place, and tightens it until the wall of her eye is brought close enough to the detached retina for it to reattach itself. For the procedure to work, your baby's retina, although detached, still has to be fairly close to the wall of her eye.

Outcome and possible complications

A scleral buckle is effective in reattaching the retina in about 70% of babies, although good vision is restored in somewhat fewer, about 50%. It can take a few months to know whether your baby's retina has successfully reattached, as hoped, or not. Although the thought of eye surgery is scary for parents, it is reassuring to know that complications from a scleral buckle are extremely rare.

Recovery and healing

After a scleral buckle, your baby will get pain medicine, and for a day or two she will probably remain on a ventilator. Her eye will be covered with a special ointment containing antibiotics and steroids, to prevent infection and to limit inflammation, and will be patched overnight. When the patch is removed the following day, you'll notice some swelling and redness, but within a few days, these should disappear, and your baby's eye will look fine.

About six months later, after her retina has had ample time to reattach, your baby will have another surgery to cut or remove the belt around her eye. This is usually a quick procedure, with a shorter recovery time than the first one, and is necessary so that your baby's eye can grow normally.

If a scleral buckle doesn't work, or if it can't be done because your baby's retina has pulled too far away from the back of her eye, there is another option: a procedure called a vitrectomy.

How a vitrectomy is performed

A vitrectomy is also performed under general anesthesia. The surgeon opens up your baby's eye, and removes some of the jelly-like substance that fills it (called the vitreous humor), so he can reach the detached portion of her retina. He then cuts out the scar tissue that is pulling on the retina and causing its detachment. That allows the retina to lie back against the wall of the eye. Finally, he injects a material into her eye to substitute for the vitreous humor that was taken out.

Outcome and possible complications

The retina reattaches in 30 to 40% of babies who have vitrectomies, but useful vision is restored in only 10 to 15%. Still, without surgery, there is no hope for visual recovery, so a vitrectomy gives your baby a chance to achieve that. Complications are rare—just a small chance of bleeding or infection.

The younger your preemie is when she undergoes the procedure, the more sight you can hope for, because her retina, most likely, has not been detached for long. (Studies indicate that this is an important factor in the success of a vitrectomy.) Restoring even a little vision, for instance enough to discriminate stationary objects from objects in motion, or to perceive light, can be crucially important in helping a child to become independent.

Recovery and healing

Recovery after a vitrectomy usually takes longer than after scleral buckling. Antibiotic and steroid ointment will be placed on your baby's eye, and she will wear an eye patch. To allow her retina to heal better, she may need to lie facedown for about 48 hours following surgery. Because retinal reattachment can take several months, your child will get regular eye exams in the weeks and months after her surgery, to check on the recovery of her eye and the success of the operation.

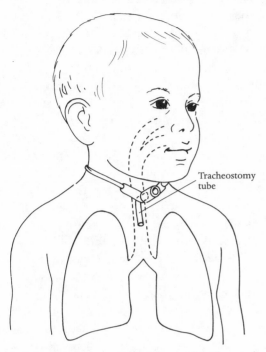

Tracheostomy tube

The L-shaped tracheostomy tube is inserted in the windpipe through a small incision in the neck.

TRACHEOSTOMY

Why it may be needed

When it becomes clear that a premature baby will be on a ventilator for many more weeks or months (usually because of BPD), or when there's an obstruction of her airway that needs to be bypassed (usually because of scarring from an endotracheal tube, or because her upper airway is weak, and collapses inward when she takes a deep breath), her doctors will consider giving her a tracheostomy. A "trach," as it is called for short, is an opening in the neck,

through which a ventilation tube is inserted directly into your baby's windpipe (trachea).

A tracheostomy will allow your baby to be free of the endotracheal tube that is now taped to her face, and is passing through her nose or mouth and throat. Finally, she will be able to practice all kinds of facial expressions (including smiling at you!), to eat through her mouth, to freely move her head around and discover the world, and eventually to sit up and move around, despite needing a ventilator. All of those experiences, which are crucial for an infant's normal development, are severely limited by having an oral or nasal endotracheal tube. If your baby is getting a tracheostomy, you can look at it as a developmental step forward, truly in her best interest, despite the anxiety that surgery may cause you. And it's reassuring to know that a trach doesn't have to be permanent. As soon as a child no longer needs it, her tracheostomy can be closed.

How a tracheostomy is performed

A tracheostomy is a delicate but quick procedure, performed under general anesthesia. The surgeon first makes a small, horizontal incision near the base of your baby's neck. He sews two strings, called "stay sutures" on each side of her windpipe, and makes an even smaller vertical incision between them. Pulling on those sutures widens the incision in the trachea to form a small hole, through which the surgeon inserts the tracheostomy tube, and connects it to the ventilator. As you can see in the illustration, a tracheostomy tube is L-shaped, and is secured by "trach ties," or strings, tied around your baby's neck. The long threads of the two stay sutures are brought out of the incision and taped to your baby's chest. They are important until her tracheostomy has completely healed: if her trach tube is accidentally dislodged, gently pulling on those sutures will reopen her windpipe enough to reinsert a new tube.

Outcome and possible complications

A tracheostomy is nearly always successful, and fortunately, surgical complications are rare. They include an accidental tear in the nearby lung, which usually heals in a few days, and injury to the vocal cords or airway. If your baby's trach tube is accidentally dislodged in the first week after surgery, before her neck and airway have completely healed, and her doctors are unable to reinsert it safely and quickly, they may have to temporarily re-intubate her through her nose or mouth. (Once her tracheostomy has healed, this isn't a problem, as the trach tube should slide easily in and out of her windpipe.)

Infections of the windpipe and lungs are more common in children with tracheostomies. The most serious complication can occur if a baby's trach tube gets blocked with mucus and isn't promptly cleaned out. Any child who has a tracheostomy is dependent on the tube staying open, so air can flow through it in and out of her lungs. If the tube gets blocked, she could suffocate. (To make sure that doesn't happen, the nurses will carefully suction your baby's trach tube every few hours, and will replace it with a fresh one weekly. You'll be taught how to suction and replace your baby's tube, too.)

Although you've probably been aching to hear your baby's voice, at first you still won't hear her cry or talk. Eventually, most children who need to keep their tracheostomies for more than a year or two do learn to talk around the tube, but they tend to be delayed in their speech, understanding more than they can express. Once your child's tracheostomy is removed, her language skills should rapidly catch up.

Recovery and healing

Most babies are kept immobile and heavily sedated for about a week after a tracheostomy, so they don't move their heads or arms and accidentally dislodge the tube. At that point, when the tracheostomy has usually healed and a good track formed, the surgeon will take out the trach tube and change it for a clean, new one, and remove the stay sutures. From then on, your baby's trach tube will be changed regularly, about once a week. If your preemie goes home with a tracheostomy, you'll be taught how to take care of it, and what to do if her tube gets blocked or dislodged. Many families will have some home nursing support for several hours a day or more initially, until they get used to taking care of their baby by themselves at home.

Remember that a tracheostomy, although demanding to live with, is almost always a temporary measure, to allow your child to grow and develop as normally as possible, while her lungs and airways heal. Within a couple of years, and often before their first birthdays, most premature babies no longer need their tracheostomies. When that happy time comes for your child, her doctors will schedule an elective surgery at your convenience, to remove her tracheostomy. The opening in her windpipe and the hole in the skin of her neck will be closed, leaving only a small scar, which will be hardly visible to those who don't know it's there.

SURGERY TO REPAIR A HERNIA

Why it may be needed

An inguinal hernia (see page 248) occurs when loops of intestine—or sometimes in girls, an ovary and fallopian tube—slip down from the abdomen where they belong, through an open canal into the groin. Having a hernia doesn't usually cause a baby any discomfort, but it's dangerous, because the bowel could suddenly get stuck ("incarcerated") down there, resulting in a bowel obstruction, which carries with it a high risk of infection and damage to the intestines, testicle, or ovary.

Surgical repair is the only available treatment for an inguinal hernia. If your preemie's hernia is not incarcerated, surgery will be scheduled when he is stable, and big enough for the operation to be done safely and successfully. If the hernia is incarcerated, the operation becomes urgent. Since repair of an incarcerated hernia carries different risks and requires a more demanding procedure, you should rely on your baby's doctors for more specific information about it.

How a hernia repair is performed

An uncomplicated hernia repair can be performed under general or regional anesthesia. (With regional anesthesia, a baby can breathe on his own and avoid being put on a ventilator; general anesthesia is a longer lasting and more guaranteed form of pain control.) If the hernia is incarcerated, general anesthesia will be used. The surgeon makes an incision in the fold of skin at the base of your baby's belly, right above his groin on the affected side. He locates the open hernia sac, makes sure it's free of the bowel, testis, or ovary, and then cuts the sac and sews it closed.

If you want your preemie circumcised, it can be done conveniently and painlessly at the same time as a hernia repair. You can ask your baby's doctors about that possibility.

Outcome and possible complications

A hernia repair is a very safe and effective operation, with zero mortality. Any early surgical complications that arise—bleeding, infection, or apnea from the anesthesia—are usually mild and treatable. Occasionally, the hernia recurs, either because the canal could not be completely closed during the surgery, or because a child has a medical condition (like BPD or a VP shunt), that causes increased pressure in the abdomen, and pushes the intestines down. Baby boys have a small risk of being found with a smaller than normal testicle after a hernia repair, or of future infertility, due to an injury to the sperm duct. All of these complications are more likely after surgery for an incarcerated hernia than for an uncomplicated one.

Recovery and healing

Recovery is usually very fast after a hernia repair, even if the hernia was incarcerated. Most preemies who were well before the operation are alert and eating several hours later, and Tylenol is enough to ease their pain. You'll notice some swelling and redness of your baby's groin, which will resolve in a few days. There usually aren't any stitches to remove, just some "steri-strips," or tiny bandages, to peel off when his wound is healed. His scar will turn into a thin, barely visible line.

After a hernia repair, a premature baby will be observed closely in the hospital for postoperative apnea for forty-eight hours. Former preemies often have their hernias repaired as outpatients.

Part
III

A LIFE TOGETHER

7

Finally Taking Your Baby Home

▶ *Decisions and preparations for the moment you've been waiting for.*

THE PARENTS' PERSPECTIVE   330

THE DOCTOR'S PERSPECTIVE   333

QUESTIONS AND ANSWERS

Preemie-Proofing   338
Diapers and Clothing   340
Choosing a Pediatrician   341
The End of Apnea   343
Car Seat   343
If You Want to Take Your Preemie on
   an Airplane   345
CPR   346
Home Nursing Care   347
House Rules for Home Nurses   349
Getting Acquainted With: Home Oxygen   350
Giving Medications   357
Reflux   358
Special Formula or Breast Milk   360
Obsessed with Baby's Weight   362
Whom to Call with Questions   363
Missing the NICU   363

Older Siblings   364
Questions about Your Baby's Age   365
Daycare   366
The Right Stimulation   367
If You Are Adopting a Preemie   369
Fussiness   373
Is Baby Remembering Pain?   376
Baby's Appearance   377
Do Preemies Have Scars?   378
Shouldn't I Feel Happier?   379
Feeling Protective   380
Parental Responses That Are of
   More Concern   380

MULTIPLES

One Twin Home Earlier   382
Daily Schedule for Multiples   383

IN DEPTH

The Cardiorespiratory Monitor: A Noisy
   Companion for Weeks to Come   385

The Parents' Perspective: Finally Taking Your Baby Home

By the time of discharge, most families have adjusted to the unusual task of caring for their infant in the hospital. The huge effort and fatigue involved may feel to them like a fair price to pay to keep their baby safe. So, when they are told that they can take their baby home, some parents react with incredulity. Happiness mixes with anxiety. They leave the hospital with their baby, delight and relief on their faces. But what they have lived through in the NICU can't easily be left behind.

I don't know these young parents' names, but I know their preemies: Eddie and Eve, who have been sharing my daughter's nursery room for many weeks. They are popular babies here in the hospital, beloved by some nurses. And I have become fond of them, too, of their shiny eyes, the color and shape of coffee beans. Their parents, who both work, usually come in the evening, when I'm gone. But today they are both here, smiling, excited, and nervous, busily talking to doctors and nurses, trying to get everything in their heads. All parents, on discharge day, look like students who have to take the most important test of their lives. Today it's Eve's turn to go home, while Eddie still needs to stay. It's strange to see him feeding in his mother's arms, wearing his usual white hospital T-shirt—which makes all preemies look alike—while his sister, all dressed up in the cutest baby outfit, is napping in a car seat on the floor. Eve's already out of here. She might be taken for any other newborn leaving the hospital with her family, the day after delivery. But, to more experienced observers, this mother and father look different. Not as newly un-pregnant, not as innocently exultant, weary—but not as acutely exhausted. There's something about the way they hold that car seat that says there's so much already invested in this little baby lying here. After a last good-bye to Eddie in his isolette, his parents and sister are now leaving. A nurse tells them it won't be long before Eddie can go home, too. She also says the same about my daughter. But until that day arrives for your baby, you don't let yourself picture it, you don't feel entitled to believe it. You never know.

For parents, taking their preemie home from the hospital is not only psychologically demanding, it involves practical difficulties as well. Their schedules, their housing arrangement, their health, their jobs—all may pose problems. In some cases, guilt about the premature birth and its effects on the rest of the family can compound these obstacles.

"We're not ready!" This is what I should have told the doctor today. Instead, I said, "Oh, great!" on hearing the news that they will discharge my daughter Gillian tomorrow, six days before Christmas. She's been doing so well lately, every day putting a little weight on her still diminutive frame. As a result, she's coming home much earlier than anybody would have predicted three months ago when she was born, an extremely premature baby. Now we're so relieved and proud of her, we're looking forward to taking her home with us. But for this Christmas . . . well, my wife and I had other plans. We wanted to make up to Cooper for all that Gillian's birth has taken away from his life. Cooper is our older boy, six

years old. He has spent weeks with relatives and friends, been picked up in the evenings by parents who have just come back from the hospital, without any energy or cheerfulness left for play and bedtime stories. After all that, Cooper deserves the best Christmas ever. But how are we going to manage it now? How can we do the rest of the shopping, bake cookies, decorate the tree, pack all the presents, cook for the relatives and friends we wanted to be here for Santa's arrival (I haven't even rented the costume yet!) if Gillian comes home? Maybe we're ungrateful, I know. But this Christmas was meant to be only Cooper's.

All of the mixed emotions parents may feel at the time of discharge usually melt into a sea of joy, an immense sense of blessing, when they actually take their premature baby home, into their life. The hardships of the recent past make every sensation clearer, and stronger.

Now that, for the first time, I'm stepping into our doorway holding you in my arms, my baby, I feel the intensity of this moment, I know its meaning. This is your home, where we have been missing you so badly, for long weeks after your rushed birth. Look, this is the phone we feared we might hear ring in the night, calling us back to the NICU. This is your parents' bed and your father's shoulder, where you can be consoled, cuddle, and nap. This is the hand of your grandmother, who has finally arrived from far away to touch you. Here there's no hurry, no sharp noises, no smell of alcohol. This is the sound of our voices, of our family life. This is your mother's breast you couldn't latch onto in the hospital. There was no privacy there, there were too many worries to deal with first, and we did. Now you can take your time getting acquainted with this breast: it belongs to you, with the milk coming from it. This is how you breastfeed, my baby. I knew you would be able to do it, here at home. This is how we all rejoice.

Leaving the hospital nursery to head into family life involves another major change for already stressed parents, who may have little resilience left. Particularly in the first days and weeks at home, some parents find caring for their preemie a truly overwhelming responsibility. Anxiety about the baby's condition and demands can grow out of control without the safety net of the medical staff.

Ted has been home for one week now. The much expected moment has come and gone, leaving me all alone with him—his father travels a lot. The weather is bad, I can't take him out, and it's best that friends don't come to see him yet, keeping their germs and colds away. I feel too tired to have visitors anyway! When I should sleep, I'm half-awake, ready to jump up at the first shrill of the apnea monitor. It's ringing two or three times a night, all false alarms so far. But sooner or later a real one will come. What if I shake Ted and he doesn't breathe? Will I be able to do CPR, if he needs it? I read the instructions they gave me, trying to memorize the steps I performed on a doll. But I can't concentrate, I can't remember. Then, although he's feeding, I can't tell if Ted is growing. To me, he looks as if he's getting smaller. But maybe that's because of his big clothes. I remember how good and reassuring it felt to hear the nurse announcing Ted's weight gain each day. Our pediatrician visit is next week. In the meantime, maybe I can go back to the hospital to weigh him again, as I already did once. The nurses were so happy to see us! They put a scale for us in the family room, since you can't take babies from outside into the nursery. How weird that Ted could not go back to where he lived for so long! He was safe there. I felt safe, too. Could it be possible that I'm missing the NICU?

Going home with a premature baby also means facing the world together for the first time. Your baby may not fit other people's expectations about how big an infant should be for her age. To avoid telling their stories to total strangers, for the sake of privacy as well as simplicity, many parents of preemies eventually try a shortcut. Nothing's wrong with that. But you should first test your new version with some predictable questions you may be asked. And stick to it, consistently, to the end.

—*Hi! I haven't seen you in a looong time! How are you? Is this your baby in the carriage? A girl, I assume!*

—*Sure . . . this is our Melissa . . .*

—*She's so cute, so little and perfect . . . How many days?*

—*Mmmm . . . she's . . . over two weeks now. We've come home from the hospital exactly two weeks ago.*

—*Oh! You know, I thought somebody in the building told me she was born some time ago. But I must be wrong, she's obviously a new baby! How much did she weigh?*

—*She was . . . very small. She's now about six pounds.*

—*Really? She doesn't look that tiny . . . But she must be totally fine if they sent her home right away! Are you breastfeeding her?*

—*Yes. I breastfed her for six weeks, then I started supplementing her with formula . . .*

—*Six weeks? . . .*

—*What did I say? I'm sorry, of course I meant six days! Melissa doesn't let us sleep much . . . I think I'm losing my mind here. . . .*

After the trepidation, perplexity, and confusion of the initial time at home, parents begin to accept that things can now be normal, that their baby's well-being is under their control. Some of them even discover a new identity: the different person their baby's premature birth has made them.

I look at my baby sleeping in her bassinet, the phone rings and I don't answer, the clock ticks and I don't rush. Time had to be stretched before her birth, more had to be squeezed out of my life. For what, I think, had she not survived? All that mattered before is still appealing, but with a paler tint, there in the background. How will I do without my eager grip on the world? How am I going to balance this unreserved love I never felt before? My friends find me well and seem surprised, knowing the peaks of anguish I climbed when my baby was born, sick and small. I look at myself in the mirror, and wonder why pain doesn't leave more visible traces. Inside, I'm more aware now, yet detached, as if nothing could ever hurt me anymore. I've reached the top already, and returned. My baby's sleeping quietly. I'm at peace.

The Doctor's Perspective:
Finally Taking Your Baby Home*

It's the question parents ask most often: "When will my baby come home?" And it makes me wish I had a crystal ball! Usually, I tell parents to expect that their baby will come home around his due date. But it's not until certain things start—and stop—happening, that we really know the momentous day is nigh. Here's what we're looking for before saying that joyful good-bye, and great good luck, to you and your baby.

PHYSICAL EXAM AND LABORATORY ASSESSMENT

To discharge your baby home, we need to be certain she's outgrown the problems of prematurity that require skilled nursing care or a doctor's immediate intervention. That means, above all, that your baby's vital signs (her blood pressure, temperature, breathing, and heart rate) are consistently normal. We monitor babies to make sure of that, gradually tapering off the frequency and kinds of monitoring we do, as a preemie becomes more stable.

The first thing to go is usually blood pressure checks. Once healthy preemies without blood pressure problems are out of intensive care, we usually stop checking their blood pressure routinely, as we expect it to remain normal. A baby who's been off oxygen for a week or so usually no longer needs continuous monitoring of her oxygen saturation. (It will be checked if there's a problem.) When a preemie has been out of an isolette, and warm and comfortable in an open bassinet for a day or two, we stop monitoring her temperature so frequently, and just check it a few times a day. Most preemies will remain on a cardiorespiratory monitor to detect changes in their breathing or heart rate patterns until they're close to discharge. But if your baby has stayed in the hospital for reasons other than prematurity (say, she's convalescing but stable after surgery), even the cardiorespiratory monitor may be discontinued, and her vital signs checked just several times a day.

We'll also want to see that your baby is eating well enough to grow and thrive. She should be gaining an average of 15 to 30 grams (one-half to one ounce) a day—and doing that without heroic measures on the part of whoever is feeding her! A preemie who's a very slow eater usually just needs a little more time in the hospital to develop the alertness and skill she needs to take in enough nourishment.

Most preemies will continue to have their blood counts followed weekly until discharge, to make sure they're not getting too anemic. And babies who are on medication may need to have their blood drawn periodically, to make sure the doses remain appropriate as they grow.

---

*"The Doctor's Perspective" describes how your doctor may be thinking about your preemie's condition, and what she may be considering as she makes medical decisions. All of the medical terms and conditions mentioned here are described in more detail elsewhere in this book. Check the index.

Toward the end of her stay, our daily notes in the medical record will get shorter, and there may not be much of import in her condition to talk about. There's only so much you can say about a baby who's just growing! That's what we're looking to see—not much excitement, just some nice, boring days.

COMMON ISSUES AND DECISIONS

Apnea and bradycardia: Because "A's and B's" are often the last remnants of instability to go away before a preemie is ready to be discharged, parents often ask if their preemie should go home on an apnea monitor. You can read about home monitoring in this chapter on page 385, so I won't repeat it all here. Always, the decision to institute home monitoring is one that you and your baby's doctor would make together, after much discussion of the pros and cons.

Doctors' opinions about home monitoring differ, but most of the time, I would rather wait until a preemie outgrows her apnea before sending her home. Apnea of prematurity usually doesn't take much longer to go away after a preemie becomes able to eat on her own and maintain her body temperature—both of which have to occur before she's ready for discharge, anyway. Monitors are clumsy and inconvenient, not proven to do much good, and can increase parents' anxiety if the alarm goes off a lot. And I wouldn't want to send a baby home—apnea monitor or not—if it takes more than mild stimulation to get her to breathe again. (In the hospital nursery, she can get rapid and expert intervention if she needs it.)

There are some exceptions, though. Sometimes, a preemie's breathing pattern does take much longer to mature than her other vital func-

tions, and her apnea, although present, is mild. In that case, I think that the developmental benefits for her, and the increased ease for her family of being out of the hospital, probably outweigh the burdens of home monitoring. If a preemie is going home on medication for apnea, even if she hasn't had any A's or B's recently, I prefer to monitor her, because if the medicine is missed or her dosage outgrown, her apnea may worsen. And if you feel very strongly that you just couldn't sleep without your baby being on a monitor, after all she's been through, then I think it's probably worth it, for your peace of mind.

Another question we get asked a lot is whether a particular episode that a preemie has had "counts" as significant apnea or bradycardia or not—meaning, will it hold up her discharge home. Often, a preemie's last week in the hospital is spent counting down the days without apnea. (We want to see eight apnea-free days, to feel comfortable that her apnea of prematurity has truly resolved.) Not infrequently, there will be occasional blips on the monitor, or changes in her heart rate or breathing while she's eating, that make one wonder if her breathing pattern has sufficiently matured. The answer isn't always straightforward, and will depend on the circumstances and the judgment of your baby's doctor. In general, I consider an episode significant if a baby requires stimulation to start breathing again, or if her heart rate falls to less than 60 beats per minute. A's and B's that occur with feeding, because of spitting up or choking, I don't count. Babies tend to recover from these spontaneously and quickly, and whoever is feeding the baby at home will be watching her closely, and be able to help her out if need be.

BPD and home oxygen: Some preemies with BPD are actually quite well—growing nicely, their medical problems adequately treated, just needing some extra oxygen—and they can potentially be discharged home. But before that happens, there are several things I would need to determine. First, that your baby will be needing oxygen for at least a few more weeks—if not, it's not worth the effort and anxiety to set up oxygen at home. I'd try to judge that by looking at her breathing patterns and chest x-ray, together with how much oxygen she's currently getting and how rapidly it's been weaning. (Here's another time I wish I had that crystal ball!) Second, the amount of oxygen and medication she needs should be stable and predictable, so we can tell you what to give. Adjusting therapies up and down to respond to frequent or erratic changes in your baby's condition is not something you can do reliably at home. Third, your family and home must be suitable and safe. There should be adequate room to store the oxygen equipment, so it's not inadvertently knocked or spilled, and it's away from fire hazards. There should be no smoking in the house, because the oxygen is flammable—and because breathing second-hand cigarette smoke can significantly worsen your baby's respiration. Parents and caregivers must be willing and able to be trained to use the equipment, recognize and respond to signs of a problem, and provide CPR, if necessary. There must be a telephone in your home, in case of an emergency, and assurance of good follow-up care with a local pediatrician and a clinic for babies on oxygen. Finally, you must agree to accept some help from a home health care agency, who will supply the equipment, and periodically check on you and your baby, to see how things are going.

You'd be amazed at how routine having your baby home on oxygen can seem once you're used to it. Some parents have said, for instance, that although their first impression was that the oxygen canister looked like a missile, after living with it for a while they were surprised when other people noticed anything odd. We'll certainly try to allay your fears. Still, you shouldn't hesitate to tell us if providing oxygen at home is too much of a burden for you, and you don't think you can handle it. Discharging babies with this amount of medical equipment is a fairly recent thing, and there's no reason to believe that all families should want or be able to do it. If home oxygen isn't for you, we can keep your preemie in the hospital nursery a while longer. (If you're still not ready to take her home, after she's been very stable for a long time, we may start looking at other places, such as rehabilitation hospitals, where she will be able to grow and recover in a more relaxed environment that's better suited for her development.)

Feeding: If your preemie is still getting special formula, we'll be deciding whether to change her feedings before she goes home. Most preemies who are big and healthy enough to go home are ready for transitional formula, which has higher concentrations of calories, salts, and minerals than regular, term formula, but is more available and cheaper than preemie formula. I'd usually make this switch a few days before discharge, to see that your baby keeps feeding and growing well. On the other hand, if your preemie has had lots of feeding intolerance in the past, and has finally settled into a good, growing routine on special formula, I may not want to rock the boat right before discharge. In that case, I may send your baby home on special formula, with the idea of making the switch in several weeks, once she's more mature and doing well at home. The exact timing of that decision would be up to your baby's pediatrician, who will be weighing and measuring her, and keeping close tabs on her progress. Mothers who will be exclusively breastfeeding at home, but haven't nursed their preemie much in the nursery, may be asked to room in for a night or two before discharge, to make sure that mother and baby do fine with round-the-clock breastfeeding.

Medications: Preemies are commonly treated with medicine for apnea, BPD, or reflux. These problems gradually resolve; in fact, outgrowing them is one sign that a preemie is ready to go home. So, as discharge day approaches, your baby's doctor will be deciding which medications to try to stop, and which your baby should go home on.

I usually try to minimize medications (it's not like there isn't enough to do in a parent's day without having to remember and then give medicine to an often uncooperative child!), stopping them at least several days before discharge, to make sure your baby doesn't relapse when the medication wears off. For intravenous medicines that she can't do without we'll switch to oral dosing. You can't be expected to adjust medications frequently at home, so I'd want to see your baby stable on constant doses for about a week or so, before I'd feel comfortable discharging her. If your baby is sent home on medicine, her doctor may intend for her to gradually outgrow her current dose (which allows the medicine, in effect, to be tapered off), or be planning to increase the dose as she grows. You can ask him to clarify what he's expecting to do.

Follow-up: Before discharging your baby, we'll want to make sure that all of her urgent medical problems are corrected, and that follow-up of non-urgent ones is arranged. For example, if your preemie has retinopathy of prematurity, we'll check with the ophthalmologist before sending her home to make sure she doesn't need very frequent eye exams or imminent therapy. We'll arrange for your baby to be seen or fol-

lowed by any specialist who diagnosed or treated an ongoing problem, to make sure the condition is being handled properly.

For preemies at risk for developmental delay (specific risk criteria will differ somewhat among hospitals and doctors, but usually have to do with age and size at birth, medical problems, and difficult social situations), we'll arrange follow-up appointments in clinics specially designed to evaluate the growth and development of premature infants. Our hope is to catch any problems early, and hook parents up with resources and services that can help. For the infants at highest risk (such as babies with PVL or severe BPD), we may, in addition, set up home visits by a "child service coordinator" (a public health nurse or social worker employed by the state). Child service coordination programs are a tremendous benefit to families, and if you qualify for this service, I would strongly recommend that you accept it. Some parents feel insulted or nervous—thinking that we believe they can't adequately take care of their preemie themselves, or fearing that their home or parenting skills will be evaluated and judged by outsiders. That isn't at all what we have in mind when we arrange for these services. We see them as opening your family and child to opportunities and expertise that even the very best parents can't provide themselves.

We'll be asking you to choose a pediatrician, and suggesting a time to bring your baby in for her first visit. For most preemies, this will be a week or two after discharge, to make sure no new problems have arisen, and that they're eating and growing well. Sometimes, we'll want your baby to be seen by her doctor sooner—perhaps to do a blood test, or to make sure that any medical conditions she has are stable or improving. You may want to meet with your baby's new doctor even before she's discharged from the hospital, to get acquainted, and to go over your concerns and understanding with the physician who, in a short time, will be responsible for most of her care.

Many parents wonder whom to call, the nursery or their baby's new doctor, when they have questions soon after discharge. We don't mind answering questions—and would enjoy hearing from you—but the answer, usually, is "your pediatrician." Please be assured that we're not trying to avoid you—just trying to manage your concerns appropriately, and to assure continuity of care in the future. Unless your question is directly related to a problem that we followed in the nursery, or you're calling to clarify instructions that we gave you, her new doctor should be able to handle it—and needs to hear about your concerns so he can get to know you and your baby. He may call us for more information or our opinion. But we need to hand over the mantle of care to your baby's own doctor at home.

Special requirements: Sometimes, caring for a former preemie takes some special skills and practice. If your baby is going home with equipment (say, a monitor or oxygen) or will be getting tube feedings or other special treatments or medications, we may ask you to room in, or at least to spend a certain number of consecutive hours with your baby in the nursery before going home together. The idea is to give you a chance to care for your baby yourself, with lots of supervision and help readily available. We may also ask you to learn CPR, so if any equipment or medication your baby is dependent on doesn't work properly, you can support your baby until help arrives. Most parents welcome these opportunities for teaching, but some are taken aback, interpreting our requests to mean that we don't trust them as parents. On the contrary—most often, we're training you so care-

fully because we are willing to entrust a fragile newborn to your responsible and loving care. We wouldn't do that unless we thought she could be safe and thrive.

FAMILY ISSUES

Parents occasionally think they should continue the hygiene or isolation practices from the nursery to keep their preemie healthy at home. While it's true you shouldn't expose your nearly-newborn to people with obvious illnesses, or take her into crowds of people during winter cold season, remember that she's going home just so that she can be exposed to lots of things that are missing in the hospital. We're discharging your preemie because that's what's good for her now—not just for your sake, or because of hospital or insurance policies. Children develop better at home than almost anywhere else because that's where they're stimulated with all sorts of different sights and sounds and smells, get lots of loving and playful touch, and mingle with family and friends as part of a community. Your natural environment is a good environment for an infant. Use common sense to protect her—as any parent would—but don't think that your home is second best. If you make it too much like a hospital, you'll diminish how wonderful it is for your baby.

Some parents become extremely anxious about what they think is a too-sudden switch from constant monitoring of their preemie in the hospital nursery to less-than-perfect vigilance at home. I promise you, we won't discharge your baby until we think she's strong and healthy enough to flourish away from the ever-observant gaze and ministrations of nurses and doctors. To show you that the cardiorespiratory monitor is no longer needed, we usually try to turn it off a day or two before going-home day; but, to be honest, sometimes we forget! I'm sorry if this adds unnecessarily to your tension and anxiety. You can try to see those extra days on the monitor as just another sign of security.

Oh, one last thing. Be sure to come back and visit us sometimes—and send pictures. We're more attached to her than you know. And who doesn't love to see their babies grow?

Questions and Answers

Preemie-Proofing

They say my baby's ready to go home. But what should we do to be ready for him? I feel like I should put him in a bubble to keep him safe!

Matching the bedding with the wallpaper, shopping for a cute mobile to hang over the crib, and having enough clothes and diapers are the kinds of things parents usually worry about in getting their household ready for a newborn. But taking a preemie home is a different story. Many families become concerned about the adequacy of their home environment and caregiving practices. After seeing their preemie tended to in a hygienic hospital nursery by specialized professionals, moving him from that safe haven to their house can cause them to fret.

Here is a first piece of advice. Your loving presence is what your baby needs, now that he's ready to begin home life with you. There are only a few precautions, easy to remember and apply, for "preemie-proofing" your habits and house. Most are aimed at helping him avoid colds and other infections, to which he's still more vulnerable than other newborns in the first weeks or months after leaving the hospital.

A few basic do's and don'ts

✻ Do take your preemie outside, but don't expose him for long to strong drafts or direct sunlight. When he's out and the sun is shining, protect him with a wide-brimmed hat or parasol. Don't apply sunscreen: unless your pediatrician advises you differently, sunscreen isn't safe to apply until a baby is around six months old, when he'll have thicker skin.

✻ Avoid bringing him into churches, movie theaters, shopping malls, or other crowded indoor places, where there's a higher risk of catching a cold or other infection.

✻ When you schedule visits with the pediatrician, ask for the earliest appointment. If you're the first patient of the day, you're less likely to be kept waiting in a crowded waiting room with sick kids.

✻ Ask relatives and friends who visit to make sure their small children keep some distance from your preemie, and not to visit if they have a cold, the flu, or any other contagious illness. If you or somebody else in the family has a respiratory infection, avoid face-to-face contact with your preemie, or wear a disposable paper mask when you're spending time close to him, like during feedings. (Inexpensive, disposable face masks can be bought at any hardware store, or you can order them from one of the vendors of allergy products listed in the appendix, page 521.) Older siblings should wash their hands when arriving home from school, sports, or play dates. When sick, they should be kept away from the baby until they're no longer contagious.

✸ Wash your hands after blowing your nose, diapering siblings, and handling raw food. (Be careful about handwashing, but don't let it become an obsession. You don't have to replicate the hygienic measures of the NICU.)

✸ When you and your baby are away from home, a small package of baby wipes comes in handy for more than cleaning little backsides. You can use them to wipe off toys or pacifiers that drop on the floor, infant seats in supermarket carts, and so on. They're also great for keeping your own hands clean.

✸ The usual tips for cleaning and storing bottles, nipples, pacifiers, breast pump equipment, and milk or formula are perfectly apt for preemies as well as term babies.

✸ Post signs around the house, if you need to, and be absolutely rigid with your family and friends: yours is a no-smoking household, for your baby's sake. All preemies, but particularly those with BPD, shouldn't be exposed to smoke, dust, animal fur, aerosol sprays, or paint fumes. These irritants can cause wheezing, coughing, and difficulty breathing.

✸ Make sure you have a car seat appropriate for preemies (see page 343).

✸ If your baby is on apnea monitor, be sure that you can hear the alarm from every room of your house. (And read the In Depth on monitors, page 385, for more safety tips.)

Babies who have BPD are more susceptible to respiratory infections, which can be severe enough to cause them to be rehospitalized. For them, the precautions above should be continued through the first year or longer (ask your pediatrician). Other special tips:

✸ Parents and caregivers of preemies with BPD should get the flu vaccine every year.

✸ If your baby is on oxygen, observe the cleaning requirements, particularly for the humidifier, and the safety recommendations (see page 350).

✸ If your baby has severe BPD, consider instituting the following precautions recommended to prevent development of allergies and asthma.

To fight dust mites: eliminate or minimize carpets, any bedding that isn't machine washable in hot water, upholstery, curtains, stuffed animals; cover pillows and mattresses in plastic casing under pillowcases and sheets; use a vacuum cleaner equipped with a special high-efficiency particulate air (HEPA) filter; wash linens at least once a week, and always in hot water. (See the appendix, page 521, for companies from which you can purchase allergy control products ranging from special mattress and pillow casing to HEPA vacuum cleaners, mold control sprays, and even special stuffed animals for allergic children.)

To fight animal dander: find your pets another home, if possible. If you can't part with them, keep them outside the house, or at least far from your baby's bedroom and any carpeted areas.

To fight cockroaches (roach proteins can be extremely irritating to reactive airways): exterminate them and carefully clean all surfaces where the insects were roaming. (But make sure you follow safety instructions when you use exterminating chemicals in your house.)

To fight mold: use a dehumidifier and carefully clean all bathroom mildew.

Besides what's listed above, and any special instructions your doctor gives you, your preemie doesn't need anything different from what you'd normally do for a full-term baby. Most parenting books offer a review of what parents should do, at various ages, to try to prevent injuries. Your preemie simply requires that you follow the same baby-proofing schedule, for his corrected age (the age he would be if he'd been born on his due date.) Isn't it refreshing to be following the same advice as all new parents, after the special circumstances and consequences of your baby's premature birth?

Diapers and Clothing

Where am I going to find preemie diapers and clothes for my baby?

Finally, you're ready to shop for your beautiful baby. She deserves to be treated royally after all she's been through, and you deserve to indulge in the adorable outfits you've been admiring from afar for so long. But before you spend a lot of time and money shopping for special, preemie-sized clothes and diapers, remind yourself of one thing: preemies grow quickly. Your baby probably won't get much use out of them before she's ready for regular, newborn sizes.

So try to resist the urge to invest in a complete preemie wardrobe. Consider buying just a few preemie outfits that your baby can don on special occasions. Remember that newborn-sized clothes can vary a lot in size from one brand to another, and that the smallest of them may almost fit your baby. The rest of the time, just roll up the sleeves and ankles, and notice how within a few weeks your baby's arms and legs start to fill them out. All newborns, after all, spend most of their time dressed for casual comfort, in billowy nightgowns with drawstring bottoms, stretchy sleepers, and T-shirts, all of which are often bought a size too big. The roomy look seems to suit them!

Many hospitals send parents home with a package of preemie diapers. (If nobody mentions this, be sure to ask.) Once those are used up, try moving on to the standard, newborn size, rolling the diapers down at the waist to make them fit better. They may be roomy for a while, but chances are they'll work just fine.

The following are a few sources of preemie diapers and clothes for the more tailored look, and for those babies who are especially small at discharge:

Diapers: Two of the most popular brands of diapers, Huggies and Pampers, make preemie sizes. They are available by the case (about a three- to four-week supply), can be ordered easily by telephone, and usually arrive within a week. For a case of Huggies (180 diapers; approximately $30 as of this writing), call (800) 447–9423. For a case of Pampers (240 diapers; approximately $46), call (800) 543–4932. For smaller quantities, you can call Children's Medical Ventures at (888) 766–8843, which claims that its WeePee diapers are designed with thinner pads to minimize the tendency of some preemies' hips to turn slightly outward.

Clothing: As the number of premature babies born in the U.S. has increased, so has the interest of retailers in selling clothes for them. For instance, some Wal-Mart stores have a large selection, and some sell preemie diapers. The Gap has introduced a line of preemie clothes, sold through a few of its Baby Gap stores and its on-line store. And there are quite a few, smaller retailers that now sell clothes for preemies by mail, telephone, or e-mail. You can call for catalogs, or check their Web sites to see their selection. Among them are: The Preemie Store and More!, (800) 676–8469, http://www.preemie.com; Le Petite Baby, (770) 475–3247, http://www.no-odor.com/preemie; premie-wear, (800) 992–8469, http://www.premiewear.com; and Tiny Bundles, (619) 451–9907, http://www.tinybundles.com.

If you decide to make clothes for your preemie, remember to use soft fabrics, and avoid scratchy seams or accessories.

And remember, no matter what your preemie wears—she'll always look pretty darn cute.

Choosing a Pediatrician

How do I choose the right pediatrician for my preemie?

When your baby has been cared for, since birth, by highly-trained neonatologists and around-the-clock neonatal nurses, it can make any parent nervous to transfer her care to a plain old family physician or pediatrician who (a) isn't a specialist in preemies, and (b) isn't going to live with you, standing next to your baby's crib 24 hours a day. Imagine!

What's hard to realize now is that your preemie is rapidly growing out of the phase in which she needed constant, specialized attention, and into one in which she can safely be treated like other newborns of the same corrected age. If that weren't the case, her doctors wouldn't feel it's time to send her home from the hospital.

Nevertheless, some preemies will finish making that transition sooner than others. The challenge for parents of a preemie, then, is to select a doctor who will take excellent care of their baby both in the short run, while she still may face some special vulnerabilities or needs, and the long run, when you will want what everyone wants in a pediatrician: someone who will effectively and sympathetically guide you through the long, normal years of teething, sore throats, fevers, booster shots, sprained ankles, growth spurts, and teenage acne.

Before choosing a specific doctor, you should decide whether to look for a pediatrician or family physician. Pediatricians specialize in children, usually from babyhood into adolescence, while family physicians have a broader practice, taking care of entire families, children and adults alike. Family physicians don't consider themselves second best at taking care of children, but they do have less training in neonatology and pediatrics. (While the length of their post–medical school training is the same—three years of specialized residency—family physicians divide that time among surgery, obstetrics, and gynecology, internal medicine, and psychiatry, as well as pediatrics. So, during their training, family physicians usually spend two to four weeks in a neonatal intensive care nursery, while pediatricians spend about four months.)

Which kind of physician is right for you—and your baby? That depends. If your baby is a big, healthy preemie with no special medical needs, then either a pediatrician or a family physician should be fine.

However, if you have a more vulnerable preemie—either because she is receiving ongoing, specialized medical treatment (such as home oxygen, or follow-up care after major surgery), or because she was sick in the hospital (for example, with BPD or hydrocephalus) and is therefore at higher risk for certain future problems—then we would advise that you select a pediatrician, if possible. Being more specialized, they generally will have a better understanding of what your preemie (and you) have been through, and what kinds of problems to look out for when they see your baby. The first few years are crucial ones for your preemie, to catch any possible problems early. So even if you have a family doctor you love, you still may want to find a pediatrician for the first year or two. Later, your preemie can graduate to your family physician's practice.

Some parents become so attached to the doctors in the nursery, or so nervous about walking away from their expertise and extensive experience with premature babies, that they want to continue using the hospital staff as their baby's pediatricians, even after discharge. In many hospitals, it's possible to do this by taking your baby to the hospital's outpatient clinic. You might be able to see the doctors you already know, or others on the staff.

A word to the wise: while that can work very well for families who live within a thirty-minute drive of the hospital, it probably won't if you live farther away. A pediatrician is someone you should feel able to pop in on quickly whenever you're worried about a stuffed nose or high fever, someone you can pick up the phone and reach without thinking about long-distance charges when you have a question you want to be answered right away, someone who can meet you in the emergency room or their office (or maybe even come to your house) in the middle of the night, if your baby is crying inconsolably and you're scared, someone who is a knowledgeable guide to dentists, schools, and other providers and resources in your community. Remember that more and more, your concerns are going to revolve around these basic matters that are part of the daily life of a pediatrician, not an intensive care nursery.

Having made these choices, it's time to gather names and phone numbers, or to sort through the various doctors your insurance plan will cover. Some ways to do this:

❋ Ask your neonatologist for advice. She will be familiar with the doctors who are affiliated with your baby's hospital, and many others who know preemies.

❋ If you live some distance from the hospital, it may be even better to ask around in your community, to find a physician who is locally respected and who'll know the other local doctors and social service providers you'll eventually want to contact.

❋ Find out if there are support groups for parents of preemies in your area, or ask other parents of preemies you know. You'll probably tap into a great, useful reservoir of experience.

❋ Once you've focused in on one or two individuals, you may want to make an appointment to meet them in person. Most of the things to learn from the visit—such as whether your style and the physician's seem to be compatible, how night and weekend calls are handled, whether you feel more comfortable with a solo practitioner or group practice, and so on—are no different than for a full-term baby. Many parenting books contain lists of questions and issues that may be helpful to consider.

❋ If your baby has special medical problems or needs, there's one issue you should not overlook: some doctors welcome these patients, and others, unfortunately, do not. It's best to find that out now, rather than by being treated poorly later. When you talk to a prospective doctor, describe your baby's circumstances, and ask straight out whether he's comfortable taking her on as a patient. He may or may not answer your question directly, but chances are, you'll be able to read between the lines. If your baby has transportation problems, also ask whether the doctor will make house calls. Even today, some physicians, under some circumstances, do.

The doctor you choose will probably see your baby within a week or two of discharge. Don't expect to feel as comfortable with him right off the bat as with the neonatologist who cared for your baby since birth. Give him a chance to show you that he knows a lot about babies, and will get to know and take good care of yours.

Within a few visits, you should start to trust him, and to feel that you've made a good choice. If not, go with your instinct, and don't hesitate to make a change. Even if it's hard to break up at first, you'll be better off if you do. A pediatrician is someone with whom you're going to have a long, intimate relationship, and it should be a good one.

The End of Apnea

They say my baby can go home next week, but just last week she had some apnea. What makes her ready to go home now?

There are many factors that go into the careful decision of when to send a preemie home; you can read about them in The Doctor's Perspective, on page 333. One common one is that a baby's apnea of prematurity must have resolved. That's determined by a baby's having gone for a certain number of days—often eight, but practices at different nurseries vary—without any apnea or bradycardia.

But how can a doctor ever be sure that an episode of apnea or bradycardia is the final one? What if there's another, unexpected one at home?

The first thing you have to understand (though many parents of preemies find it hard to believe) is that apnea of prematurity never goes on forever. It gradually gets better as a premature baby matures, with the episodes of apnea becoming milder and the intervals between them longer—until it's completely gone. A re-

cent research study indicates that when a baby goes for eight days without apnea, it's safe to conclude that her apnea of prematurity has ended: after eight apnea-free days, none of the babies in the study had another episode again. (Remember that this applies to simple apnea of prematurity. If a baby's apnea is due to other health conditions, they may need to resolve before the apnea will go away.)

Therefore, many nurseries perform an apnea "countdown," requiring a certain number of apnea-free days before discharging a baby. Don't be surprised if during the countdown period, your baby sets off the apnea or bradycardia alarm, and her doctors don't count it. It may be that they realize her heart rate is just slowing as she matures (as it should), and her monitor settings need to be lowered. Or perhaps she choked during a feeding, and some fleeting apnea or bradycardia occurred—which has nothing to do with how well she's breathing. On the other hand, if your baby has apnea that her doctors do consider significant, the countdown will have to be started all over again. It wouldn't be surprising for that to happen a couple of times, either.

Sometimes, a preemie's parents and doctor become frustrated, because she's otherwise ready to go home, but isn't making it through her apnea countdowns. In that case, the doctor may decide to send her home with an apnea monitor. If that's the plan for your baby, you can read all about home monitors on page 385.

Car Seat

Why is a car seat test so important? Is a baby so much more likely to have breathing problems there than anywhere else?

It is well known that car accidents are the top cause of injury and death of children in the U.S., and that car seats can prevent many of these tragedies. Unfortunately, preemies riding in a car sometimes face a catch–22: some of them have trouble breathing in a car seat, even if their breathing is perfectly fine when lying down or being held in an adult's arms.

The problem stems from the fact that most car seats are designed for bigger infants, who weigh more than seven pounds. In big seats, little preemies don't get much support, and tend to slump down, their heads flopping forward or sideways. Thus, more than one out of five pre-

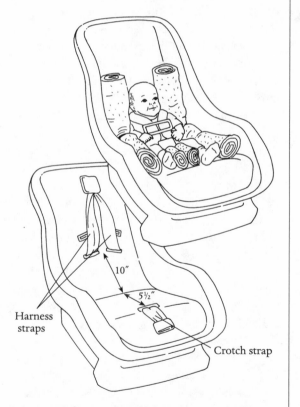

Harness straps

10″

5½″

Crotch strap

In a car seat for a preemie, the harness straps should come out of the seat no more than 10 inches up from the bottom of the seat back. The crotch strap should come out no more than 5½ inches from the bottom of the seat back. To prop up your baby, use rolled blankets or cloth diapers.

mature babies have apnea, bradycardia, or oxygen desaturation in car seats, according to research.

That's why the American Academy of Pediatrics now recommends that all infants born before 37 weeks of gestation be monitored in their car seat before leaving the hospital. If your baby passes her car seat test with flying colors, you won't have to worry. If she shows signs of breathing problems, there are some things you should consider:

✳ Make sure you have provided her with the most optimal conditions. It could help to choose a different car seat, since a small baby is least likely to slump forward in one that has a distance of less than five inches from the crotch strap between her legs to the bottom of the seat back (see illustration). It often helps to prop up your baby with rolled blankets or cloth diapers, as shown. If her head keeps flopping forward, try tilting the car seat back, so it reclines at a 45-degree angle.

✳ If she still has breathing problems in the car seat, your baby may do fine in an infant car bed that allows her to lie down when she travels. Most nurseries have one available for testing preemies. Cosco makes one that also converts into a rear-facing car seat. You can order it by calling the company at (800) 544–1108.

✳ Until you're confident that your preemie has outgrown her breathing difficulties, minimize car trips, and have an adult sit next to her in the back seat whenever possible, to keep an eye on her. (Remember that it is always safest for a child to ride in the back seat. Infants in rear-facing car seats should never be placed in the front seat of a car with a passenger-side airbag.)

A few additional tips are important for all preemies—reliable breathers or not. They sound like small details, but they make a huge difference in your baby's safety:

✹ A preemie should be in a rear-facing car seat that is designed to accommodate small babies (not one designed for children weighing over 20 pounds). The distance from the lowest harness straps coming out of the seat back to the bottom of the seat should be no more than 10 inches, for the straps to fit a preemie well.

✹ A preemie's car seat should have a three-point harness system (if it's an infant-only seat) or a five-point harness system (if it's a convertible baby/toddler seat)—not a shield or abdominal pad. During an impact, these could come into contact with a small infant's face and cause injury.

✹ Make sure the harness fits your baby snugly, and the retainer clip is positioned at the middle of her chest, not at her stomach or neck.

✹ Finally, you'll be happy to know that according to the American Academy of Pediatrics, a higher price does not mean a safer seat, and there's no "best" brand.

If You Want to Take Your Preemie on an Airplane

A word of caution: some preemies may be well enough to go home, but not ready to ride in an airplane yet. This is because even airplanes with pressurized cabins (virtually all commercial passenger airplanes today) don't achieve an oxygen concentration as high as typical room air at sea level. That means one needs to breathe more deeply or rapidly to take in the same amount of oxygen.

For a preemie whose oxygen saturation levels have been measuring close to 100%, flying should be no problem. But for babies whose saturation levels in the hospital have been sufficient, but lower—say, 93% to 95%—the further drop on the plane could be dangerous. Many neonatologists would advise parents not to take these babies on airplanes for several months after leaving the nursery. It would be equally unwise to take them to high-altitude places like Denver; or Jackson, Wyoming; or the Alps, where air pressure is lower, also.

Another reason why planes may not be preemie-friendly is that they increase the possibility of catching a cold or other respiratory infection. A few years ago, for economic reasons, commercial flights began recycling all or part of the air circulating in the cabin and since then, a higher risk of transmission of infections among passengers has been documented. Considering that all preemies are vulnerable to these illnesses, particularly in the first winter of their lives, it could be advisable to wait a few more months before flying.

If you are taking your baby on a plane ride, you'll face the decision of whether to buckle her into a car seat in the seat next to you—where she'll be safest in the event of a severe jolt—or to hold her in your arms, where she's least likely to have breathing problems. Your baby's doctor, who knows how strong her breathing is, can help you weigh the two choices.

CPR

I learned CPR, but could I really do it? Or even recognize if my baby is having apnea?

Like Olympic divers demonstrating a perfect flip, experts in CPR always make it look so simple. But it's not simple when you're a parent learning it for the first time, trying to remember all of the precise moves involved. Breathing may come naturally, but trying to make somebody else breathe doesn't come naturally at all!

Most parents who've just learned CPR feel like you: they aren't sure they could do it the right way in an emergency. Here's what we suggest.

✽ *Try to keep your memory of CPR fresh by practicing every couple of weeks.* Research has shown that parents who refresh their memory with hands-on practice, using a doll (you should never use an actual baby), retain their CPR skills the best.

✽ *Don't expect too much of your memory.* Even in NICUs, charts of emergency medications are sometimes posted near babies' beds so doctors and nurses don't have to rely on their memories in the heat of an emergency. Since your memory may not function perfectly when you're under pressure, you may feel more secure if you keep a copy of the CPR guidelines the hospital gave you (or make copies of the guidelines on page 520) in several places where you spend a lot of time with your baby—near her crib, in the kitchen, and in your purse, diaper bag, or even glove compartment, if you do much traveling.

✽ *Be assured that although it's important to learn how to do CPR right, you probably will help your baby even if you don't do everything exactly right.* You'll most likely succeed in giving your baby some breaths (which will deliver oxygen into her lungs), and pressing on her chest (to pump the oxygen-rich blood to the rest of her body). Meanwhile, someone near you will be calling for help. If you are alone, start doing CPR before rushing to the phone. Then, after giving some breaths and chest pumping, you can take a brief pause and call 911.

How can you recognize whether your baby is really having apnea? First, look for a change in her color. If she stops breathing or her heart pumps too slowly, her color will begin to change from pink to bluish/gray. It's easiest to see a change in color by looking at her lips and tongue, since they're usually rosy. (Babies who are very fair can sometimes look a little blue around their mouths, because the veins show through their thin skin. As long as the inside of her mouth is pink, you don't have to worry— she's OK.) To check that she's breathing, you can look at her chest to make sure it's moving, and put your ear next to her nose and mouth to listen for breathing sounds.

If your baby's pink and you can tell she's breathing, she's fine. If you aren't sure, stimulate her a little with some gentle pats or rubs on her foot, belly, or back. You can also try changing her position, since there are occasions when a baby may be breathing, but because her neck is kinked the air isn't getting into her windpipe. If she's eating at the time, take the nipple out of her mouth and give her a few seconds to recover and breathe. In case her airway is blocked, look to see if any food or other object is in her mouth and, if so, remove it. (Don't just sweep her mouth with your finger blindly, since you could push an obstructing object farther down.) You can also suction out her mouth and nose with your bulb syringe, or with a suction device, if you have one.

If these simple maneuvers don't work, try turning her over and patting or rubbing her back a little harder. The important thing is never to shake her so hard that her head moves back and forth, like a rag doll. If more vigorous stimulation than you've already done is needed, that's the time to start CPR.

Home Nursing Care

The hospital wants to set up home nursing for my baby. What am I in for? I'm not sure I really need it.

If the doctors have told you that they want to organize professional home nursing for your baby, you should accept the offer. Your preemie is ready to leave the hospital, thankfully, but his care is still complex. Some temporary medical help from professional nurses can greatly ease the transition from hospital to home, assuring your baby's well-being until you're fully trained and comfortable enough to perform all of his care yourself. For many families, that will be in a matter of a few weeks; for some, it may be longer.

Today, increasing numbers of families are offered the option of home nursing care, which can shorten a hospitalization considerably. Your premature baby may need home nursing for respiratory care, such as mechanical ventilation or supplemental oxygen; for alternative feeding methods, like parenteral nutrition or tube feedings; or because his medications or other special treatments are very complicated to administer.

Depending on your child's needs, his nurses will be in your home from a few hours once or twice a week, to many hours a day. Most commonly, the nurses come more frequently in the first several weeks after discharge, to make sure you are becoming familiar with the medical equipment and procedures. Then, as you gradually take over your baby's health care, the nurses come less often; eventually, they'll come only for periodic supervision. In less common, more serious medical situations, the nurses will keep coming to your home every day for a much longer time, but at some point their hours will decrease, too, as your baby recovers.

Despite the great advantage of allowing your preemie to leave the hospital much sooner, home care is not a stroll in the park. Here are some of the issues that may arise:

❋ *Pressure and demands on you.* First, you will have to deal with many organizational issues, to make sure your home is ready for your baby, and remains safe and hospitable. You'll be discussing everything with the home health care agency assigned to you—from time schedules, to the technical details of the medical equipment, to the floor plan of your baby's room. They'll expect you to learn enough about your baby's care to give the nurses the feedback they need, and to take it over, little by little. As a result, there will be a lot of pressure and demands on you. But the beginning is the hardest: most parents describe an initial stressful, even chaotic, adjustment period lasting about four to six weeks. After that, most feel they've gotten their baby's care down to a comfortable system.

❋ *Frustration and guilt.* Keeping up your self-esteem by reminding yourself of your unique and valuable parental role is very important right now. It will help you to control the frustration or guilt that home nursing can generate in some parents, who wrongly think they are not good enough to take care of their infant on their own. That's irrational, of course: the doctors' decision to set up a home nursing service is dictated by your baby's medical condition—not by any judgment about your ability as a parent. Despite the nurses' interventions and presence in your home, you are, as you always will be, your baby's primary caretaker.

❋ *Loss of privacy.* Having a nurse in their house, sitting at their baby's bedside, and observing their family life, makes some parents uncomfortable. You may become self-conscious about your personal habits, the appearance of your house, your lifestyle. One father told us that he was most bothered by not being able to come downstairs in the morning in his pajamas. Others find that the loss of privacy disrupts intimate moments with their baby, since not everyone is able to express love and tenderness in front of a stranger.

Home health care nurses know this is difficult, and most try to be supportive, nonjudgmental, and respectful of your privacy. One thing that can help is to designate certain rooms of your house as private areas, and to develop, together with your home care agency, a set of "house rules" regarding such things as where the nurse should store her food, and what your policy is on television viewing. (There's a list of suggested topics for house rules on page 349.) Remember, though, that a flexible and friendly attitude can help ease the initial discomfort of living alongside a stranger. To help make your house a good work environment, remember to ask the nurses what they may need from you. Over time, most parents succeed in de-

veloping a companionable and trusting relationship with their baby's nurses.

❋ *Psychological consequences.* Negative feelings, like anxiety and depression, can affect parents for a long time after a premature baby's birth, and are even more common if a baby has a medical condition like BPD, which may take long months to get better. Along with the practical problems of dealing with your preemie's special medical needs, having a nurse in your home is a constant reminder of your baby's ongoing health problems. Not being able to forget is an additional source of stress that you may attribute to the nurse's presence—but in reality, it's mostly due to worries about your baby.

If you have older children, they may resent the presence of the nurse, the disruption of family habits, or the tension they perceive in their parents. Their anxiety, jealousy, or anger can be expressed in temper tantrums or other aggressive behavior, health complaints, a regression in speech and behavior, or school problems. But they also may genuinely love their sibling, and feel proud of themselves for helping out. (See page 364 for advice on responding to your older children's needs.)

❋ *When parental reactions are extreme.* Occasionally, a parent will develop what has been called "parent drop-out syndrome." It happens when mothers or fathers become so dependent on the nurses that they completely withdraw from their child's care, not even participating in routine acts like feeding, or changing clothes and diapers. Less extreme, and much more common, are cases in which parents simply resist learning the medical care techniques they should be able to perform on their own, because they are too over-

House Rules for Home Nurses*

Here are some points you may want to cover in a list of "house rules" for your baby's nurses. Let them know your preferences about:

1. *Entering the house:* Where to enter (with keys or not), where to store coats or personal belongings, where to park the car.
2. *Food:* Where the nurse should store her food, where she should eat in the house.
3. *Rooms:* What bathroom the nurse should use, which rooms are private family areas, not to be entered.
4. *Phone calls:* Whether and how the nurse should answer your telephone, whether she can receive or make personal calls.
5. *Visitors:* What visitors you allow—coming to visit the nurse or your baby—in your absence.
6. *Television and music:* How often, when, and where is watching TV, and listening to the radio or other music, OK? Can the nurse watch more TV at night, when she has no other distractions and needs to stay awake?
7. *Duties:* What you expect the nurse to take care of. Home nurses generally are responsible for keeping your baby's room tidy. Who will change your baby's clothes, change his diaper, feed him, bathe him, and put him to bed? When should these routines take place? Make clear what tasks you want to take over, and how often.
8. *Discipline:* When and how the nurse may discipline your older children if they interfere with her work—be specific! (Note that a caretaker other than the nurse must always be present to watch other children in your absence.)
9. *Information:* What kind of feedback and information about your baby do you expect from the nurse, and how often?

*Adapted with permission from *Pediatric Nursing* 19(4):375, © Jannetti Publications, Inc., Pitman, NJ, 1993

---

whelmed to focus and concentrate. If you notice that you're reacting this way, you should tell your nurses that you don't feel sure of your skills in caring for your baby. Home nurses are familiar with these parental reactions, and generally handle them with patience and understanding. Since they know that you should be at the center of your baby's care, they will certainly help you to become more competent and overcome your insecurities. Open communication is essential for family members and home nurses to work together, in the best interests of the baby.

❋ *Financial pressure.* Financial pressure on a family can obviously add to worries and resentment. Before your baby is discharged, you should talk to the social worker in your nursery, to find out what costs you should anticipate for his home care, and how you might meet them. Most of the direct costs, including nurses' and physicians' fees, and medical equipment and supplies, will be covered by your health insurance plan or Medicaid. But you should also plan for some indirect costs, such as additional electricity and other utility bills, home remodeling, and loss of time and income for you, your partner, or another member of your family, since caring for a baby at home is demanding, even with the help of a nurse. The social worker can help you find out what additional financial resources are available, and which agencies in your community to contact for aid. Sometimes, premature and sick babies are eligible for Medicaid even if their parents aren't, and for Supplemental Social Security income. Your home health nurse, who can see where you have extra expenses, can also be an advocate with your HMO or government agencies.

✳ *Impact on your baby.* Having ongoing health problems, and needing prolonged medical care, can sometimes exacerbate a baby's tendency to cry, fuss, and overreact or underreact to stimulation. (You can read more about preemies' behavioral patterns on page 373.) Still, letting your baby complete his recovery in his own home, where you can give him the attention, love, and stimulation he needs to develop well, can greatly reduce the negative psychological consequences of spending many, early months in a hospital nursery.

Although it may feel pretty daunting now, most families cope well with home nursing, appreciating that it is less disruptive than a longer stay in the hospital. For many parents, it is also a great learning experience, allowing them to become better caregivers. But those who benefit most, of course, are their babies, who get the opportunity to heal faster, and develop normally, in the warm, nurturing environment of their family home.

GETTING ACQUAINTED WITH: HOME OXYGEN

Some babies with BPD or other medical conditions go on needing supplemental oxygen after they're otherwise ready to be discharged from the hospital. The extra oxygen is usually a temporary measure, to be gradually eliminated, together with other medications the baby may be on, as his lungs gradually heal. If your preemie is in this situation, the good news is that, while this process takes place, he can be at home with you, getting all the love, attention, and stimulation an infant needs to develop normally. And be assured, you're not alone: recent studies show that about 5% of preemies who have been put on a ventilator need to be sent home on oxygen.

Although this prospect might initially worry you, it doesn't mean that you have to turn your home into a hospital, or become a professional nurse. You will be provided, before and after discharge, through a home nursing service, with all the coaching and assistance you need. Most parents find they can lead a normal family life, quickly becoming familiar with the oxygen equipment, which is less intrusive than you may think. A baby on extra oxygen can go out for strolls (most home oxygen comes with its own carrying case or portable, rolling rack) and even travel, provided you get properly organized. True, oxygen is one more thing you have to handle now. But most parents find that nothing is insurmountable (see "Useful tips from parents to parents," page 355).

Sooner than you expect, your baby is likely to leave supplemental oxygen behind: studies have shown that in most cases, this therapy is not needed for longer than six months. If your child needs supplemental oxygen for longer, extra long tubing will allow him to crawl or walk

Thanks to long tubing, a supervised toddler on supplemental oxygen can move around freely.

Adapted with permission of Pediatric Services of America

freely around a room, although he'll need supervision to make sure he doesn't get tangled in the tubing, and that it doesn't get caught on furniture and dislodged.

HOW YOUR BABY'S HOME OXYGEN THERAPY IS ORGANIZED

Starting before discharge and continuing at home, you'll be carefully instructed in:

* the type of equipment you're getting, including an oxygen source, a humidifier, a device to deliver the oxygen, and possibly, a pulse oximeter or cardiorespiratory monitor;
* how to use, adjust, clean, and check the equipment for proper functioning and prevention of infections;
* how much oxygen to give your baby;
* how much humidity to provide with the oxygen;
* when to give the oxygen—continuously, or just at certain times;
* how to tell if your baby is getting enough oxygen and whether to increase his oxygen during more stressful activities, like feeding or playing;
* what to do in case of an emergency, including how to handle technical failures of the oxygen equipment, and how to do CPR.

Although it sounds like a huge task now, you'll be getting lots of teaching, support, and practice. You'll have several practical, hands-on training sessions before your baby is discharged from the hospital. And once you get home, you'll be able to count on the support of a home health service, routinely assigned to any baby discharged on oxygen. A nurse will be available to answer your calls twenty-four hours a day, and to come to your home if problems arise. The home nursing team will also make routine home visits, to ensure that you become progressively more confident in managing your baby's supplemental oxygen.

Because your teaching will be tailored to your baby's particular situation and equipment, you should rely on your hospital and home health nurses for specific information. But here's an overview of some of the most common, important issues that parents of preemies on home oxygen face.

GENERAL SAFETY ISSUES

Thousands of families have used oxygen safely in their homes by observing some basic safety measures. Because oxygen is highly flammable, no smoking, burning fire, or sparks (including gas stoves) should ever be allowed in the same room with it, and radiators and heaters should be kept at least five feet from the oxygen source and your baby's bed. The room (or car, if your child is traveling) should always be well ventilated. Some parents like to put "Caution: No Smoking" signs on their portable oxygen tanks, to warn passersby.

OXYGEN EQUIPMENT FOR INDOORS AND OUTDOORS

There are three possible sources of supplemental oxygen for use at home. Your baby's doctor will suggest the kinds that probably will work best for you. Most families end up using more than one, for different circumstances.

Oxygen cylinders. These are tanks filled with oxygen gas. They are the most cost-effective source if a baby needs oxygen only intermittently, up to twelve hours a day. The tanks come in different sizes, and can be stored for a long time. The largest are for use at home; the smallest, which are lightweight and easily portable, allow you to take your baby out for a walk, on a car trip, or on public transportation.

Once it is connected to a regulator (the device controlling the flow of oxygen out of the cylinder), a portable oxygen tank should be kept upright whenever possible. The regulator and its connection to the tank should be protected from being accidentally knocked off, because if gas at high pressure leaks out, the oxygen tank could propel itself forward dangerously.

When you travel by car, keep the oxygen tank vertical on a seat, well-secured with a belt or strap to protect it from any shock. Never put it in the trunk, where it may get knocked or overheated. If you want to walk with your baby, a backpack is a good way to carry a portable cylinder around. The tubing running from the cylinder to your baby should be safely taped in place (for instance from the backpack to your shoulder, the handle of the stroller, and your baby's face), but not stretched tight. Some parents find it more comfortable to lay the cylinder down in a basket or rack under their baby's stroller. Just make sure that it's well-shielded from any jolts or shocks. If you want to avoid people's stares or questions, you can both protect and conceal the oxygen tank with a blanket.

You'll be getting information from your oxygen supplier stating how many hours of oxygen each tank size can provide at a given flow rate. You'll learn to monitor and keep track of how much oxygen is left. Never leave the house without more oxygen than your baby needs, in case of a car breakdown, traffic jam, or other unpredictable delay.

Liquid oxygen. Oxygen at very cold temperatures (more than 300°F below zero) is a liquid, and can be maintained that way under pressure in special containers. Liquid oxygen is the most convenient for continuous, low-flow oxygen therapy. It's more compact than oxygen gas, so more of it fits in a tank. But because it will evaporate, it can't be stored for as long. Liquid oxygen tanks, like oxygen cylinders, come in different sizes. The smaller, portable ones can be refilled as needed at home. They require the same safety precautions as oxygen cylinders: they must be kept upright to avoid leakage, protected from shocks, and their remaining oxygen supply monitored so it doesn't unexpectedly run out. If some liquid oxygen spills, it should be kept away from the skin and eyes to avoid dangerous freeze-burns. For the same reason, you should never touch the frost that may form on the tank.

Oxygen concentrator. This electrical device takes oxygen from room air and concentrates it. It's the most convenient source for a baby who needs continuous oxygen at a high flow rate, because the oxygen can't run out, and you're spared the hassle of oxygen deliveries. (It will raise your electrical bills, though.) A concentrator is a bulky machine that can be loud. But you shouldn't put it in a closet or storage place, or use it with an extension cord or in outlets being used for other appliances, because of the risk of overheating and fire. If you get a concentrator, you'll need to have a portable cylinder or liquid oxygen tank available for when you want to take your baby out, and as a backup in case of a power failure or machine malfunction.

SOURCES OF HUMIDIFICATION

Each oxygen delivery system is equipped with a humidity source. Adding water to the oxygen prevents drying and irritation of a baby's airways.

HOW YOUR BABY GETS THE OXYGEN

Nasal cannula. As you've probably seen in the nursery, a nasal cannula won't interfere with your baby's movements, feeding, speech, or interaction with the environment. It can be connected to long tubing, allowing you to carry your baby easily around the house, and later, when he begins to roll over or crawl, allowing him to move freely. (If you get extra long tubing, be sure to tell your nurse or doctor, because sometimes the oxygen flow rate will need to be increased.) The clear, small tube can be held in place under a baby's nose with a headband, and, if necessary, taped to his face with soft surgical

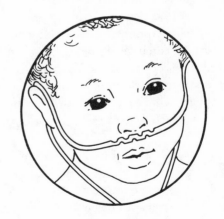

Clipping off the prongs and cutting extra holes in a nasal cannula can make it less irritating for a child's nostrils.

tape. (You may want to do this, particularly at night.)

If your baby sometimes pulls at his cannula, it may help to run the tubing over and behind his ears, then slip it inside his clothes—but don't restrain his hands, because being able to reach for and manipulate things is important for his development. Nasal prongs that don't fit right—because they're too big or spaced too close together—can be irritating, and your child may need a bigger cannula as he grows. If he is between sizes, a little lubricating jelly around his nostrils can ease the discomfort. If that doesn't work, and if your doctor gives you permission, you can clip off the prongs and cut additional holes in the cannula (see detail in illustration on page 353), so it can still deliver oxygen without entering his nose.

Tracheostomy collar. Babies with BPD who have had a tracheostomy (see page 323) usually will need extra oxygen for some time after they've been weaned from the ventilator. The oxygen can be connected to the collar that holds the tracheostomy tube in place. As with a nasal cannula, babies on "trach collar" oxygen can move about relatively freely, so their development is not impeded. At night, to prevent the oxygen tubing from being displaced when the baby turns, it can be anchored with a chest belt secured with Velcro. In addition to learning about home oxygen, parents of babies with tracheostomies will be taught how to suction and change the trach tube to prevent blockage and infection.

Ventilator. A baby with a tracheostomy may be discharged home on mechanical ventilation, as well as oxygen. Home ventilators are electrical machines similar to those used in hospitals. If your baby goes home on a ventilator, you'll be extensively trained to use the equipment and troubleshoot problems. You'll also have a nurse assigned to assist you in your home for at least several hours a day, until you feel more comfortable.

CLEANING THE OXYGEN EQUIPMENT

To prevent infections, it's crucial to clean all of the oxygen equipment regularly, following the instructions provided by your home health agency. The filter of a concentrator, for instance, should be washed with hot water and mild soap at least once a week. It's particularly important to keep the humidification tubing clean, since bacteria love to grow in its warm, humid environment.

IN CASE OF EMERGENCY

When a baby goes home on oxygen, the hospital or home health agency should inform the local electric and telephone companies to put his family on a special priority list, in case of a blackout or rationing of service. Near your telephone, for quick reference, you should post a list of emergency telephone numbers: 911 or the local rescue squad; the fire department; the closest emergency room; your baby's doctor; the home health agency and oxygen equipment supplier; and the electric company's emergency service line.

FINANCIAL CONSIDERATIONS

Insurance plans and Medicaid usually pay for oxygen equipment, but not for the higher electrical bills generated by an oxygen concentrator. They also cover home nursing care for babies with more complicated BPD who need a lot of special care and medications, but only for a limited number of hours a day and for a short time after discharge from the hospital. Most parents find that home oxygen alone poses little extra financial burden for them. But if your baby has lots of other medical needs and equipment, you may have expenses that aren't covered—you may have to buy a van, for example, or even move to a different house. Be sure to check with the social worker in your hospital to see if you're eligible for any other government or private assistance programs that provide financial help or give you access to more services.

USEFUL TIPS FROM PARENTS TO PARENTS

There's nothing like direct experience to teach a parent how to deal with a baby on supplemental oxygen. Here are some tips from families who have "been there":

* Choose a stroller with the biggest possible basket (to fit the oxygen tank), and with a canopy where you can store other things you have to carry.

* Some parents find they rest easier having their baby on a pulse oximeter, so you may want to talk to your doctor about getting one. If your baby's oxygen tube gets squeezed or twisted during the night, and he isn't getting enough oxygen, this alarm will go off earlier than an apnea monitor.

* Once a baby on oxygen becomes able to roll over, it's possible for him to wrap the tube around his neck. An easy way to prevent this

is to dress him in one-piece, long-legged outfits, and run the tube down his back, under his clothes, letting it out below the last button on the leg, at his ankle.

* Most parents find that using very long tubing, about 50 feet, allows them to move freely around the house with their baby, and is easier than switching back and forth between tanks in different rooms. Just make sure that the path is kept clear, and the tube doesn't get shut in a door.

* If your house has two floors, you may want to use two large tanks, one on each floor.

* Ask for a connecting piece, between the nasal cannula and oxygen tube, that can turn 360 degrees. That way, the tube is prevented from twisting too much as your baby moves.

* Some parents warn about the importance of having only metal pieces in the tank regulator. Plastic ones can break more easily, creating an emergency. For the same reason, you may want to keep extra parts handy (nasal cannula, prongs, tubing), at home and in the car, and bring some spares with you when you travel.

* Some babies on extra oxygen (usually those with other equipment as well, such as a portable ventilator or an apnea monitor) may qualify for a handicapped parking permit. You may not like the idea, but it can be a boon when you have a lot to carry. Ask the NICU's discharge planner what papers you have to fill out in order to get one.

* Daycare centers don't usually accept babies on extra oxygen, which can be a problem if parents need to work and don't have relatives or friends to help them. If you contact a parent support group, they may know of a baby-sitting pool, or be able to help you set one up. This may involve some organizational work at first, but it may work well for you, and give

your baby the opportunity to interact with other kids. Another option is to ask at your local hospital's special care nursery or pediatric nursing department whether any of the nurses would like to do some baby-sitting or child care. Pediatric or neonatal nurses already have the training and experience to handle a baby on oxygen—they'd just need to become familiar with your equipment. Often you can find a few nurses who enjoy the variety and fun, as well as the extra income, of taking care of a healthier baby at home.

✸ Some parents find it difficult to allow themselves to trust anybody to baby-sit for their baby. They end up very tired and stressed out, which isn't good for anyone in the family, their baby included. If you have somebody who is willing to help you and to be trained on your baby's oxygen equipment, you should try to accept the idea, and allow yourself to get some much-needed respite.

✸ If you qualify for more than a couple of hours a day of in-home nursing care, consider asking the nurses to come at night, so you can sleep.

ASSESSING YOUR BABY'S RESPIRATION

In time, you'll become a good judge of your baby's respiration, able to detect any evidence of distress. The most frequent signs are a change in color (the baby becomes pale or blue), fast and hard breathing, pronounced flaring of the nostrils, or wheezing. Some parents may be taught to check their baby's oxygen saturation with a pulse oximeter. Your baby's doctor will tell you what to expect from your child, and when you should be concerned.

Your baby will thrive on plenty of feeding, handling, and play, so you shouldn't restrict them unless the doctor has told you to do so. Occasionally, you may need to take a brief pause, to give your child's breathing a chance to return to normal. (Be sure to tell the doctor if you notice that your child has any respiratory distress, because he might want to prescribe an increased amount of oxygen during certain activities.) It won't be surprising if your baby needs to have his oxygen increased when he gets sick with colds or other respiratory illnesses. But you shouldn't change your baby's oxygen settings on your own, either raising or lowering them for long, unless you've been instructed to do so by your doctor. Sometimes, parents turn off the oxygen because their baby looks fine. But even if a baby isn't blue, his oxygen saturation can be too low, potentially causing his growth to be slowed, or injuring his lungs, heart, eyes, or brain.

Taking your baby off oxygen, therefore, must be your doctor's call. He will evaluate your baby's status, probably performing pulse oximetry or blood gas tests during different activities and times of day. If he concludes that your baby is ready to be weaned, he'll decrease the extra oxygen slowly, usually over several months. Finally, the time will come when you turn off your baby's oxygen once and for all, with thanks for its help, but understandable relief.

Giving Medications

I'm supposed to give my baby medicine with feedings every eight hours. It's going to be such a hassle.

Yes, dealing with medications is going to be a hassle. But once you get used to it, within just a few days, it should be a little hassle, not a big one. It will become part of your regular routine, not much different than changing diapers, giving baths, doing feedings, or giving daily vitamins. These tips may help things go smoothly:

✸ *Before your baby leaves the hospital, make sure the nurses show you how to give your baby her medication, and that they watch you do it yourself, to check that you're doing it right.* There are certain things you definitely will need to know, in addition to how much medicine to give and how often to give it. If there's anything on the following list that the nurses haven't mentioned, be sure to ask:

- How to position your baby when giving the medicine, and where to place the syringe or dropper inside her mouth;
- Whether to give the medicine before, with, or after meals;
- Whether there's a little flexibility in the schedule;
- What to do if your baby vomits right after receiving a dose, or you forget to give one;
- Whether to keep the medication in the refrigerator;
- Whether to expect side effects, and what to do if they appear;
- What the plan is for stopping the medication.

✸ *Usually, there's some flexibility in the medication schedule.* If you're told to give the medication to your baby "every eight hours," for example, it may be equally fine for her to get it three times a day—in roughly eight-hour intervals, but not exactly. That little fact will provide you with a lot of freedom. Instead of having to say, "Oh no, it's noon. I have to wake my baby up," you'll be able to relax, finish whatever you're doing, and let her wake up on her own.

✸ *Look on the bright side: many people believe schedules are good for babies, anyway.* For some parents—especially those whose babies have to get their medicine with feedings—it's being tied to a clock-driven routine that feels most burdensome. It's true, this means you're going to lose some spontaneity. But on the positive side, many experienced parents and experts believe strongly that babies are happier and less cranky if they're on a schedule—you prevent them from getting overtired by sticking to a regular nap schedule, and from getting too hungry by feeding them at regular, routine times. Some people even think that structure in infancy is the beginning of promoting self-discipline.

Schedules aren't all negative for parents, either: you'll know you can set aside specific times for other things, rather than always being at your baby's beck and call. It may mean you can look forward to sitting down every morning with a mug of coffee at ten o'clock, or every evening to a precious dinner alone with your partner, relatively undisturbed.

✸ *Don't panic if your baby throws up right after getting her medicine.* It happens to everyone. Here are some general guidelines to follow, but only after you've asked the nurse or doctor whether they apply to your baby's medication. If a baby throws up right after getting the medicine, you should give that dose again. (If it is colored, you'll be able to see that the medicine has come out.) If a baby throws up around one hour after getting the medicine, and you can see that some has come out, it may be right to give another half-dose, or to give no more and just wait until the next dose, depending on how crucial the medication is and what the risks of overdose are. If a baby throws up after more than an hour, you shouldn't give that dose again—she got it. Remember that these are general guidelines only. It's important to check with your doctor about them first.

✳ *If you're very late with a dose of medicine, give it when you remember, then gradually modify the schedule back to the original times.* The idea is to keep the time when the dose was missed as short as possible, then give the next doses a little earlier or later than eight hours afterward, until you've gradually readjusted the schedule back to normal. However, if the new schedule is fine for you—for instance, if it means you won't have to give the medicine in the middle of the night—you can stick with subsequent, eight-hour intervals, and leave the schedule at the new times.

✳ *If you miss a dose, never double or increase the next dose unless your doctor has specifically told you to do so.* This could be harmful to your baby.

✳ *Ask the nurses if you can take home a bunch of syringes with removable needles from the hospital.* These syringes are perfect for measuring out infant doses. You can use each one many times, if you wash them after each use.

✳ *Don't give medicine to your baby when she's lying down.* She could choke.

✳ *Don't give medicine in the dark.* It's too easy to make mistakes in measuring the dose, and too hard to see whether your baby actually swallowed the medicine. In fact, if at all possible, try to schedule things so you don't have to give the medicine in the middle of the night, when you're groggy.

✳ *Prepare your baby's medication for a day or two at a time, storing it in a safe place where it won't spill, and labeling it if your baby gets more than one kind.* When it's time for a dose of medicine, and you're rushing around with a crying baby, or stumbling around half-asleep, you'll be glad that you took a few quiet minutes in advance to do some planning.

✳ *Keep a running checklist of all the times you give your baby her medicine, and hang it on the refrigerator or medicine cabinet.* Believe us, you're going to be glad you have this. Even the most organized parent occasionally forgets whether she just gave the medication a few minutes ago. If you aren't the only one who will be giving the medication, keeping things straight with a careful record is especially crucial.

✳ *At your baby's checkups, ask the doctor whether the dose needs to be increased.* As your baby gains weight, she may need more for the medication to remain as effective—and her doctor may need a reminder.

✳ *Don't decide when to stop giving the medication yourself.* If it's important enough for your baby to be sent home on, it's not something to fool around with. If your baby is having great difficulty taking the medication, or you have the sense she doesn't need it anymore, you can certainly suggest to the doctor that you'd like to stop. He may make this decision on his own, or may consult with the neonatologist who took care of your baby, or a specialist. But this has to be the doctor's call.

Reflux

My baby has reflux. Any advice for dealing with this at home?

While reflux is rarely a serious health problem, it can be an uncomfortable and messy one. Many parents of preemies with reflux say it can be draining to care for their babies.

Fortunately, most babies outgrow their reflux within the first year, and very few still have the problem beyond age two. In the meantime, here is some distilled advice from doctors and parents who've been down this road before:

❋ *Buy a whole stash of cloth diapers, and always keep them handy.* You can use them to drape over your shoulder when you're holding your baby, to protect your clothes, and to cover the upholstery of the chair you're sitting in. When your baby spits up, they're big and soft enough to clean her.

❋ *Don't move your baby around too much during, or immediately after, feedings.* This means no bouncy seats, baby swings, or physical exercise for an hour or so after meals.

❋ *When you put your baby down to sleep, lie her on her side.* Young preemies and babies with severe reflux are exceptions to the recommendation that a baby be put to sleep on her back. On her back, it may be easier for refluxed food to get into her airway or lungs, causing her to choke or have breathing problems. When you put her on her side, you can help her stay in that position by placing rolled-up blankets around her, or using the special, positioning cushions sold by some baby stores.

❋ *Some parents find it helps to raise the head of their baby's bed about 30 degrees.* You may find that your local baby store sells foam wedges to place under the head of the crib mattress, but a cheaper alternative is to prop big books or towels under one side of the crib mattress or bassinet.

❋ *Hold your baby in as vertical a position as possible, rather than a reclining one, when you are feeding her and for a little while afterward.* Gravity will help keep the food from coming back up. Many parents find this position less natural at first, but for babies with reflux, it's the most comfortable position there is.

❋ *Give your baby smaller, more frequent meals.* This often works wonders. But keep in mind that reflux is aggravated by long periods of crying, because the stomach fills up with air. So this tip can quickly backfire if your baby dissolves in tears every time you end a feeding before she's completely full.

❋ *During bottle feedings, burp your baby often.* Babies often swallow air from the bottle when they feed. A common guideline is to stop for a burp after every ounce or two.

❋ *If you are bottle feeding your baby, and she is gulping down her formula rapidly, she may do better with a different nipple that delivers the formula more slowly.* It's also worth trying one that is designed for babies to swallow less air. Choosing the best nipple for each baby is usually a matter of trial and error.

❋ *If your baby's neonatologist or pediatrician approves, you can try thickening her feedings with rice cereal.* Eating thicker feeds improves reflux in some babies. Add one tablespoon of rice cereal per ounce of formula. (You can also try this with pumped breast milk, but it may not work well, because an enzyme in breast milk breaks down the cereal before it can thicken the milk.) If you notice that this isn't helping your baby, it could be because she is sucking more vigorously to get the thicker feedings through the nipple, and taking more air into her stomach.

❋ *Some babies with reflux keep solid foods down better than liquids.* In some countries, it's traditional to introduce solid foods within the first month of life, although American physicians have worried that this may contribute to food allergies. If you want to try it, be sure to talk to your pediatrician first about safe foods he recommends to get started.

❋ *If you notice that your baby is turning dusky or blue during a feeding, remove the nipple from her mouth, and remind her to breathe with a little pat or rub.* If you find that gentle stimulation isn't enough to keep her breathing well during meals, call your pediatrician right away. On the other hand, if your baby remains pink, and her nostrils open and close slightly while she sucks, you can be sure she's breathing just fine.

❋ *Ask your pediatrician whether he recommends Baby Mylanta.* It's an over-the-counter medication that reduces stomach acid, so it may help with any heartburn your baby may be feeling. There are other, prescription medications for reflux that your doctor may consider if he thinks the reflux is severe. If your baby is taking medicine for reflux, check with the doctor to make sure that you're giving it at the best times of day, and in the right amount (the dose may need to be increased as your baby grows).

❋ *Keep in mind that reflux can be hard on a baby's teeth.* Over time, stomach acid that comes into contact with a baby's teeth can eat away at the enamel. Dentists suggest brushing your baby's teeth regularly, never putting her to bed with a bottle of milk or juice, and making sure she gets fluoride, through your water or fluoride supplements, once her teeth come in. All parents should follow these guidelines, but it's especially important for you.

❋ *Infant seats and car seats tend to worsen reflux, because they cause a baby to slump down, putting pressure on her stomach.* If this seems to be a problem, you may want to look into getting an infant car bed. (You can order one from the manufacturer, Cosco, by calling (800) 544–1108; it also converts into a rear-facing car seat.) Or try a seat that reclines slightly, to keep your baby from slumping down.

❋ *When you're with your baby, don't wear clothes that must be dry cleaned, or that are irreplaceable.* You'll feel a lot less frustrated when your baby spits up if you can just toss your clothes into the washing machine—or easily replace them if they're beyond washing.

❋ *Keep several changes of clothes for your baby handy.* If you want her to look and smell nice, you're going to be changing her outfits more often than other parents do. White clothes are actually some of the most practical, because stains can be bleached out. Don't splurge on gorgeous baby clothes that you'll be pained to see stained after just one wearing, but don't put away all of your favorite clothes, either. If your baby doesn't wear them now, she'll grow out of them before you have a chance to enjoy them. She may wear each piece of clothing for only a few hours at a time—but she'll look adorable while she does.

During moments of frustration, remember two things. First, all babies spit up, cry, and occasionally seem uncomfortable or irritable. While your baby may do more of these things, they're not as uncommon—and you're not as alone—as you may sometimes think. Second, your baby's body is maturing every day, gradually working to eliminate the problem. In just a few months, you'll probably notice that her reflux is better. And not long after that, it may well be gone.

Special Formula or Breast Milk

How long do preemies need to be on special formulas or fortified breast milk?

Today, most preemies who are bottle fed are discharged from the hospital on a special kind of infant formula, called transitional formula. The currently available brands are Enfamil 22 and Neocare (by the company that makes Similac). They were introduced only a few years ago, to improve premature babies' nutrition and growth during the transition between preterm formula and regular formula.

Transitional formula provides 22 calories per ounce, less than the 24 calories per ounce found in preterm formula, but more than the 20 calories per ounce in regular formula. It also has more vitamins and minerals than regular formula, and a special kind of fat that's easier to digest and assimilate. Studies have shown that preemies' bone growth and mineral levels are better if they're fed transitional formula for a few months after discharge. The companies that make transitional formula suggest using it for six months. But how long your baby needs special formula will depend on her size at birth and how well she's growing. You can ask your pediatrician when she thinks it's the right time for your baby to graduate to regular formula. It will be a milestone—a happy sign that your baby, after his special beginning, is settling into much-welcomed, plain-old infanthood.

Preemies who, after discharge, take all of their feedings from their mothers' breasts and are growing well, generally don't need the extra minerals and calories from breast milk fortifier. So it's not worth interrupting or changing your nursing patterns to add it to your milk. But if you're pumping your milk and sometimes giving it to your baby in a bottle, you may be instructed by the doctor to add fortifier to the pumped breast milk. This usually isn't advised for longer than a few weeks. As long as your baby is being exclusively breastfed, he'll be prescribed multivitamin, iron, and maybe fluoride drops, to supplement the few nutritional elements that are relatively lacking in breast milk. These can be discontinued when he's eating adequate amounts of solid food—ask your pediatrician when that is.

Some babies, such as those with BPD or heart problems, need lots of energy to grow, but do poorly if they get too much fluid. If that's the case for your preemie, your pediatrician may tell you to prepare regular formula with less water, to increase its caloric content. This is a convenient alternative to buying special formulas, which are often unavailable in grocery stores or pharmacies, and can be very expensive to order.

Here's what you may be told to do by your baby's doctor:

With powdered formula:

* to make regular, 20-calorie-per-ounce formula, mix 1 scoop of powder with 2 ounces of water
* to make 22-calorie-per-ounce formula, mix 3 scoops of powder with 5½ ounces of water
* to make 24-calorie-per-ounce formula, mix 3 scoops of powder with 5 ounces of water

With liquid, concentrated formula:

* to make 20-calorie-per-ounce formula, mix 1 ounce of concentrate with 1 ounce of water (or mix the usual 13-ounce can of concentrated liquid formula with 13 ounces of water)
* to make 22-calorie-per-ounce formula, mix a 13-ounce can with 10½ ounces of water
* to make 24-calorie-per-ounce formula, mix a 13-ounce can with 8½ ounces of water

If your baby needs even more calories, the pediatrician can decide to further enrich his formula with special oils or powdered supplements containing carbohydrates. Whatever instructions you receive from your doctor about your baby's nutrition, you should follow them carefully, never taking the initiative and changing the concentration or doses on your own. Overly concentrated formula is difficult to digest, and can cause dehydration and other serious problems. Supplements can be very dangerous if not given according to your doctor's prescription.

Obsessed with Baby's Weight

My husband thinks I'm obsessed with feeding my baby. But I've got to make sure she keeps gaining weight.

To her parents, a preemie's small size often comes to represent everything that is unhealthy or dangerous in her condition. With the daily weighings in the hospital, the jubilation or consternation over ounces gained or lost—well, no wonder you're obsessed with feeding her! Even a small spit-up can upset you, as if those few, lost calories could be the precious ones that make a difference. But now, even your husband, who has gone through all of this with you, is telling you to relax. How can you do that?

First of all, you may need to acknowledge and accept that you're going to have special feelings about your daughter's nutrition for a long time. In fact, when the time comes to make the transition from breast milk or formula to baby foods, you may feel more anxious, since it means leaving a reassuring, known feeding schedule for a new one. Many parents of preemies continue paying special attention to how their child eats for a long time—and nobody should blame you for that. It's something practical you can do to ease your fears and assure that she's getting good nutrition.

But you also need to realize that it's perfectly normal for your baby to eat more at one meal and less at another. It's one way her body regulates itself, matching her fuel intake to her energy demands. If you consistently overlook her signals of hunger or feeling full, you can short circuit this important regulatory function. So try hard not to ignore your baby's cues, even if she's saying (heaven forbid!) she's not hungry. Rather than thinking that you have to get your baby to eat a certain amount at each feeding, try to see her food intake as averaged over one- to two-day cycles. Chances are, the varying amounts she eats at each meal will balance out over time. Your baby's doctor can tell you the minimum amount of food she should eat each day, on average, to grow and develop well. As long as she takes in that much, you don't have to press for more.

Ask her pediatrician to go over your baby's growth chart with you, to assure yourself that she's feeding well and gaining weight. She's doing fine if she's growing at a steady rate along a standard growth curve, and great if she's gradually catching up to her full-term peers. It might also help to ask the doctor how important it is for you to continue doing your utmost to feed her, or if you can relax your vigilance. Some preemies, such as those with severe BPD, often have trouble eating and need all the calories they can get, while others do just fine on their own. Tell your doctor if there's something about the way your baby feeds that is worrying you (such as how she sucks, swallows, or reacts to eating from a spoon). But if he reassures you, and says that a bottle or a baby food jar occasionally left unfinished is not the end of the world—believe him.

If you can, try to look at this attitude of yours with some sense of humor. A self-deprecating joke here and there, about your constant attempts to stuff the poor baby like a Thanksgiving turkey, can lighten your spirits, and give your relatives and friends better insight into your reaction to one of the most stressful issues for parents of premature children.

Whom to Call with Questions

I've already called the NICU twice because I was worried about my son, and it turned out to be nothing. Now I'm nervous again, and I don't know if I should call.

If you're often tempted to call the NICU, or have already done it, you're certainly not alone. Studies have found that a great number of parents make telephone calls to their baby's hospital caregivers for several weeks after discharge. The NICU staff understands this need. Some nurseries even have a specially assigned nurse to deal with families of discharged babies.

But acknowledging a common behavior doesn't mean it's the best thing to do. Your baby's pediatrician, with whom you should schedule a visit within two weeks after discharge, at the latest, is the one who should field most of your questions and worries. Don't hesitate to call him with any concerns about your baby's behavior, daily activities, breathing, feeding and sleeping patterns, digestion, or possible illnesses. Actually, your baby's doctor needs this information to get to know his new little patient, and you need to begin to interact with him, to develop a comfortable, trusting relationship. The time to call the NICU is when you have questions about instructions you received at the time of discharge—regarding your baby's medications, for instance—and then only until your pediatrician has had an opportunity to review your baby's caregiving schedule, and to

take over the responsibility of confirming or adapting it.

You should definitely not hesitate to call a doctor, whether it's your pediatrician or the NICU, if a problem you know your baby has is getting worse, or if she has a fever, is very lethargic, exceedingly irritable, isn't eating, or is having difficulty breathing. Many times, you'll find that your worries are false alarms. (One of us called the NICU terrified about her son's high temperature, only to have it pointed out that it was due to at least two layers of excess clothing!) But parental instinct can also detect the first signs of a real problem. It's better to get your concerns addressed, and suffer a little embarrassment if it's "nothing," than to let an important problem pass.

Missing the NICU

I thought I couldn't wait to take my baby home. But now that we're here, I think I actually miss the NICU!

It may seem strange to you, to miss a place you wanted so much to leave. But think of it this way: you couldn't wait for your preemie to be discharged from the hospital mostly because that meant he was finally safe, a normal infant going home with his family. What you couldn't picture in advance was the tremendous weight of responsibility you would feel, taking care of a fragile and demanding baby at home. Looking back, the NICU doesn't seem so scary anymore, but like a safe haven where they knew what to do to make your baby well and, as a result, to make you feel good, too.

It's true that the dozens of daily questions you have about your baby's breathing, crying, feeding, spitting up, and sleeping cannot be answered right away by a reassuring doctor or nurse anymore. You have to screen through your concerns, and choose only those which really need to be addressed. There are no monitors to tell you, with their silence, that everything is fine with your baby here at home. You have to rely on your judgment. Or if your baby is on a home monitor, the sense of security you get from it may be confounded by the stress of false alarms, and the hassle of managing it, on top of everything else.

Loneliness can add to your frustration. Most premature babies are discharged around their due date or before, so they're still not very responsive—or respond mostly with negative signals, like crying, fussing, or refusing to sleep. Here at home, there are no other mothers or fathers with whom to interact, tell your story, distract yourself with their problems, feel you're not alone in dealing with a preemie. Although the social interactions you had in the NICU may not have seemed very important to you at the time, now you may realize that they added a brightness to your day. And since it's safer not to take your preemie to public places, and to curb visitors for a while, you don't have many chances for distraction.

Not least, there's the sheer fatigue of caring for a young baby. There are no quiet nights, and few quiet moments, anymore. Who wouldn't miss that?

The important thing to realize is that your reaction is completely normal. You need some time to develop confidence (and competence) now that your baby is home with you. Give yourself a chance to adapt and settle down, and you'll see your insecurities slowly disappear. Although giving birth to a preemie leaves indelible marks on a parent's soul, these initial difficulties caused by his homecoming are, we promise you, quick to pass. They will, sooner than you may expect.

Older Siblings

I've read it's good for an older child to be a helper with a new sister or brother. But I'm so afraid that my daughter will hurt my preemie.

After all that your baby has been through, you probably have a tendency to think of him as more fragile than he really is. Unless your baby has special medical needs or equipment, such as home oxygen or a tracheostomy tube, for example, you can treat him pretty much the same as a full-term newborn—except for being a little more vigilant in protecting him from colds and infections.

Still, unless your older child is nearly a grown-up herself, she probably isn't capable of handling any baby on her own. Toddlers and children simply don't have the coordination—or power of concentration—to keep an infant's neck supported at all times, to watch him every second he's on a high changing table or bed, or to hold both bottle and baby comfortably and safely during a feeding filled with countless squirms and distractions. No matter how eager your older child is to help, or how much you want to make her feel included, your most important job is to keep both of your children safe—and right now, that means drawing the line at anything she could do that could be harmful to your newborn. You can be sure that your daughter counts on you to set these limits, which she has no way of knowing on her own.

But she still wants to help, and there are plenty of more limited, safe ways that older siblings can. Here are some, and you'll think of many others:

❋ You can ask her to help get the baby's room ready for his homecoming, and to give him a "tour" of his new home when he arrives.

* During diapering, she can bring you the diaper, coo and talk to the baby while he's on the changing table, and help attach the diaper's tabs once you have them in place.
* When the baby is unhappy, you can suggest that she try making funny faces, singing songs, or caressing him. If he stops crying, be sure to point out how successful she was.
* You can ask her to choose the baby's clothes or bibs.
* She can hold the bottle for a few seconds during feedings (or longer, if it's going well).
* She can hold the baby in her lap when she's sitting down, and you're supervising.
* She can help you push the baby's stroller when you go out for walks. Remember, though, to supervise her closely, because out of enthusiasm, she could pull down the handle and tip the stroller backward.
* You can ask for her opinion when you're trying to interpret the baby's gibberish or cries.

It's a small thing, but will count for so much: if you give your daughter positive feedback by pretending to talk for the baby and thanking her for being a great big sister, you'll probably see her face light up with pride. If she does something wrong, try not to criticize her. Instead, gently show her the right way to do it, or find some other role for her to play.

Your daughter will probably get even more out of helping with the baby than most older siblings. Some researchers have suggested that siblings of preemies, having felt powerless during the family crisis, want to help take care of the baby and even their parents, as a way of "sharing the burden." Also, given your entirely natural feelings of protectiveness toward your baby, and wanting to make up for his separation from you, you're probably spending even more time with him than most mothers of second

children do. It's easy to keep postponing your older child's needs. But it isn't easy on your daughter, who may have felt left out, or less loved, during all of the weeks or months of hospitalization, and may have expected the homecoming to put things finally right.

So, stop and check yourself every few days: Are you spending as much time as you can with your older child? Have you spent some time alone with her today? Are you helping her to feel how much she's loved and valued? Are you viewing your baby as overly vulnerable and fragile, as many parents of premature babies have a tendency to do?

No matter what you do, of course, you aren't going to be able to make your family exempt from some inevitable sibling rivalry and acting-out. Just consider it part of your welcome to normal life with two children!

Questions about Your Baby's Age

People keep asking me how old my baby is, and I don't know what to say!

Most kids would find it awesome to have two birthdays, as preemies sort of do—the date they were born, which is their legal birthday, and their due date, which you could call their developmental birthday. To preemies' parents, though, the situation is just confusing. The simplest questions, like "How old is your baby?" or "At what age did your son start crawling?" are, well, not so simple.

From the standpoint of developmental milestones—when your baby should be rolling over, reaching for objects, sitting up, babbling, walking, and so on—what counts is his due date, not his birth date. Nobody notified mother nature to reprogram his innate, developmental schedule when he came out a little early. Thus, for the first couple of years, when assessing whether a preemie's behavior and size are appropriate for his age, experts use his "adjusted" or "corrected" age. To calculate this, figure out how old he'd be if he'd been born on his due date. Or take his actual age, and subtract however many weeks or months he was early. Thus, if your baby is four months old, but was born two months early, his corrected age would be four minus two, or two months.

Nothing is simple, though. Some characteristics and abilities of a baby do develop based partly on experience, such as his ability to eat (food in the digestive tract speeds up its maturation), his immune system (exposure to germs gears his body up to fight off certain infections), the maturity of his skin (its tough, outer layer develops more quickly on exposure to air), and his familiarity with language and objects. These, and any other traits that respond to stimulation and postnatal experience, may be more advanced in your baby than in a two-month-old, term baby.

OK. How to answer those questions? That depends on what, if anything, the inquirer is really getting at (is it just passing, small talk by an admiring stranger in a supermarket, or someone trying to figure out if your baby should be crawling by now?), and how long an answer you're in the mood to give. The appropriate answer to any question concerning your baby's development is: "His adjusted age is two months." Of course, that may lead to further questions and explanations. If you want to avoid them, don't feel dishonest about simply saying: "He's two months." It's the truth, if not the whole truth—and there's no reason that parents should be expected to tell their baby's whole, private life story to everyone they meet!

But when you're in the mood to open up and reminisce about your baby's monumental experiences, the most accurate—and intriguing—answer you can give is: "He's two months going on four." Like people who are said to be 16 going on 30, because they're biologically young, but emotionally and experientially older, your baby is a rich, fascinating interweave of two ages.

Daycare

I'm thinking of going back to work. Is daycare safe for my baby?

From a medical standpoint, it's best to avoid daycare if your premature baby has been home for just a short time. Anyone who has watched the way children transfer toys from one mouth to another, and hover intimately within a few inches of each other's little faces, runny noses and all, can see why. Every child picks up more germs—and therefore comes down with more mild infections, from colds to ear infections, conjunctivitis, diarrhea, and rashes—once she enters daycare or school. That's unavoidable, no matter how carefully the program is run.

How risky daycare will be for your premature baby depends on how fragile your baby is. If she's a big, healthy preemie, you can figure that her immune system is about on par with, or a little more advanced than, her adjusted age. So if on an adjusted basis she's at term now, it would be like sending a newborn to daycare. However, if she was born before 32 to 34 weeks of gestation, she lacks some or all of the infection-fighting antibodies that normally pass through the placenta from the mother in the last trimester of pregnancy. Most of these maternal antibodies pass to the fetus between 28 and 34 weeks of gestation, and give older preemies and term babies some extra protection. They're gradually cleared from their systems over the first year or so of life, after which the baby's immune system is on its own.

One particular problem for preemies is a common respiratory virus called RSV (short for respiratory syncytial virus). Most children and adults who catch RSV simply have the symptoms of a cold. But infants, and especially preemies, are particularly susceptible to getting seriously ill from it. In some cases, RSV worsens into pneumonia or bronchiolitis, and can cause breathing difficulty severe enough to require rehospitalization. So if you have to send your preemie to daycare, be sure to ask her pediatrician whether she should get treated with preventive immune therapy for RSV (see page 438). The virus is especially common during the late fall, winter, and early spring. After your baby gets through her first cold season, or is more than six months old, her special vulnerability will be much less.

If your baby has BPD (or some doctors say a VP shunt), she is more fragile, and the risks of sending her to a daycare center are much greater. At least for the first year or so, you should try to find another option. Remember: even when it looks to you like your baby's BPD has gone away—she is no longer on oxygen and is not acting sick—she has less reserve in her lungs than other babies, and when she catches something, she'll have a tendency to get a lot sicker. For a baby with BPD, many common childhood diseases can require rehospitalization and even become life threatening. This won't be the case forever; most children outgrow their BPD, and your pediatrician can help you decide when daycare is safe.

What should you do if you decide that a large daycare center isn't safe? If you have to return to work now, and it isn't possible to arrange one-on-one care for your baby, the next best option would be to find someone who cares for a small

number of children in her own home. For referrals, check pediatricians' bulletin boards, ask your friends and neighbors, and look in the Yellow Pages for childcare referral services. Just as you would do with a large daycare center, make sure to visit and see it in action (arriving at a time when you aren't expected, if possible), and check several references before sending your child.

Every extra month you give your preemie in the relative protection of her home will allow her immune system to become more mature and better at fighting off infection. You can help by keeping up to date with her immunizations, getting a flu shot for yourself—and your baby, once she's older than six months—at flu season, and asking all of her baby-sitters to get one, too. Be patient if you can. Even if you can't put your baby in daycare now, you'll have a lot more flexibility soon.

The Right Stimulation

I want my baby to have the best chance. How can I stimulate her in just the right ways?

No developmental expert or pediatric neurologist can tell you exactly what to do with your baby and when, because a simple prescription isn't available. But don't let that worry you: you won't need one. To quote Dr. Spock, "You know more than you think you do"—and your own parental sensitivity and intuition are your greatest, most effective tools.

Just keep in mind the following, general guidelines:

❋ Your goal should be to stimulate all of your preemie's senses, without overloading them. A baby's brain and body develops as it's used. Stimulation provides fuel for her development by giving her the kinds of everyday experiences she needs to sense, move, learn, and think, and to practice her evolving skills.

❋ The best time to interact with your baby is when she has her eyes open and looks calm and attentive. This "quiet alert" state, as it's called, is more likely to occur when she's well fed and burped, but before she becomes drowsy again or starts crying because she's too tired. This is when she is most receptive to stimulation.

❋ At first, your preemie may have only two or three periods a day when she's in a quiet alert state, open to stimulation. If your baby is often irritable and overloaded, you may be able to increase her quiet alert time by keeping her swaddled more. If she tends to be a sleepy baby, you may find that she's more receptive after an activity that is gently arousing, like a bath. But don't press too hard, or get concerned if she isn't ready for much interaction just yet. Every infant has a different threshold for stimulation. Being sensitive to your preemie's responses when you interact with her is one of the keys to helping her flourish.

❋ When you notice that your baby is quiet and alert, try approaching her slowly, and place your face about eight inches away from hers, where she can focus best. You can lie down on a bed or the floor with her, on your side, so she can see your face well. (Your baby's brain is programmed to prefer human faces to any other interesting objects.) Smile, and change your expression often. You can also stimulate her vision by showing her bold, black and white toys or pictures.

❋ By the time she gets home, your preemie should be mature enough to handle having more than one sense stimulated at a time. So, while lying face to face, you can also talk to her softly, in a high-pitched voice (infants can hear higher pitched sounds better, and seem to prefer them), sing a calm song or play some music, or read her a simple nursery rhyme (babies like rhythmic sounds). At other times, you can add touch, by giving her your finger to hold or stroking her body while she's looking at you.

❋ By moving her neck, arms, and legs gently, exercising and stretching her shoulders, hips, elbows, wrists, knees, and ankles, you can help her overcome any stiffness that may have occurred from lying in only a few positions in the hospital nursery. Now may even be the time to try some infant massage (see page 250), if you haven't done it already. Remember that babies find light touch arousing, and deeper, slower strokes calming.

❋ One of the best kinds of stimulation is also one of the most natural: holding your baby. Try carrying her around the house in a soft, fabric sling, close to your stomach and chest. She will enjoy the movement and close contact with your body, and she will begin to get acquainted with the different people, lights, sounds, views, and smells in the house. The sling will hold her body in a flexed position, which is good for calming her, and also for relaxing the splayed-out shoulders and hips that many preemies develop after prolonged lying on their backs in the hospital.

❋ When you are holding her without the sling, you can keep her shoulders flexed by placing her arms together in front of her chest. Similarly, instead of laying your baby down flat in her bed or on the floor, make a little nest of rolled blankets around her, to keep her shoulders and hips from turning outward. This will make it easier for her to bring her hands forward later on, when she wants to reach for things, and will help her get into the position she needs to learn to crawl and walk.

(You'll only need to do this until she's able to assume a flexed position by herself—usually when a preemie is three to four months adjusted age. Her adjusted age is how old she would be if she'd been born on her due date.)

✱ Tummy time can help your preemie develop a stronger neck and shoulders. Her crib or, even better, a blanket on the floor, will provide a good, flat surface for this kind of exercise. Place her on her stomach with her arms forward, elbows not wider than her shoulders, an interesting toy six to eight inches in front of her, to get her attention. In the beginning, she may last only a minute or less before getting tired. You can slowly increase the time of the exercise. Occasionally, you can also place her on her tummy when she's in your lap.

✱ The single, most important guideline we can give you about stimulating your baby is to proceed slowly and carefully with each new kind of interaction, always looking carefully at how she reacts, to see if she appreciates what you're doing. Your preemie will give you clearer clues than she used to about what she likes and what she finds too stressful. If she goes on looking at you without averting her gaze, continues to breathe smoothly, doesn't grimace, strain, arch her neck or back, or begin crying, you'll know that she likes what you're doing. At around six to eight weeks corrected age, your baby's smile, and her cooing, will show up to light up your days, and tell you that you're doing the right things.

From her due date on, there's not much different that your preemie needs, compared to a term infant. You can consult a regular parenting book to find strategies that foster infant development. There are many things to do to help her reach and explore the world with her hands, grasp objects, and discover new textures, sounds, shapes, and forms. More complex body movements and postures, like rolling and sitting, that now may seem to you so incredibly advanced, will be within your baby's reach before you know it. Just remember always to correct her age when you consult developmental charts, to avoid unrealistic expectations. Also remember: by showing her how pleased and proud of her you are, you'll foster her autonomy and self-esteem, and support her efforts to master new tasks.

IF YOU ARE ADOPTING A PREEMIE

If you're adopting a preemie, most of this book applies just as much to you as to a biological parent. But you'll have other issues and emotions as well, arising from the special nature of your parenting experience. Although these can't be predicted exactly from your point of view, below are some of the most common, along with some ideas to help you deal with them.

FEELINGS OF GUILT

A sense of guilt is something that goes with the territory when you have a premature baby. Birth mothers berate themselves for things they did or didn't do during their pregnancy, which they imagine contributed to the premature birth. Although people may assume that adoptive parents are free of that burden, not all are. You may find lots of reasons to blame yourself: for choosing the "wrong" birth mother, for example, or not giving her more money for food, or not checking carefully enough on her behavior during the pregnancy, or doing something that led to your having to adopt in the first place. Some adoptive parents identify so strongly with the birth mother throughout the pregnancy that they simply have a general sense of failure, like most biological mothers of preemies do.

The thing to realize is that these feelings of guilt surrounding a premature birth, although natural, are often overly self-critical and unfair. One out of ten births in the U.S. is premature, occurring in many instances when parents took all precautions. If you are blaming yourself, try to remember that your response is normal, but not necessarily rational, and as soon as you can, shift your energies to taking the best possible care of your wonderful child. Your baby's doctor can help put in perspective any specific doubts that you have.

FEELING TRAPPED

Legally, adoptive parents have the freedom of an option that biological parents lack: to back out of the adoption before the waiting period ends, deciding that they are not ready or able to take into their family a baby who was born prematurely and could have future problems. Emotionally, however, you may feel differently. Some adoptive parents have been through years of trying to conceive and then adopt a child. They may feel trapped in the situation because of their long, difficult struggle and intense desire to have a child, or because they feel responsible for the commitment they've made.

Few would argue that it's best to go into parenting willingly, with one's eyes open. One great resource for you is the social worker in the NICU, who is very concerned with getting the baby placed in the right home. Talk to her directly, or, if that's not possible, ask your adoption agency to be your intermediary. Ask questions about your baby's medical and developmental outlook, and be very honest about your own needs and what you think you can handle. Remember, most premature babies grow up healthy and normal. But don't feel callous or irresponsible if you decide that the adoption is not the best thing for you or your family; in that case, it wouldn't be the best thing for the baby, either. If your baby faces significant risks, it may help you to know that there are many families who are willing to adopt babies who have, or may have, special needs. Your baby will find a home.

If, on the other hand, you feel "stuck" mainly for the same reason that biological parents do—you already feel that this baby, a bundle of uncertainties and hopes, is all yours—then your preemie is one lucky baby. In that case, your strong commitment and love is going to get you through these early, anxious days to happier family times ahead.

BONDING WITH A DIFFICULT PREEMIE

If their premature infant is irritable and fussy, as preemies frequently are in early infancy, some adoptive parents wonder whether they have more trouble than biological parents do in bonding with their baby early on. Many assume that biological parents feel immediately loving and attached to their babies, starting with a magical moment in the delivery room. Maybe they do in fairy tales! But in real life, it often takes longer for love to grow. Many birth parents feel guilty about this and worry that something is wrong with them, while in fact, what they—and you—are going through is entirely normal.

A popular, simplistic concept of "bonding," which was supposed to occur instantly the first time you held your baby in your arms, is now considered an inaccurate representation of the parent-child relationship. The deep, lasting attachment that binds parent and child takes time and nurturing to grow. It develops over weeks, months, and even years, as each responds to and returns the other's caring and love. Just as falling in love at first sight (or for that matter, how the first few dates go) is a poor predictor of the depth of a couple's love later on, the same is true of babies and their parents—biological or adoptive.

Interestingly, some social workers who work with premature babies and their parents observe that adoptive parents often feel more positive about their babies than birth parents, perhaps because they've had to work so hard to get a baby. But that doesn't mean you won't have negative feelings—everyone does. Anger, anxiety, disappointment, and detachment are all typical feelings of parents of premature babies. Many of these feelings arise from grief, as parents, adoptive or biological, go through the emotions of mourning. It would be very unusual not to mourn something when your baby turns out to be a preemie—the loss of the roly-poly infant you imagined, the joys you would have had in the early days or months, your fantasy of perfect, radiant health, now and in the future. It's also normal to feel anger toward your baby, for being this way and putting you through all this, although parents find it hard to admit, because it feels so unacceptable. But don't assume that you're feeling negative emotions any more strongly than biological parents. You probably aren't.

It's of greater concern if your feelings remain predominantly negative for several months, or you have thoughts about harming your baby or yourself. In that case, you should talk to a mental health professional or to your baby's pediatrician. Some professional help may make all of the difference in how you feel about your baby, and how your relationship develops.

AN IMMEDIATE MATERNAL OR PATERNAL RESPONSE

Many adoptive parents are amazed at the opposite reaction: how immediately they feel a profound protectiveness toward their infant. Even on early visits to the NICU, an instinctive urge to shout, "Don't hurt my child!" may surface whenever a doctor or nurse goes near their baby with a needle. The intensity of love for a child is an incredible feeling, and adoptive parents aren't immune to that neon emotional light inside, flashing: "This is MY child." If you're wondering if you're strange to have such a forceful attachment—well, welcome to parenthood.

NEEDING TO BE "PERFECT" PARENTS

Some adoptive parents say they feel pressure to prove that they're "perfect" parents. That's really impossible to do, and you certainly shouldn't feel you have to, in order to justify your place in this baby's life. Unfortunately, no one can criticize themselves like new parents—especially ones with high standards for themselves. Most new birth mothers and fathers are riddled with self-doubts, too.

The thing is, all parents make mistakes—usually, lots of them. First children are especially stressful, because no new father or mother comes to them with any parenting experience, and everybody learns through trial and error. Make that child a preemie, and you have even more opportunity to torture yourself, as you deal with a variety of medical, behavioral, and parenting challenges that parents of term babies don't have to face. If you're a caring enough parent to be worried about this issue, the chances are that you're an excellent one. Time will bear that out.

NOT TREATED EQUALLY IN THE NICU

Some adoptive parents find they're prevented from visiting their newborn preemie in the hospital, or not given much medical information by the NICU staff. If you're lucky, you won't encounter these obstacles. But as you know, every adoption takes place under difference circumstances. While there are many agencies, lawyers, birth mothers, and hospitals that encourage adoptive parents to get involved with their babies as soon as possible, others insist they keep some distance until the waiting period has passed.

One reason for this reserve toward the adoptive parents is to avoid pressuring the birth mother, who can still change her mind about giving up the baby. Another is to protect the adoptive parents from becoming too attached, and possibly suffering severe loss and disappointment if the birth mother revokes her decision.

Also, some birth parents have an agreement that their confidentiality will be maintained, and that's hard to do in a hospital, where babies wear nametags. (The adoption agency or lawyer will tell the hospital when the baby's name can be changed to yours.) And there's an important legal issue involved: until guardianship of the baby has been officially transferred, the birth parents are the only ones who can get confidential medical information or consent to medical and surgical procedures. Once you become your baby's guardians, of course, you can neither be kept away from your baby nor denied information about him, and you'll participate in decisions about his care. If anyone on the hospital staff is confused about this, talk to the social worker, or your agency or lawyer, and ask them to help clear things up.

It can be incredibly frustrating if you're kept away from your baby at a time when you think he needs you. If you're encountering limits that you think are unreasonable, approach the unit's social worker (the staff member who will most likely be able to fight your case), either directly or using your agency or lawyer as an intermediary. Even if you're told that you have no rights to see your baby until he is discharged from the hospital, the social worker may be able to arrange an exception for just one or two visits. Ask her for a photograph, to keep close to you until you can be with your baby. Also, ask whether the hospital has a program of volunteers who are assigned to hold and cuddle babies, and if so, whether your baby can be included until you'll be able to be there often yourself. And remember that the waiting period is usually over within a few weeks, and your baby will benefit from your presence even more as he gets a little older (see page 252).

BREASTFEEDING AN ADOPTED BABY

It's not easy to induce lactation if you haven't recently been pregnant; it takes hard work and perseverance, and even then, many mothers are not able to do it. But a few do manage to produce enough milk to partially breastfeed their infants, and feel a tremendous sense of satisfaction in giving the advantages of breast milk to their babies. (You can read about how these advantages apply to preemies on page 125.) If you're interested, ask La Leche League (telephone [800] LA-LECHE) for literature and a referral to a specialist in lactation induction, to discuss what's involved. But keep in mind that breastfeeding is by no means mandatory—either as good nutrition for your preemie, or as a way to show her you love her—and only a tiny fraction of adoptive mothers try to do it. You should carefully consider the tremendous physical and emotional effort involved before you go down that road. The important thing is to get enough information so that you can make the right choice for you.

There are other, much easier ways of getting most of the advantages of breastfeeding. One is to arrange for your preemie to get breast milk from a milk bank, as explained on page 153. If it's the physical intimacy of the experience that you crave, you can consider trying a supplemental nursing system (see page 231), or holding your baby skin-to-skin (see kangaroo care, page 221), which will provide much of the same closeness.

Living day by day with your premature baby, you'll find plenty of other useful things you can do to enhance his development, growth, and happiness. Many are covered in the rest of this book, which is for all parents, no matter how their baby comes to them.

Fussiness

Is it true that preemies are a lot fussier than other babies?

Yes, several studies have found that preemies are more likely than term babies to behave in ways their parents find difficult to deal with. Premature infants have been described as less adaptive to new people and situations, less regular in their feeding and sleeping patterns, more difficult to soothe, and more withdrawn. In other words, fussy babies! But generalizations are always of limited value. While fussiness may be more common among premature babies, that doesn't make it true for all of them.

Even a preemie who had serious complications and a difficult hospital course can turn out to be a no-fuss, self-calming baby, and an excellent feeder and sleeper. So try not to be influenced by warnings about preemie fussiness, and to understand your baby's behavior and temperament without preconceived ideas. Much of his demeanor will depend on how you react to his cues, and behave toward him.

A simple reason that explains a lot about preemies' behavior is their immaturity. It's no wonder, since most preemies leave the hospital a few weeks before their due date. As a result, their sleeping and waking times are often unpredictable; their feeding patterns irregular; their responses limited or disorganized; and their energy levels low. It's not surprising then, that preemies as a group are reported to be less adaptable and sociable, and to get upset more quickly than term infants. Just give them a little time!

Environment plays a role, too. A difficult temperament is more common among preemies who were smaller and younger at birth. These infants have gone through long hospitalizations, and are more likely to have suffered severe illnesses and complications. When stimulation is excessive or painful, as it can be in the NICU, some preemies become prone to startles and extreme agitation, or become absent and withdrawn to block out the stimulation. These behavioral patterns can linger for a long time, even after a baby goes home and is no longer subjected to disturbing medical procedures, but only to his parents' loving attention.

Thus, what you notice in the first weeks or months can be misleading, just a passing stage before your baby shows you his real nature. While you've probably heard your friends say that their newborns' personalities and temperaments were immediately obvious, from their very first hours, research has shown that a premature baby's behavior is less stable during his first years of life than a term baby's. It's not until at least 18 to 24 months that preemies are rated by their parents to be as stable in temperament as children who were born full-term. (According to parents, the vast majority of preemies achieve a stable and easy temperament by the time they enter preschool.)

The so-called "goodness of fit" between a baby and his family is also important. More sensitive, attentive parents are likely to rate their babies as less "difficult," and to find them more responsive and less irritable. How much is a baby's behavior shaped by his family's positive or negative attitude, rather than the other way around? That's hard to assess. But a parent-child relationship is a circle of mutual influence, leading to change and development not only on the baby's part. What counts is finding a common behavioral rhythm, through better understanding and communication. In the beginning, this is what parents of preemies struggle with most.

It may help you to adapt more quickly, and ease your stress, if you know what's normal in a premature baby. Be prepared to encounter some difficulties in these daily activities:

* *Sleeping.* Healthy premature babies are expected to wake up and fuss about every two hours until they're three to four months corrected age. (A long time, if you ask us!) By about six to eight months corrected age, they will have settled into longer periods of sleep, to everybody's understandable relief.

* *Feeding.* Nearly half of all parents of preemies complain about some feeding problems during their baby's first year, ranging from the infant's getting tired too easily while feeding, to difficulty reading his hunger signals, to persistent reflux. These problems can be particularly frustrating to parents of preemies, because of their concern about their baby's need for catch-up growth.

* *Crying.* Premature babies' crying reaches a peak of frequency and intensity at three to four months corrected age, which is later than in term babies. Although the first months at home with a baby who fusses a lot can be really vexing, over time you will learn how to interpret all the different meanings of your baby's cries. In the meantime, you should try to feed your baby immediately when you think he may be hungry, let him sleep undisturbed as long as he can, and play with him, or engage in active interaction, only when he seems completely awake.

Parents who find their preemies fussier most commonly complain that they don't know when to do what. They find their baby's cues unclear, so they don't know when to play or quietly cuddle, to feed or put him to sleep, to soothe or leave him alone. It can appear to be a constant series of misunderstandings: their baby crying inconsolably (when his parents expect him to sleep), then suddenly falling asleep at the wrong times (for instance, during feedings), or turning away (when his parents try to comfort or play with him). Feeling like you don't know how to care for your baby can be extremely frustrating, and you may come to feel incompetent and rejected.

What can you do about it? First of all, recognize that preemies are less predictable, and harder to read, than term infants. It's not just you, or your child. Then, gradually try to learn to decipher your preemie's behavioral signals (see page 203): that's something not all parents learn in the hospital, overwhelmed as they are by other worries. Then, follow your baby's cues, and allow him to call the shots when you can. Don't worry that you're spoiling him now—it's way too early for that to happen. To feel comfortable and secure, he needs to know that his needs will be recognized and met, and that his family can be trusted to be available, gentle, and empathetic (unlike much of his experience in the hospital, unfortunately).

To soothe your baby and help him to sleep, try the following techniques, to discover what works best for him:

❋ Calm him with your touch, by holding him quietly, and providing him with physical boundaries or swaddling that make him feel secure. Let him suck on his hand or a pacifier. (See page 202 for more details of calming techniques.)

❋ Don't think that a quiet room with dim light is what your baby necessarily needs to fall asleep. After the constant noises of the NICU, he may be better appeased by background music, the soft sound of a TV, or a monotonous, constant noise like a hair-dryer or vacuum cleaner.

❋ A ride in the car (always in a car seat), or a walk in the stroller, can provide your baby with just the right level of noise and movement he needs to console himself and fall asleep.

❋ For the same reasons, in the first months, some parents end up carrying their preemie everywhere, keeping him close to their body in a sling or baby-carrier.

❋ Firm rocking in a low baby seat, swing, or car seat placed on the floor soothes some babies, but can make others more nervous. If your preemie doesn't like this, you may want to try it again in a few weeks—his preferences may have changed.

❋ Vigorous, rhythmic touch, which is arousing for some babies, can be pacifying for others. Some parents confess they feel weird when they pat their baby hard in public. But hard back-patting, or strong tummy-rubbing, works marvels to calm down many preemies.

❋ Try to control your frustration and anger at your baby's crying, by using breathing or other relaxation techniques. Instead of getting agitated and nervous along with your baby, which may just prolong the outburst, try to slow down your movements, lower your voice, and talk in a sweet, loving tone. That can help, as a sign of a general, more positive attitude. (Psychologists believe that showing that you understand his distress, and are there for your baby, will also help with his future emotional development.) To prevent a dangerous burnout, take turns with your partner, and get any help you can from relatives, friends, and other caregivers.

Every time you find yourself thinking how difficult and exhausting it is to care for this infant, just stop for a second, rewind your mental tape, and say instead: "My baby needs more help from me than I expected." Does being aware of the special behavioral characteristics of preemies change your perspective? It probably should. And remember that although this especially fussy time can feel very long, it will pass, and you'll gradually come to enjoy your baby more and more.

Is Baby Remembering Pain?

Every time my baby smells an alcohol wipe, he starts to cry. Is he remembering pain from the NICU?

Some parents of preemies say they've noticed that their babies have unusual reactions to pain. They may say their babies are oversensitive to pain, or undersensitive. Just as you wonder whether your child is associating the smell of alcohol with the pain he felt during medical procedures in the nursery, where disinfectants were used, other parents say their preemies are scared by the sound of tape being torn, as it would have been before an IV or endotracheal tube was put in, or by the sight of doctors in scrubs or white coats.

There's no sure way to tell whether your child is simply disturbed by the irritating smell of alcohol, or is actually associating it with the pain he felt in the hospital nursery. The study of pain in premature babies is so new that researchers are still concentrating on how to properly treat pain in the NICU. Few have started investigating whether preemies remember pain, or if it has any long-term effects.

But a few things are known that make parents' concerns plausible. We know that a preterm baby's senses are functioning from a

very early age, and that preemies find certain sensations pleasurable (for example, sweet tastes) and others distasteful (like the smell of ammonia). By about 28 weeks or so, preemies are even more sensitive to pain than full-term infants. We also know that newborns can recall some sensations from the past. Studies of full-term newborns have shown that they can recognize the sound of their mother's voice, or music they heard while in the womb. Since touch develops even before hearing, it's quite possible that pain could be remembered, too.

However, the little research that has been done on the specific question of whether preemies remember pain is inconclusive. For example, one study found that 32-week preemies who had already been in the NICU for four weeks were more apt to have racing pulses in response to painful heel pricks than newly born 32-weekers (as if the earlier-born ones were already traumatized by medical procedures performed during their hospital stay). But on the other hand, they grimaced less, as if their NICU stay had muted their behavioral response to pain.

In another study, eight year olds were shown pictures and asked to rate how painful they thought the events in them were. Children who had been born very prematurely rated the pictures of painful recreational activities—such as falling off a bicycle, or out of a tree—as more painful than those who had been born at term. The longer the preemies had spent in the nursery, the worse they rated the pain. But this group of former preemies had more motor delays, and so, perhaps, more everyday accidents, than their full-term peers. Also, to confound things further, all of the kids rated pictures of medical pain about the same.

Another quandary on the subject of remembering pain: it's not uncommon for babies who have been on ventilators for a long time to have difficulty nipple feeding, and this could be because they associate the pain or discomfort of the endotracheal tube, or being intubated, with anything that is put into their mouths. But it may also be that the critical period when the brain was open to learning to nipple feed was bypassed. (Luckily, for most of these babies, the developmental gap isn't permanent and they eventually learn to enjoy eating.)

Since Developmental Care experts have pointed out that excessive light, noise, handling, and painful events can negatively affect a baby's early development, you might also worry that early pain could affect your baby in the long run, resulting in emotional problems. Yet, one psychologist who specializes in research on pain in preemies, and also follows preemies as they grow up, points out that what amazes her most is not how burdened they seem by their early experiences, but how strikingly happy and well-adjusted they turn out to be. It's hard to be pessimistic if you see these children later, and witness their incredible resilience and ability to recover.

To be sure, there are rare, severe situations when long months of pain, especially in preemies who lack the persistent presence of a loving caregiver, seem to leave permanent scars on a child's personality. But if your baby went through the average hospital course of most preemies—if he was on a vent for a while, got his share of needle sticks and suctioning, even had some complications that needed surgery but have since resolved—you shouldn't be afraid of these severe emotional consequences, because they're unlikely to happen. More likely, you'll be taken aback by the gleeful and indomitable child your preemie turns out to be.

Baby's Appearance

Will my preemie ever look like other babies?

Most of us have a baby image in our head that's based on the Gerber ads and the picture-perfect cherubs on newborn diaper packages. While incredibly cute, they're about as similar to most real-life infants as gorgeously turned-out fashion models are to your next-door neighbors: not very. Most real babies have some of the following, common imperfections: a conehead, birthmarks, infant acne, protruding ears, receding chins, and too much or too little hair, to name just a few. And yet, they're undeniably beautiful—just not perfect.

Some preemies who are on their way home, though by no means all, have a few of their own characteristic traits. One is a particularly oval-shaped rather than circular head, so their face is long and narrow. (This may come from lying on their sides in the hospital, when they would have been floating freely in the womb.) They may also have wide-set eyes, and a pale complexion. Some have a somewhat less indented belly button than usual, from umbilical catheters they had in the NICU. Although most people would see them as just typically cute kids, no different than anyone else, based on these traits neonatologists might be able to point out an occasional former preemie in a crowd. These "preemie" characteristics generally go away gradually as a child matures, but sometimes last throughout childhood.

A premature baby who was on a ventilator for a long time may have a higher than usual arch or groove to his palate—probably from the pressure the endotracheal tube exerted. This lessens as a child matures, too, and is nothing to worry about. It shouldn't affect his speech (though it may make for difficulty eating foods like peanut butter, which will stick to the roof of his mouth—but who's never had that problem?), and nobody but his dentist would notice. Later, usually when a child is seven or eight years old, and has his permanent teeth and a well-developed jaw, if a palate groove disrupts his bite or causes teeth overcrowding, it can be treated by an orthodontist. You should be reassured, though, that former preemies don't seem to need braces much more frequently than term children.

Premature babies—especially smaller ones who spent time on a ventilator, or those with high bilirubin levels—may have some minor imperfections in the enamel of their baby teeth, making them look discolored or imperfectly shaped. Since teeth with enamel imperfections are more susceptible to decay than normal, it's important to take your child for his first dentist appointment before he turns one year old or not too much later, and to follow the usual, dental hygiene rules as carefully as possible (see page 431). Luckily, good dental care can help prevent decay, and most of the time only the baby teeth are affected.

As for size, some preemies always remain small, but the vast majority attain normal height and weight sooner or later. You can read more about growth on page 409.

Your baby may well have none of these traits. In that case, people will just have to take your word for it, and marvel that he was a preemie.

Do Preemies Have Scars?

Yes, many preemies are left with some physical reminders of their days in the NICU, but in most cases the scars are so small that only their parents notice them.

Tiny, pinpoint scars are common where intravenous needles were placed, usually on the back of the hands, or elsewhere on the arms or legs. There can be pinpoint scars on the heels, also, where blood was drawn with heel sticks. These tiny scars fade even more with time. Occasionally, a spot will harden into a firm bump, but that doesn't do any harm.

Very young preemies, whose skin was particularly immature and sensitive at birth, may have light-colored scars where removal of tape or the monitor leads abraded their skin. These become less noticeable over time. If your child is prone to getting raised scars, these and other scars may be raised and bigger.

If your baby had any tubes inserted—for example, a tracheostomy or gastrostomy tube, or a chest tube—there may be small scars that follow the typical course for any surgical scar: they start out reddish and raised, then fade to white, and finally become flat lines or dimples. If your child had multiple chest tubes, and some had to be placed close to her breast tissue, her adult breast could be somewhat abnormally shaped. If the problem is severe, cosmetic surgery could be done to correct it.

If fluid or medication infiltrated deeply from an IV line, your baby may have a scar where it occurred. Since scars tend to pull the skin tighter, if one is directly over her ankle, wrist, or elbow joint, it could hamper her movement somewhat. Most of the time, exercising the joint gently and regularly will alleviate the problem.

These are the most common scars—that is, until your preemie starts climbing jungle gyms, riding bicycles, and running on concrete sidewalks!

Shouldn't I Feel Happier?

Everyone assumes I'm ecstatic now that my baby is home. The truth is, I feel relieved, but I can't say I feel happiness.

Some parents of premature babies, during their first weeks and months at home, find themselves wondering: how come I'm feeling sad when I should be rejoicing? Why isn't my baby's presence and well-being enough to make me feel happy?

You may feel uneasy, or just numb: a legacy of fear about what the future might bring. If you can't answer a resounding "yes," when friends ask if you're overjoyed or blissful about being a new mother or father, you may wonder whether something is wrong with you, or with your feelings about your baby. There isn't. Some parents, when their child has just escaped danger, are simply too wounded, and carrying too much baggage, for that. Of course, there are plenty of joyful and tender moments, when you hold your baby in your arms, or watch him peacefully sleeping. You may feel relieved, yes. Grateful, yes. Even that you have grown wiser, with a new perspective on what's truly important in life. But you don't feel that elation, that lighthearted pleasure so many parents of term babies experience when they bring their infant home. You've been through too much, and still feel too vulnerable, for innocent, shiny-eyed happiness.

Having a very premature baby has been likened by some experts to experiencing the death of a child. Parents grieve the loss of the healthy full-term newborn they pictured they'd take home, as well as of the normal pregnancy, delivery, and birth they were expecting. Don't forget that your parenthood, too, was premature, and you probably missed out on some important and meaningful social rituals that would have helped prepare you to take your baby home. You may not have completed your parenting class, had a baby shower, exulted in a celebration after delivery with your family and friends. Most parents of preemies don't realize how deep their deprivation is, or if they do, they may feel guilty about it. It doesn't feel right to mourn an imagined baby, or your own unmet needs, when you have a baby alive, and at home.

If you just came back from the hospital, it's also natural for you to feel burdened, or even overwhelmed by the responsibility of taking care of your preemie. A long and painful NICU experience sometimes interferes with the timing of the normal deepening of attachment between parent and child, and anxiety and fears may weigh down your joy. All of this doesn't mean that you don't love your baby! But acknowledging what you've lost can help explain some of the ambivalence and confusion you may feel surrounding your preemie's discharge.

The good news is that, in general, these negative reactions gradually subside. Researchers have found that by eight to twelve months after a preemie's birth, most parents have regained their emotional balance. In the meantime, just be wary of a deep state of bereavement that interferes with your normal functioning, and lasts longer than a few weeks. It could be a postpartum depression (see page 255), which should get treated before it becomes a threat to you or your family relationships.

Of course, you also shouldn't forget that you don't need to be a parent of a preemie to feel less than elated after your baby comes home. Some parents of term babies, even though they may have had far easier experiences than yours, find that they don't experience storybook bliss, either. Perhaps they get scared or put off by their first whiff of what parenthood means, don't fall in love with their child as soon as they expected, or suffer from an unexplained case of the "baby blues." Most end up feeling the great joy of parenthood eventually—as you most likely will, too.

Feeling Protective

Now that my baby's home, I want to envelop her constantly in my arms, just the two of us, perfectly safe.

After putting your desire to take care of your baby on hold during her hospital stay, now you can finally let your maternal instinct pour over her. If you don't feel like doing anything but staring at your baby, if you just want to be alone with her, to protect her from any possible danger or disturbance, if you resent your family's demands because you don't want to be distracted, that's understandable. You're making up for lost time.

Some parents of preemies get worried by

Parental Responses That Are of More Concern

A few parents remain unable to adapt to their preemies, developing worrisome, long-lasting responses that can be disruptive to their child's development and well-being. These extreme parental responses are not common. But many mothers and fathers of preemies can recognize some hints of what they feel in them, although in lighter forms.

✳ *Vulnerable child syndrome.* There's no doubt that preemies are vulnerable at the beginning of their lives, and their parents rightfully worry a lot about them. But when a former premature infant goes home, and is growing and developing well, his parents should gradually relax. If, over the first months or years of a child's life, his mother or father continues to worry excessively about his health, taking him to the doctor at the slightest sign, discouraging his desire to actively discover the world, denying him contact with other people to avoid illnesses, and limiting his participation in activities to

avert possible dangers, this overprotectiveness can impede his normal development. Kids growing up in such an atmosphere can become very insecure, shy, dependent, and lacking in self-esteem. Later, in school, they may have poor social skills, a childish demeanor, and academic and health complaints. Vulnerable child syndrome is not a direct consequence of an infant's prematurity. Rather, it is an abnormal parental reaction that is probably due to personality traits in the parent, who becomes convinced that the premature birth justifies her or his own attitudes and behavior.

✳ *Super parent syndrome.* Premature babies can be less responsive and more withdrawn than term babies in their first weeks at home. Noticing a lack of responsiveness in their child, some parents increase their level of stimulation, trying hard to get the baby's attention. But because preemies don't handle excessive stimulation well, this can do more harm

what they perceive as disturbing feelings in themselves, such as resentfulness toward their family, irrational fears, excessive protectiveness toward their baby, and a desire for isolation. If you respond like that, you're not weird. And you're going to regain your balance soon. What you're going through now is normal, and temporary. Studies have shown that the level of anxiety among parents of preemies is highest one week after discharge, and already begins to diminish by the second week at home. Any

heightened negative emotions that you have should subside within nine months after discharge. Over the next few months, you should become gradually less distressed regarding your baby, and more attentive and responsive to the rest of the world. You'll get back to your old emotional self, although painful memories of the NICU and negative feelings may periodically come back for many months or years to come.

In the meantime, talk to your partner about how you feel, so he can try to understand what

than good. To defend himself, a preemie may become even more withdrawn, further increasing his parents' efforts to get him to respond. This cycle can lead to hyperactive, frustrated and disappointed parents, and a withdrawn, unresponsive baby. The antidote is to try to adapt your reactions to your baby's cues, being sensitive to signals that she's either ready to interact or overloaded with stimulation. (Some descriptions of preemies' signals that may help you are on page 203.)

❉ *Parental burnout.* In some mothers and fathers, this follows the super parent stage when, after having tried so hard to interact with their baby without positive results, parents just burn out, and stop almost any stimulation. In other cases, the initial, normal period of low stimulation (appropriate for a preemie who's easily overwhelmed), never evolves into the more interactive relationship that a preemie becomes ready for as he matures. Whether the parents have wilted from lack of reinforcement from their young preemie, or simply don't expect their premature baby to be reactive and don't try to engage him, burned out

parents act cold or absent toward their babies. They hold, touch, talk to, look at, and smile at them much less than other mothers or fathers. It's hard to tell what comes first, the baby's lack of responsiveness or the parents' bias. But developmental psychologists warn that an absent and withdrawn parental attitude can impair a child's development if it continues as the preemie grows older.

❉ *Risk for child abuse.* Preemies are more apt to be abused than other children, mainly due to a combination of parental risk factors (such as a lack of social and family support, and a history of violent experiences and reactions to stress), and the common behavioral characteristics of premature babies (who can be fussier, more difficult to console, and more withdrawn). Put these types of parents and children together, and the situation can sometimes degenerate into a serious crisis.

If you think that you or your partner fits one of these descriptions, it's important to talk about it with your pediatrician or a mental health professional.

you're going through, and to be patient. Try to avoid cutting him out completely from your baby's and your private nest. If you have older children, make sure your partner or their grandparents give them extra love and attention while you adjust, and start spending time with them yourself as soon as you can. Soon, you'll be ready to face the world—and all of the relatives and friends that now you'd like to keep out—again.

After this initial period of adaptation, you'll be able to look at your baby more objectively, too. Preconceived ideas can be damaging: If you expect your premature baby to be frailer, less responsive, or more demanding than a term baby, that can influence the way you interact with her, inhibiting her now and affecting her future behavior.

Right now, your feelings are probably normal and healthy. But if you ever become uncomfortable with them, thinking they're excessive or not subsiding appropriately, you may want to consider the intervention of a mental health professional. Behavioral therapy (a kind of short-term, focused psychotherapy) has been beneficial for other parents in such circumstances. Joining a parent support group or arranging for a neonatal nurse to baby-sit (ask in your nursery if any of the nurses do this), can also help. You can get precious clues about your premature baby's needs, behavioral patterns, and habits, as well as valuable insight into your own feelings. Being alone with your baby and doing everything by yourself might be most appealing to you right now, but later on, isolation is exactly what you should try to escape, to be the excellent parent that you want to be.

MULTIPLES

One Twin Home Earlier

One of our twins came home two weeks before the other. Does this mean he'll always be more advanced?

Being discharged from the hospital is not a race, in which the premature twin who's first out of the starting gate is also the one who'll likely pull ahead in the long run. In stable premature babies, the physical requirements for discharge—like being free from apnea for a reassuring number of days, eating well and gaining weight steadily, and maintaining their body temperature in an open crib—are usually achieved somewhere between 34 and 38 weeks of gestation. There's no known connection between the age that a preemie develops these maturational abilities, and the time when he reaches his later cognitive or motor developmental milestones, like smiling or sitting up. In the future, you'll get used to seeing your twins perform differently: one might be able to talk earlier, while the other might be a more adventurous and active toddler. Still, you won't be able to predict whether the first one will be more eloquent in sixth grade, or the second one more drawn to sports. So long as both twins, according to the doctors, are doing well, it's misleading to interpret a slightly shorter or longer hospital stay as indicating that one is generally more advanced or physically gifted than the other.

It's a different situation when a difference in

growth or development between premature twins is due to a serious medical condition in one of them. If one twin has to stay longer in the hospital because he has more severe BPD, or because he had to undergo surgery for NEC or hydrocephalus, for example, then he may be at higher risk than his sibling for later health problems, or a developmental delay. But since babies have amazing resilience and an extraordinary capacity to recover, you shouldn't label one baby as weaker or more vulnerable at such an early age. Time will tell you whether you should acknowledge a developmental difference between your twins or not.

In the meantime, it can be a real hassle for parents to take care of one twin in the hospital and the other at home. Parents often don't trust anybody else to take care of their newly discharged preemie, yet bringing him back to the nursery with you for visits can feel overwhelming, and may not even be allowed. The hospital staff expects—and you should accept without guilt—that you won't be able to visit as often as before. If you can find a relative, friend, or volunteer who'll regularly spend time with your preemie in the hospital, it may help reassure you that you're not abandoning your little one in the nursery. Some parents find that their babies' staggered discharges, if they're only separated by a week or two, can be beneficial, allowing them to adapt to the home routine with just one preemie at first. If you look at your experience from this point of view, you might even be grateful to your baby who took his time, for the extra time he gave you, before making your hands really full.

Daily Schedule for Multiples

Any suggestion for a daily schedule to take care of triplets?

What could sound better to parents like you, whose life is a never-ending waltz around feedings and diaper changes, than the mere possibility of a daily schedule? You already know that taking care of three babies at the same time requires commitment and strength. But organization and experience can help a lot, too, to conserve your precious energy, and spare you some worry.

During the first weeks at home, when your triplets are still waking up for at least one feeding in the middle of the night—and maybe at different times—you need as much help as you can get from your family and friends. Don't be proud: ask if it's not offered. You can return the favor later, when your life is more in control.

To know what's going on with each of their babies, some parents of triplets find it useful to keep track of each baby's daily events. One way to do this is cut out the feeding and changing form in the appendix, on page 519, make copies, and use one for each day. Or you can take inspiration from it and draw up your own version, adding in other activities like bath time or one-on-one time with Mom and Dad. Parents say it can be a lifesaver, when you feel so tired that you're afraid you'll lose your mind and forget essential information.

Getting your three babies to follow a regular and possibly uniform routine, and to sleep through the night, is going to be a slow work-in-progress. Some lucky parents of triplets say it's possible to have them on a feeding, playing, and sleeping schedule by the time they're about twelve weeks corrected age, and not long after that to see them sleeping six to eight hours a night. But some other families don't get to that blissful point, when parents can finally enjoy a good night's sleep, until their babies are ten months or older. A great place to give and get advice, to and from other parents like you, are Web sites and forums organized by nonprofit organizations like MOST (Mothers of Super Twins), which you can find at http://www.mostonline.org, or The Triplet Connection, at http://www.tripletconnection.org.

Here's what some families of triplets, quads, and quints have to say about the crucial issue of scheduling:

✳ If you are trying to get your triplets into a uniform routine, slowly try to encourage them to follow the same timing, by letting one cry longer before a feeding, or putting one down earlier. If one baby has woken you up at night for a feeding, wake the others up to feed them, too. (You'll be reluctant to do this at first, but, believe us, it will save you sleep in the long run.)

✳ The "assembly line" method will help you get organized and perhaps free up some spare time, while training your triplets to adapt to a regular routine. You can apply it to everything from daily tasks like diaper changing, to bathing, nail clipping, and more fun activities like one-on-one time, reading or playing with each of your babies, as long as it doesn't become too rigid or obsessive. (Speaking of bathing your babies, you need not do it every day. In fact, many parents of triplets, and even some parents of twins or singletons, give their babies a bath only once or twice a week, which, as long as you're cleaning his diaper area when you change his diaper, is perfectly adequate to keep a young infant clean.)

✳ Accept the fact that when a child is sick, his schedule will probably change. Try to be patient, and return to the schedule as soon as possible after he's better.

✳ If one baby seems to want to play, feed, or sleep at a different time, put the little maverick in another room if you can, to avoid disrupting his siblings' more uniform schedule.

✳ If you're nursing and supplementing with formula, always feed your babies formula for their last meal before bed. Formula takes longer to digest than breast milk, so your babies' stomachs should be full longer. (This also works out well for mothers who have plenty of milk in the morning, but then see their supply dwindle as the day goes by.) When your babies begin eating solids, they'll sleep even longer between feedings.

✳ To further encourage a longer night's sleep, you can try keeping them awake, with lots of lights on, for several hours before the last evening feeding at 10 or 11 PM. For some other babies, instead of keeping them awake in the evening, it works better to put them to bed about thirty minutes earlier than usual, after a relaxing bath. (There's no harm in trying both ways.)

✳ Use only disposable, top of the line, "premium" diapers in the night. Some babies wake up just because they feel wet.

✳ Once they're about three months corrected age, try keeping them awake for a longer time after each feeding, to wear down their energies a bit more, and encourage longer intervals of waking and sleeping. (This works for some babies; others just get crankier and sleep less. You can try it and see.)

✳ Remember that babies' schedules tend to change a lot, with seasons and growth spurts, so even if you think they're finally settled, don't cry victory until they're nine or ten months old.

✳ You're asking too much of yourself if you also try to fit in extra things like making a home-cooked dinner every night, keeping your house spotless, or grooming and dressing your kids (or you) to look ravishing. Give yourself a break: right now, safe and loving childcare is enough.

Even if you do all the right things, sometimes babies just aren't ready to follow a consistent schedule yet. So don't blame yourself if your little ones don't cooperate. At a certain age, due to a combination of development and growth, something will click in, and they'll "magically" become more consistent and easier to care for. According to many parents of triplets, despite the fatigue, it all happens too fast.

THE CARDIORESPIRATORY MONITOR: A NOISY COMPANION FOR WEEKS TO COME

Is it an intrusive nuisance, or a gift that will keep your child safe? Will it add to your stress, or to your peace of mind?

A lot will depend on your mindset going in. Some parents resent their home monitors, because they had been eagerly looking forward to walking away from the hospital and leaving all aspects of having a sick or fragile baby behind. They wanted to move on to a normal family life, an image that didn't include a high-tech machine next to their baby's crib. Other parents cherish their monitors, because they feel so nervous after all they've been through that normalcy isn't their top priority anymore: it's security. The monitor allows them to relax during the day, and sleep at night, without being plagued by worries about whether their baby is breathing and fine.

In truth, for most parents, it's a mixed, love-hate relationship. If the doctor has recommended that you take a monitor home with your baby, read on, to understand more about what's in store.

WHY THE DOCTORS ARE RECOMMENDING A MONITOR FOR YOUR BABY

One of the most common reasons for a preemie to go home with a monitor is that she's otherwise ready to leave the hospital, but is still having episodes of apnea or bradycardia. Although apnea of prematurity usually disappears by the time preemies are 36 to 38 weeks of gestational age, occasionally it persists even after their due date. Doctors know it will go away eventually, and that an otherwise healthy baby is better off at home with her parents, where she can get the physical contact, positive stimulation, and love that they are best at providing.

Other reasons a home monitor may be recommended include: apnea due to other causes, such as reflux or seizures; the baby has had an apparent life-threatening event, or ALTE, as doctors call it (an incident when her breathing unexpectedly faltered, for reasons that may have been identified, or may not); the baby has BPD and needs home oxygen; the baby has a tracheostomy tube; there is a family history of SIDS (Sudden Infant Death Syndrome, or "crib death," as some people refer to it). Often, parents' needs are taken into consideration, too. If you have been through a lot since the birth of your baby, and still have lingering anxiety about her health, the doctor may weigh strongly the sense of security that a monitor can provide.

While a home monitor doesn't prevent a problem from occurring, it does alert you if there is one. An alarm will sound if your baby takes an overly long pause in breathing, or her heart rate slows down or speeds up too much, allowing you to intervene and help.

WILL A HOME MONITOR PROTECT YOUR BABY FROM SIDS?

Home monitoring has not been shown to prevent SIDS, even though it alerts you to the fact that your baby has stopped breathing. Researchers still don't fully understand SIDS—in fact, SIDS is defined as an infant's sudden death that remains unexplained, even after all possible causes have been investigated. Respiratory problems may be one mechanism that leads to SIDS, but we know it's not the only one.

Simply having apnea of prematurity does not put a baby at increased risk for SIDS. While prematurity itself is a risk factor (18% of all infants with SIDS are preemies), only 2% to 4% of SIDS babies have a hospital record of apnea of prematurity. Bronchopulmonary dysplasia doesn't put a baby at increased risk, either. A baby's risk is higher if she has had an ALTE, was exposed in the womb or in her home to cigarette smoke or drugs like opiates or cocaine, if she's put to sleep on her stomach, in

an overheated room or on very soft bedding, and, possibly, if she's from a family with a history of SIDS.

Researchers understand so little about SIDS that even though they can't demonstrate that home monitoring reduces the incidence, they also can't say for sure that it hasn't helped some infants. Since home monitors also give anxious parents some peace of mind, many doctors do recommend them for babies at risk.

WHY HOME MONITORING MAY BE A HASSLE

So, you want the real scoop on the disadvantages of home monitors? Here are the main complaints that come up:

❋ You're going to get occasional false alarms. They're inevitable. They're also scary—and incredibly frustrating when they wake you in the middle of the night. What's important to realize is that while some families get false alarms several times a day (tempting them to smash their monitor against the wall), others get them only once a week or less. Read about how to cut down on false alarms below, to give yourself a much better chance of being among the lucky ones.

❋ You can't sleep with your baby when she's on an apnea monitor, because your movements, around her or the wires, could make the monitor think she's breathing when she isn't, and miss a problem if one occurred.

❋ Trips to the store are going to be harder. But you'll do it: a home monitor, which is generally smaller than a VCR, can run on a battery pack while you're away from home, and comes with a carrying case that can go right into the car or fit into the basket under a stroller.

* If your baby is on a monitor all the time, you won't be able to carry her casually in one arm while using the other to make coffee, set the table, or do laundry. And you won't be able to take her in a snuggli or a sling as you walk around the house. (Of course, you will be able to do those things any time she doesn't need to be hooked up to the monitor.)

* You may have to postpone daily tasks that are so noisy that they'd prevent you from hearing the monitor and getting to your baby quickly. Vacuuming and showering, for example, may have to wait until your partner or someone else is at home.

* Finding, and trusting, a baby-sitter is going to be harder. You'll need to find a steady baby-sitter who isn't scared off by the monitor, and who you're confident can learn to use it reliably.

* Having a home monitor can be expensive: generally between $200 and $400 a month, but almost all health insurance plans, and Medicaid, cover the charges. It's important to find out if your plan covers only certain, specified equipment providers, so you can tell this to the hospital's discharge planner.

* A home monitor promotes the image of your baby as a fragile, vulnerable child. This can affect how you perceive her and interact with her, and how your friends, relatives, and strangers do. All new mothers have to put up with their share of intrusive looks and questions, but the monitor may make your share a little bigger than most. Just remember that most infants on apnea monitors are healthy, with a very manageable, temporary problem. Your baby just has an extra, high-tech companion to keep her company, along with her stuffed animals and dolls.

WHY HOME MONITORING MAY BE WORTH IT, ANYWAY

Simply put, a home monitor can offer you peace of mind. Even parents of full-term newborns sometimes find it hard not to rush out of bed during the night to check whether their babies are still breathing. Parents of preemies carry a lot more emotional baggage, and often find it even harder to sleep well, or to relax and enjoy their babies. With the extra safety provided by an apnea monitor, some of their fears may fade more quickly. In fact, one study found that far more parents continued to use the monitor beyond the time recommended by the doctor, than stopped early. The vast majority said they found home monitoring to be reassuring, helping them to conduct a normal life.

You'll be especially grateful to have the monitor when your child gets her first cold, and, like all congested babies, she is struggling noisily to breathe. As you leave her in her crib at night, and when you enter her room again the next morning, the sight of those little, flashing lights that blink with her breaths and heartbeats will do your own heart good.

GETTING ORGANIZED

Don't worry if you're inexperienced with machines, or if you simply have so much to do before your baby comes home that the thought of organizing one more thing seems impossible. You'll find that almost everything concerning your baby's apnea monitor will be well organized for you.

The machine. Home monitors are generally not supplied by the hospital, but by an outside provider of home health care. Your discharge planner will arrange for a representative of the provider to meet you at the hospital, give you complete training in how to use the machine, and leave it with you a few days before your baby is discharged. The provider's representative will also give you a telephone number where you can reach someone twenty-four hours a day, in case you have questions or problems once you get home. (Although you'll be encouraged to call during office hours, don't hesitate to call at any time, if you have a question that seems urgent.) Some hospitals encourage parents to spend one night rooming-in with their babies, to make sure they're able to use the monitor properly.

The machine may seem complicated and daunting when it is first introduced to you. But with the help of patient, thorough trainers, even the most technologically challenged parents (we know from personal experience, since that includes one of us) become familiar with their apnea monitor quickly. You'll master it, too.

Home monitors sound an alarm if: your baby stops breathing for more than a certain number of seconds; her heart rate is too fast or too slow (your baby's neonatologist will tell the home health care provider what settings to put in your baby's machine); or there's an equipment problem. You should know that there is one kind of apnea, called obstructive apnea, that won't set off the apnea alarm, but will set off the slow heart rate (bradycardia) alarm. This kind of apnea, which is common among babies with reflux, happens when a baby is moving his chest to breathe, but because his airway is obstructed, little air is getting through, and his heart slows down as a result.

You'll be asked to keep a record of all alarms. This, along with any data that stays in your monitor's memory (some machines can print out or download all of the data they've recorded), will be a valuable tool when you and your baby's doctor are deciding when to discontinue the monitor, or whether to adjust medications.

Instructions from the doctor. Your baby's neonatologist will tell you exactly when—at what times of the day or night—you should keep your baby on the monitor. For some babies, it's recommended that they be on an apnea monitor almost all the time. Others need it only while sleeping. Also ask the doctor how long she thinks your baby should stay on the monitor, and what the criteria are for discontinuing it.

CPR training. Most hospitals give CPR training to all parents and caregivers of babies being sent home on a monitor. Make sure to ask about this, if no one has mentioned it. If you have a regular baby-sitter, arrange for her to attend a training session, too.

Getting set up at home. There isn't much you have to do to get set up for an apnea monitor at home. You must have a telephone, in case of questions or an emergency. You'll have to choose a good place for the machine. It should go on a hard surface near your baby's bed, close to an electrical outlet but at least one foot away from any electrical appliances that could cause interference or safety problems: television sets, radios, air conditioners, portable telephones, and electric blankets. (Clocks are OK.) Try to choose a place where older children or pets are unlikely to touch it. (If you can't keep your older children's fingers, or pet's paws, away from the monitor, ask your provider if they can get you a childproof panel.)

After you set up the machine, test to see

whether you can hear its alarm (which sounds something like a smoke detector) from all the rooms in the house. If it isn't loud enough, call the provider and ask for a remote alarm, which runs on a long wire to the monitor, or better still, pick up an infant intercom from your local baby store.

Important safety precautions. Home apnea monitors are extremely safe, as long as you follow the safety precautions you're given. Most important: never bathe your baby when she has the monitor on, because of the risk of electric shock. And keep the wires from getting wrapped dangerously around your baby's neck by running them inside her clothing, to emerge between two snaps or buttons near her ankles, or if it's a short outfit, near her crotch. If her outfit has no snaps or buttons there, just poke a tiny hole in the fabric yourself, to bring the wires through.

Planning for emergency. The vendor will give you some letters to mail to your local electric and telephone companies, asking them to put your family on a special priority list in case of a blackout or rationing of service. Post a list of emergency numbers near all of your telephones: 911 or the local rescue squad, the closest emergency room, your baby's doctor, the equipment provider, and the electric company's emergency service line. And post a copy of CPR guidelines (the ones you get from the hospital or on page 520) in several places around the house: next to your baby's crib and changing table, in the kitchen or anywhere else she spends a lot of time.

THOSE PESKY FALSE ALARMS

Like most machines, apnea monitors are not perfect. No matter how hard you try, false alarms can't be completely avoided. When babies squirm (which they do more and more as they get older), leads can slip out of place. Activities like stretching or a bowel movement can cause natural, trivial bouts of bradycardia. Sometimes, the sound of the alarms themselves (or the baby's own, slightly late-acting, natural regulatory systems) stimulate a baby who's having apnea to breathe again, so that by the time parents reach their baby's crib, it seems like the alarms were false.

Here are some ways to keep false alarms to a minimum:

✳ False alarms often arise when leads are in the wrong place, either because they weren't placed properly, or because the belt was too loose to keep them from sliding around. (You can tell that a belt fits right if you can fit a finger snugly, but comfortably, between it and your baby's chest. If a belt is too tight, it might restrict your baby's chest movements.) So, follow your trainer's instructions precisely when placing the leads and putting the belt on. If you're not positive you put them on right, don't be lazy: start over and do it again.

✳ Every time you turn the monitor on, take a few seconds to check that all wires are firmly connected.

✳ If you have any doubts about whether a lead or wire is still in good shape, don't hesitate to throw it away and use one of your spares. That's what they're for. Call the home health care provider right away, and ask for a replacement, since you should always have spares on hand.

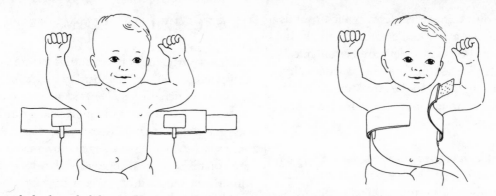

Place the leads on the belt according to the instructions you received, and fasten it snugly, but not too tightly, around your baby's chest.

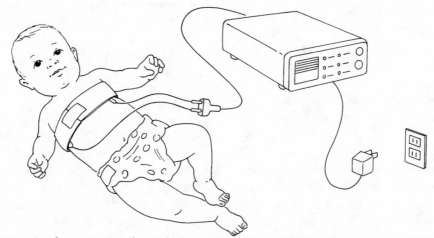

Before turning the monitor on, always check to make sure that all of the wires are properly connected.

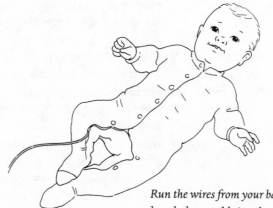

Run the wires from your baby's chest down to her crotch or leg, under her clothes, and bring them out between two snaps or buttons.

Adapted with permission of Mallinckrodt Inc., Pleasanton, CA

* When you're in the house, plug the monitor into a wall socket, rather than using the battery. Low battery alarms are almost completely avoidable!
* Don't apply oil, lotion, or powder to the areas of your baby's chest where the leads go. The leads may slide around, or not function properly.
* As babies get older, their heart rates naturally slow down, setting off more bradycardia alarms. If you notice that you're getting more false alarms, ask your doctor whether the alarm settings on the monitor should be lowered. Most babies have their settings readjusted at some point.
* If you get a lot of false alarms, ask your provider to help you figure out why. If your baby is an abdominal breather, meaning she moves her stomach more than her chest, the leads may not be picking up her chest movements, and it may help to place them a little lower. (If leads are too high, they can also get stuck under a baby's armpits, where they won't detect chest movement as well. As a baby gets older, the leads may have more of a tendency to rise under the armpits.) Also, if your baby tends to breathe shallowly, the leads may miss some of her chest movements. Your home health care provider will be able to tell if she's a shallow breather by looking at a download of your monitor's memory.

Remember: never, never ignore an alarm and assume it's false, without checking on your baby. If you get a lot of false alarms, that can be tempting—but there have been sad cases proving it's dangerous.

HOW TO RESPOND TO AN ALARM

If you have any questions about how to recognize whether your baby is breathing, or what to do about it, turn to page 346 for a quick summary. Although it's important for you to know and practice CPR, it's also reassuring to realize that most babies on monitors never need it.

If you respond to an apnea alarm, but you see or feel your baby breathing and she looks fine, it probably means that her breaths were too shallow for the monitor to detect. That's nothing to worry about, and aside from talking to your provider about how to minimize these false alarms, you don't need to do anything.

USEFUL TIPS FROM PARENTS TO PARENTS

Here are some additional tips from parents who have been in the trenches with a home monitor, for those who are just starting out:

* After your baby falls asleep in your arms, you won't want to wake her up again by putting on the monitor. So, place the leads and wires on your baby before it's her bedtime, ready to just plug in quietly after she falls asleep.
* Although some parents try keeping the leads and wires on almost all the time, there are disadvantages. For one thing, as your baby is picked up, put down, and moved around, the leads can slip out of place, subjecting you to more false alarms. For another, many babies have sensitive skin. They may need a rest from the leads and belt, which can be irritating. Most babies can take a monitor break when you're watching them closely, like

during playtime. If you're uncertain about whether this is safe, ask your doctor.

✵ Some babies' skin gets particularly irritated by stick-on leads. If you notice this, ask your provider about switching to nonadhesive leads held on by a belt. If you stay with adhesive leads, try varying the locations on your baby's chest slightly. Since stick-on leads can pull, or even tear, at the skin when you remove them, try this gentle way to do it: place your baby in the bath with the leads on (but, of course, *never* with the wires attached!), to let them soak and loosen, and remove them while she's in the tub. If any bad sores develop, talk to your pediatrician about them.

✵ Some parents say they get more false alarms with stick-on leads, others that they get more with the ones that are held on with a belt. If false alarms are a problem for you, it's worth trying the other method to see if the situation improves.

✵ When your baby has a cold or a fever, expect her to set off a few more apnea and bradycardia alarms, simply because she's weaker and breathes more shallowly than normal, or has a stuffy nose. You only need to worry if the alarms are frequent or significantly increasing, and then you should call your pediatrician immediately.

✵ Always keep the monitor plugged in at night. That way it will be fully charged whenever you want to use it in the daytime, away from home.

✵ Choose a stroller with a basket underneath, and make sure it's big enough to hold the monitor.

✵ If you're flying with your baby, allow extra time at the airport. Security may want to inspect the monitor. On the airplane, ask a flight attendant whether you can use the monitor at all times, or if it must be turned off for takeoff and landing.

✵ If you're having trouble finding a baby-sitter whom you trust, ask a local, preemie support group if you can contact other parents with babies on monitors. They may know of a baby-sitter you can try, or you may be able to take turns baby-sitting for each other's babies. If you don't have a local preemie support group, your monitor's provider may be able to put you in touch with other parents.

WHEN TO STOP USING A MONITOR

Unfortunately, although parents would find it reassuring, there's no precise formula for determining when a baby no longer needs to be monitored. Many doctors recommend monitoring until a baby is six months old, after which time the risk of SIDS, or serious apnea, usually is very small. Some doctors wait until babies have been off all medications for apnea, and had at least two months without any serious episodes of apnea or bradycardia, before discontinuing the monitor. Others also wait until the baby has shown that she can tolerate stress, by smoothly enduring immunizations or an illness. Occasionally, a doctor will request a sleep study called a pneumogram before recommending discontinuing the monitor. A pneumogram records a baby's respiration, heart rate, and oxygen saturation, usually for twelve hours. Pneumograms can sometimes help to figure out the pattern of a baby's apneic or bradyardic episodes, but there's no evidence that they can predict which babies will encounter life-threatening apnea or SIDS, so they're done much less than they once were.

Based on his clinical judgment, your baby's doctor will at some point decide that it's time either to stop the monitor completely, or to wean your baby from it gradually, perhaps by using it only at night. Actually, it's often more a matter of weaning the parents, who've come to rely on the monitor for their sense of security. The first few nights without the monitor may be hard for you, as it is for many parents. But after that, it will become clearer and clearer that your baby is safe for one simple reason: not because of the monitor, but because she is healthy. The machine has served its purpose well, but has become, thankfully, superfluous.

8

From Preemie to Preschool (and Beyond)

▶ *A time to watch your baby's health and development— and gradually begin to relax and enjoy!*

THE PARENTS' PERSPECTIVE   395

THE DOCTOR'S PERSPECTIVE   399

QUESTIONS AND ANSWERS

   Turning Out "Normal"   403

   Adjusting Age   403

   Rehospitalization   404

   Through the Doors of Preemie Follow-up
     Clinic   406

   Developmental Delays   408

   Growth Predictions   409

   Picky Eater   410

   Flu Vaccine   411

   Daycare   411

   Leading a Normal Infancy and
     Childhood with a VP Shunt   412

   Possible VP Shunt Problems   414

If Your Child Has a VP Shunt: What Should
     Concern You, and What Should Not   415

When to Call the Doctor about the
     VP Shunt   417

Seizures   418

Worrying about Cerebral Palsy   419

Typical Characteristics of Cerebral Palsy:
     What's Worrisome and What's Not   421

Eyesight after ROP   425

Risk of Future Developmental Problems   426

Troublesome Behavior   428

Clumsiness   429

Teeth   431

Emotional Aftershocks   432

Thinking about Another Pregnancy   434

IN DEPTH

   What You Need to Know about RSV   435

The Parents' Perspective: From Preemie to Preschool

People say babyhood goes by so fast. "Enjoy her now, soon she'll be six months old and you won't know how she got there," new parents are told. But if you have a preemie, common truths may not apply. When a baby comes home from the hospital she may be only a few days older than her due date—but she already has a history that weighs like years on her little shoulders, and on her parents'. Once they bring their baby home, mothers and fathers must squeeze out the little energy they have left after weeks or months in the NICU, to take care of a baby who's often more demanding than they ever thought. First months flying by? Forget it. A mother posted this note on the Internet, where some parents seek companionship and advice from other parents of preemies who understand what they're going through:

Date: Tue, 08 Nov 1999 09:22:42–0700
From: WXXXX <WXXXI@XXXX.com>
Subject: Ticia update

Hi everyone, winter's come so early in our area that Ticia and I had to go under cover sooner than expected. I'd already planned to keep Ticia home until the chill is gone, but I was really convinced when our pediatrician warned us about the risk of RSV and bad respiratory problems. Here's my list of rules: no trips to the mall, no eating out, no visitors allowed at home, strict handwashing and safe distance from Ticia for everyone who dares to come over (basically, only my mother-in-law and my sister. But not her kids!). DH says I'm crazy. [Note: many Internet talk group participants use acronyms, and DH stands for "dear husband."] *I'm not crazy yet, although I may go insane by the end of the season. I'm so lonely! My only pastime is reading your messages. I'm so thankful to all of you for sharing your thoughts and experiences with your babies.*

Here's an update on Ticia: she's 5 months corrected age now and weighs almost 10 pounds. She's smiling and reaching for things. It's so cute! The problem is with her weight. Her doctor doesn't seem very concerned, as long as she's growing regularly, which she does, just very slowly. We're feeding her solids, and adding in oil for calories, but she's not taking much, like she never has. Let's keep our fingers crossed, and hope she puts on a bit more weight. Sleeping through the night, also, we're not there yet. She fusses and fusses, four hours is the longest time she can go without a bottle. Any suggestions about that? I wish I could take her out for a walk. But it's snowing. Love to you all :-)

Wendy (mother to Ticia, 28-weeker, now 5 months old CA), Minnesota

Just when they thought they'd escaped the stethoscopes and uniforms, a few parents have to face what they fear most: a rehospitalization. It's scariest when an unexpected illness or emergency surgery brings a former preemie back to that dreaded place. But even if the trip back to the hospital has been planned in advance, and the stay is short, the shock it creates is still enormous. The hospital hits deep, to the core of a parent's heart, where it hasn't had time to harden yet.

It's 2 AM, and I'm walking in the corridors of "our" hospital, like a ghost with too much caffeine in his veins. I've spent a few hard hours. Sitting by my son's bed, I've been staring at the pulsing lines of his heartbeat on the monitor until my eyes hurt. After 11 months, a bad dream from the NICU has come true. But there's nothing to worry about now, everything went well, the surgeon said. Shaun woke up three hours after surgery and cried only a little bit, still drowsy from the anesthesia. A nurse helped me change him and lift him off the bed without disconnecting his IV. He's so big and heavy, nobody could tell he was only 3 pounds when he was born. He took his bottle in my arms, then went peacefully back to sleep. A small bandage on his head is all you can see from the surgery. They shaved a patch of hair, but left the rest of his locks intact. He's doing fine. So I came out to stretch my legs, under the glaring fluorescent lights that can turn days and nights into the same, suspended time. That's the entrance to the NICU we went through so many times. Somebody's washing his hands. Is he a father? If he had to come back in the middle of the night, maybe there's bad news about his baby. I follow him. I don't see any nurses or doctors I know well, and that's best, since I would probably break down if someone asked me why I'm here. I look through the glass doors into the large rooms, at the rows of isolettes, at the babies and the nurses handling them. There's where Shaun spent most of his six weeks in the NICU. And here's the father I just saw coming in. He's holding an infant not much bigger than his fist, close to his chest. He's smiling. Maybe he's just catching up with his preemie, taking a night turn. I feel relieved for him. I feel relieved for myself, too. Tomorrow morning Shaun will go home, you know?

When a preemie's first birthday arrives, his family may be taken by surprise. "Aren't you going to have a party, a family gathering?" relatives and friends ask. But parents often have mixed feelings. Yes, it should be an occasion for rejoicing. But they may not feel like celebrating. Why is that?

New York, June 9, 2000

Dear L., today is your first birthday, but it doesn't look like a special day at our house. There are no balloons, no children with their parents coming in for a party. You don't know that they should be here, busy as you are crawling around, tasting the new thrill of independence, and that's fine for now. I'm writing you this birthday card for when you're grown, and you'll ask to see a picture of your first birthday. You know, in the last few days summer has come. Exactly a year ago, I was ready to stop working, to go to the beach to enjoy my growing belly. I was dreaming of swimming like a seal, with you swimming inside me. How perfect. I needed a maternity swimsuit, but didn't have time to find one. When I walked into the hospital with your dad, feeling contractions, they made me lie down on a bed without even letting me take off my shoes. That evening, you were born. This morning, a year later, I took you for a stroll in the park. People were looking at us, smiling. But if they knew that today was your first birthday, they would ask me: Why aren't you home making a party? Did you get him presents? A birthday cake? I'm afraid I don't have the strength to light that candle. Maybe next year, or the following one. But it will always be the beginning of summer.

Happy Birthday. I love you. Mommy

Many couples say that after their children's births, they had to give up some things they enjoyed doing before. Some parents of preemies, though, take that normal process too far. Parenthood, if achieved with a lot of struggle, can grow absorbing and exclusive, shutting out the rest of the world, including even one's partner, or closest friends. For a while, that can help keep emotions under control.

After the premature birth of our twin girls two years ago, my wife Sarah changed so much. Before, she had a great business and social life. "Boy, what a woman you found," my old friends would say. Not to mention my parents, who seem to like her more than they like me. When Sarah got pregnant with twins, she decided that when they were born, she would leave her partner in charge of the store for a year. More than two years have gone by now, and she's still home. All she wants to do, she says, is be with the girls. Her friends call me to find out why she's disappeared. She's become detached from everything— sometimes, I'm afraid, even from me. And tonight on the phone with my sister Judy, she freaked out. Judy called to tell her something about her baby, who's just three weeks old. I heard Sarah saying: "How dare you complain about him? You're so ungrateful." Then she hung up. "Nobody understands how incredibly lucky they are," she cried angrily, fighting the tears. "I feel the same way you do about Judy's baby," I said. "What do you mean?" Sarah inquired. "Seeing them handling that chunky baby so casually annoys me. We couldn't enjoy our girls when they were little," I explained. "But we're enjoying them now, aren't we?" she whispered. There was so much love in her voice, that I felt I could be a part of it. Wouldn't it be nice if I could always count on a soft, emotional side of myself, to reach out to Sarah? Tonight I did great.

At some point, a child's premature birth fades into the background. A time comes when parents become self-conscious about mentioning that event, unless specifically asked. Despite the fact that their memories are still vivid, mothers and fathers begin to live a life in which their child's prematurity has, apparently, disappeared.

I'm here in the playground, watching Ricky play with Dave and Martin. Ricky is my son. He's two and a half now. (Although I don't say it anymore, I really consider him a little younger than that, because he was a preemie born 9 weeks before term.) Dave and Martin are Ricky's pals. Dave is the oldest of the trio, he's tall and strong, he just turned three. I tried to lift him the other day, but he was almost too heavy for me, much heavier than Ricky. Ricky is at the 15th percentile for weight and height, so he's on the small side for his age, but I don't worry about it as much as I used to. He loves to jump in the sandbox with Dave, they can't stop giggling while they bounce. I'm still terrified that Ricky might hurt himself, but I know he needs his share of bumps and bruises, so I let him do the things he likes. Martin, who's just two months younger than Dave, is a quieter little guy. He always brings a fire truck to the playground, to trade with the other kids' toys. He speaks very well, and now is saying something to Ricky, who's sitting in the sand pushing his truck. Ricky knows it's a red truck: all of a sudden, he's learned all the colors, putting to rest my anxiety that he might be color blind. He's not different from the other kids, we know that. But to us, there's always something that we never felt with his sister, who was born at term. It has to do with our secretly comparing him to the other children, checking on his speech, his movements, his achievements. To us, Ricky walks around with a big sign on his shoulders that says: "I was a preemie. Everything that seems predictable and uneventful to you, is not. I'm an extraordinary child." What strikes me most is that people can't see it.

Many adult former preemies are oblivious to their difficult starts, blissfully unaware of the obstacles they had to overcome. But memories of that tiny baby remain alive within their parents, usually hidden and muffled by time and life events, occasionally to reemerge when nobody would expect.

In December 1998, astronaut Robert Cabana successfully led a historic space shuttle mission: the first to carry material into space to build the international space station. Bob Cabana's parents were so proud of their son—a brilliant Navy pilot, flying his fourth shuttle mission, ". . . especially," as his mother tearfully told a local television news station, "since we didn't know if he'd make it past his first year." Mrs. Cabana spoke of her son's premature birth fifty years before. Great men can be born premature too, you see? And parents of preemies may not know if they're crying from remembered pain, or present joy.

The Doctor's Perspective:
From Preemie to Preschool (and Beyond)*

Although I'll gladly give you "the doctor's perspective" once again, you'll probably find that it carries a lot less weight now, as your preemie is growing up. Just before her birth, or when she was in the hospital nursery, her doctor's assessments were so revealing—and necessary—for you to understand how your child was faring. But now doctors don't loom so very large in your world. You, her community of family and friends, and a few other professionals, like teachers or child development specialists, have taken over most of that role. Of course, some health risks may be higher for her, and she may still have some conditions that relate to her prematurity, but most of the medical problems that older, former preemies have are those we can see in any child.

PHYSICAL EXAM AND LABORATORY ASSESSMENT

How often your preemie is seen, and by what kind of doctors, will depend on the problems she's had so far. Most bigger preemies, born at 33 weeks of gestation or later, who sailed through their hospital stays, will be treated just like term babies. We'll ask you to schedule regular "well-baby" checkups and immunizations with her pediatrician, and you'll be instructed to call the pediatrician for the same illnesses or questions that any new parents would. Except for social calls (many NICUs have reunions, and we're always hoping for a visit from our graduates!), your baby's neonatologist probably won't be seeing her again.

Preemies at higher risk for developmental problems will, in addition to regular pediatrician visits, be followed in a clinic for NICU graduates. There, neonatologists and other specialists in child development will be paying spe-cial attention to areas that ex-preemies may have problems with. Because preemies often have growth delays, we'll be asking you about her eating, and we'll carefully plot her length, weight, and head circumference on her growth chart. Because preemies can have difficulty with respiratory infections, we'll be evaluating her breathing, and inquire how she handled any colds. Since most preemies are still anemic when they leave the hospital, we'll be looking at her color to see if she's pale, and may check a blood count. If your preemie had any particular problems—an oxygen requirement or reflux, for example—we'll be assessing whether to escalate or back down on any treatments for them.

In particular, we'll be evaluating your child's development, sometimes with formal examinations, or by simply observing her behavior. (Does she focus on objects, and react to loud noises? Are her movements fluid and easy? Does she use both hands, or favor one—maybe because it's stronger, or more flexible than the

---

*"The Doctor's Perspective" describes how your doctor may be thinking about your preemie's condition, and what she may be considering as she makes medical decisions. All of the medical terms and conditions mentioned here are described in more detail elsewhere in this book. Check the index.

other? If she's playing with a truck, is she simply spinning its wheels, or is she pretending it's going somewhere?)

Any concerns that you bring up, I'll consider carefully, even if you try to dismiss them yourself. For instance, if you say your preemie doesn't hear what you tell him to do half of the time, but it's probably just because he's stubborn—I'll still want to investigate his hearing. Parents, we've found over and over, are usually right about their child, and doctors who listen to parents are much better at picking up problems early.

Some preemies will also be followed by other medical specialists or professionals. Preemies who had ROP will be checked regularly by an ophthalmologist. Infants who didn't pass their hearing screens in the nursery will be reexamined, and a few will end up needing therapy for hearing loss. Infants who had surgery will be seen by their surgeons a few more times, to make sure all is going well. Those with other problems, such as seizures or BPD, may be seeing neurologists or pulmonologists. As your baby recovers and grows, he'll be shedding therapies and physicians—so, what may seem like an overwhelming number of doctor appointments now will soon be honed down to a more manageable number.

COMMON ISSUES AND DECISIONS

Stopping medications and therapies: When we know that recovery is going to be a long, gradual process (in children with BPD, for example), we'll taper therapies slowly, and decrease medications little by little. (Usually, I would wait a few weeks after stopping one med-

icine before discontinuing another.) Of course, you'll be asked to report back if there's any worsening in your baby's condition after a therapy is decreased or discontinued. For other conditions, which have a risky period that will pass (such as apnea of prematurity, or certain kinds of seizures), we'll usually stop therapies more abruptly. Your doctor will decide to do that when she thinks your baby is out of the danger zone.

You should know, there's always some trial and error to this. Your baby may show us that he's not tolerating the weaning from a medication, or that he hasn't yet reached the critical time when he no longer needs a therapy. If that happens, I would probably just wait awhile, and try again later. How much later? You and your doctor will work that out, but often there's little science to it; it's what some call the "art" of medicine.

If your baby doesn't come off his therapies in the broad time frame we expect, then we'll wonder if some other problem could be complicating things. For instance, a baby with BPD who's anemic, or has reflux, may have trouble weaning off his oxygen. So we might do some tests, and maybe add a new medicine, hoping that will speed up his recovery. If you find a particular medication or therapy especially onerous, let us know. Sometimes—although not always—there will be a substitute, or a different way of doing things, that's easier for you to live with.

Growth: It's OK if your preemie remains smaller than his full-term peers, as long as his rate of growth is normal. A normal rate of growth corresponds to good nutrition, which is necessary to build strong and healthy muscles, bones, lungs, brain, and all the other organs he needs to develop well. "Catch-up" growth, which is faster than normal, is great; but as long as your preemie continues growing along his own growth curve, we'll be able to reassure you that he's doing fine.

If your preemie's size is falling farther behind his peers, though, we'd worry about something called "failure to thrive." Failure to thrive is not uncommon in kids who are chronically ill, particularly those with severe BPD or cerebral palsy, because they tend to burn up a lot of calories with their illness, but often don't eat well. The treatment, usually, is more nutrition. We may recommend a special, high-calorie formula, adding certain nutrients to his diet, or even suggest tube feedings during the night while he sleeps (this can work well, and help with severe reflux, too).

Sometimes, more food isn't the only answer. A preemie with BPD won't grow well if he needs more oxygen. Kids who are anemic may grow faster if their blood counts are raised. If your preemie's poor growth isn't simply a matter of his taking in too few calories or having a medical problem that we already know about, then we'll do further evaluations (possibly including a brief hospitalization, where his activity, diet, and elimination can be closely monitored), to try to get to the bottom of the problem.

Development: An important part of a pediatrician's job is recognizing which children are developing normally and which are not. But actually determining whether your preemie has a significant, permanent disability can take months, or even years. As you'll read later in this chapter, many preemies have abnormal muscle tone in their first year of life, which gradually goes completely away. It's common for kids who have been ill to have some mild delays, in both growth and achievement of skills, that of-

ten resolve. Sometimes a problem in attaining a developmental milestone is actually a behavioral problem in disguise: a child may be extremely passive, or hyperactive, or an overprotective caretaker may be interfering with his learning.

Even if your child has a delay that is mild and probably temporary, we may still refer him for special services, so he can improve his skills right now. It's important for him to catch up as soon as possible, so he can continue to move forward in his development. If you can, you should try to see a referral for special services as a positive opportunity for growth, not a disheartening comment about your child's future. In fact, most children's future abilities and achievements will still be wide open.

Starting school: If your preemie was born at less than about 30 weeks of gestation, even if he's been discharged from preemie follow-up clinic as normal, you might still want to have him tested by a developmental psychologist at around age four or five, before he enters kindergarten. Many people would consider this unnecessary. But I suggest it, because quite a few of these youngest preemies will end up with subtle learning disabilities or attention problems. It can take a while for teachers to realize that a child's poor performance, or lack of confidence, or disruptive behavior, doesn't reflect his intellect or personality, but the fact that he's having trouble at school. If you catch the problem early, you can assist your child before he begins feeling like a failure, or a bad kid. There are lots of techniques to deal with learning disabilities and attention problems, and most kids can do very well in school, with a little help. You can ask your pediatrician, or the public health department, where and how to make an appointment.

FAMILY ISSUES

Making time for discussion: If you have a lot to talk to your baby's doctor about, you should consider scheduling a special, longer appointment just to discuss things. It's very frustrating if you're hoping to get your concerns addressed in detail, and the doctor is trying to rush out of the room, seeming to brush you off with superficial answers and reassurances. (Hopefully, that's not because you have an insensitive doctor, but because of the time constraints in every pediatrician's schedule. Think about how you would feel if you had one of the subsequent appointments, and were kept waiting a long time, because the doctor was running late.) You may even want to leave your child at home, if the doctor doesn't have to observe her directly. You'll both appreciate the more relaxed atmosphere, where you can concentrate without feeling guilty for taking up too much time, and he doesn't feel pulled in multiple directions.

Waiting to find out if there's a problem: The long, drawn-out process of waiting to know whether your child has a permanent developmental disability or not can be extremely nerve-wracking, and many parents wonder if their doctor is holding back important information along the way. I can assure you that most doctors do not. Most of us believe that would be unfair to parents, who deserve, and want desperately, to know their own child. But a doctor may not share every tiny bit of uncertainty with parents, either. That, too, would be unfair, putting you through emotional agony over often trivial or nonexistent issues. If we don't say everything we're thinking or wondering about, usually it's not to hide anything: when my judgments are really indefinite, and

can go either way, I sometimes don't even know if I should be worried or not! That profound uncertainty can be very hard to express, without generating unnecessary fear in a parent. On the other hand, if you're worried about something, like mental retardation or cerebral palsy, and I don't address your concerns, please ask! I'm perfectly willing to discuss my observations and conclusions, even without being clear or definite, if talking about those things can help you organize your thoughts, or put your fears in perspective.

Your doctor shouldn't be offended if you ever want to get a second opinion. Judgments about something as weighty as your child's future deserve exploration and confirmation. Hearing from different doctors may help you understand or accept a diagnosis or recommendation for treatment; and if opinions differ, you'll have an idea of the range of uncertainty we're dealing with.

Vulnerable child syndrome: The tremendous caution which may have once saved your preemie's life has probably now lost its value and become counterproductive. So take a deep breath—now's the time: you've got to stop thinking of your child as a preemie!

It's hard, of course, because the perception of your child as extremely vulnerable doesn't necessarily go away, especially if he has lingering medical needs. You may feel an overwhelming desire to keep him away from anything risky, or to give him everything he wants, so he doesn't suffer any more than he already has. Although this is a natural parental impulse, it can get out of hand. We'll be asking you where your child sleeps, how you manage discipline, who besides you takes care of him. Not that there's a right or wrong answer to any of those questions. But if, for example, you don't want your child in your bed, yet he stays there because "he refuses" to sleep by himself, there's a problem. If you can't place limits on your child's behavior because, as some parents fear, "if he cries too hard he'll get sick," then you've abandoned an important aspect of your parental role, and he's become a far too powerful child. By treating your child as though he's fragile and vulnerable, you close off some very important opportunities—both physical and psychological—for him to grow and develop at his best.

It's every parent's burden that the future of their children is uncertain. You worry about the possible, bad outcomes of prematurity; we all worry about highway accidents, sex, and drugs. But, like every parent, you should try hard to keep your fears in perspective. If your child doesn't have a chronic illness (and even if he does, in every way you can), you should start treating him normally. Because that's what you want him to be, and what he probably already is—a normal, or better than that, an extraordinary, wonderful, unusual and precious child, who will gradually make his own way out into the world.

Questions and Answers

Turning out "Normal"

How could we be so lucky? Our daughter, who was born so early, seems to be totally normal.

Actually, as amazing as it may seem, you aren't unusually lucky. The vast majority of today's preemies turn out to be healthy, normal children, no different than their friends or schoolmates—except, of course, that not many kids had the same kind of start they did.

So, unless their baby is at especially high risk because of an early health problem, a good outcome is exactly what most parents of premature babies should expect.

To you, though, your child will never cease to be a walking and talking miracle. Like other parents of former preemies, you may find that you stare at her in awe, as she does perfectly normal things that other parents would hardly notice. You may know every little inch of her face and body by heart, every hair and joint and scar. It's not that you love your former preemie more than other parents love their children, but that you never take her, or her good health, for granted. So, maybe you are especially lucky, after all.

Adjusting Age

When should I stop adjusting my preemie's age?

The general rule of thumb, used by many pediatricians and preemie follow-up specialists, is to stop correcting a preemie's age when she is two to three years old. The rationale is that a difference of a few weeks or months (depending on how early your baby was born) is very significant during infancy. Put a three-month-old and a six-month-old next to each other, and it's easy to see they have little in common. But by the time a baby grows into a toddler, the difference becomes less and less meaningful. It's hard to tell a twenty-six-month-old from a twenty-nine-month-old—and whatever differences in behavior or appearance there may be, at that point, are just as likely to be due to the wide range of individual characteristics as a few months in age.

But a rule of thumb shouldn't be taken too

literally, and this is no exception. There's no magic, or scientific, reason for preemies to catch up at precisely age two, or age three, or at any other point in time. Some of your child's attributes that develop based on experience rather than just an innate developmental timetable will catch up with term babies sooner. (See page 366 for some examples). Others may do so later. For example, some researchers who've studied the long-term growth patterns of preemies have suggested that, in evaluating a preemie's height and weight, it's misleading to stop correcting so soon. Catchup growth can take much longer. So professionals may decide how long to correct your child's age depending partly on what aspect of her development they're looking at.

And remember, the two-year mark applies to an "average" preemie. If your child was one of the youngest-born preemies, born at 24 weeks, her big age gap may remain significant for longer. If she was a 34-weeker, her smaller age gap may become unnoticeable way before her second birthday arrives.

Actually, you are probably the best judge of when to stop correcting your child's age, because you're the one who sees where she falls in relation to her full-term peers. If your child's development is progressing normally, but she's still generally lagging by a few months, you probably still need to correct.

Of course, you may have doubts as to whether some lags are due to developmental delays, rather than simple prematurity. Just remember that there's a wide range of "normal" when it comes to the timing of childhood achievements. Every parent harbors worries, openly or secretly, about something their child is doing a little later than other children her age. It would be nice if all preemies could reach every one of their milestones sooner, rather than later, to save their parents some worry. But since no children do that, talk to your pediatrician or the experts at your preemie follow-up clinic. If they tell you that your child is developing normally, believe them!

The truth is that your child is *always* going to be several weeks, or months, younger than her full-term peers. So, it's not that you'll ever really stop adjusting. There may be times, even later on, when it may make a difference—for example, when it comes time for kindergarten. If your child is just on the edge of age eligibility for a given school year, some developmental experts suggest that you use her adjusted age to determine when to enroll her. (Since some preemies have minor learning disabilities or problems that show up only when they get to school, this is one circumstance in which it may be best for them not to be the very youngest in the group.) But most of the time, after a while, it just won't make much difference anymore.

Rehospitalization

My baby is back in the hospital. I feel like I failed to take care of her.

It's natural for you to feel that way, but you're probably being unfair to yourself. Unfortunately, it isn't rare for premature babies to be rehospitalized. Researchers have found that one out of three preemies has to go back into the hospital at some point during their first two years of life, because of respiratory illness. Even excluding those with chronic lung disease, who are most fragile, the number is still steep: one out of four.

So rehospitalization is just one more hill that many preemies and their parents have to climb. Parents sometimes suffer almost as much as their babies, with the following, common emotions:

❋ *Guilt.* Nothing can cause more self-doubt than having something happen to your baby on your watch. But you can only do what's possible. It's not possible to shield your baby from germs that are everywhere, or to will her health problems away. You also can't be expected to do everything right, all the time (no parent does!). So don't blame yourself for some real or imagined mistake that you can identify now, with 20–20 hindsight. And don't assume that other people—your spouse, relatives, or even the doctors and nurses—are wondering if you took poor care of your baby. People realize that preemies are more fragile, and not subject to pat advice and judgments. In fact, it's very likely that what you deserve is praise—for recognizing when your baby needed medical help, and getting her to the doctor or hospital, the right place for her to be. That is exactly what a good parent should have done.

❋ *Anger at your baby's doctors and nurses.* Anger is a natural reaction when you're feeling frustration and pain, but try to be fair, too. You may be angry that the hospital staff, in your opinion, discharged your baby before she was ready, didn't tell you how vulnerable she was, or didn't do more for her in the first place. There may be some truth in any of these, but most likely, the staff made the best decisions possible under the circumstances. Discharging babies home helps their development by placing them in a loving, enriching environment with their parents, removes them from the infection risks that are present in all hospitals, and makes places in intensive care nurseries available for critically ill infants. If you're feeling bad about blowing up at one of the doctors or nurses, be assured that you aren't the first parent in this situation to do so, and the staff probably understands what you're going through.

❋ *Physical and emotional exhaustion.* Some parents find the second hospitalization harder, in some ways, than the first one, feeling like they have no strength left to handle another round of anxiety and stress. Make sure to pace yourself: take breaks from the hospital, even if you just go to a coffee shop for a few hours, or go home and sleep for the afternoon. Tell your partner, who may not realize how much you need his help, how you're feeling. You could ask him to fill in for you at the hospital for a while, or just go there with you, and hold your hand. If you feel that you need additional support, contact a parent support group, whose members understand what you're going through, or talk to the hospital social worker.

❋ *Worry that this additional hospitalization is "too much" for your baby to take.* One thing parents of preemies come to realize, over time, is how strong and resilient babies are—sometimes, more so than their parents! Although it's painful for us to see our babies having to struggle, you can be sure that premature babies are tough little fighters. Once your baby is home again, you'll give her plenty of time to rest and get the comfort she deserves, in your arms.

❋ *Feeling less confident and more worried after your baby gets home.* It may take time for you to relax again. Your baby is probably stronger than ever—she's older and more physically mature, after all—but it's normal for you to have more of a sense of vulnerability. Parents who have gone through this say it can take weeks or months before they regain the sense that everything is going to be OK. As time passes, you will, too.

One thing that can be extremely productive, after this crisis is over, is to ask yourself whether you handled your baby's illness or emergency as best you could. Do you feel you need any additional information on how to care for your baby, or to detect a problem? Would you do anything differently next time, if there's ever an emergency again? Asking these questions constructively is a great approach, since parenting of any baby is a life-long process of learning.

THROUGH THE DOORS OF PREEMIE FOLLOW-UP CLINIC

For some parents whose preemies have been home for a few months, taking them back to the hospital's follow-up clinic can be like a nostalgic trip back to an old home with old friends. For other parents, having to go back to *that* hospital, if only for a follow-up visit, can be a source of anxiety and painful memories. If you're not at ease, be assured that the doctors and nurses can understand that, and will try to make you feel more comfortable. Your baby will probably be greeted warmly by a clinic staff that is proud to see one of their growing graduates, and genuinely concerned about her progress.

While every preemie follow-up clinic is a little different, and they all go by different names, the basic idea is always the same: for a team of doctors and specialists across a broad range of disciplines, all of whom have experience with preemies and understand your baby's start in life, to look closely at her to make sure she's healthy and developing well.

Around the time your baby is discharged from the hospital, you'll be told about preemie follow-up clinic, and scheduled for a first appointment. If you aren't, that's because, happily, your baby is not considered at risk for developmental problems. On the other hand, it shouldn't make you nervous if your baby is asked to come. It simply means that she met one of the standard criteria set by the hospital—possibly relating to her weight or gestational age at birth, or a medical problem she had—designating which babies are at a somewhat higher than normal risk for a persistent complication of prematurity. Most follow-up clinics include more babies than necessary, so they don't risk missing any.

What can you expect at your first visit? It will take place a few months after your baby's discharge, usually when she's two to six months of adjusted age. Don't figure on being there briefly, as if for a quick half-hour doctor's appointment. Block off your whole morning or afternoon, just in case, and bring a snack and bag of toys, to pass the time in waiting or exam rooms that may not be well-stocked.

Your baby will be seen by several professionals. A doctor (usually a neonatologist) will do a medical exam. An expert in child development, who may be the same doctor or another specialist, will evaluate your child's cognitive development (thinking and learning), motor skills, and behavior. The most widely-used, standardized test of a baby's development between the ages of birth and two years is called the Bayley Scales of Infant Development. It involves giving your baby a variety of objects and tasks to perform, so the tester can assess her performance relative to other babies her age. (Don't feel bad if she can't do some of the things she's asked to do. It's part of the test to give her some tasks that are above her age level, which she won't be expected to perform.) Other professionals, possibly including a physical therapist, occupational therapist, audiologist, or a speech therapist (see page 445 for a brief explanation of these fields), may also be involved in giving the test or examining your child, with a particular eye to their specialties.

Based on these evaluations, the experts will assess whether your child is developing normally, or whether there are areas in which she needs extra help. If you are receiving any early intervention services already, they will talk to you to evaluate how they're going. A social worker or discharge planner will help to coordinate whatever services your child needs with the organizations that supply them. He can also help you to get government or other funding for which you may be eligible. (Keep in mind that you may qualify for additional funding if there's a new diagnosis, or a change in your family situation.) Not least of all, he'll ask how your family is doing, and whether you need any other assistance.

Finally, you'll be told about specific, next steps you should take, including any other medical tests your baby may need, and when to return for her next appointment. Every clinic has a standard schedule for visits, though extra appointments can always be inserted to meet a child's needs. At some point, your preemie will "graduate" from preemie follow-up clinic. Some clinics prefer that all preemies keep coming until they reach a certain age, while others dismiss babies earlier, if they are developing normally, to be followed by their pediatrician as a normal child. Even if a child continues to need special services, she will out-

grow the preemie follow-up clinic at about two or three years of age, depending on the clinic's policies. At that point, she will start going to a developmental clinic for older children, which might be part of the same hospital, or a state-run center with similar resources. Or, if a child has one particular, overriding medical problem, she will be dismissed to be followed at a specialty clinic (for example, a neurology clinic for a child with seizures, or a pulmonary clinic for a child with bronchopulmonary dysplasia). The specialists there will be expected to pick up any developmental problems that might arise in the future.

Many parents wonder whether their baby needs to go to a regular pediatrician, as well as the follow-up clinic. The answer is yes. Your baby still needs her immunizations and regular, pediatric checkups, when her doctor will do some things that are out of the scope of the follow-up clinic—from checking for ear infections to getting routine blood or urine tests. She still needs a doctor who will treat her normal, childhood illnesses. The staff of the clinic will be concentrating on any medical problems that are specifically related to prematurity, and on assessing your baby's development. So, while she will get double the weighings and measurings, and there will be some other overlap, much of what's done in the two kinds of checkups will be different.

If you live far from your follow-up clinic, either because you've moved, or had been traveling to the hospital in the first place, your neonatologist can tell you whether there is another preemie clinic closer to you. But it may still make sense to go back to your original hospital's clinic, at least for the first appointment, to tie up any loose ends—and, as an added benefit, to get the chance to show off your growing baby to her fans on the staff.

Developmental Delays

When they say preemies sometimes have developmental delays, do they mean temporary or permanent ones?

The term *developmental delay* (which means that a child isn't reaching certain developmental milestones as quickly as most of his peers) can mean either one, and preemies get both. Permanent developmental delays, or disabilities, are often not diagnosed for sure until a preemie is a year old or more. That's because in preemies, a delay is often truly transient, causing their parents some temporary hand-wringing, then fading into memory, with no lasting consequences.

For example, it's common for preemies to have developmental delays resulting from temporary abnormalities of muscle tone—and then to grow out of them. Some preemies are a little weak early on, and may be slower to roll over, or sit without support. Others develop stiff joints or tight muscles, causing them, perhaps, to be stiff when they stand up, or to be unable to bring their hands together to hold their own bottle. Preemies who aren't grasping their bottles at six months are often doing it perfectly normally at twelve months. And preemies who don't begin walking quite as early as other children, if they don't have a permanent motor disability, will walk perfectly well when they do.

Nobody knows exactly why these transient muscle tone abnormalities occur so often in premature babies. They may be related to different patterns of brain maturation in preemies. Or they may be related to a preemie's experience—for example, a long stay in a hospital bed can make certain muscles weak and joints tight, from lack of movement.

Experience might also play a role in delays in acquiring other skills, such as eating with a spoon, or making speech sounds. Preemies who are on ventilators for several months, or who have tracheostomies, for example, may not have gotten any early practice in eating or speaking. Any illness, even a relatively mild one, that makes a preemie less active in working her muscles and exploring the world, can cause a temporary developmental delay.

In general, temporary problems usually cause only mild delays. Permanent disabilities often cause more significant lags, of many months or years. A child with a motor disability such as cerebral palsy, for example, with practice and training might walk at the age of 30 months. Some milestones might never be achieved. (Keep in mind that a child who has an impairment in one area will often reach milestones in other areas a little late, but perfectly well—with or without the help of special therapy. For example, a baby who doesn't see well may learn to walk later than other children, but may eventually walk just as smoothly and quickly. A child with a mild or moderate hearing loss may be delayed in her speech, but learn to talk well, with appropriate intervention.)

If you are concerned about a delay in your child's development, don't keep it to yourself! In some cases, a pediatrician or physical therapist will be able to reassure you that the "quality" of your child's movements or play is normal, so the delay is most likely temporary. (You can read about getting a developmental evaluation through your state's early intervention program, or local school district, on page 443.) If they suspect that there could be a more serious problem, or can't draw any conclusions until they observe your child's progress over time, you may still feel better, getting support and help for your child from experts, rather than stewing about the problem alone.

Growth Predictions

I'm average in height, but my two-year-old preemie is only at the 5th percentile. Will she always be small?

Everybody is enchanted by toddlers who come in adorably small packages, calling them "peanut" or "pipsqueak" in the most admiring and affectionate way. But your daughter won't necessarily be keeping those nicknames forever. The only thing anybody can say for sure about her eventual height is that it's still too early to predict. Many preemies start out small, and then catch up, partially or fully, later on.

Medical researchers are still studying the long-term growth of preemies, so we're bound to learn more over time, but here's a snapshot of what's known to date. By the time their due dates arrive, preemies are smaller, on average, than full-term newborns: in one large sample, at 40 weeks, slightly more than half were below the normal range in weight and height (meaning below the 3rd percentile, and so below the normal range covered on the regular growth charts). Some preemies are born small for their gestational age, so have further to go to catch up. But even the others find it hard to take in enough calories to grow as fast in the outside world as they would have in the womb. That's especially true if they're sick, because sick infants need even more calories to grow, but take in fewer.

This picture gradually changes. Some preemies, especially those with chronic lung disease or feeding disorders, continue to lag in growth even after their due dates, but most begin to grow just as fast as their full-term peers. Then, at some point, many preemies begin growing even faster than other babies, making up for their slow start. Because of this "catch-up growth," by eight months of corrected age, only about one-third of the preemies in the study were still below normal in weight, and about one-quarter were below normal in height. By eight years of age, although the preemies overall were still somewhat smaller than their full-term peers, only 8% of them were below normal in weight or height. Those who were born small for their gestational age, had shorter mothers, or had neurologic abnormalities, were more likely to remain small. Standard growth charts for preemies, that reflect their different growth patterns through age three, can be found in the appendix on pages 515–518. (To see how your baby "measures up," be sure to use the right chart: there are different ones for boys and for girls, as well as for preemies who were born weighing more, or less, than 1,500 grams.)

Some researchers think the story doesn't end there. A recent, intriguing study—too small to be conclusive—followed 32 preemies with birth weights less than 1,000 grams all the way through adolescence, and at latest measurement, these preemies (who earlier measured below normal in size) had reached the average heights and weights of the general population. In fact, the researchers concluded from the heights of their mothers and fathers that preemies eventually do achieve their true, genetic potential, although it may not be until after their teenage growth spurt. Further research may or may not bear this out. But one thing is clear: you shouldn't try to predict your child's future height from her early measurements.

In the meantime, enjoy her, and don't assume that being small will ever stop her. Maybe she'll be a gymnast instead of a basketball player. Maybe she'll be the smallest of her friends, but have the biggest personality. One of our preemies was a tiny toddler, and we used to quote a line from a song about Madeline, the famous, gutsy little French girl of children's books. "Though she's very small," the song goes, "inside, she's tall."

Picky Eater

My tiny toddler has never been a good eater, and now he's getting worse: all he wants is Cheerios. Is there something I can do to make his diet more nutritious?

As long as your pediatrician reassures you that your child is consistently growing at a pace that's adequate—even if he's still smaller than other kids his age—you shouldn't worry too much about his diet. A rich, varied diet would be nice, but kids have an amazing ability to grow on what seems to their parents like far too little food.

To be sure, there are some former preemies who develop serious feeding problems that prevent them from growing adequately. Most of the time, severe feeding problems are related to other medical conditions, such as reflux or cerebral palsy. If this is the case for your child, he should be evaluated by experts who can diagnose his specific problems and give you advice on how to deal with them (see page 457).

More likely, though, your preemie is afflicted with the same pickiness that's common in full-term toddlers and children. If that's what you and your pediatrician think you're dealing with, the best thing is to present your child with foods that are rich in calories, without making eating into a battleground.

Here are some practical suggestions:

✳ *Establish a schedule.* Toddlers and young children usually do well with three meals and two to three snacks every day. Try not to give your son juice and sweets as snacks, to prevent him from taking in relatively empty calories that can ruin his appetite for more nutritious food. Save sweets for after a good meal.

✳ *Make experimentation possible.* At meals, present him with different options (two or three kinds of food) and let him experiment with new foods.

✳ *Be persistent (but cool).* If your son seems to hate some foods (green vegetables?), keep putting that kind of food on his plate, meal after meal, but don't insist that he taste it, and don't be discouraged if he doesn't. Some children need to get used to the sight and smell of some foods before actually trying them. Patience and coolness in the face of rejection, some parents say, is the key to success.

✳ *Don't serve too much.* A good rule of thumb is to serve a child one tablespoon of each food for each year of age, and then give a little more if he likes it. At 18 to 24 months, typical serving sizes for some common foods are:
- 4–6 ounces of whole milk
- ¼–½ cup hot or dry cereal
- ½ slice of cheese
- ½ cup yogurt or cottage cheese
- ½ slice of bread; 2–4 crackers
- 3–4 tablespoons of pasta, or rice, or beans, or egg, or fruit or vegetable
- 2–4 tablespoons of chopped meats or fish

✳ *Try adding calories to the foods your child likes.* To increase the calories your child takes in, try such tricks as:
- Adding a little butter, cream, oil, or grated Parmesan cheese to foods
- Adding cheese sauce to vegetables
- Adding finely chopped hard-boiled eggs to pasta or rice
- Adding condensed milk or powdered whole milk to yogurt, cream cheese, or hot cereals
- Spreading crackers or bread with peanut butter (if your child is not allergic to it).

❉ *Limit the length of meals.* Some parents have found that limiting mealtime to thirty minutes helps make a child's eating pattern more regular and structured. Let him play around a little with his food and feed himself as he pleases, without getting upset about messiness, but after 30 minutes, even if he didn't eat enough, take his plate away and let him leave the table. Don't worry that he might get too hungry before the next snack or meal: he needs that experience to help him establish a schedule.

❉ *Avoid nagging or conflict.* Try not to let your anxiety turn each meal into a conflict. Don't talk too much about food, don't punish or scold your son for not eating, and try not to bribe him into eating. (A sweet treat to reward him after a healthy meal, though, is fine.) Otherwise, you're giving him the message that when he wants to assert his control, food is a good arena in which to do it.

Flu Vaccine

Should my preemie get a flu vaccine?

Yearly flu vaccines are a good idea for children who may not handle a respiratory infection as easily as other kids. Doctors recommend that preemies with BPD and members of their family (who could catch the flu and give it to their baby) get flu vaccines, and they may recommend them for any other child they think is at high risk for breathing problems or getting extremely sick from the flu. You should ask your pediatrician whether he recommends flu vaccines for you and your baby.

A baby can get a flu vaccine once she's six months old, when her immune system is mature enough to react to it. Keep in mind that even though many people say they have the flu whenever they're suffering from a bad cold, influenza is really one, specific virus. A flu vaccine will protect your baby against influenza, but not against every winter cold.

Daycare

I purposely kept my daughter out of daycare because I was afraid of her getting infections. Now that she's two years old, is daycare safe for her?

It's an unavoidable fact that any group of little ones is a perfect set-up for the quick spread of germs, and children in daycare or preschool come down with more colds and minor infections than children at home with their parents. So, if you mean will your daughter be "safe" from getting sick often, the answer is no. But will she handle the colds and illnesses as well as any other child? If she is otherwise healthy, there's no reason she shouldn't. Once a preemie is a year old, and has gotten through her first winter, you no longer have to worry about her being especially vulnerable. She has roughly the same amount of infection-fighting antibodies as full-term kids of her corrected age, with an immune system that is as mature.

The one thing it's important to realize is that preemies who are still on medications or oxygen for BPD are more fragile. They have less reserve in their lungs, so if they get a cold or respiratory infection, they will get sicker than other children. They also need more calories to grow, so diarrhea (one of the other, common things that kids in daycare come down with), may cause them more problems. If your daughter has BPD, you'll have to make a trade-off between the advantages of daycare (the social and developmental stimulation she'll get from being around other children and adults, and the time it frees up for you), and the more frequent sicknesses that she'll undoubtedly get. Make sure to talk this decision over with her doctor, who can help you understand the benefits and risks.

Also talk to the doctor if your child has a history of BPD, but is no longer being treated for it. She may still tend to get a little sicker than other children when she catches something, because her lungs may not have fully recovered—but in most cases, she won't be so fragile that she can't lead a perfectly normal life, including going to daycare.

You may have read that the latest, reassuring research has found that high-quality daycare programs can actually be beneficial in promoting a child's language and learning abilities. Especially if your child is getting early intervention services because of some developmental risks or delays, you may want to look for daycare programs with "developmental" curricula, offering more organized, skill-developing activities. If you don't know of any, ask at your child's preemie follow-up clinic, or look in the Yellow Pages for childcare referral services.

No matter what kind of program you choose, make sure to observe it in action, check references, licensing (a state or local license generally provides some safeguards, at least in terms of safety, sanitation, and caregiver-child ratio), policies on medical checkups and immunizations for the staff and kids, and enforcement of health rules (for example, whether toys are regularly disinfected, caregivers wash hands after diaper changes and before serving food, and pacifiers and bottles are labeled and kept separate). Since some of the good programs have waiting lists, it's never too early to start looking at them, and applying for a spot.

LEADING A NORMAL INFANCY AND CHILDHOOD WITH A VP SHUNT

All parents have mixed feelings about their child's VP shunt, but some have an especially hard time accepting it. Although they understand that there's no other good option, they may become overly concerned about the presence of the shunt, and its effect on their child's life. But keep in mind that the shunt is not an impairment in itself; on the contrary, it is a very effective way to prevent the possible consequences of hydrocephalus on the brain, and even to reverse some of them, greatly improving the chances that your child will grow and develop normally.

From personal experience, we can reassure you that you're going to feel a lot better when your premature baby becomes a toddler. By then, many of your initial uncertainties about your child's development will be resolved. Even if he has some delays, you'll be settled and familiar with early intervention and follow-up specialists, and know what to expect.

Medically, the first year of life of a premature baby with a VP shunt is delicate, since the risk for a shunt infection is highest in the first six months following surgery. You should consider this when making a choice about childcare (see below). Most complications requiring a shunt revision also tend to occur within six to twelve months after the first operation. Although you have to be prepared for the possibility of a shunt revision in the future, the bigger and stronger your baby is, the less anxious you should be about seeing him go back to the operating room.

Emotionally, you're going to be particularly vulnerable during your child's first year, still feeling the afterwaves of stress and sorrow caused by his premature birth and illness. The shunt inside his body, which initially you may not even want to acknowledge with your touch, will become, little by little, more familiar and acceptable to you, just as it disappears from the sight of anyone who doesn't know it is there. Actually, the time will come, sooner than you expect, when you realize that the shunt is no longer a threatening presence in your thoughts. It's very important for you to let that natural adaptation happen. If somebody in your family, or a friend, has a tendency to revive your anxiety about your child's shunt, be firm and tell that person that you don't need to be aggravated. You need, instead, to be calm and optimistic, to allow your child to live his life to his maximum potential. There's nothing he can't do, because of his VP shunt.

Here's a brief overview of some other issues that parents of children with VP shunts often wonder about:

✺ During your baby's first year, some doctors recommend that you avoid daycare (see page 366) to reduce the chances of a shunt infection, or frequent shunt infection "scares." If you can't arrange for baby-sitting in your own house, you should consider sharing a sitter with a few other parents, or choose a small family day-care setting, so your baby is exposed to only a few other children.

✺ To avoid infections, your child will need to take antibiotics before dental procedures and surgeries. Be sure to inform his dentist about his VP shunt.

✺ It is recommended that your child get periodic vision and hearing screens, as well as developmental evaluations (these are done routinely in many preemie follow-up clinics), so as to catch and correct any problems early.

✺ If you have to move to another city or state, and you're worried about leaving behind your trusted neurosurgeon, ask him for advice before you go. He will suggest how to organize your child's follow-up, and refer you to a colleague or medical center close to your new address. If a child has only mild symptoms, he might be able to travel back to his original neurosurgeon, to have him revise his shunt, but be sure to inquire about this—and any limitations on your choice of doctor or hospital—from your insurer. Your concerns are not uncommon: some families even consider moving to be near a particular doctor or hospital.

✺ Don't treat your child differently because of his condition. The shunt won't be dislodged or damaged in the course of daily activities, so your child can play, run, do team sports, swim, and dive, as all other children do, even become a competitive athlete, if he has a passion and gift for it. Some doctors discourage direct-contact sports like football; but if he wears a helmet, you can even allow him to do that. A helmet is necessary when he bicycles, skies, or rides a skateboard. But what otherwise wise parents would allow their child to do without one?

✺ Your child needs to know about his VP shunt. As soon as he is able to understand a simple explanation, you should tell him. Have him touch the little bump of the valve on his head, and the tube tunneled under his skin down to his belly. At the same time, you should give him a lot of reassurance that everything is OK. Don't scare him about the possibility of surgery for a shunt revision, but if it happens, tell him that it's normal, and he's going to recover fast.

✳ As long as you understand your child's condition and are confident about the VP shunt's effectiveness and safety, you'll be able to explain it to his siblings, friends, and teachers. Don't fear that he might be treated differently because of it: since the shunt isn't visible, most acquaintances quickly forget about it. You'll find that their attitude toward your child will depend almost entirely on yours.

Possible VP Shunt Problems

I worry so much now that my child has a VP shunt. What could go wrong with it?

Parents of a child with a VP shunt have wrenching doubts every time their kid gets sick, as all kids do. Is it just a virus, an innocent upset stomach, or the shunt, they wonder in anguish. You may find it reassuring to go over some things that your baby's neurosurgeon and pediatrician have already told you about how to recognize a shunt problem (see page 415), as well as some thoughts from families of children with VP shunts (see page 413)—parents like you, who know how hard it is to live with the knowledge that their child's well-being depends on that essential, but still foreign, object implanted in his body.

Despite its reliability and resistance to damage, a shunt system can occasionally fail and need to be changed. When a malfunction is only partial, meaning some cerebrospinal fluid is still being drained by the shunt or absorbed by the body, the pressure inside the brain from hydrocephalus rises slowly. A toddler may not show any symptoms other than his head enlarging more quickly than normal over a few weeks or months. In other cases, the shunt malfunction is total, and the rapidly increasing pressure in the brain can make a child feel very sick, with headache and vomiting. In the most serious cases, a doctor may find that a child's blood pressure is high, his heartbeat slow, and his breathing irregular. When that happens, it is a medical emergency.

The most common reason for shunt failures are breaks in the tubing, blockages (by blood clots, scarring, or other tissue in the ventricles or abdomen), or because a child has grown so tall that the shunt tubing is no longer in the proper position in his abdomen. VP shunts for tiny preemies are necessarily short, and despite the fact that neurosurgeons use extra-long tubing and coil it inside a baby's abdomen, to allow for future growth, the catheter may still need to be replaced with a bigger one, at some point.

Another possible cause of a shunt malfunction is a shunt infection. Most infections are seen in the first six months following shunt surgery, but they can happen at any time. Even if a shunt infection doesn't interfere with how well the shunt is working, it may not resolve until the shunt is removed (temporarily), because bacteria can hide in the plastic tubing, and evade efforts to eradicate them.

Both partial and total shunt malfunctions have to be corrected with shunt revisions. On average, a child will need from two to three shunt revisions during infancy and childhood. A revision gives your child a new, functioning shunt and almost always returns him to his previous wellness.

IF YOUR CHILD HAS A VP SHUNT: WHAT SHOULD CONCERN YOU, AND WHAT SHOULD NOT

Symptoms of Shunt Malfunction

Up to one year of age:
* full fontanel
* enlarging head

Sometimes also:
* vomiting
* poor feeding
* irritability
* lethargy or excessive sleepiness
* abnormal gaze and eye movements
* seizures

Toddler or older child:
* enlarging head
* headache
* vomiting
* lethargy
* abdominal pain
* irritability
* behavior changes
* loss of previous motor or cognitive abilities
* seizures

Symptoms of Shunt Infection

* Fever over 101°F, together with any other symptom of shunt malfunction

Sometimes also:
* redness and tenderness around the valve and along the catheter
* abdominal distension
* headache
* abdominal pain
* diarrhea

Fever. Always call the pediatrician if your child has a fever higher than 101°F. Most of the time the doctor will end up diagnosing a viral infection, or another common illness, rather than a shunt infection. Remember that in an infant, particularly a preemie, it's possible to detect a "fake" fever caused by a hot room and too many clothes. Undress your baby, leave him undisturbed for fifteen minutes, and then check his temperature again.

Full fontanel. A puffy, bulging fontanel (the soft spot on a baby's head) when the baby is held upright and not crying or straining is a typical sign of hydrocephalus in infants who still have open skull bones (a natural protection against pressure on the brain). If you notice tension in the fontanel when your infant is lying down, but it disappears when you put him in a vertical position, it's a false alarm. So don't panic, wait until your baby is calm, and pick him up and check again. Very large and visible scalp veins, and wide-open spaces where the skull bones should come together, can also be signs of increased pressure. But keep in mind that the shape of your infant's head will change a lot in the first months after surgery, even if his shunt is functioning perfectly.

Enlarging head. Even after the fontanels close, a toddler's skull bones are not tightly fused together, so his head can still enlarge quickly if the shunt malfunctions. (As a child grows older, this leeway gradually disappears.) Few neurosurgeons or pediatricians advise parents to check their children's head circumference, since it's common to obtain false readings, and the measurements performed at the pediatrician's office, and plotted on your child's growth chart, are sufficient. If you feel compelled to do it, though, you should use a flexible tape measure divided into centimeters. Place it across your child's forehead over the eyebrows, then wind it around his head at the widest point. Take three measurements, one after the other, to make sure of your result.

The normal rate of head growth will vary depending on the age of your child, faster (about one centimeter a week) for infant preemies, and slower (about one centimeter a month) for toddlers. To know if your child's head is growing at a normal rate for his age and sex, you'll need to plot your measurements over several days to weeks on the appropriate head circumference chart on pages 515–518. (A single measurement made at only one point in time is not an accurate guide, since a child who had hydrocephalus may have a bigger head to start with, but one which is growing normally over time.)

Headache. Many parents are greatly relieved when their child begins to speak. While an infant can only cry, or become fussier, a toddler is able to point to where he has pain, and an older child can describe what he feels. A headache caused by a shunt malfunction can be severe or mild, intermittent or persistent. Be particularly wary of a headache or sense of heaviness that wakes your child from sleep, is worse when lying down or in the morning, or that is accompanied by vomiting or nausea. In that case, you should call the doctor.

Vomiting. Babies spit up for a million reasons that don't have anything to do with shunt malfunctions. Over time, you'll get to know your child well, and usually be able to tell if he vomited because he ate too fast or too much, or because you bounced him, or for some other reason. In an older child, vomiting is more un-

usual, and therefore more worrisome for a shunt malfunction. A single episode of vomiting or nausea, though, should concern you only if it's accompanied by any of the other signs of shunt malfunction or infection. In cases of repeated vomiting, you should always call the doctor. In the vast majority of cases, after having seen your child, the doctor will be able to reassure you that the vomiting is most likely caused by a flu or common virus.

Abdominal pain, diarrhea, constipation. A bloated or painful abdomen, sometimes with fever or diarrhea, can signal a shunt infection, and should immediately be reported to the doctor. A VP shunt can cause bowel blockage, but this is a very rare complication, and you needn't be concerned about mild constipation without pain or vomiting. In general, though, your child should try to maintain regular bowel movements, with a diet rich in fiber, fruit, and vegetables, because persistent constipation can cause problems with the VP shunt tubing in the abdomen.

Lethargy. Lethargy can be a hard symptom to ascertain in an infant, particularly in a sleepy, premature infant who tires easily, falls asleep in the middle of feedings, and needs to get all the rest that he can. But if your baby doesn't wake up at his regular times or doesn't seem hungry, then you should watch him more carefully, to see if that pattern continues. In an older child, difficulty waking up, or excessive sleepiness, is more telling. Don't get anxious, though, about one longer nap or night's sleep, since your child probably is simply tired and replenishing his energies. Do worry about a consistent trend, particularly if accompanied by headache and vomiting, and call the doctor.

Poor feeding. This is another confusing one for parents of premature babies, who often need to be encouraged to eat. Often, if a baby eats less at one meal, he'll balance it out by eating more at the next one. But if your baby seems much slower in his sucking than usual, and doesn't seem hungrier over the course of several feedings, call the doctor.

Abnormal gaze and eye movements. A shunt malfunction can give a baby "sunset eyes," so-called because the gaze is deviated downward. If you notice this, you should call the pediatrician. Children with hydrocephalus can also have mild visual problems, even with a properly functioning shunt. They range from nystagmus (rapid, involuntary eye movements) to difficulty focusing on or visually following objects. After an evaluation by an eye doctor, which your baby should have at about six months of age, you'll know if your child has any of these problems, and you can look out for any change from what's normal for him.

Seizures. Children with VP shunts are also more likely to have seizures, which are usually treated with medication. But seizures can be a symptom of shunt malfunction or infection. Therefore, even if your child has already had other seizures, you should call the doctor to see if he needs to evaluate your child.

Irritability and changes in behavior. A baby or child with a subtle, persistent headache or nausea due to a shunt problem can become fussier or more difficult. Sometimes, a change in temperament or behavior, like increased irritability or

problems at school, are caused by pressure from hydrocephalus. But what toddler doesn't have a temper tantrum every now and then? What kid doesn't occasionally show decreased attention span at school? Overreacting to these subtle, common swings in behavior is unfair, to yourself and your child. A significant change in your child, one that could indicate a shunt problem, will become evident to you even if you take a more relaxed and optimistic attitude.

Loss of previous motor or cognitive abilities. Sometimes a shunt malfunction can impair a child's normal development, without other acute symptoms. If you realize that your child is no longer able to do something he used to do well, like sitting up, pulling himself to a standing position, walking steadily, or naming a familiar object, you should watch him more carefully. But also remember that ups and downs are a normal pattern of development. A child doesn't reach a milestone once, and then have it mastered—rather, he needs to practice a new skill a lot, before he can perform it consistently. So you should inform his doctor only if you continue to see a change. If your child does develop an impairment caused by a shunt malfunction, you'll be understandably anxious; but he has a good chance of overcoming it when the shunt is revised and the hydrocephalus is again under control.

When to Call the Doctor about the VP Shunt

When I see something I fear might be caused by a problem with my child's VP shunt, I never know when it's time to call the doctor.

If your child doesn't look sick, a wise approach is to wait until your first impression is confirmed, rather than calling the pediatrician right away. For your peace of mind, though, remember that you're justified in making as many phone calls and visits to your baby's doctor as you need, even if they result in false alarms, to avoid missing a real emergency.

When you call the doctor, make sure to say that your child has a VP shunt, before describing his symptoms: doctors and nurses will give your call immediate priority. Your pediatrician will refer you to the neurosurgeon if that's what's needed. But there's nothing wrong with calling your neurosurgeon directly, if you have a particular concern or question. A pediatric neurosurgeon who cares for children with VP shunts has made a long-term commitment to each of his little patients, and is well aware of their families' practical and emotional needs. Knowing that he's always there, ready to revise your child's shunt if necessary, can make you feel much safer.

Your baby's doctor will do a careful physical exam, and if he thinks that a shunt malfunction is a possibility, will obtain various kinds of x-rays. If he suspects a shunt infection, he will also do tests of your baby's blood and cerebrospinal fluid. These tests will usually reveal whether there is a problem with the shunt. But sometimes, doctors can't definitively prove, or disprove, that there is a shunt malfunction or infection. In that case, they may observe your child closely, and wait to see if he improves or worsens. Or, if their suspicion of a shunt malfunction is high, even if they're not certain, the doctors may recommend surgery, to prevent complications, which are more likely the longer an infection or hydrocephalus persists. Although it's heartbreaking to see your child going back to the operating room, you'll soon realize how fast you can put the crisis of a shunt malfunction behind you.

Seizures

My daughter had a seizure in the NICU, and recently she had another seizure with a high fever. Does this mean that she'll have more?

In most parenting books, you'll find a section on febrile seizures (as the convulsions that children can get with high fevers are called), for the simple reason that they're fairly common. About one out of every 25 toddlers gets one. And though they're terrifying to parents, doctors don't worry about them much at all. Not only are febrile seizures harmless, but children who get them have only a tiny risk of developing epilepsy, which is a disorder in which seizures recur without fevers. Up to 98% of these children will never have to worry about seizures again after outgrowing their febrile ones, usually well before their fifth birthday. (The peak period for febrile seizures is between 18 months and 24 months of age.)

But of course, if your preemie also had a seizure in the hospital nursery, it's natural for you to wonder whether the outlook for her is different. The answer is: it depends, but there's a good chance you're worrying unnecessarily.

There are only three factors that make a young child who has a seizure with fever more likely to develop epilepsy. One is if she has a cognitive or motor impairment, since this would indicate that there is some underlying injury in her brain. If your child has no cognitive or motor impairment, the great news is that neither her neonatal seizure (which can occur for all kinds of temporary reasons) nor her febrile seizure, nor even the fact that she had both, make her any more likely to have epilepsy. In fact, even if she had more than one neonatal seizure, or she has recurring febrile seizures (about one-third of toddlers who get one seizure with a fever go on to have at least one recurrence), it won't make any difference. On the other hand, if your daughter does have cerebral palsy or a developmental delay, then it could be that both her seizure in the NICU and her seizure with a fever at home were triggered by the same, underlying brain injury—and the likelihood of future seizures does rise.

The second factor that would increase your

child's risk is if her febrile seizure was "atypical." Typical, or so-called "simple," febrile seizures last for less than fifteen minutes (although most commonly, they last for just a minute or two, and some can be as brief as a few seconds), and affect a child's whole body. The child would stiffen up and arch her back, her arms and legs would jerk repeatedly, and she would briefly lose consciousness. A seizure is atypical if it lasts longer, affects only portions of the body, such as just an arm or a leg, or just the right side, or recurs within twenty-four hours.

The third factor that would increase your child's risk is if you have a family history of epilepsy.

Now, if your child has one of these three risk factors, please be warned against excessive pessimism! The odds that she'll have epilepsy are still small. Even if she has two of them, there's only about a 10% chance.

In any event, you should read up on febrile seizures, to make sure you know what to do if she gets another one. It's important to prevent any accidental injury or choking. And you should talk to your daughter's doctor, who, to be safe, may want to do some tests to make sure that the seizure wasn't caused by any problem other than the fever itself.

Worrying about Cerebral Palsy

Everyone tells me I don't have to worry, but I still keep dreading that my child will have cerebral palsy.

Like many other parents of preemies, you may not even have known what cerebral palsy was before your baby was born. Once you learn that it is one of the most feared consequences of prematurity, though, it can be hard to get out of your mind. If your baby isn't sitting up by herself on the very day she turns six months of age, you ask yourself: will she sit up tomorrow? When you see her clench her hands into little fists, you worry: is this simply an adorable gesture, or a bad sign of things to come?

Cerebral palsy, or CP, simply means that a person's muscles don't move in a naturally strong, coordinated way. It's due to a permanent injury to the brain—which may have occurred before, during, or after a baby's birth—that prevents it from sending the signals the muscles need for well-coordinated movement. CP ranges from very mild (sometimes almost imperceptible) to severe, from affecting only one limb to affecting the whole body. Movement problems that are temporary, that infants grow out of, are not cerebral palsy.

As a rule, cerebral palsy can neither be diagnosed, nor definitively ruled out, until a baby is eighteen months to two years of age. If your baby is already one-and-a-half to two years old, and the way she moves is normal for her age (according to you and her doctors), you can put your fear right out of your mind. She does not have cerebral palsy. It should reassure you to know that if your baby is younger, and doesn't have visible signs of brain damage on tests, or other risk factors for cerebral palsy, like hydrocephalus or birth asphyxia, the chances that she will have cerebral palsy are tiny. Even if she has a known risk factor, she still has a chance—possibly a good one, depending on her situation— of being normal.

It's important to realize that abnormalities of muscle tone and reflexes are extremely common in preemies during their first year. At least two-thirds of babies born at less than 1,500 grams have them—while only about 10% will actually have cerebral palsy. It's not known whether these problems are due to long hospital stays that weaken muscles and joints from lack of activity, early brain injuries that are healing, or different patterns of brain maturation in babies who are born early. But in most cases, these abnormalities are transient, gradually resolving by the time a baby is twelve to eighteen months old. On the other hand, it's also possible for an infant to have normal muscle tone early on, and then develop abnormalities later in the first year.

Because a preemie's abnormalities are so often fleeting, a diagnosis of cerebral palsy is generally made before twelve months only if a premature baby had a known brain injury, such as a severe intraventricular hemorrhage or periventricular leukomalacia, and she moves some parts of her body very differently from others. Between twelve and eighteen months, a diagnosis of CP is usually made if a child has different movement patterns in different extremities, delayed motor skills, movements that are abnormal in quality, and reflexes that persist beyond the expected age. (You can learn about these characteristics, and what they look like, on page 421.) In general, premature babies with cerebral palsy have increasingly obvious abnormalities of muscle tone, movement, and reflexes, and increasingly long delays in meeting motor milestones, especially between six months and eighteen months of adjusted age. It's not that their CP is worsening, but that as a child grows, more complex movements are expected of her, and abnormal tone interferes more.

Even the most sophisticated brain imaging, such as ultrasound or MRI scans, are of limited help in predicting which preemies will get CP. Cerebral palsy is frequently associated with a grade 3 or 4 intraventricular hemorrhage or periventricular leukomalacia, because the part of the brain controlling movement lies right next to the ventricles. But a brain scan can't accurately predict the future for an individual baby. Early head ultrasounds or MRIs that show no brain lesions don't definitely rule out a later disability. (There could be an injury that isn't visible on the scans.) And early ultrasounds or MRIs that do show abnormalities don't rule out normal development. (An infant's brain has an amazing capacity to recover from injury. Until the healing process is complete—and the timing of that is not very predictable—you can't tell whether there will be a permanent problem.)

So don't assume, as many parents do, that the doctors are hiding something when they say that they need to observe your baby's progress for a while, before giving a diagnosis or a thumbs-up. And don't think it's ominous if physical or occupational therapy is recommended to help with your baby's muscle tone problems. Although many muscular abnormalities will resolve on their own, it's better to work on them early, so they don't interfere with your baby's achieving other developmental milestones. For example, a mild amount of "toe-walking" might eventually go away on its own, but could delay a child's starting to walk independently. Stiff shoulder muscles can prevent a child from reaching for objects well. Not only is this frustrating for a baby, but motor delays can even impede cognitive development if they go on for too long, by restricting the range of a child's experiences.

We urge you to try not to look at every behavior of your baby as a possible diagnosis: you will risk missing out on the joys of this wonderful period of parenting, and possibly even transmit your anxiety to your baby. On the other hand, if you are really worried that your baby fits into the categories on page 421, by all means talk to your pediatrician about your concerns. You know your baby better than anybody, and your concerns should always be taken seriously.

The doctor may put your fears to rest, telling you that your child's movements are a lot more normal than you think. If he tells you that he needs to keep an eye on your baby's motor development over time, or suggests that she get a thorough developmental evaluation, remember that these are not necessarily bad signs, or reason for pessimism. Even if your preemie's movement problems are only temporary, as is often the case, she'll benefit from being watched carefully, to see if she needs a boost from physical therapy. If you do learn that your baby has a lasting problem, you'll get the benefit of expert advice, and she will get the benefit of early intervention, giving her the best chance of reaching her full potential. (You can read about living with cerebral palsy on page 458.)

TYPICAL CHARACTERISTICS OF CEREBRAL PALSY: WHAT'S WORRISOME AND WHAT'S NOT

Typical characteristics of cerebral palsy are: abnormal muscle tone in some, or all, parts of the body; infant reflexes that last beyond the time when they should disappear; delays in reaching motor milestones; and abnormal "quality" of movements (meaning they're not as fluid and varied as they should be). If your baby has one or two of the characteristics described below, join the club—most preemies do, and it rarely indicates a long-term problem. When a baby has many of them, the possibility of CP increases. It may reassure you to have your baby's doctor discuss with you what kinds of delays or symptoms are more significant than others.

MUSCLE TONE ABNORMALITIES

When muscle tone is abnormal—either too rigid and stiff, or too limp and floppy—some movements can become difficult.

One abnormality seen often in preemies is high muscle tone in their legs, causing them to keep their knees stiff, toes pointed, and hips rigid when they're lying or standing. Typically, this is evident by three months of adjusted age, and begins to resolve by twelve months. A little bit of toe-walking may last until 18 months, and if it does, your child may start to walk late, but isn't likely to have a long-term impairment. If the high tone lasts beyond 18 to 24 months, though, particularly in a child who has other neurologic problems, cerebral palsy becomes more likely.

Many preemies have temporarily stiff shoulders, especially those who spent a long time lying on their backs in the hospital, on a ventilator, without moving much. Called "retracted shoulders," they're held back, like an exaggeration of good posture. If a baby's stiff shoulders go along with stiffness of her whole upper body, she has a good chance of some developmental delays (when doing things that involve bringing her arms and hands forward, for example), but not cerebral palsy. If stiff shoulders are accompanied by a limp upper body, though (the stiff shoulders may be a baby's way of compensating for her limpness, to improve her head control), she does face a significantly higher risk of having cerebral palsy. In either case, physical therapy to relax her shoulder muscles may help a baby bring her hands together to hold a bottle, reach for objects in front of her, sit, and crawl.

Abnormally low muscle tone (most often, limp trunk muscles) is less common than abnormally high tone, but more concerning. If your baby has it, you would notice her head flopping back when you pull her by the arms into a sitting position; even after two or three months of age, her head would bob when she was sitting up; and even after six months of age, she would slump when sitting supported. You may see your baby compensate for this floppiness with retracted shoulders, or by locking her knees and hips when she is held in a standing position. Low muscle tone can make achievement of many milestones—from rolling over to sitting, crawling, and standing—more difficult. Some babies with low muscle tone will be just fine, but others will end up having cerebral palsy or, even if the muscle tone problems later resolve, cognitive problems, like learning disabilities or retardation.

A child with high muscle tone may keep his knees stiff, and toes pointed, when lying or standing.

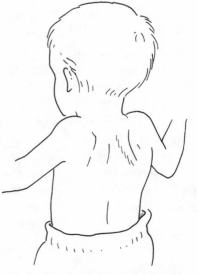

A child with retracted shoulders, held out and back.

Adapted with permission of Judy Bernbaum, M.D., from *Primary Care of the Preterm Infant* by Judy C. Bernbaum and Marsha Hoffman-Williamson, Mosby 1991

Delays in Reflexes and Balance Responses

There are numerous reflexes that are programmed to appear, and disappear, in a certain, normal time sequence in infants. (One example is the palmar grasp: place your index finger across the inside of a newborn's palm, and she will automatically flex her fingers around your finger. Another is called the Moro, or startle, reflex: when a newborn feels like she is falling, she throws out her arms, and then brings them back to her chest a few seconds later. Both reflexes are programmed to disappear by about four months of adjusted age.) In babies with CP, infant reflexes may last many months longer than normal. So-called balance responses, which help infants keep their position when their balance is threatened, also normally appear on a pre-programmed schedule. For example, most infants develop "head righting," the ability to keep their head upright when their position changes, at about four months. Balance responses may be lacking in some babies, such as those with CP, who don't have appropriate muscle tone.

Many perfectly normal babies have delays in the disappearance of some reflexes, or the appearance of some balance responses. Only if this goes along with other symptoms is it considered worrisome.

Delays in Reaching Developmental Milestones

Because there is a wide range of normal timing, even if your preemie isn't rolling over, reaching out for objects, sitting up, walking, or otherwise meeting some motor milestones as early as other babies you know, she may still be within the normal range. To pediatricians, the following delays in motor development would typically be of concern:

* *At three months:* poor head control
* *At six months:* cannot sit, even with support; keeps hands clenched in fists; does not bring objects to her mouth; only grasps an object momentarily
* *At eight months:* cannot sit without support
* *At twelve months:* is sitting but can't move from sitting position onto hands and knees, or to standing, without falling
* *At eighteen months:* does not walk; tries to walk on toes

Just remember that in full-term babies, long delays are often more worrisome than in preemies, who may have some temporary abnormalities of muscle tone that make certain kinds of movement more difficult. Also remember that for a preemie, adjusted age is what counts.

Quality of Movement

A child who has stiff muscle tone, or developmental delays, can still be perfectly normal. Often, a skilled pediatrician or physical therapist can tell parents that the "quality" of their child's movements is normal: fluid, varied, and coordinated.

Although all children deviate from normal movements when they're still learning new skills, once they master them, they should use their muscles, and move, in standard ways. Some examples of movements that are abnormal in quality:

* Rolling over in one direction only, or stiffly extending the trunk and neck to start and

complete a roll; sitting only in a W position, or sitting only back on tailbone, with legs stiff and straight in front of them;

❋ Lying, sitting, or standing only in frog-legged position, with legs splayed wide apart;

❋ Crawling with hands fisted, or in an asymmetrical pattern (using one side of the body differently than the other);

❋ Pulling to stand stiffly, or using arm strength only, without coming up one foot at a time;

❋ Only capable of reaching for things well with either the right hand or the left (a preference for using one hand is OK, though);

❋ Standing on toes most of the time, or overly stiff at the knees;

❋ Cruising (walking while holding on to furniture) with legs stiff at the knees.

There are certain motor skills that children may achieve early because of movements that are abnormal in quality. Babies with stiff muscle tone may be able to roll over as early as two months of age, or to stand holding on to something as early as four months. To be safe, mention to her doctor any motor milestones that your baby reaches long before you'd expect. And even though it's easy to feel proud of your baby's accomplishments, you shouldn't encourage them if they rely on atypical movements. They could interfere with her developing the right muscle and movement patterns for other motor skills.

W-sitting may indicate abnormal muscle tone, although all children occasionally sit in the W position.

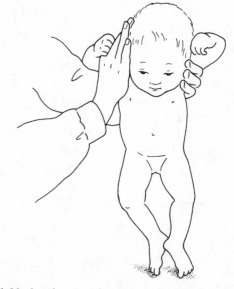

A child whose legs are splayed apart, frog-like, may have abnormally low muscle tone.

Adapted with permission of Judy Bernbaum, M.D., from *Primary Care of the Preterm Infant* by Judy C. Bernbaum and Marsha Hoffman-Williamson, Mosby 1991

Eyesight after ROP

*My 3-year-old had ROP, and wears glasses.
What can we expect for her vision?*

That depends on your daughter's unique medical history, including how mild or severe her ROP (short for retinopathy of prematurity, see page 268) was and why she needs glasses now. The best person to ask, therefore, is your daughter's eye doctor. He will undoubtedly tell you that it's impossible to make accurate predictions about any child's future vision, but should be able to describe to you any increased risks your daughter faces because she had ROP.

Because eye problems in preemies can be complex, and diagnosing problems in very young children—who aren't articulate about their eyesight (or anything else!) yet—can be tricky, your child's eye exams should be done by a specialized, pediatric ophthalmologist, or at least one who is very experienced with young children. During the first few years of a child's life, when the visual pathways between the eyes and the brain are being established, eye problems that go uncorrected for too long are more likely to cause some permanent loss of vision. So, making sure that your daughter gets follow-up eye exams will be very important.

In the meantime, you can get a sense of where your daughter might fit within the general possibilities outlined below.

✳ *Mild ROP* (stage 1 or 2) heals itself without treatment. If your child had mild ROP, you can feel relieved that the outlook for her future vision is excellent. If she's wearing glasses now because she's nearsighted, you do have to keep in mind that many people's nearsightedness worsens as they get older, but genetic factors (whether thick glasses run

in your family) are likely to p[...] than her past ROP when it [...] course your daughter's nearsight[...] take. In any case, she'll have lots of c[...] nearly one-third of all high school gra[...] are nearsighted, and the usual options for glasses and contact lenses will be available to your daughter for correcting it.

Nevertheless, it's very important for parents not to get complacent during their child's early years, because any preemie, and even more so a preemie who had ROP, faces a higher risk of developing two of the most common, childhood eye problems: strabismus (crossed eyes) and amblyopia (a lazy eye). These problems can almost always be treated successfully when they're caught early, with eye patches for amblyopia, or simple surgery for strabismus. (Treatment may be harder if factors other than ROP are contributing to your child's vision problems, which they may be if she has evidence of a brain injury.)

So, any child who had ROP should have her eyes reexamined, at a minimum, before her first birthday, and again when she turns three—and even sooner if her parents notice anything unusual. The doctor will also pay careful attention to whether she is developing better vision in one eye than the other, since this is how amblyopia can arise.

By the time your child is about four years old, if there's no sign of strabismus or amblyopia, it's unlikely she'll ever get them. Of course, she should continue to wear her glasses and, like any child who had ROP, she should get yearly eye exams, to find and treat any problems early. But chances are you're home, and there will be no further complications from her ROP.

✳ *Moderate ROP* (stage 3) is likely to leave

a child's retina with some scarring or distortion. Even if it is microscopic, and does not affect her vision, it does mean there's a higher risk of future eye problems to look out for. Many children with moderate or severe ROP have more complicated vision problems, because they're more likely to have had a brain injury in the nursery (from an intraventricular hemorrhage, for example) that contributes to their difficulty seeing.

If the doctor tells you that your daughter's retinopathy of prematurity went away without causing noticeable injury to her eye, follow the guidelines for mild ROP mentioned above—eye exams when she turns one year old, three years old, and annually thereafter. If the doctor can see some leftover scars or changes in your daughter's retina, either from laser treatment or the ROP itself, he'll give you guidance on her additional, follow-up care.

Feel assured that if you are careful about checkups, the chances of any further complications are small. Still, although the vast majority of children with moderate ROP won't get them, you should be aware of two serious conditions that can arise in the future: glaucoma and late-onset retinal detachment. Glaucoma occurs because scar tissue can interfere with the drainage of fluid from the eye, causing pressure to build up. There are various treatments to try for glaucoma, although none, as yet, have been very successful. A late retinal detachment occurs if, despite the best medical treatment, there is pulling on the retina as the eye grows, because a scar keeps some part of the retina firmly fixed to the wall of the eye. Thankfully, if retinal detachment occurs in a teenager or adult, the prognosis is far better than when detachment occurs in infancy, es-

pecially if it is repaired quickly. Thus, to be safe, it's important for your daughter to continue going for her annual retinal exams throughout her adolescence and early adulthood.

* *Severe ROP* (stage 4 or 5) affects the structure of the back of the eye differently in every individual. Most children who had severe ROP will have serious visual impairments, even with glasses, although some will have enough vision to help in walking around and daily activities. In some children, eyesight will be stable over time, while others will have progressive changes, or even need further surgery later. If your daughter had severe ROP, she should be followed by an ophthalmologist who specializes in children with retinopathy of prematurity. The ophthalmologist will tell you how often she should come for checkups. Also, make sure to read, on page 452, about how to give your child the best opportunity to develop normally and happily with her visual impairment.

Risk of Future Developmental Problems

My toddler is perfectly healthy. Is he still at risk for the developmental problems that premature babies get?

A premature baby who, by 18 to 24 months of corrected age is healthy and doesn't show any signs of "major" disabilities (cerebral palsy, mental retardation, vision or hearing loss), is no longer at risk for the most severe developmental problems caused by an early birth. So you can relax about that.

There are some milder developmental delays—or "minor" disabilities, as doctors classify them—that may show up only later: subtle difficulties with balance and coordination;

slightly lower than normal intelligence; learning disabilities; or problems with attention or behavior. Frequently, these minor impairments aren't discovered until a child is in school, when he's faced with different kinds of pressures and demands than at home. For example, learning disabilities may not show up until a child is required to do complicated mental tasks, like reading, spelling, or arithmetic; hyperactivity or attention problems may become obvious only when a child is asked to sit still in school for many hours; and the lack of motor precision needed to write legibly, or play team sports well, can point up problems with agility and coordination.

One thing to realize is that minor disabilities are harder to identify and quantify than major ones. If your child is eventually diagnosed with one, you may wonder why it wasn't found earlier. One reason is that many children can compensate for mild impairments so well that they're not readily apparent. And if they're noticed at all, they may be considered just a variation within the normal range. Another reason is that a baby or toddler can't be tested for the kinds of sophisticated information processing that he'll be required to do at school.

According to recent studies, up to 50% of premature babies with birth weights under 1,500 grams will develop one or more minor disabilities. Not all preemies are at equal risk: as usual, the smallest and youngest, and those who had the most medical complications, are most susceptible. But keep in mind that doctors call these impairments "minor" for a reason. It's not because they're not important, but because children who have them, given appropriate strategies and interventions, can adapt very well. Although these problems may transiently disturb a child's academic progress or social interactions, they need not significantly affect his long-term accomplishments or quality of life.

If you have any concerns about your toddler's development or behavior, don't hesitate to talk to his pediatrician. If she says your child is functioning at his peers' level, you should let your anxiety go, allowing him to develop skills, and his own character traits, at his own pace, as any full-term child does.

No matter how well your former preemie is doing, if you need more reassurance, you can ask your doctor to schedule him for a full multidisciplinary developmental evaluation. This is often done at age three, before a child enters preschool, or at age five, before he enters kindergarten. A multidisciplinary evaluation is usually performed by a developmental psychologist, a speech-language pathologist, a special educator (who can evaluate a child's learning skills), an occupational therapist, and a physical therapist. It is an extensive, and therefore expensive, kind of testing, that may or may not be covered by your health insurance plan or by the government, depending on your child's circumstances. So, you may want to inquire about that first.

If you decide not to have your child evaluated, try not to feel regret in the future, if a learning disability or other minor consequence of prematurity shows up when your child is in school. There will still be time for effective intervention.

Actually, if you're reasonably watchful, don't see any worrisome signs, and your pediatrician is telling you that your preemie is doing well, he has a very good chance of being perfectly normal. Most available data on long-term outcomes come from studies on preemies born in the 1980s. Given the ongoing progress in neonatal medicine, if your preemie was born after that, he may have an even better chance. And remember that the environment in which a preemie is raised has an effect on his development.

Enriching stimulation from a nurturing, attentive family, or from a good quality daycare program, can balance out some biological risk factors, enhancing a premature child's intelligence, and making behavioral problems less likely. In the meantime, try not to transmit to your child a sense of anxiety, or to let apprehension about the future deprive you of the daily surprises, hopes, and pleasures that make parenting such a wonderful experience.

Troublesome Behavior

My toddler can be really impossible. Does that come from his being born prematurely?

Possibly, but more likely it comes from his being a normal toddler. Toddlers specialize in being impossible, no matter how much time they spent in the womb. If you have any doubt about that, just open the nearest parenting book, and notice how much advice it contains for parents who worry that their toddlers are hyperactive, or overly moody, or negative, or rigid, or aggressive. Or, alternatively, for parents who are concerned that their toddler is the opposite of everyone else's: hypersensitive, fearful, passive, and shy.

No matter how much you know about the common behavior patterns of young children, they can still surprise you close-up in your own child. Toddlers flip-flop from sweetness to violent tantrums at the flick of an invisible switch. They go through periods of extreme negativism, and can lash out when they're frustrated, sometimes biting, scratching, and hitting like young animals. Some seem like bundles of frenetic energy, with an irresistible need to run until they're exhausted. Many resist any changes in their cherished, daily routines, making parents yearn for the good old days, when they could

still vary their lunch and dinner menus, or go to a different playground. You should remember that even from a very young age, personalities differ, so your child may exhibit some of these characteristics more than his playmates or siblings, while still behaving like a normal toddler.

However, if your child's behavior is so extreme or long-lasting that it worries you, or interferes with your relationship and feelings for him, then you should talk to your pediatrician about it. Even though the behavioral development of the majority of preemies is entirely normal, studies have documented a higher incidence of behavior problems among smaller preemies (those born under 1,500 grams) than among children born at term.

In the first year of life, preemies are reported to be more irritable, less responsive, and less predictable than other infants. (You can read about this, and how you might deal with it, on page 373.) Fortunately, many of these "fussy" babies grow into perfectly normal toddlers. Parents of premature toddlers who do have behavior problems typically describe their children as being excessively fearful (separation from parents, in particular, can cause great insecurity), or having a higher than normal activity level, with difficulty staying still for quiet play or meals. Some parents mention poor self-control, coupled with a stubborn willfulness, making the "terrible two's" battles extreme. Of course, it is hard to draw a line between normal temper tantrums and overly aggressive outbursts, so you shouldn't automatically assume that your child's behavior is a reaction to his early birth.

In many cases, difficult behaviors in early childhood soften or vanish spontaneously, without any lasting effect. On the other hand, some former preemies are found, at school age, to have shorter than normal attention spans, which may be accompanied by hyperactivity, or alternatively, by passivity and withdrawal. (You can read about dealing with attention deficit disorder and other learning disabilities on page 467.) At school age, parents and teachers are also more apt to report poor social skills among former preemies than among their term peers. These older preemies are often said to be less assertive, more anxious and irritable, and shy.

A variety of biological and environmental factors have been blamed for preemies' being less adept socially. Brain injuries in the newborn period, both obvious ones that result in cognitive difficulties, and more subtle disruptions in brain development, may play a role. Some complications of prematurity, like severe respiratory distress syndrome, bronchopulmonary dysplasia, and intraventricular hemorrhage make some difficult temperamental traits more likely. Parents may also contribute, by overprotecting their preemies because they view them as fragile or vulnerable. Some parents may be less willing to discipline their children, not wanting to deny them anything after their suffering in the NICU. Some may allow their preemies to rule the roost, because they've labeled them as "stubborn," "strong," or "fighters" because of their early will to survive. If you think you fit these descriptions, just being aware of it, and perhaps talking to a friend or counselor, may help you control your anxiety and change your behavior.

Thankfully, prematurity is not associated with any severe social problems or psychiatric illnesses. People who are less social and more introverted can make excellent friends, form wonderful, intimate relationships, be highly creative, and excel in many professions. What's most important now is feeling good about your child, and helping him learn to control himself and adapt.

If your child is withdrawn and resistant to change, you should try to expose him to different experiences and people, in secure environments. You can probably help a lot, but you shouldn't expect to change his personality, or feel frustrated if he doesn't become the captain of the sports team. If your toddler is particularly aggressive, impulsive and impetuous, your goal now should be to channel his growing autonomy in the right direction. Experts suggest using firm, but noncoercive methods to manage his behavior, such as giving time-outs or withdrawing rewards when he becomes disruptive, and giving token rewards, like points toward a special, desired activity, to reinforce good behavior.

If social problems at school go along with a learning disability, or if you feel your child's behavior significantly frustrates his need to interact with other children and his teachers, then it may be worth having him evaluated by a pediatric psychologist, who will judge what kind of therapy can be beneficial to him. You can ask your pediatrician for advice, or a referral. Together, you and the experts may be able to lessen his behavioral difficulties, and help him put his personal qualities to best use.

Clumsiness

My three-year-old is constantly bumping into things and falling over his feet. Are former preemies clumsier than term children?

Some are, but by no means all. Chances are, your child is like every other three-year-old—so busy exploring the world that he doesn't pay enough attention to obstacles in his path, like furniture and walls. That's often true of toddlers, who are very energetic, not aware of their still imperfect control of walking, running, or other movements, and most of all, not afraid of the painful consequences of their falls!

If your preemie has not been diagnosed with a motor problem like cerebral palsy, affecting his strength, muscle tone, or agility, and if he's been reaching his developmental milestones at the normal times, then you shouldn't worry that he'll have some serious chronic problem with coordination. Toddlers tend to refine their gross motor skills, like running, skipping, jumping, or climbing, at their own pace, so young children of the same age can differ markedly in how fast, agile, strong, and balanced they are. Among preschoolers, there's also a wide range of coordination in fine motor skills, involving the small muscles of the face and hands. Fine motor skills determine visual-motor control (needed, for instance, to catch a ball, or to eat without making a mess), and hand and finger dexterity (affecting writing and drawing abilities). Only in later childhood do kids' motor skills tend to level out.

Still, there are several reasons why some, although not all, former preemies can be clumsier than children born at term during the early childhood years:

* Some preemies have slightly turned-in or turned-out legs and feet, making them a little pigeon-toed or duck-toed. This usually goes away by school age. In the meantime, those whose feet turn in tend to be clumsier, and those whose feet turn out tend to be slower. (Being pigeon-toed, by the way, runs in families.)

* Clumsiness can result from the temporary abnormalities of muscle tone that are so common in premature infants. Even if a former preemie's tone is now normal, if his muscles were tight when he was learning to roll over, stand up, or walk, he may have gotten used to shifting his weight differently, and developed ways of moving that are less fluid or graceful. Because these awkward movements aren't due to an ongoing disorder, former preemies will naturally imitate and practice more graceful movements as they grow older, gradually becoming indistinguishable from their peers. (If your baby was often in an infant walker or jumper—not recommended by pediatricians and physical therapists—it could have made things worse, as those devices accentuate some of the excessive tone that preemies tend to have.)

* The natural exuberance of toddlers can be heightened in preemies, who can have even shorter attention spans, and be more impulsive. As a result, they may just run into things more!

If, when your child is five, you notice that he's still not keeping up with the other children in games or sports, or seems to have problems with his writing or drawing, then you should mention it to your pediatrician, and consider getting a developmental evaluation. (Your doctor can give you a referral, or you can get one from the local health department or education agency for your school district.) Delayed motor skills can occasionally be due to attention deficit disorder, or problems with vision or coordination that were so subtle they escaped earlier diagnosis. In most cases, there won't be any clear neurological basis, but some recent, inconclusive research suggests that there is a higher rate of persistent clumsiness among former extremely premature babies. It may be that your child is simply a little less dexterous than some other kids. Physical activity may just not be his thing. What counts most, then, is not the cause of your child's awkwardness, but what can be done to counteract it, so he can keep up in gym at school, and not worry about being teased.

A school-age child may be able to improve his coordination with physical or occupational therapy. Physical therapy is aimed at gross motor skills, improving balance, muscle tone, strength, and endurance. Occupational therapy focuses on fine motor skills, enhancing a child's eye-hand coordination, and his ability to use a pen, spoon and fork, or any other tools. If your child's developmental evaluation shows some delays in gross or fine motor skills, your local education agency should arrange for him to receive any needed physical or occupational therapy. Or you can ask your pediatrician to refer you to a private therapist, whose fees might be covered by your health plan.

Even if your child is clumsy, you should try to accept it and deal with it gently. Don't emphasize his awkwardness, at least in front of him, and reassure him if he has any concerns about it. To enhance his coordination and self-confidence, encourage him to do noncompetitive sports, and enroll him in a relaxed, extracurricular physical education program, if you can. Sports and exercise, music, dance, and any activity involving rhythm, body movement, and coordination can do marvels for his well-being and self-esteem. To help him grow into a well-adjusted, social young person, you and he should focus on his strengths—even if athletic strength isn't one of them.

Teeth

Our baby's teeth are coming in late, and a few of them look funny. Does being premature affect a baby's teeth?

A delay in tooth eruption is seen in many premature babies, even after their age is corrected. For instance, a baby's bottom front teeth are usually the first to come in, at about six to ten months of age. But in preemies, those first teeth may appear several months later than six to ten months past her due date (her corrected age). As long as her teeth are not missing—a doctor or dentist can tell—slower than normal eruption should not concern you. Later on, a preemie's delay in dental maturation can show up as a later than usual loss of her baby teeth, so you might want to disregard the tooth fairy's usual calendar. Most former preemies have caught up by the time they are nine years old.

Many children who were born early also have slightly irregular development of the enamel (the hard, white coating) of their baby teeth. According to studies, from 40% to 70% of preemies have some enamel "hypoplasia" (underdevelopment), which can cause irregular shapes, discoloration, or an opaque look. The upper front teeth are most often affected. The younger and sicker a baby was at birth, the more likely she is to have these minor defects, which experts attribute to oxygen deprivation and scarcity of some minerals in the early days and weeks of life. Early trauma to the gums can also be a cause of enamel underdevelopment, particularly if the teeth are more affected on one side. Some researchers think that when a baby is intubated to be put on a ventilator, the instrument (called a laryngoscope) used to insert the breathing tube can press against her gums and damage the developing teeth inside. A high bilirubin level (jaundice) has also been associated with some tooth discoloration.

A primary tooth with an imperfect coat of enamel is more prone to cavities, so you have to be especially careful about brushing your daughter's teeth twice a day, and never put her to bed with a bottle, unless it contains plain water. Ask your pediatrician to refer you to a pediatric dentist, if he hasn't done so already: former preemies need to schedule their first dental visit early, around their first birthday. The dentist will be able to reassure you about the effectiveness of good oral hygiene: a recent study found that former preemies, despite their common enamel defects, have only a slightly higher incidence of tooth decay than children born at term.

Some traces of enamel underdevelopment and discoloration can be found in former preemies' permanent teeth, but much less frequently than in baby teeth, and pretty much only in those children who were smallest at birth. Frequent dental checkups will help you pick up any problem soon, and get the maximum possible protection (such as fluoride treatments and sealants) for your daughter's teeth.

The little imperfections in your baby's teeth are probably barely noticeable to anyone but you. If they recur in her permanent teeth (which is unlikely) and are really bothersome, they can be capped when she's older. Remember that several modern beauties with irregular front teeth, Isabella Rossellini and Lauren Hutton, for example, refused to fix theirs, preferring their own, special look.

Emotional Aftershocks

My daughter is two years old now, happier and healthier than ever, but I'm still feeling the aftershocks of her premature birth and hospitalization. Will I ever be able to recover my old self, and put my life back together?

You're certainly not alone in suffering the lingering effects of a premature birth. Plenty of parents of former preemies have said that although much of the distress caused by their baby's birth receded after a few months, it never vanished completely. Having seen their newborns so frail, struggling to live and not being able to help them, can leave many parents with an enduring sense of insecurity.

The aftershocks can take many forms. Some parents report recurring dreams, intense reactions to certain sounds, images, or smells that remind them of the NICU, or a reappearance of pain and fear when their children are sick, even with trivial illnesses like colds. Just hearing about a child's illness may bring uncontrollable tears. Some parents can't deal with the issue of becoming pregnant again, because of the painful memories it stirs up, or the fear of having another preemie. Others admit that they've given up friends, hobbies, or jobs, so they can spend all of their time with their precious children, who have become the sole focus of their lives.

Another ripple effect can be marital problems, particularly if partners have different ways of coping with emotional distress. If one parent was unable to talk about her grief or fear, the other may have felt isolated and abandoned. One partner may have resented the other's anger, or guilt, or obsession with medical details, or retreat into work. Turning the page, forgiving and reconciling, may be harder than usual because the painful episodes occurred when both parents were particularly vulnerable and needy. A couple may not even be completely aware of the role that their premature child's birth played in their eroding relationship.

Parental suffering that lingers underneath the surface, and is periodically refueled by changes or anxiety-provoking events in a child's life, has been called chronic sorrow. The expression *chronic sorrow* was first applied to parents of children with special needs. Those parents struggle, often for their whole lives, to gradually let go of various plans and dreams, and come up with others that are meaningful. For parents of premature infants, chronic sorrow can last through infancy and for several years afterward, while preemies are still perceived as fragile and at risk for health and developmental problems. During this period, an illness, a rehospitalization, a developmental evaluation, even a banal situation like walking out the door and leaving your child with a baby-sitter, can revive old anxieties and sorrow.

Some psychologists have compared the reactions of parents of preemies to post-traumatic stress disorder (PTSD). That comparison makes sense to the many parents who have been haunted by nightmares or terrifying flashbacks brought on by an innocent thing like the phone ringing in the middle of the night. Some mothers of former premature babies report that they have difficulty falling or staying asleep, are jumpy and irritable, and have problems concentrating: reactions that are typical of both post-traumatic stress disorder and depression.

You would not be diagnosed with PTSD, or clinical depression, unless you suffered from a sizable cluster of severe, frequently recurrent, or persistent symptoms. But even if you're having a milder reaction to your premature baby's birth, that doesn't mean you aren't suffering, or that you wouldn't benefit from some kind of professional counseling.

Although the psychological aftershocks of a premature birth can last through your child's toddler years, you should expect them to become progressively milder. Psychologists studying the reactions of parents of preemies have found that by the time many preemies are 8 to 12 months old, their mothers, on average, are no more depressed or anxious than mothers of full-term babies. Mothers of preemies who have more health problems tend to have longer-lasting psychological distress, at least until their preemies are two years old. (Remember that you're experiencing some things that all parents go through in raising a child. Ripples in a child's health or happiness can make any mother or father emotionally vulnerable.)

To make your recovery easier, it's important to communicate with relatives, friends, and trusted counselors, who can understand your feelings and help you make sense of them. Spending all of your time with your children may soothe some of your anxieties, but it will give rise to others. Remember that to be a good parent, you need to enjoy yourself, and to be able to show your children how partners, friends, and meaningful pastimes can enrich one's life.

If you don't feel that you're making emotional progress—or if your recovery is too slow for comfort—counseling can often help to resolve some lingering issues. Definitely seek counseling if you find that your fears are getting out of hand, if you can't function at home or work, or if you find yourself in a deep state of bereavement that doesn't abate. You can get treatment for what could be a bout of depression. If your partner is the one who's suffering, don't hesitate to ask your family doctor to refer him to a therapist.

Couples counseling can be beneficial if you're experiencing marital problems. Don't be skeptical—it really can work. Sometimes just by committing to work on their union, a couple realizes how much their relationship still means to them, and can take the first crucial steps toward each other. Counseling can help point out how elements in both partners' histories and emotional makeup influenced their reaction to their child's premature birth. Don't lose hope: many couples, with or without the help of therapy, succeed in working their way out of this crisis, and reconcile. Parents who cling to each other during the hardest times, or who are able to get back together after a crisis, often build the strongest families.

Most parents say that giving birth to a premature baby has deeply changed them, modifying their attitudes toward other events and life choices. Everyone's path is different, but you'll probably also realize that your suffering has not been useless, and that you've grown in awareness, maturity, ability to assign things their proper value, and basic human understanding. Although it may not feel soon enough—time will heal you, too.

Thinking about Another Pregnancy

We've always wanted to have another child, but we're scared of having another preemie.

It is true that you have a higher risk of delivering prematurely next time, now that you've had one premature baby already. But every case is different. If your first premature delivery was caused by something that you or your obstetrician can do something about, you may be able to reduce your risk significantly.

Some of the main risk factors for preterm birth are things you may be able to change: smoking or drug use, being underweight at the start of your pregnancy, not gaining enough weight during the pregnancy, doing heavy physical labor, or becoming pregnant again less than four to six months after a previous delivery. You can read in more depth about these and other risk factors in Chapter One.

If it looks like there was a medical reason for your premature birth, there may be things your obstetrician can do to make a difference. If you have a so-called incompetent cervix (a weak cervix that tends to open before term), it can often be treated by a procedure called a cerclage, in which your cervix is stitched closed early in your next pregnancy. Infections that can cause a premature delivery (especially uri-

nary tract infections or sexually transmitted diseases) can be treated before or during pregnancy with antibiotics. Anemia, which can be a factor, sometimes responds to iron supplements or other therapies. If you have an anatomical abnormality of your uterus (something especially worth looking for if your mother took the drug DES when she was pregnant with you, possibly during the 1950s), it may be able to be corrected surgically. And if you have a chronic illness, such as diabetes or high blood pressure, closer medical surveillance may lengthen your next pregnancy.

If you had premature twins, triplets, or more, you already know that multiples carry a higher risk for premature delivery. Since the risk rises steeply with an increasing number of fetuses, if you get pregnant with just one this time, you're much less likely to have another preemie. If you conceived twins or triplets naturally last time, even though you may have a family predisposition for multiples, or erratic ovulation (which tends to occur more as a woman gets older), the chances are that it's not going to happen again. Overall, the odds of having twins naturally are roughly 1 in 90, of triplets 1 in 7,500. Women who had twins in their last pregnancy, and those who are over 45 years old, are about five times more likely to have multiples next time. But that still means the chances are pretty small.

The likelihood of another, multiple pregnancy is also higher if you're planning to conceive through fertility treatments. But, fortunately, there are things that can be done to reduce that risk. For example, if your hormones are being stimulated with drugs, you can be monitored very closely with ultrasound for the number of eggs you are releasing in each cycle, and you can make sure not to get pregnant during any cycles in which you release more than, perhaps, two. Or, if you are planning to do in vitro fertilization, you can have fewer embryos implanted in your uterus. Although these things may slightly decrease your chance of becoming pregnant, the trade-off may be worth it. Be sure to talk to your fertility specialist about them.

The other possibility, if you get pregnant with multiples, would be to have a selective reduction—an abortion of some of the fetuses, to give the one or two that remain the best chance of being born on time and healthy. But that option may not be acceptable to you for personal reasons, and also carries a higher risk of miscarriage for the remaining fetuses, so you should carefully weigh it beforehand.

Of course, a great many women deliver prematurely for reasons that are never known. And some risk factors just can't be changed or fixed. Women who are over 40 have a higher incidence of premature deliveries. In almost all age categories and educational levels, black women have a higher risk than white women. (Researchers are not sure how much of the difference relates to higher rates of other risk factors, like smoking or medical illnesses.) Teenagers also deliver more preemies, probably due to social factors, like poor nutrition and inadequate medical care, and, in girls under 15, biological immaturity. Family factors may even play a role: some studies suggest that women whose mothers or sisters have given birth prematurely are at an increased risk of giving birth prematurely themselves.

So, by all means, before you become pregnant, find an obstetrician who specializes in high-risk patients, and talk to her about your desire for another child. Ask her what she can tell you about your risks, and what you should do to minimize them. It's natural that you'll feel nervous during your next pregnancy. But by following her recommendations, you'll give yourself and your baby the best possible chance.

In Depth

WHAT YOU NEED TO KNOW ABOUT RSV

You've probably had RSV many times in your life. Short for respiratory syncytial virus, RSV is a very contagious virus that gives most people a plain, old, common cold. (A cold you catch may be from RSV or from one of a few dozen other cold viruses.) Most children get RSV at least once before they're two years old.

While RSV isn't discriminating in whom it infects, it does affect some people differently than others. In older children or adults it usually triggers a trivial cold, but in infants it can be more serious. The virus may cause not just an upper respiratory infection, with symptoms like sniffles, sneezes, and fever, but also a lower respiratory infection, such as pneumonia or bronchiolitis (an infection of the small airways in the lungs), with breathing problems that can be serious enough to require hospitalization. Some babies even need to go on a ventilator while they fight off the virus. In a small minority of cases, it can be fatal.

Although the chances of the average preemie having such a serious problem is very small, it's worth knowing about RSV, and the preventive therapies that are available, in case your child is at high risk.

WHICH BABIES ARE AT RISK

RSV is a seasonal virus that you don't need to worry about much during the warmer months. It's mainly around during the cold season, which typically lasts from November through April.

The two groups that are most likely to be hospitalized with RSV are preemies and full-term infants with chronic respiratory conditions. Both are prone to breathing problems, and preemies have two additional disadvantages. Their immune systems are immature and they lack some or all of the protective antibodies against RSV that they would have received from their mothers during the last trimester of pregnancy. Also, their airways are very small, so any swelling or mucus there is more apt to cause problems with breathing.

Not all preemies are at equal risk, though. Most vulnerable are those who are under two years old, with bronchopulmonary dysplasia (BPD) or congenital heart disease. Next come other preemies, who don't have BPD or heart conditions, but are less than six months old when the cold season starts. As preemies get older and bigger, their vulnerability declines. Once they are past their first winter, if they are healthy, the chance that they'll get seriously ill from RSV is remote.

These numbers may help put things in perspective. Among 500 premature babies who were followed for one cold season, about 8% of those who were healthy and younger than six months old, and about 12% of those who had BPD and were younger than two years old, were hospitalized with RSV.

Other risk factors that come into play are:

❋ Preemies who were born earlier, especially at less than 28 weeks of gestation, are more vulnerable than those who were born later;

❋ Boys are more at risk than girls;
❋ Formula-fed preemies are more at risk than those who are breastfed;
❋ Preemies who have a smoker in their household are at greater risk of being hospitalized if they catch RSV;
❋ Preemies who are in daycare, or have school-age siblings, are more likely to be exposed to the virus.

HOW TO RECOGNIZE IF YOUR BABY HAS RSV

The first symptoms of RSV are usually those of a cold, such as a runny or stuffed nose, sneezing, coughing, or fever, along with general symptoms of sickness like irritability, lethargy, or poor feeding. If your preemie has BPD, or is less than six months old, or if you're just feeling worried, don't hesitate to take her to the doctor at this point. He'll make sure she's handling the cold OK, and can also do a simple test to find out if she has RSV, by swabbing her nose with a tiny Q-tip. If he has the necessary laboratory equipment, he may even be able to give you the results on the spot. Some parents find it's worth going to the doctor to find out that their baby doesn't have RSV, just so they can relax. But even if your baby does have RSV, it probably won't progress beyond a slight cold. You and your doctor will most likely just watch your baby more closely.

If RSV does get worse and becomes a lower respiratory infection, you'll notice that your baby will have more trouble breathing: she may wheeze, suck in her chest deeply, her nostrils may flare widely with each breath, and she may breathe rapidly and have spells of apnea. If you notice any of these symptoms, call the doctor right away. He's the best judge of whether your baby needs help with her breathing, or other medical support, while she fights off the virus.

TREATMENT OF RSV

Just as there's no cure for the common cold, there's no cure for RSV. When a baby gets the virus, the important things are to keep her adequately breathing and nourished while her body's immune system does the job of fighting it off. If your child has cold symptoms, you can help her breathe more easily by keeping her room humid, with a humidifier or vaporizer, and by elevating the head of her bed a little. (You can place some towels or a stack of books under one end of her mattress.) Try to keep your baby well hydrated—which at her age, doesn't have to mean large quantities of fluids. Even a few teaspoons of liquid every hour, whether milk, water, or Pedialyte (a liquid that contains salts and sugar and is sold in many drugstores and baby stores), goes a long way.

If your child is wheezing, it probably indicates that she has bronchiolitis. The doctor may try treating her with a bronchodilator (the same kind of medication that might be used for asthma), to help open up her airways so she can breathe easier. Studies have been mixed on whether this helps with RSV, so if your child develops more than very mild respiratory distress, the doctor will probably recommend that she go to the hospital, where her breathing can be monitored carefully. She may not need much more than monitoring and plenty of fluids through an IV. If she's having a lot of trouble breathing, she'll also get supplemental oxygen,

or, in rare cases, will be put on a ventilator. Some doctors may try a medicine called Ribavirin, which is supposed to keep the virus in check, but it has not had great success in changing the course of RSV infections.

Having your preemie rehospitalized, when you've had her home so briefly, can be heartbreaking. For parents whose baby had a rough hospital course the first time, it can also be terrifying. But if you can, try to see the hospital as the safest, most comforting place for her to be, where she'll be supported, enabling her to do the best possible job of battling the virus. You can read more about rehospitalization of preemies on page 404.

Keep in mind, so you won't worry excessively, that it's normal for babies with RSV to get sicker before they get better. Within a week or so, most babies recover enough to go right back home with their parents.

SHOULD YOU ISOLATE YOUR CHILD?

All of this makes it tempting to want to build a protective wall around your child, isolating her from the sneezes, coughs, hands, and kisses of well-meaning, but germ-ridden people. That's understandable. If your child is still at a point when she's at risk of getting very sick from RSV, taking a certain amount of precaution, especially during the late fall, winter, and early spring, is wise—such as keeping her out of daycare, forbidding visits by friends or relatives who have colds, and washing your hands frequently. But also remember that there's a limit to how much isolation is good for you or your preemie. You'll find some suggestions on page 338.

PREVENTION OF RSV: ARE THE NEW THERAPIES RIGHT FOR YOUR BABY?

Vaccines can prevent illnesses like measles, mumps, and whooping cough, but unfortunately, there is not yet a vaccine for RSV. The way a vaccine works is to stimulate the body's immune system to produce its own infection-fighting antibodies against an illness. A second best, but still valuable, measure is to get the antibodies from somewhere else. That's what two new preventive treatments for RSV provide—substances containing RSV-fighting antibodies. Research has shown that these treatments don't stop babies from getting the virus altogether, but do cut by about half the number of babies who get so ill that they need to be hospitalized.

The preventive treatment that came out first, called RespiGam, is given in such a large quantity of fluid that a child must get it intravenously, in a hospital or clinic, over a period of several hours. More recently, a more concentrated drug, called Synagis, was introduced, which can be given to a baby as a shot, in a doctor's office. Since the antibodies in RespiGam or Synagis wear off after about a month, babies must go for monthly infusions, or shots, usually from October to May.

Although Synagis makes more sense for most preemies who are already at home, RespiGam has the advantage of offering some extra protection against ear infections and other respiratory infections in addition to RSV, so it may be given to preemies who are still in the hospital.

It's up to you, and your baby's doctor, to decide whether the advantages of these treatments outweigh the disadvantages for your child. According to the American Academy of Pediatrics, RespiGam or Synagis should be considered for your baby at the start of RSV season if:

* she was born at 28 weeks of gestation or less, and is younger than twelve months old;
* she was born between 29 and 32 weeks of gestation, and is younger than six months old;
* she has BPD, is less than two years old, and has received medical treatment for respiratory problems within the past six months.

(Children with symptoms from congenital heart disease should not get these RSV treatments, because of concerns about their safety for that group.)

What are the pros and cons? On the positive side, there is the chance that these treatments could help avoid a serious illness and hospitalization. On the negative side, there is the fact that the protection they offer is far from perfect—some babies will still need to be hospitalized, and among those who are, there is little evidence they will have a less serious illness than they would have otherwise. Moreover, there is a minor risk of adverse reactions, such as fever or pain at the site of the shot; and you'll have to make monthly trips to the doctor (where it's possible your baby could pick up some germs that she would have avoided if she'd stayed home!). The cost of the treatments is steep, up to $1,000 per month, so make sure to find out whether your insurance will cover it, as most do.

Many parents also find it excruciating to expose their baby to a little extra pain each month. If your baby is going to be getting monthly, anti-RSV injections, you may want to ask your baby's doctor about a relatively new, local anesthetic, called EMLA, that comes as a cream or a patch. If you apply it in a thick layer to your baby's skin at least an hour beforehand, it can reduce the pain. (Since it has to be applied directly over the spot where the injection will be given, be sure to ask the doctor where that will be.) Be forewarned, though—if you have a toddler who is constantly moving and can't easily be convinced to leave it alone for an hour, you could be in for some mess! Although EMLA isn't given out routinely, your doctor may have some samples on hand, or be willing to write a prescription for you. And if it seems to help your child, you can also use it for any other shots or blood drawing she might need, as well.

For most preemies, there's no obvious, right or wrong decision. Talking the issue through with your baby's doctor, and perhaps even her former neonatologist, will help you become comfortable with whichever path you choose.

9

When Parents Have Something Special to Worry About

▶ *Learning more about some possible consequences of prematurity.*

INTRODUCTION   441

QUESTIONS AND ANSWERS
   Why Do We Need Early Intervention?   442
   Getting Acquainted With: Early
      Intervention Services   443
   Hearing Loss   446
   Language Education for Children
      with Hearing Loss   448
   About Hearing Aids   449
   What Is a Cochlear Implant?   451
   Visual Impairment   452
   Does Your Child Have Cortical
      Visual Impairment?   454

   Sensory Integration Problems   455
   Feeding Problems   457
   In Plain Language: What Is
      Cerebral Palsy?   458
   Predicting Intelligence   462
   Prematurity and IQ   464
   Detecting Learning Disabilities   466
   Preemies and Learning Disabilities   467

MULTIPLES
   One Twin with Disabilities   470

IN DEPTH
   Parenting a Child with Special Needs   473

Introduction: When Parents Have Something Special to Worry About

If your child has special needs, you are going to need more detailed information and support than this chapter can give you, but it is a good place to start. You may need to learn to deal with a radical change in perspective, practical problems you never thought about, and new, powerful, and contrasting feelings—possibly without role models to follow. You and your baby will need time to adjust, to find your own path, advisors, special sources of information, and support. Learning more about a disability may frighten you initially, but may also make you feel better, because reality is often more reassuring than what you fear. Most of all, you will discover that there's a lot you can do to help your child live well with his condition and to develop his full potential.

Much as it might comfort you, you shouldn't think of early intervention and other special services as a cure. What they do is help a child work with and around his disability, so the disability doesn't unnecessarily impede his development in other areas. For example, a child with very poor sight will be given special lenses, to improve his vision as much as possible. But providing him with nonvisual ways of taking in information will probably make a greater difference. A child with a motor disability affecting his face and mouth will be given exercises to build up his strength and flexibility. Some children may never be able to speak clearly, but they may be taught to communicate extremely well with a computerized board. By giving a child alternative ways to develop knowledge and skills, special services can be the impetus that gets a child's development back on track, helping him do his best.

You are likely to find that doctors (except those who specialize in child development) are not the best source for locating and negotiating the maze of possible resources for your child. The school system, the public health department, your child's service coordinator, your hospital's social worker, and other parents with children in similar situations will often be a lot more helpful and informed. A word of warning, though: be sure to be careful about things you hear from nonprofessional sources. Claims of miracle cures, or the opposite—major problems that pop up suddenly and unexpectedly—are often not based entirely in fact. In particular, the Internet—a great resource for opening up possibilities and pointing you in interesting directions—is also littered with inaccuracies. When you come across a promising lead, by all means follow it up, and be aggressive and innovative in looking for resources, but don't leave your critical faculties behind.

You are probably going to find it easier than you might think to accept your child's limitations. Just consider examples from your own life. You may never speak a foreign language, or climb a mountain, or paint a portrait—and by now, that's probably OK with you. It's just not part of who you are. What you do often and well, though, probably means a lot to you and to the friends and loved ones who know you well. You'll find a similar thing happens with your child—you'll help him hone some skills, come to value the things he can do, and dismiss the things he can't. Every child, with or without special needs, has weak areas and strong ones. Your responsibility will be to provide your child with opportunities for growth, by helping him improve his weaknesses, for sure; but, mainly, by focusing on his strengths. That is what most parents naturally do, anyway.

Your attitude will rub off on your child. It may surprise you to know that in a survey asking disabled people what one thing they would change about themselves if they could, most chose something other than their disability. It just shows how one can celebrate the person one is, and be fulfilled in the life one has.

Questions and Answers

Why Do We Need Early Intervention?

I'm energetic, I read a lot, I'm going to be home with my child. What can an early intervention program possibly do that I can't?

If your child has been referred to an early intervention program, you shouldn't think that your parental skills or dynamism have been underestimated or disregarded. On the contrary, your personal qualities are going to be put to good use, because a main tenet of early intervention is that nobody has a more powerful effect on a baby than his parents.

According to government regulations, early intervention services are family-centered, meaning they are there to assist a baby and his family, providing them with information, skills, and support. Moreover, the service coordinators are expected to collaborate with parents, and, if needed, siblings and grandparents, in planning a child's intervention program and administering his care.

Convincing data on the efficacy of early intervention services in premature babies come from a nationwide study called the Infant Health and Development Program, involving nearly a thousand preemies who were randomly assigned to get either routine medical care or intensive early intervention services until they were three years old. The early intervention services consisted of parent support group meetings, home visits several times a month (to help families better understand child development, provide appropriate toys and activities for their infant or toddler, and deal with behavioral or other problems), and attendance at a developmental day-care center for at least four hours a day, five days a week, beginning when the child was 12 months old. Compared to preemies who got just regular, pediatric follow-up, at three years of age those who also got early intervention had, on average, higher IQs, and were rated by their parents to have fewer behavior problems. The improvement in intelligence was greatest for preemies who weighed more than 2,000 grams at birth, although smaller preemies benefited, too. The improvement in behavior was significant only for preemies whose mothers did not have a college education.

Early intervention services are usually provided by an infant-toddler development specialist (a specially trained psychologist, social worker, or graduate of a school of education). The infant-toddler development specialist will work with you and your child, to help him develop at his best, and may also get help from professionals from other disciplines (see page 445 for a summary of what each one does). They will bring additional valuable experience and expertise, as well as knowledge about useful resources.

You'll be counted on to practice exercises at home, as that's the best way for your child to learn new skills. You can also make up creative games that build on the exercises or make them more fun. So you'll have ample opportunities to help your child take his developmental steps forward. And since you'll be the main source of information on your child's situation and progress, and be involved in any decisions concerning your child, you should always feel in charge.

According to many parents, you should beware of one pitfall: it can be hard to tell people about shortcomings you perceive in your own child. So, not surprisingly, some parents find themselves exaggerating to the therapists what their child can do, or practicing things they know he'll be evaluated on, so he'll "perform" better. Although this is a natural reaction, try hard to combat it. It may make you feel more comfortable, briefly, to present your child as more polished than he actually is; but it won't do him any good, if he doesn't get the help he needs.

On the whole, you should feel glad that you're not your preemie's therapist, and that the early intervention team is there to fall back on. If you were the sole provider, it would be easy to let a home therapy program completely take over your daily routine. But constant pressure and excessive attention aren't beneficial to your child in the long run, and they can drain you of energy, causing frustration, and making the rest of your family feel neglected. Free play, activities, and interactions with family and friends are just as important as planned intervention for your child's development. With professional support, when the time for exercises and therapies is over, you can forget them—letting your child be just a child, with you, just his loving, committed parent, by his side.

GETTING ACQUAINTED WITH:
EARLY INTERVENTION SERVICES

The idea behind early intervention is that when it comes to children's development, preventing is better than correcting. Whether a child has a diagnosed developmental delay, or is simply considered at risk for one, the earlier an intervention program is begun, the better the results.

The reason is that every individual skill or ability can influence a child's overall developmental progress. For instance, a baby who has a motor impairment may not be able to explore his environment freely. As a result, his learning will be more limited, so he may understand fewer things. Even his language skills can suffer, because his lack of exposure provides him with fewer concepts and words for objects and activities—and he may have additional trouble communicating because, with a movement disorder, his body language may be less expressive. As he grows older, his independence and sense of self-worth could be affected, too. Fortunately, many developmental delays can be prevented, corrected, or at least lessened if the right stimulation and exposure occur.

WHO IS ENTITLED TO EARLY INTERVENTION

Early intervention services for babies and toddlers are funded by the federal government, and organized by each state. States are not mandated to provide these services, but receive grants and assistance to develop them, if they follow federal guidelines. Currently, all fifty states offer early intervention programs, which differ somewhat from state to state. In every state, infants and toddlers between birth and two years of age are entitled to early intervention services if they have a diagnosed developmental delay (meaning they lag behind other children their age in their physical or mental abilities, or communication and social skills), or if they have a condition that carries a high probability of future developmental delay, such as periventricular leukomalacia, severe BPD, or hearing loss. Each state, though, has its own interpretation of "developmental delay" and its own list of "high probability" conditions. In some states, all premature babies with birth weights of 1,500 grams or less, who don't have developmental delays but are at somewhat higher risk for them, are included, as well as bigger preemies with complicated medical histories and difficult family situations.

To find out more about your state's early intervention program, you can call the state agency in charge of the program. In your state, it may be part of the Department of Education, or Health and Human Resources, or may be a distinct division of its own. Your county health department can tell you where to call. Another excellent source of information on early intervention services (as well as special education programs for preschoolers) is NEC-TAS, or National Early Childhood Technical Assistance, a consortium of national organizations that support special education programs for young children. You can reach it by phone at (919) 962–2001, or visit the Web site at http://www.nectas.unc.edu/index.html.

REFERRAL AND EVALUATION

Premature infants are usually referred for early intervention services by their hospital at discharge, a preemie follow-up clinic, or some other medical professional. Parents, relatives, or anyone who's in close contact with a child can request a referral from his pediatrician, or even initiate one themselves. (For information, call your state agency, or NECTAS, see above.) Don't be intimidated by the paperwork that might be required, and don't let anybody or anything discourage you, if you think your child needs to be evaluated: developmental experts are convinced that a parent's concern is the most powerful indicator of developmental delay. On the other hand, parents have the right to refuse evaluations and services, so you can step out of the program at any time.

Once your child has been referred, he'll be assigned a child service coordinator. The child service coordinator's job is to decide what kinds of developmental services a child needs, and to arrange for them to be provided. Premature babies who are eligible usually are evaluated by the child service coordinator soon after discharge from the hospital. If your baby is doing well, and doesn't have a condition that is known to cause developmental delays, the service coordinator may decide simply to reevaluate him periodically, or conclude that no follow-up is necessary. (A second referral can always be made in the future, if you or your baby's doctor see a need for it.)

If the child service coordinator decides that your child does qualify for early intervention services, she will work out with you an Individual Family Service Plan. This written document will include:

❋ your child's medical history
❋ the results of his latest developmental evaluation
❋ information about your resources, concerns, and developmental goals for your child
❋ an overview of any early intervention services your child needs
❋ a list of the public or private professionals who will provide them, how often, and where
❋ any applicable financial arrangements

Eligible children and their families are entitled to a child service coordinator at no cost. Other early intervention services beyond that are usually free for children on Medicaid, but most private insurers don't cover them. Many early intervention providers will help out by charging for their services on a sliding scale, based on a family's income.

At any time, parents, the child service coordinator, or another medical professional can request an extensive, formal evaluation of a child's development, including his cognition (thinking and learning), motor skills, language, and social and emotional development. Most early intervention programs schedule a full developmental evaluation at around 18 months of age if it has not been requested before then, although some states arrange for it earlier and some later. This full evaluation can be conducted at your preemie's follow-up clinic, or at your county's public health department or child developmental evaluation center. (These public developmental evaluations are usually excellent, so you shouldn't feel that private is necessarily better. Plus, they're free for all children.)

MEET THE EARLY INTERVENTION TEAM

Your child's early intervention team may include, along with the infant-toddler development specialist, professionals from such diverse fields as:

❋ *physical therapy:* to help with his gross motor development—strength, balance, coordination, and the ability to control his movements and get around;
❋ *occupational therapy:* to improve his fine motor and self-help skills—the ability to manipulate things with his hands, and to feed, dress, clean, or otherwise care for himself. Occupational therapy can also help if your child has so-called "sensory integration" problems, see page 455;
❋ *audiology:* to assess his hearing and provide hearing aids;
❋ *speech and language therapy:* to help him understand and develop speech, or to address feeding problems;
❋ *vision services:* to assess his vision, and provide glasses or special lenses;
❋ *special education:* including sign language classes for hearing-impaired children, early education for blind children, and stimulation-enriched environments for infants at risk for cognitive delays;
❋ *psychology:* to facilitate cognitive and behavioral development, given a child's particular temperament and activity level;
❋ *nursing:* to provide home health care and specialized medical services;
❋ *social work:* to assess the impact of a fragile child on a family, and to help locate and arrange for special resources, such as financial aid, transportation, specialized schooling, and respite care.

Several professionals may work with your child, individually or together. Alternatively, one therapist (usually, the infant-toddler developmental specialist) will be assigned to your child, and will provide a wide range of interventions, under the periodic supervision of her colleagues. The child service coordinator is responsible for encouraging communication and sharing of expertise among team members, and for flexibly addressing the family's needs and preferences.

The best setting for early intervention services is an environment that is natural for the child—for example, his home or a childcare center. Since the main occupation of a child is playing, which is crucial for his overall development, age-appropriate and skill-appropriate play is an intervention tool, as well as one of the primary goals of therapy. Some children may benefit from the presence of other kids, while others may respond better to therapy if they are alone. The choice of setting is worked out by the service coordinator and the family, with the family having the right to modify the location, and to choose public or private specialists.

WHEN DOES EARLY INTERVENTION END?

The opportunity to assess whether the goals for your child have been reached comes every six months, when his Individual Family Service Plan is reviewed, and also at the time of your child's complete developmental evaluations. When these take place, the majority of parents feel that early intervention is a success story, because the benefits, whether small or large, all can mean an improvement in a child's quality of life.

When a baby or toddler is consistently reaching the developmental milestones that are appropriate for his corrected age, he'll be discharged from early intervention. If at thirty months, six months before a child's third birthday, he is still receiving early intervention services, his child service coordinator will refer him to a public preschool in his school district, with his parents' consent. There, he'll be evaluated for preschool readiness. School officials, consulting with the family, will make plans for the child to get special education, or just the extra services he needs to participate in a mainstream preschool classroom. If you are considering sending your child to a private preschool with special education programs, you should discuss this with your child service coordinator.

This important step of facilitating the transition to preschool is the last one in a child's Individual Family Service Plan, since early intervention services stop when a child turns three. The right preschool program will step in to give him expert attention and services, and to provide him with the interactions with other kids that he needs to blossom.

Hearing Loss

How well can a hearing aid restore my child's hearing?

A hearing aid amplifies sounds, making them louder, but can't restore hearing as thoroughly and immediately as glasses can restore vision. Since making sounds louder doesn't always make them clearer, hearing and speech therapy is also needed to help a child understand what he hears.

As soon as your preemie is fitted with a hearing aid, he should begin working with a speech and language therapist, who will follow him throughout childhood. The therapist will help him learn how to listen to sounds and make the most of the hearing he has (95% of hearing impaired children have some), and to develop his language skills, using spoken language only or a combination of speech and sign language.

Although hearing loss is a life-long condition, with patience and training an infant can benefit greatly from a hearing aid. If you've never met people with hearing loss before, and seen what successful, enjoyable, normal lives they lead, you may not be imagining your child's future to be as open and bright as it is. Very few endeavors will be closed to him.

On the other hand, you shouldn't underestimate your child's needs. The sooner a baby is fitted with a hearing aid and begins hearing and speech therapy, the better he will be able to talk and understand spoken language. If a hearing loss is not discovered and compensated for by about six months of corrected age, a toddler can develop significant speech and language delays, and over time his cognitive abilities may be affected. In some cases, the isolation caused by an unrecognized hearing impairment may lead to behavior problems, like lack of attention, hyperactivity, aggressiveness, or poor social skills.

Thus, if your preemie failed his hearing tests in the nursery, you should have him evaluated as soon as possible by a doctor who specializes in the ear (usually an ear, nose, and throat doctor), to try to detect any conditions that might be improved with medicine or surgery. You should also take him to a pediatric audiologist (a professional who is trained to diagnose and treat hearing impairments), who can get a complete picture of his type and degree of hearing loss, and determine what kind of amplification or other special intervention he needs.

If your child has a mild hearing loss (difficulty hearing soft or distant speech) he may not need a hearing aid while he's still an infant, since adults will mainly talk to him from close by, while holding him. When he grows into a roaming toddler, however, he'll probably need a hearing aid or FM system (see page 449), to hear well from a distance. Children with moderate hearing loss, who can understand face-to-face conversation but have trouble with group discussions, or those with severe hearing loss, who can hear only very loud, close voices and sounds, are the ones who benefit most from amplification and hearing and speech therapy. Children with profound hearing loss, who can perceive only very loud sounds or vibrations, don't get as much from amplification as children with a less marked hearing impairment. But if a cochlear implant is a possibility for your child later (see page 451), he should be fitted with a hearing aid and/or an FM system as soon as possible, and followed with therapy now, to get the best results in the future.

It's very important to keep in mind that time matters. Most children with hearing loss can learn to talk well, provided they get therapy early. Young children develop speech by imitation and practice, so they have to be exposed to language in order to learn it. By eight weeks of age, normal infants can distinguish the sounds of their own language from other languages, and by six months, all of the basic sounds have been memorized. Up to six years of age, children can acquire complete linguistic fluency, but after that, their ability quickly fades. (If you've ever studied a foreign language as an older child or adult, you know that struggle!) This prime period for language development should not be missed if your child is to master either speech or sign language. People with hearing loss who are not exposed to sign language early enough can still learn it, but don't totally master it.

Several recent studies found that children diagnosed with hearing loss and treated before six months of age achieved much better speech than children who were diagnosed later, from the seventh month on. When tested at one to five years, the earlier-identified children showed language skills in the normal range, even when their hearing loss was severe. So, if your preemie goes home by about three to four months of corrected age, you can wait until after discharge to address his hearing problem. But if a baby with hearing loss is going through a very long hospitalization, his family and doctors should consider getting him hearing aids and speech and language therapy while he's still in the hospital nursery, so the crucial window for intervention is not missed.

Language Education for Children with Hearing Loss

Is it true that children who are hearing impaired should learn sign language before speech?

If your baby has hearing loss, it is important to make up your mind soon about the educational program you want for her. There are two main options:

❋ The total communication approach, in which a baby is taught to use a combination of sign language and speech at the same time. Children wear hearing aids, but more importance is given to sign language than to speech;

❋ The auditory-oral approach, in which a child

is taught to use only oral speech, with the help of lip-reading or other cues. A variation is the auditory-verbal approach, which discourages lip-reading, and stresses the importance of learning to understand words by listening to their sounds.

Total communication allows a child with hearing loss to learn sign language very quickly and easily, and to fit in well in the Deaf community. A child using total communication will attend a school for the deaf, or special classes where the teacher and the other students use American Sign Language (ASL, the official language of the Deaf community). His parents and the people who interact with him often, such as siblings, grandparents, and regular baby-sitters, should also learn sign language. But while he will become perfectly fluent in ASL, which is as rich and expressive as any spoken language, his understanding of spoken language and speech will often lag far behind. Why? Because it's extremely hard to master two languages with totally different grammar, such as sign language and English, at the same time. Since sign language has no written form, he'll eventually need to be taught to read and write English as a second language, so he can advance academically, and the world of books will not be closed to him.

Auditory-oral education requires more from a child. It can take great patience, time, and effort for a hearing impaired child to learn to understand and speak fluently. "Bathe your child in sounds," the League for the Hard of Hearing recommends to parents who have chosen auditory-oral education for their children. If, later in life, he wants to join the Deaf community, he will have to learn sign language as a second language, and that will never come as naturally to him as if he had learned it as a baby:

a regrettable thing, according to the Deaf. Experts from the auditory-oral field, though, argue that only with this kind of education is a child with hearing loss really free to choose between the mainstream culture and Deaf culture, or to participate in both, because if sign language is taught first, most hearing impaired children will lose the motivation to struggle to learn to hear and talk. With the auditory-oral approach, children can attend special classes with other hearing impaired kids, or can attend mainstream schools, with or without the help of a special educator for extra tutoring.

Not all children will do equally well with both approaches, and each choice has advantages and disadvantages. You should carefully weigh these with your child's audiologist, speech, and language therapist, and experts from organizations for the deaf (see references in the appendix, page 525). Your choice for your child's type of education will be influenced by their opinions, and by the programs that are available in your area. Be assured that either choice can be excellent, provided that your child is given a chance to develop at least one kind of language very well, and that the significant people around him are able to talk to him using the same kind of communication.

If your child hasn't already been evaluated by a child psychologist, you can ask your doctor for a referral, to assess his development and other needs. It may also help you to talk to a counselor yourself, to make sense of your own reactions to your child's hearing loss. You may have a hard time, particularly at first, accepting the sight of your beautiful baby wearing a hearing aid (which, though not obtrusive, is not invisible), and adjusting your expectations for the future. You'll need to be very patient, since it may take a long time for your child to learn to use a hearing aid and begin to talk. To succeed, he needs all of the optimism, reassurance, and stimulation that you can give him. As soon as you realize that your baby is becoming, day by day, more responsive to the sound of your voice, and talking back to you with his developing communication skills, you'll know that your efforts are being adequately compensated.

ABOUT HEARING AIDS

Modern hearing aids, thanks to microchips, digital technology, and sound processors, have some very sophisticated features. For example, they can be programmed to amplify only certain sounds—the softest ones, or those of a certain pitch; to automatically adjust very loud and disturbing noises, to protect the wearer from the discomfort they can cause; or to diminish background noise, making human speech coming from in front and close by easier to hear and understand. Still, a regular hearing aid doesn't help much when it comes to understanding somebody speaking from more than three feet away, because other background voices and noise will get amplified as well.

An FM system can help solve those problems. An FM system consists of a wireless microphone worn by a person who's speaking, and a receiver worn by the hearing impaired listener. With an FM system, a child with hearing loss can listen to his parent's or teacher's amplified voice, avoiding most of the background disturbance. Most children with hearing loss do best with an FM system when they're in school, because classes can be very noisy. But many infants and children will also benefit from wearing an FM system at home—when the family is having dinner, watching TV, or even all of the time.

The audiologist will choose the most appropriate kind of hearing aid for your baby. The smallest and most invisible ones, which fit inside the ear, are not used for young children for practical and safety reasons: they would need to be changed too often, to properly fit a rapidly growing baby's ear, and their hard plastic cases break too easily with falls and knocks.

Young children can be fitted with a BTE (behind the ear) hearing aid or a body aid (short for body-worn hearing aid). A BTE consists of a plastic hook holding a small case that goes behind the ear, and a tiny tube that conveys the amplified sounds into a soft mold that fits in the ear canal. A body aid is contained in a case that can be carried in a pocket, or in a small purse or backpack worn by the child. The case is connected to the ear through a small wire and earmold. Earmolds are custom-made after taking impressions of your child's ear, a simple process that only takes about fifteen minutes. They will need to be periodically readjusted throughout childhood, and particularly frequently in infancy (every six to eight weeks, when your baby is growing rapidly and his ear canal is changing

a lot in size and shape). Some BTE hearing aids and body aids also contain FM systems. A child can use either the hearing aid function, or the FM function, or the two together (for instance in a classroom, when he's listening to the teacher wearing the FM microphone, but also wants to hear other sounds or voices).

The choice between a BTE and body aid depends on a child's age and degree of hearing loss. A BTE can create feedback (an unpleasant whistling sound) when a baby is lying down, or if his ears are very soft, preventing a perfect seal. A body aid generates less feedback, and is a better choice for an infant who is not sitting up yet. Body aids are also more appropriate for children with severe to profound hearing loss, because they can provide more powerful amplification.

To help your child with his hearing aid:

* Make sure that the earmold fits snugly in his ear, to avoid feedback noise.
* Keep an eye on your baby's hearing aid, to make sure that it hasn't been dislodged during movement or play, or that little fingers haven't been tampering with it.
* Check the volume several times a day, and remember to have your child put his hearing aid on as soon as he wakes up. When he's old enough to understand what it does, he'll be asking for it.

What Is a Cochlear Implant?

If, after being equipped with a hearing aid, your child still isn't able to understand speech without lip-reading, he may be a good candidate for a cochlear implant. A cochlear implant is a device, implanted surgically in the inner ear, which picks up sounds from the environment and directly stimulates the auditory nerve. A person with a cochlear implant wears a device similar to a body aid, usually placed in a harness on the chest, containing a microphone and a transmitter that electronically codes the incoming sounds and transmits them to the cochlear implant.

Cochlear implantation is now considered a standard treatment for profound deafness by the National Institutes of Health, the American Medical Association, and most associations of hearing specialists. Cochlear implantation is also used in some milder forms of hearing loss. Its results are best in people who were deafened as adults and have a memory of sounds; the effects are more variable among children who have been hearing impaired since birth. But if surgery is performed early, and a child receives intensive hearing and speech therapy and has a very committed family who supports and stimulates him, he is likely to develop an understanding of speech and to learn to talk. Before being able to speak intelligibly, though, a child may need a long course of therapy. (Many continue to show improvement even three years after surgery.)

Experts point to some potentially beneficial social and cognitive effects of cochlear implantation, even when speech doesn't fully develop. Many children's first reaction is an increased interest in learning sign language. And a better awareness of voices and sounds coming from the environment can greatly improve cognitive development and social responsiveness.

Despite its positive effects, cochlear implantation remains controversial in the Deaf community, particularly when it is performed on children who can't choose for themselves whether they want it or not. Some deaf adults, who argue that they know better than any hearing person what it's like to be deaf, criticize cochlear implantation as an invasive procedure that doesn't cure deafness, and, because it is only partially effective, prevents a child from leading a normal life among either the hearing or the Deaf. They also believe that deafness is not a disability, but an alternate way of life, and that a deaf child can grow up without feeling or being in any way handicapped, if he is nurtured in American Sign Language and allowed to participate fully in Deaf culture. (If your child is profoundly hearing impaired, it is worth learning about and understanding these arguments, so that you can make the best choice for your child. See page 525, for some references to organizations for the hard of hearing.)

If cochlear implantation is a possibility for your child, his ear doctor will give you the information you need, discuss the pros and cons of the procedure with you, and refer you to a specialized medical center. A child becomes eligible for a cochlear implant only after he's 18 months old, and has tried hearing aids, together with hearing and speech therapy, for at least three to six months. So, you will have enough time to make an informed decision.

Visual Impairment

We just found out that our child has very little sight. We're completely lost.

To be told that your child is legally blind is to feel a devastating sense of loss. To help parents get through this, it's important for them to know that an infant won't have the same sense of loss of vision that an older child or adult would feel. We don't want to minimize the present and future difficulties, for you and your child. But remember that few activities in life involve just one sense, and your baby will have a chance to enjoy all of the others. Bathing, for example, involves the smell of soaps, the sound of running water, the feel of rough sponges or light water splashing against one's skin, and the loving touch of being cleaned and rubbed by one's parents. Even small amounts of vision, that you might consider almost useless, can be a source of tremendous enjoyment to your child. Even the perception of light and dark can be worthwhile, enhancing her sensory enjoyment of the world.

Most children who are legally blind still have some sight. A person is legally blind if she can see clearly at 20 feet away an object that someone with normal vision can see at 200 feet away, or if her visual field is limited to 20 degrees, compared to over 180 degrees provided by normal sight. In many cases a child who is legally blind can still read large symbols, see her hands, and perceive forms and light.

There are many organizations that offer programs and expert advice on how to help your child profit from whatever vision she has, and ensure that she doesn't miss valuable opportunities for intellectual, motor, and emotional development. You'll find that they can help address your many, unanswered questions and fears, and give you information on getting financial support for your child's needs. If no one has mentioned these developmental services yet, ask your eye doctor, pediatrician, or preemie follow-up clinic for a referral to the right kind of organization for your daughter. If they aren't good sources of referrals, your county's public health department, or your state's division that handles services for the blind (every state has one, although they go by different names) should be able to point you to both state-run and private organizations. Keep in mind that some organizations specialize in children whose only impairment is visual, while others work with children who have multiple disabilities. If you're having trouble finding an organization, the National Association for Parents of the Visually Impaired may be able to help. You can write to them at P.O. Box 317, Watertown, MA 02272, or call (800) 562–6265.

The sooner a specialist starts working with your baby, the better it will be for her development. The development of infants who can see is inextricably tied to their sense of vision. By noticing that people and things can move from place to place, they learn about object permanence (that objects continue to exist, even when they disappear from view), by reaching out to grasp something and watching it move, they learn about cause and effect, and so on. What is fascinating, and gratifying, for parents of blind babies to realize is that in the absence of other disabilities, and with people to help them learn how to interact with their environment in nonvisual ways, blind children are able to progress through the same, developmental stages, along almost the same timetable, as infants who can see.

For example, by about six months of age, both blind and sighted babies can recognize their parents (who, by that time, are very ready to be recognized and appreciated for all of the nurturing they've been doing!), and tense or cry when they're held by a stranger. Blind and sighted babies are able to sit up at about the same age. If someone is teaching them how to explore their environment, they develop comparable language skills. (An exception is that blind children often have temporary confusion with personal pronouns like "I" and "you" between the ages of two and three).

There are a few, significant differences in the typical development of a blind child that are important for you to be aware of, so they won't worry you. Early on, many parents worry about their baby's often-blank facial expression and rare smiles, wondering if this is a sign of either unhappiness or lack of intelligence. Most often, it is neither, and simply results from not having the opportunity to imitate other people's varied expressions. You can help your baby by allowing her to feel your face with her hands—and by looking out for other signs, such as body movements, of her emotions.

For a blind infant, some motor milestones also come later. Sighted infants start reaching out for things they see, almost automatically, at about four or five months of age. Blind infants have to wait until they have learned a lot about objects through sounds, and are then motivated to reach out and grasp things, at around nine months. Similarly, independent walking often comes later, typically at around one-and-a-half to two years of age. You can help your baby by playing games involving the way that sounds, the feel of things, and their position in space relate. For example, you can shake your keyring in front of her, then to one side and the other. Have her grab your jangling keys, to see where they are, and to help her realize that hard, metal things clink when they hit each other and are silent when their movement is stopped.

Most commercial toys are fine for visually im-paired babies, especially those that do more than one thing, or play music, or have various textures. You can also look at the American Foundation for the Blind's catalog of recommended toys for blind children (call [800] 232–5463), or contact specialized companies, such as Dragonfly Toy Co. ([800] 308–2208, or http://www.dftoys.com), that sell toys especially for children with disabilities.

Despite many parents' instincts to the contrary, you won't be helping your daughter by exposing her for long periods to the sounds of TV, or radio dialogue. This kind of auditory stimulation—words that just go on, without being tied to any apparent cause and effect—can actually hurt, rather than help, by teaching your child that words are meaningless and irrelevant to communication. Music is great, though, and children's songs can be a good way to teach your child some language and early concepts (that animals make sounds, wheels on a bus go around, and so on).

If you notice that your child has certain repetitive mannerisms, such as rocking her body, rubbing her eyes, or swinging her head back and forth, don't worry: experts believe that blind children may resort to this kind of self-stimulation at times when there isn't enough external stimulation to be satisfying. You can try to distract your child, by encouraging her to focus on people or objects around her. Even if that doesn't always work now, be reassured that these mannerisms usually go away as a child grows up. (The more disabilities a child has in addition to visual impairment, the longer they may last.)

As she grows, your child will be able to lead a rich life, to enjoy books (which she can read in Braille), become adept on computers (there is an extensive library of software for the visually impaired), and play sports (such as climbing jungle gyms or playing t-ball, which can be adapted with a beeper ball), depending on her abilities and interests. You'll weigh the pros and cons of regular, neighborhood schools, where she'll be in the "mainstream," versus specialized schools for blind children, where she probably will have an easier time socially, especially as she gets older. Many professions will be open to her, because of great advances in the field of technology for the blind, and the willingness of more companies to provide it.

Experts suggest that ideally, a blind child have both a certified teacher of the visually impaired (who specializes in helping her use her remaining vision and other senses to optimize all areas of development), and a certified orientation and mobility specialist (who specializes in helping her understand and safely move through spaces). They might teach your child directly, or be consultants to the early intervention specialist who works with her. You can view them as pretty much lifetime needs. Early on, for example, the orientation and mobility specialist might help your toddler move from her room to the kitchen, where she'll play with your pots and pans, and at the start of high school might teach her how to take public transportation, or become familiar with the layout of her new school.

One piece of advice that is most stressed by experts is that you shouldn't give in to your normal, parental instinct to be overprotective of your young child who is visually impaired. Yes, she will bump into things and fall more often than many other children. It's not easy to sit back and let this happen! But it's important to start looking at gentle knocks and bruises as good things, not bad. They're a sign that your child is getting around and exploring her environment—rather than suffering from the much worse consequences of passivity and under stimulation—and that through your loving ef-

forts, you're giving her the confidence, desire, and trust to do so.

Does Your Child Have Cortical Visual Impairment?

Some preemies have trouble seeing, temporarily or permanently, due to a disruption of the visual pathways of their brain. Even though their eyes may send good pictures to their brain, their brain isn't able to process or understand them well. Most commonly, so-called cortical visual impairment results from a serious intraventricular hemorrhage, or some other injury to the brain.

You can ask your pediatrician or ophthalmologist whether your baby's vision problems appear to be due partly to cortical visual impairment, which is present in some preemies who also had ROP. Children who have it often love looking at lights, and prefer peripheral vision; you may notice them trying to look at objects out of the corners of their eyes. Their vision may seem better one day, or hour, than the next.

If your baby's main problem seems to be cortical visual impairment, rather than damage to the eye itself, there's reason to be hopeful: this condition often improves gradually over months or years. No one can predict how much sight an individual child will recover. The resulting vision may not be good, but it may be much, much better than before.

Sensory Integration Problems

Our daughter, who was a preemie born at 32 weeks, hates the noise of the vacuum cleaner and the touch of wool or fur. I was told she could have sensory integration dysfunction. What is that?

The term *sensory integration* refers to one of the functions of everybody's brain: organizing and interpreting signals from our senses—noises, sights, smells, tastes, body movements, textures, and temperatures—so we can respond to them appropriately. A person who doesn't process sensory signals in quite the right way might not tolerate some kinds of touch or sound well—as you've noticed in your daughter—or alternatively, might be unusually oblivious to them. This is what is meant by sensory integration dysfunction, which some experts believe can result in unusual behavior, and social and emotional difficulties.

Of course, all of us find some sensations disturbing (you might be bothered by a scratchy, wool sweater, the squeaking of a knife against a plate, or lumps in your mashed potatoes), and different people are disturbed by things to different degrees. But while a lot of people, like your daughter, hate the noise of the vacuum cleaner, most know how to defend themselves against it, simply moving to another room, or shutting it out by concentrating on something else. The theory is that some former preemies don't learn to do that as well, or as early as their peers. Your daughter, for example, may not know how to "modulate"—in this case, dampen—the signal coming through her ears, and her negative responses to it. (Along with sensory integration, you may also hear about sensory modulation problems.) Overwhelmed by the noise, she flies off the handle. The same thing could be happening when she touches something that gives her an unpleasant sensation.

Professionals who deal with sensory integration problems say they can take several forms:

* Some children with sensory integration problems find more sensations, and milder ones, grating, and often react inappropriately. They may be unable to tolerate certain noises (for example, the sound of air conditioners or people singing), smells (like perfumes or detergents), movements (like swinging or rocking), textures (things that are very soft, like a stuffed animal's fur, or coarse, like brushes), or sights (like rapidly changing facial expressions). These hypersensitive babies may cry a lot and be difficult to soothe, or may simply "shut down," responding less and less to their increasingly frustrated parents. Older children with hypersensitivity may respond with crying, terror, lashing out, or avoidance and withdrawal.

* Some young preemies can't tolerate two different kinds of sensation at the same time. For instance, an infant may feed well only if his mother is not looking at him, or not holding him, and accept a bottle only when it's propped in his crib.

* Other children may be unusually underresponsive, or unaware of sensations. For instance, a baby may not suck readily because she's less aware of a nipple being put in her mouth. Underresponsiveness can lead to a craving for particularly intense stimulation, like deep touch, fast swinging, or spinning. A toddler may make himself fall on purpose, or frequently lift and throw heavy objects. Both overresponsiveness and underresponsiveness can be present in the same child.

Feeding problems believed to relate to sensory integration range from an aversion to foods with a certain taste, temperature, or texture (for instance, all soft foods like pasta or Jell-O, or all crunchy foods like pretzels or crackers) to an absolute insistence on eating only them. Some babies refuse all finger foods or anything with chunks, taking only smooth, processed food for a long time. Others reject smooth foods, and will eat only finger foods. Frequent gagging or spitting up, when not due to a condition like reflux, can be related to what some call tactile defensiveness in the mouth and throat.

You should know that many physicians and educators still consider sensory integration dysfunction a controversial concept. Doubters say that the problems it describes are too varied and fuzzy, overlapping with those of learning and behavioral problems like attention deficit disorder, hyperactivity, or autism, or even with perfectly normal differences in temperament. Moreover, there haven't been large studies to support it.

Other professionals—occupational therapists, in particular—have found sensory integration problems to be a useful way to understand what might be going on with some of these "difficult" or "fragile" kids, who are fussy and easily stressed by too much stimulation.

Why might preemies have sensory integration problems? One theory blames overstimulation in the NICU. Invasive medical therapies, a noisy, overly bright environment, and overly frequent contact, all at a gestational age when a baby is supposed to be getting only dampened sensory signals in the womb, could lead to a subtle brain imbalance that forms the root of sensory integration problems. But no one really knows if this is the case.

Experts believe that in most cases, these sorts of problems can be solved within the family, without a lot of outside help. Remember that your daughter, through her sometimes exaggerated or unusual responses, is sending you clues. By picking up on them, you'll help her avoid the things that disturb her, and little by little, over time and with patience, you should be able to help her become accustomed to them.

However, if you don't know what to do or feel stuck, occupational therapists have developed some strategies for dealing with sensory integration issues. For example, you might be advised to keep a stable facial expression, what therapists call a "still face," when you are feeding or dressing your baby, if she becomes easily agitated when she is stimulated in more than one way at once. Some preemies respond well to particularly deep touch, or the repetitive, intense movements of a rocking chair or swing, to calm them. Some tips for feeding issues might include:

* Desensitizing a gag reflex by swabbing a child's tongue with lemon ice or a lemon lollipop;
* Rubbing a child's hands and cheeks with a washcloth before food is presented, to stimulate the body parts involved in feeding;
* Blending food more effectively, to make it absolutely chunk-free;
* Adding textures (perhaps with Cheerios) or tastes (with cinnamon, spicy sauces, or pickles) to make food more intensely flavored and interesting.

Often, an occupational therapist can evaluate a child once and give her parents advice on how to minimize her strange reactions.

You can call Sensory Integration International, a non-profit association of therapists, teachers, and parents who believe in sensory integration dysfunction, at (213) 533–8338, for more information. The American Occupational Therapy Association (AOTA), at (301) 948–9626, can give you a list of occupational therapists in your region.

Most of all, keep in mind that even if your child is diagnosed with sensory integration dysfunction, it doesn't mean she's sick, although living with her can sometimes be difficult. Adapting the environment to her needs or quirks could be all that's needed to smooth out her peculiar behavior, and progress to a more relaxed daily life.

Feeding Problems

The doctor says that if my 8-month-old daughter's eating and weight gain don't improve, she might need a feeding tube.

It's very hard when your child has difficulty eating, and you're dealing with feelings of frustration, anxiety, and guilt at every meal. Former preemies with more serious, long-term complications of prematurity are more prone to develop feeding problems. In particular, they are:

* children with severe lung disease;
* children who have a tracheostomy;
* children with severe GE reflux;
* children who have cerebral palsy.

Luckily, most feeding difficulties can eventually be overcome, but it often takes time, patience, and expert advice.

The first thing to realize is that the way your child eats is affected by her medical problems and her physical and neurological development, as well as her personal preferences and tastes. For instance, a baby with BPD may have trouble breathing while she eats, and may not be able to eat solids successfully until her lungs have more

fully recovered. Eating may cause pain in a preemie who suffers from reflux. Preemies with cerebral palsy may have difficulty coordinating the complicated movements of their tongue, lips, jaw, and neck that are needed to suck, chew, and swallow. And some preemies who have temporary developmental delays may just reach their feeding milestones later than other babies do.

Sometimes, preemies who were on a ventilator for months, and had a lot of medical procedures performed in and around their mouths (intubations, suctioning, taping, for example) may develop a reaction that doctors call oral aversion. Instead of associating eating with pleasure, they associate it with medical treatment and discomfort. Often, babies with oral aversion refuse to suck on a nipple, and need to be fed by tube temporarily, but are willing to eat from a spoon and cup when they're older. Some experts believe that these, and other preemies who had long hospitalizations, are especially prone to sensory integration dysfunction (see page 455), causing them to intensely dislike and avoid certain food textures, tastes, or temperatures.

You should certainly have your baby seen by experts who can diagnose her specific feeding problems and offer advice on how to deal with them. Your doctor may already have arranged for this. If not, here are some specialists who could help:

* *A pediatric nutritionist or dietitian* can do daily calorie counts, and estimate how much more your child needs to eat to meet her nutritional needs. She can also help enrich your child's current diet, to get the most out of every mouthful.
* *A pediatric gastroenterologist* can assess whether your baby has reflux, isn't absorbing nutrients adequately, or whether any other medical conditions might be contributing to her feeding problems.

✻ *An occupational therapist* looks at whether the muscles needed for eating are working properly, and are well-coordinated. An occupational therapist can also assess whether sensory integration issues are interfering with your child's eating.

✻ *A speech-language therapist* also focuses on diagnosing and treating problems with oral-motor coordination—all of the movements needed for sucking, chewing, moving food in the mouth, swallowing, and breathing. To be seen by a speech-language therapist, a baby doesn't need to be talking yet.

In fact, the earlier you get help, the better—for your baby's growth, and your peace of mind.

Whether or not to get a feeding tube (called a gastrostomy tube, or "g-tube") placed in your child's stomach, to allow you to supplement the amount of food she takes by mouth, is a decision that you usually don't need to rush into. Most doctors won't recommend it if there's still a good chance that your child's eating and growth will improve soon. To help with the decision, you can read about g-tubes on page 320, consult with a feeding specialist to find out whether your child's eating is likely to improve anytime soon, get a second opinion from a pediatric gastroenterologist on whether a g-tube is medically advisable, and talk to other parents who have a child with a g-tube, to learn exactly what is involved and how they feel about it.

Some of the things you will find out are that a g-tube is only a temporary measure, that most children continue eating by mouth after getting one, using the tube only for supplemental feedings, often during the night, and that many parents fight for a long time against a g-tube, but change their minds about it afterward when they see their child's growth blossom.

IN PLAIN LANGUAGE: WHAT IS CEREBRAL PALSY?

Although the idea that their child has cerebral palsy initially brings pain and anguish to a family, it's wrong to be overly pessimistic. Many people imagine someone with CP as mentally retarded, tied to a wheelchair, and unable to live an independent life. But in fact, most people with CP have normal (and sometimes even very high) intelligence, and the severity of their physical problems can vary greatly, making a world of difference for a child's future. CP can be so mild that it is barely noticeable, apparent only when someone is doing certain, specific tasks, like brushing her long hair or pouring from a heavy coffeepot. While a child with mild CP can't be expected to be a professional football player or pianist, she is likely to lead a virtually normal life, going to school, playing recreational sports and games, getting married, having children, and working like all of her peers. At the other end of the spectrum, CP can be so severe that it leads to poor control over most movements, including speaking and eating. In between are many people who use a wheelchair, or need ongoing physical therapy and medical treatment, but still lead fulfilling lives.

Your own child's situation will become

clearer over the next few years, as it becomes apparent what she can and cannot do. A lot will depend on whether she suffers only from this disability, or from other disabilities and problems, as well. If a larger area of her brain was injured, she might be mildly or severely retarded. Children with CP also are more likely than other kids to suffer from hearing or visual impairments, seizures, sleep disorders, reflux, behavior problems, or learning disabilities. Remember that CP is not something you grow out of, but it is also not progressive, meaning it doesn't get worse. If your child has mild CP, she is not at risk of having more severe CP later on.

You'll learn that cerebral palsy is classified into different types, depending on what part of the child's body it affects most, and what kind of muscle tone or movement problems it causes.

✻ *Spastic diplegia:* This is the most common type of CP among preemies. *Spastic* refers to stiff muscle tone, and *diplegia* to the fact that the legs and feet are mainly affected. (Preemies with spastic diplegia can have some trouble with hand movements, but to a much lesser extent.) This means that walking and running might be hard for them—they may, for example, not walk independently until the age of two or three, perhaps with the help of braces on their lower legs—but they'll probably be able to use their upper body well, holding themselves upright, and using their hands and arms for everything from eating to writing. Many preemies with spastic diplegia can speak well, and, fortunately, are spared many of the other medical problems that often go along with CP.

It's also possible to have spastic hemiplegia (stiff tone affecting the arm and leg on one side of the body, but not the other) or spastic quadriplegia (affecting all limbs, and often the head and trunk, as well). Quadriplegia can often be diagnosed within the first six months of life.

✻ *Athetoid CP:* Preemies who do not have spastic cerebral palsy may have what is called athetoid CP, in which muscle tone is changeable, and varies between too low and too high. Children with athetoid CP, who are often very bright intellectually, may have trouble holding themselves in an upright posture while walking or sitting, getting their hands to the right spot to grasp something, or holding on to things. They often make involuntary movements of the face and upper body.

✻ *Ataxic CP:* A few preemies have ataxic CP, which is characterized by clumsy, uncoordinated movements, and poor balance.

One thing many parents worry about is their future feelings for their child with cerebral palsy. As with any special needs child, you may wonder: Will you love her? Will you ever be able to accept what has happened to her, and you? These are normal fears, and we can assure you: you almost certainly will. Parents who have children both with and without CP say their feelings for them are not that different. In both cases, they range across the typical parental spectrum from anxiety, frustration, and fatigue to delight and pride. Just as their love for their children who don't have CP is not related to their IQ scores or school grades, their love for their child who does have CP is not related to the results of her developmental evaluations.

Treatment of cerebral palsy focuses not on curing it—it is a life-long condition—but on helping a child achieve her maximum potential. The earlier treatment begins, the more chance there is of improving abnormal movements and developing normal abilities. If your child has been diagnosed with CP, she should be referred by her pediatrician or preemie follow-up clinic to your state's early intervention program, whose job it is to do a complete, developmental evaluation, and arrange for the appropriate, specialized interventions for your child. Therapy for a child with cerebral palsy may include:

* *physical therapy:* to help with gross motor skills, such as standing, walking, running, and sports, and to recommend any special equipment, such as shoe inserts or braces (to keep the foot and ankle in normal positions);

* *occupational therapy:* to help with fine motor and self-help skills, such as eating, dressing, toileting, writing, and drawing, and to recommend any special equipment, such as adapted silverware or pencils. Occupational therapy can also help with any sensory issues, such as aversion to certain textures (in clothing or food, for example) or kinds of touch, which some preemies with CP will have (see page 455);

* *speech and language therapy:* because CP sometimes affects the way a child moves her lips, jaw, tongue, and respiratory muscles, all of which are necessary for speaking;

* *medical treatments:* including medications or procedures to reduce high muscle tone, and treatments for joint problems that can result from abnormal tone or movements;

* *family support:* to help parents or siblings cope with the emotional and practical challenges of caring for a child with CP.

Fees for physical therapy and medical treatments are often covered by private insurance plans or Medicaid. Other kinds of therapy are less often covered, but if your child's doctor provides good documentation of medical necessity, you may have a better chance of being reim-bursed. Many therapists also help by adjusting their fees based on a family's ability to pay.

One of the advantages of starting therapy early is that therapists can help parents learn how to understand and relate to their child better. This can be tremendously valuable, since muscle tone problems interfere not only with the way a child does various tasks, but also with the way she responds to and communicates with her parents. A child with CP may have trouble giving non-verbal cues about her wants and needs. For example, she may not be able to turn away from her parents when she needs a rest from stimulation, and instead, may be frequently irritable, making her parents feel rejected. A therapist can help parents by teaching them that some of their child's responses and symptoms are due to her cerebral palsy, not to lack of love for her parents.

As time goes on, and if the need arises, your child's doctor will tell you about medical treatments that are used to help children with spastic CP. Most involve attempts to loosen stiff joints and muscles. One, a relatively new treatment called Botox, is a medication that is injected into tight muscles to reduce the high tone and make them more pliant. It is effective in many cases of mild or moderate CP, helping a child improve her leg positioning and walk better. The effects are temporary—from three to six months—and provide a good opportunity for physical therapy, or casts that aim to correct positioning problems.

Another fairly new treatment for spastic CP is a Baclofen pump, a small pump that is inserted surgically under the skin of the abdomen and releases doses of the medication Baclofen, a muscle relaxer, into the spinal fluid every few hours. This treatment has the advantage of relaxing a broad range of the body's muscles, rather than just a few, specific ones, but is generally not used in children under the age of three.

A surgical procedure used to decrease high tone in the legs is called rhizotomy. In the lower back area, nerves that lead to the legs and are functioning abnormally are identified and cut. The effects are permanent, but months of intensive physical therapy are needed after the procedure, to strengthen the legs that have been weakened, and to train them to make new movements.

All of these treatments have pros and cons that you should discuss in detail, along with other treatment options, with your child's doctor and therapists before making any decisions. When the time comes, keep in mind that high muscle tone is not the only thing that prevents good motor function in children with cerebral palsy. (Abnormal balance reactions and weakness of muscles can, also.) Thus, reducing spasticity will improve some children's function more than others.

While the effectiveness of physical therapy is hard to prove in research (one problem is that it's difficult to do controlled studies, in which some children are denied physical therapy for the experiment's sake), it is generally believed to improve quality of movement, to decrease the eventual occurrence of muscle contractures that might require orthopedic surgery, and to give parents a better understanding of how best to help their children. Some experts, although not all, believe that motor skills, like cognitive skills, can be enhanced by enriching stimulation—compensating for some biological deficits.

Most people with cerebral palsy and normal intelligence reach high levels of function and independence. Children with disabilities have a legal right to public education through high school, and a significant number go on to study at colleges and universities, including some of the nation's best. An adult with moderate CP should be able to do almost any job that involves intellectual more than manual dexterity; you'll find lawyers, doctors, and teachers, among others. An adult with severe CP is more likely to live at home longer, or in an apartment with a personal aide or a group home set up for people with disabilities, but may be able to work, utilizing new breakthroughs in assisted technology, such as voice-activated computers.

In most cases, children with CP outlive their parents, although the survival rate to adulthood is lowest, about 70%, for children with quadriplegic cerebral palsy and severe retardation.

According to experts, there are certain periods of particular stress in the life of a family with a child with cerebral palsy. The first, of course, is at the time of diagnosis, and for a while afterward, when parents are dealing with their own grief, while having to meet the practical and emotional demands of starting various kinds of treatment. The second period of particular stress comes when the child enters school. Next are the adolescent years, when children with CP, even if it is mild, struggle with particularly tough social and self-esteem issues. Finally, there's the advent of adulthood, when parents have to figure out living arrangements, how to get any needed special services (which were available through the school system or pediatric clinics in the past), and how their child will cope, in general, in the less protective, adult world.

As you make your way through the first period, we suggest that you take a few minutes to read In Depth: Parenting a Child with Special Needs on page 473, where you may find some answers to questions you have about the journey you are facing. One question shared by many parents is: will our lives ever be the same again? The answer is no, as it would be for any parents with a new baby. What is hard to realize now, but what most parents gradually do, is that the change won't necessarily be for the worse. Just as childless couples have never experienced the joys of children, and don't realize how worthwhile it is, on balance, to be awakened at dawn every morning or to lose the opportunity for nightly, romantic dinners, couples without disabled children can't possibly understand the joys and profound meaning that they bring to their parents.

A study of the impact of cerebral palsy on families was revealing. Asked about the negatives, about 65% of the parents interviewed said they lived on a "roller coaster," about 40% said they had trouble finding good childcare, and about 35% said they had had to quit a job at some point. Asked about the positives, about 90% of the parents said that the experience had increased their self-esteem and brought the family closer together. "Again, we learn that having a child with a disability means hard work for parents, but it is rewarding work," concluded United Cerebral Palsy, the study's sponsors.

As your child grows, experts advise that you allow her to do everything she's capable of, avoid overindulging her, listen to her opinions and feelings, and above all, recognize and value her efforts and achievements. Keep in mind that the most valuable thing you can give your child is not a new developmental skill, but an environment of unconditional love, and a strong foundation of self-esteem.

Predicting Intelligence

My one-year-old son is doing some things later than his twin sister, and at preemie clinic they told us his mental development is slower than it should be. Does this mean he's mentally retarded?

Of course you're anxious. But don't necessarily come to that conclusion yet. First of all, keep in mind that some of the differences you are noticing in your twins may be due to the fact that one is a boy and one is a girl. Because of differences in brain development, baby girls tend to acquire language more quickly than boys do, and are usually more interested in social interactions. (Boys tend to have a better sense of spatial relations and mechanics, but those skills emerge later, when toddlers begin to play with puzzles and blocks.) Also, although severe mental retardation can usually be diagnosed in early infancy, experts often can't tell which infant preemies will end up with milder problems, and which will be normal. Minor developmental delays often come and go. It's hard to predict whether a young child will end up being a quick or slow learner, with a higher or lower IQ, before he reaches school age.

Overall, former preemies do have slightly lower IQ scores, on average, and a higher rate of mental retardation, than children born at term (see page 464). But averages don't tell you anything about your individual child.

Parents whose children have mild cognitive delays in the first couple of years have many good reasons to be optimistic. Here's why:

✳ The younger a child is, the less likely it is that his score on a developmental test will persist over time. The most commonly used developmental test for babies and toddlers is the Bayley Scales of Infant Development, which has a mental and a motor component. The Bayley assesses the development of a child up to about two years of age—but is not actually an IQ test. It is useful because it allows delays to be picked up early, and helps identify infants and toddlers who can benefit from early intervention services.

But a Bayley score doesn't reliably predict how a child will develop in later years. First of all, normal development can proceed in different children at very different rates. Also, infants have only a small repertoire of behaviors and skills that can be assessed. For instance, a baby can reach for things he wants, and find sights or sounds amusing, but no baby can build a model airplane or write a funny story. As a child gets older, there are more skills and abilities that should emerge and can be measured. Finally, you can't tell what experiences an infant is going to be exposed to as he grows, and those, in addition to his innate abilities, are going to contribute significantly to his learning.

When a Bayley test is given at six months of age, only one in four scores corresponds to a child's IQ at three years of age. When a Bayley test is given at two years, the predictive value increases: three in four scores are confirmed by an IQ test a year later.

* An exception to this is severe mental retardation, as indicated by an extremely low Bayley score. Very low scores are more likely to stay low over time, and to be confirmed later by IQ testing. Significant cognitive impairments can usually be diagnosed before 18 to 24 months of age. If this happens with your child, it's important to know that the vast majority of children who are mentally retarded can still learn a lot—probably much more

than you think they can—and steadily progress over the years.

* When an infant or toddler has Bayley scores that are only slightly lower than average, his delays may be only a temporary consequence of his prematurity. Preemies can develop more slowly than full-term babies in their first 18 months, because long hospitalizations and medical treatments can interfere with normal stimulation and learning, some may still be recovering from the effects of illness, and some may have transient problems with muscle tone (see page 408).

Mild cognitive delays are the developmental problems that are most responsive to early intervention, and many of these children, with appropriate education and stimulation, improve over time. By the time they're four or five years old and ready to enter preschool, quite a few of these slow developers have caught up, and have IQ scores in the normal, or even high, range.

After a child turns three, there are several tests that can measure his IQ (the Stanford Binet Intelligence Scale, the Wechsler Preschool and Primary Scale of Intelligence, the McCarthy Scales of Children's Abilities, and others). These tests evaluate a wide range of cognitive abilities that normally develop before a child enters preschool. They can also determine a child's strong and weak points in particular areas of learning. But they have limitations, as well:

* The presence of a motor or sensory impairment (like cerebral palsy or a hearing loss) can make a child perform at a level lower than his intellectual capabilities. An IQ score can also be biased by the behavior of a child during testing (if he doesn't pay attention, for example), his language and culture (if he's

Prematurity and IQ

The normal range for IQ scores is from 85 to 115. About three in four preemies have scores in this range, indicating that they have average intelligence. Within the normal range, though, premature children who were born smaller and younger tend to score lower. One large study of eight- to ten-year-old former preemies found:

❋ a mean IQ of 103 with birth weight over 2,500 grams;

❋ a mean IQ of 96 to 97 with birth weight between 1,000 and 2,500 grams;

❋ a mean IQ of 88 with birth weight under 1,000 grams.

It is believed that loss of cognitive faculties in preemies may result from numerous factors that can interfere with a developing brain, such as medical complications that cause a lack of blood flow or oxygen, very poor nutrition over a long period of time, infection, or exposure to drugs or stimulation that adversely affect the brain.

About 10% to 15% of the total population have IQ scores between 70 and 80, indicating borderline intelligence, or slow learning abilities; in preemies born under 1,000 grams, the prevalence is somewhat higher, about 15% to 30%. Borderline intelligence is not mental retardation, and can go unrecognized if a child is enrolled in a class in which the mean IQ of the other students is in the low average range. But if a child who is a slow learner is in a more demanding school environment, he may fail, or may be wrongly reproached for laziness. When given adequate early intervention and educational support, children with borderline intelligence can learn and progress in mainstream schools at an almost normal rate.

An IQ score below 70 is classified as mental retardation. About 5% of preemies with birth weights greater than 1,000 grams, and 10% to 15% of preemies with birth weights less than 1,000 grams, have IQs in this range. Mental retardation in former preemies frequently goes along with other handicaps,

bilingual, or not a white American), and the skills of the examiner.

❋ IQ scores can change over time. A child's intelligence can improve, thanks to his parents' and teachers' efforts. The IQs of many children who come from disadvantaged families, for instance, rise once they're enrolled in a good quality preschool program. (The reverse is unfortunately true, too. Children who are not appropriately stimulated can lose IQ points over time.)

❋ True, a high IQ is usually a good indication of a child's future academic success. But human intelligence is too complex to be described by one number. The capacity to learn and apply knowledge encompasses a vast range of abilities, some of which are measured by IQ scores, like memory, language comprehension, and the ability to discern patterns, and others that are not, like creativity, and how well one understands emotions. There may be only one Albert Einstein

like cerebral palsy or loss of vision, and most children who are affected do best with multidisciplinary interventions, as well as special education.

Different degrees of retardation lead to dramatically different developmental outcomes and quality of life. Most former preemies diagnosed with mental retardation will have a mild (IQ 55 to 70) or moderate (IQ 40 to 55) degree of cognitive impairment, and will be able to dress and feed themselves, use the bathroom, talk, learn, make friends, find work, and carry on a productive life. Family environment and participation, together with special education, can have a great impact on the cognitive abilities of children with mild or moderate mental retardation. Those who are mildly retarded can usually reach a sixth-grade academic level, and develop enough social and vocational skills to live semi-independently. Those with moderate retardation can usually be educated to a second-grade level, and function independently in environments that are orderly and familiar, like their home or a sheltered workshop. Children with mild or moderate men-

tal retardation may be slow to learn, but their emotional responsiveness is often normal or better, bringing deep joy to their families and friends.

Children with severe mental retardation (IQ 20 to 40) can develop language, but usually not until after age five, and can think very simply. Those with profound mental retardation (IQ below 20) usually need constant aid and supervision.

The statistics on mean IQ scores in former preemies should be interpreted with caution. For one thing, the studies that have correlated birth weight with IQ haven't taken into account the relative IQ scores of the preemies' parents. Genetics, not just premature birth, may play a major role in these babies' IQs. Moreover, studies on mean intelligence levels refer to large groups of children, without taking into consideration individual factors—the educational level of the parents, their active and loving involvement at home, and the quality of the early intervention and education a child receives—that can greatly affect his cognitive outcome.

(a student considered "slow" who was later recognized as a genius), but huge numbers of children who start out as poor students become very successful later, in school and in life. (Some provocative, recent research suggests that emotional intelligence may be even more important for success at work than the intellectual abilities that are measured by IQ.) IQ scores that are classified as low average, borderline, and mildly retarded should be interpreted with particular cau-

tion, before jumping to pessimistic conclusions.

Developmental psychologists often use more than one test to assess a child's thinking and learning abilities. Specific learning disabilities can frequently be improved with special educational techniques. Families should take each test result as a piece of information that may be useful, but can sometimes fail to reflect a child's real abilities for personal growth.

Detecting Learning Disabilities

We think our son is really bright, yet he's slower in learning to read than his friends. Are preemies at special risk for learning disabilities?

If you asked around among a group of normal adults, you would find that some of them learned to read earlier than average, and others later. You would also find that some who eventually became the most successful students were late readers. Some kids just aren't neurologically ready, or interested in reading, as soon as others. It could be that your son is more focused on mastering jungle gyms, or exploring the world of dinosaurs or action toys, than on sitting down to read at this point in his life, and that he'll catch up as soon as he gets around to it.

Nevertheless, since your child was a preemie, it's important not to just wait and see. Former preemies are at greater risk for learning disabilities than other children, and if your son does have one, an early diagnosis could help him a lot. The academic problems caused by learning disabilities can be a source of great frustration to a child, particularly if they're mistaken for lack of intelligence, talent, effort, or interest in school. So, talk to your pediatrician and your child's teacher about your concerns. If either agrees that it's warranted, or you remain concerned, ask for a referral to a professional who specializes in learning disabilities, and arrange to have your son evaluated.

Learning disabilities are quite common in the general population, affecting approximately one in ten children. When preterm and term children with normal IQs are compared, though, learning disabilities occur approxi-

mately twice as frequently in preemies,—mostly affecting those with smaller birth weights and gestational ages, more medical complications of prematurity, and more social stresses (like poverty, low parental education, and unstimulating or chaotic home environments). They're also more common in preemies with a family history of learning disabilities.

Although a few kinds of problems that affect learning, such as hyperactive behavior, short attention span, or problems with fine motor coordination (which can later affect a child's penmanship), are sometimes evident earlier, most learning disabilities aren't picked up until elementary school, when children are challenged with the demanding tasks of reading, spelling, writing, and arithmetic. A learning disability is diagnosed when there's a significant gap between a child's intelligence and the skills he's achieved in one or more academic areas. Children with learning disabilities may have more difficulty than other kids their age with spoken or written language, math, memory, and reasoning, or attention and self-control. Besides delaying academic achievement in one or more areas, learning disabilities can also be a cause of social problems.

Even if he does turn out to have a learning disability, your child's long-term prospects may be very good. Because these deficits affect only specific aspects of development, they usually don't limit a child's general potential to learn. Special education programs, tutoring, counseling, or medication can often help a lot. Young people with learning disabilities can aim to achieve a college education or higher, and to find professions in which they make the best use of their gifts, becoming successful, fulfilled, and well-adjusted adults.

PREEMIES AND LEARNING DISABILITIES

What is a learning disability? It is a wide, umbrella term that covers many kinds of problems in the key areas of learning:

❋ *Reading disorders.* Difficulty with reading is called dyslexia. Dyslexia can refer to problems with any of the steps involved in reading, such as being able to recognize letters as symbols (rather than as meaningless shapes), perceive the different sounds that make up words, or remember words that one has read before. Other reading disabilities, involving difficulty with comprehension of concepts rather than identification of single words, may be found in later grades. These might arise if a child has difficulty forming mental images from a written sentence, or relating a concept she's reading about to one stored in her memory.

❋ *Writing disorders.* If a child has difficulty reproducing shapes and symbols (including letters, words, and numbers) in writing, dyslexia may be to blame (if she has trouble recognizing or remembering them), or you may be told that your child has a problem with "visual-motor coordination." Delayed fine motor skills—for instance, holding and controlling a pencil with precision, to write and draw—may also contribute to this difficulty. Children with disorders of visual-motor coordination, in early as well as later grades, often produce less in writing than their peers, because they can't write as fast or as well.

❋ *Arithmetic disorders.* Problems with math can arise from difficulty distinguishing numbers and symbols, memorizing facts like the multiplication table, aligning numbers (a task requiring visual-motor coordination) and understanding abstract concepts.

Some learning disabilities, because they're so broad, hinder performance in more than one subject, and can also affect a child's social interactions:

❋ *Difficulty understanding speech, despite normal hearing (central auditory processing or receptive language disorder).* These children may be unable to distinguish one sound from another, or to understand a complex sentence they hear, making it difficult for them to follow instructions.

❋ *Difficulty articulating sounds (articulation disorder), using words (expressive language disability), pronouncing words,* or *stuttering.* These children may lack fluency in expressing themselves and what they've learned, orally and in writing. Many have difficulty retrieving words they know from their memory.

❋ *Difficulty focusing and concentrating (attention deficit disorder, or ADD).* ADD can show up, especially in preemies, as excessive daydreaming, easy distractability, and a tendency to mentally drift off. Or it can be accompanied by the fidgety, hyperactive, and impulsive behavior more commonly associated with ADD (in which case it's called attention deficit/hyperactivity disorder, or ADHD). Not surprisingly, any difficulty paying attention can make the consequences of other learning disabilities worse. Boys are more frequently diagnosed with ADD or ADHD than girls.

* *Difficulty with cognitive functioning.* This can include problems with logic, abstract thinking, or memory. It also can include problems with so-called executive functions: planning, problem solving, and being able to work independently. A child may have difficulty handling new information, remembering assignments, or planning a course of action. He may show poor judgment, lack common sense, or have problems with decision making. Delays often appear in the later grades, as more activities that involve abstract reasoning are required. Young people with this kind of cognitive learning problem can show normal or even higher than normal intelligence in other areas.

* *Non-verbal learning disabilities.* These children have difficulty with space and time. They may have trouble understanding how much space things take up (including their own body, which can result in clumsiness), or in telling time and planning within a time frame (which can lead to problems doing homework). They often have trouble with the big picture: they know a lot, but struggle to write an essay with a beginning, middle, and end, and learn rote arithmetic skills well but struggle with math problems. They are at risk for social problems, also, since they don't perceive or use facial expressions as skillfully as other kids do.

Mostly because of learning disabilities, up to half of preemies with a birth weight under 1,000 grams, and one-third of those with a birth weight under 1,500 grams, will need some kind of special tutoring or educational services.

If a child in elementary school has a two-year or greater delay in some area (for instance, if a fourth grader is writing only at a second-grade level), his parents and teachers should suspect a learning disability, and have him evaluated. Of course, not all children with normal intelligence who fail in school have a learning disability. Some of them have emotional disturbances, previously unrecognized visual or hearing losses, are just slower to develop a skill, or may simply lack motivation. Diagnosing and identifying learning disabilities is done by a psychologist (ideally, a child neuropsychologist, if there is one in your area) or a pediatrician, sometimes with the help of other specialists, like an audiologist, speech-language pathologist, occupational therapist, or special educator.

The origin of learning disabilities is not yet certain. It is believed they are caused by problems in the way that different areas of the brain are linked together, perhaps because of an insufficient supply of some substances in certain brain structures, or because of damage to nerve cells as their connections were developing. The result is difficulty interpreting and using information coming through the senses or from another part of the brain. Neuroscientists, who are trying to pinpoint what goes wrong in the brain of a child with a learning disability, hope that future discoveries will also bring the keys to effective treatment.

Preemies may be at higher risk for learning disabilities because a premature birth and unusual early experiences might interfere with the way that brain cell networks would normally form in the third trimester of pregnancy. Sometimes, the cause of a premature birth (for instance, a mother's use of cigarettes or other drugs during pregnancy, or a medical complication) may also be the cause of the learning disability. In other cases, prematurity is unrelated to a child's learning disability. Disorders like dyslexia tend to run in families, and scientists suspect there is a genetic link to some subtle brain dysfunctions.

You should realize that kids with learning disabilities are often bright and, with help, can succeed academically—or even excel. Public schools are required by federal law to provide special programs for learning disabled children, either in separate, all-day classrooms, or in extra classes that a child attends in addition to his regular ones. Some parents hire a private tutor to help their child. (If you decide to do that, be sure to check the tutor's qualifications to teach a learning disabled child. See page 527 for a list of resources on learning disabilities, including organizations that can provide references for private special educators.) By giving a child individual attention, and focusing on ways to overcome or work around his particular deficits (for instance, a child with a writing disorder may benefit greatly from writing on a computer, even from an early age), special education can have remarkable success.

Specialists other than teachers may also be called on to help:

* *Audiologists* can help children develop better strategies for listening to and understanding what they hear (sometimes by using technologies like hearing aids or amplification, even for kids who aren't hard of hearing, or computer programs that slow down words, making it easier to understand their sounds).
* *Speech pathologists* can work with children who don't articulate well, practicing specific sounds through imitation, play, and exercise.
* *Occupational therapists* can help with fine motor delays, improving hand movements for writing and drawing, and coordinating them with visual attention.
* *Doctors* can treat attention and hyperactivity disorders with medications like Ritalin.

* *Psychotherapists* (usually using a combination of behavioral therapy and family therapy) can help to decrease a child's restlessness and improve his concentration and ability to learn.

No matter what kind of learning disability your child has, the therapists following him should also teach you the best strategies for interacting with him, stimulating his interest with activities and toys, and encouraging appropriate behavior and skills. Since some kids with learning disabilities can't read facial expressions well, they may do or say the wrong thing and turn people off, so parents should also try to help their child learn how to make friends by teaching him how to understand people's attitudes and feelings.

If your former preemie is diagnosed with a learning disability, remember that he's not alone. These problems are found every year in millions of school-age children, often relieving them from the pressure and stigma of being considered lazy, difficult, or unintelligent. A parent's unconditional support and optimism are crucial to help a child take a positive attitude toward his problems at school, and lessen their possible psychological consequences, such as withdrawal, anger, depression, and loss of self-esteem.

It takes great patience to sustain a child with a learning disability, and many parents find comfort in talking to a counselor, at least initially, when they're still searching for solutions. Support groups, books, and Internet resources can also help parents better understand and face their child's learning disability, connecting them to the many other families who are dealing with a similar problem.

MULTIPLES

One Twin with Disabilities

What can I do to help my twin who has a disability? She's going to feel so bad when she compares herself to her sister.

As a parent, nothing is more difficult than seeing a child of yours in pain, physical or emotional. You would take it onto yourself, if you could. But pain is a part of every person's life, whether she has a disability or not. All parents learn that the most important thing they can offer is to help their children develop the emotional strength and inner resources to deal with it—and perhaps even to be strengthened, rather than weakened, by it.

Although it's natural to be most concerned about your daughter who has a disability, make sure not to overlook your other twin's needs, also. It's difficult, and occasionally painful, growing up with a sibling who has a chronic illness or disability. But try not to get discouraged or depressed about her situation. There is a hidden, but profound, positive impact of these problems. In many growing children, they give rise to unusual amounts of compassion, responsibility, and self-confidence. In fact, biographers have noticed that among the prominent, historically important people in our century, more of them than usual faced adversity—of this kind and many others—in their childhoods, not the idyllic childhood that we all strive to give our children and assume is best for them. Strong children who are "fighters" can overcome a lot, and profit from doing so.

Still, it's sometimes difficult to know how to help your children. First, some advice from experts concerning your daughter who has a disability:

* *Affirm her feelings.* As your daughter gets older, and has a growing awareness of being different, there will be many times when she will feel sad, embarrassed, angry, lonely, fragile, and discouraged. When she does, acknowledge her feelings and let her cry about them, holding her and letting her know that you realize things are hard for her. Don't say things like, "Buck up," or "Other children have even worse problems." No matter how well meaning you are, you'll give her the impression that you find her feelings unacceptable, or just don't want to hear about them.

* *Don't pity her.* Even though you are empathizing, don't convey pity. Once you've let her know that you understand her feelings, you can teach her that everyone feels pain and has struggles—and that no disability defines her, or limits her future. It's important for you to believe this, too.

* *Be open and honest about her disabilities.* Openly discuss your daughter's disabilities with her—what they are, how they happened, and whether they are likely to get better or worse in the future. But find clear, simple, age-appropriate explanations, rather than telling her more details than she really wants to know at one time. Also practice with her some answers she can give to kids at school, if they ask questions or make comments.

* *Be a model of acceptance.* Model for her,

through your daily actions, that you accept all aspects of every child, and admire every child for what he is. When you meet new children (say, in social settings or at the doctor's office, comment on their strong points, not their weak ones. If they have disabilities, don't treat them any differently than other children—be just as open and engaged. If you think they have beautiful eyes, say so. If they're really good at something, or have accomplished something that required effort, mention your admiration.

❋ *Show her respect by being firm and demanding of her.* Whenever possible, apply to her the same rules, discipline, and expectations for being a responsible member of the household that you apply to her sister. At times this may seem overly demanding (to you or to her), as she will have to struggle and find alternative ways of doing things. But over time, it will build her self-respect. Overprotecting and indulging her will diminish her sense of competence. However, it's also important to let her know often that you're aware of the extra effort she has to expend, and you treasure it.

❋ *Show clearly that it's the amount of effort that you value in your children, rather than the extent of their specific achievements.* It's important that your daughter who has a disability realize that you would not admire or love her more if she were free of her disability. Keep in mind that all of the therapy and medical treatments can send the wrong signal: that you are desperately trying to make her normal, and will be disappointed with anything less.

❋ *Go out of your way to find an activity at which your daughter can excel.* Everyone needs to feel successful, and to have pride of accom-

plishment. It may be anything from horseback riding to swimming, computers, or reading. Pay attention when your daughter tells you she particularly enjoys something, and get tips from her therapists or special education teachers about things she may be able to excel in. Do whatever is needed to facilitate her involvement, and share her pleasure!

❋ *Don't discourage her from mixing with other children who have disabilities.* While you may want to give your daughter a mainstream education, and as normal a life as possible, find some arena in which she can interact with others who have disabilities. It will help her social self-confidence to meet other children with disabilities, and give her direction and ambition to meet adults who can become mentors and role models.

What about your other daughter? Most studies show that children who have siblings with a disability or chronic illness are well-adjusted, on average, and some indicate that they are more likely to develop positive qualities like strong social skills, sensitivity, and compassion for others. But that doesn't mean things are easy for them. Their lives are different, and more challenging, than other children's. You can expect a number of normal reactions.

Your daughter who does not have a disability will feel understandably jealous of all the attention her twin is getting from you and other caregivers. As she gets older, it will dawn on her that you may repeatedly have to cancel your plans to attend her events, or anticipated family events, to cater to her twin's needs. Also, she may have to cope with an unusual amount of early separation from you, because of hospital visits and doctors and therapists appointments.

It's common for children with siblings who have a disability to feel anger, blaming their sibling or parents for the fact that they don't get enough attention, or even for somehow causing their sibling's condition (before they are old enough to understand it). When they're young, it's typical for them to fear that they may get the condition, too, or that they did something to cause it. When they're a little older, they often feel embarrassed about having a sibling who is different, and may want to hide her from schoolmates—only to get hit by another negative feeling, shame, for doing that. And some feel guilty just for being healthy themselves.

Some ways to help your child who does not have a disability:

❉ *Be open and honest about her sibling's disability and ongoing problems.* Give her as much information as she wants, but communicate it in age-appropriate ways. For example, a young child whose sibling has cerebral palsy and wears braces could be told, "It's hard for her to keep her legs in the right position for walking, the way we do. The doctor gave her these to help her." When she's older, it may help to give her an update after each of her sibling's visits to the doctor, when there's most family stress. Be sure to assure your young child that her twin's condition is not contagious, and that she didn't cause it. These are common misconceptions that you may not even realize your child has.

❉ *Spend time alone with her.* Set aside some time each day, even if it's just at bedtime, and a longer period of a few hours each week. Siblings of children with disabilities often get very little time alone with their parents— when it's easiest for you to show her, and her to realize, how much you love her.

❉ *Take the time to listen to her feelings.* Acknowledge that you understand that her life is different, and more stressful, than that of other kids, and encourage her to share her feelings with you. Don't criticize them as selfish or mean. When it's appropriate, let her take part in family decision-making, and take her feelings into account.

❉ *Make sure to treat her like a child, not like a helping hand.* Involving your child in her sister's care can be a very positive thing—she may feel extremely proud of being able to help her disabled twin and the family—but only to the extent that she likes it. When she's young, simple tasks like handing you diapers, singing, and playing with her sister may be appropriate. Above all, follow her cues. The aim is to make her feel included and helpful, but never burdened. Also beware of putting pressure on her to behave much more responsibly than a child of her age naturally would.

❉ *Teach her how to respond to comments about her sister.* As she gets older, unfortunately, she's going to get both questions and barbs from her peers, and she's going to be at an age when they will hurt.

❉ *Clearly demonstrate that you accept and admire both of your children exactly as they are.* Researchers have found that when parents appear to be unaccepting of their child who has a disability, siblings are more likely to have problems adjusting.

❉ *Consider a sibling support group.* There are many support groups for siblings of children with disabilities, where they can freely voice their feelings, and see that others have them, too. If you think your daughter would benefit, you can call the organizations listed on page 531 to see if they know of a group that is convenient for you.

Try to remember that every single sibling relationship is different, and being a twin is always complex, whether or not a disability is involved. There are siblings who are close from childhood through adulthood, some who never are, and some who start out close and grow apart as they grow up, and vice versa. Even if you do all you can, your children may fall into any of these categories—just like everyone else's.

PARENTING A CHILD WITH SPECIAL NEEDS

A TRIP YOU NEVER PLANNED

In 1987 Emily Perl Kingsley, a writer for *Sesame Street* and the mother of a child with special needs, compared her parenting experience to being forced to take a trip to a place you never planned to visit. Parents who are going to have a baby feel like they are planning a fabulous vacation to a dreamland like Italy, she says. But if their child has a disability, they find out that their plane has landed, instead of in Italy, in Holland.

> . . . *So you must go out and buy new guidebooks. And you must learn a whole new language. And you will meet a whole new group of people you would never have met. It's just a different place. It's slower-paced than Italy, less flashy than Italy. But after you've been there for a while and you catch your breath, you look around and you begin to notice that Holland has windmills . . . and Holland has tulips. Holland even has Rembrandts. But everyone you know is busy coming and going from Italy . . . and they're all bragging about what a wonderful time they had there. And for the rest of your life, you will say, "Yes, that's where I was supposed to go. That's what I had planned." And the pain of that will*

> *never, ever, ever, ever go away . . . because the loss of that dream is a very very significant loss. But if you spend your life mourning the fact that you didn't get to Italy, you may never be free to enjoy the very special, the very lovely things about Holland.*

HOW FAMILIES REACT TO THE BIRTH OF A CHILD WITH SPECIAL NEEDS

Many parents of children with disabilities have responded to Kingsley's words, not denying that their paths have been difficult, but affirming that over time, they also have found the "very lovely things about Holland."

Sociologist Rosalyn Benjamin Darling, co-author of *Ordinary Families, Special Children* (Guilford Press), points out that although personal details may differ, most parents in this situation follow similar paths, before being able to bring their lives back to normal. The steps along the way include:

✳ *Anomie, or disorientation.* When a baby's disability is diagnosed, and for some time afterward, his parents can be disoriented, confused, and uprooted from their normal habits and frame of mind, since so many of their plans and expectations have been shattered. Anomie is a mainly passive stage. Psychologists suggest that during this period, parents experience the normal process of grief for the loss of a healthy baby. First comes the initial shock, accompanied by numbness, and sometimes denial or disbelief. It may be too overwhelming, at first, to deal with the truth. For some parents, offers of information or emotional support can set off waves of panic, anger, and despair. Even those parents who want more information on their child's disability, in order to help him, may not know where to find it and, as a result, feel powerless. Self-pity may alternate with guilt, and parents may feel lost, not knowing what to think or where to turn to get their bearings again.

✳ *Seekership.* Seeking answers to make sense of one's experience is a natural human reaction to the stage of anomie. To reestablish order, and find meaning and solutions, most parents begin searching for resources that can help them with their child. They may look for medical treatments, intervention programs, educational and social support. They may also begin to ask openly for their child to be loved by family members, respected by friends, and accepted socially. By focusing their energies on meaningful tasks, most parents gradually begin to modify their expectations, and come to accept their situation.

The stage of seekership may never end completely, as new problems or obstacles may arise at any time, particularly when a child with a disability has a health or developmental setback, or when new challenges arise in adolescence and adulthood. Psychologists and parents report that flashbacks of the negative, passive feelings from the stage of anomie can periodically reappear (in a process that some experts have called chronic sorrow, see page 432), but they become easier to deal with, through experience.

✳ *Normalization.* Once they've discovered or created solutions to their problems, and if they receive good medical, social, and educational support, most families of children with disabilities succeed in reorganizing and normalizing their lives. In most cases, their lifestyle is not very different from that of families with normal children, although their expectations have been modified. Most parents still worry about their child's future, and many cope by adopting the philosophy of taking one day at a time. At the same time, most also feel hope. Although, given the choice, many families would not bring a baby with a disability into the world again, they all say that they deeply love their child, and that their parenting experiences have been fulfilling.

A LONGER PHASE OF ANOMIE, FOR PARENTS OF PREEMIES

A permanent disability in a premature baby is often diagnosed only after months have gone by, prolonging for his parents the initial stage of anomie. Their "plane" doesn't land in Holland right at birth, but is forced to make an emergency landing in an unexplored place.

For these families, the first reason for grieving is the loss of a normal pregnancy and full-term baby to take home right away. In addition, if their preemie is very small and fragile, or very sick, the fear that he might not survive makes them experience anticipatory grief over the possibility of losing him. Worries about a future disability may only lurk in the background, during the hospitalization. Even when a premature baby is finally ready to go home, his future development may still be uncertain, and doctors only able to tell his family about an increased risk of a future disability. Some parents deal better with this uncertainty than others; some can maintain an optimistic outlook, while for others, having to wait and see is pure torture.

When a definite diagnosis of disability is finally reached, it's a hard blow. Painful questions are faced for the first time: "Will my child ever walk, or will he always use a wheelchair?" "Is my baby ever going to see my face?" "Why did this have to happen to us? What did we do to deserve it?" Mothers and fathers who already felt guilty about their child's early birth, blaming themselves or their doctors for not preventing it, may find their remorse grow to unbearable heights. Parents who are unprepared, because their preemie had an easy hospital course and seemed to be OK, may feel acutely betrayed. Some other families, who suspected all along that there was something wrong with their child, may actually feel relieved that their impressions are affirmed at last.

If you have just discovered that your premature baby has a disability, you're probably still disoriented, in the stage of anomie. Be reassured that your feelings, even if they're extremely negative, are normal: you need to feel them deeply in order to move on. But try not to despair. Ask for help from your partner, a close friend, or relative. Even if your friends are worried about you, they may need a word or sign from you to feel entitled to reach out and talk about the painful things that are happening to you. If you're afraid you're sinking into a depression, you should talk to a therapist (you can ask your pediatrician or your own doctor for ad-

vice on finding one) or a religious advisor. With some support, you'll find yourself learning day by day what can help you cope, slowly leaving the climax of your crisis behind.

MOVING ON: THE ROLE OF SOCIAL RELATIONSHIPS

Before and shortly after their child's birth, many parents may share some of the negative, or ambivalent, societal attitudes toward children with special needs. People often consider having a child with a disability to be one of the worst tragedies that can happen to a family. When first hit by the harsh reality of their baby's condition, a mother and father have to review their ideas from a personal perspective they never imagined they'd have, and really think: "Exactly how bad is this? What, specifically, is no longer possible for us, and what is?" Bonding with a baby with a disability is sometimes more difficult, and can take longer, because the infant may not respond to his parents' attention and loving gestures with predictable and rewarding behavior, such as smiling, cuddling, or becoming soothed. (Many preemies, with or without disabilities, can be fussier and more difficult to handle than term infants, because of their still immature senses and neurological responses. See page 373.)

Fortunately, barriers and obstacles are usually swept away by the strong bond that develops between parents and their baby, no matter how he looks or behaves. "As time goes by, you fall in love. You think, this kid's mine and nobody's gonna take her away from me," said one mother interviewed by sociologist Darling. Like any parent, you notice and relish your baby's unique beauties. You feel the urge to hold and protect him. Your love, nourished by the love you'll get in return, will steadily grow. It will be your primary source of strength, helping you to abandon most of your initially negative feelings.

Especially at first, some parents may not talk openly to relatives and friends about their child's disability, out of shame, self-protection, or fear of causing pain or worry to people they love. But later, when they fully understand the nature of their baby's problem, parents begin to ask for attention and consideration for their child from significant others, and then from the rest of the world. In Darling's interviews, most parents described their close relatives, friends, and work colleagues as generally sympathetic, and a great source of emotional as well as practical help. Only in a few cases did some relatives or friends react negatively, not wanting to get involved with a child who is disabled, or treating him differently from his siblings or cousins (sometimes in an overly affectionate, but not genuine, fashion).

If this happens to you, don't be too surprised. People who react oddly, out of self-defense or ignorance, often change their behavior over time. But even if some relationships become impossible for you to carry on, you won't be abandoned. Your loyal friends will be supplemented by some families of other children with disabilities, whom you'll meet through your child, and will become meaningful friends and soulmates for you, like a second family.

Initially, facing strangers or acquaintances with a child who has a disability can be hard. If a baby doesn't look different, his parents may choose not to mention his condition, or tell a white lie about his age, to make it match his behavior or size. Don't feel bad about doing that— you have no obligation to open yourself up to everyone you meet. Questions can make a mother or father feel uncomfortable, and lead

to isolation, to avoid conflicts or embarrassment. That's also an understandable reaction. But after some time, most parents begin to feel stronger and more secure when they take their child out in public. They find the right answers to give even to indelicate questions, and find that explaining their situation to others helps them put it in perspective themselves. Slowly, families begin to resume old habits, like going to restaurants or shopping malls with their child, without feeling that people's eyes are pointed at them. If somebody stares, they eventually learn not to be hurt by it, or to lash out in anger, but simply to ignore it.

Sometimes, a family risks isolation because of their child's restrictions—he has to avoid infections, it's difficult to move him around with his equipment, or he just can't enjoy certain activities. Parents may not get out much because they can't find competent baby-sitters and are scared that their child will get sick while they're gone, or are simply too tired to want to leave home. In time, you'll feel more comfortable getting your child out and about, or going out without him. In the meantime, it can help to hire nurses as baby-sitters, or to form a baby-sitting co-op with other parents of children with disabilities. (Try contacting local early intervention and disability agencies, or even advertising in the local paper.) You can also train several, willing relatives and friends to take care of your child. Your child service coordinator or hospital social worker may know of possible options for "respite care," or help you find financial resources to help pay for it.

A significant interaction is the one with doctors. Many parents in Darling's studies say their doctors were tactful and supportive, pointing out positive aspects of their child's condition without minimizing their concerns, and helping them to overcome their initial grief and immobilization. But many parents say they've also dealt with medical professionals who were lacking in compassion, concern, and bedside manners. If a doctor uses the wrong words or tone in communicating a child's risk for disability, confirming a diagnosis, or even recommending institutionalization to parents who would never consider that, he can deeply hurt them, leaving an open wound that won't heal for a long time. If you're not happy with your baby's doctors and therapists, you should find the courage to leave them, looking for other medical professionals who make you feel good about your child. All parents eventually find them, and cherish those relationships.

HOW PARENTS BECOME RESEARCHERS AND EXPERTS

A powerful way for parents to move out of anomie, and on to normalization, is to seek answers to their questions and become well informed about their child's disability. A mother or father can feel particularly isolated because nobody around them is concerned with their concerns or is available to answer their questions. Supportive relatives and friends just can't provide a lot of practical advice about a child with a disability. Good books and written sources of information do exist, but they're not so easy to find. Pediatricians and general practitioners may be good doctors, but not know much about a child's particular disability and its most up-to-date treatments or possible interventions. A few parents have the shocking revelation that their pediatrician can't (or worse, doesn't want to) manage their child's condition, or one of its complications. As a result, many families decide to look for medical information on their own, and for a doctor who specializes in their child's condition.

If you don't have that drive for knowledge, or can't take the initiative yet because you feel empty or overwhelmed, be assured that you don't have to do everything alone. You can think of it as embarking on a new career—a venture that isn't easily undertaken without the help of others in the field, who can educate and guide you, and share their accumulated wisdom. In this case, the other "professionals" are other parents of disabled children who have gone through the experience before you. Look around you, and you'll find them. You'll meet them in a support group or parents' association that you can get in touch with through your child's school or early intervention program, or one of the many national or local organizations on disabilities (see the list starting on page 521).

The sense of empowerment, of deep mutual understanding, that another parent can offer you is unequaled. It's one thing to get advice from a counselor or developmental expert, which is indeed useful, and another to see how someone has put it into practice. You'll be able to ask or answer questions, share experiences, agree or disagree, as a peer. Through other parents' eyes, you'll also learn how to better appreciate your child with his special needs and special gifts. (He certainly has many!) And breaking your isolation, you'll be able to normalize your life more quickly.

A new place that's developing right now around us, where hundreds of parents reach out to other parents, is cyberspace. The families of children with special needs, organized in support groups, as well as all the major national organizations for the disabled, have claimed for themselves a chunk of the Internet (you will find a list of a few Web addresses starting on page 521). If you are not familiar with this world, you should ask a friend or colleague to help you get acquainted with it. Another possibility is to ask at the local public library if they offer workshops or demonstrations on how to access the Internet and search the World Wide Web. Alternatively, you can borrow or buy one of the popular reference books for beginners, like *The Internet for Dummies* (IDG Books Worldwide), *10 Minute Guide to the Internet and World Wide Web* (Que Corp.), or *The ABCs of the Internet* (Sybex).

You'll be surprised by the vast and rich human network that's living and developing online. Chat groups and e-mail discussion lists allow you to "listen" to parents like you freely describing their daily joys and battles to each other. You can participate in discussions, sending your own messages, or just be a silent reader. Many families, and children with disabilities, have created their own personal Web sites, where they post pictures and notes, to share their experiences with anybody who's interested. Emotional support, guidance, and valuable information can be only a few seconds away, just by touching a few keys on a computer, connected to a modem and an Internet server. If you don't have one, it may be a good investment to make now, for you and your child.

FROM SEEKERSHIP TO NORMALIZATION

Many parents become excellent advocates for their children, thanks to other families' support and suggestions, and their own efforts. Your goal should be to learn as much as possible about your child's condition, finding out about existing medical treatments, the effectiveness of developmental interventions and therapies, and any available educational and financial help.

Today, thanks to early intervention programs, developmental and educational support for infants and young children is usually readily available, right after, or even before they have been diagnosed with a disability. (You can read more about early intervention on page 442). But despite the fact that legislation has also aimed to secure free and appropriate public education for older children with disabilities, parents may still face some difficulties during the preschool and school years. Inappropriate settings, lack of qualified staff for special education and health services, and inadequate transportation can still create challenges for families, particularly if they live in an underserved or rural area. As a result, it is extremely important for parents to be well informed and persistent in claiming their child's right to get help to grow to his maximum potential.

In other words, you should be a squeaky wheel, and never take no for an answer, if it means getting your child the help he needs. That doesn't mean you should become unnecessarily confrontational or aggressive, since the school and public health officials you'll have to deal with are not your enemies, and are often the route to what you want. But since some of them may not be as forthcoming as they should be, you had better be prepared to find a way around them, talking to their supervisors, and making your voice clearly heard.

Many parents and experts offer advice on establishing fulfilling lives for you and your child, and a normal routine for your family. Try to switch off your worries about your child's delays or limitations when you're with him, to really play and relax together. Learn how to praise him frequently, but without exaggerating, as you would any other child. As much as possible, apply the same rules and discipline to him that you expect from your other children. Set challenging goals for him, avoiding overprotectiveness or overindulgence, so he can truly do his best.

Keep in mind that kids with disabilities, like all children, don't have fixed skills, but need to be exposed to activities, and helped to master them, in order to move forward. Much of what any child can accomplish will depend on his education, the expectations he's trying to live up to, and the resources at his disposal. No one is born knowing how to swim, or read, or use the toilet, or act politely. These come with education, and a lot of hard work and practice. So, you should nurture and educate your child as you would any child (although sometimes with different techniques), so that you can recognize his potential and help him reach it.

Talk to your child openly about his condition, as soon as he can understand it, so he can accept himself without embarrassment. Let him mingle with other children, with and without disabilities, to help him be comfortable in both spheres and get the best educational opportunities—without denying the limitations that go along with his disability, or implying that other children with disabilities are less desirable friends. Thanks to your efforts, along with early intervention and special education, you should see your baby make progress, and develop into a happy, well-adjusted child. That will give you an incredible sense of accomplishment: the most significant reward you could ever get. You'll soon realize that you too can be a proud and happy parent. And that your family's life can be wonderful.

Darling's studies indicate that the vast majority of families with a disabled child adapt well to the demands of their situation, and some even seem to function better in some ways than before. Most parents say they feel that their other children have not been negatively affected by a sibling with special needs. On the contrary, many say that they have seen their children becoming more responsible, aware, and compassionate, often assuming the role of protectors and defenders of their special brother or sister, and taking over caregiving tasks without complaining. Parents often find that they have become better people, and achieve a sense of growth and mastery through their experience. Many couples are rewarded with a deeper, more fulfilling relationship, after going through this experience together.

But in some situations, a mother and father can get entangled in their different emotional reactions, particularly in the stage of anomie, or become so busy dealing with seekership, that they grow apart. Often, these couples were already troubled before the birth of a special child. Awareness of possible marital problems, extra efforts to keep communication alive, and, if needed, prompt marital counseling, can help you address difficulties at the first sign, overcome them when possible, and make your bond stronger.

HOW FORMER PREEMIES WITH DISABILITIES VIEW THEIR LIVES

When parents of a child with special needs realize they have overcome their own acute sense of loss, and are enjoying life again, they still have wrenching doubts about their child's future. "The world can be cruel." "How will he feel when his friends begin to date?" "Will he be miserable that he can't do sports?" In early childhood, parents can provide reassurance, encouragement, protection. But what about later, in adolescence, when peers become so important in shaping a child's self-image?

An encouraging answer comes from a landmark study conducted by a pediatrician in Canada, looking at how former preemies judged their quality of life at adolescence. One hundred and forty-nine former preemies—83% of all premature babies with a birth weight under 1,000 grams born between 1977 and 1982 in central west Ontario—were interviewed when they were 12 to 16 years old. In addition, parents of nine severely impaired teenagers gave responses for them. Due to their extreme prematurity, more than a quarter of the interviewed adolescents had some serious impairment, like cerebral palsy, mental retardation, blindness, or deafness. Yet—to the surprise of the researchers and the public—the vast majority of these young people, including those with disabilities, thought their lives were very good, and certainly worth living. As a matter of fact, their ratings of their "quality of life" were similar to those of a group of full term-born adolescents of comparable age and socioeconomic background, none of whom had disabilities.

This research study—published by one of the major U.S. medical journals, and praised for its design—is particularly meaningful because, for the first time, former preemies are speaking for themselves. How heartening and encouraging it is to learn that they have a much more positive perspective on their lives than society, health professionals, and even some of their parents may have. When reporting on these findings, one newspaper told the story of a former preemie who was in the study: a sixteen-year-old girl who weighed 640 grams at birth. She is blind. But she can play the flute (and hopes to be a professional musician), is a downhill skier, and rides a tandem bicycle. The portrait is that of a vibrant, spirited, proud young woman, who is in love with life.

Of course, we must ask: Is it possible that some of the children with disabilities in this study were hiding their true feelings, out of defensiveness? While that cannot be completely ruled out, the evidence doesn't support it. Other research on adolescents with disabilities has found their self-worth and quality of life ratings to be high, too. The authors of the Canadian study pointed out that these children, and their parents, should get credit for how well they learned to cope with their disabilities. That may be the most important message coming from this research.

You are a mirror for your child. The way you see him will mightily shape his body image and sense of self. That is why you shouldn't deny his disability, try to change it or hide it, but make an effort to accept it, work with it, and even love it, as a part of your child's whole identity. Listen carefully to what so many others like him have to say about their lives—those who know firsthand what it's like to live with a disability. They say their lives are full and good. So, convince yourself that he can be happy, and that he will be able to fulfill his dreams. That, after all, is what really matters.

Part IV

OTHER CONSIDERATIONS

10

Losing a Baby

▶ *Helping you deal with a profound grief, and guiding you through the necessary arrangements.*

INTRODUCTION   484

QUESTIONS AND ANSWERS
  *When You Lose Your Baby: A Parent's
    Grief*   484
  Dying at Home or in the Hospital   487
  Naming and Birth Announcements   488
  Funeral   489
  Blessings and Benedictions   490
  Donating Organs and Breast Milk   491
  Autopsy   492

  How to Help Older Siblings   493
  *As They Grow: A Child's Understanding
    of Death*   495

MULTIPLES
  Loss of One Twin   496
  The Effect on Your Surviving Twin   498

IN DEPTH
  Making the Hardest Decisions   498

Introduction: Losing a Baby

Of all of the issues we cover in this book, this is the one for which words are most inadequate. Facing the loss of a child shatters all of a parent's expectations of how birth, and life, are supposed to go. You may feel shaken to your core right now, struggling to get your emotional bearings and keep going.

In this chapter, you can find some answers and guidance to help you deal with some of the questions, feelings, issues, and choices you are now confronting, many of which you may never have thought about before. Some parts of this chapter may be useful to you now, and others you may want to come back to, as time passes, and you find that new feelings and questions come to the surface.

While everyone must make his or her own way through this intensely personal experience, we hope that reading this will help you feel a little less lost, and a little less alone.

Questions and Answers

WHEN YOU LOSE YOUR BABY: A PARENT'S GRIEF

Nothing hurts like the loss of a child. Maybe the observation that comes closest to expressing what it means to a parent is that when your child dies, part of you dies, also. You can never "get over it," or go back to what you were. To be sure, you will eventually recover from the grief, in the sense that you will become happy, and work and play normally again. But you will never forget the part of you, your child, who should have been with you.

Infants die so infrequently in our society that most parents have no role models for what they are expected to feel or do. Many wonder whether the excruciating pain they are feeling is abnormal, since they knew their child so briefly. Because someone who hasn't lost a baby themselves cannot truly imagine what you are feeling, friends and family don't know how to react, and may say the wrong things. Another reason a parent's grieving over a newborn child is lonely is that hardly anybody knew and loved your baby but you. While everybody else will soon forget his importance to you, you will still be aching to hold him in your arms.

HOW YOU MAY FEEL IN THE INITIAL, ACUTE PHASE OF GRIEF

Grieving for your baby may involve more intense and longlasting feelings than you expected. Try to remember that while grief is painful to live through, psychologists say it is healthy and necessary: only by facing your feelings, and expressing them, will you be able to heal your wound and adjust to your loss.

Grieving is as individual as people are. A lot has been written on the typical stages and nature of grief, but remember that nobody's feelings follow a fixed formula or neat progression. More likely, you will have good days and bad days, good moments and bad moments—and you may feel a vast range of emotions at the same time.

Many bereaved parents have both emotional and physical symptoms. Physical symptoms may include: extreme fatigue; pain, nausea, or a feeling of emptiness in your stomach; loss of appetite; headaches; heaviness in your chest with rapid or deep breathing; difficulty sleeping; and sleeping all day or not wanting to get out of bed. Some mothers even say their arms ache (as though they are aching for the baby they want to hold). You may cry a lot, or you may cry a little. This doesn't indicate how much you're suffering inside, but how much you're openly releasing your pain.

Emotionally, you may feel: depression; numbness; helplessness or fear; anger at yourself, your doctors, or even your baby; emptiness and longing; disbelief that this really happened; and guilt. Be assured that most grieving parents feel guilty—for things they did or didn't do, during the pregnancy or their baby's life, that might have made him healthier or happier. The instinctive drive to protect one's child is so strong that many bereaved parents feel an underlying sense that they failed their child—even if protecting him would have required miracles. Always remember that no parent is perfect, and whether our children live a short time or a long time, we all do some things we're proud of, and some things we aren't. Try to ban yourself from thinking the inevitable "if only" thoughts, because they are unfair and harmful.

You may find that you can't concentrate, and are uninterested in things you spent time on be-fore. You may spend tremendous amounts of time replaying every detail of your baby's life in your mind. You may feel like you are in a trance-like state, invisible to the people around you, because they cannot see your pain. You may wonder how the world around you can be going on as if everything were normal.

With all of these disturbing reactions, it's common for mothers and fathers who have lost a child to wonder, at some point, whether they might be going crazy. You aren't. Your baby has died. You are experiencing one of the greatest losses that anyone can, and grief is a lot more complicated than mere sadness.

Even if what you are going through is normal, however, you may find it a comfort to get professional counseling. Your obstetrician or hospital's social worker may be able to recommend a psychologist or family counselor who specializes in grief. There are also support groups especially for parents who have lost babies (a couple are listed on page 528), where it can be a relief to talk to people who really understand what you are going through. Some hold meetings, while others bring parents together by telephone or on the Internet.

You should definitely seek professional help if serious marital strains arise, you have persistent thoughts about committing suicide, you are doing things that are harmful to yourself (including overusing alcohol or drugs), or if, after several weeks, you are still having trouble sleeping, aren't eating much, or can't carry out normal, daily activities.

As Time Passes

When can you expect to start feeling better? Thankfully, as with a physical injury, the most acute, searing pain may ease fairly soon. But most people find that the gradual process of healing, and making peace with the loss, takes longer than they expected. Researchers who looked at how bereaved parents were doing two months, and then eight months, after their infant had died found that although mothers' symptoms of depression and anxiety eased a lot, compared to other mothers they still had significantly higher rates of depression and anxiety after eight months. Bereaved fathers had significantly higher levels of depression and anxiety than other fathers two months after the death, but by eight months they had recovered a lot, and that was no longer the case. (It's possible that these fathers still had some other grief symptoms; anxiety and depression were the only ones measured in this study.)

Most parents find that there are ups and downs over the months, when their pain seems to worsen or ease for a while, for no obvious reason. But at some point, whether it's seven months, or one year, or two years, you will adjust to the loss, and realize that it doesn't hurt as much as it did before. Some psychologists say the goal of mourning is to allow you to get to the point when you can remember everything about your baby, from conception through his brief lifetime, but without acute suffering.

Later on, you may find that the weeks leading up to your baby's birthday or the anniversary of his death are hard. Like some parents, you may want to start a tradition of doing something special on these occasions, such as lighting candles, or giving a children's book to your library in your baby's name, or having everyone in the family write a note to your baby.

Because you will be your baby's parent forever, a little portion of your grief may reappear at times, for the rest of your life, when something provokes a memory. But this "shadow grief" won't be debilitating. In fact, many parents feel that far from being diminished by their loss, they've become better people—more sensitive, to both the riches of life and the suffering of others—and stronger than they ever expected.

THE IMPACT ON A MARRIAGE

It's important for you to know that the death of a baby can be very tough on a marriage. More than half of all couples who lose a child get divorced within a few years.

One reason that grieving doesn't always draw partners closer together is that there is something inherently lonely about it. Even when you are mourning the same person, your suffering can't really be shared. Each partner has to deal with his own acutely personal feelings. Each is unable to alleviate the other's pain. Another reason is that a couple may be so weary from grief that they forget to be nurturing to each other.

Men and women also tend to grieve differently—often without awareness or respect for the differences. It goes without saying that no two men or women are the same. But in general, it has been observed that fathers tend to cope with grief by keeping busy. They may throw themselves into physical activities, work, or hobbies that distract them from the pain. Mothers are more likely to cope by talking about the loss, reading books about grief, seeking out support groups, and going back over every memory and question about their baby in their mind. Fathers are frequently more logical, mothers more intuitive and emotional. This can easily result in a woman's doubting her partner's love for their child, or feeling like her partner is bullying her to get over the loss. Or, in a man's complaining that his partner is running away from life.

Sexual tensions also can arise, if one partner wants the comfort and closeness of making love, while the other feels guilty about seeking pleasure at a time of sadness, or associates it with memories of creating the baby who died.

Just by keeping these things in mind, you'll have a better chance of avoiding the strains that build up and divide some couples. Try to respect differences as just differences, not as right or wrong ways of feeling or acting. Try to understand that they don't relate to how much love you or your partner had for your child. Be patient with each other. Above all, when tensions do arise, talk them through openly and as soon as possible, so they don't build up over time.

Dying at Home or in the Hospital

We've been told that our baby does not have long to live, and that he can stay in the hospital or come home with us until then. We're afraid we couldn't bear watching him die at home.

When you can no longer hope that your precious baby will live, being afraid is one of the most natural emotions. Afraid of feeling too much like a mother or father to your baby, and loving him too much when he is going to be stolen away from you. Afraid of not being able to alleviate his suffering. Afraid of your own pain, which is nearly unbearable already, and will become even worse.

If you also feel afraid when the doctor says that you can take your baby home with you, don't think that your initial reaction is strange, or cold-hearted. Just the opposite, it probably reflects the vulnerability that you feel. The important thing, though, is to think this decision over carefully, so you don't look back on this time with regret, feeling that you lost precious opportunities in your fleeting time with your child.

Not many premature babies who are dying can go home with their parents. It is possible only for a baby who has an illness or condition that is incurable, but who can survive for a while, usually several days or more, independent of a ventilator or other intensive care technology. Most often, these are preemies who have genetic or other congenital problems, like severe heart or kidney disease, or brain abnormalities. It may also be possible, for instance, for a premature baby with short gut syndrome (which can result from severe NEC, the intestinal disease that afflicts some preemies), who can live for a week or two on regular feedings at home. If you feel that your baby fits this description and his doctor hasn't asked whether you would like to take him home, make sure to ask whether it is an option. Some hospitals don't think to offer this choice to parents, but may be willing to consider it.

You may fear that caring for your beloved, dying baby at home would open the door to more suffering and pain, just when you are trying desperately to protect yourself against it, and that you simply couldn't handle it. You know yourself and your family best. For some parents, it may truly be the best decision to have their baby cared for in the hospital, with them coming to visit as they have been.

We want to be sure you know, though, that many parents with the same initial concern end up caring for their baby at home with much more confidence than they expected, and are very glad they did it. Most parents find that they treasure the moments of being a mother or father to their baby in the traditional ways, holding him when he cries, wiping his mouth or nose when he needs it, diapering him and scheduling his feedings, and putting him to sleep in his crib or beside them in their bed, as they always had planned. Later, they treasure these memories forever.

Some parents who have older children worry that it would be harmful to them to have the baby at home. Research has shown, though, that it may actually help children to spend time with their sick sibling. In one study of terminally ill children with cancer, children whose siblings died at home seemed to show less fear and to adjust better to the loss, than those whose siblings spent their last days in the hospital, out of view.

Your baby's doctor and nurses will teach you how to care for your baby, and what to do as his health worsens. Ask whether your baby is likely to be in any pain or discomfort, and what you should do to keep him as comfortable as he would be in the hospital. Many babies, with certain health conditions, won't suffer. But if there is a chance that your baby will, the NICU may arrange for a hospice nurse, whose expertise is in pain control and other comfort measures for dying patients, to come and help you. Or they may teach you to give your baby drops of oral morphine when he needs it. Of course, if you are ever concerned that your baby is suffering, you can always bring him back to the hospital.

If you are specifically worried about the last moments, and afraid for your baby to die at home alone with you, you can arrange with your family doctor or a hospice nurse to come to your house and be with you at the end (ask your hospital's social worker or your neonatol-ogist to help you with these arrangements), or you can take him back to the hospital at the end. (You shouldn't call 911, though, because the emergency medical team may have to try to resuscitate him, even though you don't want them to do that.) If you take him to the emergency room, tell the staff right away that your baby is there for comfort care, not to be resuscitated. Your neonatologist or family doctor can call your local emergency room in advance, so that they'll know to expect you.

No matter which choice you make, whether your baby stays in the hospital or comes home with you, nothing can take away your pain. The question to ask yourself is whether one course of action will bring you more peace.

Naming and Birth Announcements

We don't know what to do about naming our daughter, who lived so briefly. Should we give her our favorite girl's name, as we had planned? Should we send out birth announcements?

True, your daughter lived briefly. But in your memory, she is going to be alive for as long as you are, always your child. A decade from now, if you have two other children, and someone asks you how many children you have, you will find that you think, "I have three children. One died ten years ago."

For that reason, it is very important to name your baby, and to consider giving her the name that you always intended. You will think of her by her name, you will talk to friends about her life and death using her name, and you will talk with your partner or other children about her place in your family using her name. You will want it to be a very beautiful name, to represent the profound feelings you have for her.

While there is no set tradition on whether to send out birth announcements, from personal experience we can say that you'll be happy if you give your cherished baby this recognition, also. Experts on grieving say that parents of babies who die often feel extremely lonely in their grief, since there were so few people who knew, and remember, their child. A birth announcement is one way of including other people in your baby's life and death. It can be very simple, giving your baby's name, birth date, death date, and some expression of your feelings. Your friends and family will probably be deeply moved by your open demonstration of love and loyalty to your child.

'A name and a birth announcement are among the few things you had time to give to your baby. If you had only had the chance, you would have given her so much more.

Funeral

Our baby was so young, and our friends and family never even got to meet her. Is a funeral really appropriate?

When you lose a baby, you learn that there is no greater trauma than the loss of a child, whether tiny or big, young or old. Love can't be calculated on the basis of ounces or years.

For a long time, it was thought that parents would recover fastest if all signs and memories of their infant were erased as quickly as possible. But now experts understand that parents don't forget their baby, and never put the loss "behind" them. They recommend strongly that parents attend to their grief, and express it. In the long run, it will be important for you to feel satisfied with the way your baby's death was recognized, and by the way you said goodbye.

In the initial devastation or numbness of your grief, it is easy to decide that it is too difficult, or too costly, to make funeral arrangements. Or that a formal service isn't necessary, and there are many, different ways to say goodbye. That's true, but many parents do feel later that a funeral or memorial service was an important element. It can be as big, or as small and private, as you wish. You can introduce your baby to your family and friends, or just have your immediate family send off your darling child with love. If you start by talking to your clergyman or the hospital's social worker, you'll discover that it really isn't so hard to arrange, and can be done inexpensively. If you're a member of a religious congregation, your church or synagogue may even make many of the arrangements for you.

To help you decide whether to have a funeral and burial, a funeral and cremation, or a memorial service alone, here are some things to consider:

✳ *Burial.* Think about where you want to bury your baby. Remember that if you bury her where you live now, and move away later, it may be very hard to leave her. There is a wide range of cost among cemeteries. You can choose one for its location, or beauty, or because some of your family members are buried there. If cost is a concern, many religious denominations have low-cost or free cemeteries, and some hospitals will bury a baby with no charge. Your nursery's social worker may have a list of options in your region, or be able to help you locate them. Be sure to ask whether your baby would be buried in a common or an individual grave, and whether you'll be able to visit her, and put a marker where she is buried.

Unless the hospital is handling the burial, you will need a funeral home. If you don't know of one, you can ask the social worker or your clergyman to suggest one, or you can find one in the Yellow Pages. Many funeral directors are extremely considerate of parents who have lost babies. Some even provide funeral services for babies free of charge, or for much less than their normal fees. If you find a funeral director unpleasant, or if he is quoting prices that are high for you, don't hesitate to call another one.

One possibility is to ask the funeral home to handle everything for you (they will pick up your baby's body at the hospital, take it to the funeral home, prepare her body and lay her in the casket you choose, and manage the burial). But if that is too expensive, or you simply want to be more involved, you can take over some of these tasks. Some parents take their baby's body from the hospital to the funeral home. If you want to do that, make sure to ask the social worker whether you need to take along a special permit or certificate of death. Some parents even build their own little caskets, or ask a friend who does woodworking to do it for them.

❋ *Cremation.* Some parents are drawn to cremation's sense of finality, and it is generally much less expensive than burial. Most of the time, all of the arrangements and the cremation are handled by a funeral home. (Just as with burial, you can be the ones to take your baby's body to the funeral home if you prefer.) Think about where you would like to place the ashes. You may want to buy a special urn from the funeral home, or bring in a pretty container from home, and keep it at the funeral home, at home or buried in a special place. Or you may prefer to scatter the ashes in a place that is meaningful to you, or beautiful and peaceful for your baby.

Some hospitals offer cremation at no charge to parents, but you should find out be-

forehand whether you will be given your baby's ashes. If not, take into consideration that many parents say they're sorry if they don't have a specific place to go to visit their deceased baby—on her birthday, holidays, or whenever they feel the need.

❋ *The service.* A service can be a funeral, which is performed with the burial or cremation, usually at the funeral home or gravesite. Or it can be a simple memorial service, separate from the arrangements you make for your baby's body. Your baby's funeral or memorial service can take any form you wish: it can follow religious traditions and be directed by a clergyman, or it can be one that you adapt or

---

Blessings and Benedictions

For some parents, it is important to bless or baptize their baby in the hospital, before she dies. NICUs are used to doing this, and you shouldn't hesitate to ask. A small service can be held right in the nursery, by the hospital chaplain or your own clergyman. In most nurseries, parents are able to bring some close friends and family members for the service, as long as the nursery doesn't become too crowded. Often, a screen or a curtain can be put up, so you can have some privacy during the service. This expression of spirituality and love can be very meaningful for a family whose child is dying and, if you want to include them, for the doctors and nurses taking care of your baby. Just talk to your baby's doctor or nurse, or the social worker, to make the arrangements.

create yourself, and have directed by your clergyman, a friend, family member, or you and your partner.

You shouldn't feel inhibited about incorporating some loving, parental touches. This is your baby, and you still have the same need that any mother or father has to take care of your child. Some parents bury their baby with a blankie, a family photograph, a stuffed animal, or a toy. Some drape a quilt over the coffin. You could dress your baby in a special outfit that you had waiting for her, but she never got the chance to wear. Instead of flowers, you can ask your family and friends to bring stuffed animals, toys, or balloons that your baby would have loved.

There's no right or wrong, of course. With all of these choices, it's a matter of what feels right to you. If at all possible, both you and your partner should be involved in planning your baby's goodbye, so that neither regrets the choices that were made.

Donating Organs and Breast Milk

We want to give something of our baby, so she can live on in some way and do some good. What can we do?

Nothing can make up for the loss of your lovely baby, but some parents hope that their child can leave a legacy that lives on, or gives some other sick child a better chance in life.

If you would like to donate your baby's organs, you should know that unfortunately, this is rarely an option for parents of premature babies. Organ donation, which is subject to strict guidelines, is possible only when someone dies in a way that is unusual for preemies—when brain death occurs, but the body's other organs are still functioning normally. Occasion-

ally, a baby who is not eligible to donate organs is able to donate corneas or other tissues. But there are age and weight requirements, which rule out most premature babies who die soon after birth. However, if you are interested in making this extraordinarily generous gift, you should certainly ask your baby's doctor about it. She will know whether your baby is eligible.

There is another valuable donation you may be able to make: the breast milk that your body made for your baby. All preemies get health benefits from being fed breast milk. For some, whose health is particularly fragile, it can be an especially important advantage. But not all mothers of premature babies are able to provide it for their own children, so there are breast milk banks that collect breast milk from mothers of preemies who can spare it, and send it to premature babies who need it. (As you can read on page 125, milk produced by mothers of preemies is different from milk produced by mothers of full-term babies.)

If you have been pumping already, the easiest thing to do is to tell your nurse not to throw away the breast milk that you had stored for your baby. Then, you or someone from the NICU staff can contact the closest breast milk bank, and make arrangements to send them your milk. If your nursery staff does not know of the nearest milk bank, you can find out by calling the Human Milk Banking Association of North America at (919) 350–8599. Some mothers whose babies have died even continue to pump their breasts for several days or weeks longer, to send as much milk as possible to the breast milk bank. They say this helps them as they grieve, and assures them that something good is coming out of their tragedy. Since breast milk banks sometimes run short of milk for preemies who need it, your milk would be a very precious gift.

Autopsy

Our baby just died, and we've been asked whether we want to have an autopsy done. Why would we do that?

The last thing you're ready for now is decisions, yet a few of them have to be made. Whether or not to have an autopsy needs to be decided quickly, because an autopsy must be performed within a day or two of your baby's death in order to provide the fullest answers.

Usually, parents are asked whether they want an autopsy if there is uncertainty about the cause of their baby's death. Some hospitals have a policy that parents are always asked. In a few situations, an autopsy may even be legally required, such as when there was no doctor or nurse attending to the baby, and her death was sudden and unexpected. (This might arise, for example, if your baby died unexpectedly at home.) Even if the doctor doesn't mention it, parents always have the right to request an autopsy.

You may have been told that one reason for an autopsy is to help medical science and future preemies, by clarifying the exact cause of your baby's death and helping doctors learn more about how to prevent it in the future. That's true. But what matters more, at this terribly painful time for you, is whether an autopsy would be emotionally helpful or hurtful to you. Some doctors recommend autopsies because they find that for many parents, questions tend to surface a few weeks or months after their infant's death. If there are questions in your mind as to why your baby died, whether it was preventable by the doctors, or whether you were in any way to blame, the answers provided by an autopsy might provide you with peace of mind. While the reassurance or answers won't alleviate your grief—because nothing can—they may allow you to grieve without unnecessary, extra doubts or guilt. You should also consider, with your doctor's help, whether you might want the information for future pregnancies, to know whether this might happen again.

On the other hand, you may find the idea of subjecting your innocent baby to an internal examination to be disturbing, or even inconceivable. For you, the additional information isn't worth it. Be assured that many parents skip an autopsy and never regret it.

Autopsies are usually done at the hospital by a staff pathologist. If your hospital doesn't have a pathologist who does autopsies, it will be done elsewhere. (Ask about this, since you'll want to know exactly where your baby is.) Incisions are required, so the pathologist can carefully examine the internal organs and tissues, but they can be completely covered by your baby's clothing, or a blanket, later. If you want to impose some limits on the autopsy, you may be able to do that. For example, some parents request that only their baby's lungs be examined, or that no incisions be made in his head. If you are told you can place limits on the autopsy, make sure that they are written on the autopsy permit before you sign it.

Generally, preliminary results are available within a week. The full report, including the results of lab tests, may not be ready until several weeks later. Once it is, parents usually meet with their baby's doctors to discuss the findings. You may find it helpful to make a list of your unanswered questions beforehand, so you're less likely to forget any. But if more questions come to mind as you reflect on the meeting later, you can call the doctor again at that point. Charges for an autopsy vary, so you'll need to ask about your hospital's policies. Many hospitals don't charge parents at all for the cost of a baby's autopsy.

As with many decisions surrounding your

baby's death, there is often no right or wrong answer on whether to do an autopsy—just the answer with which you feel most comfortable.

How to Help Older Siblings

We can't tell how our older daughter is reacting to our baby's death. We don't know how much to involve her, or what to say to her about it.

It can be hard for parents to tell how their other children are feeling about their baby's death. Often, a young child doesn't react initially when told about a death in the family, and doesn't show obvious grief. It is widely accepted, though, that children do grieve, sometimes deeply, but in their own, childlike way—a different way than yours.

Until the age of around seven or so, most children don't understand that death is permanent, and keep wondering when the baby will come back. But every child, no matter how young, can sense when something is wrong in her family, and has strong feelings—such as fear, guilt, anger, and sadness—in response. If, because of your own suffering, you are withdrawn, either physically or emotionally, your child is going to be dealing with a serious secondary loss: the temporary loss of her mother or father.

Don't expect your child to be able to verbalize her feelings. It may be too scary for her even to try. Your child's grieving will be expressed mainly through her behavior and the questions she asks. (You'll probably be struck by the directness and honesty with which your child discusses death. Parents often find it healthy and refreshing—although at first it can seem inappropriate, by adult standards.)

Every child is going to react to death and grief in her own, individual way, partly depending on her age and temperament, and partly on other factors, like how much time she spent with the baby, and how the rest of the family is grieving. Adults usually mourn a loved one from one to two years, with the most intense grief reactions occurring in the first two months. Although it hasn't been well-researched, children who lose baby brothers or sisters are thought to grieve on a similar time frame.

Here are some typical responses that you should be prepared for:

❋ *Fear.* Probably the most frequent and powerful feeling for a child when there is a death in her family is fear. These questions loom: "Who is going to die next?" "Who will take care of me if my parents die?" "Where will I go if I die?"

You can help your child by helping her to understand why your baby died, and reassuring her that you and she are not going to die for a long, long time. You can tell her that most people die when they are very old, or very sick. In explaining your baby's death, use truthful language that is simple enough for her to understand. To a young child, you might say: "He was born too soon, so he was too small," or "He was born too soon, and so he became very sick." A slightly older child may understand: "His lungs were not ready to breathe yet." Answer all of your child's questions honestly and directly, but with explanations that do not provide unnecessary or complex information. Be prepared for her to ask them, and for you to answer them, again and again.

As you do, don't forget that children generalize from specifics. For example, if you say that your baby died because he was sick, your child may think that people die every time they get sick. Point out the huge difference between everyday sickness and a severe illness that won't get better, and remind her of this distinction repeatedly.

Don't assume that it will be easier on your child if you resort to fairy-tale descriptions of death. To the contrary, they almost always cause increased fear. For example, if you say, "Our baby went to sleep forever," your child may become afraid of going to bed at night. If you say, "Our baby went away on a long, long trip," your child may become afraid whenever you leave her.

* *Guilt.* Many children, unable to fully understand what happened, feel guilty when there is a death in their family. They worry: "Did I cause the death?" "Did I make him sick?" "Are my parents upset because of me?" Your child may be especially worried because of the jealousy and anger she felt when you were in the hospital visiting your baby.

Even if your child doesn't verbalize those doubts, it's safe to assume that she has them, and important to address them. Reassure her that there was nothing she did or thought that made the baby sick, and nothing that anybody could do to save the baby. Make sure you tell her that you are distraught because the baby died, not because of something she did.

* *Behavior problems.* It's common for children to have some sort of behavior problems when a sibling dies. Misbehaving may be a way of getting your attention, which they've been craving while you've been remote and distracted by your grief. Regressive behavior, such as bed wetting, thumb sucking, or baby talk, may be a way of asking for reassurance, by having you care for them the way you did when they were smaller.

Sometimes, just giving your older child more attention can make a difference, by boosting her sense of security. If you're finding it too hard to talk and play as much as usual, make a point of holding your child more, and communicating through touch.

* *Taking on too much responsibility.* Some children think it's up to them to resolve this family crisis. They may think that if they're perfectly well-behaved the trouble will go away, or they may search for a way to alleviate your pain. One of our small children concocted a plan to bring the baby back from heaven by climbing a tall ladder, then boarding a jumbo jet for a flight from the top step. She would eagerly look at her mother and ask, "That's what I'll do. Then you won't be sad anymore?" If you have older children, they may even take upon themselves the responsibility to keep the household running, or offer their shoulder for you to lean on. Small gestures of this kind are giving and appropriate, but they shouldn't go too far.

For a child to parent her parents, or to feel that she needs to be a superachiever, is a heavy burden. Try to relieve your child of it by reassuring her that you love her no matter whether she's naughty or nice, that she doesn't have to do anything special, because she already helps make you happier just by being herself, and that although you're sad now, you won't be forever.

In general, be prepared for the fact that a child's grief behavior is different from an adult's. A child is likely to spend almost all of her time acting as if nothing had changed, and then for no apparent reason, become contemplative or sad. She may try to lose herself in noisy, active games. She may use imaginative play to work through what happened, pretending that her stuffed animals die, or playing dead herself. At moments when she can't handle your feelings or her own, she may transform the scene into

As They Grow: A Child's Understanding of Death

Your children's ages will largely determine how they understand death, but there are variations, based on a child's experience, religious training, and family's beliefs. Here are some general guidelines.

* *Children under four:* Most children under four have no real understanding of death. They do, however, absorb the pain of others around them. Three- and four-year-olds may think of death as a temporary condition that is reversible, or as a similar way of living, but in another place. They also may believe that their feelings or actions can cause death.
* *Four to seven:* Many children of this age are able to understand some of the biological aspects of death: the absence of breathing, heartbeat, seeing, or thinking. They are also better able to talk about death. Some, by six or seven years of age, understand that death is permanent, but others continue to think of it as reversible. They may

also still think that a death in their family is a punishment, or their fault. Preschoolers often fear that death is "catching," and may need to be reassured that no one else is going to die.
* *Seven to eleven:* Over these years, children generally make the transition to a more adult understanding of death. They become interested in what happens to the body after death, and may be fascinated by bodily mutilation, graveyards, and coffins. They are also concerned with how their world may change, because their sibling died.
* *Twelve and older:* By this age, most children can think abstractly and have an adult understanding of death. They may be less revealing of their own feelings and reactions, though. During their teenage years, children are apt to start searching for meanings, and to want to explore religious or philosophical interpretations of death.

something more familiar by, say, giggling foolishly at silly things, or misbehaving.

Most experts agree that parents should not try to shield children from the fact that their sibling died, or from the mourning rituals and grief that follow. If there is a lot of tension and sorrow in the family, but no one is explaining it to them, it can be a lot more frightening than if they are included.

Try to take cues from your child on how much to talk about your baby's death. Most psychologists suggest that if your child is seven years or older, you should allow and even en-

courage (but never force) her to go to the baby's funeral. Make sure to explain what will happen in advance, so she knows what to expect. If your child is younger, you'll be the best judge. If you don't want her to be present at the funeral, partly because your own reaction may be upsetting to her, try to include her in other ways—by having her attend some other service for the baby, or devising a way for her to say her own, personal goodbye. You may want her to choose a toy or draw a picture for the baby to be buried with, something that will mean a little to her now, and a lot in the future.

When you lose a baby, having an older child can be difficult for a while, when you wish that you could grieve for your baby undisturbed. Try not to blame yourself if you aren't the best mother or father to your older child immedi- ately after your baby's death. That's inevitable, given what you are going through. But as soon as possible, your older child needs your help. She'll also help you, giving you love that lifts your spirits immeasurably.

MULTIPLES

Loss of One Twin

One of our twins died. I feel torn apart, grieving for her while needing to care for her brother.

Although one of your babies has died, you are and always will be the mother of twins. If you had been given the chance to raise both of your twins, you would have had to juggle the time and attention you gave to each of them. Now, you are also faced with juggling, in the deepest, emotional way, as you mourn one of your twins, while trying to be a happy, loving parent to the other.

There is no map that will lead you through this, but some advice may help you decide how to navigate your own, personal way:

❋ *Don't cut short your goodbye to your baby who is dying or has died, or feel that you need to go straightaway to taking care of your surviving twin.* Many parents feel it is important to divide their time equally among their babies, but that's not what you should be concerned about now. Thankfully, you will have time ahead of you to shower your healthier baby with undivided love. With your baby who has died, however, you won't get another chance again. If you don't take all the time you need now to hold her, say goodbye, and grieve— peacefully, to the temporary exclusion of your other baby—you will probably regret it later. Don't feel guilty about giving your surviving twin some loving caresses, and telling him that you'll be back in a day or two. If he is already home with you, ask his grandparents or someone else close to you to help by taking care of him and giving you this much-needed break. Dealing with the pain of having just lost a baby, and giving your surviving baby the happiness and support he deserves, are opposites that are just plain impossible for most people to do at the same time.

❋ *Try not to worry if you feel some resentment or distance from your surviving twin, for a little while.* At first, your surviving twin may seem like a painful reminder of your loss, or even an intruder in the world of your memories and grief. Consciously or not, you may also keep some distance from him because of the fear of losing a loved child again. Don't worry; these feelings are normal. They should start gradually to diminish soon. If you didn't take the time you needed to grieve, apart from your surviving baby, consider doing it now.

When you do start to relax and become more attached to your surviving baby, don't worry, as some people do, that you're being disloyal to your child who died. You can be sure that she will never be out of your thoughts for long. When she is, try to accept the relief, which you badly need. It is said that both laughter and tears are necessary in recovering from grief.

✳ *Be prepared for the ignorant things some people will say.* You can be sure that at least one of your relatives or friends, not knowing any better, will say something foolish that may offend you, such as: "At least you have one baby left" or "Be glad you only have one baby to take care of instead of two." When parents who have lost a twin hear these kinds of statements, they feel that no one understands what they are going through. In fact, studies have consistently shown that parents who lose a twin suffer the same level of grief as parents who lose a singleton. However, they also show that family, friends, and hospital staff sometimes downplay the death of a twin, assuming that a parent's grief would be less. Try to forgive them, and realize that they don't mean to hurt you, they probably just don't have any experience with this. If you are feeling particularly alone, you will find that other bereaved parents best understand your loss, and what you are going through. If you are interested, ask the NICU's social worker about support groups for bereaved parents near you, or see page 528.

✳ *Parents often become extremely attached to their surviving twin, so beware of becoming overprotective.* Many parents develop an extremely close attachment to their surviving twin, never taking any of the wonderful things about him, or their luck in having him, for granted. At the same time, they may find themselves terrified that he will be the next to die, and are unable to shake this feeling even as their child grows older and more robust. Some parents find that it takes two or three years before they finally believe, deep down, that their child is going to survive. These re-

actions are natural. If you feel this way, just beware of overprotecting your child, and discouraging him from exploring the world. Children who are overprotected can become fearful, insecure, and have difficulty with social relationships.

✳ *Expect to feel uneasy, for a while, when people ask you how many children you have.* Since you will certainly be asked, the key is to plan in advance what you feel comfortable saying. At the beginning, you may feel most comfortable including your deceased baby in your count, even though ensuing conversation may lead you to have to explain what happened. As time passes, you may prefer to avoid that subject by including only your surviving children—even though, inside, most parents never reach a point where they feel that is the accurate number.

✳ *Don't feel that you need to remove all traces of your baby who died, but don't make your surviving twin grow up in her shadow.* For some parents, it feels better to remove their deceased baby's furniture and clothes right away, while for others, it seems like they're negating their baby if they do that immediately. Do what feels right to you right now. Just remember that over time, you can let your deceased baby be a natural part of your family and life, one whom everyone in the family knows about and remembers, without being an inescapable presence for your surviving twin. Tell your child about her twin who died as early as possible, never making it a secret. But find a way to keep your celebrations of your surviving twin's birthday joyous, by separating them from your recognition of the anniversary of your baby's death. As time passes, and your pain lessens, it will become easier to rejoice and mourn at the same time.

The Effect on Your Surviving Twin

Many parents wonder whether their surviving baby has a sense that he's alone now when he wasn't before, and whether the loss of his twin will have a psychological effect on him later in life. The answer is that we just don't know. No systematic research has been done on the impact of losing a twin in the womb or in infancy. There are adults whose twin died just before or after birth, who say that they have lingering feelings of sorrow, anger or guilt, and still introduce themselves as twins. There are parents who say that their surviving twin needs an unusual amount of physical closeness, perhaps seeking something that is missing. Some grown-ups even say they have the feeling they lost a twin, but have no proof—just a lifelong sense that someone who should be there, isn't. Of course, there are many perfectly happy and well-adjusted children who seem to have no memory of their early loss. Twin researchers don't dismiss the notion of a lasting impact out of hand, but they do caution that, at this point, there is no reliable evidence to support it.

In Depth

MAKING THE HARDEST DECISIONS

There are some decisions that no parent should ever have to make.

If your baby's outlook is very poor, the time may come when his doctors ask you, or you ask yourself, whether you want to limit or stop his medical treatment: whether it is better and kinder to allow him to die, rather than aggressively trying to keep him alive for as long as possible.

Any parent faced with this question knows the deep, searing pain it causes. You search for the "right" answer, but unfortunately, there isn't one. The doctors are probably telling you that your baby's future is not absolutely certain, and even if it were, no doctor or expert could answer the paramount question: whether living the life your child is expected to have—maybe a short one, or a long one that involves medical struggles and disabilities—will be a good thing for your child or not.

It is amazing to think that not long ago, you and your partner were discussing the color of sheets for the crib, or debating when a child should start daycare. Now, those concerns seem like part of a fairytale world that you no longer inhabit.

It's common for parents to feel overwhelming guilt or shame when they even begin to think about a decision like this. That's because parents have an instinct, virtually hard-wired into them, to save their children's lives. Certainly, in most situations, this is a wonderful, protective reaction. But when one's baby is severely ill, things are more complicated. If all that medical technology can do is to uncomfortably postpone an infant's inevitable death, or to enable a premature baby to survive but with debilitating physical or mental disabilities, parents may be offering the greatest protection to their child by not using it. Try to remember that the guilt you feel is natural, and understandable for the deepest emotional reasons, but it doesn't mean you are doing something wrong.

LOOKING FOR ANSWERS FROM ETHICS AND RELIGION

Doctors, judges, and specialists in medical ethics agree that in this technological era, just because something *can* be done to prolong an infant's life doesn't mean that it *should* be done. The decision whether to use life-sustaining treatment is intensely personal, based on values about what makes life worth living, and what kind of suffering is intolerable. Because a baby cannot speak for himself, his parents have to decide for him.

If you are confronting this decision, you will find that you need to examine your most fundamental values. There are very few people who believe that life is good no matter what. Think of an elderly person who is terminally ill, with unremitting pain; a person with severe brain damage, who is permanently unconscious; a martyr who fights and dies for a noble cause. Most people believe that life is precious because it enables us to "live out" the things we really value—interacting with other people and the world around us, through language and our senses, being able to make plans and work toward our goals, feeling more pleasure than pain, and loving and being loved.

If you, too, believe that life is not always better than death, considering whether to limit medical treatment for your baby is a matter of assessing whether that tragic point has been reached for him. Where the turning point lies is going to be different for different parents. You may believe it has been reached if your baby has little chance of surviving, or if in surviving, he is probably going to be physically or mentally unable to do most of the activities that kids do. Or, you may feel that it doesn't matter whether your child is "normal" by societal standards, as long as he doesn't have to endure repeated medical problems, hospitalizations, and pain. Of course, babies don't always do what they are predicted to do, and a child with a high likelihood of dying or having long-term disabilities still has a chance, even if it's small, of beating the odds. So, some parents may feel that life is worth battling for, at all costs, until they are told that medical care is absolutely futile, and that their baby has no hope of surviving.

Determining where the turning point lies for you is going to take tremendous strength on your part, no matter what your values and choices. You may have to be strong enough to recognize that it has not yet been reached for you, even if it has been for your baby's doctors. Or vice versa: that it has been reached for you, even though the doctors are inclined to do everything possible to keep your baby alive. If you feel that point has been reached for you, you will need to be strong enough to act on your intuition and conviction, and to let go of the person you least want to let go of, your child.

If parents decide to limit their baby's medical treatment, they authorize what is called a Do Not Resuscitate order (you may hear it referred to as a DNR). For a baby who is just being delivered, a DNR means that the doctors will do everything they can to make your baby comfortable, including drying him off, wrapping him in warm blankets, and giving him to you to hold close. But they won't put him on a ventilator, take blood, or put in IV lines. For a baby who is in the intensive care nursery, a DNR may mean withdrawing the medical support your baby is already on (for example, taking him off a ventilator), or taking the slightly lesser step of withholding any further life-sustaining treatment that turns out to be needed (for example, if his breathing weakens, not putting him on a ventilator if he isn't on one, and not giving CPR).

Some parents, and some doctors too, instinctively believe that withdrawing treatment that a baby is already on, such as a ventilator, which may be keeping him alive, is very different from withholding new, additional treatment. They think that not adding treatment is morally justified when a baby is too sick for it to do much good, but that stopping medical treatment that a baby is already receiving would be actively "killing" their baby. It's important for you to know that most experts in medical ethics don't view these options as morally different at all. They explain that parents often think of them in terms of other situations in life, which aren't really comparable. For example, if you are walking across a bridge and the person in front of you falls off and drowns, even if you don't jump in to try to save him you aren't to blame for his death, because you didn't actively cause it. But if you push the person who is walking in front of you off the bridge, you have done something terribly wrong, and you are to blame if he dies.

There are two reasons this analogy doesn't apply in the NICU. First of all, it is your baby's disease, his prematurity, that has "pushed him off the bridge" and will be the cause of his death—not you, no matter what medical treatments you authorize or stop. Second, parents

and doctors are not like innocent bystanders on the bridge, who don't have any responsiblity to jump in after a stranger. Rather, they have special roles and relationships that morally obligate them to help their babies and patients when they're in trouble. But "helping" can mean different things. Sometimes, stopping medical treatment is the most helpful, and continuing it is harmful. Your obligation, and your baby's doctor's, is to figure out what you believe will most help your baby, and to do that.

Some parents who are religious express concern about whether making life and death decisions is taking over God's role. Although you should talk to your clergyman or the hospital chaplain if this is a concern for you, we can assure you that there are many different ways, even within the same faith, that devoutly religious people perceive God's will, and how medicine fits into God's plan. Some people believe that since God gave us medical technology, it is God's plan for us to use it. Others believe that since God gave us not just medical technology, but also the knowledge and experience to recognize when it will work and when it won't, it is God's plan for us to use medicine wisely. One belief is that we should treat premature babies to the very end, because God will take the baby when God is ready. Others think that God's plan will be revealed after a baby is taken off technological support, in whether the baby then lives or dies.

Many religious and nonreligious people alike find comfort and peace in letting nature take its course, rather than fighting something so essential.

One thing many parents worry about is whether it is selfish or inappropriate to consider their family as a whole in making their decision. Raising a child with chronic health problems or disabilities will change parents' and siblings' lives, and involve physical, emotional, and financial burdens. It's possible to imagine these kinds of considerations being selfishly motivated in some cases. But it's also possible to imagine them arising from parents' deep sense of responsibility to all of their children, including their sick one, and a realistic view of the care they are capable of providing to them all. In fact, many theologians have said that Christian moral tradition, for one, requires weighing everyone's needs, and taking the common good, as well as what is good for any one individual, into account.

TIME AND INFORMATION TO HELP YOU MAKE A GOOD DECISION

If it isn't absolutely necessary for you to make a decision immediately, take your time, and make it only when you are ready. Psychologists have noted that parents are less likely to feel regret or guilt about their decision later, if they had good information and time to reflect on their alternatives beforehand.

For many reasons, doctors and nurses are often several steps ahead of parents in believing that the time has come to limit medical treatment. Parents who just gave birth to a premature baby may still be in shock, or filled with an understandable, stubborn hope that they aren't ready to abandon yet. Also, experienced doctors and nurses know many things about a preemie's condition and prospects that are not obvious to parents, who may never have been in this situation before. They know, for instance, that a newborn who weighs only 500 grams and needs 100% oxygen has little chance of surviving for long. Parents have to listen to the unfamiliar information the doctors give them, digest it, and

decide whether they accept it or not. And, of course, time passes very differently when you are contemplating the death of someone you love than when you are a medical professional with more distance.

Unfortunately, bad feelings can arise between parents and the NICU staff when parents are slower to decide to limit treatment. While conflict is the last thing you need right now, be assured that whether you agree with the doctors and nurses or not, both you and they have your baby's best interests at heart.

Before making a decision, make sure you have a clear understanding of what is wrong with your child, what his medical treatment might entail, and what his prospects are with and without treatment, both now and in the future. Many parents find that they're in such a state of shock that they can't absorb or remember much. Don't be embarrassed: the doctors understand this, and it is their role to answer as many questions as you have, as many times as you need to ask them, until you have all the information you need.

You may discover that different doctors and nurses have varying opinions on your baby's condition and future quality of life. Different opinions can be terribly confusing when you are making life and death decisions, but try to listen to them, and to understand that they reflect uncertainty about your baby's future, and what the right path is to take. Getting a better sense of the uncertainties will help you make a better, more realistic decision.

If you and your partner are in conflict about the decision, it may be helpful to talk together to the nursery's social worker or the hospital chaplain. Talk to other people you trust, also. Then, weigh all of the information and views you hear, listening to your own, internal voice. Most hospitals have ethics committees or consultants, who have experience making difficult ethical decisions about medical treatment. Usually, a hospital ethics committee offers only advice, not binding decisions, and can be a resource for you, as well as for the medical staff. You should feel free to ask the chaplain, social worker, or your baby's doctor to set up a meeting for you with the ethics committee at any time, if you think it might help with your decisions.

DECIDING HOW TO SPEND THE REMAINING TIME

If you do decide to limit medical treatment, think about what you want for your baby's precious, remaining minutes, hours, or days. There are still a lot of things to hope for, even if a long life isn't one of them. One thing to hope for is that your baby feels love. Many parents treasure the memories of the time they had together at the end, when they could finally envelop their baby in their arms, free of wires and tubes and beeping monitors, whispering and singing to him, and giving him the blissful feeling of being loved.

You can also hope that your baby feels at peace. Ask whether he has been given medicine to eliminate any pain or discomfort. The medications that most intensive care nurseries use will make him feel comfortable and serene.

The doctors and nurses will want to help with any other requests you have, so be sure to tell them. If you want privacy with your baby, they may have a separate room the two of you can sit in, or will put up a curtain or screen within the nursery. You can tell the nurses whether you would feel most comfortable if they check on your baby frequently, or if you would prefer to have longer periods of time with him alone. Also tell them if you want your baby to remain on a monitor or not (the alarms can be turned off, so you'll have peace and quiet, but you'll see exactly when his heart stops beating). If you cannot leave your hospital room and your baby is being brought to you, you may want to ask that he get breathing assistance until he gets to your room, so he will be sure to feel your arms around him in his last moments.

Both before and after your baby dies, you can hold him, cuddle him, kiss him, rock him, and tell him some of the things you want him to know—about you, his siblings or cousins or grandparents, the places you would have taken him, and, of course, about your everlasting feelings for him. You can ask the nursery staff if there is someone who can take photographs: whether you look at them often or not, you will treasure them, as keepsakes of your baby, later.

Don't be ashamed if you feel afraid of holding your baby while he dies, or afraid of seeing him afterward, thinking that you would rather remember him alive. There are no rules for what you should do, and many other parents have the same feelings. We want you to know, though, that parents who do are usually relieved to find that it is like holding your baby close to you as he falls asleep, or sleeps. The moments together feel peaceful, intimate, and far more natural than you would imagine. And they provide a valuable sense of finality and closure. Some parents spend a few minutes with their baby after he dies, while others want to spend hours. There's almost no limit—just tell your doctor what you want to do, and he'll let you know if it's possible within your hospital's guidelines.

Some hospitals will put together a collection of mementos for you, but if yours doesn't, or there are more things you'd like, don't be embarrassed to ask. Among the things that parents often want, in addition to photographs, are: their baby's blanket, T-shirt, and hat; a lock of hair; a set of footprints and handprints; their baby's I.D. bracelet; the name card from his bed or isolette; a record of their baby's weight and measurements, and any presents or personal items that decorated their baby's bed. Some hospitals give all parents copies of their child's birth certificate or certificate of death, but others don't. Your hospital's social worker can tell you how to get these if you want them.

Always remember that if you feel guilty or have doubts about your decision later, it doesn't mean you made the wrong decision. Parents who decide to stop medical treatment can't help but wonder whether their baby might have beaten the odds and recovered. Parents whose children went on to have problems after they continued treatment can't help but wonder whether they did the right thing for their family and child.

As a parent, you try to make the right decision out of love, and then you revisit it out of love. If you can say that after much soul-searching, you made the best choice you could, you should try to accept your decision, and live with it in peace.

11

I Was a Preemie, Too

▶ *Famous people who were born premature and thrived,*
even before the recent advances in neonatal medicine.

Despite the hurdles that premature babies have to face, there's never been a better time than today to be born before term. Still, prematurity has always been a part of the human experience, and some babies who were born early have always been able to survive. We can find traces of illustrious preemies in historical biographies—some whose prematurity is certain, thanks to precise records, and others for whom it can only be inferred, because an infant was very small, or had some typical complication of prematurity. The list includes some of the most famous names imaginable—scientific and artistic geniuses, great athletes, entertainers and statesmen—all of whom attest to the vastness of a preemie's potential, despite, and sometimes because of, his shortened gestation.

Take a look at the amazingly big footsteps that our children are following in:

Isaac Newton (1642–1727): English natural philosopher and creator of modern physics. According to tradition, a ripe apple falling in Newton's garden led him to discover the law of gravity. He, instead, fell out of his mother's womb too green, small enough, he later said, to fit into a quart mug, and to raise considerable worry for his survival.

Jean-Jacques Rousseau (1712–1778) and **Voltaire,** pseudonym of François Marie Arouet (1694–1778): Two of the most famous French writers and philosophers, they lived at the same time, and had extremely influential but opposing ideas. Voltaire believed that education and reason were what elevated humankind above beasts. The egalitarian Rousseau thought that education was corrupting, separating humans from nature. Both tough characters, they despised each other. Yet, they had something in common: each came into the world as a tiny preemie. Rousseau was born almost dead, Voltaire so sick that he received last rites—and was christened only when he was nine months old.

Johann Wolfgang von Goethe (1749–1832): German poet, dramatist, and novelist, and one of the greatest figures in world literature, Goethe was born prematurely, "a puny waif whose life was despaired of." His birth became the catalyst for instituting better training for midwives in the city of Frankfurt, thanks to Goethe's powerful grandfather, who was mayor at the time.

John Keats (1795–1821): English Romantic poet, widely celebrated for his poetry despite dying young, at the age of 26, of tuberculosis. A premature birth, a short life truncated by a very premature death, Keats was truly a "fair creature of an hour," who nonetheless left a lasting mark with his poems.

Mark Twain, pseudonym of Samuel Clemens (1835–1910): American author and humorist, Twain wrote two masterpieces of American literature, *The Adventures of Tom Sawyer* and *The Adventures of Huckleberry Finn*. Born two months premature, he didn't appear fit to grow up. "A lady came in one day," his mother wrote later, "and said, 'You don't expect to raise that babe do you.' I said I would try. But he was a poor looking object to raise." Still, the night of his birth, Halley's Comet had been seen in the sky, and his family rightly thought it was a good omen.

Winston Churchill (1874–1965): Born of a British lord and an American heiress, Churchill was Great Britain's Prime Minister during World War II. He secured an alliance with the United States and Russia and masterminded the strategy that led to Hitler's defeat. Churchill was born a month and a half early, at his parents' country home, far from London's excellent doctors. "The boy is wonderfully pretty ... very healthy considering his prematurity," his father wrote to his mother-in-law. A born fighter, impetuous and courageous, in his first statement as Prime Minister Churchill would say, "I have nothing to offer but blood, toil, tears and sweat."

Albert Einstein (1879–1955): Discoverer of the theory of relativity, Einstein revolutionized contemporary physics, and became a synonym for human genius. He was a lonely and shy child, who hardly spoke until age three, and was never successful in school. He said: "I sometimes ask myself how it came about that I was the one to develop the theory of relativity. The reason, I think, is that a normal adult never stops to think about problems of space and time. These are things which he has thought about as a child. But my intellectual development was retarded, as a result of which I began to wonder about space and time only when I had already grown up."

Anna Pavlova (1881–1931): Beautiful Russian ballerina Pavlova was the most celebrated dancer of her time, who became famous as the dying swan in a solo that was choreographed for her in the ballet *Swan Lake*. She never became physically strong, despite the wrenching practice required by ballet. "You must realize that your daintiness and fragility are your greatest assets," young Pavlova was admonished by a teacher. And she did, developing rare qualities of expressiveness, delicacy, and fluidity of movement that enchanted audiences.

Willie Shoemaker (1931–): The legend of American jockeys. Shoemaker was born too early and too small, and he didn't grow much afterward, either. But at 4-feet-11 inches and 96 pounds, he used his small size, smarts, and strength to great advantage. In an amazing career of 42 years, Shoemaker won eleven Triple Crown horse races and earned more than $123 million in prize money. It is said that his grandmother put him in a shoebox next to an oven to keep him alive the night he was born.

Stevie Wonder, pseudonym of Steveland Morris (1950–): Hugely successful American soul singer and songwriter, a natural talent and child prodigy who sang and mastered the piano, harmonica, and drums before the age of ten. Wonder was among the thousands of preemies who, in the 1940s and early 1950s, were blinded by ROP (retinopathy of prematurity). Blindness didn't prevent Wonder from doing what all of the kids his age were doing, he once said, and perhaps enhanced his exceptional musical gift. He celebrated life, freedom, love, and his newborn baby, Aisha, with the song "Isn't She Lovely?"

Patrick Bouvier Kennedy (1963): Third child of Jacqueline Bouvier Kennedy and John F. Kennedy, 35th President of the United States. Patrick was born prematurely at 34 weeks of gestation, and died only two days later of RDS (respiratory distress syndrome), one of the most common complications of prematurity. Patrick's brief life had a tremendous impact. The loss of a First Family's baby deeply moved the nation, and led to an outpouring of public and private resources for medical research and special newborn care units. Thanks to that support, and to the many new medical treatments that followed, the lives of today's 34-weekers are not at risk from RDS. Patrick rests in Arlington Cemetery, beside his parents.

The list of alleged premature babies goes on. It includes an emperor, **Napoleon Bonaparte,** and a king, **Farouk** of Egypt; the father of evolution and natural selection, **Charles Darwin**; the French writer **Victor Hugo**; the impressionist painter **Pierre-Auguste Renoir**; and actors and comedians **Joey Bishop, Richard Simmons, Sidney Poitier,** and **Michael J. Fox.**

Who knows how many towering figures are being born among our preemies of today?

APPENDICES

APPENDIX 1

Conversion Charts

HOW MANY POUNDS? HOW MANY GRAMS?

Weight Conversion from Pounds to Grams

	Ounces 0	1	2	3	4	5	6	7	8	9	10	11	12	13	14	15
Lbs. 0	—	28	57	85	113	142	170	198	227	255	283	312	340	369	397	425
1	454	482	510	539	567	595	624	652	680	709	737	765	794	822	850	879
2	907	936	964	992	1021	1049	1077	1106	1134	1162	1191	1219	1247	1276	1304	1332
3	1361	1389	1417	1446	1474	1502	1531	1559	1588	1616	1644	1673	1701	1729	1758	1786
4	1814	1843	1871	1899	1928	1956	1984	2013	2041	2070	2098	2126	2155	2183	2211	2240
5	2268	2296	2325	2353	2381	2410	2438	2466	2495	2523	2551	2580	2608	2637	2665	2693
6	2722	2750	2778	2807	2835	2863	2892	2920	2948	2977	3005	3033	3062	3090	3118	3147
7	3175	3203	3232	3260	3289	3317	3345	3374	3402	3430	3459	3487	3515	3544	3572	3600
8	3629	3657	3685	3714	3742	3770	3799	3827	3856	3884	3912	3941	3969	3997	4026	4054
9	4082	4111	4139	4167	4196	4224	4252	4281	4309	4337	4366	4394	4423	4451	4479	4508
10	4536	4564	4593	4621	4649	4678	4706	4734	4763	4791	4819	4848	4876	4904	4933	4961
11	4990	5018	5046	5075	5103	5131	5160	5188	5216	5245	5273	5301	5330	5358	5386	5415
12	5443	5471	5500	5528	5557	5585	5613	5642	5670	5698	5727	5755	5783	5812	5840	5868
13	5897	5925	5953	5982	6010	6038	6067	6095	6123	6152	6180	6209	6237	6265	6294	6322
14	6350	6379	6407	6435	6464	6492	6520	6549	6577	6605	6634	6662	6690	6719	6747	6776
15	6804	6832	6860	6889	6917	6945	6973	7002	7030	7059	7087	7115	7144	7172	7201	7228

HOW MANY DEGREES FAHRENHEIT?
HOW MANY DEGREES CELSIUS?

Temperature from Fahrenheit to Celsius

To convert from °F to °C: (°F − 32) ÷ 1.8 = °C		To convert from °C to °F: (°C × 1.8) + 32 = °F	
Degrees Fahrenheit	Degrees Celsius	Degrees Fahrenheit	Degrees Celsius
93.2	34.0	101.5	38.6
93.6	34.2	101.8	38.8
93.9	34.4	102.2	39.0
94.3	34.6	102.6	39.2
94.6	34.8	102.9	39.4
95.0	35.0	103.3	39.6
95.4	35.2	103.6	39.8
95.7	35.4	104.0	40.0
96.1	35.6	104.4	40.2
96.4	35.8	104.7	40.4
96.8	36.0	105.2	40.6
97.2	36.2	105.4	40.8
97.5	36.4	105.9	41.0
97.9	36.6	106.1	41.2
98.2	36.8	106.5	41.4
98.6	37.0	106.8	41.6
99.0	37.2	107.2	41.8
99.3	37.4	107.6	42.0
99.7	37.6	108.0	42.2
100.0	37.8	108.3	42.4
100.4	38.0	108.7	42.6
100.8	38.2	109.0	42.8
101.1	38.4	109.4	43.0

APPENDIX 2

Growth Charts

WEIGHT AND GESTATIONAL AGE AT BIRTH

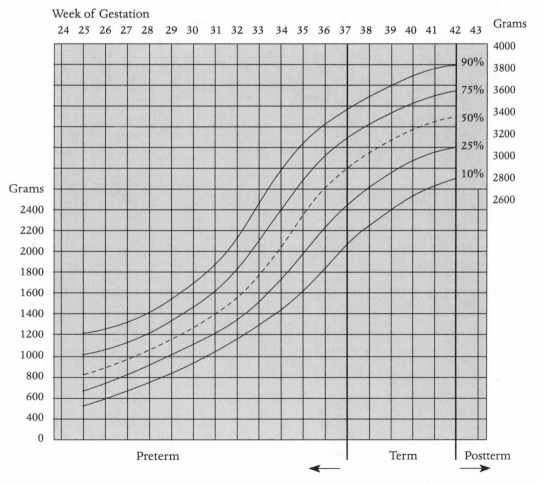

Adapted with permission from Lubchenco LO, Hansman C, and Boyd E: *Pediatrics* 37:403, © American Academy of Pediatrics 1966, and from Battaglia FC and Lubchenco LO: *Journal of Pediatrics* 71:159, © Mosby 1967

GROWTH IN THE WOMB

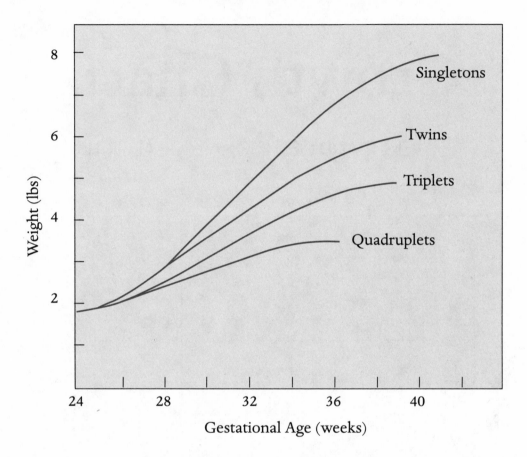

Adapted with permission from McKeown T, Record RG: Observation on foetal growth in multiple pregnancy in man, *Journal of Endocrinology* 8:386, 1952

GROWTH FROM BIRTH TO AGE 3 FOR PREMATURE GIRLS WHO WEIGHED LESS THAN 1,500 GRAMS AT BIRTH

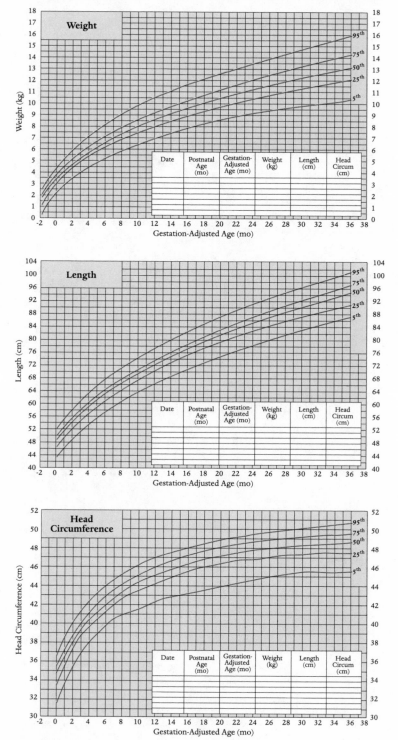

GROWTH FROM BIRTH TO AGE 3 FOR PREMATURE GIRLS WHO WEIGHED 1,500–2,500 GRAMS AT BIRTH

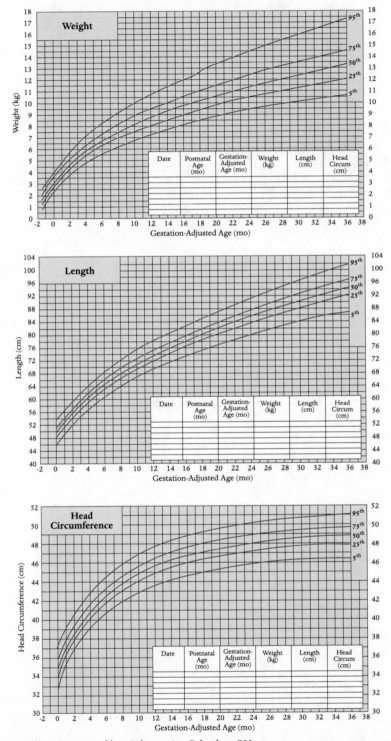

Chart provided by Ross Products Division, Abbott Laboratories, Columbus, OH

GROWTH FROM BIRTH TO AGE 3 FOR PREMATURE BOYS WHO WEIGHED LESS THAN 1,500 GRAMS AT BIRTH

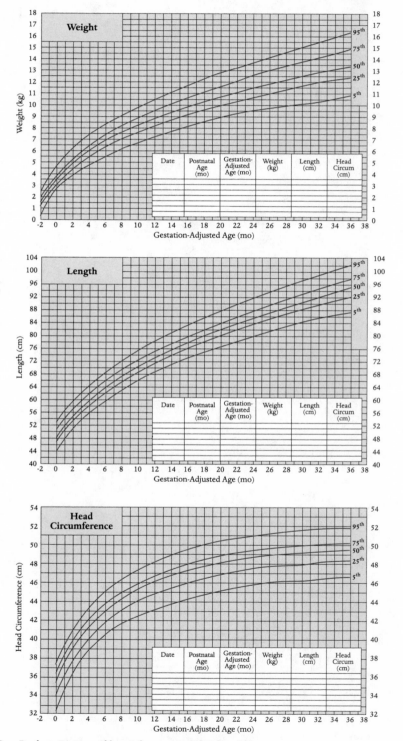

Chart provided by Ross Products Division, Abbott Laboratories, Columbus, OH

GROWTH FROM BIRTH TO AGE 3 FOR PREMATURE BOYS WHO WEIGHED 1,500–2,500 GRAMS AT BIRTH

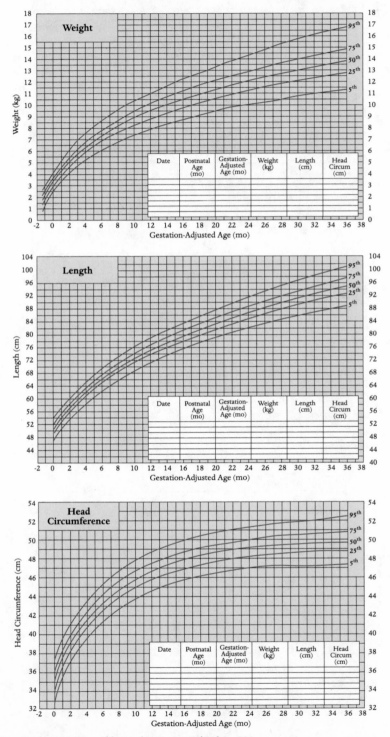

Chart provided by Ross Products Division, Abbott Laboratories, Columbus, OH

APPENDIX 3

A Schedule for Multiples

Date:_____

Triplet A

Time	Feeding			Diaper	
	Nurse	Food	Formula	Urine	Bowel
12:00					
1:00					
2:00					
3:00					
4:00					
5:00					
6:00					
7:00					
8:00					
9:00					
10:00					
11:00					
12:00					
1:00					
2:00					
3:00					
4:00					
5:00					
6:00					
7:00					
8:00					
9:00					
10:00					
11:00					

Triplet B

Time	Feeding			Diaper	
	Nurse	Food	Formula	Urine	Bowel
12:00					
1:00					
2:00					
3:00					
4:00					
5:00					
6:00					
7:00					
8:00					
9:00					
10:00					
11:00					
12:00					
1:00					
2:00					
3:00					
4:00					
5:00					
6:00					
7:00					
8:00					
9:00					
10:00					
11:00					

Triplet C

Time	Feeding			Diaper	
	Nurse	Food	Formula	Urine	Bowel
12:00					
1:00					
2:00					
3:00					
4:00					
5:00					
6:00					
7:00					
8:00					
9:00					
10:00					
11:00					
12:00					
1:00					
2:00					
3:00					
4:00					
5:00					
6:00					
7:00					
8:00					
9:00					
10:00					
11:00					

Reprinted with permission of MOST (Mothers of Supertwins), Inc., Brentwood, NY

APPENDIX 4

Birth to One Year

Step 1   **Does baby respond . . .**

Support the head.
Tap the infant gently.
Speak loudly to establish a startle response (this may be all that is necessary for breathing to return).
Check for response.
If no response, shout for help.
DO NOT PICK UP AND SHAKE THE INFANT.

Step 2   **Is the airway open . . .**

This is the most important.
Place hand on the infant's forehead. Tilt the head back into a neutral position and lift chin. Keep head in this position. With hand on the head at all times, clear the airway if a foreign body or vomitus is present.

Step 3   **Is there breathing . . .**

LOOK for the rise and fall of chest.
LISTEN for breathing.
FEEL for air flow at the mouth.

Step 4

If NO breathing . . .
Open your mouth widely and inhale deeply.
Cover infants mouth and nose with your mouth.
Give 2 slow breaths (puff of air 1.0–1.5 seconds per breath).
Pause after the first breath to take another breath.
Watch for an adequate rise of the chest.

Step 5   **Feel for pulse . . .**

Place index and middle finger over the brachial pulse (located on the inside of the upper arm, midway between the elbow and shoulder.)
Do not use thumb.
Feel for heartbeat.

If there IS a pulse . . .
Provide rescue breathing alone at a rate of 20 breaths per minute (every 3 seconds) for the child until breathing resumes.
After giving approximately 20 breaths, call the Rescue Squad.

Step 6

If NO pulse . . .
Use one hand to maintain the child's head position.
Place your index finger on the sternum just under the nipple line.
Place your third and fourth fingers on the sternum. Compress at this location. Using 2 fingers, compress the breast bone 1/2 to 1 inch.
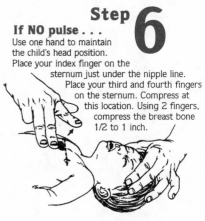

Step 7   **Count out loud . . .**
Count for compressions:
1, 2, 3, 4, 5 BREATH
1, 2, 3, 4, 5 BREATH
1, 2, 3, 4, 5 BREATH, etc.
After every 5th compression, pause and give one breath.
Maintain compression rate at 100 per minute (minimum).
After 20 cycles (or one minute), check for breathing and pulse, if both are present – stop CPR. If absent – continue CPR.

Step 8

Calling the rescue squad . . .

If alone, you should call the rescue squad after the first 4 cycles (5:1 or one minute). After calling, check for infant's pulse and respirations. If present, monitor infant and await the rescue squad. If absent, continue CPR. If two people are present, send one to call while the other is performing CPR.

Remember, in ALL cases requiring CPR, the infant should be transported by the rescue squad to the hospital and the physician should be contacted.

APPENDIX 5

Resources for Parents of Premature Babies

These are some organizations, Web sites, and books that may be helpful to you, depending on your and your baby's experiences. We do not endorse these listings, but merely offer them to give you some leads to the many resources that are available. The phone numbers, street addresses, and Web site addresses are correct as of the time of writing this book, but are subject to change.

ALLERGY PRODUCTS

Allergy Clean Environments (company that sells a wide range of allergy control products)
San Rafael, CA
(800) 882–4110
http://www.allergyclean.com

Allergy Control Products (company that sells a wide range of allergy control products)
Ridgefield, CT
(800) 422–3878
http://www.allergycontrol.com

Breastfeeding

Ameda/Egnell Inc. (breast pump company)
Cary, IL
(800) 323–8750
http://spiker.net/betz/pumps.htm

Avent America, Inc. (nonelectric breast pump)
Elkgrove, IL
(800) 542–8368
http://www.aventamerica.com/home.html

Human Milk Banking Association of North America (to locate the breast milk bank nearest you)
Raleigh, NC
(919) 350–8599

International Board of Lactation Consultant Examiners (to locate a breastfeeding consultant)
Falls Church, VA
(703) 560–7330

International Lactation Consultants Association (to locate a breastfeeding consultant)
Raleigh, NC
(919) 787–5181
http://www.ilca.org

La Leche League (information and support for breastfeeding mothers, and for help locating a
    breastfeeding consultant)
Schaumburg, IL
(800) LA–LECHE
(847) 519–7730
http://www.lalecheleague.org

Medela (breast pump company)
McHenry, IL
(800) 435–8316
http://www.babiesbestchoice.com/medcatalog.htm

Mother's Milk Bank at Austin (Web site with information on milk banking, and referrals to the
    milk banks in the U.S.)
Austin, TX
(512) 494–0800
http://www.mmbaustin.org/links.htm

BRONCHOPULMONARY DYSPLASIA

Bronchopulmonary Dysplasia page from Children's Hospital of Eastern Ontario (Web site providing detailed information on what BPD is, how it is treated, and what problems parents should look out for)
http://www.cheo.on.ca/bpd/BPDindx.html

CEREBRAL PALSY

Cerebral Palsy, from University of Minnesota's Disability Specific Web Sites (list of recommended Web sites relating to cerebral palsy)
http://www.disserv.stu.umn.edu/disability/Cerebral_Palsy

United Cerebral Palsy Association (broad information and support for people with CP and other disabilities)
Washington, DC
(800) 872–5827
http://www.ucpa.org

CHILD CARE

Child Care Aware (for help and advice in finding good child care, and to locate a local child care referral agency)
Washington, DC
(800) 424–2246
(202) 393–5501
http://www.naccrra.net

DEVELOPMENTAL CARE

World Health Organization Kangaroo Care Network (updated information on kangaroo care)
http://www.nursing.ab.umd.edu/mch/kc.htm

Tender Touch (parent education program for touching and massaging premature infants)
Melissa Thomas, nurse specialist at St. Luke's-Shawnee Mission Health System
Kansas City, MO
(816) 932–5174
http://www.saint-lukes.org/edu/ceu/tendertouch/

Touch Research Institute (research on massage, and to order video demonstrating how to massage preemies)
Miami, FL
(305) 243–6781
http://www.miami.edu/touch-research/home.html

EARLY INTERVENTION

NECTAS (National Early Childhood Technical Assistance) (for information on early intervention services and preschool special education, or for the organization to contact for specific information on your state's programs)
Chapel Hill, NC
(919) 962–2001
http://www.nectas.unc.edu

FEEDING PROBLEMS

New Visions (information and specialists on children with feeding problems)
Faber, VA
(804) 361–2285
http://www.new-vis.com

FINANCIAL ASSISTANCE

Social Security Administration (to apply for or get information on Supplemental Security Income, or SSI, for which you may be eligible, based on your child's medical history and your financial resources)
Washington, DC
(800) 772–1213

For other information on financial assistance, including Katie Beckett Funds (a federal program) and any public or private sources within your state for which you might be eligible, the best approach is to contact your hospital's social worker, even after your baby has left the NICU.

GE REFLUX

PAGER (Pediatric/Adolescent GE Reflux Association) (information and support on reflux)
Germantown, MD
(301) 601–9541 (eastern U.S.)
(760) 747–5001 (western U.S.)
http://www.reflux.org

HEARING IMPAIRMENTS

Alexander Graham Bell Association for the Deaf (broad information and support for parents
and educators of children who are deaf or hard of hearing)
Washington, DC
(800) HEARKID
(202) 337–5220
http://www.agbell.org

American Speech, Language and Hearing Association (to locate a pediatric audiologist or language pathologist in your area)
Rockville, MD
(800) 638–8255
(301) 897–5700
http://www.asha.org

Auditory-Verbal International (information on listening and speaking as a way of life for children who are deaf or hard of hearing)
Alexandria, VA
(703) 739–1049
http://www.auditory-verbal.org

Gallaudet University (university and research center for the deaf and hard of hearing; Web site
provides broad information on hearing loss)
Washington, DC
(202) 651–5051
http://www.gallaudet.edu/

League for the Hard of Hearing (information for parents of children who have hearing loss)
New York, NY
(917) 305–7700
http://www.lhh.org

HIGH-RISK PREGNANCIES

Complications from Childbirth (Web site offering information on a broad range of possible complications of pregnancy)
http://www.childbirth.org/articles/comp.html

Post Preemie Pregnancy Group (Internet support group for parents who are pregnant again after having had a premature birth)
http://www.cyg.net/~hewitt/PostPreemiePregnancyGroup.html

Sidelines (support group and resources for women going through a complicated pregnancy or on bed rest)
Laguna Beach, CA
(714) 497–2265
http://www.sidelines.org

Twin to Twin Transfusion Syndrome Foundation (information about TTTS, or to get in touch with other parents whose babies have had it)
Bay Village, OH
(440) 899–TTTS
http://www.tttsfoundation.org

HOME HEALTH CARE

Aaron's Tracheostomy Page (information and advice for parents of a child with a tracheostomy)
http://www.twinenterprises.com/trach

Access to Respite Care Help (ARCH) (information on respite care, and to locate respite services in your area)
Chapel Hill, NC
(800) 473–1727
http://www.chtop.com/archbroc.htm

Bronchopulmonary Dysplasia Page (Web site with advice if your child goes home on oxygen or a monitor)
http://www.geocities.com/HotSprings/Spa/8100/bpd.html

Gastrostomy Support (Web site with information and advice on gastrostomy tubes and many feeding issues)
http://www.challengenet.com/~g-tube/index2.html

United Ostomy Association (information, teaching materials, and support network, if your child has an enterostomy)
Irvine, CA
(800) 826–0826
http://www.uoa.org

HYDROCEPHALUS

Hydrocephalus Association (information, resources, and parent support on hydrocephalus)
San Francisco, CA
(888) 598–3789
(415) 732–7040
http://neurosurgery.mgh.harvard.edu/ha

LEARNING DISABILITIES

International Dyslexia Association (formerly called the Orton Dyslexia Society, offers information and support on dyslexia)
Baltimore, MD
(410) 296–0232
http://www.interdys.org

Learning Disabilities Association of America (information and support relating to learning disabilities)
Pittsburgh, PA
(412) 341–1515
http://www.ldanatl.org

National Attention Deficit Disorders Association (information and support relating to attention deficit disorders)
Highland Park, IL 60065
(847) 432–ADDA
http://www.add.org

National Center for Learning Disabilities (broad information and support related to learning disabilities)
New York, NY
(888) 575–7373
(212) 545–7510
http://www.ncld.org

LOSS AND GRIEF

Compassionate Friends (support group and resources for parents who have lost a child)
Oak Brook, IL
(630) 990–0010
http://www.compassionatefriends.org/

Mothers in Sympathy and Support (support group and resources for parents who have lost a child)
http://www.misschildren.org/

When Bad Things Happen to Good People by Harold Kushner, Avon, 1997 (a former bestseller, written by a theologian and father who confronted his son's fatal illness, and addressed the question so many parents ask: "Why us?")

PREEMIE CLOTHES AND SUPPLIES

Children's Medical Ventures (isolette covers, special pacifiers, and a wide range of other products designed especially to enhance the development of premature babies)
South Weymouth, MA
(800) 377–3449
http://www.childmed.com

Komfy Ride (car seat inserts for premature babies, to help them stay positioned correctly and reduce the risk of apnea)
Jacksonville, FL
(904) 398–6485
http://www.komfykids.com/home.html

Le Petite Baby (clothes for preemies)
Alpharetta, GA
(770) 475–3247
http://www.no-odor.com/preemie/

Preemie Store . . . and More! (preemie clothes and other supplies)
Fountain Valley, CA
(800) 676–8469
(714) 434–3740
http://www.preemie.com/

premiewear (clothes for preemies)
Auburn, CA
(800) 992–TINY
http://www.premiewear.com

Smart-Start Baby Boutique (preemie clothes and other supplies)
http://www.cadvision.com/lawrencc/

Tiny Bundles (preemie clothes, special pacifiers, car seat inserts)
San Diego, CA
(619) 451–9907
http://www.tinybundles.com

PREEMIE ISSUES (VARIOUS)

American Association for Premature Infants (organization engaged in advocacy, and offering a
newsletter and other resources)
Cincinnati, OH
(513) 522–8040
http://www.aapi-online.org

Comeunity Premature Baby—Premature Child (Web site offering information and resources for parents of premature babies)
http://www.comeunity.com/premature/

Dear Zoe by Max De Pree, HarperCollins, 1996 (book of letters from the author to his premature granddaughter, sensitively exploring issues of love, perfection, and faith)

For Parents of Preemies (Answers to Commonly Asked Questions) (Web site offering a wide range of information on medical and other topics, by the University of Wisconsin)
http://www2.medsch.wisc.edu/childrenshosp/parents_of_preemies/index.html

Neonatology on the Web (teaching files from medical schools on neonatology topics)
http://www.neonatology.org/syllabus/syllabus.html

Preemie-L (Internet support group for parents of premature babies)
http://home.vicnet.net.au/~garyh/preemie.htm

Text of speeches, by a psychologist and father of a preemie, on how parents cope emotionally with a high-risk birth (by Michael T. Hynan, University of Wisconsin-Milwaukee)
http://www.uwm.edu/~hynan/MINNAEP.html and
http://www.uwm.edu/~hynan/MINNAEP.html

RSV

The RSV Info Center (Web site offering comprehensive information on RSV)
http://www.rsvinfo.com/

SENSORY INTEGRATION DYSFUNCTION

Sensory Integration International (information for parents on sensory integration issues)
Torrance, CA
(310) 320–2335
http://home.earthlink.net/~sensoryint/faq.html

SIBLING ISSUES

The Dougy Center, The National Center for Grieving Children and Families (information and publications to help parents understand their older child's reaction after loss of a baby)
Portland, OR
(503) 775–5683
http://www.dougy.org

Sibling Support Project (a national program offering information, resources, and support groups for siblings of children with special needs)
Children's Hospital and Regional Medical Center
Seattle, WA
http://www.chmc.org/departmt/sibsupp/

SPECIAL NEEDS (VARIOUS)

Dragonfly Toy Co. (toys for children with special play needs)
http://www.dragonflytoys.com/

Families with Special Needs Children (Web site providing information on alternative therapies for some disabilities)
http://www.mondenet.com/~chrisck/Welcome.htm#Alternative%20Therapies

Family Support Network (helps parents find services, agencies, and other resources for your child's specific disability; has some national resources, or can direct you to a central directory of resources in your state)
Chapel Hill, NC
(800) 852–0042
(919) 966–2841
http://www.med.unc.edu/commedu/familysu/fsnframe_main.htm#mission

Family Village (Web site that brings together Internet resources, on topics ranging from recreational opportunities to laws to helpful products to medical information, for people with special needs)
http://www.familyvillage.wisc.edu/index.htmlx

Internet Resources for Special Children (Web site that provides links to Internet sites for numerous disabilities)
http://www.irsc.org/disability.htm

March of Dimes (information, research, and advocacy relating to improving health of babies, including information on prenatal care and specific disabilities)
White Plains, NY
(888) 663–4637
http://www.modimes.org

National Information Center for Children and Youth with Disabilities (information, referrals, and support for parents of children with special needs)
Washington, DC
(800) 695–0285
(202) 884–8200
http://www.nichcy.org

Special Child Magazine (online magazine for parents of children with special needs)
http://www.specialchild.com

TWINS AND OTHER MULTIPLES

Mothers of Supertwins (MOST) (support group and resources for parents of triplets, quadruplets, or more)
Brentwood, NY
(631) 859–1110
http://www.mostonline.org/welcome/index.htm

National Organization of Mothers of Twins Clubs (advice regarding multiples, and referral to a club near you)
Albuquerque, NM
(800) 243–2276
(505) 275–0955
http://www.nomotc.org

Triplet Connection (information, resources, and networking for parents of triplets, quadruplets, or more)
Stockton, CA
(209) 474–0885
http://www.tripletconnection.org

Twins Magazine (a national magazine that focuses on topics relating to multiples)
Englewood, CO
(888) 558–9467
(303) 290–8500
http://www.twinsmagazine.com

Twin Services (to request brochures and publications for parents of twins or multiples)
Berkeley, CA
(510) 524–0863

Twinspace (Web site offering information, resources, and referrals to organizations for parents of twins)
http://www.twinspace.com

VISUAL IMPAIRMENTS

American Foundation for the Blind (information, resources, publications, talking books, and toys for children with visual impairment)
New York, NY
(800) 232–5463
http://www.igc.org/afb/

American Printing House for the Blind (catalog with aids and appliances, Braille and recorded materials)
Louisville, KY
(800) 223–1839
(502) 895–2405
http://www.aph.org

Association for Education and Rehabilitation of the Blind and Visually Impaired (membership information and up-to-date information for those who provide services to people with visual impairment)
Alexandria, VA
(703) 823–9690
http://www.aerbvi.org

Blind Children's Center (instructional guides for parents)
Los Angeles, CA
(800) 222–3566
http://www.blindchildrenscenter.org

Braille Institute of America (source for large print, braille, and recorded materials)
Los Angeles, CA
(800) BRAILLE
(323) 663–1111
http://www.brailleinstitute.org

Hadley School for the Blind (free correspondence courses to learn Braille, for families of visually impaired children)
Winnetka, IL
(800) 323–4238
(847) 446–8111
http://www.hadley-school.org/index.htm

National Association for Parents of the Visually Impaired (practical support for parents, and help locating an organization near you)
Watertown, MA
(800) 562–6265
(617) 972–7441
http://www.spedex.com/napvi

ROPARD (association concerned with retinopathy of prematurity and related diseases, providing information for parents and caregivers of children with visual impairment)
Franklin, MI
(800) 788–2020
http://www.ropard.org

Seedlings Braille Books for Children (source for braille books, ages 1 to 14)
Livonia, MI
(800) 777–8552
http://www.seedlings.org

V. I. Guide (Web site providing broad range of information and resources for parents of visually impaired children)
http://www.viguide.com

GLOSSARY

AGA (appropriate–for–gestational age): A newborn is considered appropriate-for-gestational-age if her birth weight is between the tenth and the ninetieth percentiles on the standard growth curve for her age.

Amniocentesis: A procedure to obtain a sample of amniotic fluid, by passing a needle through a pregnant woman's abdomen and into her uterus. The fluid can be analyzed to detect some birth defects (such as Down syndrome), signs of infection, or to assess a fetus's lung maturity.

Amnioinfusion: A procedure in which liquid is infused into the womb through a catheter, with the goal of reestablishing a sufficient amount of amniotic fluid.

Anemia: Fewer red blood cells than normal. In preemies, anemia can cause breathing problems, low energy, and poor growth.

Apgar score: A test to quickly assess a newborn's need for resuscitation at birth. Points are assigned beginning at one minute after birth, and at five-minute intervals thereafter, for heart rate, respiration, reflexes, muscle tone, and color, until an infant is stable.

Apnea: A pause in breathing that lasts for more than 20 seconds, or is accompanied by a slow heart rate (bradycardia) or a change in skin color. Apnea is common among preemies, who still have immature control of their breathing.

Arterial line: Similar to an intravenous, or IV, line, an arterial line goes into an artery instead of a vein. A tiny catheter in an artery can be used to measure blood pressure, draw blood, or give fluids.

Asymmetric (head-sparing) growth restriction: When an SGA, or small–for–gestational age, baby is born with a normal head circumference. Asymmetric growth restriction is believed to occur when nutrients are in short supply in the womb and nature preferentially gives scarce nourishment to the brain—a vital organ—compared to the rest of the body.

Ataxic CP: A type of cerebral palsy that is characterized by clumsy, uncoordinated movements and poor balance.

Athetoid CP: A type of cerebral palsy in which muscle tone is changeable, varying between too high and too low, and there are often involuntary movements of the face and upper body.

Bacterial vaginosis (BV): An infection caused by the overgrowth of common bacteria normally living in the vagina, it is believed to be a risk factor for preterm delivery.

Bilirubin: A yellow substance that the body makes all the time, as red blood cells are broken down. When bilirubin builds up in the body, it turns the skin a yellowish tinge, called jaundice.

BPD (bronchopulmonary dysplasia): Chronic injury and scarring in a preemie's lungs, caused by supplemental oxygen and mechanical ventilation.

Bradycardia (or "brady"): A slower than normal heart rate, in preemies it most often results from apnea (an overly long pause in breathing).

Bronchoscopy: A procedure that involves looking inside a baby's trachea and bronchi (the large airways of the lungs) with a fiberoptic scope, to see whether there is a problem that is making breathing more difficult.

Cath toes: Temporary discoloration of a baby's toes due to a blood clot from her umbilical catheter.

Central line: A long-term intravenous catheter placed in a large, deep blood vessel close to the heart.

Cerclage: A surgical procedure in which the cervix is sewn shut, to prevent its opening at an early stage of pregnancy.

Cerebral palsy (CP): A condition in which a person's muscles don't move in a natural or coordinated way, because of a permanent injury to the brain.

Chorioamnionitis: An infection of the amniotic fluid and sac.

Cochlear implant: A device that is surgically implanted in the inner ear, it picks up sounds from the environment and directly stimulates the auditory nerve. A cochlear implant is one approach to dealing with a profound hearing impairment.

Colostrum: The first milk that comes out of a mother's breasts, until about a week after delivery. Colostrum looks yellow and thick, and is particularly rich in proteins and antibodies.

CPAP: Short for continuous positive airway pressure, it is a method to keep the air sacs in a baby's lungs open, by preventing them from collapsing after each breath. Preemies are usually given CPAP through prongs in their nose.

Cyanosis: A bluish or grayish discoloration of the skin caused by insufficient oxygen.

Developmental Care: An approach to caring for premature babies that places an emphasis on their individual needs, and on keeping them as free from stress as possible.

Developmental delay: A delay in reaching certain developmental milestones, relative to most other children of the same age. In preemies, developmental delays may be temporary or permanent.

Dizygotic twins: Fraternal twins, who don't share all of the same genes.

Dyslexia: A learning disability, dyslexia means difficulty with reading. It can refer to problems with any of the steps involved in reading, such as recognizing letters as symbols, perceiving the different sounds that make up words, or remembering words that one has read.

Eclampsia: Seizures, occurring in a pregnant woman with preeclampsia.

Endotracheal (ET) tube: A tube, inserted through the nose or mouth into the windpipe (trachea), that can be attached to a ventilator, to send air directly into the lungs.

Enterostomy: Or "ostomy," for short. The medical term for the open, unconnected ends of a baby's intestines, which are brought out during bowel surgery, through a small incision in the skin of his belly.

Erythropoietin: Pronounced *"a-RITH-ro-po-it-in,"* this is a natural hormone that stimulates the body to produce red blood cells. It can be made in the laboratory, and given to preemies to help prevent anemia.

Fetal fibronectin: A protein helping to keep the placenta and membranes attached to the uterine lining. Low free levels of fibronectin detected on a swab of the vagina or cervix can help reassure that a preterm delivery is not imminent.

Gastroesophageal reflux: Often referred to as "GE reflux," or just "reflux," this is a condition in which food in the stomach comes back up into the esophagus, and sometimes all the way out of the mouth.

Gavage feeding: Feeding a baby by way of a soft tube inserted in his nose or mouth, going down into his stomach.

Guaiac: Pronounced *"GWY-ak,"* this is a test performed on a sample of a baby's stool, to see whether there is any blood in it that isn't visible to the naked eye.

HELLP syndrome: Short for *h*emolysis (destruction of red blood cells), *e*levated *l*iver enzymes, and *l*ow *p*latelets, HELLP syndrome is a severe form of preeclampsia. It involves dangerous abnormalities of blood clotting with liver damage, and carries a risk of stroke or even death.

Hydrocephalus: A buildup of cerebrospinal fluid inside the ventricles of the brain. In preemies, hydrocephalus most often occurs after a severe intraventricular hemorrhage (IVH).

Hypoglycemia: A dangerously low level of sugar in the blood.

Hypothermia: A body temperature below normal.

Indomethacin: Pronounced *"in-do-METH-ah-sin,"* this medication may cause a patent ductus arteriosus (PDA) to shrink and close. It is also known as indocin.

Interleukin 6: A protein whose high levels in amniotic fluid or in an expectant mother's blood can signal a uterine infection, possibly leading to preterm delivery.

Intrauterine growth restriction (IUGR): The medical term for a fetus's poor growth in the womb. When diagnosed during pregnancy, it may lead to a medically indicated preterm delivery.

Isolette: A transparent plastic box, equipped with a heating system, to keep premature babies warm. Isolettes used to be known as incubators.

IVH (intraventricular hemorrhage): Bleeding occurring in an inner part of the brain, near the ventricles, where premature babies have blood vessels that are particularly fragile and prone to rupture.

Jaundice: A yellowish discoloration of the skin caused by a buildup of bilirubin in the body.

Kangaroo care: A way to hold your naked baby skin-to-skin, against your bare chest, inside your shirt or covered by a blanket, like a baby kangaroo in his mother's pouch.

Lanugo: Soft and fuzzy fetal hair, generally heavier on a baby's back, upper arms, and shoulders, which some premature babies are born with. It will be shed later.

Monozygotic twins: Identical twins, who have the same genes.

Moro reflex: One of the many automatic reflexes that babies have. When startled by a sudden noise or fear of falling, the Moro reflex leads them to throw out their arms, and arch their back.

Nasal cannula: A set of plastic prongs and tubing that can deliver extra oxygen into a baby's nose.

NEC (necrotizing enterocolitis): An intestinal disease, most common in young preemies, in which portions of the bowel are damaged or destroyed because of poor blood flow, inflammation, or infection.

Neonatologist: A pediatrician with specialized training in newborn intensive care.

NG (naso-gastric) tube: A soft tube that goes through a baby's nose down into his stomach. It can be used for feeding or to empty the stomach of gas.

NICU: Short for Neonatal Intensive Care Unit. An NICU is a hospital ward where preemies who require complex medical care are taken care of, along with other critically ill or medically unstable newborns.

Obstructive apnea: A pause in breathing that occurs because a baby's airway is obstructed and little air can get through. It can happen even when a baby is moving his chest to breathe.

OG (oro-gastric) tube: A soft tube that goes through a baby's mouth down into his stomach. It can be used for feeding or to empty the stomach of gas.

Oligohydramnios: An insufficient amount of amniotic fluid. When resulting from insufficient blood flow to the fetus, it can lead to a medically indicated preterm delivery.

Oscillating ventilator: Also called a high-frequency ventilator, it works differently than a conventional ventilator. An oscillating ventilator keeps a baby's lungs continuously inflated by providing tiny quantities of air at extremely rapid rates.

Oxytocin: A hormone that stimulates the uterus to contract. Its synthetic form, pitocin, can be given to a woman in labor to speed up a vaginal delivery.

Parenteral nutrition: Nutrition that is given intravenously, rather than through the stomach and the intestines.

PDA (patent ductus arteriosus): An open blood vessel near the heart and lungs which is a necessary part of a fetus's circulation, a PDA should normally close a few days after birth. If it lingers, as it often does in premature babies, it can cause breathing difficulties and some heart failure.

Perinatologist: An obstetrician who specializes in high-risk pregnancies.

Periodic breathing: An irregular breathing pattern. Because of immaturity, it's normal for a preemie to take some deep breaths, and then pause for five or ten seconds before taking the next one.

Peripheral IVs: Intravenous lines that go into "peripheral" veins, meaning small blood vessels near the skin's surface, usually in the baby's extremities or scalp.

PIE (pulmonary interstitial emphysema): A complication in which there are many tiny tears in the air sacs or small airways of a baby's lung, causing air to leak out of them.

Placenta previa: A pregnancy complication, usually signaled by bleeding, in which the placenta partly or completely covers the cervix, so that when the cervix dilates, or during labor, it can tear and bleed. A preterm delivery may be necessary to prevent a serious maternal hemorrhage.

Placental abruption: A pregnancy complication, commonly signaled by vaginal bleeding and abdominal pain, in which part of the placenta detaches from the wall of the uterus, affecting the blood and oxygen supply to the fetus. When the area of abruption is large, it may require an emergency, preterm delivery.

Pneumothorax: A tear in the air sacs of a baby's lung, causing air to leak out into the space between the lung and the chest wall.

Polycythemia: An excess of red blood cells. In babies, it can cause breathing difficulties, low blood sugar, and jaundice.

Polyhydramnios: An excessive amount of amniotic fluid, which can overly distend the uterus, and lead to preterm labor and delivery.

Preeclampsia: A disease of pregnancy, signaled by high blood pressure, protein in the urine, and fluid retention, which can limit the blood flowing to the fetus and to the mother's vital organs. When preeclampsia is severe, a medically indicated preterm delivery may become necessary.

PVL (periventricular leukomalacia): Cysts in the white matter of the brain near the ventricles, indicating areas that have been permanently damaged.

Radiant warmer: An open bed with an overhead heater, on which a premature infant who needs frequent medical attention can be kept warm.

RDS (respiratory distress syndrome): Also called hyaline membrane disease, it is the result of a preemie having immature lungs. A baby with RDS is not able to breathe well on her own.

ROP (retinopathy of prematurity): An eye disease of premature babies, in which new, abnormal blood vessels grow near the retina, and temporarily or permanently damage it.

RSV (respiratory syncytial virus): A common virus that gives most people a cold, but can be more serious in premature babies, causing infections such as pneumonia or bronchiolitis.

Scleral buckle: A surgical procedure used to repair a detached retina, it involves placing a band of silicone—like a belt—around the sclera, or white of the eye.

SGA (small-for-gestational-age): A newborn is considered small-for-gestational-age if her birth weight is below the tenth percentile on the standard growth curve for her age.

Spastic diplegia: The most common type of cerebral palsy among preemies, it is characterized by stiff ("spastic") muscle tone, affecting mainly the legs and feet ("diplegia").

Surfactant: A natural substance in the lungs that helps keep the air sacs expanded, it is deficient in premature babies who suffer from RDS. Replacement surfactant can be given to babies who don't produce enough of their own.

Symmetric growth restriction: When an SGA, or small-for-gestational-age baby, has a head circumference, as well as birth weight, that is below the tenth percentile for her age.

Tocolytics: Drugs to relax the uterus and halt uterine contractions. They can be given to a pregnant woman to treat preterm labor.

TPN (total parenteral nutrition): A nourishing solution—containing protein, vitamins, minerals, and other nutrients—that is given to a baby intravenously.

Tracheostomy: A "trach," as it is called for short, is a surgical opening in a baby's neck, through which a ventilation tube can be inserted directly into his windpipe.

Twin to twin transfusion syndrome (TTTS) A complication in which identical twins in the womb share not only the same placenta, but also placental blood vessels, causing excessive blood flow in one fetus and insufficient blood flow in the other.

UAC (umbilical artery catheter): An arterial line that goes into a baby's umbilical cord, or belly button, it can be used for withdrawing blood, monitoring blood pressure, or delivering fluids and nutrition.

Vitrectomy: This surgical procedure, used to repair a detached retina, involves removing some of the jelly-like substance that fills the eye (the vitreous humor), so the surgeon can reach and reposition the detached portion of the retina.

VP (ventriculo-peritoneal) shunt: A long-term treatment for hydrocephalus. A VP shunt is a long, plastic tube that is inserted surgically, to carry excess fluid from the ventricles in the brain, where it builds up, to the abdomen (or "peritoneum") where it can be reabsorbed.

INDEX

Page numbers referring to illustrations are indicated in italics.

A

"A, B, C" designation of multiples, 68

abdominal cramps (maternal)
  and preterm labor, 13

abdominal pain (baby's)
  tense and tender, and feeding intolerance, 151
  and VP shunt, 416

abortion
  prior, and cervical incompetence, 15
  prior, as risk factor for prematurity, 33
  selective reduction, 29, 435

abrasions on baby
  and use of tape in NICU, 145

abstract concept difficulty
  as learning disability, 467

acceptance
  and child with disability, 470, 473
  and sibling of child with disability, 472

accidental extubation, 144, 265

acid in blood (baby's)
  at first day, doctor's perspective, 81
  and resuscitation, 62

ADD. *See* attention deficit disorder

addiction to pain medication, 111

ADHD. *See* attention deficit hyperactivity disorder

adhesive tape. *See* tape

"adjusted" age, 365–66
  when to stop adjusting age, 403

adolescence of a preemie with disabilities, 479

adoption of preemie, 369–73

afraid to hold baby on ventilator, 144

afraid to leave baby, 160

afraid to see baby, 88

African-American ethnicity
  and baby's viability, 47
  and prematurity rate, 37
  and SGA, 71

AGA. *See* appropriate-for-gestational age

age (maternal)
  as risk factor for prematurity, 37

age of baby. *See also* gestational age
  "adjusted," 365–66
  when to stop adjusting, 403

aggressive care
  decision regarding, 46–47, 498–502

AIDS. *See* HIV

air leaks, 160–64. *See also* pneumothorax, pulmonary interstitial emphysema

air travel. *See* plane travel

airway inflammation, 258–60

airway suctioning, 173–74

alarms. *See also* monitoring; breathing difficulty
  and home monitors, 385–86, 389–92
  nurses' response to, 158–60

alcohol, maternal use of
  as SGA cause, 71

alertness
  in babies 26–29 weeks gestational age, 139
  in babies 30–33 weeks gestational age, 140

allergy
  prevention tips, 339
  resources list, 521

altitude, high, 345
  as SGA cause, 71

amblyopia, 425

American Foundation for the Blind, 453, 533

American Occupational Therapy Association, 456

American Sign Language, 448

aminophylline medication, 135, 219
  and reflux, 246

amniocentesis
  for fetal health assessment, 25
  following membrane rupture, 22

amnioinfusion, 21, 35

amniotic fluid. *See also* chorioamnionitis
  and fetal growth restriction, 72
  infection of, as risk factor for PVL, 284
  and membrane rupture, 19–22
  production, and bed rest, 5
  too little or too much, as risk factors
    for prematurity, 35
  in twin to twin transfusion syndrome, 30–31

amplification. *See* hearing aids

analgesics
  and pain reduction (baby's), 109, 310

anatomic abnormality, 36
  and prognosis, 73

anemia (baby's), 276
  and BPD, 262
  causes, prevention and treatment, 116, 215, 276–77
  during first week, 137
  and growth, 401
  and low blood pressure, 179
  in twin to twin transfusion syndrome, 31, 122

anemia (maternal)
  and getting pregnant again, 434

anesthesia (baby's)
  for surgery, 308–10

anesthesia (maternal)
  and C-section delivery, 58
  and effect on baby, 60

anesthesiologist, 304, 308–10

anger (parents'), 193, 256
    and fussy baby, 374–75
    and nurses, 279–82
    and rehospitalization, 405
animal dander minimization, 339
anomie and disorientation phase
    in parent with special needs preemie, 473–75
antibiotics (baby's)
    on first day, 83
    for infection, 182–83
    for NEC, 239
    and pneumonia, 180
    risks of, 274
    before surgery, 308
antibiotics (maternal)
    in a high-risk pregnancy, 4, 17–18
    and membrane rupture, 21
    side effects, 18
anticipatory grief, 297, 487
anti-inflammatory drugs
    for pain, 110
    steroids, 258–59, 262
anti-labor drugs, 12–14
antiseptics
    and thyroid function, 278
anxiety (baby's), 82, 109–11, 202–04
anxiety (father's), 296–97
anxiety (mother's)
    after baby comes home, 363, 379–81, 415, 419, 432
    while baby is in hospital, 88, 98, 158, 160, 193–95,
        255–57, 304
    during pregnancy, 8, 19, 22, 434
Apgar scores, 62–63
apnea of prematurity, 99–101, 135, 218–20. See also
        bradycardia; breathing difficulty
    at baby's gestational age, 84, 86
    end of, 334, 343
    and feeding intolerance, 151
    how to recognize and respond, 158–60, 346
apparent life-threatening event
    and home monitoring, 385–93
appearance
    of newborn preemie, 88–91
    of preemie in early years, 377–78, 409
    and SGA, 72
appropriate–for–gestational age (AGA), 70
arithmetic disorder
    as learning disability, 467
arterial line, 95, 146–47
articulation of sounds, difficulty with
    as learning disability, 467
A's and B's. See apnea; bradycardia
asked to leave baby's bedside, 191

ASL. See American Sign Language
asphyxia at birth, 61
    and jaundice, 156
aspirin
    and preeclampsia prevention, 10
assessment
    at delivery, doctor's perspective, 45–48
    early years, doctor's, 399
    first day, doctor's perspective, 80–81
    first week, doctor's perspective, 133–34
    at home-going, doctor's perspective, 333–34
    during hospital stay, doctor's perspective,
        212–13
asthma prevention tips, 339
asymmetric growth retardation, 72, 75
ataxic CP, 459
athetoid CP, 459
at-home monitors, 385–93
    stopping use of, 392
Ativan medication, 110
atosiban medication, 14
at risk babies, 399, 401–03
    early intervention for, 442–46
    follow-up clinic for, 406–07
    when to rule out problems in, 426–28
at risk mothers, 4, 33–37, 434–35
attachment, 252–54. See also bonding; time with baby
attention deficit disorder
    late appearing, 427
    as learning disability, 466–67
    and motor skill delay, 430
attention deficit hyperactivity disorder, 466–67
audiological exam. See hearing exam
audiologist, 445, 447, 450, 469
auditory-oral education, 448–49
automatic reflexes
    in baby 30–33 weeks gestational age, 141
    in baby 34+ weeks gestational age, 142
    and cerebral palsy, 419, 423
autopsy considerations, 492

B
"baby blues," 255–57
baby feeling loved, ways to help, 198–205
baby-proofing the home, 338–40
baby-sitter
    vs. daycare, 366–67, 411–12
    and home oxygen use, 355
back pain
    and preterm labor, 13
back-transfer of baby, 216, 288–89
Baclofen pump
    for CP, 460

bacterial vaginosis
  and preterm birth, 17
"bagging" the baby, 159
balance responses
  delays in, 423
Ballard examination, 81
banks, for breast milk, 153–54
baptism of baby, 490
barbiturate medication, 110
barium swallow, 245
bathing baby, 247
Bayley Scales of Infant Development, 406, 463
bed (baby's), 91–92, 93
  personal decoration of, 188–91
  position in, 219, 243
bed rest, 5–8
  and delayed interval delivery, 67
  and membrane rupture, 21
  and preeclampsia, 9
bedside nurse, 97
behavioral expectations
  and child with disability, 471
behavioral factors (maternal)
  as risk factor for prematurity, 37
behavior in toddler, 428–29
behavior of siblings
  of child with disability, 472–73
  after loss of baby, 493–95
behind-the-ear hearing aid, 450
benediction service in NICU, 490
betadine antiseptic
  and thyroid function, 278
betamethasone administration (maternal),
    27–28
bililights
  as jaundice treatment, 157
bilirubin
  and direct hyperbilirubinemia, 242
  and jaundice in newborn, 155–57
biophysical profile
  for fetal health assessment, 24–25
birth announcements, 142
  when baby has died, 488
birth date prediction, 10–12
  after membrane rupture, 19–22
birth defect, 36
  diagnosis, at first day, 73, 100
birth order
  and labeling of multiples, 68–69
birth process
  and delayed interval delivery, 66–68
  infections during, 183
birth weight

difference in twins, 122–23
  and IQ, 464
  normal variations in, 72
  predictions of, 63–64
  and SGA, 70–75
Bishop, Joey, 507
blackened toes, 148
bleeding in brain, 136, 164–69, 285
  and air leak, 162
  and C-section, 56
  and prenatal steroid treatment, 28
  risk according to gestational age at birth, 84–88
bleeding in lungs, 175
bleeding (maternal)
  and bed rest, 5
  and delayed interval delivery, 67
  as risk factor for prematurity, 34
blessings service in NICU, 490
blindness, 452–54. See also retinopathy of prematurity;
    visual impairment
bloated abdomen (baby's), 151
blood donor, parent as, 116
blood flow (baby's)
  and IVH, 165
  and PDA, 176–78
  and resuscitation at delivery, 61
  in SGA baby, 73
blood flow (fetal)
  and bed rest, 5, 21
  and PDA, 176
  and preeclampsia, 9
  and twin to twin transfusion syndrome, 30–31
blood flow (mother's). See circulation
blood in stools, 151, 155
blood pressure, high. See high blood pressure
blood pressure, low. See low blood pressure (baby's)
blood tests (baby's)
  at delivery, doctor's perspective, 45
  on first day, doctor's perspective, 81–82
  during first week, doctor's perspective, 133–34
  and IVs, 147
  and nutritional shortages, 234, 241
  and routine newborn screenings, 278
blood transfusion (baby's), 116
  vs. alternative treatment for anemia, 276
  parent as donor, 116–17
blood type
  and jaundice, 156
bluish lip or skin color
  as sign of breathing difficulty, 159, 346–47
blurry vision (maternal)
  and preeclampsia, 9
body hair, 90. See also lanugo

body temperature, 91–92, 101
　as cause of apnea, 218
　and infection, 182
　and kangaroo care, 221–22
　NICU equipment to regulate, 93
　and readiness to go home, 92, 121
　in SGA baby, 73
body-worn hearing aid, 450
Bonaparte, Napoleon, 507
bonding. *See also* time with baby
　and adoptive parents, 370
　attachment, 252–54
　and breastfeeding, 126
　after delivery, 64–65
Botox
　for CP, 460
bottle feeding, 149, 152, 227
　vs. breastfeeding, 124–28, 226
　and nipple confusion, 228
　special formula or supplements, 234–37, 361–62
　techniques for, 232–34
bowel disorder, 237–40. *See also* necrotizing enterocolitis
　and narrowing or obstruction, 240
　risk according to gestational age at birth, 84–88
　and short bowel syndrome, 240
　and surgery, 313–15
BPD. *See* bronchopulmonary dysplasia
bradycardia, 214, 218–20. *See also* apnea of prematurity
　and feeding intolerance, 151
　and home monitor, 385–93
　monitoring for in the hospital, 93–94, 158–60
　and readiness to go home, 120–21, 334, 343
　and reflux, 245
brain bleed. *See* bleeding in brain
brain cysts, 284. *See also* periventricular leukomalacia
brain damage. *See* brain injury
brain development
　and breast milk vs. formula, 125–26
　and Developmental Care, 198–200
　and developmental delays, 408
　varying by gestational age at birth, 138–42
brain injury
　and detection of, 164–69, 336, 399, 401–02, 407, 408, 419–24
　from hydrocephalus, 168, 316
　from infection, 184
　and intraventricular hemorrhage, 164–69
　and making decisions about treatment, 46–47, 136, 498–503
　and movements baby makes, 98
　parenting a child with, 441, 473–80
　and PVL, 284–87
　and resuscitation of baby, 60–61

risk of, according to gestational age at birth, 49–52, 84–88
　and seizures, 170–71, 418–19
　and SGA babies, 74
brain swelling
　and IVH, 167–69, 285
Braxton-Hicks contractions, 12–13
　and activity during pregnancy, 5
breasts at birth, 90
　and determining gestational age, 81
breastfeeding. *See also* pumping breast milk
　and adoptive mother, 373
　advantages of, 125–26
　and baby's nutrition, 213, 228, 235–37, 290
　breast milk banks, 153–54
　burping during, 233
　difficulty in starting, 112–13
　donation of breast milk, 154, 491
　vs. formula feeding, 124–28
　fortification of breast milk, 235, 360–62
　and fortifiers after baby goes home, 361
　hassles of, 127
　how and when baby gets started, 85, 87, 113–14, 149–53, 226–28
　mother getting ready for, 124, 127–28, 222–26
　and NEC, 85, 87, 238
　and nipple confusion, 228
　partial, 127, 235
　and quantity of milk production, 115, 223–25, 229–31
　resources list, 522
　and rooming-in before baby goes home, 335
　stopping and re-starting, 230
　with twins or triplets, 290–93, 384
breast milk. *See* breastfeeding; pumping breast milk
breathing difficulties. *See also* alarms; apnea of prematurity; bronchopulmonary dysplasia; respiratory distress syndrome
　and car seat, 343–45
　at delivery, doctor's perspective, 45
　at first day, doctor's perspective, 81–82
　during first week, doctor's perspective, 133–35
　and going home, doctor's perspective, 334–35
　and high-frequency ventilator, 163
　and home monitoring, 385–93
　and home oxygen use, 350–56
　during hospital stay, doctor's perspective, 213–14
　and monitor alarm accuracy, 158
　and pain reduction drugs, 110
　and resuscitation at delivery, 59, 60–62
　risk for, according to baby's gestational age at birth, 84, 86, 87
　as RSV symptom, 436
　in SGA baby, 74
　after surgery, 310

and trouble coming off ventilator, 257–58
breech position
  and C-section delivery, 56
bronchiolitis
  and RSV, 435, 437
bronchodilator
  for BPD, 214, 262
bronchopulmonary dysplasia, 261–65. *See also* breathing
     difficulty
  and daycare, 411–12
  and early years, doctor's perspective, 400–01
  and feeding problems, 457
  and going home, doctor's perspective, 334
  and home oxygen use, 350–56
  and pulmonary interstitial emphysema, 162
  resources list, 523
  risk according to gestational age at birth, 84, 86,
     87
  and steroids, 259
bronchoscopy, 260
broviac catheter, 147, 275
  surgery to place, 315–16
bruises on baby
  and jaundice, 156
  from tape in NICU, 145
bubble, VP shunt, 317
bulb syringe
  for suctioning, 347
burial arrangements, 489–90
burnout, 381–82
burping baby, 233
  with reflux, at home, 359
BV. *See* bacterial vaginosis

C

caffeine medication
  as apnea treatment, 219
calcium
  and preeclampsia prevention, 10
caloric intake, 236
  and special formulas, 361
car bed, 344, 360
carbon dioxide monitor, 94
cardiorespiratory monitor, 93, 385–93. *See also* breathing
     difficulty; monitoring of baby; monitors
carrying baby
  and home monitors, 387
car seat use, 339, 343–45
  and reflux, 360
car travel
  and home monitors, 386
  and home oxygen, 355
  to soothe baby, 375

catheters (baby's), 95, 146–48
"cath toes," 148
Caucasian ethnicity
  and baby's viability, 47
  and prematurity rate, 37
caudal anesthesia, 309
cellophane "blanket," 92
centigrade to Fahrenheit conversion chart, 512
central auditory processing difficulty
  as learning disability, 467
central line catheter, 147, 275
  surgery to place, 315–16
cerclage procedure, 15–16. *See also* cervical incompetence
cerebral palsy, 458–62
  and assessing IQ, 463
  and BPD, 264
  and brain cysts (PVL), 286
  and chorioamnionitis, 60
  and feeding problems, 457
  and intraventricular hemorrhage, 169
  resources list, 523
  and resuscitation at delivery, 60
  risk for, according to baby's gestational age at birth, 50,
     51
  and SGA history, 74
  typical characteristics of, 421–24
  worrying about, 408, 419–21, 426
cerebrospinal fluid, 166
  and hydrocephalus, 168–69, 316–19
cervical incompetence. *See also* cerclage
  and bed rest, 5
  diagnosis of, 16
  as risk factor for prematurity, 33
cervical length
  and birth date prediction, 10
cervix problems. *See* cervical incompetence
chaplain
  help with decisions about limiting treatment, 501
  and loss of baby, 490
  role, in parents' coping, 195, 256
chest (baby's)
  compressions, for resuscitation at delivery, 61
  indented, 243
  RSV and sucked in while breathing, 436
chest physiotherapy, 174, 262
chest tube, for air leak, 161–63
chicken pox vaccine (before pregnancy), 18
child abuse, risk for preemies, 381–82
child care—resources list, 523
children with special needs, 441–80
child service coordinator
  and early intervention, 336, 444–46
child's understanding of death, 495

chlamydia (maternal)
and risk of preterm birth, 18
chloral hydrate medication, as sedative, 110
choices. *See* decision-making
chorioamnionitis, 183
and delayed interval delivery, 67
and resuscitation of baby, 60
choroid cysts, 284
chromosomal abnormality, 36
as SGA cause, 71, 73
chronic disease (maternal)
as risk factor for prematurity, 36
chronic sorrow, in parents, 432–33
Churchill, Winston, 505
circulation. *See also* blood flow
assessment of, doctor's perspective, 45, 80–81,
133
and preeclampsia, 9
circumcision
timing of, 192, 325
cisapride medication
and reflux, 246
classical C-section, 57
clinic, follow-up for NICU graduates, 399, 406–07
clot formation (from umbilical catheter), 148
clothing for preemie 340, 528–29 (resources list)
while in isolette, 190
and reflux, 360
clumsiness, 429–31
and difficulty with space, 468
CMV. *See* cytomegalovirus
cobedding (twins), 197
cocaine use (maternal)
as risk factor for preterm birth, 37
as SGA cause, 71
testing for, 119–20
cochlear implant, 451
cockroaches and breathing problems, 339
cognitive function, 462–65. *See also* intelligence; learning
disabilities
and BPD, 264
and gestational age at birth, 50–52
and intraventricular hemorrhage, 166, 169
and PVL, 284, 286
and SGA history, 74–75
colds and flu
exposure to, after baby is home, 338–39, 366, 381
exposure to, in the hospital, 181, 184–85
and home monitors, 392
and RSV, 435–39
color (baby's)
and apnea recognition, 158–59, 346, 360
at delivery, doctor's perspective, 45

at first day, doctor's perspective, 80
at first week, doctor's perspective, 133
and home oxygen use, 356
and jaundice, 155, 242
of newborn preemie, 90
of stool, 155
of teeth, 378, 431
of toes, 148
colostrum, 127, 225–26
comfort level (baby's). *See* pain
communication
with bedside nurses, 280
at delivery, doctor's perspective, 48
with doctors and nurses, 55, 105–07
at first day, doctor's perspective, 81, 83
during first week, doctor's perspective, 137
questions—whom to ask, 105–06
at time of surgery, 306–07
comparisons with other babies, trap of, 216–17
complications
and baby's surgery, 304–25
and cerclage, 16
and terbutaline, 14
concentrated formula, 236, 262–63, 361
concentrating, difficulty in
as learning disability, 467
concentrator (oxygen), 353
concepts, comprehension of
as learning disability, 467
confusion (parental), 193, 256
and child with special needs, 473–75
congenital conditions
and elective preterm delivery, 23
heart disease, and RSV preventive treatments,
438
infection, 183–84, 242
as SGA cause, 71, 73
conjugated hyperbilirubinemia, 242
constipation (baby's), 155
and feeding intolerance, 151
and VP shunt, 416
containment
positioning baby to give sense of, 202
contentment signals, 203
continuous positive airway pressure (CPAP), 96,
103–04
contractions
Braxton-Hicks, 5, 12–13
and delayed interval delivery, 67
and membrane rupture, 19–22
and preterm labor, 12–14
contraction stress test, 24
convulsions. *See* seizures

coordination. *See also* clumsiness
    loss of, and VP shunt, 417
    poor, and worries about cerebral palsy, 419–24
coping emotionally. *See* emotions (parents')
cortical visual impairment, 454
cost of care
    and CP, 460
    early intervention services, 445
    and home monitors, 387
    and home nursing, 349
    and home oxygen, 354
    during hospital stay, 192
counseling. *See* therapy
"countdown"
    for end of apnea, 334, 343
CP. *See* cerebral palsy
CPAP. *See* continuous positive airway pressure
CPR (instructions and diagrams), 520
    parents' ability to do, 346–47
    parents' learning, 335, 388
cramps (maternal)
    and preterm labor, 13
cremation arrangements, 489
crossed eyes
    in newborn, 141
    risk of, after ROP, 425
crowds
    whether to avoid after homecoming, 338
crying
    and baby on ventilator, 96, 266
    at birth, 45, 60
    by fussy baby at home, 373–76
    by parents, 255–57
cryotherapy
    for ROP, 271
C-section delivery, 56–58
    and identification of multiples, 69
cues baby gives, recognizing, 203–04
cuts on baby. *See* abrasions on baby
cyanosis, 159. *See also* color (baby's), and apnea recognition
cylinder, oxygen, 352
cysts in the brain, 284. *See also* periventricular leukomalacia
cytomegalovirus
    and safety of blood transfusions, 116–17
    as SGA cause, 71

D

Darwin, Charles, 507
daycare, safety of, 366–67, 411, 413, 436
    and child with BPD, 367, 411
    and child on home oxygen, 355
    and RSV, 436
    and VP shunts, 413

day-night cycling
    and Developmental Care in the NICU, 200
    after going home, 373–75
Deaf community, 448–49
    and cochlear implants, 451
deafness. *See* hearing exam; hearing aids; hearing loss
death of baby, 484–503
decision-making
    asking doctor about parents' role in, 55
    breastfeeding vs. formula feeding, 124–28
    whether to deliver immediately after membranes
        rupture, 21
    and dying baby, 487, 502–03
    whether to limit or give aggressive care, 46–47
        (doctor's perspective), 498–502
    and surgery, 306–08
degrees conversion chart, 512
dehumidifier (for home oxygen), 339, 353–54
dehydration
    and low blood pressure, 179
delayed interval delivery, 66–67
    one twin in distress, 31–32
delivery room
    large staff in, 58
dense patch on chest X-ray, 83
dental health (baby's), 377–78, 431–32
    and reflux, 360
dental health (maternal)
    and preterm birth, 18
depression (parents'), 193–95, 255–57. *See also* emotions
    (parents')
    and bed rest, 8
    and loss of baby, 484–87
desatting, 158–60, 220
    and home oxygen, 356
development. *See also* growth; growth charts;
        growth (fetal)
    adjusting age for, 365–66, 403–04
    delays in, 408. *See also* long-term health issues
    and early intervention, 442–46
    during early years, doctor's perspective, 401
    right stimulation for, 367–69
    risk of future problems, 426–28
    and turning out normal, 403
development (fetal). *See* growth (fetal);
        small–for–gestational age
Developmental Care, 198–205
    and baby with BPD, 262
    helping baby feel loved, 198
    and personalization of isolette, 189–91
    resources list, 523
    and time spent with baby in hospital, 253, 204–05
developmental evaluation, 427

diabetes
    and preeclampsia, 9
    as risk factor for prematurity, 36
    and steroid treatment, 28
diaper rash, 247
diapers
    examination of baby's, 154–55
    for preemies, where to find, 340
diarrhea (baby's)
    and feeding intolerance, 151, 154
    and VP shunt, 416
diarrhea (maternal)
    and preterm labor, 13
diet (baby's). *See* breastfeeding; feeding; nutrition
diet (maternal)
    as risk factor for preterm birth, 37
dietitian 457
digestion (baby's), 151–52. *See also* feeding
dilation
    and cervical incompetence, 15–17
    and predicting birth date, 10
diptheria, tetanus and pertussis vaccine, 290
"directed" donation
    for blood transfusion, 117
    of breast milk, 154
direct hyperbilirubinemia, 242
disability. *See also* brain injury; hearing loss; learning
        disabilities; long-term health issues
    parenting a child with, 473–80
    preemies and special needs, 440–80
    risk according to gestational age at birth, 49–52
discharge from hospital. *See also* home care; home
        monitoring; home nursing care; home oxygen
    doctor's perspective, 333–38
    requirements for discharge, 121
discharge (vaginal)
    and preterm labor, 13
discolored toes, 148
discomfort (baby's). *See* pain
"disorganized feeders," 153
disorientation (parents') and special needs, 473
diuretics for baby with BPD, 214, 262
DNR (Do Not Resuscitate) order, 47, 55, 498–503
dobutamine medication, 180
doctor (baby's). *See also* communication
    change of, 282–84
    for child with disability, 476–77
    choosing a pediatrician, 336, 341–43
    doctor's perspective at delivery time, 45–48
    doctor's perspective during early years of growth,
        399–403
    doctor's perspective on first day, 80–83
    doctor's perspective during first week, 133–37

doctor's perspective on going home, 333–38
doctor's perspective during hospital stay, 212–17
    first meeting with, 54–56
    and questions in the NICU, 105–06
    several, with multiples, 123
    vs. surgeon's role, 305–06
    trouble understanding, 105
    two, disagreement between, 283
    and whom to call after baby is home, 363
doctor's perspective. *See* doctor (baby's)
donor of blood, parent as, 116–17
donor of breast milk. *See* banks for breast milk
Do Not Resuscitate order, 46–47, 55, 498–503
dopamine medication, 180
Doppler flow studies
    for fetal health assessment, 25
double pumping, 224, 291
drug abuse (maternal)
    as risk factor for prematurity, 37
    and SGA, 71
    test for, 119
drugs (baby's)
    possibility of addiction, 111
DTP. *See* diptheria, tetanus and pertussis
Dubowitz examination, 81
duck-toed toddler, 430
dust mite minimization, 339
dying at home or in hospital, 487
dyslexia, 467

E
early birth. *See* elective preterm birth; premature birth
early intervention, 442–46
    and child with CP, 459–60
    end of, 446
    evaluation for, 444
    resources list, 524
    team members, 445
earmold fitting for hearing aid, 450
ears. *See also* hearing ability; hearing loss; hearing exam;
        hearing aids
    folded over, 90
    stiffness, 81
eating. *See* feeding
echocardiogram, 171
eclampsia seizures, 9
education, right to, for children with special needs,
        461, 469, 478
EEG
    for seizure diagnosis, 170
Einstein, Albert, 506
elective preterm birth, 4, 22–23
    after membranes rupture, 21

and preeclampsia, 10
electrolytes, 134, 170
    and low blood pressure, 179
emergency power outage, at home, 354, 389
emergency surgery, vs. scheduled, 306
emergency, with baby in the NICU, 160
EMLA cream or patch, 110, 438
emotional intelligence, 465
emotions. *See also* decision-making; family issues; parents;
        siblings
    and adoption of preemie, 369–72
    afraid to see baby, 88–89
    and bed rest, 8
    and BPD, 263–65
    and children with special needs, 441, 459, 462, 473–80
    desire for privacy, 143
    doctor's perspective, 255–57, 379–82
    extreme reactions, 380–82
    father of preemie, 296–302
    and feeling aftershocks, 379–80, 432–34
    and fussy baby, 373–76
    and loss of baby, 484–87
    parents', 193–95, 216–17
    and rehospitalization, 404–06
    and surgery, 304–05
    symptoms of depression, 256
employers
    and bed rest, 8
    and leave of absence from job, 254–55
endotracheal tube, 95
    and pain, 108
Enfamil 22 formula, 361
enterostomy, 313–15
epidural anesthesia
    baby's, 309
    maternal, 58
epilepsy, 418–19
    and seizure differentiation, 171, 418–19
equipment. *See also* monitors; home monitoring; isolette;
        home oxygen; nasal cannula; alarms
    in NICU, 92–96
erythropoietin medication, 215 (doctor's perspective), 276
esophageal irritation, from reflux, 245
estriol, salivary
    and birth date prediction, 11
ethnicity (baby's)
    and viability, 47
ethnicity (maternal)
    as risk factor for prematurity, 37
exchange transfusions, for jaundice, 157
exercise (maternal)
    and false labor, 5
    and risk of prematurity, 37

during bed rest, 7
experimentation on preemies, concern about, 117–18
expressing breast milk. *See* pumping breast milk
extremely premature baby, 49–50, 84, 89
extubation, 96
    accidental, 144, 265
eye exam, 213
    doctor's perspective, 267
eyelids fused, 90, 139
eye movement
    abnormal, and VP shunt, 416
eye problems (maternal)
    and anti-labor drugs, 13
eyesight. *See* retinopathy of prematurity; visual
        impairment

F
face masks
    use at home, 338
facial expression
    and blindness, 453
    difficulty with, as learning disability, 468
Fahrenheit to centigrade conversion chart, 512
"failure to thrive," doctor's perspective, 251,
        253, 401
false alarms. *See also* alarms
    and home monitors, 386, 389–92
    on newborn health screening tests, 279
false labor, 5–6, 12–13
    and monitoring cervix with ultrasound, 10
family issues. *See also* emotions (parents')
    adjustment to disability, 479
    and child with disability, 471–72, 475–77
    and CP, 460, 461
    at delivery time, doctor's perspective, 48
    and early intervention, 442–43
    during early years, doctor's perspective, 402
    on first day, doctor's perspective, 83
    during first week, doctor's perspective, 137
    when going home, doctor's perspective, 337
    and home nursing care, 347–50
    during hospital stay, doctor's perspective, 216
    loss of baby and impact on marriage, 486
    marital, 298, 432–34
    resilience after time, 257
    siblings, 185, 299
    stress, during hospital time, 255–57
    stress, during maternal bed rest, 7
    at transfer time, 54
family physician
    vs. pediatrician, 340
Family Service Plan, 444–45
famous preemies, 505–07

Farouk, King of Egypt, 507
fasting (baby's)
    and surgery, 308
father (baby's), 296–302
    feeling faint in NICU, 112
    role in delivery room, doctor's perspective, 48
    role in transfer of baby, 65
    role in transfer of mother, 53–54
fatigue (baby's)
    as apnea cause, 218
fatigue (parents')
    when baby comes home, 364, 381
fats in breast milk, 125
fear
    and dying baby, 487–88
    father's, 297
    of holding baby, 144
    of leaving baby, 160, 380–81
    of seeing baby, 88
febrile seizures. *See* seizures
"feeders and growers," 134
feeding. *See also* nutrition issues (baby's); bottle feeding;
        breastfeeding; diet
    and apnea, at home, 346
    whether baby getting enough milk, 228, 234–37, 362–63
        multiples, 290–91
    baby with reflux, 359–60
    and BPD, 262–63
    breastfeeding vs. bottle feeding, 124–28
    gavage feeding, 150–51
    at home, concern about growth, 362–63, 410–11,
        457–58
    how a preemie is fed, journey from intravenous to
        breast or bottle, 149–53
    intolerance, 73, 151–52, 154–55, 236
    multiples, 290–93
    and NEC, 85, 87, 238–40
    nipple confusion, 228–29
    not feeding newborn, 113–14
    oral aversion, 263, 377
    parenteral nutrition, 113–14, 149–50, 242
    picky toddler, 410–11
    poor, and VP shunt, 416
    problems with, at home, 374, 410–11, 456–58
    resources list, 524
    and sensory integration problems, 455–57
    special formula and supplements, 234–37, 360–62
        doctor's perspective, 335
    starting breast or bottle, 152–53, 226–28, 232–34
    working up on feeds, doctor's perspective, 136–37,
        214–15
feeding tube, 95, 320, 457–58
feeling loved (baby), 198–205

feelings. *See also* emotions (parents'); siblings of twins if
        one has disability, 470–72
    of child with disability, 478–80
    of surviving twin, 498
fees. *See* cost of care
fentanyl medication, 110
fertility treatment
    and risk of prematurity, 28, 33, 434–35
fetal distress, 22, 23–26, 61
    and C-section delivery, 55
fetal fibronectin
    and birth date prediction, 11
fetal growth rate. *See also* small–for–gestational age;
        twins, and twin to twin transfusion syndrome
    as risk factor for prematurity, 22, 35
fetal health, 22–23. *See also* fetal monitoring
    and bed rest, 5
    birth defect as risk factor for prematurity, 36
    and membrane rupture, 19–22
    and one twin having trouble, 31–32
    and preeclampsia, 9
fetal monitoring, 23–26
fetal movement, 23–25, 26
fever
    and VP shunt, 415
fibronectin. *See* fetal fibronectin
fighting spirit, 26
financial assistance. *See also* cost of care
    resources list, 524
fine motor skills
    and learning disability, 467
flu
    exposure to, 338
    vaccine, 411
fluid in scrotum, 250
fluid intake (mother's)
    and breast milk quantity, 229
fluid loss, in newborn preemies, 92, 100
fluid management
    and BPD, 262
fluid retention (maternal)
    and preeclampsia diagnosis, 8
FM system (hearing aids), 447, 449–50
focusing difficulty
    as learning disability, 467
focusing eyes, in newborn preemie, 140, 141
folded ears, 90
follow-up care, 406–07
    choosing a pediatrician, 341
    doctor's perspective, 336, 399–400
fontanel
    full, and VP shunt, 415
forceps

and preemies, 56
forgetting to breathe. *See* apnea of prematurity
former preemies
    alternative to today's high-tech NICUs, 118–19
    famous, 505–07
    self-image of, with special needs, 479–80
formula feeding. *See* bottle feeding
Fox, Michael J., 506
fractures in baby, 241
fragility of baby, 98
fraternal twins vs. identical, 69–70
freezing breast milk, 225–26
frog-legged position
    and CP, 424
fundoplication, 246, 319–21
funeral arrangements, 489–91
fussy baby, 373–76
    and sensory integration problems, 455

G
gag reflex
    desensitizing, 456
    and gavage feeding, 150
    and ventilator tube, 108
galactosemia
    and inaccuracy of screening test for, 279
gas, excess (baby's)
    and feeding intolerance, 151
gas bloat syndrome
    and surgery for reflux, 321
gastroenterologist, 457
gastroesophageal reflux. *See* reflux
gastrostomy tube, 320. *See also* feeding tube
    need for, 457–58
gavage feeding, 95, 149, 150–51
    and breast milk, 124
    and nipple confusion, 228–29
gaze
    in child with hydrocephalus, 417
    downward, and VP shunt malfunction, 417
    as preemie's signal, 203–04
gels, adhesive, 145–46
gender
    and IQ prediction, 461
    and one twin doing better, 121
    and respiratory distress syndrome, 102
    and RSV risk, 436
genital formation, 90–91
genital tract infections
    and cerclage, 15–16
    and preterm birth, 17–18
germinal matrix
    and intraventricular hemorrhage, 166

gestational age
    and breastfeeding, 124
    and cerclage, 17
    and delayed interval delivery, 67
    and effectiveness of prenatal steroid treatment, 27–28
    evaluation of, 81
    and lung growth after membrane rupture, 20, 21
    SGA, 70–75
    and viability, 46–47
    and weight at birth, 513
    23–25 weeks
        behavior and sensing, 138–39
        survival and long-term health, 49–50
        top health concerns, 84–85
    26–29 weeks
        behavior and sensing, 139–40
        survival and long-term health, 50–51
        top health concerns, 86–87
    30–33 weeks
        behavior and sensing, 140–41
        survival and long-term health, 51
        top health concerns, 87–88
    34+ weeks
        behavior and sensing, 141–42
        survival and long-term health, 51–52
        top health concerns, 88
gestational diabetes. *See also* diabetes
    as risk factor for prematurity, 36
glaucoma
    after ROP, 426
glossary, 537–43
gloves, worn by NICU staff, 185
glycerin suppository
    and constipation, 155
    and feeding difficulty, 151
von Goethe, Johann Wolfgang, 505
going home (baby). *See also* family issues
    and BPD, 263
    family issues, doctor's perspective, 337–38
    preparing for, 337, 338–40
    requirements for, doctor's perspective, 333–37
    timing of, 120–21
gonorrhea
    and preterm birth, 18
government, state
    and early intervention services, 444
grams to pounds conversion chart, 511
grief. *See also* depression (parents'); emotions (parents');
        chronic sorrow; sadness
    anticipatory, 297–98, 474
    and having a special needs child, 474
    losing baby, 484–87
    siblings, and loss of baby, 493–97

growth. *See also* growth charts; growth (fetal); nutrition issues; weight
  and changes in weight, length and head circumference, 235
  early years, 400–401
  monitoring in hospital, 212–13
  and obsession with, 362–63
  predictions concerning future height, 409
  and SGA baby, 75
growth charts
  fetal growth, multiple gestation, 514
  premature boys born between 1,500 and 2,500 grams, 518
  premature boys born under 1,500 grams, 517
  premature girls born between 1,500 and 2,500 grams, 516
  premature girls born under 1,500 grams, 515
  weight and gestational age, 513
growth (fetal). *See also* growth charts
  and bed rest, 5
  poor, reasons for, 71–72
  poor, as risk factor for prematurity, 22, 35
  and SGA baby, 70–75
g-tube, 320. *See also* feeding tube
guaiac test, 155, 239
guilt, 193. *See also* emotions (parents'); feelings
  and adopting a preemie, 369–70
  and death of baby, 485
  and decision to stop or continue medical treatment, 503
  and dividing time between twins, 294
  and home nursing care, 347–48
  and rehospitalization of preemie, 405
  of sibling, and loss of baby, 494
gum disease (maternal)
  and preterm birth, 18

H
hair, 90
handling baby. *See also* holding baby; touching baby
  and fathers, at home, 302
  and fathers, in NICU, 301
  fracture, and concern about rough handling, 241
  frequency in NICU, 201
handwashing
  in hospital, 184–85
  after preemie comes home, 338–39
"hand womb," 202
handwriting
  as learning disability, 467
headache (child's)
  and VP shunt, 414, 415, 416
headache (maternal)
  and anti-labor drugs, 13, 14

and preeclampsia, 9
"head righting," 423
head size
  evaluation on first day, 80
  and hydrocephalus, 168–69, 316–17
  and intraventricular hemorrhage, 168
  ongoing evaluation of, 212
  and VP shunt, 414, 415–16
head-sparing growth retardation, 72, 75
head-turning
  30–33 weeks of gestation, 141
head ultrasound, 85, 136. *See also* ultrasound
health concerns (baby). *See also* development; health concerns (expectant mother and fetus); long-term health issues
  and accidental extubation, 265–66
  according to baby's gestational age at birth
    23–25 weeks, 50, 84–85
    26–29 weeks, 50–51, 86–87
    30–33 weeks, 51, 87–88
    34+ weeks, 52, 88
  and alternatives to the NICU, 118–19
  and antibiotic use, 274
  and autopsy, 492–93
  and baby on ventilator for a long time, 257–58
  and baby turning out normal, 403
  and being afraid to leave baby, 160
  and childhood seizure, 418–19
  during childhood, doctor's perspective, 399–403
  and clumsy child, 429–31
  and daycare, 366–67, 411–12
  at delivery, doctor's perspective, 45–47
  and early intervention, 442–43
  and feeling protective, 380–82
  on first day, doctor's perspective, 80–83
  during first week, doctor's perspective, 133–37
  during hospital stay, doctor's perspective, 212–16
  and infection control measures in NICU, 184–85
  is baby sick or immature?, 99–101
  and IV in scalp, 274–76
  and lingering effect on parents' emotions, 432
  and making decisions about continuing or stopping treatment, 498–503
  and medical tests on multiples, 293–94
  and meeting with neonatologist, 54–56
  and need for longer-term feeding tube, 457–58
  and need for rehospitalization, 404–06
  and need for resuscitation at delivery, 60–62
  and NICU environment, 198–205
  and obsession with baby's weight gain, 362–63
  and older siblings, 364–65
  and parenting a child with special needs, 473–80

and preparing to take baby home, 338–40
and risk for developmental problems in healthy toddler, 426–28
and risk of prematurity in subsequent pregnancy, 434–35
and RSV, 435–39
and SGA baby, 72–75
and sibling visits to NICU, 185–86
and smaller vs. bigger twin, 122–23
and surgery, 304–05
around time of hospital discharge, 330–37
and transfer of baby to another hospital, 65–66
and transfer to community hospital, 288–89
and transfer to intermediate care unit, 287–88
and VP shunt, 412–18
and vulnerable child syndrome, 380, 402–03
and whom to call with questions after hospital discharge, 363
and worrying about cerebral palsy, 419–21
health concerns (expectant mother and fetus). See also health concerns (baby)
and assessing fetal well-being, 23–26
fetus doing poorly, 22–23
and medications to help prevent complications of prematurity, 26–28
and multiple gestation, 28–29, 30–31, 31–32
and need for C-section, 57–58
risk factors for prematurity, 33–37
and transfer to another hospital, 52–53
hearing ability
at 23–25 weeks of gestation, 139
at 26–29 weeks of gestation, 139
at 30–33 weeks of gestation, 141
at 34+ weeks of gestation, 141
hearing aids, 446–48, 449–51
hearing exam, 213, 272–73, 447
screening, and VP shunts, 413
hearing loss, 446–51
and IQ, 463
resources list, 525–26
heartbeat. See heart function; heart rate
heart function, 133, 179–80. See also circulation; heart rate; low blood pressure
and blood flow, 61–62, 80–81
and CPR (cardiopulmonary resuscitation), 61
at delivery, doctor's perspective, 45
and PDA, 176–79
response to resuscitation at delivery, 61, 62
heart murmur, 277
and PDA, 178
heart rate (baby's). See also blood flow; circulation; bradycardia; heart function
and Apgar scores, 62

apnea and bradycardia, 218–20
assessment at delivery, doctor's perspective, 45
high, 133
and monitors, 93–94
and need for resuscitation at delivery, 60–62
normal, 94
heart rate (fetal)
and elective preterm delivery, 22
and fetal distress, 56
and monitoring fetal well-being, 24–25
heart rhythm (maternal)
and anti-labor drugs, 13, 14
HELLP syndrome, 9
helplessness, 193, 256, 298. See also emotions (parents')
hemiplegia and CP, 459
hemophilus influenzae b vaccine, 290
hemorrhage (maternal)
as risk factor for prematurity, 34–35
heparin and blood clots, 148
hepatitis B virus (maternal), 18
herbal medicines
and breast milk quantity, 231
hernia (baby's), 248–49, 249
as late-appearing problem, doctor's perspective, 212
surgery for, 324–25
heroin addiction (maternal)
and SGA baby, 71
herpes, 71, 183–84
high blood pressure (baby's), 266–67. and BPD, 262
in lungs, and pulmonary hypertension, 171–72
high blood pressure (maternal). See also preeclampsia
and bed rest, 5
and pregnancy, 8–10
as risk factor for prematurity, 36
high-risk pregnancy, 4
resources list, 526
risk factors for prematurity, 33–37
Hispanic women
and prematurity rate, 37
HIV (mother), 183–84
and breastfeeding, 126
hoarseness, 265, 266
holding baby. See also touching baby
afraid to touch baby, 98
asking doctor about, 55
at delivery, 46, 59
not allowed to, and worry about loss of bonding, 64–65
positioning and stimulation, 368
skin to skin (kangaroo care), 221–22
and on ventilator, 144

home care
    and dying baby, 487–88
    father's role, 301–02
    and feeling protective, 380–82
    and fussy baby, 373–76
    and giving medication, 357–58
    and not feeling happy, 379–80
    and older siblings, 364
    and preemie-proofing, 338–40
    requirements for discharge, 121
    resources list, 526
    and the right stimulation, 367–69
    and schedule for multiples, 383–85, 519
    and whom to call with questions, 363
    and worrisome parental responses, 380–81
home monitoring
    cardiorespiratory, 334, 385–93
    fetal, 6
home nursing care, 347–50
    house rules for home nurses, 349
    resources list, 526–27
home oxygen, 350–56
hopelessness, 256. See also emotions (parent's)
hospice nurse, 487
hospital, back in, 404–06, 437
hospital chaplain
    role, in parents' coping, 195
hospitalization (maternal), 4
    and membrane rupture, 20–22
    and preterm labor, 12
hostility, 256, 298. See also emotions (parent's)
hot flashes
    and anti-labor drugs, 13
Huggies, toll free number, 340
Hugo, Victor, 507
human milk fortifier, 235
    and feeding intolerance, 152
humidification, and oxygen, 353
hydrocele, 250
hydrocephalus, 168–69. See also intraventricular
        hemorrhage; VP shunt
    and high blood pressure, 267
    resources list, 527
    surgery for, 316–19
hygiene
    at home, 337, 338–40
    in NICU, 184–85
hyperactivity. See also development; disability
    and clumsiness, 430
    and developmental delay, 401
    as disability, 401, 427, 466, 467
    and parenting a child with special needs, 441, 473–80
    risk for, according to baby's gestational age, 50, 51

and sensory integration problems, 456
    and troublesome behavior, 428–29
hyper-alertness
    and brain injury, 62
    and infant signals, 204
hyperbilirubinemia, 155–57, 242–43. See also jaundice
hypersensitivity, 455. See also overstimulation
hypertension, 266–67. See also high blood pressure
    and pregnancy, 5, 8–10
hypoglycemia
    in SGA baby, 73
hypotension See low blood pressure
hypothermia. See body temperature
hypothyroidism, 278–79

I
identicality of twins, 69–70
identification of multiples by alphabet, 68–69
imminent delivery. See also preterm labor
    medications for, 26–28
    and meeting with neonatologist, 54–56
    tests for, 11, 26
    and transfer to another hospital, 52–54
immunizations. See vaccination
incarcerated hernia, 248–49
incompetent cervix. See cervical incompetence
incomplete emptying of stomach, 151
incubator, 205. See also isolette
indentation of chest, 243
Indocin, 110. See also indomethacin
indomethacin
    and IVH prevention, 165
    and PDA, 135, 178–79
    and preterm labor, 14
infant seats. See car seat use
infant-toddler development specialist, 442, 446
infection (infant and child), 99, 182–84
    and antibiotics, 274
    and bronchoscopy, 260
    and daycare, 411–12
    on first day, doctor's perspective, 83
    and flu vaccine, 411
    and handwashing, 184–85
    as health concern, according to baby's gestational age, 85, 86, 87
    and home care, 338–39
    during hospital stay, doctor's perspective, 215
    and jaundice, 156
    and need for resuscitation at delivery, 60
    from other babies, 181
    and pneumonia, 187, 260
    RSV, 435–39
    and seizures, 170

as SGA cause, 71
and sibling visits, 187
and VP shunt, 413, 414, 415
infection (maternal)
    and incompetent cervix, 15, 16
    and membrane rupture, 19–22
    and preterm birth, 4, 11, 12, 17–19, 36
    risk, and prenatal steroid treatment, 28
    and testing for, with amniocentesis, 25
    transmitted to fetus, 183–84
infertility
    and prematurity, 29, 33
    and twins, 69
inflammation
    and preterm birth, 11
"informed" consent for surgery, 306–07
inguinal hernia, 248–49
    surgery for, 324–25
injection pain, and EMLA use, 438–39
insurance coverage
    and cost of care, 192–93
intelligence
    and cerebral palsy, 458, 459, 461
    and learning disabilities, 466, 468
    measurement and prediction of, in preemies, 462–65
    and prematurity, 464–65
    and SGA baby, 74–75
intensive care. See neonatal intensive care unit
interleukin 6, 11
intermediate care
    moving baby to, 287
internet, 477–78
intestinal tract. See also feeding; necrotizing enterocolitis
    development of, 149
    maturation of, and feeding intolerance, 214
    and necrotizing enterocolitis (NEC), 237–40
    obstruction, after NEC, 240
    and prenatal steroids, 27–28
intravenous feeding, 113–14, 149–50
    and breathing difficulty, on first day, 82
    and NEC, 238
    in SGA baby, 73
intravenous lines, 95
    central lines, 275
    and holding baby, 144–45
    kinds of, 147–48
    need for more than one, 146
    scalp, 274–76
intraventricular hemorrhage, 99, 164–69, 167
    and brain cysts (PVL), 285
    doctor's perspective on, 136
    and forceps or vacuum extractor, 56
    and jaundice, 156

and pneumothorax, 162
and prenatal steroid treatment, 27–28
and seizures, 170
top health concern, according to baby's gestational age
    at birth, 85, 86
intubation, 96. See also endotracheal tube; ventilator
in vitro fertilization. See also infertility
    and premature delivery, 28–29
iodine and thyroid function, 278
IQ scores. See intelligence
iron. See also nutrition issues (baby's)
    and anemia, 277
    and EPO (erythropoietin), 215
    nutrition and growth, 235–36
    and preterm breast milk, 125
    relative concentrations of, in preterm formula
        vs. breast milk, 126
irritability (baby's)
    and adoptive parents, 370–71
    and BPD, 264
    and reflux, 360
    and relation to prematurity, 368, 373–76, 428–29
    and sensory integration problems, 455
    similarity to pain, 109
    and VP shunt, 417
irritability (parents'). See emotions (parents')
isolation
    and parents' need for privacy, 143, 380–82
    and preemie at risk for RSV, 437
    unwanted, and child with disability, 476
isolette, 91–92, 93
    covering, 189, 200
    personalization of, 188–91
IVH. See intraventricular hemorrhage

J
jaundice, 155–57, 242
jerkiness. See twitchiness
jitteriness and preterm labor medication, 14
    normal, 98–99
    and seizures, 170
joint flexibility, 20
judgment, poor
    as learning disability, 468

K
kangaroo care, 65, 205, 221–22
    and breastfeeding, 125, 227, 230
Keats, John, 505
Kennedy, Patrick Bouvier, 506
kick counts, 23
kicks
    and baby's fighting spirit, 26

kidney disease (maternal)
    and preeclampsia, 9
    and risk for prematurity, 36
Kingsley, Emily Perl, 473
kitty litter and hidden infection, 18

L

labeling multiples, 68
labor. *See also* false labor; preterm labor
    and C-section delivery, 56
    and IVH, 165
    true labor, compared to false, 5–6
laboratory assessment of preemies. *See* monitoring of
        baby, 399
lactation, 223. *See also* breastfeeding; pumping breast milk
    counselor, and getting help with, 113
    later-onset, 230
    natural cycle of, 229
lactose intolerance, 236
La Leche League, 223, 522
language delay
    and cerebral palsy, 458, 460
    and hearing loss, 447–49
    and intelligence, 462, 465
    and learning disabilities, 466, 469
language education
    and hearing loss, 448–49
language therapy. *See* speech and language therapy
lanugo, 88, 89, 90
laser surgery
    for ROP, 271
    and twin to twin transfusion syndrome, 31
laser therapy. *See* laser surgery
late with medication, 358
laxative, for feeding difficulty, 151
leads
    and cardiorespiratory monitors, 93–94, 94, 389–92, 390
    and false alarms, 158, 389, 391, 392
leakage of air in lungs, 161–64
learning disabilities, 466–69. *See also* disability;
        development; hyperactivity
    and late appearance of, 427
    and PVL, 286–87
    resources list, 527–28
    risk of, according to baby's gestational age at birth, 50,
        51
    and SGA babies, 74–75
leaving baby
    difficulty of, with special needs child, 476
    and dividing time between twins, 294–95
    and fathers working excessively, 298
    fear of, 160
    to go back to work, 254–55

and how much time to spend in hospital, 252–54
    and parents asked to leave nursery, 191
leg swelling, 8
length of baby, 212
let-down reflex, 228, 229–31. *See also* breastfeeding
lethargy
    as symptom of infection, 436
    and VP shunt, 415, 416
Level 1–3 hospitals, 52–53
life support decision-making. *See also* decision-
        making
    at delivery, 46–47, 55
    and making the hardest decisions, 498–503
light
    altering, for Developmental Care, 200
    baby loves looking at, 454
    as jaundice treatment, 157
limpness. *See also* muscle tone; lethargy
    and cerebral palsy, 422
    at delivery, 60
    as troublesome sign, 62, 159
line. *See* central line catheter; catheters (baby's);
        intravenous line; tube
listening. *See* communication
liver and jaundice, 155–56, 242–43
    and TPN, 150
local anesthesia, 110
    and surgery, 309
long-term health issues. *See also* children with special
        needs; development
    according to baby's gestational age at birth, 50, 51, 52
    and apnea, 220
    behavioral issues, 428–29
    and BPD, 264–65
    and brain cysts, 284, 286–87
    cerebral palsy, 419–21
    developmental delay, 408
    disability, 441–42
    and fractures, 241
    and home nursing care, 348–50
    and intraventricular hemorrhage, 169
    and jaundice, 157
    late appearing, 426–28
    learning disabilities, 466, 467–69
    and making decisions about continuing treatment,
        498–503
    mental retardation, 464–65
    motor, 430
    and NEC, 240
    and need for resuscitation at delivery, 61–62
    and NICU environment, 198–99
    and PDA, 177–78, 179
    and RDS, 104–05

and reflux, 246
and ROP, 271–72
in school years, 428–29
and seizures, 171
and SGA baby, 74–75
slow diagnosis of, 402
in twins of different size, 122–23
loss and grief—resources list, 528
loud noise. *See* noise
low birth weight. *See also* gestational age; growth charts;
        growth; growth (fetal)
    and multiples, 28–29
    and preeclampsia, 9
    and small–for–gestational age, 70–75
low blood flow. *See also* circulation; heart function; low
        blood pressure
    and apnea and bradycardia, 220
    to the fetus, as risk factor for premature birth, 22
    and intraventricular hemorrhage, 164–65, 169
    and oligohydramnios, 35
    and PDA, 178
    and placental abruption, 34
    and preeclampsia, 9, 35
    and PVL, 285
    and resuscitation at delivery, 60–62
    and smoking during pregnancy, 37
low blood pressure (baby's), 179–80
low-grade infections
    and preterm birth, 17–19
low maternal weight, 37
low oxygen flow. *See* oxygen; oxygen deprivation
lumbar puncture
    and hydrocephalus, 168–69
    and infection, 83, 167, 182
lung disease, 82, 84, 86, 87, 134–35, 213. *See also*
        bronchopulmonary dysplasia; respiratory
        distress syndrome
    chronic, 162, 261–65
    and feeding problems, 457
    and immaturity, 99, 101–05
lung maturity, 84, 86, 87, 88. *See also* respiratory distress
        syndrome; lung disease
    assessment of, 25
    and prenatal steroids, 27
    and resuscitation at delivery, 60
    in SGA baby, 74
    and twins, 121
Lyme disease, 18
"lytes," 134. *See also* electrolytes; monitoring of baby

M
magnesium sulfate, 10, 13, 60
malacia, 260, 323

malformation of the uterus, 33
malnutrition (maternal)
    as risk factor for prematurity, 37
    as SGA cause, 71
mask
    worn by staff, 181
massage
    of baby, 250–52
    of breasts, and breast milk quantity, 230
maternal response
    and adoptive parents, 371
    and bonding, 64–65
maternal transport. *See* transport; transfer of mother
maternal weight (low)
    as risk factor for prematurity, 37
math difficulty
    as learning disability, 467
maturation
    and differences between twins, 102, 121, 461
    and prenatal steroid treatment, 27
McCarthy Scale, 463
meconium drug test, 120
    and fetal distress, 62
    and timing of first bowel movement, 154
Medicaid
    eligibility, 192
medical costs. *See* cost of care
medical specialists. *See also* early intervention;
        pediatrician; doctor (baby's)
    for high risk pregnancies, 4
    in the NICU, 96–97
    and transport to another hospital, 52, 65–66
medication. *See also specific brands and types*
    giving to baby at home, 357–58
    at home-going, 336
    and pain reduction, 109–11
    stopping, 358, 400
medication (maternal)
    for low-grade infections, 17–18
    need for, as reason for elective preterm
        delivery, 36
    for preeclampsia, 9–10
    and preterm labor, 12–14
membrane rupture, 19–22
    and bed rest, 5
    and cerclage, 16, 17
    and cervical incompetence, 15, 16
memorial service for baby, 489, 490
memory of pain (baby), 376–77
memory of words
    and learning disability, 467
meningitis, 99, 182–83
    and seizures, 170–71

mental health. *See* emotions (parents'); feelings
  in children with disabilities, 480
  and coping emotionally, 193–95
  and extreme parental responses, 380–81
  and long-term emotional effects of a preterm birth,
    432–34
  maintaining, while on bed rest, 6–8
  and post-partum depression, 255–57
mental retardation, 462–64, 464–65. *See also* intelligence
  and BPD, 264
  and brain cysts, 284
  and hypothyroidism, 278
  and learning disabilities, 466
  and PVL, 286
  and SGA baby, 74–75
metabolic problems. *See also* monitoring of baby
  and jaundice, 242
  and seizures, 170–71
methadone, 110
mildew elimination, 339
milestones. *See also* development; developmental evaluation
  and blindness, 452–53
  and cerebral palsy, 420, 421–24
  and clumsiness, 430
  delays in reaching, 401, 408, 457
  and discharge from early intervention services, 446
  and feeding, 457
  and hearing, 447
  and IQ, 461–65
  and teeth, 431
milk allergy, 236
milk production. *See* breast milk; lactation; pumping breast
    milk; breastfeeding
minerals, 241. *See also* iron
  and assessment of baby's nutritional status, 212–13,
    235
  and intravenous feeds (TPN), 150, 241
  and preterm breast milk or formula, 126, 235, 361
  and supplementing baby's feeds, 235–36, 361
  and supplementing during pregnancy, 37
"minor" disabilities, 426–27. *See also* development;
    disability; hyperactivity; learning disability; sensory
    integration dysfunction; special needs children
  and late appearance of, 426–28
  risk of, at various gestational ages, 50, 51
missed medication, 358
modified biophysical profile, 25
moisturizers for baby, 247
mold elimination, 339
monitoring of baby
  Apgar scores, and assessing need for resuscitation at
    delivery, 62–63
  for apnea and bradycardia, 93–94, 220

"blood gases," 95
blood pressure, 94, 179
cardiorespiratory function, at home, 385–93
and common issues and decisions during childhood,
    doctor's perspective, 400–402
and common issues and decisions at delivery, doctor's
    perspective, 46–47
and common issues and decisions on first day, doctor's
    perspective, 82–83
and common issues and decisions during first week,
    doctor's perspective, 134–37
and common issues and decisions during hospital stay,
    doctor's perspective, 213–16
and common issues and decisions around time of
    hospital discharge, doctor's perspective, 334–37
for developmental delays, 427
diaper output, 154–55
for feeding intolerance, 151
head size, after IVH, 168
nutritional status, 235
oxygen and carbon dioxide, 94–95
physical examination and laboratory assessment in
    childhood, doctor's perspective, 399–400
physical examination and laboratory assessment at
    delivery, doctor's perspective, 45–46
physical examination and laboratory assessment on first
    day, doctor's perspective, 80–82
physical examination and laboratory assessment during
    first week, doctor's perspective, 133–34
physical examination and laboratory assessment during
    hospital stay, doctor's perspective, 212–13
physical examination and laboratory assessment around
    time of hospital discharge, doctor's perspective,
    333–34
monitoring of fetus. *See* fetal monitoring
monitors. *See also* monitoring of baby
  and alarms, 158–60
  and blood pressure, 94, 95
  carbon dioxide, 94
  cardiorespiratory, at home, 334, 385–93
  cardiorespiratory, in the hospital, 93–94
  pulse oximeter, 94
Moro reflex. *See* startle reflex
morphine, 110, 111–12, 310
mother's scent
  infant's preference for, 139, 141
  in isolette, 190
motor development. *See also* movement; development;
    developmental delays; developmental evaluation
  and blindness, 453
  and BPD, 264
  and cerebral palsy, 419–24, 458–62
  and clumsiness, 430–31

and evaluation of, 406–07
and minor disabilities, 426–28
normal pattern of, 98–99, 138–42
and outcomes at various gestational ages, 50–52
and PVL, 286
and stimulating a preemie "right," 367–69
and temporary delays in, 408
motor milestones, 423. *See also* motor development
Motrin, 110
mourning. *See* grief
movement (baby's), 91. *See also* motor development
and appropriate stimulation, 368–69
and CP diagnosis, 420
and reflux, 359
movement (fetal). *See also* kick counts; kicks
lack of, 22
and membrane rupture, 20
moving baby. *See also* holding baby; transfer of baby
to another hospital, 65–66, 216
on home oxygen, 351, 352, 355
to intermediate care, 287–88
moving mother to another hospital, 52–53, 53–54
to baby's hospital, 66
multidisciplinary evaluation, 427. *See also* developmental evaluation
multifetal pregnancy reduction, 29
multiples
babies in different hospitals, 196
babies in different rooms in NICU, 197
breastfeeding triplets, 293
breastfeeding twins, 290–92, *292*
and C-section delivery, 57
and co-bedding, 197
and death of one twin, 496–97, 498
and delayed interval birth, 32, 66
at delivery, attention to, 46
dividing time with, 294–95
famous examples, 295–96
and fertilization and gestation process, 30
and fetal reduction, 29
and growth in womb, 28–29, 514
and health of mother during pregnancy, 29
home-going, 383
identical or not?, 69–70
and labeling by alphabet, 68
and likelihood of prematurity, 28–29, 34
and multiple doctors, 123
one twin with disability, 470–73
one twin going home earlier, 382–83
one twin initially doing better, reasons for, 121–22
one twin needs early delivery, 32
and outcome, 29

planning for future pregnancies after, 434–35
and preeclampsia, 9
resources list, 532–33
as risk factor for prematurity, 34
and ROP, 269
and SalEst test, 11
schedule for, 383, 519
as SGA cause, 71
and size discrepancy, as it relates to health, 122–23
and space in womb, 28
and tests ordered, 293–94
twin to twin transfusion syndrome, 30–31
mumps vaccine, 18
muscle tone
and cerebral palsy, 419–20, 421–22, 459–61
transient abnormality in premature infants, 408
and clumsiness, 430
development of, 91, 139–42
and maternal treatment with magnesium, 13
music, listening to
and blindness, 453

N

nails, development of, 90
naming
avoidance of, and anticipatory grief, 298
when baby has died, 488
narcotics, 110. *See also* addiction; pain
nasal cannula, 96
and home oxygen, *351, 353,* 353–54, 355
naso-gastric tube, 150. *See also* gavage feeding
National Association for Parents of the Visually Impaired, 452, 534
National Early Childhood Technical Assistance, 444, 524
nausea (maternal)
and anti-labor drugs, 13–14
NEC. *See* necrotizing enterocolitis
neck straightening
and holding head up, 142
necrotizing enterocolitis, 237–40
and breast milk, 125
and feeding intolerance, 151
and prenatal steroid treatment, 28
and risk for, at various gestational ages, 85, 86–87
surgery for, 313–15, *314*
negative feelings, 379–80, 381–82 . *See also* anger; anxiety; depression; emotions (parents'); fear; feelings; grief; hostility; sadness
Nembutal, 110
Neocare formula, 361
neonatal fellows and residents, 97

Neonatal Intensive Care Unit. *See also* Level 1–3 hospitals
  and adoptive parents, 372
  alternatives to, 118–19
  and baby remembering pain from, 376–77
  environment, and Developmental Care, 198–205
  equipment, 92–96
  father's behavior in, 301
  follow-up services of, 289, 406–07
  infection control in, 181, 183, 184–85
  missing NICU after discharge, 363–64
  parents' first visit to, 88–89
  parents' presence in, 191, 252–54
  and relations with nurses, 279–82
  religious services in, 490
  return to, after baby's surgery, 310
  and rotation of doctors, 282–84
  sibling visits in, 185–86, 186–88
  staff, 96–97
  telephoning, 107, 363
  types of, 52
neonatal nurse practitioner, 97
neonatologist, 97
  first meeting with, 54–56
  and multiple doctors, 123, 282–84
  parents' questions for, 54–55, 105–06
neurological problems. *See also* development;
     developmental evaluation; disability; hearing loss;
     intelligence; mental retardation, motor
     abnormalities; visual impairment
  and behavior problems, 429
  and BPD, 264–65
  and brain cysts, 284
  and cerebral palsy, 419–21, 421–24, 458–62
  and clumsiness, 430
  and cortical visual impairment, 454
  and early intervention services, 442, 443–45
  evaluation for, 401, 406–07, 444–45, 463, 465
  fear of, and baby's jittery movements, 98–99
  and feeding problems, 457–58
  and intraventricular hemorrhage, 166, 169
  and IQ score, 463, 464–65
  and learning disabilities, 468
  and need for resuscitation at delivery, 62
  and PVL, 286–87
  risk of, and healthy toddler, 426–28
  risk of, in babies born at 23–25 weeks of gestation,
    50
  risk of, in babies born at 26–29 weeks of gestation,
    50–51
  risk of, in babies born at 30–33 weeks of gestation, 51
  risk of, in babies born at 34+ weeks of gestation, 52
  and seizures, 171, 418
  and sensory integration, 455–57

  and SGA baby, 74
  and VP shunt, 318–19, 417
neuropsychologist, 468
neurosurgery
  for hydrocephalus, 168, 317–19
Newton, Isaac, 505
nicotine
  as risk factor for prematurity, 37
NICU. *See* Neonatal Intensive Care Unit
nifedipine, 14
nipple confusion, 228–29
nipple feeding. *See also* breastfeeding; bottle feeding; feeding
  difficulty with, 377
"nippling," 152
noise
  baby overwhelmed by, 455
  and hearing aids, 449–50
  and home monitors, 387
  and irritable baby, 375
  levels of, in NICU, 201
  from oxygen concentrator, 353
  reducing, for Developmental Care, 200–201
  to wake up fetus for monitoring, 24
non-nutritive sucking, 140
non-steroidal anti-inflammatory drugs, 110
nonstress test
  for fetal health assessment, 24
non-verbal learning disabilities, 468
"normal" child from preemie, 403, 404
normalization phase
  parental, and child with special needs, 474
normal pregnancy, 4
nostrils flared while breathing
  as sign of breathing difficulty, 356, 436
nourishment. *See* nutrition issues
NPO (nothing by mouth) order, 113
numbers and arithmetic learning disability, 467
numbers and comparisons
  calculating baby's caloric needs, 236
  conversion table, degrees celsius to fahrenheit, 512
  conversion table, grams to pounds, 511
  feeling bad about famous multiples, 295
  trap of, 216–17
nurse practitioner
  in NICU, 97
nurses, 97
  asking parents to leave, 191
  in the delivery room, 58–59
  and help with breastfeeding, 228
  home care, 347–50
  and infection control in NICU, 185
  and parents calling NICU, 107
  parents' relationship with, 279–82

questions to ask, 105–06
response to alarms, 158–59
rules for home nurses, 350
nursing. *See* breastfeeding; pumping breast milk
nursing care. *See also* nurses
    and Developmental Care practices, 201–02
    and early intervention services, 445
    and fracture of baby's rib, 241
nutrition issues (baby's), 136, 214–15, 335–36. *See also*
        bottle feeding; breastfeeding; growth; weight
    and baby not being fed, 113–14
    baby's caloric needs, 236
    and bone weakening, 241
    and BPD, 262–63
    and breathing difficulty, on first day, 82
    comparison of breast milk and formula, 125–26
    and going for surgery, 308
    and insufficient weight gain, 234–37
    monitoring status, ongoing, 134, 212–13
    need for nutritional supplements, 234–37, 360–62
    and parent's obsession with baby's weight, 362–63
    and picky eater, 410–11
    and types of feeding, preemie's progression through
        149–53
nutrition issues (maternal)
    and risk for prematurity, 19, 37
nutritionist, pediatric, 457
nutritive and non-nutritive sucking, 227. *See also* sucking

O

object permanence concept
    and blindness, 452
obstetric history. *See* pregnancy history
occupational therapist, 456, 458, 469
occupational therapy
    for CP, 460
    and early intervention, 445
    and motor skill delay, 431
    and sensory integration problems, 456–57
oligohydramnios
    and fetal monitoring, 23–24, 25
    and lung growth in fetus, 20
    as risk factor for prematurity, 35
    in twin pregnancy, 31
open ductus arteriosis. *See* patent ductus arteriosis
opiate narcotics, 110
    and addiction, 111–12
oral aversion, 377, 457
oral education. *See* auditory-oral education
Ordinary Families, Special Children, 473
organ damage
    and low blood flow, 62
organs

donation of, 491
orientation and mobility specialist, 454
oro-gastric tube, *94, 95,* 150. *See also* gavage feeding
ostomy and NEC, 313–15, *314*
overprotection, 380–82, 402
    of blind child, 454
    after loss of a twin, 497
overstimulation, 188–91
    and apnea, 219
    and baby's signals, 203–04
    in NICU, and Developmental Care, 198–205
    and sensory integration problems, 455–57
overweight
    and preeclampsia, 9
oxygen. *See also* home oxygen; monitoring of baby;
        monitors; oxygen deprivation
    and baby's position, 243
    and BPD, 213–14, 261–63
    as cause of lung damage, 258, 261–62
    expected need for, at various gestational ages, 84, 86, 87
    and high blood pressure in baby's lungs, 171–72
    increase of, during feeding, 152
    and respiratory distress syndrome (RDS), 101–05
    and ROP, 269
    and steroids, 259
    supplementary, 95–96, 213–14
oxygen deprivation (baby). *See also* ventilator; blood flow
    and anemia, 276
    and apnea, 219, 220
    and NEC, 238
    and PVL, 285
    and resuscitation at delivery, 60–62
    toleration of, 61–62, 220
oxygen deprivation (fetus)
    and anemia, 137
    assessment of, 22–23, 23–26
    and bed rest, 5
    and need for resuscitation at delivery, 61
    and obstetric complications, 34–37
    and preeclampsia, 9
    and SGA baby, 71, 73, 74, 75
oxygen desaturation, 158, 220
    and air travel, 345
    and apnea, 219–20
    and car seats, 344
    and reflux, 245
oxygen hood, 96
oxytocin and contraction stress test, 24

P

pacifier
    and feeding start, 228
    special kind for preemie, 202

pain, abdominal (maternal)
   and preeclampsia diagnosis, 9
pain (baby's), 109–12
   and chest tubes, 164
   dilemma of treating, 110
   evaluation at first day, 82
   medical treatment, 109–10
   memory of, 376
   non-medical treatment, 110
   and surgery, 308–09
   and ventilator, 108
pain (maternal)
   and pumping breast milk, 114
palmar grasp
   delay in the disappearance of, 423
palpitations (maternal)
   and anti-labor drugs, 13, 14
Pampers toll free, 340
paranoia
   and anti-labor drugs, 13
parents. See also coping emotionally; family issues
   and alarm scares, 160
   asked to leave NICU, 191
   burnout issue, 381
   child abuse risk issue, 381
   and child with special needs, 441–80
   and CPR, 335, 388
   and emotional aftershocks, 432–34
   father's role, 296–302
   and home nursing care, 347–50
   immersion in baby's care, 204
   perspectives of
      at delivery time, 42–44
      at first day, 77–79
      at first week, 130–32
      during early years of growth, 395–98
      at home-going, 330–32
      during hospital time, 208–11
   presence in NICU, 205
      and baby's rehospitalization, 404–06
      and staff relationships, 279–82
      and twins in separate hospitals, 196
      worry about cost, 192
partial breastfeeding, 127. See also breastfeeding
   and multiples, 291
partial exchange transfusion, 73. See also polycythemia
past pregnancy. See pregnancy history
patent ductus arteriosus (PDA), 84–85, 176–79
   in babies born at 26–29 weeks gestational age, 86
   in babies born at 30–33 weeks gestational age, 87
   and BPD, 262
   at first week, doctor's perspective 135
   surgery for, 311–13

paternal response. See also father
   and adoptive parents, 371
paternal role. See father
Pavlova, Anna, 506
paying attention, difficulty with
   as learning disability, 467
PDA. See patent ductus arteriosus
pectin barriers, 146
pediatric gastroenterologist, 457
pediatrician
   choosing a, 336, 340–43
   safe office visits to, 338
   taking over baby's care, 399
pediatric nutritionist, 457
pelvic pressure
   and preterm labor, 13
penmanship. See writing disorders
pneumonia, 180–84
   and BPD, 262
   diagnosis of, 180
   and infections in preemies, 182–84
   prevention of, 181
percucaths, 147, 275
percutaneous umbilical blood sampling
   for fetal health assessment, 25
perfection in parenting
   myth of, 371
perinatologist
   definition of, 4
periodic breathing, 218
   and monitoring alarm accuracy, 158
peripheral pulmonic stenosis, 277
peripheral vein IVs, 147
peripheral vision, baby prefers. See cortical visual
      impairment
peristalsis
   in younger preemies, 149
peritoneal drainage
   and NEC, 314
periventricular leukomalacia (PVL), 85, 284–87
   in babies born at 26–29 weeks gestational age, 86
   and BPD, 264
   and high-frequency ventilators, 163
permanent developmental delay, 408
persistent pulmonary hypertension, 171
personal care (maternal)
   during bed rest, 7
personality issues
   baby's, 374
   staff and parents, 279–82
   toddler's, 428–29
phenobarbital,
   as sedative, 110

as seizures treatment, 171
as steroid alternative, 27
phenylketonuria
screening test for, 279
phoning. *See* telephoning
photo for baby, 189
photo of baby, 89
phototherapy
as jaundice treatment, 157
pH probe
and reflux test, 245
physical exam
and birth weight prediction, 63
at delivery, 45
during early years of growth, 399
at first day, 80
at first week, 133
at home-going, 333
during hospital time, 212
physical exercise. *See* exercise
physical exertion
as risk factor for prematurity, 37
physical therapy
for CP, 460
and early intervention, 445
physiotherapy, chest (baby), 174
for BPD, 262
PIE. *See* pulmonary interstitial emphysema
pigeon-toed, 430
pitocin medication
and contraction stress test, 24
PKU
screening test for, 279
PL. *See* periventricular leukomalacia
placental abruption, 34
and cocaine use, 120
and preeclampsia, 9
and resuscitation, 61
as SGA cause, 71
placental health
blood flow, and bed rest, 5
and inflammation, 11
insufficiency, as SGA cause, 71, 73
placenta previa, 34–35
plane travel, 345
and home monitors, 392
plug episode, 174
"plus disease"
in ROP, 270
pneumothorax, 108, 161–64
Poitier, Sidney, 507
polio vaccine
schedule for, 290

polycythemia, 73
polyhydramnios
as risk factor for prematurity, 35
in twin to twin transfusion syndrome, 31
poor judgment
as learning disability, 468
portrait of a newborn preemie, 89
position (baby's)
and apnea of prematurity, 219
comforting and calming, 202
and developmental stimulation, 369
for pulmonary hygiene, 174
and SIDS, 243
position (fetal)
and C-section delivery, 56
post-operative care (baby's), 309–10
postpartum depression, 256
post-traumatic stress disorder
and parents of preemies, 433
posture. *See also* position
in babies born at 23–25 weeks gestational age, 139
in babies born at 26–29 weeks gestational age, 140
in babies born at 30–33 weeks gestational age, 141
in babies born at 34+ weeks gestational age, 142
pounds to grams conversion chart, 511
powdered formula
recipe for higher calories, 361
power outage
and home oxygen, 354
PPS. *See* peripheral pulmonic stenosis
precautions
to reduce risks of prematurity, 4
prediction of birth date, 10–12
preeclampsia, 8–10. *See also* high blood pressure
and bed rest, 5
as risk factor for prematurity, 35
preemie clothes and supplies
diapers, 340
resources list, 528
preemie issues—resources list, 529
preemie-proofing the home, 338–40
pregnancy. *See also* normal pregnancy
and bed rest, 5–8
and high blood pressure, 8
pregnancy history
and causes of preterm birth, 33
and cerclage, 16
and hidden infection, 18
and preeclampsia recurrence, 10
pregnancy reduction. *See* multifetal pregnancy reduction
pregnant again, 33, 434–35

premature birth
  elective, 4, 10, 22–23
  and hidden infections, 17–19
  and multifetal pregnancy, 29
  risk factors and prevention, 3–37
  spontaneous, 4
premature labor. *See* preterm labor
prematurity. *See* premature birth
prenatal care
  lack of, as risk factor for prematurity, 37
preschool years, 395–99
preterm birth. *See* premature birth
preterm formula, 126, 235–37
  as breast milk supplement, 235
preterm labor
  and bed rest, 5
  diagnosis and treatment of, 12–14
  effectiveness of anti-labor medications, 14
  signs of, 13
prevention
  of prematurity, 3–37
previous pregnancy
  and cervical incompetence, 15
  and preeclampsia recurrence, 10
  as risk factor for prematurity, 33
prior pregnancy. *See* previous pregnancy
privacy
  and home nursing care, 348
  parents' desire for, 143
procedures. *See* tests
prolactin, 223
prone sleeping position. *See* position
pronoun confusion
  and blindness, 453
protein in urine
  and preeclampsia diagnosis, 8
psychological evaluation
  and behavior of child, 429
  before entering school, 401
  and hearing loss, 449
psychotherapist
  and learning disabilities, 469
PUBS. *See* percutaneous umbilical blood sampling
puffiness of face/hands
  and preeclampsia diagnosis, 8
pulmonary edema (maternal)
  and anti-labor drugs, 13
pulmonary hemorrhage, 175
pulmonary hypertension, 171
  and low blood flow or oxygen before delivery, 62
  and severe apnea, 220
pulmonary hypoplasia
  and membrane rupture, 20–21
pulmonary interstitial emphysema

  and pneumothorax, 162
pulsating bed, 219
pulse (baby's), 94, 218
pulse oximeter
  NICU equipment, 94
pumping breast milk. *See also* breastfeeding
  best pump for, 223–24
  frequency and timing, 224
  hints for first attempts, 114–15
  hints to increase milk supply, 229–32
  at home, 223
  in the hospital, 223
  and pain, 114
  practical advice, 222–26
  and quantity, 225
  weighing pros and cons, 124–28
PVH. *See* intraventricular hemorrhage
PVL. *See* periventricular leukomalacia

Q
quadriplegia
  type of CP, 459
quality of movement
  in preemies, 423–24
questions—whom to ask, 105. *See also* telephoning
"quiet alert" state
  and developmental stimulation, 368

R
race (maternal)
  and BV rate, 17
radiant warmer (bed), 91
radiation
  and X-rays, 172
rapid breathing (baby)
  and BPD, 261
Rapid Eye Movement (REM)
  in babies born at 26–29 weeks gestational age, 139
rash
  and diaper, 247
RDS. *See* respiratory distress syndrome
reaching out
  as method to cope with stress, 194
reactions of friends and strangers
  and child with special needs, 476
reading disorder
  as learning disability, 467
real labor. *See* true labor
receptive language disorder
  as learning disability, 467
record-keeping
  for medication schedule, 358
red blood cells
  and bilirubin, 155

excess of (polycythemia), in SGA baby, 73
    monitoring count, 213
    shortage of in anemia, 276
reduced activity prescription
    compared to complete bed rest, 6
reduction transfusion (or partial exchange transfusion), 73
"re-exploration"
    and NEC surgery, 313
reflexes. *See also* startle reflex
    delays in disappearance of, 423
reflux, 244–46
    and BPD, 262
    and long-term feeding problems, 457
    practical advice for home care of, 358–60
    resolve of, doctor's perspective, 214
    resources list, 525
    surgery for, 319–21
reglan medication, 214
    and reflux, 246
regret
    as parental feeling, 193
rehospitalization, 404–06
    for RSV, 437
religion
    help for end-of-life decisions, 499
religious service for baby, 489
REM. *See* Rapid Eye Movement
remembrances
    and loss of a baby, 491, 497, 502
removal of IVs, 148
Renoir, Pierre-Auguste, 507
repetitive mannerism
    and blindness, 453
reproductive organs
    problems with, as risk factors for prematurity, 33
research on preemies. *See* experimentation
resentment
    toward surviving twin, 496
reservoir (shunt component), 317–18
residents, neonatal
    in NICU, 97
resources for parents, 521–34
RespiGam medication
    and RSV, 438
respirator. *See* ventilator
respiratory difficulties. *See also* breathing difficulties;
        respiratory distress syndrome
    in babies born at 26–29 weeks gestational age, 50
    in babies born at 30–33 weeks gestational age, 51
    in child on home supplemental oxygen, 356
    at delivery, 45
    as first symptoms of RSV, 436
respiratory distress syndrome (RDS), 101–05. *See also*
        breathing difficulty

    in babies born at 26–29 weeks gestational age, 86
    in babies born at 30–33 weeks gestational age, 87
    benefits of prenatal steroids, 27
    evaluation at first day, 82
    evaluation at first week, 134
    and jaundice, 156
    and "lung disease," 99
    and need for resuscitation and ventilation at birth, 60
    in SGA baby, 74
respiratory infections
    and face mask use at home, 338
respiratory syncytial virus (RSV), 435–39
    resources list, 530
respiratory therapist
    in NICU, 97
restraints, 112
resuscitation of baby, 59–62
    and brain cysts, 284
    method, 61
retinal detachment
    after ROP, 426
    surgery for, 321–23
retinopathy of prematurity (ROP), 213, 267, 268, *268*, 268–72
    in babies born at 23–25 weeks gestational age, 85
    in babies born at 26–29 weeks gestational age, 87
    eyesight after, 425–26
    and severe apnea, 220
    in SGA baby, 74
    stages of, 270
    surgery for, 321–23
"retracted" shoulders, 421, *421*
rhizotomy
    for CP, 461
Ribavirin medication
    for RSV, 437
rib fractures in baby, 241
rickets, 241
rigidity
    and CP, 421–22
risk factors for premature birth, 33–37. *See also* at risk
        mothers
    and birth date prediction, 10
    for preeclampsia, 8–9
risks of surgery, 311
rocking
    and blindness, 453
rocking baby
    as soothing effect, 375
"role negotiation"
    in nurse-parent relationship, 280
rolling over stiffly
    and CP, 424
"rooming in nursery"
    before home-going, 337

rooting reflex
    appearance of at 30–33 weeks gestational age, 141
ROP. *See* retinopathy of prematurity
rotating bed, 219
rotation of medical staff, 282–84
Rousseau, Jean-Jacques, 505
routine. *See* schedule
RSV. *See* respiratory syncytial virus
rubella (maternal)
    as SGA cause, 71
    vaccine, 18
rupture of membrane. *See* membrane rupture

S

sadness
    as parental feeling, 193
safe sex
    and prevention of infection, 18
safety issues
    home monitors, 389
    home oxygen, 352
SalEst test
    and prediction of premature labor, 11
scalp IV, 147, 274–76
scars of preemies, 378
    and BPD, 261–62
    and ROP, 426
scar tissue
    as cerclage result, 16
    in lungs, and bronchoscopy, 260
schedule for multiples, 382–85
    chart, 519
school
    and children with visual impairment, 454
    decision to start, 401
    after discharge from early intervention, 446
    and language education for children with hearing loss,
        448–50
    and later onset of minor impairments, 426–28
    and learning disabilities, 466–69
scleral buckle surgery, 321
scrotum
    fluid in and hydrocele, 250
"second look," or re-exploration
    and NEC surgery, 313
second opinion
    about developmental problems, doctor's perspective,
        402
    before surgery, 307
sedatives
    and apnea, 218
    and baby on ventilator or CPAP, 108
    and pain treatment, 109–10
    and surgery, 309–10

types of, 110
seeing baby
    at delivery, 59
    at delivery, doctor's perspective, 46
    parental feelings at first time, 88–89
seekership phase (parental)
    and child with special needs, 474
seizures, 170–71
    and low blood flow or oxygen before delivery, 62
    and PVL diagnosis, 286
    recurrence of with fever, 418–19
    and severe IVH, 167
    and SGA history, 74
    uncertainty in diagnosis, 170
    and VP shunt, 417
seizures (maternal)
    and preeclampsia, 9
selective reduction. *See* multifetal pregnancy reduction
self-assessment
    of preterm labor, 13
self-image
    and child with disability,, 479–80
    and twin with disability, 470–71
self-stimulation
    and blindness, 453
sense of failure
    and adoptive parent, 370
    and parent of child with disability, 474
sensor taped on baby, 93
sensory development
    at 23–25 weeks gestational age, 138–39
    at 26–29 weeks gestational age, 139–40
    at 30–33 weeks gestational age, 140–41
    at 34+ weeks gestational age, 141–42
sensory integration dysfunction, 455–57
    strategies for dealing with, 456
    resources list, 530
Sensory Integration International, 456
separation, sense of, 77, 79. *See also* holding baby
sepsis (baby's), 182–83
    and general infection at first day, 99
sexual activity
    and BV rate, 17
    as risk factor for prematurity, 37
sexual intercourse
    and cerclage, 15
    and membrane rupture, 19
sexually transmitted disease
    and premature birth, 18
sexual organs
    appearance, in newborn preemie, 88, 90, 91
SGA. *See* small–for–gestational age
shaking
    and high-frequency ventilator, 163

shallow breathing
    and monitoring alarm accuracy, 158
sharing emotions
    as method to cope with stress, 194
shock
    as parental feeling, 193
Shoemaker, Willie, 506
short bowel syndrome
    as consequence of NEC, 240
    risk for, after NEC surgery, 314
shoulders stiff, 421
shunt, VP. *See* ventriculo-peritoneal shunt
siblings, 186–88
    of child with disability, 471–72
    and dying baby, 487
    and father's role, 299
    as helper with baby's home care, 364–65
    and home nursing care, 348
    and loss of baby, 493
    one with disability, 470–73
    planning for future pregnancies, 434–35
    resources list, 531
    safe exposure to, 338
    visits from, in the hospital, 185
sickle cell anemia
    screening test for, 279
side effects (maternal)
    anti-labor drugs, 13, 14
    terbutaline, 14
SIDS. *See* sudden infant death syndrome
sight. *See* vision
signals from baby, 203–04
sign language, 448–49
Simmons, Richard, 507
simple febrile seizures, 419
sitting posture
    and CP, 424
size of baby. *See also* growth
    and fitness for surgery, 304–05
    prediction for future, 401
    and preemie's appearance, 378
    in SGA baby, 75
skin (baby's), 88, 90
    and assessment of gestational age, 81
    in babies born at 23–25 weeks gestational age, 138
    care of, 246–48
    and home monitors, 392
    physical exam at first day, 80
    and use of tape in NICU, 145
sleep (baby's)
    in babies born at 23–25 weeks gestational age, 138
    in babies born at 26–29 weeks gestational age, 139
    in babies born at 30–33 weeks gestational age, 140

in babies born at 34+ weeks gestational age, 142
    best position for in baby with reflux, 359
    and home monitors, 391
    interruption for handling, 201
    normal at-home pattern, 374
sleeping too much
    and VP shunt, 416
sleeping with baby
    and home monitors, 386
sling use, 368
slow breathing (baby's)
    caused by magnesium sulfate, 10
slow heartbeat. *See* bradycardia
small–for–gestational age (SGA), 70–75
    and congenital infection, 184
    definition, 70
    long-term effects, 74–75
    reasons for, 71–72
    short-term effects, 72
smell, sense of
    in babies born at 23–25 weeks gestational age, 139
    in babies born at 26–29 weeks gestational age, 139
    in babies born at 30–33 weeks gestational age, 141
smells
    parental, for baby's stimulation, 190
smoking
    and breast milk quantity, 229
    and home oxygen, 335
    and home preemie-proofing, 339
    and learning disabilities, 468
    and membrane rupture, 19
    as risk factor for prematurity, 37
    as risk factor for RSV, 436
    as SGA cause, 71
SNS. *See* Supplemental Nursing System
soap for baby, 247
social factors
    and cognitive outcome in preemie, 465
    as risk factor for prematurity, 37
social problems and prematurity, 429
social relationships
    and child with disability, 475–77
    and learning disabilities, 467
social worker
    and early intervention, 445
    in NICU, 97
    role in parents' coping, 195
soft spot, 80. *See also* fontanel
    bulging, and VP shunt, 415
soothing
    self, baby, 203
    techniques for, 375
sores on baby. *See also* skin
    from tape, 145

sound. *See also* hearing ability
   and baby in isolette, 189
   and blindness, 453
   reduction of, Developmental Care principles, 200–201
space, difficulty with
   as learning disability, 468
spastic diplegia, 459
special education
   and early intervention, 445
specialists
   for preterm birth, 4
special needs children. *See also* children with special needs
   resources list, 531
speech and language delays
   and hearing loss diagnosis, 447
speech and language therapist, 458
speech and language therapy
   for CP, 460
   and early intervention, 445
speech pathologist, 469
spinal anesthesia
   and baby's surgery, 309
   and C-section delivery, 58
spinal cord
   and infection, 99. *See also* meningitis
spinal tap (or lumbar puncture)
   and IVH, 167
spontaneous preterm birth, 4
squirming
   and monitoring alarm accuracy, 158
stabilization
   and gestational age, at delivery, 46
staff
   in delivery room, 58
   in NICU, 96
staff relationships, 279–82. *See also* doctor for baby; nurses
      for baby
Stanford Binet IQ test, 463
startle reflex, 91, 273
   in babies born at 34+ weeks gestational age, 142
   delay in disappearance of, 423
STD. *See* sexually transmitted disease
step-down unit
   definition of, 117
   moving baby to, 287–88
   and older newborn preemie, 134
steroid treatment (baby's)
   for BPD, 262
   to wean baby from ventilator, 258–59
steroid treatment (maternal), 4, 22, 26–28
   alternatives to, 27
   and amniocentesis to test baby's lung maturity, 26
   and anti-labor drug regimen, 14
   and risk for IVH, 165

   and tests to predict delivery, 26
stiff shoulders, 421
stimulation of baby,
   and at-home care, 366–69
   in babies born at 26–29 weeks gestational age, 140
   in babies born at 30–33 weeks gestational age, 141
   in babies born at 34+ weeks gestational age, 142
   craving for, and sensory integration problems, 455
   to end apnea or bradycardia episode, 219
   excess, effect on breathing pattern, 214
   and extreme parental responses, 380–81
   and monitoring alarm accuracy, 159
   and outcome with BPD, 264
   and preemie's stress, 188
stitch removal (maternal cerclage), 15
stool (baby's), 154
   blood in, 155
stopping medication
   doctor's perspective, 400
   hints for parent, 358
storage of breast milk, 225–26
strabismus, 425
strep infection (maternal), 183
stress (baby's)
   as apnea cause, 218
   and benefits of touch, 250–52
   reduction of, Developmental Care principles, 202
   signals of, 204
   from too quick transitions, 201
stress (parental)
   and delayed interval delivery, 67
   and home nursing care, 347–50
   marital, during maternal bed rest, 7
   reduction, and bed rest, 6–8
   and staff relationship issues, 279–82
stricture
   of bowel after NEC, 240
stroke
   and preeclampsia, 9
stroller selection
   and home monitors, 392
   and home oxygen, 355
stuffed toys
   in isolette, 190
subarachnoid cysts, 284
sucking
   in babies born at 26–29 weeks gestational age, 140
   in babies born at 30–33 weeks gestational age, 141
   and breastfeeding start, 227
   development of reflex, 227
   as stimulus for breast milk production, 223
   as stress reduction, 202
suction device
   in case of blocked airway, 347

suctioning baby, 173–74
    first week, 173
sudden infant death syndrome, 243
    and home monitoring, 386
    and sleeping position, 220
suicidal thoughts, 256
sunscreen
    safe use of, 338
sunshine
    safe exposure to, 338
super parent syndrome, 380
Supplemental Nursing System, 231
supplemental oxygen
    and ROP, 269
supplements (baby's)
    to breast milk, 235
    to formula, 235–37
    required by medical conditions, 236–37
    and tests to detect need for, doctor's perspective, 213
supplements (maternal)
    and social-behavioral risk factors for prematurity, 37
support groups, 195
    role, after discharge from NICU, 382
    role, in finding a pediatrician, 342
    role, for parents of child with disability, 477
    role, in parents' coping emotionally, 193–95
    role, for siblings of child with disability, 472
surfactant
    lack, in RDS, 101
    use, and air leaks, 163–64
    use, as treatment for RDS, 103
surgery, baby needs, 304–25
    and anesthesia, 308–10
    and apnea, 220
    and baby's size, 304–05
    and common risks, 311
    to decrease high muscle tone in CP, 461
    for GE reflux, 246, 319–21
    for hernia repair, 247–48
    to insert tracheostomy tube, 323
    to insert VP shunt, 168–69, 316–19
    and medical decisions, 305–07
    for NEC, 240, 313–15
    and pain, 308–10
    and parents' information, 306–07
    for PDA, 135, 179, 311–13
    to place Broviac catheter or other central line, 275,
        315–16
    to place gastrostomy tube, 320–21
    and recovery, 309, 312, 315, 316, 319, 321, 322, 324, 325
    for ROP, 271, 321
    and second opinion, 307
    to treat hydrocephalus. See to insert VP shunt
    for VP shunt revision, 412, 413, 414, 418

survival. See also viability
    at delivery, doctor's perspective, 46–47
    before delivery, prediction of, 21, 55
    and long-term health, 49
        in babies born at 23–25 weeks gestational age, 49–50
        in babies born at 26–29 weeks gestational age. 50–51
        in babies born at 30–33 weeks gestational age, 51
        in babies born at 34+ weeks gestational age, 52
    and loss of twin, 498
    in SGA babies, 72
swaddling
    and bottle feeding, 233
symbol manipulation
    as learning disability, 467
symmetric growth retardation, 72. See also
        small-for–gestational age
    long-term effect of, 75
Synagis medication
    and RSV, 438
syphilis (maternal)
    and preterm birth, 18
    as SGA cause, 71
syringes for home, 358

T
tactile defensiveness,
    and sensory integration problems, 456
"tag," vaginal, 91
taking baby home, 330–93
tape
    sores from, 145
taped down (baby), 112
    reasons for, 146
"tapping chamber." See reservoir
taste, sense of
    in babies at 23–25 weeks gestational age, 139
teacher of the visually impaired, 454
teaching hospitals
    and delivery room staff, 58
    and experimentation, 117
teeth
    problems in former preemies, 377–78, 431–32
    and reflux, 360
telephoning officials
    and parent advocacy, 478
telephoning the doctor
    and VP shunt, 417
telephoning the NICU, 107
    after home-going, 337, 363
television sound
    and blindness, 453
temperature. See body temperature
temporary developmental delay, 408
tender abdomen (baby's), 151

tense abdomen (baby's), 151
terbutaline medication, 13, 14
tests, 119. *See also* ultrasound
  of baby's urine for maternal drug abuse, 119
  for congenital infection, 184
  at delivery, doctor's perspective, 45
  for fetal health assessment, 23–26
  first week, doctor's perspective, 133
  at home-going, 333
  during hospital time, doctor's perspective, 212
  for infection, 182
  for IQ, 463
  ordered with multiples, 293
  for PDA, 178
  for pneumonia, 180
  for prediction of birth date, 10–12
  reasons for false alarms on, 279
  for thyroid levels, 278
theophylline medication, 219
  and reflux, 246
therapy (psychotherapy)
  and loss of baby, 485
  and negative feelings, 382
  role, in parents' coping, 195, 433
thinning baby's blood. *See* partial exchange transfusion
throwing up. *See* vomiting
thyroid
  levels, testing, 278–79
tied-down baby, 112
tight chest sound, 214
time
  and crisis decision-making, 502–03
  difficulty with, as learning disability, 468
  as healer, after loss of baby, 485
  and loss of one twin, 496
time in hospital (baby's), 41–325
time with baby
  balancing with multiples, 294
  balancing with other duties, 252–54
tocolytics, 12
toe discoloration, 148
toe-standing
  and CP, 424
toe-walking, 421
too soon pregnancy
  as risk factor for prematurity, 33
total communication
  and child with hearing loss, 448–49
total parenteral nutrition (TPN), 113–14, 149–50
  during hospitalization, doctor's perspective, 213–14
  and jaundice, 24
touch, sense of
  at 23–25 weeks gestational age, 138
  at 26–29 weeks gestational age, 139
touching baby, 98
  and Developmental Care principles, 201–02

  and infection transmission, 181
  and kangaroo care, 221–22
  massage, 250–52
  and sensory integration problems, 455
  as soothing effect, 375
toxoplasmosis (maternal)
  and PVL, 284
  as SGA cause, 71
toys
  in isolette, 190
"trach." *See* tracheostomy
tracheostomy, 263, 323–24
  collar, and home oxygen, 354
  and feeding problems, 457
traditional medicine
  and breast milk quantity, 231
transcutaneous measuring device
  and monitoring carbon dioxide, 94
transfer of baby, 65–66
  "back-transfer," 288–89
  to step-down unit, 117
transfer of mother, 52–54. *See also* moving mother
transfusion for baby, 116
  compared to medication, 215
  as jaundice treatment, 157
  safety of, 116
transitional formula
  and at-home care, 361
"transitioning" stage, 81
transport
  of breast milk, 226
  of mother. *See* transfer
transport (baby's). *See* transfer of mother
transverse C-section, 57
"trapped" feeling
  in adoptive parent, 370
trembling
  in babies 23–25 weeks gestational age, 139
Trendelenburg position, 6
triplets, 29. *See also* multiples
  breastfeeding of, 293
  daily schedule for, 383
  and ROP, 269
trust
  medical relationships, 4
tubes
  chest, 161–64, *161*
  for bronchoscopy, 260
  endotracheal (ET), or breathing, 61, *94*, 95, 104, 108, 265–66
  feeding, 95, 150–51. *See also* gavage feeding
  G-tube, *319*, 320–21, 457–58
  nasal cannula, 353–54, *351*, *353*
  oxygen, *351*, *352*, 355
  shunt tubing, *317*, *316–18*, 414
  tracheostomy, *323*, 323–24

tummy time, 369
turned-in legs, 430
turned-out legs, 430
turning out "normal," 403
Twain, Mark, 505
twins. *See also* multiples
    breastfeeding, 290–93
    and cobedding, 197
    identical, and PVL, 284
    identical or fraternal designation, 68–70
    interval delivery of, 66
    keeping them close to each other, 197
    and loss of one, 496
    one bigger, 122
    one doing better, 121
    one home earlier, 382
    one needing early delivery, 31–32
    resources list, 532
    and ROP, 269
    in separate hospitals, 196
    sharing a placental blood vessel, 30–31
    twin to twin transfusion syndrome, 30, 122
    and vaginal delivery, 57
twitchiness, 91
    in babies at 23–25 weeks gestational age, 139
    and seizure differentiation, 170
Tylenol medication, 110
typical febrile seizures, 419

U
UAC. *See* umbilical arterial catheter
ultrasound
    and birth weight prediction, 63
    and cervical evaluation, 10, 16
    and CP diagnosis, 420
    as fetal health assessment, 23
    head, for IVH, 85, 162, 165
    and membrane rupture, 22
    and twin to twin transfusion syndrome, 31
umbilical arterial catheter, 147
umbilical cord
    assessment at delivery, 45
    health, and inflammation, 11
    position, and membrane rupture, 20, 21
    and resuscitation, 61
umbilical venous catheter, 147
underresponsiveness
    and sensory integration problems,, 455
understanding speech, difficulty with
    as learning disability, 467
uneasiness
    as parental feeling, 193
unresponsivity (fetal)
    and elective preterm delivery, 22
upper GI series, 245
urinary tract infection (baby's)

and jaundice, 242
urinary tract infection (maternal)
    and preterm birth, 17
urine
    monitoring (baby's), 119, 155
uterine infection
    and prematurity, 11
UVC. *See* umbilical venous catheter

V
vaccination, 289–90
    of caregivers, 339
vaccine for flu
    for toddler, 411
vacuum extractors
    and preemies, 56
vaginal delivery
    and breech position, 56
    and cervical incompetence, 15
vaginal discharge
    and preterm labor, 13
vaginal infections
    and prematurity, 11
vaginal "tag," 91
values
    help for end-of-life decisions, 499
ventilator, 95
    and babies born at 23–25 weeks gestational age, 84
    and babies born at 26–29 weeks gestational age, 86
    and babies born at 30–33 weeks gestational age, 87
    baby put on, at delivery, 60
    baby "stuck" on (having trouble coming off), 214, 257–58
    and BPD treatment, 263–64
    and feeding problems, 457
    first day, doctor's perspective, 82
    high-frequency, 162, 163
    and holding baby, 144
    at home, 354
    and pain control, 108
    and RDS, 104
    removal from, doctor's perspective, 134
    role in BPD, 261–62
    slow weaning from, 263–64
    and steroids, 258–59
ventriculo-peritoneal shunt (VP shunt). *See also*
        hydrocephalus
    guide to living with, 412–16
    surgery, 316
ventriculostomy, 318. *See also* surgery, to insert VP shunt
Versed medication, 110. *See also* sedatives
vestibular stimulation, 140. *See also* stimulation
viability. *See also* survival
    babies at the edge of, 46–47
    when water breaks before, 21
violent thoughts
    as signal of postpartum depression, 256

viruses (baby's)
  and infections, 182–84
viruses (maternal)
  and premature birth, 18
vision. *See also* visual impairment
  in babies born at 23–25 weeks gestational age, 139
  in babies born at 26–29 weeks gestational age, 139–40
  in babies born at 30–33 weeks gestational age, 141
  screens, and VP shunts, 413
vision service
  and early intervention, 445
visiting baby (home)
  hints to prevent infections, 338
visiting the NICU, 92, 252–54
  asking doctor about, 55
  and being asked to leave, 191
  during hospitalization, doctor's perspective, 217
  siblings, 185
visual impairment, 85, 452–54. *See also* retinopathy of
       prematurity
  resources list, 533
  risk for in babies born at 23–25 weeks gestational age, 50
  risk for in babies born at 26–29 weeks gestational age, 50
  risk for in babies born at 30–33 weeks gestational age, 51
  after ROP, 425–26
  and SGA, 73
visual-motor coordination
  as learning disability, 467
visual problem (maternal)
  and anti-labor drugs, 13
  and preeclampsia diagnosis, 9
vitamins
  and breastfeeding, 235–36
  D, and bone health, 241
  K, as steroid alternative, 27
  and risk factors for prematurity, 37
vitrectomy, 321, 322. *See also* surgery, for ROP
vocal quality, 266
vomiting, 151
  and home medication, 357
  and VP shunt, 415
VP shunt. *See* ventriculo-peritoneal shunt
vulnerable child syndrome, 380, 402

W
waking up
  in babies at 23–25 weeks gestational age, 138
  in babies at 26–29 weeks gestational age, 139
  in babies at 30–33 weeks gestational age, 140
  in babies at 34+ weeks gestational age, 141
wandering eye, 141
washing baby, 247
water breaking. *See* membrane rupture
weak cervix. *See* cervical incompetence

weakness (baby's muscle tone abnormalities)
  temporary vs. permanent, 408
  in trunk and legs as early symptom of PVL, 286
weakness (maternal)
  and anti-labor drugs, 13
Wechsler Preschool and Primary Scale, 463
WeePee diapers toll free, 340
weight (baby's). *See also* growth
  below normal, in first years, 409
  and birth announcements, 142
  at delivery, doctor's perspective 45
  and differences in twins, 122
  gain, and caloric needs, 236
  gain, after discharge from hospital, 362
  gain, during hospitalization, doctor's perspective,
       212
  at home-going, doctor's perspective, 333
  insufficient gain, and feeding problems in first years,
       457–58
  insufficient gain, and need for supplements, 234–37
  loss, in first days of life, 113, 213
  and need for special services, 468
  and SGA designation, 70, 71–72
  and surgery, 304
  and viability, 47
weight (maternal)
  and birth weight prediction, 64
  and preeclampsia diagnosis, 8
  as risk factor for prematurity, 37
"well preemie," 134
wheezing sound, 214
  and BPD, 261
  as RSV symptom, 436
withdrawal symptoms
  and urine analysis (baby's), 120
withdrawing life support
  decision regarding, 498–502
womb
  compared to NICU, 198–99
  as "hand womb," Developmental Care principle, 202
Wonder, Stevie, 506
work
  father's, 298
  going back to, 254–55
  mother's, and bed rest, 8
"working up on feeds," 214
worry
  as parental feeling, 193
wrapping baby, 202
writing disorders
  as learning disability, 467

X
X-ray tests (baby's), 172